The Evolution of Economic Diversity

The traditional role of evolutionary theory in the social sciences has been to explain the existence of the object of their study in terms of the survival of the fittest. In economics, this approach has acted as a surrogate justification for hypotheses such as profit maximization or to justify the existence of institutions in terms of their overall efficiency.

This volume challenges this view and argues that one of the first tasks of economic theory should be to explain the enormous diversity of institutional arrangements that has characterized human societies. The issues covered include:

- evolution in the natural sciences and its implications for economics
- learning and evolutionary theory
- the evolution of institutional arrangements
- equilibrium selection and the evolution of norms

The Evolution of Economic Diversity unravels the remarkable two-way traffic between economics and biology that has characterized the history of the two disciplines, and develops a notion of "economic evolution" that is able to explain the diversity of economic institutions which is to be found in human societies. It will be welcomed by students and researchers of economics, economic methodology and the philosophy of social science.

The Siena Summer School hosts lectures by distinguished scholars on topics characterized by a lively research activity. The contributions collected in this series offer a clear account of the alternative research paths that exist within a particular field. The Routledge Siena Summer School Series presents the findings of the School, emphasizing the common methodology employed in organizing the different workshops.

Antonio Nicita is Assistant Professor, Department of Economics at the University of Siena. **Ugo Pagano** is Professor of Economics at the University of Siena.

Routledge Siena studies in political economy

The Siena Summer School hosts lectures by distinguished scholars on topics characterized by a lively research activity. The lectures collected in this series offer a clear account of the alternative research paths that characterize a certain field. Former workshops of the School were printed by different publishers. They include:

Macroeconomics: A Survey of Research Strategies
Edited by Alessandro Vercelli and Nicola Dimitri
Oxford University Press, 1992

International Problems of Economic Interdependence
Edited by Massimo Di Matteo, Mario Baldassarri and Robert Mundell
Macmillan, 1994

Ethics, Rationality and Economic Behaviour
Edited by Francesco Farina, Frank Hahn and Stafano Vannucci
Clarendon Press, 1996

New Theories in Growth and Development
Edited by Fabrizio Coricelli, Massimo Di Matteo and Frank Hahn
Macmillan, 1998

Published by Routledge:

The Politics and Economics of Power
Edited by Samuel Bowles, Maurizio Franzini and Ugo Pagano
Routledge, 1998

Forthcoming titles:

Cycles, Growth and Structural change
Edited by Lionello Ponzo

Legal Orderings and Economic Institutions
Edited by Fabrizio Cafaggi, Antonio Nicita and Ugo Pagano

The Routledge Siena Studies in Political Economy Series gives a comprehensive access to the publications of the School, which emphasizes the common methodology employed in organizing the different workshops.

The Evolution of Economic Diversity

Edited by

Antonio Nicita and Ugo Pagano

London and New York

First published 2001
by Routledge
11 New Fetter Lane, London EC4P 4EE

Simultaneously published in the USA and Canada
by Routledge
29 West 35th Street, New York, NY 10001

Routledge is an imprint of the Taylor & Francis Group

Typeset in Baskerville by
HWA Text and Data Management, Tunbridge Wells
Printed and bound in Great Britain by
MPG Books Ltd, Bodmin

British Library Cataloguing in Publication Data
A catalogue record for this book is available from the British Library

Library of Congress Cataloging in Publication Data
A catalog record for this book has been requested

ISBN 0-415-22192-7

Contents

Contributors

Samuel Bowles, Depatment of Economics, University of Massachusetts at Amherst, Massachusetts, MA 01060, USA

Robert Boyd, Department of Anthropology, University of California, Los Angeles, California, CA 90024, USA

Vincent Crawford, University of California, San Diego, 9500 Gilman Drive, La Jolla, California, CA 92093-0508, USA

Paul A. David, All Souls College, Oxford OX1 4AL , UK

Daniel C. Dennett, Center for Cognitive Studies, Tufts University, Medford, Massachusetts, MA 02155-7059, USA

Giovanni Dosi, Scuola Superiore S. Anna, Pisa, Italy

Giorgio Fagiolo, European University Institute, via dei Rocchettini 12, 50016 S. Domenico di Fiesole, Firenze, Italy

Marcus W. Feldman, Department of Biological Sciences, Stanford University, Stanford, California, CA 94305-5020, USA

Herbert Gintis, Department of Economics, University of Massachusetts at Amherst, Massachusetts, MA 01060, USA

Katsuhito Iwai, Faculty of Economics, University of Tokyo, Tokyo, Japan

George J. Mailath, Department of Economics, University of Pennsylvania, 3718 Locist Walk, Philadelphia, Pennsylvania, PA 19104, USA

Luigi Marengo, Department of Economics, University of Trento, Italy

Richard R. Nelson, Department of Economics, Columbia University, SIPA 420 West 118th Street, New York, NY 10027, USA

Antonio Nicita, Department of Economics, University of Siena, Piazza S. Francesco 7, 53100 Siena, Italy

Luigi Orsenigo, Department of Economics, Bocconi University, Milan, Italy

Ugo Pagano, Department of Economics, University of Siena, Piazza S. Francesco 7, 53100 Siena, Italy

Fabio Pammolli, Department of Economics, University of Siena, Piazza S. Francesco 7, 53100 Siena, Italy

Massimo Riccaboni, Scuola Superiore S. Anna, Pisa, Italy

Larry Samuelson, Department of Economics, University of Wisconsin, Madison, Wisconsin, USA

Avner Shaked, Department of Economics, University of Bonn, Bonn, Germany

Stefano Vannucci, Department of Economics, University of Siena, Piazza S. Francesco 7, 53100 Siena, Italy

1 Introduction

The co-evolution of economics and biology and the evolution of diversity

Antonio Nicita and Ugo Pagano

The traditional impact of evolutionary theories on social sciences has been to provide an explanation – in terms of the survival of the fittest – of the evolutionary phenomena observed in human societies. In economics this approach has acted as a surrogate justification for hypotheses such as profit maximization – that are typical of the traditional neo-classical approach – or to justify the existence of institutions in terms of their overall efficiency. The essays contained in this book challenge this view and argue that one of the first tasks of economic theory should be to explain the enormous diversity of institutional arrangements that has characterized human societies. The focus of this book is on those elements of evolutionary theory – such as the persistence of diversity and the co-evolution of diversity patterns – that have been relatively neglected by economists.

The book is divided in four parts. In the first part - *Natural selection and social sciences* – it is argued that there is little in natural science that justifies the orthodox interpretation. Indeed, an important task of biology is to explain the enormous diversity of living species, the complexity of the natural world and the mechanism by which this diversity can be generated. In this sense the impact of natural sciences should be to stimulate economists to turn their attention towards the general rules of structure and change that have caused the blossoming of this diversity. In the second part – *The multiplicity of learning paths* – it is argued that learning – a typical human activity that finds little room in the traditional neo-classical approach – involves a wide diversity of learning paths. The third part refers to *Technical change in organizations and economic growth.* The chapters contained in this part argue that economic and social organizations – embodying human learning in a wide varieties of routines and collective capabilities – can be characterized by multiple arrangements and do not necessarily converge towards a unique "efficient" solution. In the last part – *The evolution of norms* – it is observed that this same argument applies also to institutions, norms and co-ordination mechanisms that arise outside the realm of formal organizations.

In this introduction, before summarizing the other chapters of the book, we will give a brief account of the remarkable two-way traffic between economics and biology that has characterized the history of the two disciplines. The aim is not to provide a full account of these interactions but simply to outline the purpose of the book the aim of which is to contribute to the development of a notion of "economic evolution" that may help to explain the diversity of the economic institutions and the diversity of the complex paths followed by human histories.

1.1 From economics to biology

In a passage of his *Autobiography* Darwin wrote:

> In October 1838, that is fifteen months after I had begun my systematic inquiry, I happened to read for amusement Malthus on *Population* and being well prepared to appreciate the struggle for the existence which everywhere goes on, from long-continued observation of the habits of animals and plants, it at once struck me that under these circumstance favorable variations would be preserved and unfavorable ones to be destroyed. The result of this would be the formation of a new species. Here, then, I had a theory by which to work; but I was so anxious to avoid prejudice that I determined not for some time to write even the briefest sketch of it.
>
> (Darwin 1858: 58)

Similar passages can be found in the autobiography of Wallace – the codiscoverer of evolutionary theory – who claimed to have had the inspiration at about the same time during an attack of malaria:

> One day something brought me to my recollections Malthus Principle of Population, which I had read about twelve years before. I thought of his clear exposition of the "positive checks" to increase . . . which keep down the population. It then occurred to me that these causes or their equivalents are continually acting in the case of animals also. . . .
>
> (Wallace 1905: 51)

These two quotations are among the many that could show the influence of economic thinking on the early development of economic theory. While the idea that competition and struggle were pervasive aspects of life and they could somehow have unintended beneficial consequences was taken from political economists, Darwin added the idea of evolution – an idea that was going to backfire on economics and other social sciences inverting the flows of metaphors that in the early days of evolutionary theory had been from economics to biology.

While the influence of Malthus is clearly evident in Darwin's work, the contribution of Hume and Smith, as the prominent economists of the Scottish school, is more subtle. The basic idea absorbed by Darwin, which was a common idea in the works of Hume, Smith and Malthus was the unavoidable nature of conflict among human beings. Men are in conflict with each other following their "natural" instinct to self-interest satisfaction and by doing so they produce unintentional social outcomes. As Hodgson (1993) pointed out, Smith and the Scottish school "gave Darwin the idea of order and regularity being based on a chaotic multitude of individual units, and emerging without common intention or conscious design".

To persist as a "natural order," the social outcome reached by unintentional "rational" agents should possess those resources and distribution mechanisms necessary for its self-reinforcement. In this respect, "natural order" should be intended simply as "stable order" and not as an order determined by an oriented path of behaviors or moral oriented norms.

Natural order implies then that the social outcomes that are reinforced show some elements of "efficiency" in the sense that each part of the economic system "justifies" overall organization and vice versa. To this regard, Smith's theory of division of labor plays an essential role in determining those alignments of self-interests which produce "efficient" social outcomes. If the existence of conflicting self-interests in human environments is immediately related to natural selection, the way in which natural selection operates has to be referred to the Smithian (and Mandeville's) idea of increasing specialization. The division of labor is the way by which self-interested conflicting human beings are organized. Organization is possible because it polarizes – in a variety of skills – the natural conflicting behavior of human beings, inducing a specialization of human activity which has the ultimate effect of solving conflicts by building a chain of activities each requiring a given endowment of skills. In this respect the Smithian division of labor and the Darwinian emergence of varieties and species share the idea of a growing diversity and complexity. Within the framework of the division of labor, skills tend to enhance by learning processes, increasing the level of specialization and distinguishing sub-sets of the population with regard to the levels of skills therein developed. Departing from a homogeneous population, division of labor will shape population members by adapting their skills that follow learning processes which produce ultimately different members. However, unlike other economists like Babbage and Gioja or philosophers like Plato, Smith denied that the difference of skills are the cause of the division of labor and argued that causation flows in the opposite direction: often skill differentiation was rather the "effect of the division of labor." He explicitly argued that, unlike the case of different "varieties" of dogs:

> The difference between the most dissimilar characters, between a philosopher and a common street porter, for example, seems to arise not so much from nature, as from habit, custom and education.
>
> (Smith 1976: 19)

According to Smith, before being adapted to their tasks in the framework of the division of labor, the philosopher and the street porter differed less than two different varieties of dogs. Individuals were adapting their skills within the framework of the division of labor; a role in the division of labor was not simply adapted to their skills. However also the second notion of adaptation was well developed by the political economists: in opposition to Smith, Babbage had argued the division of labor was adapted to pre-existing skill variety and allowed the best use of the given comparative advantage of each individual (Pagano 1991, Hodgson 1993). Both directions of adaptation were perhaps useful for the development of the Darwinian notion of adaptation.

To be completely assessed, the influence of political economists must also be related to their specific concept of (very tough) competition that distinguishes them from modern economists: in the world of classical economists wages were bound to be at subsistence level and competition among workers was not far from a struggle for survival, as clearly stated by the Malthusian population theory. As Gould (1978) pointed out "the Malthusian population theory provided a general vision of crowding and struggle and enabled Darwin to identify an agent of natural selection." Darwin took from Malthus a purely logical idea: that of geometric series. Given a population of organisms this tends to replicate itself into another generation which tends to replicate itself in another generation. In a world of given resources not all the organisms generated would have access to those resources necessary to survive.

According to Mayr, what Darwin added to Malthusian predictions was the idea of the preservation of favorable traits: any variations among competitors (in the proportion of characters inside the population), that gave some advantages to a particular population sub-set would be transmitted to descendants and then reinforced in the overall population. Or, in other words, what Darwin added was the idea of evolution – a concept that was later going to backfire on the development of economics.

1.2 From biology to economics (and back)

Darwin's theory of evolution dealt with both the phenomenon of adaptive change (we refer to this phenomenon as vertical evolution) and the phenomenon of the diversity of populations, incipient species and new species (we refer to this phenomenon as horizontal evolution). Vertical evolution represents the natural and familiar idea of evolution as a phenomenon of change and mutation which occurs over time in a given species. By contrast, horizontal evolution refers to the phenomenon of the diversity of incipient species and the emergence of new species occurring in a given time unit. The innovative contribution of Darwin's theory was merging, in a complex even if not always successful way, two separate problems: the origin of adaptation and the origin of diversity or, in other words, vertical and horizontal evolution. In our area of concern, what economists did, in fact, was to keep some elements of the complex bundle of Darwin's theory of evolution (adaptation and the idea of competitiveness as a struggle for survival), while neglecting others (the persistence of diversity and the co- evolution of diversity patterns). This is somewhat paradoxical. In natural history variation is not only a matter of the "stage achieved" by a given species, but it is also a consequence of the "many divergent histories" that characterize the different species. However, in many respects, the economists could share the blame with Darwin. In the *Origin of Species* he was not only unable to explain the circumstances under which speciation (the formation of a new species) could occur, but did not even make a clear distinction between the concept of species and the concept of variety within a given species.

The confusion between species and variety is even more striking when one considers that in his early work Darwin was well aware of the definition of species in terms of reproductive isolation – a definition that is consistent with modern biology and implies a clear difference between varieties and species. As Mayr (1982) argues, it is very likely that Darwin gave up his early correct definition of species to defend his thesis against the creationists. Creationists pointed at these characteristics of species to challenge the claim that such discontinuities could be the results of the gradual adaptation due to the working of natural selection. Thus, Darwin "solved" the species problem defining them by degree of difference rather than by reproductive isolation and by denying their qualitative distinctness from varieties of the same species. In some ways, to deny the distinctness of species was a successful strategy against the creationists . "But the switch from Darwin's species concept the 1830s to that of 1850s laid the foundation for controversies that lasted for a century" (Mayr 1982: 269). Perhaps, another consequence of this switch was that it created some space for a view where "variation was a matter of stage achieved, not a consequence of many divergent histories."

When this progressive and unilinear view of evolution was accepted, humankind could be seen more as the most advanced stage of natural history than as one of the divergent histories that characterized living species. The discontinuity of speciation and the comparative understanding of the diverging histories of the different species were sacrificed to a vision where evolution could even been seen as unfolding along a single line. When the vision was transposed from natural to human history it implied something similar to what Veblen (like Marx) believed to be true: while progress and stagnation were both possible they were only occurring along a single line. This vision also had an attractive implication: the synchronic analysis of different societies existing at the same point of time allowed the diachronic reconstruction of the different stages that defined the single line of development of each society. Or, in other words, the comparisons between present societies in all their variations would have allowed a reconstruction of the past. When anthropological and historical evidence disclaimed this unilinear vision of history "the convergence of many disciplines on a 'single natural-historical model of the world' ceased and, with it, the evolutionary vision faded." (Mayhew, 1988: 452).

While the grandiose evolutionary visions inspired by Darwin faded away, the simple application of the "survival of the fittest" principle to the market economy prospered. As Winter (1987) has observed the typical application became some sort auxiliarity defense for the profit maximization. It is often claimed that under competitive conditions a business firm must maximize profit if it is to survive – an observation that is considered to defend the profit maximization assumption against the criticism related to the bounded rationality.[1] However, while economists justified often their optimizing arguments by the use of evolutionary analogies, the traffic of metaphors started to flow again also in the opposite direction. Evolutionary biologists argued that genes were treated as "as if" maximizing entities and the way was suddenly open to import many of the related tools developed by economists. According to evolutionary biologists like John Maynard Smith some of the tools could paradoxically work better in biology than in economics. In particular he argued that "it is turned out that game theory is more readily applied to biology than to the field of economic behavior for which it was originally designed."[2]

However it would be misleading to say that the use of game theory by biologists was simply marking a return of the traffic in the original direction; by that time the traffic had become so intense that it had simply become impossible to indicate clearly a dominant direction. While game theory was imported by biologists, Nelson and Winter (1982: 16–17) were claiming with reference to their well known theory of economic change that "The selection mechanism here clearly is analogous to the natural selection of genotypes with differential net reproduction rates in biological evolutionary theory. And, as in biological theory, in our economic evolutionary theory the sensitivity of a firm's growth rate to prosperity or adversity is itself a reflection of its genes." At the same time Dawkins was commenting on the success of Darwinism outside evolutionary biology by arguing:

> I am an enthusiastic Darwinian, but I think Darwinism is a too big theory to be confined to the narrow context of the gene. The gene will enter my thesis as an analogy, nothing more. What, after all, is so special about genes? The answer is that they are replicators." Or in other words the Darwinian approach could be applied well outside the realm of evolutionary biology to fields such as cultural evolution whenever some replicators could shape the dynamics of a process.
>
> (Dawkins 1976)

1.3 Toward an explanation of the evolution of economic diversity

Given the high intensity of exchanges between economics and evolutionary biology it is not surprising that also the reactions to the simple optimizing stories considered above have been strictly interrelated. Path dependency, development constraints, the importance of initial conditions are the common terms that have indicated a widespread common feeling among both economists and evolutionary biologists that (natural or human) history matters in a strong sense. In this respect it is particular instructive how Jay Gould (1992) has related Paul David's history of the QWERTY keyboard (David, 1985) to the development of the Panda's thumb. In both cases a simple optimizing story fails to explain the "inefficient" outcomes that can only be understood by referring to the numerous interactions and complementarities that characterize often both human and natural history. In this particular sense, according to Gould the QWERTY keyboard can be seen as the "Panda's thumb of technology." While, in the same spirit, the Panda's thumb could perhaps be seen as the "QWERTY keyboard of nature," the aim of this book is to advance the understanding of the evolution of economic diversity and, in some cases, also the analysis of the many different "Panda's thumbs" that characterize human societies.

1.3.1 Natural selection and social sciences

The natural selection analogy has often been used to claim that the selection processes considered by social sciences should lead to some optimal outcome. The chapters of this part challenge this idea by observing that a careful analogy with natural selection has very different implications.

To what extent it is possible to analyze the selection of "organizational equilibria," through the lens of evolutionary biology? The question is addressed in Ugo Pagano's chapter "The origin of organizational species." In contemporary evolutionary biology the competition among the members of the same species favors the emergence and the selection of gradual "efficient" mutations. At the same time, such competition may inhibit the formation of new species requiring a set of "complementary" (epistatic) mutations. In these cases the "epistatic" relations among genes involve that hybrids between the old and the new species are inferior to both species and speciation may require "allopatric" conditions – that is the new species is likely to evolve far away from the areas where the original species is more numerous and its competition is tougher. The evolution of economic systems may follow a similar path. Organizational species are characterized by such characteristics as rights and technologies that fit each other and define "organizational equilibria" superior to hybrid combinations with the characteristics of other organizational species. Competition among the members of the same organizational species, continues Pagano, may then improve its average efficiency. However, because of the complementarities between rights and technology, competition may also inhibit the emergence of new potentially more efficient "organizational equilibria." For these reason, Pagano argues that the evolution of new forms of capitalism has also often been characterized by a form "allopatric" speciation. In particular it is well known that "managerial capitalism" "speciated" in Germany and the US and not in England where the "first" industrial revolution had seen the successful development of "family capitalism." Thus, even when we restrict the analysis to the development of modern capitalist economies, no smooth improvement of "organizational species" seems to occur .

The analytical shortcomings of the optimality approach to the study of biological and cultural evolution are considered by Marcus Feldman ("Biological and cultural evolution: aspects of dynamics, statistics, and optimization") who starts by setting out the restrictive analytical assumptions under which a simple minded "survival of the fittest story" holds true. The optimality results are usually derived for a case of a single gene model where the "complementarities" (epistasis) among the different loci are necessarily ruled out by the "single gene assumption" itself. However, even in this case, when other levels of selection, especially fertility, are incorporated into the analysis or some other assumptions (for instance mating with relatives or geographical variations of selection), multiple equilibria become possible. In these cases, the actual history of the population contributes to the determination of the particular equilibrium that is going to be achieved. In general, when we move to the case of multiple genes, the possibility of "epistatic" relations among genes implies that, even if no other additional assumptions are made, the convergence to a global optimum ceases to be the necessary outcome of the evolutionary process. Thus, the trouble with the optimization arguments is that they generally fail with more than one locus and bypass the complex dynamics that may occur even with one locus. Moreover, the multiple loci argument becomes even more relevant when we consider cases of cultural transmission and the possible co-evolution of genetic and cultural traits. While any genetic contribution to human behavior is likely to involve many genes, there are multiple variants of each behavior that is culturally transmitted. It is therefore very difficult that the selection of cultural and genetic traits, and even more their joint transmission, can be usefully expressed in terms of optimality theory.

The existence of human agency seems to limit the realm of blind evolutionary forces. This point was forcefully underlined by Dawkins in the concluding sentence of *The Selfish Gene* with the following words:

> We are built as gene machines and cultured as meme machines, but we have the power to turn against our creators. We alone on earth, can rebel against the tyranny of the selfish replicators.
>
> (Dawkins 1976: 215)

This "duality" of human beings is the starting point for Dennett ("The evolution of evaluators") who considers the complex relations existing between human agency and the "selfish replicators." On the one hand, the self, who is also able to rebel against the selfish replicators, cannot be narrowly defined without considering our unique ability to extend our "self-interest" not only in space to other human beings but also in time, caring about own futures and pasts, and even about remote pasts and future centuries outside our individual lifetimes. On the other hand the "selfish cultural replicators" that replicate in our minds do not necessarily favor their host: also in the cases of the "memes" the final cost-benefit calculations must apply to the meme itself not to its carriers. The "sweet tooth" is considered as a standard example where what it is optimal in terms of the cultural fitness of some memes is different from what is optimal in terms of genetic fitness and, also, in terms of the individual agents hosting the "selfish replicators."[3]

1.3.2 The multiplicity of learning paths

The search of an optimal solution could be favored by the fact that the acquisition of human knowledge does not simply rely on the selection of genes and memes but on the active process of learning carried out by intelligent human beings. However, the chapters in this part argue that also the processes of active learning can generate phenomena like path dependency, lock in and, in general, suboptimal results. Also learning processes may well be characterized by a multiplicity of paths and, again, the path that is followed may be heavily influenced by the actual history of the processes.

Concealed ovulation is, together with menopausa,[4] one of the most distinctive aspects of human beings. While concealed ovulation has given an evolutionary advantage to making love well beyond the actual periods of fertility (a characteristic that distinguishes us from overwhelming majority of species) its evolutionary advantage puzzled evolutionary biologists for a long time.[5] Whatever the evolutionary reasons are for which concealed ovulation emerged in human natural history, it is only very recently, thanks to the advances of physiology of this century, that human beings have been able to unravel what their nature had concealed. Only now we are starting to guess with some degree of efficiency what is immediately evident to every rabbit or to every dog.

Why "learning by doing" did not allow the individuation of the ovulation time and of the related "safe period"? After a careful historical account of this dramatic "case study" of a "learning by doing failure" Paul David considers a formal stochastic simulation model which can provide a rationale for this class of phenomena ("Path dependent learning and the evolution of beliefs and behaviors"). In his model a Bayesian procedure for information processing is coupled to sequential behavioral modifications conditioned on revised beliefs on the process that is being managed. Under some assumptions concerning the cognitively bounded nature of the algorithm, simulation results reveal that surprisingly strong degree of functional behavioral adaptation is consistent with agents unable to make significant cognitive progress toward fundamental knowledge about the underlying process. Learning is characterized by a multiplicity of paths and it does not converge to the "true state" of the underlying process. Or, in other words, learning is not the same thing as becoming more learned in the sense of "knowing." As the case of concealed ovulation shows, a process of "learning by doing" may well imply that humans are trapped (for centuries) in erroneous beliefs (even if with some useful result in terms of controlled fertility). According to David, only if we unpack the "black box" treatment of learning by doing, can we successfully examine the variety of possible relationships that characterize human learning behaviors. In this way we can also understand more about the role of cognitive understanding (and misunderstanding) in the evolution of control over complex and imperfectly observed stochastic processes.

The history dependent dynamics that characterizes the process of learning is also the topic of Vincent Crawford's chapter "Learning dynamics, lock-in, and equilibrium selection in experimental coordination games." Crawford considers the leading theoretical approaches to equilibrium selection in the light of recent experimental literature in which subjects repeatedly played coordination games uncertain only about each other's strategy choices. Crawford proposes a model that gives a flexible characterization of individual behavior and allows for strategic uncertainty, in the form of idiosyncratic random shocks to players' adjustments. The model provides a framework where representatives of the leading approaches to equilibrium selection can be distinguished by different values of behavioral parameters and where the values can be estimated econometrically using the data from the experiments. The analysis shows that even when strategic uncertainty is eventually eliminated by learning, it imparts a drift to the learning dynamics, whose magnitude depends on the environment and the behavioral parameters.

Giovanni Dosi, Giorgio Fagiolo and Luigi Marengo ("On the dynamics of cognition and actions: an assessment of some models of learning and evolution") conclude their very useful selective guide to the enormous and diverse literature on learning processes in economics by pointing out that the path-dependent nature of the learning is a quite general property since new knowledge is typically accumulated on existing knowledge basis. However, they propose that more complicated and fascinating questions could be asked by considering the path-dependent outcomes driven by the correlation across cognitive, behavioral and organizational traits. Dosi, Fagiolo and Marengo maintain (like Feldman, and Pagano)that the type of interactions, that in biology come under the heading of epistatic correlation, could offer a fruitful analogy for other fields of evolutionary analysis. In the case of learning, the epistatic correlation among the learning rules imply that one is not able to say whether a rule is absolutely good or bad, since its value could be assessed only in a relative way considering the other rules and the representation and preferences that characterize the overall dynamics of the system. In this respect any learning system should typically entail the mutual adaptation and the co-evolution of the co-existing traits. Thus, with reference to a learning process, Kauffman's (1993) contribution would imply that as correlation among traits increases, learning is no longer likely to bring about a smooth path-dependent process of incremental overall changes. The "rugged fitness landscape" is more likely to imply that an improvement on the fitness of single trait will dramatically lower the global fitness of the system.

1.3.3 Technical change in organizations and economic growth

Technical and organizational changes in human societies constitute the immediate outcomes of human evolutionary learning processes. Such changes represent, at the same time, the cause and the effect of a wide range of the interactions and complementarities occurring between human societies and their environment.

In modern human societies, the economic performance generated by technical and organizational innovations acts as a benchmark justification for the adoption and the spread of a given technological paradigm. Economic growth becomes thus the engine of evolutionary technical changes and – ultimately – the outcome of the same. As Nelson and Winter (1982) have stressed, the socio-economic world is continually throwing up new situations that constitute opportunities to make profit if the situation can be comprehended and seized appropriately.

However, the way by which humankind selects the profitable business opportunities to open up or foreclose does not only depend on the economic growth expected by such changes but also on the distributional effects induced by the surrounding social and market conditions. For this reason, the emergence of different evolutionary patterns of technological and organizational change can be characterized by multiple institutional arrangements and the selection of a particular pattern will not necessarily promote a unique "efficient" solution. This suggests the adoption of a "neutral" meaning of "evolutionary change" in economics and the removal of the notion of a unique, positive and irreversible pattern of economic progress in capitalistic societies. It is from this standpoint that, in his chapter, Richard Nelson outlines the variety of evolutionary theories which have been developed both in economics and in other fields of social science in recent years.

Nelson ("Evolutionary theories of economic change") reviews evolutionary theories of economic change by distinguishing at least three principal branches of scientific theorizing about evolutionary change: the first is the common approach shared by social scientists on the meaning and the extent of cultural evolution with reference to science, technology and organizations; the second relies upon the recent developments of evolutionary game theory; the third is concerned with the analysis of dynamic processes of change and their empirical understanding. Recalling, among others, the works by Campbell, Vincenti and Chandler, Nelson notes that these theories are similar in some respects, while differ in others. While the theories differ in the details of the mechanisms generating innovation and variety, they are similar in their single-minded concern with a particular aspect of culture (science, technology, organizations) and in assuming the "blindness" of the processes that generate new cultural elements or modify old ones.

Nelson observes how the role of "out of equilibrium" behavior is also unsatisfactory. For instance, in evolutionary game theory, the analysis of out of equilibrium behaviors is mainly a vehicle for trying to understand equilibrium configurations. By contrast, the analysis proposed by Nelson and Winter is mainly concerned with the understanding of the dynamic processes and with their future evolution, stressing the historical path dependency of the economic processes. Much of the body of such evolutionary theorizing is focused expressly on variables that seem to be continuously changing, like technology, or fashions of business strategy an organizations. For this reason, the Nelson-Winter tradition of evolutionary theory can be viewed as a way of understanding economic growth. In this respect, understanding observed empirical dynamic patterns is the central focus of the kind of evolutionary theorizing proposed by Nelson.

In their chapter "Variety and irreversibility in scientific and technological systems: the evolution of an industry network" Fabio Pammolli, Luigi Orsenigo and Massimo Riccaboni propose one interesting way of developing the empirical implications of Nelson's theorizing and consider the connection between the structure and evolution of knowledge basis and the structure and evolution of organizational forms in innovative activities in science-intensive industry. The chapter characterizes some stylized structural and dynamic properties of search spaces in scientific and technological systems. The emphasis is on the nature of relevant uncertainties and the evolutionary processes which characterize the growth of knowledge and promote the division of innovative labor. They analyze the structural and dynamic properties of the network that enables and implements such a division of labor under conditions of strong uncertainty. In this perspective, the network is considered as an organizational form which allows individual agents and firms to balance the need for a variety of *a priori* plausible hypotheses to be tested and the irreversibilities associated with the cost and degree of specialization required in search activities. The authors focus on the dynamics of the network of collaborative agreements in R&D in the pharma/biotech industry after the "molecular biology revolution." Technological specialization does not only become the outcome of profitability strategies but also the result of a complex interaction between firm's strategies and market processes. In this respect the emergence of internal conflicts within the firm could not be separated from market dynamics.

Antonio Nicita ("The firm as an evolutionary enforcement device") emphasizes the two-way traffic between market and firms in the selection of a technological pattern and in the alignment of agents incentives in organizations characterized by incomplete contract relationships. According to Williamson (1985), in order to prevent post-contractual opportunism in an incomplete contract framework, economic agents have to design endogenous enforcement devices. The purpose of Nicita's chapter is to explain the firm as an evolutionary enforcement device emerging in an institutional context characterized by incomplete contracts and *cross competition*. "Cross competition" is the label given to the strategic context which emerges when, in order to enforce a bilateral incomplete contract, the agents involved try to reach a monopolistic position, *vis-à-vis* their counterpart, by "destroying" their competitors and/or by "encouraging" counterpart competitors. Nicita argues that in order to win cross competition against their counterparts or competitors, agents involved in incomplete contracts will design the institutional arrangements necessary to achieve the enforcement of contractual obligations. Still, to win cross competition against rivals (competitors and/or counterparts in a contract), parties involved in an incomplete contract could employ the degree of assets specificity as an endogenous enforcement device. To achieve the enforcement of incomplete contracts, investing in specific assets could then become an optimal enforcement strategy, rather than the cause of the failure of incomplete contracts. Whereas the main contributions of the relevant literature on incomplete contracts implicitly assume perfectly competitive markets, Nicita shows that, under the assumption of endogenous outside options, specific investments could increase or decrease counterparts' ex-post outside options and could have a strong impact on their incentives to select a post-contractual opportunistic behavior.

A consequence of Nicita's chapter is that the co-existence of alternative governance structures of the firm could be explained as a second best response to the market failures which arise in a "*cross competition*" context. The evolution of alternative organizational arrangements – such as the Fordist and the Japanese firm – may represent "second best" response to profit maximization processes in an incomplete contracts framework. In this sense the analysis may offer some sort of "microfoundations" to the explanation of alternative patterns of technical change and economic growth.

1.3.4 The evolution of norms

Behaviors in human societies are affected by norms and crystallized in institutions and co-ordination mechanisms that arise outside the realm of formal organizations. By norms we mean every long-term, frequent, personal and structured interaction occurring among individuals who shares a common environment. They are, in a wider sense, all the cultural traits governing actions and affecting group well-being. The evolution of norms in human societies represents the ultimate step toward an explanation of the evolution of economic diversity. Norms and institution constitute thus a complex bundle of rules and behaviors where genotypes and phenotypes co-evolve in a multidimensional setting and where genetic inheritance and active learning phenomena produce and maintain organizational innovations and human beliefs.

To tackle the analysis of the evolution and selection of norms Robert Boyd brings together, in his chapter "Equilibrium selection and the evolution of norms," two bodies of evolutionary theory and then applies the resulting amalgam to the evolution of norms in human societies. The two bodies are (i) evolutionary game theory and (ii) the theory of evolution in structured population. The former, originally developed by biologists, has been adopted by game theoretic models in which the assumption of perfectly rational agents is removed. The latter provides models of evolution in populations that are subdivided so that mating, social and ecological interactions are not uniform throughout the population. This approach has been developed by population geneticists interested in more basic problems such as evolution of sets of co-adapted genes. Boyd stresses that the two bodies of theory are relevant to each other because the analysis of structured populations could help in selecting one stable equilibrium among the potential set of different possible stable equilibria in a broad class of evolutionary games.

According to Boyd, evolutionary game theory helps to establish how norms are structured in population and, more important, how norms that are group beneficial are selected in sub-populations and transmitted in population. In evolutionary game theory every individual is a "type" and the outcome of players' interactions depends on the way individuals are sampled from the population to interact. However, the problem with evolutionary game theory is that it provides multiple equilibria and the selection of a particular equilibrium will depend on the initial conditions.

These difficulties of game theory make it very interesting, in Boyd's view, to model cultural evolution as a population dynamic process. Boyd reviews different models concerned with the emergence of variation among groups and the transmission of cultural traits from sub-population to overall population. Boyd applies the "shifting balance" model due to Sewall Wright to group selection by individual learning. Wright has shown that natural selection alone can't cause a population to shift from one co-adapted set of genes to a second, superior set of genes. In particular, a genetic drift causes the frequency of a gene combination to exceed the threshold frequency necessary for that combination to be focused by natural selection. Then, natural selection increases the frequency of the emphasizes gene combination to near one within the initial sub-population. Finally, because the average fitness of this sub-population is higher than that of neighboring sub-populations, the initial sub- population will produces more emigrants. As a result, the emphasizes gene combination will spread through group selection. Thus, according to Wright, emphasizes gene combinations evolved through a combination of genetic drift and natural selection in structured populations. Boyd then suggests that group selection could proceed more rapidly if group competition is driven by individual learning. Norms spread from successful groups because individuals in the less successful group imitate individuals in the more successful group. The interesting feature about these results is, according to Boyd, that group selection has nothing to do with the spread of the group beneficial trait. The group beneficial trait spreads because it is more strongly focused by individual selection.

As Boyd sets out, in order to select the evolution of norms in populations, the development of matching behaviors in populations represents an essential condition. In this respect, the chapters by Mailath, Shaked and Samuelson and by Vannucci provide interesting analytically tractable models of the evolution of social behaviors.

The chapter "Endogenous interactions" by George Mailath, Larry Samuelson and Avner Shaked, examines an evolutionary model with "local interactions," so that agents are more likely to interact with some agents than with others. After having shown the result that equilibrium strategy choices with given local interactions correspond to correlated equilibria of the underlying game, they allow the pattern of interactions itself to be shaped by evolutionary pressures. It is then shown that when agents do not have the ability to avoid unwanted interactions, then heterogeneous outcomes can appear, including outcomes in which different groups play different Pareto ranked equilibria. If agents do have the ability to avoid undesired interactions, then it is possible to derive conditions under which outcomes must be not only homogeneous but also efficient.

In a similar perspective, the emergence and the sustainability of social networks in evolutionary common interest games is analyzed in Stefano Vannucci's chapter "Social networks and efficient evolutionary outcomes in recurrent interest games." Social networks are defined by Vannucci as sets of repeated pure coordination games. The selection of efficient outcomes within recurrent common interest games acts in two different way: (i) by working as a system of reliable information transmission channels which enables the players to discriminate between co-operators and defectors within a large population or (ii) by lowering the threshold frequency of co-operators which is required for the evolution of "co-operative" playing schemas in a noisy context.

The selection of efficient rules of behavior depends also on the wide range of interactions and complementarities which perspective economic institutions, in particular markets. Bowles and Gintis, and Iwai represent economic institutions as distinct environments imparting specific direction to the evolutionary processes affecting the selection and the transmission of norms in human societies. They favors the influence of economic institutions on the evolution of norms and polarizes the impact of well-defined norms on the evolution of the behaviors of economic agents.

The first chapter by Samuel Bowles and Herbert Gintis,"Community Governance: an evolutionary analysis," focuses on the influence exerted by economic institutions on the evolution of norms. The model proposed shows how allocation rules which closely conform to idealized markets may support lower equilibrium frequencies of socially beneficial norms and otherwise militate against the prevalence of these norms, by comparison to alternative allocation rules which deviate from the market ideal. The intuition behind this result is that behaviors governed by norms are typically non-contractible, and the regulation of non-contractible behaviors through market-like interactions gives rise to coordination failures which may be attenuated by deviation from the market ideal.

The second chapter by Bowles and Gintis, "Cooperation and exclusion in networks," focuses on the reasons of the persistence of networks in a market economy despite their relative inability to exploit the economies of scale and other efficiency-enhancing elements of markets. The authors suggest that networks can foster cooperative behavior by supporting decentralized enforcement of pro-social behavior among networks members. Networks have this capacity by virtue of their ability to reduce information costs, thus permitting the emergence of "trusting" Nash equilibria that do not exist, or are unstable, when information costs are high. The capacity of networks to foster cooperation is widely attributed to their ability to foster pro-social norms through cultural indoctrination. Bowles and Gintis develop a model in which pro-social norms emerge as part of dynamically-stable Nash equilibria.

The last chapter in the book gives an account of the evolution of one of the most important institutions and norms in economic societies. In "The Evolution of Money" Katsuhito Iwai addresses the question of how money has evolved in human societies – a question intimately connected with the question of what money is. The chapter develops a simple search-theoretic model of decentralized economy which is capable of characterizing the barter system, commodity money system, fiat money system, and gift exchange system, all as different forms its equilibrium. It demonstrates that while barter system requires a well-balanced distribution of abilities and needs in the economy and gift exchange system requires an infinite memory of its every member, monetary exchange system, whether it uses a commodity money or fiat money, requires no such "real" condition and no such "informational" requirement to support itself as equilibrium.

Iwai points out how money is money simply because it is used as money. Indeed, it is this complete transcendence from "reality" and "information" that sets up a monetary exchange system, thereby throwing doubt both on economist' commodity theory explanation and on the anthropologist' gift exchange story.

Iwai observes that there is a fundamental limit on the power of the theory to explain the origin of money *ex-post facto* and asserts that path dependency in history plays a crucial role in determining the emergence and the evolution of money.

Iwai's chapter suggests that we should not confuse the fact that we take some institutions for granted with their "rational historical necessity." Even in this cases, where "*ex-post* diversity" has been reduced or eliminated, evolution could have taken *ex-ante* many diverse paths; or, in other words, we should never confuse between the *ex-post* realization of one path with its *ex-ante* necessity.

Notes

1 The argument is, however, highly conditional. "In the presence of deliberation cost, for example, survival logic may favor a cheap rule of thumb over a costly optimization." (Coslink 1996: 684).

2 "There are two reasons for this. First, the theory requires that the values of different outcomes (for example, financial rewards, the risks of death and the pleasures of a clear conscience) be measured on a single scale. In human applications, this measure is provided by 'utility' a somewhat artificial and uncomfortable concept: in biology, Darwinian fitness provides a natural and genuinely one-dimensional scale. Secondly, and more importantly, in seeking the solution of a game, the concept of human rationality is replaced by that of evolutionary stability. The advantage here is that there are good reasons to expect populations to evolve to stable states, whereas there are grounds for doubting whether human beings always behave rationally." (Maynard Smith 1982: Preface)

3 Also a convincing explanation of nationalism requires some reference to the "duality" considered by Dennett. While the self who has national feelings extends the notion of self-interest in space and time, one can also argue that the "nationalistic" memes may be increasing their fitness against the interests of their host. On this problem see Pagano (1995) who considers these and other explanations that have been given of the phenomenon of nationalism.

4 In both cases Jared Diamond (1998) shows we are much more like (very) isolated exceptions than the prevailing rule. The evolutionary advantage of menopausa is particularly counter-intuitive and it can only explained as a particular "making more by making less" strategy that is successful for a species where the risk of delivery is so high and the children are dependent on the mother for such a long time after birth.

5 According to a recent theory concealed ovulation may first have emerged as a successful evolutionary strategy of mothers to protect children against males (who had, in turn, an evolutionary advantage to kill others' males children but, when ovulation was concealed, could not tell whether this was the case). Concealed ovulation may have, then, have had the effect of "keeping daddy at home." Only in this way he could be sure that his partner would not reproduce with other males during periods of concealed fertility (Diamond 1998).

References

Coslink, J. (1996) Why bounded rationality? *Journal of Economic Literature*. XXXIV: 669–700.

Cronin, H. (1991) *The Ant and the Peacock*. Cambridge: Cambridge University Press.

Darwin, C. (1858) *Autobiography*, reprinted 1974 Oxford: Oxford University Press

Darwin, C. (1859) *The Origin of Species*. Edited by J.W. Burrow (1968). Harmondsworth: Penguin Books.

David, P.A. (1985) Clio and the economics of QWERTY *American Economic Review* 75: 332–33

Dawkins. R. (1976) *The Selfish Gene*. Oxford: Oxford University Press

—— (1988) *The Blind Watchmaker*. Penguin Books, Harmondsworth.

Diamond, J. (1998) *Why is Sex Fun? The Evolution of Human Sexuality*. London: Phoenix.

Gould, S.J. (1978) *Ever Since Darwin: Reflections in Natural History*. London: Burnett Books.

—— (1992) The panda's thumb of technology. In S.J. Gould *Bully for Brontosaurus*. Harmondsworth: Penguin Books.

Hodgson, G. (1993) *Evolution and Economics. Bringing life back into economics*. Cambridge: Polity Press.

Kauffman, S.A. (1993) *The Origins of Order: Self-Organization and Selection in Evolution*. Oxford: Oxford University Press.

Mayhew, A. (1988) On the difficulty of evolutionary analysis. *Cambridge Journal of Economics*. 22(4): 449–461.
Maynard Smith, J. (1966) Sympatric speciation. *American Naturalist* 100: 637–650.
—— (1982) *Evolution and the Theory of Games*. Cambridge: Cambridge University Press.
Mayr, E. (1982) *The Growth of Biological Thought*. Cambridge, MA: Harvard University Press.
—— (1988) *Towards a New Philosophy of Biology* Cambridge, MA: Harvard University Press.
Nelson, R.R. (1994) Economic growth via the coevolution of technology and institutions. In L. Leydesdorff and P. Van Den Besselaar (eds) *Evolutionary Economics and Chaos Theory*. London: Pinter.
Nelson, R.R. and S. Winter (1982) *An Evolutionary Theory of Economic Change* Cambridge, MA: Harvard University Press.
Pagano, U. (1991) Property rights, asset specificity, and the division of labour under alternative capitalist relations. *Cambridge Journal of Economics* 15(3): 315–342. Reprinted in G.M. Hodgson (1993) *The Economics of Institutions*. Cheltenham: Edward Elgar.
—— (1995) Can economics explain nationalism? In A. Breton, G. Galeotti, P. Salmon and R. Wintrobe (eds) *Nationalism and Rationality*. Cambridge: Cambridge University Press.
Ridley, Mark (1996) *Evolution* (2nd edn.) Oxford: Basil Blackwell.
Smith, A. (1976) *An Inquiry into the Nature and Wealth of Nations*. Edited by J Cannan. Chicago: The University of Chicago Press.
Spencer, H.G. and J.D. Masters (1992) Sexual selection: contemporary debates. In E.F. Keller and E.A. Lloyd (eds) *Keywords in Evolutionary Biology*. Cambridge, MA: Harvard University Press.
Wallace, A.R. (1905) *My Life: A Record of Events and Opinions*. London: Chapman and Hall
Williamson, O. E. (1985) *The Economic Institutions of Capitalism*. New York: The Free Press.
Winter, S. (1987) Competition and selection. In J. Eatwell, M. Milgate and P. Newman (eds) *The New Palgrave*. London: Macmillan.

Part I

Natural selection and the social sciences

2 The origin of organizational species

Ugo Pagano

2.1 Introduction

Commenting on the analogy between his own panda's thumb evolutionary story and the economics of QWERTY analyzed by Paul David (1985), Gould has observed that:

> My main point, in other words, is not that typewriters are like biological evolution (for such an argument would fall right into the nonsense of false analogy), but that both keyboards and the panda's thumb, as product of history, must be subject to some regularities governing the nature of temporal connections. As scientists, we must believe that general principles underlie structurally related systems that proceed by different overt rules. The proper unity lies not in the false applications of these overt rules (like natural selection) to alien domains (like technological change) but in seeking the more general rules of structure and change themselves.
>
> (Gould 1992: 66)

The purpose of this chapter is to argue that some of the limitations and problems that arise with the working of natural selection in the case of speciation may be one aspect of the more general rules of structure and change and may have some counterpart on the competitive selection of organizational species in human history. In biology the laws of structure and change that characterize the selection among species are very different from those that characterize the selection of the members of the same species. This may be relevant also in economics where one may want to distinguish the laws of structure and change that govern the selection of the members of a given organizational species from those that govern the emergence of new organizational species. Or, in other words, the working hypothesis of this chapter is that the problem of the "origin of organizational species" in economics may share some of the complicated intellectual challenges that characterize the "origin of natural species" in biology.

The first section considers the struggle of Charles Darwin with the concept of species. From the viewpoint of the modern definition of species, that is not based "on degree of difference" but on "absence of interbreeding," (Mayr 1988: 318)

Darwin's struggle was unsuccessful. In order to explain the origin of species as the result of a gradual adaptations Darwin ended up denying any fundamental distinction between species and varieties.

The second and third sections of this chapter consider the modern biological debate on speciation. The purpose of these sections is to show that, in this respect, modern biology has substantially departed from Darwin's theory of speciation. Competition among many members of the same species favors the emergence and the selection of fitter one-mutant variants that favor the adaptation to the environment. However, the pressure of natural selection may inhibit the formation of new species requiring a set of "complementary" mutations characterized by the fact that "hybrid combinations" between the two species are either inferior or, even, impossible. In these cases, that involve that hybrids between the old and new species are inferior to both species, speciation may require "allopatric" conditions or, in other words, some initial protection from the competition from the members of the old species. In other words while the pressure of natural selection favors the adaptation of each species to the environment and its co-evolution with other species, it may inhibit the formation of new species. The pressure of natural selection may even contribute to a stasis of the evolutionary process. A "punctuation" of this stasis is more likely to occur in "allopatric conditions" in a relatively protected periphery. By contrast, natural selection may have a stabilizing role "freezing" some parts of the genotype.

In the third section we argue that the evolution of economic organizations may be characterized by similar rules of structure and change. Organizational species are characterized by rights and technologies that fit each other and define "organizational equilibria" superior to hybrid combinations with rights and technologies of other species. Competition among the members of the same organizational species may improve its average efficiency but, because of the complementarities between rights and technology, it may also inhibit the emergence of new potentially more efficient "organizational equilibria." Thus, while the pressure of competition favors the adaptation of each organization to the environment and its co-evolution with the other organizations, it may inhibit the "speciation" of new organizational species; like in the case of natural species, speciation may again require "allopatric conditions."

In the last section we consider the "second industrial revolution" and the coming of the new species of "managerial capitalism" in United States and Germany. We argue that Britain's failure to keep the pace of organizational change was paradoxically due to the fact that it had been the main actor in the first industrial revolution developing a robust species of "personal capitalism." The speciation of managerial capitalism required the "allopatric conditions" offered by Germany and the United States.

2.2 The concepts and origin of species in Darwin

Helena Cronin concludes her book *The Ant and the Peacock* observing that:

> The two fundamental problems that Darwin's theory was designed to solve were adaptation and diversity. The riddle of adaptation he solved superbly. As for diversity, on certain aspects he was equally successful. The patterns of geographical distribution, the fossil record, the taxonomic hierarchy, and comparative embryology all fell into place under his incisive analysis. But in the mist of such success, there was one problem that remained just outside his grasp. It was poignantly the problem of the origin of species.
>
> (Cronin 1991: 430)

In some ways, Darwin's failure was made more striking by the fact that he failed to give a satisfactory definition of species. The concept of species was somehow blurred with the concept of variety within a given species. Indeed, Darwin concludes his chapter on hybrids arguing that:

> Laying aside the question of fertility and sterility, in all other respects there seems to be a general and close similarity in the offspring of crossed species, and of crossed varieties. If we look at species as having been specially created, and at varieties as having been produced by secondary laws, this similarity would be an astonishing fact. But it harmonizes perfectly with the view that there is no essential distinction between species and varieties.
>
> (Darwin 1859: 288)

This conclusion shows an adherence to a "phenetic species concept" defining species as a set of organisms that resemble one another and are, in this sense, distinct from other organisms. In terms of this definition the distinction between species and varieties becomes a matter of degree. Indeed, a great weakness of the phenetic species concept is that the distinction between varieties and species becomes inevitably subjective and arbitrary. Different phenetic measures may group into different ways different clusters of individuals attributing to one or to another characteristic the role of defining a border line among different species.

Darwin does not seem to be aware of the fact that "laying aside the question of fertility and sterility" is tantamount to ignoring the very essence of the "biological species concept" that defines species as groups of interbreeding natural populations that are reproductively isolated from other such groups.

The "biological species concept" has the advantage "that it places the taxonomy of natural species within the conceptual scheme of population genetics. A community of interbreeding organisms is, in population genetic terms, a gene pool." (Ridley 1996: 403). Moreover, the biological concept of species provides an explanation for the similarities[1] that are the main ingredient the "phenetic concept of species": the gene flow among the members of the species gives a species its phenetic coherence while the absence of this flow among the members of different species causes more pronounced differences in their appearances.

According to Mayr (1982: 265), the discovery of Darwin notebooks shows that he was well aware of the "modern" concept of "biological species." Mayr observes how "No author reflects the struggle with the species concept more vividly than Darwin." Before the publication of the *The Origin of the Species* his notebooks contained "a clear description of reproductive isolation, maintained by ethological isolating mechanisms" and moreover "Darwin emphasized repeatedly that species status had little if anything to do with degree of difference (Mayr 1982: 266).

Thus, according to Mayr, when one reads what Darwin says about species in *The Origin of species* "one cannot help but feel that one is dealing with an altogether different author" claiming that varieties have the same general characters as species "for they cannot be distinguished from species (Mayr 1982: 266–7).

"What could have brought about this complete turn around in Darwin's species concept?" asks Mayr (1982: 267).

The botanical literature had, perhaps, made Darwin aware of one genuine problem related to the biological concept of species: the difficulty and often the impossibility to rank geographically isolated populations that might (or might not) interbreed if they lived in sympatry (i.e. in the same area). However this difficulty does imply that species are purely arbitrary or invented for the convenience of taxonomists as Darwin seemed to maintain in *The Origin of Species*.

Thus, according to Mayr the explanation has to be found in "a strong, even though perhaps unconscious, motivation for Darwin to demonstrate that species lack the constancy and the distinctiveness claimed by them by creationists." (Mayr 1982: 262) Creationists pointed at these characteristics of species to challenge the claim that such discontinuities could be the results of the gradual adaptation due the working of natural selection. Thus, Darwin "solved" the species problem defining them by degree of difference rather than by reproductive isolation and denying their qualitative distinctness from varieties of the same species.

Mayr concludes his analysis observing that when species are reduced to varieties it is possible to provide a relatively simple explanation of their origin "by the means of natural selection."[2] Thus, in some ways, "it was a good strategy to deny the distinctness of species." "But the switch from Darwin's species concept the 1830s to that of 1850s laid the foundation for controversies that lasted for a century" (Mayr 1982: 269) One may add that it also laid the ground for the type of influence that Darwinism was to have on the social sciences: the fitness of organizational and cultural species was to be related to the strength of the competitive struggle while no inquiry was made on the conditions under which new "fitter" species could ever come about.

2.3 Natural selection and speciation.

If the biological definition of species is accepted how can natural selection favor the formation of new species?

If one follows the Darwinian approach, the answer should necessarily be based on the argument that natural selection should be able to discriminate against the hybrids between the old and new populations and favor the reproductive isolation necessary to give them the status of distinct species. "This process by which selection increases reproductive isolation, independently of the history of the populations is simply called *reinforcement.* Reinforcement may occur when two forms coexist, and the hybrids between them have lower fitness than crosses within each form." (Ridley 1996: 431)

Reinforcement would act by discriminating against those that mate members of the other form favoring a process of pre-zygotic isolation or, in other words, favoring those members that develop a mating preference for the individuals of their own form. When these preferences are selected the two population are completely separated and become two different species.

Reinforcement can be an important mechanism to isolate two populations living in sympatry (i.e. without being separated by geographic barriers). If they can mate and the hybrids are as fit or fitter than the two original forms, then selection will not reinforce isolation but will rather tend to decrease any pre-existing partial reproductive isolation.

Thus, reinforcement may be necessary to keep isolated in sympatry two populations that are able to produce hybrids. However, this does not imply that reinforcement favors speciation when a new genotype is emerging. By contrast, it can be easily shown that, even when hybrids are inferior, the pressure of natural selection may inhibit rather than favoring speciation.

Ridley considers a simple case that illustrates the nature of this important problem. If we have two alleles A and *a* at a locus, the inferiority of hybrids implies that AA and *aa* have higher fitness while A*a* is selected against. In this conditions the working of reinforcement means that natural selection favors AA types that have a preference to mate only with AA types and *aa* types that have a preference to mate only with *aa* types. Thus natural selection could cause the formation of two different species. However, the force of natural selection will also act against the heterozygotes (i.e. the hybrids). Assume that *a* is a much rarer allele associated to a recent mutation. Then, *a* is likely to be eliminated by natural selection because it will tend to find itself more often in the hybrid combinations A*a*. Thus the very same natural selection forces causing reinforcement cause the loss of the rarer allele. Ridley argues that the evolutionary race between these two effects of natural selection is likely to be won by the loss of the allele. This latter effect will often be faster because it does not require any new genetic variation, whereas speciation cannot happen without genetic variation for mating preferences.

Thus, when species are not defined by the "degree of difference" but by the "absence of interbreeding," it is difficult to see how natural selection may bring about the isolation of the two species: selecting against hybrids involves selecting against the rarer allele and may bring about greater uniformity instead of new species.

Besides these theoretical difficulties, evidence does not always favor the theory of reinforcement. "A theory of speciation, therefore, can avoid a theoretical and empirical minefield if, while not excluding the possibility of reinforcement, it nevertheless does not depend on it." (Ridley 1996: 433)

If the "biological species concept" is adopted Darwin's theory of the "origin of the species by means of natural selection" must, in fact, rely on the fact that reinforcement can act in situations of sympatry . The theoretical conditions under which *sympatric speciation*[3] is possible turn out to be rather special. Sympatric speciation is possible if a species first evolves a stable polymorphism and the different types are best adapted to different niches. The stability of the polymorphism rules out the possibility that reinforcement acting to eliminate the hybrids eliminates also the less common type. Once the most difficult step – the establishment of a stable polymorphism of types best adapted to different niches – is achieved, then natural selection will favor the evolution of reproductive isolation between the two types and hence speciation (Hall 1993). In order for this process to occur "habitat selection" is crucial in two respects. In the first place habitat selection is crucial to establish the initial polymorphism whose fitness is due to the fact that different forms are best adapted to different habitats. In the second place, habitat (or host) selection is important to evolve reproductive isolation. It may be in principle possible that reproductive isolation arises as a result of a "double" (pleiotropic) effect of the gene causing the adaptation to the particular niche: the same gene also happens to cause frequent mating between individuals of the same type. However, reproductive isolation is more likely to arise because the individuals that live in the different habitats tend to mate with the other individuals living in the same habitat and are likely to evolve different mating times and habitats that may isolate their re-production from that of the other individuals.

In *parapatric speciation*, the new species emerges in a territory contiguous to the pre-existing population. In this theory we assume that a population initially existed in an area to which it was well adapted, and that it then started to expand in a contiguous area in which the environment favored a different form. Suppose that the transition between the two environments is sudden. We will have a graded series of forms (a stepped cline) at the border while a new population adapted to the new environment will tend to evolve in the new area. If the new population will diverge almost to become different species, the border will be recognized as a hybrid zone. Because of the sudden change, existing between the two environments, a stable cline will be indefinitely maintained by natural selection at their border. The stability of the cline implies that reinforcement has a long time to operate against the hybrids and allow speciation to take place.

In the case of parapatric speciation the stability of the stepped cline has the same role that the stability of the polymorphism has in the case of sympatric speciation. Both the stability of the polymorphism and that of the cline imply that natural selection will not eliminate the less numerous genes and that gene flow will be unable to merge the two populations.

The conditions under which parapatric and sympatric speciation occur are rather special. In both cases speciation must rely on a mechanism such as reinforcement that we have seen to have, in general, the tendency to eliminate the less numerous new group of individuals that should eventually speciate. It is a virtue of the theory of *allopatric speciation* that it does not depend on any of the special circumstances under which reinforcement can operate. According to this theory reproductive isolation evolves in allopatry that is after that the two populations have been separated by some geographical barrier. The Darwinian natural selection mechanism against hybrids is not a (necessary) part of the theory even if it may operate in the case in which, after having evolved only partial reproductive isolation in allopatry, the two species meet again: only in this case reinforcement may be useful to complete the partial isolation initiated in allopatric conditions (otherwise partial isolation may not be completed in sympatry).

Allopatric speciation may occur in two ways. According to the "dumb-bell" model the ancestral species may be divided into two roughly equal halves, each of one forms a new species. This model must be distinguished from another model developed by Mayr where the new species emerges in a small population isolated at the edge of the ancestral species range. This process, that is obviously a form of allopatric speciation, is now denominated by Mayr *peripatric speciation*, meaning that it happens at the periphery of the ancestral population.

Since the two populations are geographically isolated, genetic drift is by itself able to differentiate the two populations. Natural selection may also lead to differentiation as long as the two populations will follow two different evolutionary paths. Stabilizing selection may be a weaker force especially in peripherally isolated small populations where a small number of founder individuals spread a considerable amount of genes that would have been eliminated by natural selection in conditions of sympatry. Because of the elimination of the force of natural selection (acting in sympatry against the less numerous forms) allopatric conditions may favor a new type of "protected" natural selection of the population leading to speciation.

The irrelevance of the "origin of species by means of natural selection" argument is reinforced by the fact that even the "protected" natural selection occurring in allopatry may be much less important cause of speciation than "sexual selection." This argument may be better understood by elaborating on the "biological concept of species" and introducing the "recognition species concept" introduced in the literature by Hugh Paterson.

According to the classical definition introduced by Mayr "species are groups of interbreeding natural populations that are reproductively isolated from other such groups" (Mayr 1988: 318). According to Eldredge, while this definition established the primacy of reproduction as the *sine qua non* of species, "it was left to Paterson to refine the conceptualization of the nature of those reproductive communities" (Eldredge 1995: 466). Paterson defines a species as an inclusive community of individual biparental organisms which share a common fertilization system. The fertilization system includes all the components, such as courtship behavior, genital structure, or attractiveness of the ovum to the sperm or pollen, that contribute to the ultimate function of bringing about fertilization with another individual having the same fertilization system.

Paterson's definition of species allows us to understand more precisely when speciation occurs. The two species become reproductively isolated when a different fertilization system evolves. Thus, reproductive isolation does not evolve because the two species have developed two incompatible "economic relationship"[4] to the environment but it is rather a mere by-product of a change in fertilization systems. A modification of the fertilization system is both necessary and sufficient for speciation to occur.

> In other words, a great deal of economic change can accrue within a polytypic species (whether through selection, genetic drift, or other mechanism of genetic change) without reproductive isolation necessarily following. The converse is also true as we know from numerous examples of "sibling" species, reproductive isolation can exist between two closely related species that are hardly to be distinguished on the basis of external, economic phenotypic attributes.
>
> (Eldredge 1995: 467–8)

Sexual selection involves such striking runaway effects such as the growth of the peacock tail that have no, or even a negative, "economic" value for the species in terms of its successful adaptation to the environment. This selection for continued mate recognition can lead to a divergence of the fertilization system – such divergence having nothing to do with successful adaptations to the environment. At the same time it has been argued that "the function of courtship in sexually reproducing animals is to facilitate syngamy, and hence the male-female communication system is subject to strong stabilizing selection. Unusual or fussy individuals (whether male or female) will be at a disadvantage, because they reject suitable mates or are themselves rejected." (Spencer and Masters 1992: 301).

It remains an open issue whether different sexual preferences develop as a consequence of "protected" natural or sexual selection. What is relevant for our argument is simply that in both cases the differentiation of sexual preferences and, in general, reproductive isolation, is likely to require allopatric conditions or, in other words, a protection from rather than the working of selection.

2.4 Stasis and epistatic interactions

Chapter 9 of *The Origin of Species* was "On the Imperfection of the Geological Record." Ever since Darwin this "imperfection" has been used to conciliate the missing steps of phylogeny with the gradual nature of the adaptation predicted by the Darwinian theory.

The allopatric theory of speciation has also the virtue that it can explain the incompleteness of the fossil records without justifying the absence of intermediate populations with the fact that some intermediate populations were not able to leave a fossil for our paleontological research.

What looks in the main territory of the ancestral species an incompleteness of the fossil record and could be interpreted as a "saltation" of intermediate evolutionary events, may be due to the fact that the evolutionary process leading to speciation has occurred far away in an isolated periphery. The new species has only later re-penetrated the main territory of the ancestral species and, for this reason, this appears to be substituted by a population showing a substantial phenetic jump.

In other words, the theory of allopatric speciation seems to provide an explanation for the long period of stasis and the "apparent jumps" – or in one word the "punctuated equilibria" – that characterize natural history.

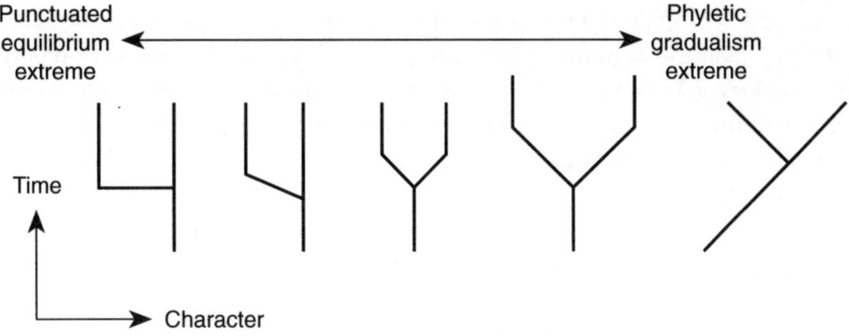

Figure 2.1

The theory of punctuated equilibria developed by Eldredge and Gould (1972) implies that most evolutionary change is associated to speciation events. However, the argument is not incompatible with the idea that gradual intra-specific events may take place while the members of a species try to adapt to environmental change and co-evolve with other species In this sense according to Turner (1995: 65) "Efforts to demonstrate that evolution is gradual by producing evidence for slow change in one or other character of a species in the fossil record simply say nothing about the deployment of speciation." In this sense "phyletic gradualism" does not make sense for the simple fact that speciation involves always a moment of discontinuity related to the break-down of a common fertilization system between two populations. The crucial distinction is not between the evolutionary speeds of speciation and within-species change, but between the different mechanisms entailed by these two types of changes. By contrast the hypothesis that within-species events do also characterize evolution can be easily compromised with the hypothesis of punctuated equilibria. In this last respect punctuated equilibrium and phyletic gradualism can be seen as extremes of a continuum as it is shown in the following Figure 2.1 taken from Ridley (1996: 562).

Even if gradual intra-specific events are not incompatible with the theory of punctuated equilibria, one important aim of the theory is to explain why, after rapid changes related to speciation events, long period of stasis characterize the history of species. This explanation is related to an "holistic"[5] view of the genotype that claims that "much of macroevolution cannot be explained by atomistic genes replacements or by selection pressures on single genes, but only by a more drastic reorganization, made possible by loosening the tight genetic cohesion of the genotype found throughout widespread populous species." (Mayr 1988: 471)

The "holistic" view of the gene focuses its attention on the epistatic interactions characterizing the genotype. Epistatic interactions are the synergistic effect on the phenotype of two or more gene loci, whereby their joint effect differs from the sum of the loci taken separately. Or, to use a term familiar to economists, the holistic view focuses on the "complementarities" existing between different gene loci implying that each part makes a fitness contribution depending upon that part and the other parts with which it has epistatic interactions.

Even when "complementary" mutations could improve the fitness of the genotype, the epistatic interactions among the gene loci imply that the genotype is characterized by a built in inertia.[6] Evolution is characterized by a succession of single mutations and natural selection eliminates those genotypes that make only one of the two complementary changes required to improve the outcome of epistatic relations.

If natural selection has been acting for sufficient time each allele is likely to be optimally adjusted to the other alleles with whom it has epistatic relations. Thus, in these conditions, single mutations are likely to lower fitness and be eliminated by "normalizing" (stabilizing) selection that acts to keep the species at a "local" fitness peak. Thus, because of epistatic relations, long period of stasis may characterize evolution.

Allopatric conditions sterilize the forces of natural selection that, together with gene flow, act to keep the "integrity" of the species. In allopatric theory speciation may occur in small isolated populations.[7] In this situations the genes of isolated founders, who change only one of the two "complementary" alleles, are not promptly eliminated by natural selection. Thus, the "exploration" of a new fitness peak, characterized by different epistatic relations, becomes possible: the "founder effect," that is typical of isolated peripheries, may break previously existing "epistatic relations" and allow the formation of a new population. When and if the two populations meet again reproductive isolation may result from the fact that hybrids have inferior epistatic interactions that may imply the impossibility or the gradual elimination of hybrids. The new species may, then, co-exist with the ancestral population. Alternatively, if it occupies the same ecological niche, the new species may displace and replace its ancestor.

The role that allopatric conditions have in punctuating long period of stasis and favoring speciation implies that the evolution of life has required some balance between the forces of natural selection and the "temporary" protection of mutants to allow them to explore new fitness peaks. A similar conclusion is reached by Stuart A. Kauffman who develops the intuition that epistatic interactions are the crucial factor for the understanding of the evolution and the co-evolution of the different species.

Kauffman's (1993) *NK* model of rugged fitness landscapes considers a model of epistatic interactions where N is the total number of parts and the fitness of each part depends upon that part and upon K parts of the N. The relatively rugged or smooth nature of fitness landscapes is defined by its "correlation structure" or the degree of similarity of the fitness value of one-mutant neighbor. In a smooth landscape knowing the fitness value of one point carries a lot of information about the other points because neighboring points in the space have nearly the same fitness value. By contrast in a maximally rugged landscape carries no information about the fitness of neighboring points because fitness values are entirely uncorrelated. Kauffman shows that in the *NK* model tuning the K parameter from 0 to $N-1$ increases the ruggedness of the landscape in a controlled manner. In other words, increasing the richness of epistatic interactions among the components of the system changes the landscape from the $K = O$ case where it is single-peaked and smooth to the $K = N - 1$ case where it becomes fully random.

When $K = 0$ and there are no epistatic interaction, the fitness of a mutant neighbor can only differ by the amount of the independent fitness contribution of an allele in a different locus. This implies that the landscape is smooth carrying maximum information about neighboring points. Any genotype can be sequentially changed via fitter one-mutant variants to the global optimum and no local optimum exists.

When $K = N - 1$ and the richness of epistatic interactions is maximum, the fitness of a mutant neighbor does not only differ by fitness contribution of the altered allele but affects also the fitness contribution of all the other genes. For this reason the fitness value of a genotype is entirely uncorrelated with that of a mutant neighbor. The landscape is maximally rugged carrying no information about neighboring points and sequential changes via fitter one-mutant variants can only lead to one of the many local optima.

In general as K increases from 0 to $N - 1$, fitness landscapes change from smooth to fully uncorrelated landscapes through a family of rugged landscapes. In rugged landscapes many local optima exist and this poses the problem of the existence of a trade-off between evolvability and sustained fitness. At sufficient low mutations rates natural selection will induce the population to climb the nearest fitness peaks and remain clustered about one or the other of these peaks; thus sustained fitness will be sacrificed. By contrast at sufficient high mutation rates the low fitness valleys will be passed and new peaks be explored but natural selection will be unable to accumulate heritable information beyond the coherence of walks due to founder effects; thus in this case evolvability is sacrificed. In other words at low mutation rates population becomes trapped on poor local peaks while at high mutation rates populations are driven far below the peaks in fitness lowlands. A delicate intermediate rate of mutation, where populations are just beginning to "melt" and come down from the peaks, could allow natural selection to optimize both evolvability and sustained fitness.

However stasis at a local peak is likely to be a normal state for parts of organisms characterized by complex epistatic interactions. These parts of the genotype are somehow "frozen" by epistatic interactions and provide an explanation for one important puzzle about stasis: while it is normally accounted for as normalizing selection which holds a phenotype at the optimum in a stable environment, the latter cannot be stable if other species are co-evolving in the same niche. Kauffman's solution of the puzzle is that frozen components imply that "species within or on the boundaries of such components have an unchanging optimal genotype and phenotype, despite changes in some of their coevolutionary partners. Thus familiar normalizing selection *can* sustain the phenotype in stasis despite changes in the niche" (Kauffman 1993: 270).

Kauffman's contribution clarifies how natural selection may contribute to the stasis of species by inhibiting the exploration of new peaks. Natural selection helps adaptation when improvements only require one by one sequential changes, but may well inhibit those changes that are such that involve that a single change lowers fitness if it is not accompanied by a complementary changes. If speciation is characterized by the inferiority of hybrids with the ancestral species, the (future) hybrid combination is a fitness valley that is hard to overcome in the presence of tight natural selection.

Even if a fast rate of mutations allows some genotypes to survive the fitness valley between the old and new peak, the selection against hybrids (or reinforcement) may not separate the two species. It may rather imply the elimination of the few mutant alleles that are likely to find themselves more often in the inferior hybrid combinations.

While selection may stabilize the parts of the genotype frozen by epistatic interactions, it can help the diffusion of those fitter one-mutant variant that stabilizing intra-specific events. However, this may help to stabilize even more the "frozen parts" of those species that happen to be more numerous and can have a higher number of one-mutant variations in the "non-frozen" parts of the genotype. Darwin himself pointed out how more numerous species would not only show greater fitness because they were less liable to accidental extermination but also because "these from existing in greater numbers will, in the aggregate, present more variation, and thus be improved through natural selection and gain further advantages" (Darwin 1859[1968]: 211).

2.5 The speciation of organizational models

Are the biological debates concerning stasis and speciation relevant to the understanding of the origin of organizational species?

A positive answer to these question might be based on the observation that the history of organizational species also seems to be characterized by those long period of stasis and allopatric speciations that occur in natural history. I will try to develop these points in the following sections whereas in this section I will be concerned with some particular theoretical reasons for which organizational species may share the same laws of "structure and change" that characterize natural species.

A simple definition of an organization of production can be based on two factors. The first is its technology and, in particular, the technological characteristics of the resources used in production. The second is the set of rights (which may be legal rights and/or customary rights supported by social norms) on the resources employed in the organization and on the organization itself.

The relationship between these two factors has traditionally been a controversial issue in social sciences: if causation exists, it can go both ways. On the one hand property rights can be seen as factors shaping the nature and the characteristics of the resources used in production. On the other hand, the technological characteristics of resources employed in production can be considered to be the cause of changes in the system of property rights.

This two-way relationship was at the very root of the Marxian theory of history and of his view of the firm. It was the source of interesting problems and contradictions within this theory. Marxist analysis has often oscillated between "technological determinism" (technology invariably gives rise to a unique set of property rights) and "property rights romanticism" (alternative property rights can invariably bring about an alternative technology).[8] Moreover, as Hirschman (1981) observes, Marx "oscillated between the grand generalization with which to stabilizing an entire epoch or process and the discriminating analysis of events which made differences between countries and subperiods stand out in richly textured detail."

In spite of these contradictions and limitations the two ways relationship considered by Marx has not ceased to be an important key for the understanding of alternative organizations and it is difficult to disagree with John Hicks when he maintains that when we come to "theories of history" "there is so little in the way of an alternative vision which is available" (Hicks 1969: 3).

The relationship between property rights and the characteristics of productive forces, which created so many interesting problems and contradictions (as well as so many wrong "predictions") in the Marxian approach became a non-issue in neoclassical theory. In a market economy workers' or capitalists' ownership would have had no effect on the characteristics of the resources (or of the productive forces) employed by the firm. At the same time, the characteristics of the resources employed in the firm had no implication whatever on the form of ownership which was going to characterize the firm.

This point of view was well expressed by Samuelson when he argued that "In a perfectly competitive economy it doesn't really matter who hires whom. . . ." (1957: 894) – a statement that contained the double implication that, while the nature of property rights has no implication on the choice of "optimal" technology, the latter does not involve that particular owners are better suited to its management.

Recently, both New Institutional and Radical Economists have re-considered the interaction between rights and technology. However, the relationship between rights and technology is still very controversial. In these two streams of literature the direction of causality runs in opposite directions. In New Institutional economics rights are endogenously and efficiently determined by the characteristics of the resources employed by the organizations:[9] namely their degree of specificity and their monitoring requirements. By contrast, in the Radical Literature the characteristics of the resources employed in the firm are in turn determined by the rights which owners of different factors have on the organization.[10]

In spite of their differences the lines of inquiries of New Institutional and Radicals are not necessarily incompatible and they can be integrated in a framework that considers the two-ways relationship between property rights and technology.

The "Radical direction"[11] of causation runs from property rights to technology. It is argued that the specificity and monitoring characteristics of the resources are due to the nature of property rights under which they are employed. For instance, individuals working in organizations where they do not have rights are likely to be characterized by a relative underinvestment in organization specific skills and by an unfavorable distribution of asymmetric information attributes that makes them "easy to monitor." Specific and difficult to monitor workers are high-agency-cost resources that are expensive for the present owner who have an incentive to substitute them with low-agency-cost resources. By contrast, no similar substitution occurs for the individuals having rights on the organization: the alignment of their objectives with that of the organization allows a considerable saving of the high agency costs that would have been paid if they were employed by other agents.

When we leave the neo-classical world with zero agency costs, the "radical direction" of causation can be justified by using a fundamental principle of economic theory: that profit-maximizing employers tend to replace high cost factors with low cost factors. This point becomes evident when one considers that a change in property rights from one factor to the other changes also the relative costs of employing these factors. The new owning factors will save on their own agency costs while they will pay the agency costs of employing the former owning factors (while this cost was saved in the former ownership arrangement). Thus the simple profit-maximizing principle allows us to state there is an influence of property rights on the combinations of productive forces that is going adopted in the precise sense that the optimal technology changes with a change in property rights.

The "New Institutionalist" direction[12] of causality, running from the nature of technology to property rights, can also be easily understood by using another fundamental principle of economic theory: that, like other economic goods, organizations tend to be owned by those individuals in the hands of which they are more valuable. This implies that for each combination of resources employed in production property rights should go those individuals that can save the most on agency costs when they own the organization: these are the most difficult to monitor and specific factors that is to the high-agency-cost factors that involve higher agency costs when they are employed by other people. Thus for each combination of resources employed by the organization there is an optimal assignment of the ownership rights on the organization.

Thus in a world of positive agency costs there is an optimal technology for given ownership rights on the organization and an optimal set of ownership rights for a given technology that is employed by the organization. Using the biological terminology we could say that organizations are characterized by epistatic interactions between rights and technology – an observation that suggests that many of the "laws of structure and change" that stabilizing the origin of natural species may be also relevant for that of "organizational species."

Like the "frozen part" of a genotype the interactions between technology and property rights has a "built-in" inertia. Pagano (1991, 1992) and Pagano and Rowthorn (1994, 1996) have tried to capture this point by introducing the concept of organizational equilibrium and investigating the characteristics of "institutional stability" that stabilizing these equilibria in the framework of simple two factors model.

An organizational equilibrium is defined by the fact that technology is optimal relative to property rights and property rights are optimal given the technology that is employed. The self-sustaining[13] characteristic of organizational equilibria comes from the fact that owning factors saving on their own agency costs tend to choose a technology characterized by high intensity of their own high-agency-cost factors – that is a technology under which their ownership is optimal.

The analogy between the epistatic relations characterizing natural species and the characteristics defining an organizational equilibrium have, of course, to be taken with some caution. Human learning may allow patterns that are not permitted to genes. On the other hand the concept of organizational equilibria entails already a considerable degree of rationality. The optimality of technology given property rights and that of property rights given technology defines a "Nash equilibrium"; it is tantamount to assuming that "financiers" are able to choose the optimal owners for each firm characterized by a certain given technology and that "production managers" are able to choose the optimal technology for a certain given ownership structure. Indeed, it is reasonable to assume that this equilibrium is rather achieved by an evolutionary process by which firms that have sub-optimal technologies given the ownership structure as well as those that have sub-optimal ownership structures given technology are gradually eliminated by competitive forces.[14]

The analogy between organizational equilibria and natural species turns out to be useful to explore the issue of the characteristics of the organizational models that come into existence as a result of the working of competition. In particular, we may ask the following question: "Does competition entail the selection of efficient organizational models?"

Indeed, the analogy with natural species may even help to clarify the meaning of this problem. In natural selection the pressure of competition helps to select the best members of a given species; however, we have seen that the effects of natural selection on speciation are much more controversial. Our question is related to the case of speciation: we are not asking whether competition can select the best member of a given species of organizations but whether it can help the formation of a new more efficient species of organization characterized by different technology-property rights "genotypes."

We have seen that epistatic interactions imply that each species is characterized by important "development constraints": the fitness of each mutation is constrained by the other characteristics of the species. This implies that many evolutionary paths may be blocked. Unfortunately, in the case of organizational equilibria these obstacles may work exactly against those changes that may otherwise lead to the formation of a superior species of organization. Suppose that there are some efficient alternative potential owners that could get a higher ownership rent than the present owners. These alternative owners are efficient because their employment by the present owners involves very high agency costs that could be saved if they own the organization. For this reason, the factors of the potential alternative owners are promptly replaced by factors that are cheaper for the present owners. In other words, an "anti-speciation" mechanism is embodied in each "species" of organizational equilibrium and it has the unfortunate characteristic that its strength is related to the efficiency of the alternative potential species.[15]

However, suppose that this "anti-speciation" factor is overcome and one of the characteristics of the old species mutates into one characterizing also a potential more efficient new species of organization. For instance, some organizations are characterized by new property rights that, if were coupled with the associated optimal new technology, could form a new more efficient organizational equilibrium. Until this new technological combination is developed and employed, we will have a situation of organizational disequilibrium or, in other words, an inferior hybrid between the new property rights and the old technology. If the pressure of competition by the members of the old species is strong, the hybrid is likely to be wiped out before it has any chance of turning into the new superior species. Or, in other words, the epistatic interactions between property rights and technology imply the existence of rugged multi-peaked fitness landscape; in these conditions the pressure of competition will act to keep the firms at the local peaks.

However, even if speciation is successful, the survival of the new species can endangered by a strong competition by many members of the old species.

In the first place, if there are few members of the new organizational species, "interbreeding" with the many members of the old species will be very frequent and will produce numerous inferior hybrids. In these conditions "interbreeding" may lead to the extinction of both mutations. When the new technology is imitated and run under the old property right system it turns out to be inferior and, vice versa, when the new rights are influenced by the old technology they also turn out to be inferior. Hybrid organizations that have imitated only one aspect of the new species will be doomed to fail and the new mutation may tend to disappear with them.

Second, in nature, the efficiency of each species depends on its frequency. Organizations also share the same characteristic. For instance, network externalities in property rights and in technologies may imply that few firms characterized by different organizational equilibria are not viable: they would be outcompeted by firms that, even if inferior when they exist with the same frequency, can better benefit from network externalities because of their present large number.

Third, as Darwin pointed out more numerous species may enjoy more mutations. Also organizations that are more numerous will share this advantage for the non-frozen part of their characteristics. Even if few organizations have succeeded speciating they may find hard to compete with the innovations of the more numerous species.

These considerations imply that, while many characteristics of organizations evolve and co-evolve with other institutions, some important aspects of property rights and technology may be characterized by long periods of stasis.

If the analogies with the origin of species may be pushed even further we should expect that while competition favors the selection of the best members of a given organizational species, it may inhibit the formation of new species. In other words we should expect that the formation of new species does not happen in sympatry but it is more likely to occur under allopatric conditions or, in general under conditions, where the members of the new species could somehow be protected from the competition of the members of the old species. Alternatively, institutional and technological shocks should be strong enough to overcome the inertia built in the epistatic relations characterizing rights and technology.

2.6 British organizational stasis and the "allopatric speciation" of managerial capitalism

In the last half of the nineteenth century "came into being a new economic institution the managerial business enterprise, and a new subspecies of economic man, the salaried manager. With their coming, the world received a new type of capitalism – one in which the decisions about current operations, employment, output, and the allocation of resources for future operations were made by salaried managers who were not owners of the enterprise" (Chandler 1990: 2).

According to Chandler, the advent of the new institutions and the "new subspecies" of economic man were strictly related to the building and operating of the rail and telegraph systems. The complexities of their operations required firm-specific organizational capabilities that could have not been developed within the members of the family owning the firm nor efficiently monitored and controlled by them. The new firms required a managerial hierarchy where to a great extent salaried managers controlled other managers. In other words the new technology required the employment of "high-agency-cost" managerial skills. In turn, this required that rights, incentives and safeguards were to be given to these managers. In particular it was vitally important for managerial effort as well as for the efficiency of the firm to know that promotions from the low to the high positions of the managerial hierarchy would be related to their achievements and unrelated to family and other social ties.

The new system came first into being in the rail and telegraph industry but it showed greater efficiency in many of the industries characterized by economies and scale and scope that could be efficiently be exploited by the use of managerial hierarchies. Indeed, the diffusion of the new organizational model characterized the coming of a new species of capitalism: "managerial capitalism." The new species had two local varieties "competitive managerial capitalism" in the U.S. and "cooperative managerial capitalism" in Germany. While in German industries family control lasted longer that in the United States, in both countries salaried managers with little or no equity in the enterprises for which they worked, participated in making decisions concerning current production and distribution, as well as in planning and allocating resources for future production. "The greatest difference, however, came in interfirm and intrafirm relationships" (Chandler 1990: 395). In the United States the new managerial firms competed aggressively for market share and profits and the anti-monopolist legislation reflected a shared belief in the value of competition. By contrast, in Germany many firms preferred to cooperate and trade associations played a much larger role in the Germany than in United States.

While the coming of these two sub-species of managerial capitalism made the U.S. and Germany the two most important actors of the second industrial revolution, Britain – the main actor of the first industrial revolution – became a late industrializer in many of the new industries. In Britain the commitment to the "species" of personal capitalism, that had been so successful at the time of the first industrial revolution, continued. While long- term profits based on long-term growth were a goal on which the managers and the major investors of the American and German managerial firms could agree, the families owning the British firms often preferred to pay out earning in dividends rather than using them to make the extensive investments required to move into foreign markets or to develop new products in related industries. "Because their firms grew slowly and because they hired only a small numbers of managers, the founders and their families remained influential in the affairs of the enterprise and so affected dividend policy" (Chandler 1990: 595). By contrast, the long-term growth of American Firms helped the managers to gain strong job rights in their firms. "Such a goal not only helped to assure tenure for the senior executives, but it also enhanced the opportunity for advancement for the more junior managers" (Chandler 1990: 595). British firm did not provide similar opportunities to non-owning managers. The key managerial positions were usually reserved for the owning family. Social and family ties were more important than competence to advance in managerial ladder. There were few opportunities for junior managers while no job security similar to those of German and American firms could be given to senior executives. It is hardly surprising that organizational capabilities that were so important for the firms of the second industrial revolution stagnated. As a result, Britain lost the world economic leadership to the countries that had "speciated" the new form of managerial capitalism.

Using the terminology of the preceding sections the coming of competitive and cooperative managerial capitalism can be seen as a form of "allopatric" speciation. The speciation did not occur in Britain, where the competition and strength of personal capitalism was the strongest, but in countries that had not participated to the first industrial revolution and had not build any form of personal capitalism as well developed as that which characterized Britain. In the U.S. and Germany the nature of productive forces required by railways and telegraph changed first the structure of rights that characterized these sectors and after few years that of the other industries where the growth of productive forces could benefit from the change. Soon, the new rights favored the widespread employment of "specific" "difficult to monitor" (and, therefore, high-agency-cost) managers while their employment had a self-reinforcement feed-back making the new rights of managerial capitalism an irreversible choice.

The U.S. and Germany saw the speciation of new organizational equilibria where the managerial rights and managerial skills were a fundamental characteristic of new "epistatic interactions" between relations of production and productive forces. On the one hand, given tenure rights for senior executives and fair promotion opportunities for junior managers, productive forces were best characterized by a relative high intensity of high-agency-cost managerial skills. On the other hand, given the employment of these skills, only a system of strong of managerial rights could ensure the commitment of managers to the organizations and save the high agency costs that should have otherwise been paid in case of a pronounced incongruence of their goals with those of the organization.

By contrast, in Britain the "epistatic relations" between the structure of rights and the nature of productive forces were not broken by the second industrial revolution. By that time the managerial skills accumulated by the British families had already made some of their members high-agency-cost factors. This reinforced the stability of their ownership rights: only under their ownership could their own high agency costs be saved. In turn these ownership arrangements had a feed-back on technology involving the continuation of the intensive employment of the high-agency-cost skills of the owning family members. In this framework, in spite of the environmental changes no tendency to "sympatric" speciation of managerial capitalism came about. In fact the vicious circle characterizing managerial skills and rights mirrored the self-reinforcing interactions that we have just considered. Since managers were not involved in the organization their agency costs could not be saved like those of the committed family members; for this reason the former were often substituted by the latter, but this damaged the managers' commitment to the organization and their accumulation of organizational skills even more. At the same time, the low intensity of high-agency-cost managerial skills implied that the (partial) saving of these agency costs (that would have occurred under managerial capitalism) could not favorably compare with the saving of agency costs of family members (that characterized British personal capitalism).

Thus, in spite of the technological shocks induced by the second industrial revolution, the "frozen part" of the genotype of the British firms did not melt. The fairly strong competition that characterized the British environment had not the effect of favoring a new species of capitalism but it acted as a normalizing selection that favored the organizational "stasis" of British capitalism. Organizational change was inhibited by the same laws of structure and change that make sympatric speciation so difficult in natural history. The inferiority of hybrids was, perhaps, again the crucial problem: a high intensity of high-agency-cost managerial skills coupled with the property rights of personal capitalism was situtated in a "fitness valley" that was too difficult to overcome under strong competitive pressure. The forces of competition favored the selection of the best members of the British species of personal capitalism but inhibited the speciation of managerial capitalism. Allopatric conditions, where the competitive pressure of "personal capitalism" was weaker, were required for the coming of the new species of capitalism.[16] In this respect the glorious contributions of Britain to the achievement of the first industrial revolution became a paradoxical disadvantage for the further development of its economy.

2.7 Conclusion

Sidney Winter has observed how biological analogies have been often used to justify the efficiency claims of neo-classical economics.

> Under competitive conditions a business firm must maximize profit if it is to survive – or so it is often claimed. This purported analogue of biological natural selection has had substantial influence in economic thinking, and the proposition remains influential today.In general, its role has been to serve

> as informal auxiliary defense, or crutch, for standard theoretical approaches based on optimization and equilibrium.
>
> (Winter 1987: 545)

With reference to New Institutional Economics a similar point has been made by Geoff Hodgson (1996) who has shown how often Williamson uses evolutionary thinking to justify the use of efficiency as a positive principle.

These uses of biological analogies are hardly surprising. The traffic of metaphors between economics and biology has gone both ways since the very beginning of the two subjects and, indeed, political economy had a considerable influence on the early development of the theory of evolution.[17] However, the influence of modern biology on economics should, perhaps, go some way to help understand some of the limitations of competition: while competition has a fundamental role in promoting gradual change, it may help "freezing" some relations between rights and technology and be a cause of organizational stasis. In a world that too often praises the advantages of global competition "the common rule of structure and change" would rather suggest that the allopatric protection from competition played also an important role in the formation of new and, some times, fitter organizational species. More generally, biological debates should help us understanding why, in spite of some common legal forms of a market economy,[18] we have a considerable diversity of species of capitalism and their histories are characterized by fast change and long periods of organizational stasis.

Appendix

We assume the existence of a standard production function $Q\ (k, K, l, L)$ such that the output Q can be produced with different combinations of low-agency-cost capital and labor (k, l) and high-agency-cost capital and labor (K, L). $Q(\cdot)$ can be interpreted as a "long-run" production function. Thus, the substitution effects induced by property rights are not immediate and it is possible to have short run mismatches between property rights and the associated technology.

We assume that when workers own the organization they pay an additional agency cost Z in order to employ a unit of difficult-to-monitor or specific capital K – a cost that is saved when K is employed under capitalist ownership . By contrast, when the capitalists own the organization, they pay an additional agency cost H when they employ a unit of difficult-to-monitor or specific labor L – a cost that is saved when L is employed under labor ownership. No such additional costs are paid for easy-to-monitor and general purpose labor and capital k and l when they are employed by either capitalists or workers.

We denote by r and w the prices of respectively easy-to-monitor and/or general capital and labor and by R and L the prices (net of agency costs) of respectively difficult-to-monitor and/or specific capital and labor. We also set the price of output equal to 1. Thus, we can formulate our "Radical assumption" as follows:

Radical assumption: Under capitalist ownership firms maximize profits equal to:

$$R^c = Q(k,K,l,L) - [rk + RK + wl + (H+W)L] \tag{2.1}$$

Under labor ownership firms maximize profits equal to

$$R^L = Q(k,K,l,L) - [rk + RK + ((Z+R)K + wl + WL] \tag{2.2}$$

This way of formalizing the "radical assumption" makes it very clear why property rights influence technology in a way similar to changes in relative prices: for instance, the relative prices of the high-agency-cost factors are $(H+W)/R$ under capitalist ownership and $W/(Z+R)$ under workers' ownership. Thus, under standard assumptions, the intensity of high-agency-cost capital relatively to the intensity of high-agency-cost labor is higher under capitalist ownership than under labor ownership. Observe that in this framework, the value of the elasticity of substitution among factors becomes a measure of the "strength" of the effects of changes of property rights on the nature of the technology.

We have seen that the "New Institutionalist assumption" runs in the opposite direction to that of the "Radical assumption"; taking as given a certain technology, the firm is supposed to be owned by that factor which can earn the highest ownership rent. This rent is equal to the difference between the cost of employing the factor in a firm that is property of the owners of the factor and the cost of employing it in a firm that is property of other owners.

New Institutional assumption:

For any given combination of factors employed in the firm, ownership of the firm will be acquired by the factor which can get the highest ownership rent. Therefore: capitalist property rights can prevail if, given the factors currently employed, $R^c \geq R^L$ or, alternatively,

$$ZK - HL \geq 0 \tag{2.3}$$

workers' property rights can prevail if, given the factors currently employed, $R^L \geq R^c$, or alternatively,

$$HL - ZK \geq 0 \tag{2.4}$$

Conditions defining organizational equilibria

There will be a capitalist organizational equilibrium (COE) if there is a technology that maximizes (2.1) and satisfies (2.3) and there will be a labor organizational equilibrium (LOE) if there is a technology that optimize (2.2) and satisfies (2.4). Let:

$$(k^c, K^c, l^c, L^c) = \text{argmax} R^c(k,K,l,L) \tag{2.5}$$

$$(k^L, K^L, l^L, L^L = \text{argmax} R^L(k,K,l,L) \tag{2.6}$$

Then a firm will be in *a capitalist organizational equilibrium* (COE) if:

$$ZK^c - HL^c \geq 0 \tag{2.7}$$

and in *a labor organizational equilibrium* (LOE) if:

$$HL^L - ZK^L \geq 0 \tag{2.8}$$

Condition (2.7) has an immediate intuitive meaning. Suppose that a firm is under capitalist ownership and the technique of production is such as to favoring profits. Condition (2.7) implies that, *with this technique*, the ownership rent occurring to capitalists is at least as great as the rent which workers could obtain if they owned the firm. Hence, *with this technique of production*, the workers would have no incentive to buy out the capitalists. This is what is meant by a capitalist organizational equilibrium. Condition (2.8) has an analogous intuitive meaning. The conditions for COE and LOE can also be written in the following equivalent ways:

$$K^c/L^c \geq H/Z \tag{2.7$'$}$$

$$K^L/L^L \leq H/Z \tag{2.8$'$}$$

Conditions (2.7′) and (2.8′) have also an intuitive meaning. Observe that K/L is the ratio of high-agency-cost (H-A-C) capital to H-A-C labor or *the H-A-C capital intensity*; observe also that H/Z is the *agency cost ratio* between the capitalist's extra-cost in employing H-A-C labor and labor's extra-cost in employing H-A-C capital. Thus (2.7′) means that a COE is feasible when the intensity of H-A-C-capital is greater than the agency cost ratio and (2.8′) means that a LOE is feasible when the intensity of H-A-C capital is lower than the agency cost ratio. For instance, high agency costs per unit of labor could be compensated by the employment of a great amount of H-A-C capital and make it feasible a COE.

Under standard assumptions, the high-agency-cost capital intensity will be higher under capitalist ownership or:

$$K^c/L^c \geq K^L/L^L \tag{2.9}$$

The value of the agency cost ratio H/Z either falls in the interval defined by these two values or outside it.

Let us first consider the case in which it falls in this interval. In this case H/Z is such that:

$$K^c/L^c \geq H/Z \geq K^L/L^L \tag{2.10}$$

Then both (2.7′) and (2.8′) are satisfied and we have multiple (capitalist and labor) organizational equilibria.

Consider now the cases in which H/Z does not fall in this interval.

H/Z may be smaller than the high-agency-cost capital intensities. Or:

$$K^c/L^c \geq K^L/L^L > H/Z \tag{2.11}$$

Then (7′) is satisfied but (8′) is not satisfied. In this case only a COE exists.

By contrast, if H/Z is such that:

$$H/Z > K^c/L^c \geq K^L/L^L \tag{2.12}$$

(8′) is satisfied but (7′) is not satisfied. In this case only a LOE exists.

Observe that since the ratio H/Z must necessarily fall in one of the three intervals considered above, for any H/Z ratio at least one organizational equilibrium must always exist.

We can visualize the three possibilities considered above in the following. For H/Z that goes from zero to infinity we have first unique COE equilibria, then multiple equilibria and, finally, LOE unique equilibria.

$$0 - -\text{COE} - -K^L/L^L - -\text{COE} + \text{LOE} - -K^c/L^c - -\text{LOE} - - \rightarrow \infty$$

This "assumes" a certain value of the elasticity of substitution and it can give us some intuition of the effects of its changes. An increase in the elasticity of substitution widens the values of the agency cost ratio for which multiple equilibria exist. It moves K^L/L^L leftwards and K^c/L^c towards the right widening the interval of multiple equilibria defined by them. Within this interval any initial set of property rights will induce technologies such that their interaction will define organizational equilibria. Thus, an increase of the elasticity of substitution widens the interval where property rights can shape technologies in a self-sustaining manner and increases the probability that an organizational equilibrium will stay such after an exogenous shock to agency costs (i.e. increases "institutional stability)." Because of the "Radical assumption," the higher the elasticity of substitution the more powerful the effects of ownership on technology .

Acknowledgments

I am grateful for useful comments to Antonio Nicita, John Earle, Frank Hahn, the participants to the Siena Summer School on Economic and Evolution and to an anonymous referee of the CBR Working Paper Series. The support from the ACE-PHARE Research Project P96-6053-R is gratefully acknowledged.

Notes

1 We will see that another relevant explanation of the "integrity of the species" is given by the forces of "natural selection" themselves.

2 The complete title of Darwin's masterpiece – *The Origin of Species by the Means of Natural Selection or the Preservation of Favoured Races in the Struggle for Life* synthesizes the main target of his research programme.

3 Models of sympatric speciation have been elaborated by Maynard Smith (1966) and Seger (1985).

4 On the relationship between "economic" and "reproductive" activity see Eldredge (1996).

5 This holistic view has been extended by Wilson and Sober (1994) who have argued that natural selection operates on a nested hierarchy of units and it is not incompatible

with group selection. As far as the fate of each gene is linked to the fate of the other genes, it cannot do anything better than maximizing the fitness of phenotype or of the other relevant vehicles of selection. The selection of the genotype is one form of group selection but also "higher" forms of group selection are possible insofar as the group is the relevant vehicle of selection.

6 Comparing the genotype to a team of rowers Dawkins claims that "It is the 'team' that evolves. Other teams might have done the job just as well, or even better. But once one team has started to dominate the gene pool of a species it thereby has an automatic advantage. It is difficult for a minority team to break in, even if a minority team which would, in the end, have done the job more efficiently. The majority team has an automatic resistance to being displaced, simply by virtue of being the majority. This doesn't mean that the majority team can never be displaced. If it couldn't, evolution would grind to an halt. But it does mean that there is a kind of built-in inertia" (Dawkins, 1988: 171–2). Sober (1984) introduces explicitly the role of epistatic reactions in Dawkins rowing example and observes that they occur when a rower's superiority in a certain position depends on which rower is occupying another position. However it is important to point our that in natural selection genes can also compete against themselves in different combinations because the object of selections is gene-kinds, not gene-instances. In natural selection the coach is like "a mad scientist who clones his favorite rowers and makes them race against each other in all combinations" (Sober 1984: 307).

7 According to the Nobel laureate John C. Eccles an important episode of our own pre-human "recent" natural history can be characterized in terms of allopatric speciation and punctuated equilibria. "Despite the very extensive distribution of *Dryopithecus* – Hungary, Greece, Turkey, India, Kenya – the next stages of hominid evolution were restricted to Africa, both the Australopithecines and *Homo habilis*. It can be asked why only the African Dryopithecines participated in the evolutionary line to *Homo*? I believe that the origin of Australopithecines represented a unique evolutionary transformation such as it is postulated by Eldredge and Gould (1972) in their punctuated equilibria. It was likely therefore to be unique to a small isolated population. The reminder of the Dryopithecines went on to eventual extinction" (Eccles 1989: 12).

8 Marx contains both types of elements and is not often able to find the right balance between them. Marxists have given different importance to the "primacy" of the productive forces or to the influence of property rights on technology. For instance Cohen (1978) defends this "primacy" whereas Brenner (1986) criticizes it. Roemer (1988) offers an useful survey of both.

9 Nelson (1994: 28) observes that New Institutional Economics has been characterized by "a broad theoretical stance that somehow, institutions changed optimally (if perhaps with a lag) in response to changes in economic circumstances that called for those changes. However he points out how some New Institutionalists have abandoned the assumption of optimality of institutional response and analyzed the interest-group conflict often involved in public responses.

10 A formalization of the New Institutional and Radical assumptions is contained in the appendix to this chapter.

11 See, for instance, Bowles (1985 and 1989) and Braverman (1974).

12 Alchian and Demsetz (1972) and Williamson (1985) are, perhaps, the two canonical examples.

13 This self-sustaining ability of property rights depends on their capacity to shape the technology in a self-sustaining manner by inducing changes in relative agency costs. It is not surprising that the elasticity of substitution σ of factors relatively to prices plays an important role in determining the robustness of organizational equilibria. A high σ acts like a good "anti-virus": it favors the rejection of the non-owning factors, that, because of the increase in their agency costs, threaten to upset the health of the existing ownership regime. Unfortunately, the "anti-virus" works particularly well with

the factors that are the most efficient potential alternative owners. They are efficient potential alternative owners because of the high agency costs that must otherwise be paid when they are employed by other factors. A high σ causes an unfortunate "preventive treatment": these factors are promptly replaced by factors that are cheaper for the present owners. Using the biological terminology a high σ can also be interpreted as an "anti-speciation" factor: by allowing adaptations of the present species it prevents major mutations that would bring about the emergence of "new species" of organizational equilibria. A high σ implies that each ownership arrangement can define self-sustaining organizational equilibria under a wider combinations of agency costs. The higher σ the wider is the ability of ownership rights to shape technology in a self-sustaining manner. For the same reason, a high σ implies that each organizational equilibrium has greater institutional stability with respect to exogenous agency cost shocks. The appendix to this chapter contains an intuitive argument relating the multiplicity and the stability of organizational equilibria to σ. A more rigorous argument can be found in Pagano and Rowthorn (1994 and 1996).

14 We are aware of the fact that the nature of learning in evolutionary environments poses very complex problems and there is no easy solution to the problem of the degree of rationality that it is proper to assume. For a discussion of this point see Dosi, Marengo, Fagiolo 2000 (in this volume).

15 The strength of this mechanism depends on the elasticity of substitution that also determines the multiplicity and the efficiency of organizational equilibria. For a formal intuitive argument see the appendix to this chapter. For a more complete analysis see Pagano and Rowthorn (1994) and (1996).

16 Also other cases seem to follow a similar pattern. Indeed, after World War II, the "speciation" of the Japanese model was another example of allopatric speciation. In this case the war and post-war institutional shocks destroyed the epistatic interactions of the *zaibatsu* version of personal capitalism. The result was not an imitation of the American model, but the speciation of a new forms of capitalism that was going to challenge the American model itself. In this sense a new allopatric speciation took place. The new species did not come about in America where competition was strongest but in an isolated periphery where institutional shocks had irreversibly weakened the preceding epistatic interactions. In the meantime no shock has yet been able to melt the frozen parts of the genotype of Italian family capitalism. On this see Pagano (1998), Barca, Pagano, Trento and Iwai (1999).

17 See the introductory chapter to this book by Nicita and Pagano.

18 Iwai (1999) clarifies how the legal form of the corporation is compatible with very different organizational and property right arrangements.

References

Alchian, A. and H. Demsetz (1972) Production, information costs and economic organisation. *American Economic Review*. 62: 777–95.

Barca, F, K. Iwai, U. Pagano and S. Trento (1999) The divergence of the Italian and Japanese corporate governance models: the role of the institutional shocks. *Economic Systems* 23(1): 35–61.

Bowles, S. (1985) The production process in a competitive economy: Walrasian, Neo-Hobbesian, and Marxian models. *The American Economic Review*. 75: 16–36.

—— (1989) Social institutions and technical change. In M. Di Matteo, R.M. Goodwin and A. Vercelli (eds) *Technological and Social Factors in Long Term Fluctuations*. New York: Springer-Verlag.

Braverman, H. (1974) *Labor and Monopoly Capital*. New York: Monthly Review Press.

Brenner, R. (1986) The social basis of economic development. In J. Roemer (1986) Analytical Marxism. Cambridge: University Press. Cambridge.

Chandler, A.D. (1990) *Scale and Scope: The Dynamics of Industrial Capitalism.* Cambridge, MA: Harvard University Press.

Cohen, G.A. (1978) *Karl Marx's Theory of History: A Defence.* Oxford: Oxford University Press.

Cronin, H. (1991) *The Ant and the Peacock.* Cambridge: Cambridge University Press.

Darwin, C. (1859[1968]) *The Origin of Species.* Edited by J.W. Burrow (1968). Harmondsworth: Penguin Books.

David, P.A. (1985) Clio and the economics of QWERTY. *American Economic Review* 75: 332–337

Dawkins, R. (1988) *The Blind Watchmaker.* Harmondsworth: Penguin Books.

Dosi, G., L. Marengo and G. Fagiolo (2000) On the dynamics of cognition and actions: an assessment of some models of learning and evolution. Chapter 7 in this volume.

Eccles, J.C. (1989) *Evolution of the Brain: Creation of the Self.* London: Routledge.

Eldredge, N. (1995) Species, selection, and Paterson's concept of the specific-mate recognition system." In D.M. Lambert and H.G. Spencer (eds) *Speciation and the Recognition System.* Baltimore: The Johns Hopkins University Press.

—— (1996) Ultra-Darwinian explanation and the biology of social systems. In E.L Khalil and K.E Boulding (eds) *Evolution, Order and Complexity.* London: Routledge.

Eldredge, N. and S.J. Gould (1972) Punctuated equilibria: an alternative to phyletic gradualism. In T.J.M. Schopf (ed.) *Models in Paleobiology* San Francisco: Freeman Cooper & Co.

Gould, S.J. (1992) The panda's thumb of technology. In S.J. Gould *Bully for Brontosaurus.* Harmondsworth: Penguin Books.

Hall, M. (1993)'Species, speciation and extinction. In E. Skelton (ed) *Evolution: A Biological and Paleontological Approach.* Wokingham: Addison-Wesley.

Hicks, J. (1969) *A Theory of Economic History.* Oxford: Oxford University Press.

Hodgson, G. (1996) Organisational form and economic evolution: a critique of the Williamsonian hypothesis. In U. Pagano and R. Rowthorn (eds) *Democracy and Efficiency in the Economic Enterprise.* London: Routledge.

Hirschman, A.O. (1981) *Essays in Trespassing: Economics to Politics and Beyond.* Cambridge: Cambridge University Press.

Iwai, K. (1999) Persons, things and corporations: the corporate personality controversy and comparative corporate governance. *American Journal of Comparative Law.* 47: 583–632.

Kauffman, S.A. (1993) *The Origins of Order: Self-Organization and Selection in Evolution.* Oxford: Oxford University Press.

Mayr, E. (1982) *The Growth of Biological Thought.* Cambridge, MA: Harvard University Press.

—— (1988) *Towards a New Philosophy of Biology.* CAmbridge, MA: Harvard University Press.

Maynard Smith, J. (1966) Sympatric speciation. *American Naturalist* 100: 637-650.

Nelson, R.R. (1994) Economic growth via the coevolution of technology and institutions. In L. Leydesdorff and P. Van Den Besselaar (eds) *Evolutionary Economics and Chaos Theory.* London: Pinter.

Pagano, U. (1991) Property rights equilibria and institutional stability. *Economic Notes* (2): 189–228.

—— (1992) Organisational equilibria and production efficiency. *Metroeconomica* 43(1–2): 227–246.

—— (2000) Transition and speciation of the Japaese model. In O. Fabel, F. Farina and L.F. Punzo (eds) *European Economics in Transition* London: Macmillan.

Pagano, U. and R. Rowthorn (1994) Ownership, technology and institutional stability. *Structural Change and Economic Dynamics.* 5(2): 221–243.

—— (1996) "The competitive selection of democratic firms in a world of self-sustaining institutions. In U. Pagano and R. Rowthorn (eds) *Democracy and Efficiency in the Economic Enterprise.* Routledge: London.

Ridley, Mark (1996) *Evolution* (2nd edn) Oxford: Basil Blackwell.

Roemer, J. (1988) *Free to Lose: An Introduction to Marxist Economic Philosophy* London: Radius.

Samuelson, P. (1957) Wage and interest: a modern dissection of Marxian economic models. *American Economic Review* 47: 884–912.
Seger, J. (1985) Intraspecific resource competition as a cause of sympatric speciation. In P.J. Greenwood, P.H. Harvey and M. Slatkin (eds)*Evolution* Cambridge: Cambridge University Press..
Sober, E. (1984) *The Nature of Selection*. Chicago: The University of Chicago Press.
Spencer, H.G. and J.D. Masters (1992) Sexual selection: contemporary debates. In E.F. Keller and E.A. Lloyd (eds) *Keywords in Evolutionary Biology*. Cambridge, MA: Harvard University Press.
Turner, A. (1995) The species in palaeontology. In D.M. Lambert and H.G. Spencer (eds) *Speciation and the Recognition System*. Baltimore: The Johns Hopkins University Press.
Williamson, O.E. (1985) *The Economic Institutions of Capitalism*. New York: The Free Press.
Winter, S. (1987) Competition and selection. In J. Eatwell, M. Milgate and P. Newman (eds) *The New Palgrave* London: Macmillan.
Wilson, S.W. and E. Sober (1994) Reintroducing group selection to human behavioral sciences. *Behavioral and Brain Sciences* 17: 585–654.

3 Biological and cultural evolution

Aspects of dynamics, statistics and optimization

Marcus W. Feldman

3.1 Introduction and terminology

The structures and functions of an organism that can be observed and measured are called its *phenotype*. Some parts of the phenotype, e.g., blood groups or enzyme concentration, require more sophisticated calibration than is amenable to direct observation. Nevertheless, they are in principle observable and are therefore phenotypes. The *genotype*, on the other hand, is defined entirely by the sequence of nucleotides that make up the DNA. For a given genotype, different phenotypes may be realized, depending on the environment in which the organism finds itself. The *norm of reaction* of a genotype is the pattern of the phenotypes that can be realized by placing that genotype in some range of environments.

The variation that Darwin perceived was phenotypic; evolution was the process of the conversion of phenotypic variation between individuals into variation between populations and species. The transmission of this variation from parent to child was assumed by Darwin and Galton to be blending in character: the expected phenotype of a child was the average of its parents' phenotypes. This produced the paradox that phenotypic variation should eventually disappear, and it was not until the rediscovery of Mendel's particulate theory of transmission that the paradox was resolved. Mendel's phenotypic differences were the result of simple genotypic differences whose transmission could be described quite precisely. Under Mendelian transmission, Hardy and Weinberg were able to show that phenotypic variation, resulting from genetic differences of the Mendelian kind, is conserved. Insofar as the genotype contributes to the phenotype (as described by the norm reaction), natural selection on the phenotype, acting via the environment, results in the conversion of genotypic differences between individuals into genotypic variation between populations and species.

Fisher (1918) was the first to demonstrate mathematically how Mendelian qualitative differences could be translated into metrical or quantitative variation. His theory allowed quantification of expected statistical relationships between the phenotypes of relatives. It was not, however, an evolutionary theory, and did not allow for the action of natural selection on the phenotype. Nevertheless, animal breeders subsequently used Fisher's theory in attempting to predict the genetic consequences of artificial selection on the phenotype (see, for example, Lewontin 1974: 15).

The serious mathematical difficulty inherent in the construction of a formal theory of phenotypic change was recognized early in the history of population genetics. The mathematical theory originated by Fisher, Wright and Haldane was genotypic in nature, and in their mathematical models, phenotypic differences were identified with genotypic differences at one or a very small number of genes. In these models, natural selection acted on the genotype, and evolution occurred as genotypic frequencies changed. Most mathematical evolutionary theory developed over the past 70 years has addressed genotypic evolution.

Two of the major tensions in modern evolutionary theory concern (1) the adequacy of simple genetic models, i.e., those based on single genes or haploid genetics to explain evolutionary phenomena, and (2) the relative importance of nature and nurture in explaining the outcome of the evolutionary process, namely observed contemporary phenotypic variation. First, many workers in evolutionary theory, particularly those from an ecological or behavioral ecology tradition, use game theoretic arguments similar to those in economics to find evolutionary "optima" as though these were the fixed points of evolutionary dynamics. For genetic systems governed by more than one locus, these "optima" are not the same as the fixed points of the dynamic, as we shall see in the first part of what follows. Second, for phenotypes that involve contributions from many loci, the usual description of the degree of genetic determination, heritability, is derived from correlations between relatives. These correlations, however, are also created by non-genetic forces of familial and other environmental origins. In order to properly describe the dynamics and the statistics of such traits, I claim that a theory of gene-culture coevolution is required. In the second part of this chapter, I outline how such a theory might proceed and cite examples from the work of our research group. Before proceeding to these analyses, it might be valuable to develop more precisely the terms mentioned in the opening paragraph before moving to properties of the dynamical systems that characterize evolutionary genetic theory.

3.1.1 Units of evolution

A *gene* is a position on a *chromosome* usually represented by a letter, e.g., A, B, C, etc.: gene $\equiv$ *locus.* A chromosome is a string of genes:

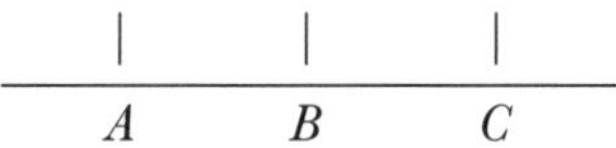

At each gene different forms may occur. These are called *alleles,* e.g., $\{A_1, A_2, A_3\}$ is a set of three alleles at the A-locus.

Inside the cell at certain times the chromosomes are seen to form pairs in most animals; for example, humans have 23 pairs and the fruit fly, *Drosophila,* has four pairs. Organisms like these in which the chromosome form pairs are called *diploid.* Bacteria and many primitive microorganisms have just one chromosome. They are *haploid.* The sex cells, spermatozoa and ova (egg cells), are also haploid and at fertilization they fuse to produce a diploid *zygote,* i.e., the fertilized egg. Often the sex cells are called *gametes.* Most population theory refers to *diploids,* but in the study of plants, polyploidy is also important. In what follows, we shall denote the set of genes by $\{A, B, C\}$ with alleles $\{A_i, A_j\}$, etc. In fact, each gene consists of a segment of heteroduplex DNA, the chemical which contains the code to produce RNA that is then translated into strings of amino acids called proteins. Many complications of this process are ignored in the idealized formulation that follows.

In the most familiar diploid species, there are two kinds of pairs of chromosomes: *autosomes* and *sex chromosomes.* In mammals and birds there is, for example, an X-Y sex-determining system: X and Y are sex chromosomes. The other pairs of chromosomes are autosomes. Genes on sex chromosomes are said to be *sex linked.*

In a diploid organism, every gene is represented on both members of the pair of autosomes; the alleles on the two copies may differ and the pair of alleles represents the *genotype* at that locus. The set of such pairs over all chromosomes is the *complete genotype.*

The individual below has its diploid genotype specified at two loci:

$$\frac{A_1 \qquad B_1}{A_1 \qquad B_2}$$

This individual is *homozygous* at the A-locus and *heterozygous* at the B-locus. For genes which are on the sex chromosomes, we may represent a homozygote at the A-locus by XA_1/XA_1. Such an individual, were it a mammal, would be a female, because it is X/X and homozygous at the A gene which is on the X chromosome. For males in such a species, the Y chromosome is usually very small and is regarded as not having any genes in the usual sense. Thus a male might be XA_1/Y.

The external manifestations of gene products and their interactions with the environment are the *phenotype.* For most traits, there is no simple rule that relates the genotype to the phenotype. In some cases, however, this can be done. For example, if A_1 and A_2 are two alleles at the A locus, and the phenotype of A_1A_1 is the same as that of A_1A_2, and different from that of A_2A_2, we say that A_1 is *dominant* to A_2 and A_2 is *recessive* to A_1. By far the majority of genetically determined diseases in humans are recessive. For more complicated phenotypes, however, it may be possible to scale the environment and for a given genotype graph its phenotype as a function of the environment. This graph is called the *norm of reaction* of that genotype.

3.1.2 Forces of evolution

It is common practice in population genetics to distinguish the forces of natural selection from other events that affect evolution but do not require renormalization of frequencies. Among the latter, the most important are mutation, migration and/or population subdivision, recombination, and random genetic drift. Mutation is simply the change of one allele into another; this may occur in a restricted set of alleles, or the new allele may be regarded as never having been seen before (Kimura and Crow, 1964). Mutation alone produces a linear dynamic in allele frequencies. Migration is the exchange of individuals or gametes between subpopulations (often called demes) of a larger population. When the allele frequencies differ among demes, the change in these frequencies due to migration, as in the case of mutation, is linear. Recombination is a process of breakage and reunion of the strings of genes in chromosomes that occurs at meiosis. The simplest description of this process, which is complicated at the molecular level, is in terms of exchange between two genes:

$$\begin{array}{llcll} & & & & \textit{frequency} \\ & & & A_1B_1 & (1-R)/2 \\ \text{diploid} & \dfrac{A_1B_1}{A_1A_2} & \xrightarrow{\textit{meiosis}} \quad \text{haploid} & A_1B_2 & R/2 \\ \text{parent} & & \phantom{\xrightarrow{x}} \quad \text{gametes} & A_2B_1 & R/2 \\ & & & A_2B_2 & (1-R)/2 \end{array} \tag{3.1}$$

Here, R is the recombination fraction. The dynamic effect of recombination is actually quadratic, but in some of its properties, it exhibits a kind of quasilinearity. Random genetic drift, made famous by Wright (1931), is the stochastic process of sampling among parental gametes in a finite population to produce the offspring generation. This sampling is usually multinomial, and the allele frequency dynamic can usually be well-approximated by a diffusion process (Wright 1931; Feller 1951, 1954; Moran 1962).

Most quantitative theory of natural selection is modeled in terms of differential survival, from zygote to adult, among the different genotypes (or phenotypes). Experimental assessments of the relative importance of different components of fitness have concluded that this level of selection, usually called *differential viability*, accounts for a much smaller fraction of the fitness variance than does fertility selection. *Fertility* is measured in terms of the number of offspring produced by different mating types and is notoriously variable (e.g., Lewontin 1974). Despite the importance of selection at the fertility level, only a minuscule fraction of the theoretical (and experimental) literature has been devoted to it, mainly because it results in extremely complicated high dimensional dynamics (Hadeler and Liberman 1975, Pollack 1978, Feldman and Liberman 1985). A final form of selection that should be mentioned because there are a few well-studied examples of it in nature, and because it relates to properties of cultural transmission discussed later, is *gametic* selection or *segregation distortion*. This occurs when, for some reason, the A_1 and A_2 gametes produced by an A_1/A_2 heterozygote do not obey Mendel's rules in being equally frequent in the effective gamete pool, but fertilize eggs at the rates k and $1-k$, respectively. The result is a strong advantage to whichever allele has the greater of k and $1-k$. In most cases, this advantage in gametic fitness is overwhelmed, or at least balanced, by reduced fitness of the diploid made up of one or two of the advantageous gametes.

3.2 Dynamics in evolutionary genetics

The modeling of genetic operations and the resulting dynamics of allele, genotype, or phenotype frequencies, may be traced (in spirit at least) to Haldane's famous series of papers in the 1920s in the *Proceedings of the Cambridge Philosophical Society*. Modern theory introduces the machinery to handle multiple allele or chromosome frequencies and to include appropriate stability theory. This mathematical population genetic theory is dynamic in its approach, and should be contrasted with theory that has its origin in the economics of fitness gains and losses, and where evolutionary outcomes are assumed to be expressible in game-theoretic terms. One of the interesting questions in modern evolutionary theory revolves around when these two approaches may be expected to make the same predictions.

3.2.1 Dynamics of selection on one gene

The theory of selection on the genotype has been most extensively studied in the case that the selection is due to differences among genotypes in their chance of survival from zygote to adulthood, i.e., viability selection. For a single gene A, its alleles will be denoted by $A_1, A_2, \ldots A_r$, and in a given generation the frequency of A_i is $x_i (i = 1, 2, \ldots, r)$ with $x_i \geq 0$ and $\sum x_i = 1$. Now, if the genotypes are haploid, each allelic type is in fact a genotype, and we may write the relative viabilities of $A_1, A_2, \ldots, A_r$ as $w_1, w_2, \ldots, w_r$. Using primes to denote the next generation, the haploid dynamics are

$$x_i' = \frac{w_1 x_i}{\sum_j w_j x_j}; \sum x_j = \sum x_i' = 1. \tag{3.2}$$

It is easy to see that continued iteration of (3.2) leads to convergence to $\hat{x}_k = 1$ where w_k is the greatest among the $\{w_i\}$. A fixed point of this kind, with only one type present, is called *fixation*, in this case fixation on A_k.

The diploid case is more interesting. We assume the population is large (large enough so that sampling problems may be ignored) and that mating among all members of the population occurs at random. It is then mathematically accurate to describe the evolution of the population of genotypes A_i/A_j in terms of the allele frequencies x_i. In the diploid case, however, we need a symmetric matrix $\|w_{ij}\|$ to describe the relative viabilities of A_i/A_j with $w_{ij} \geq 0$. Then we have

$$x_i' = \frac{x_i \sum w_{ij} x_j}{\sum_i \sum_j w_{ij} x_i x_j} = \frac{x_i w_i.}{\overline{w}}, \quad i = 1, 2, \ldots r, \tag{3.3}$$

where $w_i.$ is the marginal fitness of A_i, and $\sum_i x_i w_i. = \sum_i x_i x_j w_{ij}$ is the mean fitness of the population and is usually written as $\overline{w}$.

The properties of the system (3.2) are surprisingly nice. The following are representative.

Property 1. A *polymorphism* is a fixed point, or equilibrium, of (3.3) at which more than one of $A_1, A_2, \ldots, A_r$ has positive frequency. A *complete polymorphism* for a given set of alleles is one at which all alleles are represented. There may exist only one complete polymorphism and it is globally stable if the viability matrix $\|w_{ij}\|$ has one positive and $r-1$ negative eigenvalues (Kingman 1961a). Two polymorphisms, e.g., one with A_1 and A_2 present and another with A_3 and A_4 present may be simultaneously stable, but stability of a polymorphism with A_1, A_2, A_3, A_4 present precludes the stability of any equilibrium involving any smaller subset of these alleles.

Property 2. If the viabilities w_{ij}; $i, j = 1, 2, \ldots, r$, are chosen randomly from a uniform distribution on $[0, 1]$, the probability that there is a stable complete polymorphism decreases as a function of r according to $\exp[-\{r^2 \log r/2\}]$ (Karlin 1981). In other words, for $r \geq 5$, if viabilities were assigned randomly by the environment, complete polymorphism would be highly unlikely.

Property 3. With two alleles A_1A_2, heterozygote advantage is the condition $w_{12} > w_{11}, w_{22}$, and this is sufficient for a stable polymorphism with A_1 and A_2. In general, however, heterozygote superiority, i.e., $w_{ij} > w_{ii}$, w_{jj} is not sufficient to ensure that a complete polymorphism is stable. The following four-allele viability matrix, with $0 < s < 1$, allows stable equilibria with $\hat{x}_1 = \hat{x}_4 = 1/2$ or $\hat{x}_2 = \hat{x}_3 = 1/2$, but the complete polymorphic equilibrium $\hat{x}_i = 1/4$ is unstable:

$$\begin{array}{c} \\ A_1 \\ A_2 \\ A_3 \\ A_4 \end{array} \begin{array}{c} \begin{array}{cccc} A_1 & A_2 & A_3 & A_4 \end{array} \\ \begin{pmatrix} (1-s)^2 & 1-s & 1-s & 1 \\ 1-s & (1-s)^2 & 1 & 1-s \\ 1-s & 1 & (1-s)^2 & 1-s \\ 1 & 1-s & 1-s & (1-s)^2 \end{pmatrix} \end{array}. \tag{3.4}$$

Property 4. The "fundamental theorem of natural selection," originally enunciated by Fisher (1930), states that the mean fitness increases over time. In terms of system (3.3), we have

$$\overline{w}(\boldsymbol{x}') \geq \overline{w}(\boldsymbol{x}), \tag{3.5}$$

where $\boldsymbol{x} = (x_1, x_2, \ldots x_r)$, with equality holding only at $\boldsymbol{x}' = \boldsymbol{x}$; i.e., at equilibria. The most elegant proof of (3.5) is due to Kingman (1961b). The result makes formal the Darwinian idea that a population's average fitness should increase over time. It is also compatible with optimality arguments that would have a stable equilibrium maximize the mean fitness.

Although viability selection on one-locus genotypes produces beautiful mathematical theory, as soon as other levels of selection, especially fertility, are incorporated, the picture is much less elegant. Average fertility, for example, is not a Lyapunov function for the dynamics under fertility selection, and multiple stable equilibria or even cycling may occur. If there is some chance that individuals mate with relatives, or if selection varies geographically, multiple equilibria are possible. In such cases, the history of the population, i.e., the initial frequency vector, as well as the parameter values for selection, migration, and inbreeding, contributes to the ultimate outcome. Similar considerations apply to the case of multiple loci, even when the selection *is* at the viability level.

3.2.2 Geographic variation in selection

When the range of a species is somewhat discontinuous, random mating across the whole range is unlikely to occur. Within sub-populations, however, random mating may be a reasonable assumption, and it may also be the case that some individuals migrate between subpopulations. The resulting dispersal of genetic material is often called *gene flow*. Consider the case of two demes, and one locus with two alleles A_1,A_2 such that the viabilities in deme I are $w_{11} > w_{12} > w_{22}$ and in deme II, $v_{11} < v_{12} < v_{22}$. Clearly, in the absence of gene flow, allele A_1 would fix in deme I and allele A_2 would fix in deme II. With a small amount of migration between the demes, however, Karlin and McGregor (1972) showed that many equilibria are possible, and which one is approached depends on the history, i.e., the starting conditions. The nature and number of possible equilibrium configurations changes as a function of the degree of exchange between the demes.

3.2.3 Multiple loci

Consider a set of loci A, B, C, D etc., organized in a linear fashion along a chromosome. The corresponding haploid genotypes take the form $A_1B_2C_3D_1$ etc., while for diploids the genotypes are best written as pairs of haploid genotypes $A_1B_2C_3D_1/A_1B_1C_2D_4$ etc. Recently, the haploid representations for each chromosome have been called *haplotypes*. In the case of random mating, the frequencies of complete multilocus genotypes can be expressed in terms of the haplotype frequencies. In general, however, the haplotype frequencies may not be expressed in terms only of allele frequencies at each locus. This can be seen in the case of two loci with two alleles per locus, where the haplotypes A_1B_1, A_1B_2, A_2B_1, A_2B_2 in a given generation occur with frequencies x_1, x_2, x_3, x_4. It is straightforward to see that these haplotype frequencies may be written as p_1q_1+D, p_1q_2-D, p_2q_1-D, and p_2q_2+D, respectively, where $p_1 = x_1+x_2$, $p_2 = x_3+x_4$, $q_1 = x_1+x_3$, $q_2 = x_2+x_4$ are the frequencies of alleles A_1, A_2, B_1, and B_2 respectively. Only if $D=0$ can the haplotype frequencies be written in terms of the allele frequencies.

The quantity D is usually called the *linkage disequilibrium* and is a measure of statistical association between loci. It is, of course, generalizable to higher order measures of association among many genes. In the two-locus two-allele case, $D = x_1x_4 - x_2x_3$ reflects the difference in frequencies between the two double heterozygotes A_1B_1/A_2B_2 and A_1B_2/A_2B_1. It is these double heterozygotes whose gametes, produced at meiosis, are subject to the effects of recombination. Whereas the allele frequencies at each locus do not change under random mating in the absence of selection, D does, and in fact decreases to zero at the rate $1-R$ per generation. In the limit, then, recombination alone results in independence of the loci, and the greater the rate of recombination the faster $D=0$ is approached.

Viability selection on two loci is best represented in matrix form indexed by the haplotypes. This allows natural comparison with the corresponding four-allele system in the absence of recombination:

$$\begin{array}{c} \\ A_1B_1 \\ A_1B_2 \\ A_2B_1 \\ A_2B_2 \end{array} \begin{array}{c} \begin{array}{cccc} A_1B_1 & A_1B_2 & A_2B_1 & A_2B_2 \end{array} \\ \begin{pmatrix} w_{11} & w_{12} & w_{13} & w_{14} \\ w_{12} & w_{22} & w_{23} & w_{24} \\ w_{13} & w_{23} & w_{33} & w_{34} \\ w_{14} & w_{24} & w_{34} & w_{44} \end{pmatrix} \end{array}. \tag{3.6}$$

Again, the viabilty matrix is symmetric, and it is usual to assume that the two double heterozygotes have equal viabilities; $w_{14} = w_{23}$. The analysis is somewhat more complicated when $w_{14} \neq w_{23}$ (Nordborg et al. 1995). If we normalize with respect to w_{14} (i.e., set $w_{14} = w_{23} = 1$) then the resulting dynamics for the haplotype frequencies are given by the recursion system

$$\begin{aligned} \overline{w}x'_1 &= x_1 \textstyle\sum_{j=1}^{4} w_{1j}x_j - RD \\ \overline{w}x'_2 &= x_2 \textstyle\sum_{j=1}^{4} w_{2j}x_j + RD \\ \overline{w}x'_3 &= x_3 \textstyle\sum_{j=1}^{4} w_{3j}x_j + RD \\ \overline{w}x'_4 &= x_4 \textstyle\sum_{j=1}^{4} w_{4j}x_j - RD \\ \text{where} & \\ \overline{w} &= \textstyle\sum_{i=1}^{4} \sum_{j=1}^{4} w_{ij}x_ix_j. \end{aligned} \tag{3.7}$$

Obviously when $R = 0$, we are back in the one-locus, four-allele situation; it is the *RD* term which introduces complexity here.

A key problem in the analysis of two-locus models has been the explication of the relationship between equilibrium values of D and the viability system $\|w_{ij}\|$. In other words, can we predict the association between genes in the population from inspection of the fitnesses? One way to pose this question is in terms of specific measures of interaction in fitness between the loci. These measures have come to be called *epistasis.* Thus, in terms of $\|w_{ij}\|$ in matrix (3.6), four additive measures of epistasis are considered: $\varepsilon_i = w_{i1} - w_{i2} - w_{i3} + w_{i4}$ ($i = 1, 2, 3, 4$ with $w_{ij} = w_{ji}$). These have the flavor of interaction measures in analysis of variance. If the contributions to viability from each locus are additive, then these measures, which should rightly be called *additive epistatic* measures, all vanish. If all $\varepsilon_i = 0$, then for $R > 0$, a fixed point of (3.7) with $D = 0$ is globally stable when the heterozygotes are superior in fitness to both homozygotes at each locus. Alternative measures of epistasis on a multiplicative scale are $\varepsilon_i = [w_{i1}w_{i4}/w_{i2}w_{i3}] - 1$, but even if all of these vanish, stable fixed points of (3.7) may exist with $D \neq 0$, although the stability of these is a function of R. Generally, as R increases, the value of D at a stable polymorphic equilibrium decreases. Thus there is a tight relationship between the values of D expected in a population, R, and epistasis, but few detailed generalizations can be proven for arbitrary $\|w_{ij}\|$. The following facts are known:

1. If an equilibrium with $D = 0$ is stable for $R = R_0$, then it is stable (locally) for $R > R_0$. This is intuitive because, as mentioned above, the rate of approach of D to zero in the absence of selection is faster with larger R.

2. In general, $\overline{w}$ is *not* a Lyapunov function for the system (3.7) (Moran, 1964). If the viabilities are additive between the loci, $\overline{w}$ works as a Lyapunov function (Ewens, 1969), but it is conjectured that this is the only viability matrix for which this is so.

3. More than one complete polymorphism (i.e., all four chromosomes present) may exist and be stable, even when fixation states are also stable. Of course, this is not true of four-allele polymorphisms in the four-allele, one-locus model.

4. The dynamics are complex. Hastings (1981) found that, very occasionally, numerical iteration of Eq. (3.7) led to a cycle rather than to an isolated equilibrium point. Although this is an extremely rare occurrence, it shows the added level of complexity imparted by recombination.

3.3 Optimality theory and its alternatives

We have just seen that when the viabilities of two-locus genotypes are not additive in the separate one-locus contributions, the mean fitness in the population may not increase over time. Fitness is not maximized in this case. There may, of course, be some other function of the haplotype frequencies which has a biological interpretation and which is maximized, but to date it has not been found. There is considerable controversy in modern evolutionary analysis over the extent to which organismal traits may be regarded as having been optimized during the evolutionary process. Those who favor the position that the process of evolution is one of optimization often couch their analysis in game-theoretic terms, focusing on the economics of fitness gains and losses. This is the approach taken by the practitioners of inclusive fitness arguments.

One major difficulty with such arguments is that they generally fail with more than a single locus (as we saw in the previous section) and they bypass the problems of complex dynamics which may occur even with one locus. Typical examples of the latter occur in the kin-selection theory for the evolution of altruism (Cavalli-Sforza and Feldman, 1978; Uyenoyama and Feldman, 1981), where conditions for the initial increase of an "altruistic" allele are not the same as conditions for its ultimate fixation. The exact dynamics, revealed by detailed population genetic analysis, often place significant restrictions on the validity of seemingly heuristic qualitative conclusions drawn from optimality considerations.

3.4 Long-term and short-term selection

Short-term evolution describes the dynamics of the relative frequencies of a finite, fixed set of genotypes existing in a population at a given time, possibly including mutations among that set of genotypes. Short-term evolution proceeds by changes in the frequencies of genotypes represented in the population. For most of these genotypic dynamical systems, evolution moves the frequency vector towards one of (possibly) many stable equilibria that are possible for the given set of evolutionary parameters (e.g., viabilities, mutation rates, recombination fractions, etc.). Starting from a set of frequencies close to one of these stable equilibria, evolution takes the population ever closer to that equilibrium. The dynamic processes of one or multiple loci described above are examples of short-term evolution, and we have seen that this process does not, in general, lead to a mean fitness optimum.

Long-term evolution is used to describe a process whereby mutation continually introduces new genotypes into a population. These new genotypes are then subject to natural selection, recombination, etc., and may be eliminated, become established, or even go to fixation. Once such a mutation is established, a new process of short-term evolution is initiated the result of which would usually be approach to a new (short-term) stable equilibrium. One or more of the originally present genotypes may be lost in this process. Thus, long-term evolution is an infinite sequence of transitions from one fixed set of genotypes to another in which each of these sets is subject to short-term evolution. We assume that the rate of occurrence of these mutations that become established is low enough that after invasion by such a mutation the ensuing short-term process has time to approach its equilibrium before transition to another short-term process occurs.

It is important to recognize that most of classical population genetic theory is in terms of the short-term process. On the other hand, verbal analyses of evolutionary theory are (usually implicitly) in terms of long-term processes; this is certainly the case for evolutionary game theory as applied to evolution of populations. The terms "unbeatable strategy" (Hamilton, 1967) and "evolutionary stable strategy (ESS)" (Maynard Smith and Price, 1973), for example, address invasion by *any* new mutation, not just one from a finite set, and therefore concern long-term evolution. The dynamic analysis appropriate for short-term evolution is not relevant to the long-term process, and this explains why concepts like ESS have usually been employed in a dynamics-free context. This distinction between the two time scales of selection has its antecedents in work by Eshel and Feldman (1984) which is summarized in the following paragraph.

3.4.1 A long-term result for two-locus genetics

Suppose that the A and B loci have alleles $A_1, A_2, \ldots, A_n$ and $B_1, B_2, \ldots, B_m$, respectively, and that the viability of A_iB_k/A_jB_l is w_{ijkl} $(i,j = 1,2,\ldots,n;\ k,l = 1,2,\ldots,m)$ with $w_{ijkl} = w_{jikl} = w_{ijlk} = w_{jilk}$. Denote the frequency of the haplotype A_iB_k after selection and recombination by x_{ik}. After random mating, selection, and recombination, the recursions analogous to (3.7) are

$$\overline{w}x'_{ik} = (1-R)\sum_{jl} w_{ijkl}x_{ik}x_{jl} + R\sum_{jl} w_{ijkl}x_{il}x_{jk}, \tag{3.8}$$

where R is the recombination fraction and $\overline{w} = \sum_{ijkl} w_{ijkl}x_{ik}x_{jl}$ is the mean viability. At equilibrium, denote the haplotype frequencies by $\{x^*_{ik}\}$. Now assume that viability mutations occur at each locus, and although we make no assumption about the distribution of viability effects on the carriers of the mutations, we do assume that the rate of mutation is low enough that after an advantageous mutation arises, short-term evolution takes the population near a stable equilibrium before a new advantageous mutation appears. Thus we may restrict attention to a new allele A_{n+1} near the equilibrium $\{x^*_{ik}\}$, and the viabilities of genotypes carrying A_{n+1} are $w_{n+1,jkl}$. Near $\{x^*_{ik}\}$ write $x_{n+1,k} = \varepsilon_k$ with $\sum_k \varepsilon_k = \varepsilon$ and then linearize recursions (3.8) to give a linear system for $(\varepsilon_1, \varepsilon_2, \ldots, \varepsilon_m)$. If λ is the leading eigenvalue of the resulting local stability matrix, with associated right eigenvector $\boldsymbol{u} = (u_1, u_2, \ldots, u_m)$, then A_{n+1} increases when rare, and invades the population, if $\lambda_1 > 1$. Eshel and Feldman (1984) showed that $\lambda_1 > 1$ if

$$w^*_{n+1}(\boldsymbol{u}) = \sum_j u_j \sum_k \sum_l w_{n+1,jkl} x_{kl} > \overline{w}^* = \sum_{ijkl} w_{ijkl} x^*_{ik} x^*_{jl}. \tag{3.9}$$

If the inequality is reversed, A_{n+1} is expelled from the population. In other words, an appropriately weighted average fitness of genotypes containing $A_{n+1,k}$ must exceed the resident mean fitness for A_{n+1} to become established. This is true for all R values and constitutes one of the few mean-fitness results that work with recombination in the system. Note that this result (which has been generalized by Liberman (1988) to include any number of loci) allows mutation at only one locus at a time. It is generally false if mutations occur simultaneously at more than one gene. Nevertheless, it may be regarded as a weak long-term counterpart to the fundamental theorem of natural selection, which is a short-term result that is false for more than a single gene.

If the new mutations invade by increasing a weighted mean fitness, what happens to them later in their progress? No mathematical theory exists, but a vast number of simulations reveal that the equilibrium achieved after the invasion may actually have a lower mean viability than that prior to the invasion. This might have been expected since, after the invasion, the process is a short-term one in which $\overline{w}$ may not increase over time.

3.4.2 Long-term evolution via modifer theory

Suppose that a population is evolving under the joint effects of differential selection, mutation, migration, and recombination. One class of questions, addressed in classical population genetics, concerns the fixed points (i.e., equilibria) and their domains of attraction. A second class of questions focuses on those forces other than fitness differences that influence evolution and asks how these might evolve. Thus we have studies on optimal mutation rates (Kimura 1960, 1967), optimal levels of dispersal (Comins *et al.* 1980) and optimal rates of recombination (Fisher 1930, Muller 1932, Nei 1967, Lewontin 1971, Feldman 1972, and Feldman et al. 1997).

This second class of questions is clearly within the purview of long-term selection: given that the rate of mutation, for example, is currently μ_1, what will be the effect of changing it to μ_2? One approach has been to determine the short-term stable equilibrium value of the mean fitness as a function of the mutation rate (for example) and find its maximum. Such a mutation rate might then be said to be optimal.

A second approach is to posit genetic control of the parameter θ under study, so that its present value is due to genotype M_1/M_1 at the θ-controlling locus, which we usually call a modifier locus. Mutations then occur at the M-locus, and the evolution of θ is mathematically described by the dynamics of alleles M_i over time. We call this approach *modifier theory*. Intuitively, the end point of a process of long-term evolution might be a genotype M^*/M^* and a parameter θ^* that cannot be invaded by any other M-mutation. θ^* and the frequencies of the genotypes that produce θ^* might then be said to be long-term stable (Feldman, 1972; Eshel and Feldman, 1982; Feldman and Liberman 1986). It is not necessarily the case that critical values of the mean fitness coincide with θ^* defined via the second approach (Thomson and Feldman 1974, Karlin 1975). Indeed, to check the validity of a value obtained using an optimality argument (e.g., ESS, or unbeatable strategy), it is necessary to perform a population-genetic analysis and this will usually involve some kind of modifier theory.

3.5 Phenotypes, culture, transmission, and evolution

The basic premise of evolutionary theory is that natural selection acts on phenotypes. The problem we face in developing a predictive theory of phenotypic evolution is that the rules of transmission for phenotypes are not known. In those few cases where genotypic differences at one or two loci specify measurable or qualitative differences in phenotypes, we can use the theory from the previous paragraphs. Otherwise we do not know the structure of the function $L(x,y;z)$ which is the probability that parents of phenotypes x and y give rise to an offspring with phenotype z. Following Fisher (1918), this problem was resolved practically by the use of statistics that predicted correlations among relatives under assumptions on the relationship between genotypes and phenotypes. This is not very useful in the presence of natural selection, interaction among linked genes, population subdivision, etc. On the other hand, it was successful in stimulating a quantitative statistical theory of animal and plant breeding in controlled environments that has had important agricultural consequences.

When it comes to human behavior, however, this approach is severely limited in its evolutionary application. The important role of familial transmitted (and/or non-transmitted) environment in the form of learning from parents, relatives, or peers is not easy to include in the Fisherian variance analysis approach. This is why we developed a quantitative theory of cultural transmission and evolution (Cavalli-Sforza and Feldman 1973a, 1973b, 1981; Feldman and Cavalli-Sforza 1976; Feldman and Laland 1996).

The degree to which changes in the environment experienced by an organism affect a trait was described above by the norm of reaction. For traits that depend on teaching and learning, it might be possible to be more specific about the parameters that determine the value of a trait. We call such traits *cultural*, although anthropologists disagree vehemently on what aspects of society the term "culture" should subsume. We have found the *Webster's Dictionary* (Third International Edition) definition satisfactory: "The total pattern of human behavior and its products embodied in thought, speech, action, and artifacts and dependent upon man's capacity for learning and transmitting knowledge." By analogy with evolutionary genetics, it is more productive to focus on specific traits that may vary among individuals, change over time, and be transmitted among individuals, rather than the "total pattern," which is very hard to describe quantitatively. Careful analysis of population dynamics in terms of the rules of change and transmission may increase our understanding of societal evolution.

The kinds of cultural traits we have in mind may be discrete valued or continuous, and they may also have some degree of biological determination, although this is not necessary for the development of the theory. Cultural *innovation* and *borrowing* are analogous to the biological phenomena of mutation and gene flow. The stochastic effect of small population size (i.e., random genetic drift) has a direct analogy in an increased chance that cultural diversity is lost in small populations. Natural (Darwinian) selection is usually couched in terms of competition for food, space, mates, etc. *Cultural selection* may include a component of this kind, where one cultural variant might leave more offspring than another, but it may be a much more complex phenomenon. Thus, an idea may be more attractive than its alternatives and be preferentially transmitted or obtain adherents without physical deaths or additional births. The analogy here with segregation distortion is clear. One might go further: although attractive cultural traits may usually involve no loss of Darwinian fitness, it is completely feasible that there exist a high rate of transmission (and adoption) for a trait that increases the likelihood of morbidity, sterility, or death for those who adopt it.

The kinds of traits that our theory of cultural transmission is best suited for are preferences, biases, beliefs, attitudes, and customs. Such traits might be subject to *vertical transmission*, from parents to offspring; *oblique transmission*, from teachers or adult group members to an offspring; or *horizontal transmission*, from peers or a similar age cohort. The level of variation expected in a population will depend on the kind of transmission it undergoes. Vertical transmission, for example, is highly conservative and tends to produce slower evolution than oblique or horizontal, which can produce rapid evolution. We have also shown (Feldman and Cavalli-Sforza, 1979; Cavalli-Sforza and Feldman, 1981) that the tendency for individuals with similar trait values to meet more often than dictated by chance (which might be called assortative meeting) can have important effects on the dynamics; in particular it speeds up evolution, it can overcome deleterious fitness effects, and reduce within-population variability.

3.5.1 Three examples with cultural transmission

I have chosen three models, two purely cultural and one with both genetic and cultural transmission, to illustrate the scope of the theory described above in general terms.

Kuru

Kuru is a neuronal degenerative disease that was once prevalent among the Fore highland people of New Guinea. It has now largely disappeared but was once an important cause of mortality among women and children who participated in ritual cannibalism. The disease is caused by a prion which is transmitted from the cadaver to the eater. Our use of the name Kuru for the model comes from the combination of two evolutionary forces, vertical transmission and viability differences.

Suppose that a behavior exists in two forms, labeled 1 and 2, in frequencies u and $1-u$ at some time t. Assume mating is random (i.e., mass action) and that an offspring becomes type 1 if at least one of its parents is of type 1. Clearly, type 1 has a transmission advantage. Now assume that the viability of type 1 is $1-s$ relative to 1 for type 2 and write u' for the frequency of type 1 in generation $t+1$. We have

$$u' = \left[u^2 + 2u(1-u)\right](1-s)/\left\{1-s\left[1-(1-u)^2\right]\right\}. \qquad (3.10)$$

From (3.10) it is clear that u increases when it is small provided $s < 1/2$. Thus, type 1 may suffer up to a 50 percent fitness loss relative to type 2 and remain in the population, because the transmission bias in its favor overwhelms this viability disadvantage.

Although the simple model just described was stimulated by the disease Kuru, I suggest that the general principle it raises may be applicable to many individually disadvantageous traits that are transmitted and learned with high reliability. Thus, the kin-selection argument for the evolution of altruism, which relies on the peculiarities of genetic transmission and genetic relatedness between donors and recipients of altruism, is not the only explanation. Learning may be more plausible, especially for humans.

This simple two-state example can be used to illustrate a surprising complexity that emerges when we superimpose genetics on the transmission. Suppose now that the transmission of the advantageous type 2 trait depends on the genotype at one diallelic locus. Suppose also that A_1A_2 transmits (or receives) type 2 at a greater rate than A_1A_1 or A_2A_2. This might look, on the face of it, like heterozygote advantage. It is not, however, and the fact that the transmission is not complete necessitates a stronger condition on the rate of heterozygote transmission of type 2 than just simple heterozygote advantage for the maintenance of both A_1 and A_2 in the population (Feldman and Cavalli-Sforza 1976).

A demographic example: the fertility transition

In recent human history, as populations have increased their level of sanitation and general public health so that infant mortality drops, there appears to be a decrease in the total fertility rate which is often referred to as the demographic transition. If control of fertility is regarded as a possible behavior with the alternative being natural fertility, we may regard these as morphs of a trait that is culturally transmitted. A natural question is how strong the cultural transmission must be so that population size actually stabilizes or even drops. We have addressed this question using variants of the classic Leslie model for the dynamics of an age-structured population. I will outline the model here; the detailed analysis is in Carotenuto *et al.* (1989).

At time t, let $n_j(t)$ be the number of women in age class j ($j = 0, 1, \ldots N$). The fertile age classes are $d, d+1, \ldots, m$. Then if a_ℓ is the birth rate to women in age class ℓ, the number of newborns at time $t+1$ is

$$n_0(t+1) = \sum_{\ell=d}^{m} a_\ell n_\ell(t). \tag{3.11a}$$

If p_j is the survival rate of individuals in age class j, then

$$n_i(t+1) = p_{i-1} n_{i-1}(t). \tag{3.11b}$$

This linear system is usually called the Leslie model. Now suppose that instead of a single fertility for all members of an age class there are two classes of individuals, fertility controllers and non-controllers, with a_i, $\bar{a}_i$ the respective fertilities. Let $k_i(t)$ be the frequency of controllers in age class i, with $1 - k_i(t)$ that of non-controllers, and suppose that b_ℓ is the rate of vertical transmission from parents in age class ℓ ($\ell = d, d+1, \ldots m$). Then we have

$$k_0(t+1) = \frac{\sum_{\ell=d}^{m} b_\ell a_\ell n_\ell(t) k_\ell(t)}{\sum_{\ell=d}^{m} \left[\bar{a}_\ell + (a_\ell - \bar{a}_\ell) k_\ell(t)\right] n_\ell(t)}. \tag{3.12}$$

Horizontal transmission might occur from age peers and older members of the population at age- and frequency-dependent rates. That is,

$$\begin{aligned} n_i(t+1) k_i(t+1) &= p_{i-1} n_{i-1}(t) k_{i-1}(t) \\ &+ p_{i-1} n_{i-1}(t) \left[1 - k_{i-1}(t)\right] f_i(k_{i-1}, k_i, \ldots, k_N), \end{aligned} \tag{3.13}$$

where $f_i(\cdot)$ describes the horizontal transmission to those aged $i - 1$ who do not possess knowledge of fertility control.

The dynamics (3.12) and (3.13) have the properties of an age-structured epidemic, and the focus is on conditions under which the trait of fertility control would spread through the population. It turns out that horizontal transmission, as in (3.13), is more efficient than vertical in establishing fertility control in the population. In fact, vertical transmission alone must be extremely strong for fertility control to have a major effect on the long-term dynamics of population size.

The incest taboo

Most societies proscribe marriages between very close relatives: brothers and sisters, fathers and daughters. Westermarck (1894) proposed that "there is an innate aversion to sexual intercourse between persons living closely together from early youth" and that this is the reason for the societal proscriptions against incest. Cultural anthropologists have produced data on marriage patterns among adults reared together as children in Israeli kibbutzim (Shepher 1971) and on fertility of Chinese *sim-pua* marriages (where the wife was adopted at birth by a family with a son and eventually married to that son/adopted brother; Wolf 1970, 1995) that seem to support Westermarck's hypothesis.

We recently constructed a gene-culture coevolutionary model in which a female haploid of genotype A_i exhibited probability b_{is} of wanting to mate with a brother if her parents were sibs, and b_{ir} if her parents were unrelated (Aoki and Feldman 1997). One of the reasons most frequently offered as the basis of the incest taboo is that it is a biological adaptation to the increased likelihood that inbred offspring suffer from debilitating inherited diseases, so we propose a fitness loss d to the offspring of brother-sister mating. In this framework, the parameters $\{b_{is}, b_{ir}\}$ may be regarded as the norm of reaction for A_i. If $b_{ir} = 0$ and $b_{is} = 1$, then mate choice is completely cultural. Aoki and Feldman (1997) show that if $d > 1/3$, it is possible to achieve a stable state where $b_{ir} = 0$ and $b_{is} > 0$, which suggests that cultural (familial) transmission of the desire to mate with a sib can indeed evolve and be stable to genetic perturbations. There are few data on which to base estimates of d although Durham (1991) suggests a value of 0.45 using data from Seemanová (1971). Our analysis offers at least theoretical support for a cultural alternative to Westermarck's genetically-based hypothesis.

3.6 Conclusion

If we restrict attention to traits that are jointly determined by genetic transmission of a single locus with two alleles and cultural transmission of two variants, we have six phenogenotypes to consider: AA_1, Aa_1, aa_1, AA_2, Aa_2, aa_2. The simultaneous transmission of genotype and phenotype is described by an array of probabilities $\{\beta_{ghi,\ell mn}\}$ where $\beta_{ghi,\ell mn}$ is the probability that a mating between a mother of genotype g and phenotype ℓ and a father of genotype h and phenotype m produces an offspring of phenotype n whose genotype is i. This might be regarded as a minimal gene-culture vertical transmission system, yet it requires 60 transmission parameters. By focusing on correlations among a few types of close relatives, there has been a tendency in behavioral sciences to lose sight of the fact that even this simplest of systems is indeed extremely complex. Of course, any genetic contribution to human behavior is likely to involve many genes, and there are multiple variants of each behavior, so it is unlikely that optimality theory can be useful for evolutionary speculation. It is also unlikely that simple statistics can give us much insight into the relationships among the 60 parameters that define the joint cultural and genetic transmission in the determination of these behaviors.

References

Aoki, K. and M.W. Feldman (1997) A gene-culture coevolutionary model for brother-sister mating. *Proc. Natl. Acad. Sci. USA* 94: 13046–13050.

Carotenuto, L., M.W. Feldman, and L.L. Cavalli-Sforza (1989) Age structure in models of cultural transmission. Working paper No. 16. Stanford, CA: Morrison Institute for Population and Resource Studies.

Cavalli-Sforza, L. and M.W. Feldman (1973a) models for cultural inheritance. i. group mean and within-group variation. *Theor. Pop. Biol.* 4: 42–55.

—— (1973b) Cultural versus biological inheritance: phenotypic transmission from parents to children (a theory of the effect of parental phenotypes on children's phenotypes). *Amer. J. of Hum. Gen.* 25: 618–637.

—— (1978) Darwinian selection and "altruism". *Theor. Pop. Biol.* 14: 268–280.

—— 1981 *Cultural Transmission and Evolution: A Quantitative Approach.* Princeton: Princeton University Press.

Comins, H.N., W.D. Hamilton and R.M. May (1980) Evolutionarily stable dispersal strategies. *J. Theoretical Biology* 82: 205–230.

Durham, W.H. (1991) *Coevolution.* Stanford: Stanford University Press.

Eshel, I. and M.W. Feldman (1982) On evolutionary genetic stability of the sex ratio. *Theor. Pop. Biol.* 21: 430–439.

—— (1984) Initial increase of new mutants and some continuity properties of ESS in two-locus systems. *Amer. Natur.* 124: 631–640.

Ewens, W.J. (1969) Mean fitness increases when fitnesses are additive. *Nature* 221: 1076.

Feldman, M.W. (1972) Selection for linkage modification: i. Random mating populations. *Theor. Pop. Biol.* 3: 324–346.

Feldman, M.W. and L.L. Cavalli-Sforza (1976) Cultural and biological evolutionary processes: Selection for a trait under complex transmission. *Theor. Pop. Biol.* 9: 239–259.

—— (1979) Aspects of variance and covariance analysis with cultural inheritance. *Theor. Pop. Biol.* 15: 276–307.

Feldman, M.W. and K.N. Laland (1996) Gene-culture coevolutionary theory. *Trends in Ecology and Evolution* 11: 453–457.

Feldman, M.W. and U. Liberman (1985) A symmetric two-locus fertility model. *Genetics* 109: 229–253.

—— (1986) An evolutionary reduction principle for genetic modifiers. *Proc. Natl. Acad. Sci. USA* 83: 4824–4827.

Feldman, M.W., S.P. Otto and F.B. Christiansen (1997) Population genetic perspectives on the evolution of recombination. *Ann. Rev. Genet.* 30: 261–295.

Feller, W. (1951) Diffusion processes in genetics. In J. Neyman (ed) *Proc. Second Berkeley Symposium on Mathematical Statistics and Probability.* Berkeley and Los Angeles: University of California Press.

—— (1954) Diffusion processes in one dimension. *Transactions of the Amer. Math. Soc.* 77: 1–31.

Fisher, R.A. (1918) The correlation between relatives on the supposition of Mendelian inheritance. *Trans. Roy. Soc. Edinburgh* 52: 399–433.

—— 1930. *The Genetical Theory of Natural Selection.* Oxford: Clarendon Press.

Hadeler, K.P. and U. Liberman (1975) Selection models with fertility differences. *J. Math. Biol.* 2: 19–32.

Hamilton, W.D. (1967) Extraordinary sex-ratios. *Science* 156: 477–488.

Hastings, A. (1981) Stable cycling in discrete-time genetic models. *Proc. Natl. Acad. Sci. USA* 78: 7224–7225.

Karlin, S. (1975) General two-locus selection models: some objectives, results and interpretations. *Theor. Pop. Biol.* 7: 364–398.

—— (1981) Some natural viability systems for a multiallelic locus: a theoretical study. *Genetics* 97: 457–473.

Karlin, S. and J. McGregor (1972) Polymorphisms for genetic and ecological systems with weak coupling. *Theor. Pop. Biol.* 3: 210–238.

Kimura, M. (1960) Optimum mutation rate and degree of dominance as determined by the principle of minimum genetic load. *J. Genetics* 57: 21–34.

—— (1967) On the evolutionary adjustment of spontaneous mutation rates. *Genetical Research* 9: 23–34.

Kimura, M. and J.F. Crow (1964) The number of alleles that can be maintained in a finite population. *Genetics* 49: 725–738.

Kingman, J.F.C. (1961a) A mathematical problem in population genetics. *Proc. Camb. Phil. Soc.* 57: 574–582.

—— (1961b) A matrix inequality. *Quart. J. Math* 12: 78–80.

Lewontin, R.C. (1971) The effect of genetic linkage on the mean fitness of a population. *Proc. Natl. Acad. Sci.* 68: 984–986.

—— (1974) *The Genetic Basis of Evolutionary Change.* New York: Columbia University Press.

Liberman, U. (1988) External stability and ESS: criteria for initial increase of new mutant allele. *J. Math. Biol.* 26: 477–485.

Maynard Smith, J. and G.R. Price (1973) The logic of animal conflict. *Nature* 246: 15–18.

Moran, P.A.P. (1962) *The Statistical Processes of Evolutionary Theory.* Oxford: Clarendon Press.

—— (1964) On the nonexistence of adaptive topographies. *Ann. Human Genet.* 27: 383–393.

Muller, H.J. (1932) Some genetic aspects of sex. *Amer. Naturalist* 66: 118–138.

Nei, M. (1967) Modification of linkage intensity by natural selection. *Genetics* 57: 625–641.

Nordborg, M., I.R. Franklin and M.W. Feldman (1995) The effects of *cis-trans* selection on two-locus viability models. *Theor. Pop. Biol.* 47: 365–392.

Pollack, E. (1978) With selection for fecundity the mean fitness does not necessarily increase. *Genetics* 90: 383–389.

Seemanová, E. (1971) A study of children of incestuous matings. *Hum. Hered.* 21: 108–128.

Shepher, J. (1971) Mate selection among second-generation kibbutz adolescents and adults: incest avoidance and negative imprinting. *Arch. Sexual Behavior* 1: 293–307.

Thomson, G.J. and M.W. Feldman (1974) Population genetics of modifiers of meiotic drive. II. Linkage modification in the segregation distortion system. *Theor. Pop. Biol.* 5: 155–162.

Uyenoyama, M. and M.W. Feldman (1981) On relatedness and adaptive topography in kin selection. *Theor. Pop. Biol.* 19: 87–123.

Westermarck, E. (1894) *The History of Human Marriage.* (2nd edn) London: Macmillan.

Wolf, A.P. (1970) Childhood association and sexual attraction: a further test of the Westermarck hypothesis. *Am. Anthropol.* 72: 503–515.

—— (1995) *Sexual Attraction and Childhood Association.* Stanford: Stanford University Press.

Wright, S. (1931) Evolution in Mendelian populations. *Genetics* 16: 97–159.

4 The evolution of evaluators

Daniel C. Dennett

4.1 Whence cometh our values?

We have values and aspirations. What of other animals? Are their "values" different from ours? Animals manifestly prefer having plenty of food to starvation, and comfort to pain, and they will work hard to obtain a mate. But beyond these "creature comforts," they seem to be largely indifferent to the prospects and anxieties that make up human life. A suitable coverall term for human aspiration would be *the pursuit of happiness*, bearing in mind that happiness is many different things to different people. This already sets us aside from our fellow creatures. To put it vividly, Mother Nature doesn't care whether we are happy – but we care (and Mother Nature doesn't care that we care). That is, it would be naive to suppose that the process of natural selection has somehow endorsed our pursuit of happiness as the proximal mechanism for maximizing our genetic fitness. It is consistent with what we know of evolution to suppose that the process of natural selection – Mother Nature – would design us to experience however much anxiety and torment is consistent with making more grandchildren. Our values are, like everything else in our extended phenotypes, products of evolutionary processes, but we misread them if we see them to be just like the "values" of other animals, which can indeed be viewed as the straightforward result of Mother Nature's project of installing an optimally reliable fitness-enhancing set of preferences. The difference arises, I will argue, from the fact that we have culture, and culture provides a medium in which a radically different – indeed, orthogonal – set of selection pressures can re-direct evolutionary processes into unprecedented channels.

There is an immense gap between us and other animals, even though we are all non-miraculous products of natural selection. Whence cometh our norms, our standards against which to judge decisions? Some of them, no doubt, are created by a sharpening and extension of our animal natures: like other creatures, we can distinguish comfort from discomfort, easy from difficult, safe from risky. If all our norms had such a genealogy, economics would not only be a lot easier; it would be a straightforward branch of ecology, human foraging theory, in effect. Economics is – or ought to be – more interesting than that, because human desire is more interesting than that. The "animal model" might be appropriate for considering the welfare of severely retarded children in an institution, for instance, for they are apparently incapable of responding to, recognizing, or benefiting from the goods that matter so much to the rest of us. Keep them comfortable, well-fed and stimulated in whatever ways they care about, and that is about as good a life as they could have. It is a good life for a dog or a tiger or a chicken or a fish, but it is not a good life for a normal human being.

Consider an example drawn from a recent study of subjective well-being: "He believes that others believe that he is responsible for his unemployment." It is obvious that such a belief could play a major role in determining the (un-)happiness of a human being: it's baleful influence could overpower the positive contributions of comfort, food, health and plenty of sex. The *basis* for such an attitude might well be genetically laid down. It might, for instance, be grounded somehow in our species' history of living in groups ordered by dominance hierarchies, but in its convolution of nested attitudes it goes way beyond any factors that could play a role in the subjective well-being of any non-human creature.

Our genetic heritage gives us a biological base on which to build our values, but a base is only a base. It provides us with dispositions and preferences and organs that can then be adapted for other purposes, cobbling up ancient competences to new uses. We must not commit the genetic fallacy of assuming that we use these organs today for what they were evolved for. Consider, for instance the schematic graph in figure 1.

Let goodness be whatever you think goodness is, and look at the two life trajectories, A and B. The person on trajectory A gets off to a fine start, and has lots of goodness (whatever that is) for the rest of his life. The person on trajectory B has a life that steadily gets better, and eventually reaches the same level of goodness as on trajectory A, but the total goodness accumulated by the person on trajectory A is roughly twice as much. It would seem that life A should be preferred to life B, and yet many different studies suggest that no matter how you operationalize the positive value on the vertical axis, people tend to be happier when their lives are steadily getting better than when their lives are "stagnating" at a high level, no matter how high. Who says this is wrong? On what basis could it be demonstrated that a preference for trajectory B is irrational?[1] Is it "unnatural"? Maybe it is (on some construal of the term), but so what? Many of the things we prize are "unnatural." Consider yet another trajectory C, a roller-coaster ride of ups and downs. Any novelist will tell you that these are the lives that make the best stories, and who is to say that it would be irrational to prefer a life that makes a good story – even a tragedy – to a life of comfort, ease, and a plethora of descendants?

Who is to say? Not Mother Nature. Mother Nature doesn't care. Perhaps at bottom the reason people tend to prefer a life trajectory that gets better and better is that they have been designed by evolution to be better at detecting changes than at detecting absolute values, and they are designed to detect relevant (value-laden) changes more than others. The sorts of evaluations they are good at are "getting warmer" or "feeling better" or "hurting more" or "getting hungrier." If they come to value change for change's sake, this may well be, from Mother Nature's point of view, a mistake, but so what? Psychologists describe a personality type they

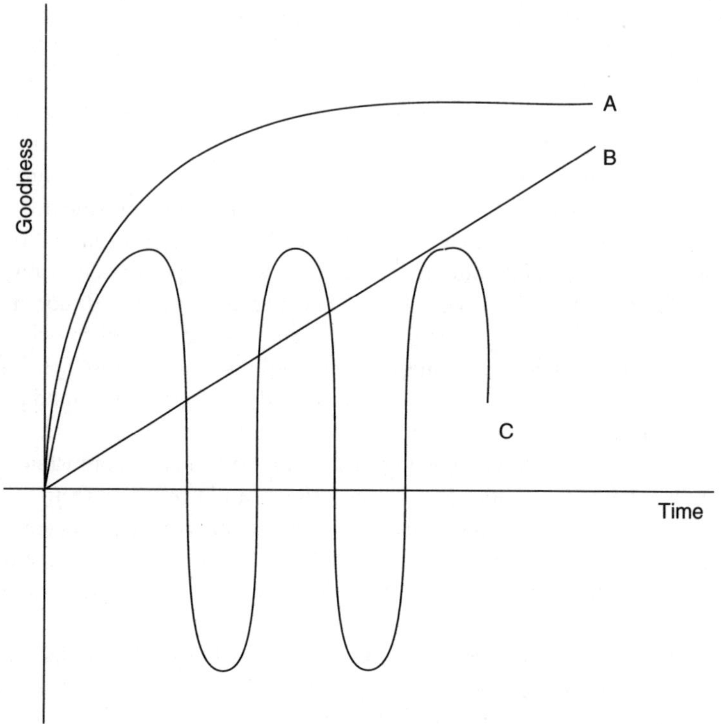

Figure 4.1

call "sensation seeker," and they tend to impose their own values on the category by treating it as a mild pathology, a subnormal or aberrant type. But if some of us want to be sensation-seekers, why shouldn't we have our heart's desire? Why should we puritanically resolve to stick to the norms that guide the other species – or the clinical psychologists? In fact, we just don't. Not only do we go our merry way, adopting a wide variety of values and life goals; we declare that very freedom to be a value.

As Cavalli-Sforza and Feldman (1981) note,

> There are people determined to risk their life to reach the top of Mt. Everest, and others that spend their life accumulating money, or attempting artistic or scientific creations, or simply trying to do as little as possible. It is difficult to subsume all of these choices under a common schedule admitting no individual variation.
>
> Control is delegated to a system of poorly understood internal drives and rewards that direct the activity of the individual, . . . (p.342)

they go on to say, and

> Our very inadequate knowledge of this steering system prevents us from making finer statements, but it is probably true that the system's overall activity is directed towards maximizing self satisfaction of the individual. Important complications arise because we can satisfy ourselves in many different, competing ways, many of which demand careful advance planning (p.364).

These important complications are the result of structures we build in our decision-making systems, structures that incorporate our values, as well as our empirical knowledge. Since we are not born with them, they have to be installed, in the course of acculturation and learning. This process, which exploits the equipment Mother Nature gave us in ways she never "intended," might seem to lead to cultural relativism of the most nihilist kind. If culture is the source of the values that Mother Nature doesn't give us, isn't one culture as good as another? Does might make right, or does majority rule? Is there any objective standpoint from which some bit of social construction could ever be judged to be a social *mis*construction?

The fear of a slippery slide into relativism should not panic us into endorsing the imperative of our genes. That would be to commit the genetic fallacy, just as surely as if we endorsed the norms of, say, the Bible. What was good enough for the reptiles or the apes, or good enough for the Samaritans or the Israelites, *may or may not* be good enough for us – that is an open question, which we must decide.

And we *can* decide, for good reasons or for bad reasons. How is it that we, alone among the creatures, have this choice point, this unprecedented opportunity to bootstrap ourselves beyond the norms of our biological heritage? Richard Dawkins closes his book, *The Selfish Gene*, with the ringing declaration:

> We have the power to defy the selfish genes of our birth and, if necessary, the selfish memes of our indoctrination . . . . We are built as gene machines and cultured as meme machines, but we have the power to turn against our creators. We, alone on earth, can rebel against the tyranny of the selfish replicators (1976, p.215).

But how is this possible? Dawkins doesn't say. I think, however, that his brief, informal account of cultural evolution presents the key ideas needed for an explanation of this fact about human nature.

What Cavalli-Sforza and Feldman call the "steering system" is something that emerges over time in a maturing human being. It differs from culture to culture, and from individual to individual. We are all agents, but we are not all the same agent; we differ in our beliefs, and in our values – and in the way we think about values. It is important to ask if we can keep this last factor distinct from the others, since there is a natural tendency for differences in ways of thinking to disappear in our models. When two agents agree on the *summum bonum*, and on the ranking of their subsidiary goals, and on the background information that is relevant, can they arrive at different courses of action? Suppose they have all the same beliefs and desires (suppose, in my terminology (Dennett 1971, 1987), that they are identical *intentional systems*). To a first approximation, at least, we predict that they will make the same decisions, choose the same actions, because they will choose to do whatever it is they deem to be most rational, given their beliefs and desires – which *ex hypothesi* are identical. This assumes that there is just one canon of rationality, an optimal decision procedure. And this assumption can be maintained, come what may, by recasting any apparent differences in canons of rationality that emerge as differences in beliefs or values. I am not deploring this possibility; just reminding ourselves of it. It may be wise to idealize to a content-free framework rationality and treat all differences as differences in beliefs and desires, information and goals.

Some such differences are more fundamental than others, of course. Consider, for instance, a question of paramount importance: *Cui bono*? Who benefits? (Dennett 1995a: 324–330) When an agent or intentional system makes a decision about which is the best course of action, all things considered, we need to know from whose perspective this optimality is being judged. A more or less standard default assumption, at least in the Western world, and especially among economists, is to treat the agent as a sort of punctate, Cartesian locus of well-being. What's in it for *me*? Rational *self*-interest. But while there has to be something in the role of the self – something that defines the answer to the *Cui bono* question for the decision-maker under examination, there is no necessity in this default treatment, common as it is. A self-as-ultimate-beneficiary can in principle be indefinitely distributed. I can care for others, or for a larger social structure, for instance. There is nothing that restricts me to a *me* as contrasted to an *us*. (This is distinct from Bowles' and Gintis' concept of community [this volume]; I am saying that, independently of any particular history of individuals or structure of community it is an open possibility that a mind – the "steering system" that gets built in a human brain – treat something other than the well-being of the body it inhabits as the touchstone of value.)

One tradition would speak here of "selfless" caring, but since this inevitably invites cavils about the purported incoherence of true selflessness, I prefer to think of this as the possibility of extending the domain of the self. I can still take my task to be looking out for #1 while including, under #1, not just myself, but my family, the Chicago Bulls, Oxfam . . . . Here is one good reason for treating the self this way: Suppose I am an agent in a bargaining situation, or in a prisoner's dilemma, or faced with a coercive offer, or an attempt at extortion. My problem is not resolved, or diminished, or even significantly adjusted, if the "self" I am protecting is other than my proper self, if I am not just trying to save my own skin, so to speak. An extortionist or a benefactor who knows what I care about is in a position to frame the situation to hit me where it matters to me, whatever matters to me.

We human beings can distribute our selves not only in "space" but also in time, caring about our own futures and pasts, and even about remote pasts and futures centuries outside our individual lifetimes. No other species has such labile boundaries on the problems of self-interest its members can define. And it is worth noting that we are quite properly concerned with the prospect of this lability moving in the other direction. As I put it in *Elbow Room*, in my discussion of the Incredible Disappearing Self, "If you make yourself really small, you can externalize almost everything." (1984: 143) Shrinking the boundaries of the self can be a way of obtunding suffering (as when an abused child dissociates and "leaves" [Dennett, 1995b]), but it can also be a way of evading responsibility. The standard Western model of the self is not as universally appreciated as we in the West often suppose. "To us in Asia," says Lee Khan Yew, Senior Minister of Singapore, "an individual is an ant. To you, he's a child of God; it is an amazing concept." (*Boston Globe*, April 29, 1994) Recognizing that this statement is itself a piece of propaganda, not remotely an accurate scientific observation, only drives home the point that selves are socially constructed (and none the less real and objective on that account), and hence pre-eminently cultural entities, not simply part of our biological equipment.

4.2 Perspectives on cultural evolution

How does culture accomplish the design work in our brains that makes all these transformations possible? Partly by restructuring the functional structure of individual human brains – creating virtual machines on the underlying hardware (for more on the mind as a virtual machine, see Dennett 1991, 1996), but also by creating structures in the public world that alter the perceivable opportunities and costs for those virtual machines. For instance, consider Bowles' definition of a norm [this volume]. "A norm is a cultural trait governing actions that affect the well-being of others but that cannot be regulated by costlessly enforceable contracts." By making norms, culture makes habits; this makes it easier for brains to be the kinds of minds they are. As Andy Clark has put it, "We use intelligence to structure our environment so that we can succeed with less intelligence. Our brains make the world smart so we can be dumb in peace!" (1996: 180)

If culture transmits and installs virtual machines in growing human brains and their surroundings, where does the software come from? Who writes the code? Nobody. Who invented Chinese? Who invented arithmetic? Who invented money? Nobody. These fine artifacts, all exhibiting impressive features that bespeak expensive histories of R and D, have evolved over long periods of time, the design work distributed among myriads of largely oblivious innovators and editors.

When one says that cultures evolve, this can be taken as a truism, or as asserting one or another controversial, speculative, unconfirmed theory. Consider a cultural inventory at time t: it includes all the languages, practices, ceremonies, edifices, methods, tools, myths, music, art, and so forth, that compose a culture. Over time, the inventory changes. Some items disappear, some multiply, some merge, some change. (When I say some change, I mean to be neutral at this point about whether this amounts to their being replaced by similar items, or their undergoing a transformation.) A verbatim record of this history would not be science; it would be a data base. That is the truism: cultures evolve over time. Now the question remains: how are we to explain the patterns found in that data base? Are there any good theories or models of cultural evolution?

The traditional model to be found in most accounts by historians and anthropologists treats culture as composed of goods, possessions of the people, who husband them in various ways, wisely or foolishly. They carefully preserve their traditions of fire-lighting, house-building, speaking, counting, justice, etc. They trade cultural items as they trade other goods. And of course some cultural items (wagons, pasta, recipes for chocolate cake, etc.) are definitely goods, and we can plot their trajectories using the tools of economics. The people, on this model, are seen as having an autonomous or independent rationality; deprive a person of his goods, and he stands there, naked but rational and full of informed desires. When he clothes himself and arms himself and equips himself with goods, he increases his powers, complicates his desires, etc.

On this way of thinking, the relative "replicative" power of various cultural goods is measured in the marketplace of cost- benefit calculations performed by the people. If Coca-Cola bottles proliferate around the world, it is because more and more people prefer to buy a Coke. Advertising may fool them. But then we look to the advertisers, or those who have hired them, to find the relevant loci of values for our calculations. *Cui bono*? The purveyors of the goods, and those they hire to help them.

Biologists, too, can often make sense of the evolution (in the neutral sense) of features by treating them as goods: one's food, one's nest, one's burrow, one's territory, one's mate[s], one's time and energy. Cost-benefit analyses shed light on the husbandry engaged in by the members of the different species inhabiting some shared environment. Not every "possession" is considered a good, however; one's accompanying flies and fleas, the dirt and grime that accumulates on one's body, are of no value, or of negative value, for instance. One's symbionts are not normally considered as goods by biologists, except when the benefits derived from them (by *whom*?) are manifest.

This perspective is not uniformly illuminating, nor is it obligatory. I would like to suggest that both biologists and economists (and other social scientists) can benefit from adopting a different vantage point on these phenomena, one which quite properly gives pride of place to the *Cui bono* question, which can provide alternative answers that are often overlooked. This is Dawkins' meme's-eye point of view, which recognizes – and takes seriously – the possibility that cultural entities may evolve according to selectional regimes that make sense only when the answer to the *Cui bono* question is that it is the cultural items *themselves* that benefit from the adaptations they exhibit.

Dawkins' theory of memes, as briefly sketched in a single chapter of *The Selfish Gene* (1976, but see also Dawkins 1993), is hardly a theory at all, especially compared to the models of cultural evolution developed by other biologists, such as Cavalli-Sforza and Feldman (1981), Lumsden and Wilson (1981), and Boyd and Richerson (1985). Unlike these others, Dawkins offers no formal development, no mathematical models, no quantitative predictions, no systematic survey of relevant empirical findings. But Dawkins does present an idea that is overlooked by all the others, and it is, I think, a most important idea. It is the key to understanding how we can be not just guardians and transmitters of culture, but cultural entities ourselves – all the way in.

Whenever costs and benefits are the issue – e.g., when Pagano [this volume] speaks of how a difference in the distribution of property rights leads to a difference in accounting the profits, or when Bowles [this volume] speaks of "group beneficial effects" and of the "efficiency-enhancing properties" of a practice, we need to ask *Cui bono*? A benefit by itself is not explanatory; a benefit in a vacuum is indeed a sort of mystery; until it can be shown how the benefit actually redounds to enhance the replicative power of a replicator, it just sits there, alluring, perhaps, but incapable of explaining anything.

We see an ant laboriously climbing up a stalk of grass. Why is it doing that? Why is that adaptive? What good accrues to the ant by doing that? That is the *wrong question* to ask. No good accrues to the ant; its brain has been invaded by a fluke (*Dicrocoelium dendriticum*), one of a gang of tiny parasites that need to get themselves into the intestines of a sheep in order to reproduce (Ridley 1995: 258). (Salmon swim up stream, these parasitic worms drive ants up grass stalks, to improve their chances of being ingested by a passing sheep.) The benefit is not to the reproductive prospects of the ant but the reproductive prospects of the fluke.

Dawkins points out that we can think of cultural items, memes, as parasites, too. Actually, they are more like a simple virus than a worm. Memes are supposed to be analogous to genes, the replicating entities of the cultural media, but they also have vehicles, or phenotypes; they are like not-so-naked genes. They are like viruses (Dawkins 1993). As with viruses, there is a phenotype/genotype distinction, but just barely. Basically, a virus is just a string of DNA (or RNA) with attitude. And similarly, a meme is an information-packet (the information, not the vehicle) with attitude – with some phenotypic clothing that has differential effects in the world that thereby influence its chances of getting replicated.

And in the domain of memes, the ultimate beneficiary, the beneficiary in terms of which the final cost-benefit calculations must apply is: the meme itself, not its carriers. This is not to be read as itself a bold empirical claim, ruling out (for instance) the role of individual human agents in devising, appreciating and securing the spread and prolongation of cultural items. It is rather a proposal that we adopt a perspective or point of view, from which a *wide variety of different* empirical claims can be compared, and the evidence for them considered in a neutral setting, a setting that does not prejudge these hot-button questions.

In the analogy with the fluke, we are invited to consider a meme as like a parasite which commandeers an organism for its own replicative benefit, but we should remember that symbionts can be classified into three fundamental categories:

- *parasites*, whose presence lowers the fitness of their host;
- *commensals*, whose presence in neutral (though, as the etymology reminds us, they "share the same table"); and
- *mutualists*, whose presence enhances the fitness of both host and guest.

Since these varieties are arrayed along a continuum, the boundaries between them need not be too finely drawn; just where benefit drops to zero or turns to harm is not something to be directly measured by any practical test, though we can explore the consequences of these turning points in models.

The main point to note is that we should expect memes to come in all three varieties, too. This means, for instance, that it is a mistake to *assume* that the "cultural selection" of a cultural trait is always "for cause" – always because of some perceived (or even misperceived) benefit it provides to the host. We can always *ask* if the hosts, the human agents that are the vectors, perceive some benefit and (for that reason, good or bad) assist in the preservation and replication of the cultural item in question, but we must be prepared to entertain the answer that they do not. In other words, we must consider as a real possibility the hypothesis that the human hosts are, individually or as a group, either oblivious to, or agnostic about, or even positively dead set against, some cultural item, which nevertheless is able to exploit its hosts as vectors.

The most familiar cases of cultural transmission and evolution discussed are innovations that are obviously of some direct or indirect benefit to the *Darwinian* – that is, genetic – fitness of the host. A better fishhook catches more fish, feeds more bellies, makes for more surviving grandchildren, etc. The only difference between stronger arms and a better fishhook in the (imagined) calculation of impact on fitness is that the stronger arms might be – might be – passed on quite directly through the germ line, while the fishhook definitely must be culturally transmitted. (The stronger arms could be culturally transmitted as well, of course. A tradition of body-building, for instance, could explain why there was very *low* [genetic] heritability for strong adult arms, and yet a very *high* rate of strong adult arms in a population.) But however strong arms or fishhooks are transmitted, they are typically supposed to be a good bargain from the perspective of genetic fitness. The bargain might, however, be myopic – only good in the short run. After all, even agriculture, in the long run, may be a dubious bargain if what you are taking as your *summum bonum* is Darwinian fitness. What alternatives are there?

First, we need to note that in the short run (evolutionarily speaking – that is, from the perspective of a few centuries or even millennia) something might flourish independently of whether it was of *actual* benefit to genetic fitness, but strongly linked to whether it was of *apparent* benefit to genetic fitness. Even if you think that Darwinian fitness enhancement is the principle driving engine of cultural evolution, you have to posit some swifter, more immediate mechanism of retention and transmission.[2] It's not hard to find one. As I noted earlier, cultural items may exploit machinery that had earned its keep in the past by embodying a "fitness-enhancing set of preferences." We are genetically endowed with a quality space in which some things feel good and some things don't, and we tend to live by the rule: if it feels good, keep it. This rough and ready rule can be tricked, of course. The sweet tooth is the standard example. The explosion of cultural items – artifacts, practices, recipes, patterns of agriculture, trade routes – that depend quite directly on the exploitation of the sweet tooth has probably had a considerable net negative effect on human genetic fitness. Notice that explaining the emergence of these cultural items by citing their "apparent" benefit to genetic fitness does not in any way commit us to the (preposterous) claim that people *think* (mistakenly) that they are enhancing their genetic fitness by acquiring and consuming sugar. The rationale is not their's, but Mother Nature's. They just go with what they like.

Still, given what they like, they choose rationally, and indeed ingeniously and often with impressive foresight, how to obtain what they like. This is still the traditional model of cultural evolution, with agents husbanding their goods in order to maximize what they prefer - and getting their preferences quite directly from their genetic heritage. A more interesting possibility is acquiring new preferences that are themselves culturally transmitted symbionts of one sort or another. Each will have to bootstrap itself into the memosphere by exploiting some pre-established preference, but this recursive process, which can proceed at breakneck speed relative to the glacial pace of genetic evolution, can transform human agents indefinitely far away from their genetic beginnings. In an oft-quoted passage, E.O. Wilson claimed otherwise:

> The genes hold culture on a leash. The leash is very long, but inevitably values will be constrained in accordance with their effects on the human gene pool.
>
> (Wilson 1978: 167)

This leash. I am claiming, is indefinitely long, in the sense that the constraints Wilson speaks of can be so co-opted, exploited, and obtunded in a recursive cascade of cultural products and meta-products that it is not clear that there are *any* points in imaginable cultural design space that could not, in principle, be occupied by some product that could ultimately be traced back, via Wilson's leash of historical processes, to the genes. Many of these imaginable points would no doubt be *genetic* cul-de-sacs *H. sapiens* would sooner or later go extinct as a result of occupying those points), but this is no barrier to their evolving in the swift time of cultural history.

Not only can we acquire tastes; we can acquire meta-tastes. That is, we can discover in the culture, and thereupon adopt, a taste for "cultivating" further acquired tastes, and so forth. At each stage we can anticipate finding parasites, commensals and mutualists - but we can classify these only by asking the *Cui bono?* question *against a new background* and making one local determination or another. One person's scholarly connoisseurship is another person's addiction to trash. Meta-memes for "traveling" or "being a collector" or "having a hobby" or "educating oneself" can themselves be viewed as either exploiters or enhancers of the pre-established *personal* (no longer genetic) preferences. It is interesting that in common parlance we often call our preferences "weaknesses," - as in "I have a weakness for strong cheese (or puns or redheads)" - deftly implying a standard to which in the same breath we deny any personal allegiance.

And this, then is the main point I wanted to emphasize in Dawkins' vision. The memes that proliferate will be the memes that replicate *by hook or by crook.* Think of them as entering the brains of culture members, making phenotypic alterations thereupon, and then submitting themselves to the great selection tournament - *not* the Darwinian genetic fitness tournament (life is too short for that) but the Dawkinsian meme-fitness tournament. It is *their* fitness as memes that is on the line, not their host's genetic fitness, and the environments that embody the selective pressures that determine their fitness are composed in large measure of *other* memes.

Why do their hosts put up with this? Why should the overhead costs of establishing a whole new system of differential reproduction be borne by members of

H. sapiens? Note that the question to be asked and answered here is parallel to the question we ask about any parasite-host relationship: why do the hosts put up with it? And the short answer is that it is too costly to eradicate, but this just means that the benefits accruing to the machinery that is being exploited by the parasites are so great that keeping the machinery and tolerating the parasites (to the extent that they are tolerated) has so far been the best deal available. And whether or not in the lone run (millions of years) this infestation will be viewed as mutualism or commensalism or parasitism, in the short run (the last few millennia) the results have been spectacular: the creation of a new biological type of entity: a person.

I like to compare this development to the arrival of the eukaryotes several billion years ago. Relatively simple prokaryotes got invaded by some of their neighbors, and the resulting endosymbiotic teams were more fit, and prospered, enabling a biological revolution. The eukaryotes, living alongside their prokaryotic cousins, but enormously more complex, versatile and competent, opened up the design space of multi-cellular organisms. Similarly, the emergence of culture-infected hominids has opened up yet another region of hitherto unoccupied and untraversable design space. We live alongside our animal cousins, but we are enormously more complex, versatile and competent. And by joining forces with our memes, we create new candidates for the locus of benefit, new answers to *Cui bono?*

4.3 Some paths not taken

In Cavalli-Sforza and Feldman's pioneering work on cultural evolution, they note the phenomena that invite the meme's-eye view, but treat them as complications best set aside. As noted before, they discuss what they call the "steering system" and observe that "it is probably true that the system's overall activity is directed towards maximizing self satisfaction of the individual" (1981: 364). But they don't go on to look at the possibilities this opens up.[3] They briefly consider the prospect of treating artifacts, such as violins and cars, as "second order organisms," and measuring *their* fitness as "cultural objects" (p.17), but they do not suggest that such fitness might be anything other than excellence of design *from the point of view of the artifact-user*, which is, as we have seen, just one of the possibilities – the analogue of the mutualist case, in effect. Thus when they speak of adaptation, they apparently have in mind only the genetic fitness of members of human cultures. For instance, "If cultural innovations are not truly random, but are designed to solve specific problems, they may increase the rate of the corresponding adaptation in evolution over that expected for a truly random process" (p.66). They go on to see that the chance that an intended improvement will be "truly adaptive in the long run is not 100%" so "a significant proportion of new cultural mutations might be truly random without any semblance of adaptiveness." But many of the mutations in this "significant proportion" might exhibit clear adaptiveness, measured from the meme's-eye perspective.

This overlooked opportunity is compounded by another. Cavalli-Sforza and Feldman correctly draw our attention to the distinction between what they call awareness and adoption. Awareness is the minimal result of exposure; adoption involves a change of phenotype as a result of that exposure. The distinction is analogous to that between testing positive for a virus and having the full-blown symptomatology of the viral disease. The growth of awareness of a meme can be much swifter than its adoption, of course. The adoption/awareness distinction is important, but by restricting their models to the spread of adoption, they submerge a major channel of cultural evolution: "However, the final test of fitness is whether the learned trait will be really incorporated into the final permanent phenotype of the individual, or alternatively forgotten, rejected or replaced. In the latter cases the trait evidently does not pass the test of cultural selection" (p.66).

Certainly memes can be widely transmitted without being "adopted." In Dawkins' terms one might say that a meme can have a limited phenotype and an "extended" phenotype. Beavers in captivity may not get to build dams, the most distinctive feature of their extended phenotype, but still they may reproduce and hence evolve. Similarly, a meme "in captivity" may reproduce without having its extended phenotype effect. For instance, Marco Polo brought the pasta meme from China to Italy in his mind-zoo; he didn't have to adopt the meme; he didn't have to become a pasta-maker. I have the idea of cannibalism, but am not a cannibal. I keep the meme alive, however, and can pass it on to others by taking about cannibalism. Many effects of cultural evolution depend on such silent transmission, transmission with negligible phenotypic effects in the carriers – aside from the all-important effects of *informing* the carriers on that topic and fostering further transmission. (A fitness-enhancing phenotypic trait for a meme is *being an interesting topic of conversation*, but it is shared by very many widely diverse memes.) By defining the presence of the cultural item in terms of the manifestation of the trait in individual phenotypes, Cavalli-Sforza and Feldman obscure these routes of cultural transmission, and hence overlook many large-scale phenomena of cultural evolution.

> With the advent of telecommunications it seems reasonable to suggest that, for many socio-behavioral traits, the teacher-leader type of transmission has come to play a dominant role. Today the audience of a single social-cultural leader can be more than continental in size. For traits under this sort of influence, evolution, as we have seen, becomes extremely fast. Since the awareness increases so quickly via the mass media, it is the rate of acceptance that limits the rate of evolution of these traits (p.354).

This is one sort of case, but just as salient, one would think, are the cases that don't involve "teacher-leaders" as their source. The Heaven's Gate suicidal cult memes recently took full advantage of the telecommunications media, and will now lie, more or less dormant in millions, perhaps billions, of minds, where they can evolve in all manners of ways with very little adoption.

It may be true that these phenomena do not really represent overlooked opportunities for science after all. Perhaps they are not paths that have been ignored, but rather stony ground on which no science could be grown.[4] Perhaps, as I have suggested (1995a, pp. 35–60), memetics cannot be turned into serious science for the relatively boring reason that the requisite data-gathering cannot be done. (If fossils were not formed and preserved in sediment, and if DNA could not be sequenced, evolutionary biology would be very largely speculative, for similarly tedious reasons.) But then at least we should acknowledge that the phenomena of cultural evolution are not exhausted by the few cases for which mathematical models of some realism can be constructed. And we shouldn't take those cases as evidence for the ubiquity of the constraints that make up Wilson's imagined leash. Suppose it were a fact that the only aspects of cultural evolution *that we can mathematically model* "are constrained in accordance with their effects on the human gene pool"; it wouldn't follow that all important phenomena of cultural evolution are similarly constrained.[5]

A confusion that misdirects the imagination of theorists in another direction derives, I suspect, from a subtle misreading of Darwin's original use of artificial selection (deliberate animal breeding) and "unconscious" selection (the unwitting promotion of favored offspring of domesticated animals) as bridges to his concept of natural selection.[6] While it is true that Darwin wished to contrast the utter lack of foresight or intention in natural selection with the deliberate goal-seeking of the artificial selectors, in order to show how the natural process could in principle proceed without any mentality at all, he did not thereby establish (as many seem to have supposed) that deliberate, goal-directed, intentional selection is not a subvariety of natural selection! The short legs of dachshunds, and the huge udders of Holsteins are just as much products of natural selection as the wings of the eagle; they just evolved in an environment that included a particularly well-focused selective pressure consisting of human agents. These phenotypes fall under the same laws of transmission genetics, the same replicator dynamics, as any others – as special and extreme cases in which the default "randomness" or noisiness of selective pressure has been greatly reduced.

Applied to cultural evolution, the implication is this: There is no conflict between the claim that artifacts (including abstract artifacts – memes) are the products of natural selection, and the claim that they are (often) the foreseen, designed products of intentional human activity. It appears that some thinkers in the newly emerging school of evolutionary archeology have made this mistake. According to a critique by Boone and Smith (forthcoming), at least some evolutionary archeologists think that the only way to be hardheaded and scientific about the Darwinian evolution of culture is to deny all intention, all rationality, on the part of human culture-makers. They opt for "selection rather than decision-making" (p.11). That is simply a mistake, for the same reason it would be a mistake to say that the fancy plumage of prize pigeons is the result of decision-making *rather than* selection. But Boone and Smith fall in the same trap, in their discussion of the interesting phenomenon of the spread of snowmobiles among the Cree in northern Canada. They are surely right that the adoption of snowmobiles by the Cree cannot be accounted for in terms of the differential biological replication of the snowmobile users, but they misread the more interesting meme's-eye view perspective. They say:

> The alternative that 'snowmobile memes' were transmitted more effectively

> than 'snowshoe memes' to non-descendant Cree (as well as offspring), while plausible, *is not natural selection* [emphasis added]; more significantly, it requires precisely the kind of adaptive decision-making that EA [evolutionary archeology] is dedicated to eliminating from archeological explanation [ms p.12].

On the contrary, if you adopt the meme's-eye perspective, in which the snowmobile meme is seen as the replicator, with *its own* fitness, then cultural evolution can be seen to be due to "adaptive decision-making" while also a variety of natural selection. Consider the fitness of the domesticated horses that spread so quickly among the Native Americans after their introduction, but then more recently, after the advent of the automobile, have dwindled sharply. These fluctuations in genetic fitness have been due to changes in the selective forces arrayed in the various environments in which the horses have existed, of course, and the fact that conscious, foresightful human agents form the key component in those selective environments does nothing to remove the phenomena from the domain of standard genetic evolution by natural selection.

Among those who have overlooked this fact is Steven Pinker, who dismisses models of cultural evolution in a brief passage in *How the Mind Works* (1997):

> Stop being so literal-minded! respond the fans of cultural evolution. Of course cultural evolution is not an exact replica of the Darwinian version. In cultural evolution, the mutations are directed and the acquired characteristics are inherited. Lamarck, while being wrong about biological evolution, turned out to be right about cultural evolution. . . . To say that cultural evolution is Lamarckian is to confess that one has no idea how it works. The striking features of cultural products, namely their ingenuity, beauty, and truth (analogous to organisms' complex adaptive design), come from the mental computations that "direct" – that is, invent – the "mutations," and that "acquire" – that is, understand – the "characteristics" (p.209).

Pinker has imputed the wrong parallel; it is not Lamarck's model, but Darwin's model of *artificial* selection (as a special case of natural selection) that accommodates the phenomena he draws t out attention in this passage. And it is ironic that Pinker overlooks this, since the cultural phenomena he himself has highlighted as examples of evolution-designed systems, linguistic phenomena, are almost certainly *not* the products of foresightful, ingenious, deliberate human invention. Some designed features of human languages are no doubt genetically transmitted, but many others – such as changes in pronunciation, for instance – are surely culturally transmitted, and hence products of cultural, not genetic, evolution.

Some memes are like domesticated animals; they are prized for their benefits, and their replication is closely fostered and relatively well understood by their human owners. Some memes are more like rats; they thrive in the human environment in spite of being positively selected against – ineffectually – by their unwilling hosts. And some are more like bacteria or other viruses, commandeering aspects of human behavior (provoking sneezing, for instance) in their "efforts" to propagate from host to host. There is artificial selection of "good" memes – like the memes of arithmetic and writing, which are carefully taught to each new generation. And there is unconscious selection of memes of all sorts – like the subtle mutations in pronunciation that spread through linguistic groups, presumably with some efficiency advantage, but perhaps just hitchhiking on some quirk of human preference. And there is unconscious selection of memes that are positively a menace, but which prey on flaws in the human decision-making apparatus, as provided for in the genome and enhanced and adjusted by other cultural innovations – such a the abducted-by-aliens meme, which makes perfect sense when *its own* fitness as a cultural replicator is considered.

4.4 Conclusion

This spectrum of possibilities, from unwitting, unconscious hosting of culture-borne viruses (of all "attitudes") to the foresightful design and promulgation of inventions and creations that intelligently and artfully draw upon well-understood cultural resources, *must* be viewable under a single, unifying perspective. It is only from such a perspective that we can make sense of the trajectories that have taken us – and only us – beyond the horizons of our selfish genes, by creating new environments of selection – persons and their projects – that in evolution doesn't *deny* the possibility of moving to what might be called a *mind's-eye* perspective of evaluation; it is precisely what makes such a transition – without any help from skyhooks – possible.

Notes

1 Perhaps we just haven't yet found the "right" definition of goodness. But if we are constraining our attempt at definition by the demand that it yield a preference for trajectory A over trajectory B in "normal people," then we are prejudging the issue in a way that itself requires motivation. Who says this is a constraint we should honor?

2 This is parallel to the familiar myopia of genetic evolution; the fact that sex, say, is good for maintaining genetic versatility in the long run is no explanation of how and why it gets maintained in the short run. The heavy and immediate costs of meiosis have to be balanced by some heavy and immediate benefit (see e.g., Ridley 1993).

3 "Coca-Cola, frisbee, volleyball and yo-yos are examples of 'innovations' that have spread rapidly through whole countries or continents. It is obvious that in none of these examples does participation appreciably alter the probability of surviving or having children" Cavalli-Sforza and Feldman (p.15).
Boyd and Richerson, similarly, make it clear that "Nonadaptive, or even frankly maladaptive, cultural variants can spread in a population under the influence of indirect bias, even in the face of selection and direct bias favoring more adaptive variants" (p.279). They do not, however, attempt to explore these possibilities.

4 In later work, Feldman and his colleagues have addressed some of the complexities they deliberately submerged in their earlier work. In a paper submitted to the Siena workshop, Feldman, Otto and Christiansen (1996) discuss models that have the potential to distinguish awareness ("a latent factor that can be transmitted culturally from generation to generation") and adoption ("phenotypic effects") [ms, p.12].

5 Aaron Lynch (1991) has attempted a mathematical formulation of some aspects of memetics, focusing on the simplest stripped down cases – which still swiftly spawn complications. Like Cavalli-Sforza and Feldman, he postpones treatment of the awareness

side of the awareness/adoption distinction, though his model permits the distinction to be expressed. Whether these tactical simplifications permit the resulting model to tell us anything surprising (and confirmed) about the real phenomena remains to be seen.

6 The following paragraphs are drawn, with revisions, from Dennett, forthcoming.

References

Boone, James L. and Eric Alden Smith (forthcoming) A Critique of Evolutionary Archeology, *Current Anthropology*. [special issue, supplement, June 1998].

Bowles, Samuel and Herbert Gintis (2000). Chapters 14 and 15, this volume

Boyd, Robert and Peter J. Richerson (1985) *Culture and the Evolutionary Process*. Chicago and London: Chicago University Press.

Cavalli-Sforza, Luca and Marcus Feldman (1981) *Cultural Transmission and Evolution: A Quantitative Approach*, Princeton, NJ: Princeton University Press.

Clark, Andy (1996) *Being There*, Cambridge, MA: MIT Press.

Dawkins, Richard (1976) *The Selfish Gene*. (2nd edn, 1989). Oxford: Oxford University Press.

—— (1993) Viruses of the mind. In Bo Dahlbom (ed.) *Dennett and his Critics*. Oxford: Blackwell.

Dennett, Daniel (1971). Intentional systems. *Journal of Philosophy*, LXVIII: 87–106.

—— (1984) *Elbow Room: The Varieties of Free Will Worth Wanting*. Cambridge, MA: MIT Press, and Oxford: Oxford University Press.

—— (1987) *The Intentional Stance*. Cambridge, MA: Bradford Books/MIT Press.

—— (1991) *Consciousness Explained*. Boston and New York: Little Brown.

—— (1995a) *Darwin's Dangerous Idea: Evolution and the Meanings of Life*. New York: Simon & Schuster.

—— (1995b) Animal consciousness: what matters and why. *Social Research* 62(3): Fall 1995, 691–710.

—— (1996) *Kinds of Minds*. New York: Basic.

—— (forthcoming) Snowmobiles, horses, rats, and memes: a comment on *A Critique of Evolutionary Archeology* by James L. Boone and Eric Alden Smith. *Current Anthropology*, [special issue, supplement, June 1998].

Feldman, Marcus, Sarah P. Otto and Freddy B. Christiansen, Genes, Culture and Inequality. Submitted to the Siena workshop.

Lumsden, C. and E.O. Wilson (1981) *Genes, Mind and Culture*, Cambridge, MA: Harvard University Press.

Lynch, Aaron (1991) Units, events and dynamics of meme replication. *Journal of Ideas* [available in revised form at http://www/mcs//net/ aaron/mememath.htm]

Pagano, Ugo (2000) Chapter 2, this volume

Pinker, Steven (1997) *How the Mind Works*. New York: Norton.

Ridley, Mark (1995) *Animal Behaviour* (2nd edn), Boston: Blackwell Science.

Ridley, Matt (1993) *The Red Queen: Sex and the Evolution of Human Nature*. London: Penguin.

Wilson, E.O. (1978) *On Human Nature*. Cambridge, MA: Harvard University Press.

Part II

The multiplicity of learning paths

5 Path-dependent learning and the evolution of beliefs and behaviors

Implications of Bayesian adaptation under computationally bounded rationality

Paul A. David

5.1 Introduction: technological learning by doing and evolutionary epistemology

Can economists and economic historians of technology usefully continue to take a black box approach in modeling the phenomena characterized as "learning by doing"? Is it sufficient for their purposes to sometimes hypothesize, and other times to document the existence of the empirical relationship between some measure of technological improvement and some measure of "experience," dubbing it "the learning curve"? I suggest that rather than continuing to go on in this way, greater efforts should be made to unpack this black box and examine distinct and interrelated processes of learning that, in practical contexts of technological management under conditions of incomplete information, are taking place in the domains of cognitive progress and behavioral adaptation. The subject of this paper can be described in abstract terms as being concerned with human learning behaviors and the roles of cognitive understanding (and mis-understanding) in the evolution of control over complex and imperfectly observed stochastic processes. This surely represents important territory for historical social scientists in general, and for students of the evolution of technological knowledge in particular. From the foregoing description one reasonably could suppose that this is an inquiry into the influences of evolutionary processes upon human cognition. If the "evolutionary epistemology" label is to be applied in a manner that will not mislead and eventually disappoint those who trust its accuracy, however, it should be read in this instance as referring simply to the proposition that conceptual change is an evolutionary process, or can be modeled usefully as such.[1] Nothing in the following pages will address the preoccupations of the other branch of inquiry in the literature so designated – the branch concerned with the epistemological implications that might follow from the fact of the human organism's evolutionary origins.[2] Nevertheless, even so delimited, the general subject matter ought to hold some considerable interest for students of the history of the interplay between ideas and material civilization.

While the larger topic would warrant a much more systematic consideration of an extensive literature to which many have contributed, what is on offer here is an idiosyncratic speculative venture into this vast and difficult terrain. These speculations are grounded in the study of a particular and very narrow tract of the broad field of experience-based technological learning, and therefore follow the approach of working from the specific and concrete, towards the general and abstract. Moreover, the starting point is an eccentric one, and the reader must therefore be asked to trust that the historical problem that motivates the following, although outwardly far removed from the usual matters on which students of technological change have focused, will lead to a quite general formulation of the issues involved in modeling experience-based learning. It is to be hoped, therefore, that this latter will be found to have much wider, paradigmatic value.

The concrete domain of research upon which I shall draw concerns the historical development of knowledge about human reproductive physiology in relationship to the intentional control of fertility within marital unions. Perhaps this is a sufficiently interesting matter to stand on its own, and it is one that has engaged my attention on previous occasions, even recently in a paper with Warren Sanderson.[3] But, here its intrinsic interest will be made subsidiary to its utility in an intellectual exercise that could be called "applied metonomy" – a mode of inquiry predicated upon belief in the possibility that significant attributes of the whole can be revealed by close examination of one, albeit small part. To be still more concrete, the historical inquiry in which Sanderson and I were engaged began quite a number of years ago as one part of a larger program of research on the efficacy of rudimentary fertility control techniques, and their possible impact in the American population's nineteenth-century transition to family limitation.[4] At the time, this entire topic lay far outside the usual ambit of economists and economic historians, and so the keen interest we developed in the efficacy of the particular class of contraceptive practices that were referred to during the nineteenth century as "safe-period" methods, must have seemed more than a little recherché – even to our colleagues in demography. Some consciousness of this attitude in others, undoubtedly, contributed to heightening our concern to not lose sight of the generalizable issues – the meta-problems, so to speak – in the welter of fascinating particulars. Of the latter there was no shortage, for, the precursors of the modern "rhythm method" had a long and curious history about which a little more must now be said, if only by way of setting the stage.

5.1.1 *Safe-period puzzles: treacherous advice or functional process?*

A part of the attraction of posing the general problem of learning in this concrete "problem context," undeniably, has to do with the inherent interest of the history of beliefs and knowledge regarding the biology of human sexual reproduction. It quite alters one's sense of the chronology of "modernity" to realize at how recent a date medical scientists succeeded in dispersing most of the pall of confusion and misapprehensions which previously had enshrouded the physiology (let alone the endocrinology) of the processes of ovulation and conception in humans. The idea that the menstrual cycle of the human female contains a period of peak susceptibility to impregnation, and the complementary notion of a "safe" or "sterile" period, has a long history. It is well known that these notions have figured more or less explicitly in the conceptual structures and patterns of behavior found by ethnographers among the peoples of various pre-literate cultures. They also appeared in the systematic gynaecological writings of Soranus of Ephesus (98–138 AD) and his followers in the West, down to the modern age.[5] The immediate legacy which this venerable tradition left to medical writers in the nineteenth century, unfortunately, was largely one of confusion about the timing of ovulation and the location of the so-called "sterile period." Given the intensity of human concerns with controlling the procreative consequences of sexual activity, one must wonder how it was possible for the basic facts about the periodicity of ovulation to have remained a mystery for so great a portion of human experience.

Soranus had started from the perfectly plausible supposition that menstruation in the human female was an estrous event, a conjecture that, however correct and well-founded it might be in observational evidence from domesticated animals, just happens to be completely wrong in the case of the higher primates. Nevertheless, the citation of ancient authority in medical writings, as in other matters, served to propagate erroneous beliefs, namely, that there was a fertile period that was coincident with menstruation, and that the period of minimal susceptibility to conception must therefore occur somewhere toward the middle of the inter-menstruum. This was only one among manifold misapprehensions concerning the physiology of reproduction, many of them tracing back to Hippocrates and Aristotle, that remained current in the West for more than a millennium.[6]

The durability of human confusion over what today we deem to be rather basic facts about the physiology of procreation, especially among the supposedly "learned" whose opinions have been recorded for us to reflect upon, is truly sobering. Coming to the early nineteenth century, one finds that the influential work by Charles Knowlton, *Fruits of Philosophy* (1833/1841), for example, reiterated Soranus' conviction that conception was most likely to occur in the days *immediately following* menstruation.[7] In England and America, the perpetuation of the belief that ovulation and menstruation were physiologically related and temporally coincident events, quite naturally, led some nineteenth-century authorities on birth prevention to instruct their readers to confine sexual intercourse to the "mid-month" period.[8]

Not all the medically-informed advice published on the subject of the safe period was quite so bad, however. Along with their mistaken belief about the timing of ovulation, some experts came to hold the equally erroneous theory that, following ovulation, the ovum survived in the female reproductive tract and remained capable of being fertilized for a very considerable span of time. The most cautious among them therefore counseled, as a method of avoiding pregnancies, complete abstention from coitus throughout the fourteen days following the cessation of the menses.[9]

When considered *in toto*, therefore, the information emanating from physicians and other "authorities" during the nineteenth and the early twentieth century as to the whereabouts of the safe period had a rather diabolical cast to it. Recipients who took to heart the urgings of extreme caution, and so foreswore coition before the eighteenth day of the menstrual cycle, would indeed have had scant chance of conceiving children; whereas, those couples who deemed it adequate to avoid only the supposed period of maximum susceptibility (in the week following the menses) would thereby be directed to resume sexual relations at just the point in the month when the woman was most likely to be ovulating.[10] The roots of this exquisitely treacherous nineteenth-century advice obviously lay in the medical profession's persisting ignorance of the parameters of the ovulatory cycle in humans. It was not until the physiological discoveries based on lapyroscopic observations by Ogino and Knaus, in 1931 and 1933, respectively, that the safe period method began to be placed on scientific foundations; these reflected a growing consensus that ovulation was a periodic event in human females, and that there was enough regularity about it to describe *the* rhythm of ovulation. In recognition of this important and comparatively recent qualitative shift, historians concerned with voluntary fertility limitation practices in the West generally have followed Norman Himes' (1936–1970) lead in supposing that the historical antecedents of the modern rhythm method essentially had no contraceptive value worthy of consideration.[11]

The reasoning upon which this conclusion seems to rest is not unassailable, as one may see by pausing to ask why anything so putatively useless as the pre-modern "safe period" should have had so wonderful a career. Current expert opinion on the diffusion of contraceptive methods might suggest that a technique that was likely to yield its users an enormously variegated set of outcomes, ranging in this case from extremely effective contraception to perversely quick pregnancies, would not be easy to promote and therefore would not be likely to establish itself even among the members of a population who actively sought means of limiting their fertility. Yet, archival records have been found of interviews conducted around the turn of the nineteenth century on American university campuses, in which some of the married female respondents to questions about their sexual and reproductive behaviors volunteered that, among the various contraceptive techniques they had employed, "the safe-period" method had been used – and, to good effect.[12]

Cast into this frame of reference, the history just reviewed presents something of a paradox, in that the treacherous nature of the practices to which it led notwithstanding, belief in the "safe period" as a method of contraception became widely diffused geographically and persisted in western societies over a very considerable stretch of time. This, however, is a paradox that is more contrived than real. It arises from the failure to distinguish explicitly between the principle of seeking the woman's period of minimal (or maximal) susceptibility to impregnation, and the various specific recommendations that have been made as to where to look first. The historians of medical contraception and family limitation have tended to identify the pre-modern safe period method as a static array of conflicting and erroneously informed recommendations, contrasting this with the modern, scientific rhythm method. In so doing, they have overlooked the possibility that the informal practice of *searching* for the elusive safe period could in itself constitute an effective means of controlling individual fertility.

A puzzle emerges, nevertheless. Inasmuch as some versions of the safe period method, when rigorously applied, would have rivaled the anovulant pill and IUD in use-effectiveness, the question one well might ask is: Why did not those "good" versions drive the others from the field? Indeed, if birth control advice that incorrectly located the safe period within the menstrual cycle could be quickly modified or discarded on the basis of personal experience of their untoward consequences, would it ultimately matter which particular version of the method people had accepted when they commenced the practice? Perhaps it was through a similar process of experience-based revision that some nineteenth-century medical practitioners had come to extend the proscribed interval, eventually advising against sexual intercourse during the two weeks following the end of menstruation, and correspondingly adjusting their theories about the viability of the human ovum. These, and some other largely unnoticed puzzles concerning the history of fertility control beliefs and practices, can be approached by treating the primitive rhythm method as a *process* – a search or learning process, to be concrete – and analyzing the opportunities it could have provided for effective, fertility-limiting adaptations at the micro-behavioral level.

5.1.2 Conceptualizing control via learning as an evolutionary process

The question thus posed is whether the sheer lack of accurate physiological knowledge had prevented women from deriving any substantial degree of contraceptive protection from safe-period methods, which some of them testified to having employed during the era before more reliable modern contraceptive techniques were available. One approach to answering that question is creating a stochastic computer simulation model of an interactive, micro-level learning process that would permit a quantitative exploration and evaluation of the possibilities of constrained experience-based ("trial-and-error") learning about the rhythm of ovulation and susceptibility to impregnation. The relevant constraints on such a process Sanderson and I took to be two-fold in nature. One set would stem from the fundamental lack of understanding about the physiology of reproduction, and the other from limitations that necessarily would be imposed on individual experimental action in this field – by the participants' other motivating concerns. Principal among the latter, we were ready to suppose for the purposes of the analysis, would be a desire to manage the "regime" of coition (and, specifically, the distribution of the times when sexual intercourse occurred within the intermenstruum) so as to minimize the expectation of a conception.

In building a model of sequential "regime adaptation," we thus were soon obliged to consider the problem of the cognitive limitations under which experience-based inferences and consequent behavioral adaptations would have to proceed. These we characterized in two ways: (i) *maintained beliefs* about the existence, and nature of a monthly interval during which a woman would be at the peak of her susceptibility to the risk of impregnation from unprotected intercourse, and (ii) *mutable and adaptable beliefs* concerning the location of that interval within the intermenstruum. The representation of cognitive evolution as the sequential updating of beliefs concerning those matters, following Bayesian principles of inference to guide the trial-and-error process of learning, was then a comparatively straightforward step to take in the formal modeling exercise. To suppose that revision of such beliefs would induce adaptations in the goal-seeking behaviors of the individuals who held them, so that the time distribution of coition might correspondingly be modified, also was (for economists) a quite natural conceptual sequel.

The upshot of this was a simple model that qualified as "evolutionary," although not so in the strict Darwinian sense. The touchstone of an evolutionary process is that whatever can exist at each point in time remains strictly bounded by that which existed previously; genetic processes of evolution are those in which the contents of the gene pool set the limits upon the genetic material that can be phenotypically expressed in the next generation. So, as often is said, in matters biological, Nature is obliged to solve her problems largely with materials that already are on hand.[13] A thoroughly Darwinian evolutionary process is one that can be said, following the usage made popular by Campbell (1960), to depend upon some mechanism involving "blind variation and selective retention" – irrespectively of whether the subject of evolution is a gene-governed biological trait, or a cultural "meme." Our simple model of behavioral optimization under uncertainty, where actions are conditioned upon beliefs concerning states of the world that are sequentially revised on the basis of the observable realization of the stochastic process, thus qualifies as "evolutionary." It also features selective retention of beliefs and consequent patterns of behavior, although the hypothesized mechanism of selection has nothing to do with the principle of "inclusive fitness" that operates in Darwinian natural selection; rather the opposite, for it involves the retention of beliefs that are consistent with consequential actions which are functionally adaptive to the extent that they serve the (myopic) goal of minimizing the monthly conditional expectation of a pregnancy. Whether or not it is more illuminating, therefore, to see the process of selection as representing Larmarckian *instructionism*, rather than strict Darwinian *selectionism*, is a matter of interpretation that will occupy me later on in this essay.[14]

What is beyond question, however, is that whether one focuses upon the individual's belief structures (concerning the timing of ovulation) or the associated behavioral regimes (concerning the timing of intercourse) as being the "memes" in this micro-level evolutionary process, from the point at which the process begins, variations in the memes over which selection takes place will not be "blind." Such evolution as may occur is driven by a conscious cognitive process of interpreting "the data," and optimizing, and re-optimizing the behavioral regime subject to the constraints of the agents' currently prevailing information states. It is of interest to ask whether there are conditions under which this kind of rational, evolutionary learning procedure could permit the user effectively to control fertility within a finite reproductive life-span. But also, we would like to know whether or not in doing so it would perform in a way that was qualitatively superior to a strictly Darwinian evolutionary process of adaptation. The possibility of answering such questions by numerical simulations, as has been intimated, motivated our efforts to construct a computable model.

When it came to trying to implement this research program concretely, by specifying our stochastic learning model, Sanderson and I soon were forced to reconsider carefully the formulation that initially had been chosen for the maintained portion of the agents' beliefs about the (physiological) "states of the world" with which they were having to contend. We had started from a suitably modern, medically-informed specification of the objective processes that our hypothetical couples would be trying to control. But we were then driven towards ever-less-complicated suppositions about "reality," in order to reduce to plausibly manageable levels the computational burden of the implied Bayesian information processing procedure. The emergence of this latter class of considerations, and the existence of an elegantly simple and intuitively appealing solution to the problem, were not at all obvious to us at the outset. Moreover, as will be seen, they present a rather interesting new way of approaching the problem of modeling "bounded rationality" in the management and adaptation of complex technological processes – and the related issue of the possible origins of "rational heuristic strategies" more generally conceived.

In the following section a model of sequential Bayesian modification of beliefs and consequent behavioral adaptation aimed at controlling conceptions is described, and this serves to clarify the existence of several distinct ways in which it is possible to characterize "learning" within this quantitative framework. (Details of the model's formal specifications, and the basis for parameterization of the objective biological component of the stochastic simulation structure, are relegated to Appendices A and B, respectively.) Section 5.3 reports and comments on what the simulation studies revealed about individual and population-level adaptation in fertility control, and the relationship of the latter to the evolution of beliefs held regarding the rhythm of ovulation and the time pattern of "susceptibility" to impregnation in the human female.

Section 5.4 takes up several broader, generic themes upon which the specific illustrative case may be seen to have a more-or-less direct bearing: (1) the relationship between cognitive and behavioral evolution in a population, and the implications of changes in conditions for experimentation; (2) deeper connections that may exist between evolutionary models that appear to feature Larmarckian "instructionism" and those that are built upon strictly Darwinian "selectionist" principles; and (3) a suggested "bounded rationality" view of cognitive progress, as involving the co-evolution of information processing capabilities and the selection of computationally expedient heuristics.

I conclude by remarking that the foregoing line of speculation suggests that potentially far-reaching, transformative implications at the epistemological level may flow from the advances in information processing technologies that are occurring around us.

5.2 Bounded Bayesian adaptation: a simulation model of stochastic learning

The following describes a Bayesian strategy for averting conceptions by selecting regimes of sexual intercourse that minimize the subjective expectation of pregnancy, doing so myopically, for each successive "trial." In this routine, prior probabilities assigned to alternative states of the world are updated on the basis of the outcome of each month's experience – a "state of the world" being a particular time-profile of the hazard of a conception, corresponding to the location of the date of ovulation in the woman's monthly cycle. We will use the term "Bayesian adaptive rhythm" (BAR) when referring to the generic method of averting pregnancies by "sampling" and using the conditional likelihoods of the observed outcomes to revise beliefs about the location of the "safe period." BAR is to be distinguished from the modern rhythm method(s), which rely upon information about basal temperature and other physiological indicators to predict the occurrence of ovulation.

Our model falls within a very broad class of statistical learning models that have been investigated by mathematical psychologists.[15] Described in their parlance, the sequence of events for each monthly "trial" of a series proceeds like this: at the beginning of each month (trial), a stimulating situation is presented, and the subject responds to the stimulus with one or another of a set of alternative actions or "responses" (which in this case correspond to the implementation of a selected regime of intercourse for the month). The trial terminates with the occurrence of some one of a set of outcomes (announcement of a pregnancy, or the absence thereof). The underlying specification of a Bayesian strategy for the choice of a regime gives rise to the possibility which is assumed in statistical learning theory, namely, that if other parameters of the situation are held fixed there will be a course of "learning" determined by the trial outcomes. To continue in the language of the so-called "stimulus-sampling models" of learning behavior, the reinforcement serves to connect elements in the set of stimuli with particular responses; stimuli thus connected are said to be "conditioned" to the response. In the mathematical formalization of these theories one major set of axioms relates the probabilities of responses to the proportion of conditioned elements in the stimulus sample. A second major set of axioms specifies how those elements change their state of conditioning as a result of the occurrence of events. The place of the latter is occupied in the present model by the (Bayesian) rules for the updating of priors, and the place of the former axioms is taken by the rules specifying that regimes be selected so as to minimize the current *a priori* expectation of a pregnancy.

Unlike the majority of the statistical learning models that have been submitted to formal analysis and experimental tests, the structure of the learning algorithm we present here does not conform to axioms of "path-independence." Being strictly Bayesian, the model is recursive: the probabilities of a response at every moment in time are functions of the preceding *sequence* of response probabilities and of the intervening consequences of each probabilistic trial. This "history" is distilled and compactly summarized by the current beliefs of the agent – her assignment of *a posteriori* subjective probabilities to alternative conceivable "states of the world."

While it is possible to set up the model so that there exists a direct mapping from the *a posteriori* distribution of beliefs (about the time pattern of ovulation) to the choice of a regime of coitus, and thence to an objective probability of conception, the "state space" of the *a posteriori* distributions is potentially infinite. Therefore, although the mathematics of homogeneous Markov chains has been used to good effect in studying other kinds of stochastic learning, it is not the best tool for analyzing the detailed properties of this Bayesian statistical learning process. To study our non-Markovian "path-dependent" dynamical system, we can more conveniently resort to numerical analysis by using stochastic simulation methods.[16]

5.2.1 Structure of the constrained Bayesian adaptive rhythm (BAR) model

Abstracting from the full complexity of biological realities, we may proceed by representing the intermenstruum as a vector comprising a fixed number of ordered elements; specifically, there will be T elements, arranged in sequence corresponding to the days of the "month"; following convention, these are numbered from 1 beginning with the day of the onset of menstruation. A "rhythm of susceptibility" is our term for the $1 \times T$ vector whose elements describe the woman's subjective estimate of the risk that (an observable) conception would result from her having unprotected sexual intercourse on that day of the month. Each such imaginable profile of susceptibility, or "rhythm," describes a state of the world. But, there will be some restrictions maintained upon conceivable, or, as we may more precisely label them, "admissible" states of the world – those to which the woman assigns positive *a priori* subjective probabilities, $A^0 > 0$. The vector(s) describing an i-th "rhythm of susceptibility," $\tilde{\theta}^i$, must satisfy some very general restrictions, but to these we add a set of further restrictions. These restrictions are set out formally in Appendix A.

Having been imposed in a specific invariant form (which is detailed in mathematical terms in Appendix A.2), these restrictions function as maintained hypotheses that consistently delimit the set of possibilities which the learning agent regards as worthy of serious consideration. One may think of them as representing a particular "model of the biology," one that has been chosen with an eye to the computational feasibility of implementing a BAR strategy. Inasmuch as we envisage such a "model of the world" being formed largely in ignorance of the actual biological processes of ovulation, fertilization and conception, there is no reason to suppose that the objectively "true" state of the world – as far as concerns the time pattern of susceptibility within a representative menstrual cycle – would necessarily be included among the subset S comprising the "admissible" rhythms.[17]

A "regime" of coitus, analogously, is represented as a $1 \times T$ vector whose ordered elements signify whether or not coitus is held on the given day of the month. Thus, in j-th regime, the time-pattern of unprotected coitus is described by a permutation of 0 and 1 elements forming the vector $\overline{\phi_j} = (\phi_1, \phi_2, \ldots \phi_t, \ldots \phi_T)$ where 1 = coition, 0 = no coition. The regime index is $j = (l, \ldots \binom{T}{\tau})$, where the number of days on which intercourse is held , is simply:

$$\tau = nT = \sum_{T}^{t} \phi_t.$$

The parameter n, namely the woman's coital frequency *rate*, will be restricted in this discrete application of the model to regular fractions in the interval (0,1); it is assumed that effectively only one act of coitus can occur on any day, and the maximum number is limited to T.

As was noted previously, we shall be concerned here with the performance of a constrained form of BAR, in which the hypothetical woman (user/experimenter) is restricted throughout the period of the experiment to choosing from among the set of all possible regimes of intercourse only those for which the monthly frequency of coitus, t is identical. If the maximum number of coition-days available in the month is $T_{\prime} \leq T$, then $n = \tau / T'$ corresponds to the coital frequency *rate*.[18] Effects of parametric variation in coital frequency (τ) can readily be studied using this model, and we will do this by simulating the performance of the constrained BAR algorithm over a standard duration of 264 months, that being taken as the "full" reproductive life-span for a woman who married at the age of 24.

Given the *a priori* probability, A_i^0, that the woman attaches to the proposition that the i-th rhythm of susceptibility depicts the "true state of her world," and given any j-th regime of coition, it is possible to ascertain the corresponding subjective probability of a conception, P_{ij}. This magnitude is the product of the two magnitudes, l_{ij}, the likelihood of a conception ensuing from choice of the j-th regime under the i-th rhythm of susceptibility (i.e., "state of the world"), and A_i^0 the *a priori* probability assigned to that rhythm. Then, the monthly expectation of a conception conditional on the selection of the j-th "regime" can be calculated by summation of the P_{ij} over all the admissible rhythms.

By evaluating these expectations for every possible regime, the hypothetical woman can choose the regime that minimizes her monthly subjective expectation of a pregnancy. For each cycle she also will observe whether or not a conception has ensued. Given that information, the conditional likelihoods $l_{ij} \in L_{ij}$ may then be used to compute the *a posteriori* probabilities of the rhythms of susceptibility – by Bayesian revision, or updating the priors A_0 to obtain A'. The formal details of this procedure are set out in Appendix A.

On the basis of the revised set of priors thus obtained, the regime for the following month can be selected, and so on. The interaction between this cognitive-behavioral algorithm and the objective stochastic process that determines the actual time-profile of susceptibility, and the probabilistic outcomes of coital acts in the regime selected, is schematically summarized by the flow diagram in Figure 5.1. As is indicated there, certain biological conditions, affecting the objective levels and timing of fecundability in the woman, must be specified for the purposes of computationally assessing the learning algorithm's efficacy. Whether the woman's *a priori* understanding of those processes allows these conditions to be represented with reasonable accuracy among the set of admissible rhythms may, of course, be a matter of crucial importance for the ultimate success of a Bayesian strategy of "learning." Hypotheses that are wholly excluded from consideration cannot be evaluated by analysis of empirical data.

It usually is not feasible to consider seriously every conceivable state of the world. Can the foregoing model of learning be thought to be plausible when we examine it from the latter standpoint? Even were one pre-disposed (as we believe most economists will be, at least for the sake of their "discourse") to accept the rationality postulates of expected utility maximization that underlie the present characterizations of the agents' motivation and behavioral constraints, there remains the problem of implementing the resulting program of control in real time. Notice that with T days in the month, of which τ might be assigned as coition-days, there would be $T!/(T-\tau)!(\tau)!$ possible regimes among which to choose. Thus, given a 28-day month in which a menstrual period taboo on sexual intercourse removed 4 days from the set of those "available," when the coital frequency rate is as low as one-sixth ($\tau = 4$), there will be 10,626 regime permutations to evaluate at the start of each month. When n is one-third, so that coitus is to occur 8 times per month (rather closer to the rate observed among married white women in the age range 25–34 in the U.S. population during the 1970s[19]) the number of possible regime combinations rises to 735,471! The computational requirements for this trial-and-error learning scheme would appear to be so burdensome that one scarcely could imagine it to have any bearing on human behavior, either in the present or the past. It has been remarked that merely having to undertake the arithmetic entailed would produce a strong anti-natal effect.

This is the issue in regard to which our inquiry took on a third intriguing aspect: the choice of the maintained, *a priori* restrictions on the "states of the world" turns out to be of critical importance in determining whether or not "information processing" *per se* becomes a binding constraint. In pursuing this point, we have proved that there exists at least one simple, and quite reasonable restriction on the admissible states of the world – i.e., on the form of the rhythms of susceptibility that would be considered – sufficient to reduce the whole procedure to a computationally trivial *heuristic* learning algorithm, and yet preserve strict adherence to the rules of Bayesian inference.[20] The trick in doing this is the choice of a simple "model of the biology" – an *a priori* structural specification that is, in effect, the maintained hypothesis for the entire learning experiment. A drastically simple conjecture is one that uniquely associates every admissible rhythm of susceptibility with a single (peak) day of susceptibility within the intermenstruum. With maintained *a priori* restrictions of that form, it can be shown that the conditional expectation of a conception, $E(c_j)$, for the month in question is minimized by avoiding coitus on the days that the woman believes most strongly to be ones of peak susceptibility.

The intuition for this is quite simple. Because each "rhythm" is associated with one possible day of peak susceptibility, the woman's "priors," or subjective probabilities on rhythms correspond to subjective evaluations of the relative "dangerousness" of unprotected coitus on the associated days of hypothesized peak-susceptibility. To implement a Bayes Exact heuristic algorithm, therefore, it is sufficient to rank-order all the days of the intermenstruum according to the woman's

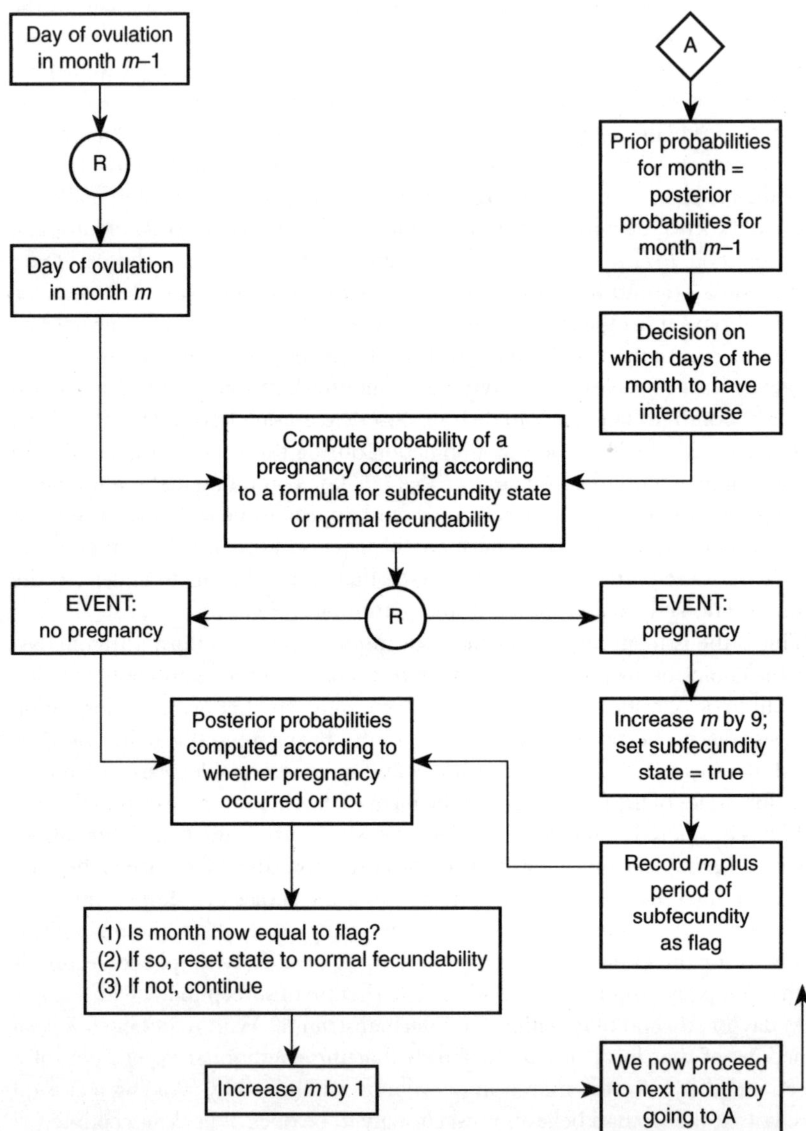

Figure 5.1 Schematic of computational model for evaluating BAR

subjective estimate of their "dangerousness," and allocate the days of coition accordingly by starting with the "least dangerous" and moving upward through the ranking as far as is necessary (see Appendix A: sections A.4–A.5).

Thus, to implement this formulation of the algorithm requires only some minimal record-keeping: a woman using BAR must keep track of the days on which coitus occurred (but only during the preceding month); and she must remember the subjective probabilities she held at the start of that month, in regard to the alternative ("admissible") rhythms of susceptibility.

5.2.2 *Specifying the objective process – the relationship of "reality" to beliefs*

To appreciate the nature of the computation-simplifying restrictions that are placed on beliefs about the nature of the stochastic process that our hypothetical agents are attempting to manage, it is best to start from the "objective" component of the model – the part that we specified with the intention of capturing at least something of the complex biological *realities*.

There is a substantial literature on the timing of fecundability in humans, which divides roughly into two branches. The biological branch focuses attention on the complexities of the interactions of egg life, sperm life, ejaculate volume, sperm motility, and the like. The epidemiological branch of the literature is concerned with attempts to infer time patterns of fecundability from observations of coital patterns and conception frequencies, without explicit reference to those underlying biological processes.[21] Unfortunately, the two branches suggest somewhat different patterns of human fecundability. The parameters of our adaptive learning model have been chosen to be roughly consistent with the picture presented by the reproductive biologists, in part because this structural approach allows us greater flexibility and realism in simulation work than could be attained by distilling the reduced-form results of the epidemiological studies.[22]

Appendix B sets out the underlying structural specifications governing the fecundability states of the hypothetical woman in our simulation model, and the resulting parameter values that are used in all the simulations. Rather than seeking to closely mimic the individual sub-processes of ovulation, menstruation, fertilization, and nidation (or "implantation" of the fertilized ovum in the lining of the uterus) leading up to a conception, this part of the model aims to capture some of the stochastic complexities governing the dynamics of the woman's fecundability state in a computationally parsimonious fashion. Thus, we make a radical simplification by assuming a menstrual cycle of invariant duration (28) days, within which there will be an invariant duration of menstruation (4 days). The date of ovulation, however, moves randomly month-by-month, always cycling within the bounds set by the 13th and 16th day of the woman's month. Because we allow, realistically, for the occurrence of a conception as a consequence of an isolated act of unprotected intercourse two full days preceding the time of ovulation, in any randomly drawn month there is a positive hazard for "fecundability" on each of the 6 days in the interval stretching from day 11 to day 16 of the standard intermenstruum.[23]

Specification 1. In any given month fertilization leading to a conception may result from coitus on any one of three consecutive days, the day of ovulation and the two days preceding.

The maintained beliefs of the women represented in our simulation experiments, however, are far simpler in their view of the way that their susceptibility to impregnation varies from day to day within any month, and from one month to the next. As has been already noted, in describing the restrictions imposed on their admissible rhythms of susceptibility, we discovered that the BAR algorithm's computational feasibility could be assured by supposing that the individuals engaged in learning remained ignorant about these details of their ovulatory cycle, and of their implications for the actual month-to-month variations of the "true rhythm of susceptibility." We assume that the woman believes she has one particularly susceptible day in her "month" when the probability of a conception is $\bar{\theta}$, and 27 days on which there is a (negligibly) low probability of conception, ϵ.

As a consequence of this greatly simplified model of the world, the task of executing a strictly Bayesian information processing routine is reduced to almost trival dimensions. The assignment of *a priori* probabilities to each member of the set of admissible rhythms is rendered equivalent to the formation of a simple index, ranking each of the 28 days of the woman's month according to her subjective evaluation of the inherent "danger" that a conception would ensue were she to have unprotected coitus on that day. Regime optimization to minimize the risk of a conception then may be achieved by following a so-called "packing" algorithm for allocating the τ days of coitus in the month, starting with the least (subjectively) "dangerous" and proceeding as far as required toward days of higher rank.

Furthermore, as is pointed out in Appendix A (section A.5), under these same conditions the conditional likelihoods for the occurrence and non-occurrence of a pregnancy also become very simple to calculate, which makes it no trouble at all to carry out the Bayesian computation of an *a posteriori* distribution. The latter operation, it will be recalled, is the equivalent of revising the woman's prior index of "inherent dangerousness" of the days in her month. To do that in a consistent and statistically correct fashion requires only the systematic application of one or the other of a pair of *constant* multipliers: one of these must be applied to proportionally raise the relative dangerousness rating of the coition days in the month when a pregnancy has ensued, and the other to proportionally reduce the relative rating of the month's non-coition days, when a pregnancy does not ensue.[24] The choice of the exact Bayesian values for those multipliers is a bit more of a challenge, as they depend in a complicated way on the woman's maintained subjective evaluation of how "easy" or "difficult" it would be for her to become pregnant by having unprotected coitus on her day of peak susceptibility – which is to say, on her belief about the level of $\bar{\theta}$ in relation to ϵ.

In the simulation experiments reported here we have set the woman's maintained beliefs to coincide with this "best approximation to the truth," and it should be borne in mind that this eliminates one potential source of confusion that could becloud the trial-and-error process of learning.[25]

Still, there are many other notable points of divergence between the assumed form of the maintained beliefs and the objective, "biological reality" specified in the model. Over the course of her reproductive life, the woman's observations of outcomes of different regime-choices (i.e. whether or not a pregnancy ensues) are treated by her as independent random events. This is the simplest way for her to process the available data, especially considering the supposition that she does not know about the mechanism governing the timing of ovulation. The objective component of the model, as we have noted, is constructed in a way that causes the assumption of independence to be violated in actuality: the day of ovulation in each month was assumed to depend in part on the day of ovulation in the previous month. This misperception of the nature of the randomness in the objective process creates a "realistic" source of confusion, making the woman's learning task that much more difficult.[26] The question that must now be considered, before turning to the results of the simulations themselves, is: What kinds of effective "learning" should we be looking for in this inquiry? In view of the tight cognitive bounds that have been placed upon the learning agent's "model" of the process they are trying to control, it will be important for us to allow for distinctions between cognitive progress and other kinds of learning.

5.2.3 Alternative characterizations of learning within the BAR model

The behaviorist approach to learning is generally one that considers any change in behavior to be "learning," whether or not it is adaptive, desirable for certain purposes, or in accordance with any other such normative criteria. Under this approach learning is taken to be "complete" simply when certain kinds of stability – not necessarily stereotypy – obtain in observable behaviors.[27] Although there are attractive aspects in such an approach, the premise of our investigation is that learning should produce changes that *are* adaptive, in the sense of being consistent with the hypothetical agent's anti-natal goals.

Proceeding in this spirit we shall speak of adaptive changes that may occur in either or both "contraceptive behavior," and "effective control," corresponding to Learning Definitions 1, and 2, respectively:

- *Learning Definition 1 (Contraceptive Behavior)*: Trial-to-trial changes in the probability of "responses" (constrained regime choices) that progressively reduce the monthly probability of conception below the levels which would obtain under a regime of randomly timed coitus.

- *Learning Definition 2 (Effective Control)*: Progressive anti-natal deviation of the sequence of actual births from that which would be expected under a regime of randomly timed coitus.

There are two points to be noticed regarding these definitions. First, both address the dynamic aspect of learning, in that they are concerned with changes that would occur over time. The conception probabilities can be viewed as an evaluation (from the anti-natal perspective) of the "dangerousness" of the regime of coitus that had been selected for the month in question, and their time-path thus provides a convenient summary indicator of *behavioral* adaptation. Of course, it is also possible to evaluate the degree of adaptive change by reference to transversal measures computed for the entire span of the experiment. In the case of Definition 1, the transversal measure would be the overall reduction achieved – at a constant, parametrically specified coital frequency – in the monthly probability of conception, starting from the level implied by randomly timed intercourse. In the case of Definition 2, the corresponding transversal measure is simply the expected number of births averted, again, with reference to the number of births expected were the monthly regimes of coitus to have been selected randomly throughout the whole time-span considered.

The second point to be noticed is that were we to undertake a very large number of replications of each (full life) simulation experiment, there would be no substantive difference between the characterizations of learning provided by Definitions 1 and 2; the Central Limit Theorem applies here, so that Law of Large Numbers guarantees these two measures would reveal exactly the same thing about the effects of learning. Looking at the sequence of monthly conception probabilities (Definition 1), rather than the average sequence of conception outcomes, however, does makes more sense when one is limited to a small number of replications. The reason is that the Definition 2 measures will contain an additional component of "noise" arising from sampling errors in the realization of the probabilistic process of conception (leading to a birth). The latter source of "noise," however, is more attenuated in its effect upon the transversal measures that correspond to Definition 2, namely, expected cumulative births, and births averted. Those summary indicators have an additional virtue, in being more readily interpreted and related to the objective of family limitation. Thus, both Definition 1 and Definition 2 type measures of learning will be worth considering.

In contrast with the focus of the foregoing notions of adaptation in behavior (and its consequences), it is possible within the framework of our model also to characterize a cognitive form of "learning." Once again we have a choice, in this case between taking a "relativist" and an "absolutist" stance in regard to "knowledge." The former might consider the assignment of higher and higher subjective probabilities to *any* small, and not internally discordant subset among the conceivable states of the world, as representing a process of "cognitive evolution." The absolutist stance, however, would insist that such evolutions be deemed "learning" only when they proceed in the direction of attaching greater credibility to states of the world that are "objectively true." Embracing this latter position, we should then be obliged to accept a third characterization of learning:

- *Learning Definition 3 (Cognitive Evolution)*: The convergence of the agent's "priors" regarding her rhythm of susceptibility to the "true" pattern in the day-specific probabilities of a conception ensuing from unprotected coitus.

Now it will be recalled that the true state of the world is more complicated than any among the set of "admissible" rhythms in our Bayesian algorithm, as a result of which the wording of Definition 3 poses something of a problem. Perfect convergence of the woman's *a posteriori* distribution of probability on her true rhythm of susceptibility is too much to expect when the admissible rhythms exclude the "true" state of the world. Movement towards significantly greater correlation between beliefs and reality is a reasonable way to assess "cognitive evolution" in keeping with the sense of Definition 3. It is quite feasible, however, to construct both sequential and transversal indicators of the degree of conformity between beliefs and reality that could be expected to emerge through the trial-and-error learning process.[28]

In the context of the present model, individual cognitive evolution in the general sense of Definition 3 implies behavioral adaptations in the sense of Definition 1, because regimes are chosen to minimize the *a priori* expectation of pregnancy. But notice that the reverse is not true. It is quite possible that within a finite reproductive life-span, a woman may "learn" to avert pregnancies precisely in the behaviorist sense captured by Definitions 1 and 2, yet not make any significant progress toward discovering the true time-pattern of ovulation and her consequent "rhythm" of susceptibility to impregnation. With this, however, there also comes the dual possibility that erroneous cognitive states can become deeply entrenched "beliefs" when they are consistent with functional adaptations in human behavior.

This latter remark should serve to underscore the point that in investigating this model we really were not interested in the possibility of a Bayesian strategy being successfully applied to the discovery of the modern rhythm method – by an epidemiological approach, rather than the physiological approach that actually was pursued successfully by Ogino and Knaus in the 1930s. Rather, we posit the Bayesian strategy because it offers a familiar and appealingly rational basis on which to develop a computationally tractable algorithm describing path-dependent stochastic learning behaviors that coevolve with a structure of beliefs about the natural world. We conjecture that qualitatively similar results also can be obtained with many other algorithms that are statistically less well founded, but which might be justified as arising from psychologically more plausible heuristic procedures for processing information acquired sequentially, in the manner of trial-and-error experimentation.

5.3 Overview of the simulation results

The simulation results enable us to address the issue of the effectiveness of learning in each of the several senses that just have been identified, and to see how behavioral adaptations and cognitive evolution are affected by parametric variation in the coital frequency rate. For this purpose six different levels of coital frequency (τ), ranging from 2 to 12 times per month in increments of 2, were specified as an invariant aspect of the regime of intercourse whose time pattern was optimized, and re-optimized, sequentially on a month-by-month basis. Every reproductive life-span in these simulations lasts for 264 months, or 22 years, representing the approximate average duration of a woman's "exposure" to the risks of childbearing if she entered an interrupted marital union at age 24–25. The statistical results reported in Tables 5.1–5.4, and also Tables 5.6–5.7, are based on the samples constituted from the first 50 simulated cases of *mothers*, that is, women for whom one or more births were recorded over the course of their reproductive life-span.[29]

Although it is possible to investigate the effects of varying other parametric settings in the model, especially those describing the maintained beliefs as to the maximum and minimum levels of the woman's inherent fecundability (θ and ϵ, respectively), these were held fixed, so that the subjective evaluation of fecundability is always $\hat{\theta} = 0.06$ throughout the simulation runs reported here. That value was chosen to coincide with the point estimate implied by the specifications of the model's objective, biological component: it is the mean probability that a single act of coitus on a susceptible day would result in a conception.[30] Loosely expressed, the latter assumption comes down to our having chosen to let the hypothetical woman correctly guess (at the beginning of her reproductive life-span) the mean level of her susceptibility to conceive when unprotected coitus occurs on a "dangerous day." At the same time, however, it should be recalled that we suppose that she begins without any particular convictions about where such a day might be situated within her "month." In every run of the simulation model, then, the woman is assumed to start with completely "diffuse priors" regarding the set of admissible rhythm of susceptibility. Inasmuch as that is tantamount to believing each day in the intermenstruum to be an equally likely candidate for being her "peak day" of susceptibility, the regime optimization routine initially allocates the days of coitus randomly over the 24 days of the cycle (the first available day, following the cessation of menstruation, always being day 5).

5.3.1 Behavioral adaptation and effective control

We may start by looking at the summary, transversal measures of "effective control" that correspond to "learning" in the sense of Definition 5.2. Table 5.1 (and Figure 5.2 which is derived from it) compares the average numbers of births to a woman who follows a BAR-guided routine consistently, at each of the alternative coital frequencies that are indicated; also shown are the corresponding outcomes that would be expected were the timing of intercourse in the regime to have been selected randomly. The difference between the two cases yields an evaluation of "effective control" in terms of the mean number of births averted. In these terms BAR is shown quite clearly to be an "effective" method: the mean number of births averted is positive, and statistically significantly so, over the whole range of coital frequencies displayed in the table.

Indeed, BAR($\hat{\theta} = 0.06$) turns out to be not simply "effective," but remarkably effective in reducing (marital) fertility when the frequency of coitus is maintained at levels below six times per month ($\tau = 6$). A woman engaging in a regime of randomly timed sexual intercourse at $\tau = 4$ could expect 8.22 births in 22 years of exposure, whereas, by adhering to BAR under the same conditions, she could expect as few as 2.12 births. Moreover, when using BAR at the lower levels of coital frequency, the standard deviation of her completed fertility is found to be just the same, if not smaller than that which would be generated by selecting the

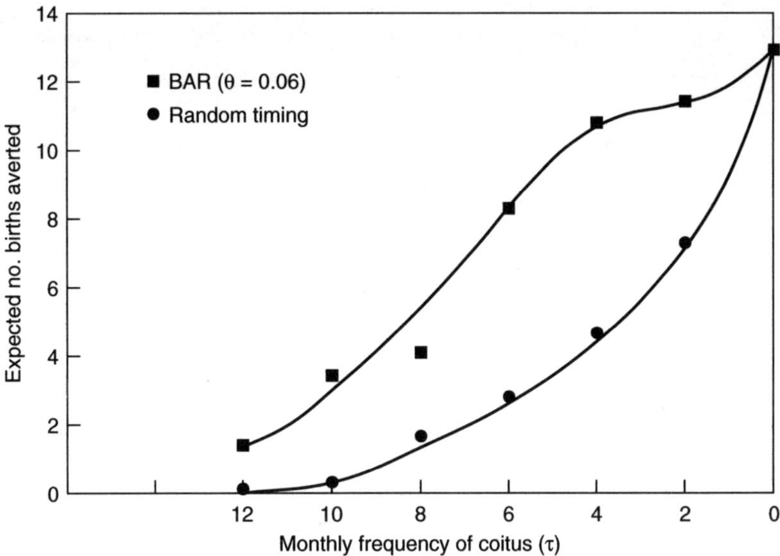

Figure 5.2 Simulation results for Bayesian adaptive rhythm method: expected number of births averted. (Runs of 50 sample lives, each of 264 months in duration.)
Note: Data plotted in the figure are averages of births averted per mother: in simulation results for regimes of randomly-timed coition, the number of mothers always equalled the number of women (50).
Source: Table 5.1

time pattern of coition in a random fashion. Although the variance is larger in relation to the mean of completed fertility, the much lower average number of children ever born is not obtained at the cost of any absolute enlargement of the margin of uncertainty surrounding the outcome.[31]

Quite obviously, fertility can be reduced by simply lowering the monthly frequency of randomly timed coitus. But the relationship between those two variables is quite non-linear – a point that is often not appreciated but shown plainly by Figure 5.2. In order for any substantial decreases in completed fertility to be achieved simply by a reduction of coital frequency, it is necessary to curtail the latter to levels ($\tau \leq 4$) far below those observed among modern married women.[32] With BAR, however, there is a powerful differential "learning effect," reflected in the rise of the mean number of births *averted* to a maximum before those extremes of conjugal restraint are reached. As may be seen from the rightmost column of Table 5.1 (and graphically in the difference between the curves plotted in Figure 5.2), the birth-averting effect attributable to BAR-guided behavioral adaption becomes strongest when coital frequency moves into the range between 6 and 4 times per month.

These simulation results substantiate a conjecture that could have been offered purely on intuitive grounds, namely, that there would have to exist a coital frequency rate in the interval between 1 and 0 that was optimal for eliciting information about the timing of the woman's susceptibility; that this "learning optimum" would be

Table 5.1 Number of births per mother during reproductive life of 264 months: Simulation samples of 50 mothers

Invariant monthly frequency of coitus	*Randomized monthly regime:*		BAR ($\theta = 0.06$)		*Incremental births averted per mother due to BAR ($\theta = 0.06$)*	
	Mean	*Std. Dev.*	*Mean*	*Std. Dev.*	*Mean Difference*	*Pooled Std. Dev.*
2	5.62	1.38	1.54	0.80	4.08	0.23
4	8.22	1,57	2.12	1.38	6.10	0.30
6	10.18	1.62	4.66	3.30	5.52	0.52
8	11.28	1.54	8.72	3.61	2.56	0.55
10	12.70	1.23	9.52	3.61	3.18	0.54
12	12.90	1.04	11.54	2.56	1.36	0.39

bounded away from rates closely approaching 0 by the infrequency with which any conceptions would occur at those levels.

The dynamic adaptation process ("learning," in the sense of Definition 1) which produces those outcomes is more directly reflected in the measures presented by Table 5.2. For every given coital frequency level, it is possible to compute a simple index of the objective "dangerousness" of the regimes that the woman selects – where the "danger" involved is that of an unwanted conception. We do this by first calculating an "intercourse regime score," IRS_m for the month in question.[33] With this measure, an intercourse regime score of unity corresponds to "maximal dangerousness," which would be obtained were the selected regime to schedule unprotected coitus on every one of the 6 days of the woman's month on which it would be possible (within her life-span) for a conception to occur. A score of zero, obviously enough, would obtain when intercourse did not take place on any of those objectively feasible days for a conception.[34]

In Table 5.2 it is seen that – with the initial regime always having been one selected at random – the index of dangerousness starts out in the neighborhood of 30–33 percent of the maximum level, regardless of whether coital frequency is at 4 or at 8 times per month. Further, some statistically significant contraceptive adaptation in behavior is achieved in both cases after 14 years (169 months) of adherence to BAR. Yet, when $\tau = 8$ no significant "learning" in this sense occurs after the 2nd month, on average; whereas with $\tau = 4$ significant adaptive changes in the regime of coitus continue to occur; even after the sixth year (73rd month). Indeed, by that point in the woman's marital history, the mean index of the dangerousness of her selected regime has been reduced to approximately a tenth of its initial magnitude, and the process does not stop there. Further statistically significant adaptations cut that monthly probability of conception again, by a factor of 5, eventually reducing it to the negligibly small level attained by the time her union has begun its 14th year (month 169).[35]

Table 5.2 Time-path of intercourse regime adaptation with BAR ($\theta = 0.06$) for simulated groups of 50 mothers all starting with diffuse priors

Month of reproductive union	*Index of regime dangerousness:*[1] *100 = Most dangerous (least safe) regime possible with given* τ			
	Coital frequency $(\tau) = 4$		*Coital frequency* $(\tau) = 8$	
	Mean	*Std Dev.*	*Mean*	*Std Dev.*
1	29.8[2]	15.8	33.0[2]	15.8
2	11.6[2]	16.2	29.6	16.5
49	5.8[2]	10.9	24.1	15.7
73	3.0[2]	6.4	23.4	15.7
97	2.6[2]	5.8	21.9	14.8
121	1.9	5.6	22.9	15.0
145	1.3	4.0	23.8	16.4
169	0.5	1.4	20.2	13.4
193	0.5	1.4	22.6	16.0
217	0.5	1.4	21.4	14.8
241	0.5	1.4	21.1	14.6
264	0.5	1.4	20.6	14.3

Notes:

1 For women pregnant at indicated date, the regime index is calculated for the following post-partum regime of intercourse.

2 Significantly greater than mean index values for months 217,241 and 264 at 95 percent confidence level.

5.3.2 Bounded cognitive evolution

The foregoing *behavioral* adaptations on the part of our simulated populations of BAR-users suggest that at the low end of the range of coital frequencies, at least, it is possible for a woman's cognitive state to evolve towards a more accurate view of her "rhythm of susceptibility," and therefore of the "true" timing of ovulation specified in our model. Given the Bayesian strategy of control being deployed, changes in the woman's regime of intercourse must be driven by changing beliefs expressed in terms of *a priori* probabilities assigned to the alternative (admissible) states of the world. Hence we should enquire directly about what the representative woman will have "learned" in the cognitive sense of Definition 3.

It is useful to distinguish between two facets of the problem of the bounded nature of cognitive evolution within the framework of our model. The first has to do with whether or not statistically significant cognitive evolution is taking place; whereas the second addresses the question of how closely it is possible to come to discovering "the truth" – remembering the maintained restrictions that information-processing constraints have placed upon the admissible set of rhythms.

Table 5.3 is designed to illuminate the first issue. Correlations can be computed between the objective rhythm of susceptibility and the subjective *a priori* probabilities assigned to the occurrence of the peak of susceptibility on the corresponding

Table 5.3 Proportion of mothers (50 cases) whose priors exhibit statistically significant positive correlation with the 'True State' (rhythm of susceptibility) after 264 months of reproductive life with BAR ($\theta = 0.06$) regime

	Statistical significance (error) levels:		
	10 percent	*30 percent*	*50 percent*
		Beginning-of-life priors[1]	
	0.14	0.24	0.44
Invariant monthly frequency of coitus		*End-of-life priors*	
2	0.56	0.78	0.98
4	0.46	0.84	0.98
6	0.46	0.82	0.96
8	0.32	0.74	0.94
10	0.48	0.72	0.96
12	0.38	0.86	0.96

Note:

1 These proportions are calculated from the first *finite* correlation coefficients (28 days of data) that can be computed for subjects who (all) start with diffuse priors.

days of the month. The columns of the table show the proportion of cases in each simulation sample of 50 mothers for which the degree of correlation is statistically significant at the beginning, and at the close of the reproductive life-span. At the end of the initial month of the process, which starts out in every instance with the woman having "diffuse priors," the proportion of women whose *a posteriori* evaluations and the true rhythm of susceptibility are correlated at a statistically "significant" level should conform quite closely with what one would expect to find purely as a result of chance. There cannot have been much opportunity for the Bayesian inferential engine to have done serious work within its first cycle of operation. So, if we picked a confidence level of 90 percent, we should expect to find that only 10 percent of the cases would, essentially by random chance, have turned out to be "significantly" correlated. From the 14 percent figure that appears in the top row of Table 5.3, it is seen that the correlation analysis of the output from all the first months in all the simulation runs does indeed come close to matching that (large sample) expectation.[36] This, and the corresponding proportions for the "beginning-of-life priors," can be taken as the benchmarks appropriate to each statistical confidence level. It is against these benchmarks that we must gauge the extent of the significant "cognitive evolution" that takes place by the time that the representative woman reaches the close of her reproductive life-span.

From Table 5.3 just such evaluations can be made for conjugal lives lived at each of the six fixed monthly frequencies of coitus. Focusing on what can be said with a reasonably high level of confidence (the 10 percent significance level), it appears that in the lower range of coital frequencies (τ in the 2–6 range) the end-of-life priors show significant correlation in about half of the cases in each simulation run, i.e., in 46 to 56 percent of the lives. Comparing that to the initial benchmark figure, one would have to say that in only 30 to 40 percent of the 50 cases simulated

Table 5.4 Proportions of mothers (50 cases) whose end-of-life priors exhibit significant rank correlation with 'True Rhythm' of susceptibility, after 264 months of reproductive life with BAR ($\theta = 0.06$) regime

Invariant monthly frequency of coitus	*Proportions for whom the probability of achieving a higher rank correlation score (Kendall's τB) is less than or equal to:*		
	10 percent	*30 percent*	*50 percent*
2	0.80	0.86	0.90
4	0.62	0.88	1.00
6	0.48	0.84	0.96
8	0.26	0.70	0.94
10	0.54	0.76	0.86
12	0.50	0.86	0.80

did the individual experience *significant cognitive evolution* in the course of trial-and error learning. Considering how remarkably well these same groups of (identical) women are found to have done by the criteria of behavioral adaptation, their poor average performance in the cognitive domain is rather a surprise. Also striking is the fact that whereas reduced coital frequency made a big difference in terms of behavioral adaptation and effective control (Learning Definitions 1 and 2), there appears to be no Learning Definition 3 counterpart of that effect in the results displayed by Table 5.3.

To get a sense of how much of "the truth" those who do learn in this way are able to uncover, we show in Table 5.4 the results of our computation of the coefficients of rank correlation (Kendall's Tau-B, corrected for ties) between the *a posteriori* probabilities associated with the admissible rhythms of fecundability at the end of each woman's reproductive life, and the "true" fecundability ranking of the days of the month (according the specification for the model's objective component). Were the women of our simulated world able to converge in their beliefs on a close approximation to the structure of the stochastic process governing their fecundability, we would expect to be able in general to reject the null hypothesis that there was no correlation between their objective susceptibilities on each day of the month and their *a posteriori*, end-of-life estimates of those inherent conception risks. The proportion of cases in which the null hypothesis ("no positive rank correlation") could be rejected at the 10, 30 and 50 percent error levels of significance are displayed, respectively, in the three columns of Table 5.4.

Once again focusing on the statistics for first and most conservative error level, it is found that only at the lowest two coital frequencies (2 and 4) was it possible in significantly more than half the cases to extract information about the rhythm of susceptibility from the trial-and-error process. The very best performance in this dimension is obtained with coital frequency drastically reduced to the twice-monthly level: 80 percent of that sample of 50 mothers attained a rank correlation score exceeding that which could be expected to occur purely by chance in 10 percent of the cases. At the higher coital frequency level ($\tau = 4$) which was found to be near-optimal for behavioral adaptation and effective control of fertility under the "guidance" of BAR, the proportion drops to only 0.62, implying that in only roughly half of the 50 cases did the correlation scores attained at the end-of-life represent an improvement upon the state of biological "understanding" that could have been arrived at purely by chance.

What these experiments have brought out most starkly is that while it is possible to use the bounded BAR algorithm quite effectively, on the average, as a method of family limitation, the practitioners as a group would remain very confused about the timing of the "fertile" and "safe" periods within the intermenstruum. A result of this kind can occur in our model because the woman is motivated to learn about the timing of ovulation only to the extent that it helps her to avoid becoming pregnant. Should she happen upon a set of beliefs (i.e., "priors") which, though far from the truth, nonetheless enabled her successfully to avert any further births, her beliefs about the safe period will never converge any closer toward "the truth." For these rational adaptive agents, the operative "truths" toward which they are myopically driven is simply "whatever works."[37]

This aspect of our finding is really most instructive. It sheds light on the history of popular and medical confusion surrounding the "safe-period," and at the same time provides some rational grounds for the historical persistence of faith in the potential efficacy of such a method of regulating marital fertility. In performing this explanatory service, however, the divergence between BAR's performance in the behavioral and cognitive domains has set a new and unanticipated question for us to puzzle over: How does cognitively bounded BAR manage nonetheless to control fertility so tightly?

This question can be given a sharper, quantitative form by considering the following illustrative calculations. It has been seen that when the coital frequency level is maintained at 4 times per month, approximately half of a population of BAR users will have "learned" something about the rhythm of susceptibility by the end of their reproductive career. Let us then suppose that the gain in "knowledge" thus acquired yielded so precise an approximation to the true rhythm of susceptibility that these "cognitive learners" were enabled to cease having any conceptions after giving birth to a first child. Further, let us suppose that at the other extreme those women whose end-of-life priors were still not significantly correlated with the true rhythm of susceptibility would have done no better to have selected all their coital regimes at random. From Table 5.1 we see that with the hypothesized coital frequency ($\tau = 4$) the latter group on average should have ended up with a completed fertility of 8.22, whereas the group of cognitive learners, *ex hypothesis*, would average 1.0 birth apiece. As the groups are of equal size, the average number of births per mother for the whole of this imagined population, therefore, ought to have been 4.61, which is just the arithmetic average of the respective group means for the number of children ever born. Yet, as a glance back at Table 5.1 will confirm, BAR at the indicated coital frequency ($\tau = 4$) actually manages to limit the mean number of births in the corresponding population of *mothers* to a mere 2.21, far below the level of average completed fertility than the foregoing calculations would lead one to anticipate.

5.3.3 How does bounded BAR do it?

How then is this mysterious power of cognitively bounded BAR to be explained? Evidently, the algorithm must be working in a way that does not entail a tight coupling at the micro-level between "correct knowledge" and "correct action"; that is, between understanding what is going on – in the sense of possessing either a good structural model of the underlying process or an accurate empirically induced reduced-form approximation of it – and being able successfully to avoid regimes in which coitus occurs during the "fertile" period of the month. The key to the mystery lies in an often overlooked generic feature of Bayesian adaptive routines, all of which have embedded within them the following primitive but powerful rule: "Stay with a winner."

Staying with a winner, which in the context of BAR means not abandoning a regime that has just avoided generating a conception, is the behavioral consequence of the fact that in response to contraceptive successes the woman's priors undergo revision in a direction that raises the subjective evaluation of the *relative* dangerousness of those days on which coitus did not take place during the month preceding. Re-optimization of the regime on the basis of the *a posteriori* evaluation, thus causes the same regime to be repeated whenever it has yielded a success in the previous trial. Regime selections that initially met with a run of successes will tend to become "locked in." Correspondingly, agents whose initial regime choices issued in unwanted outcomes, eventually, will be pushed by the revision of their priors to discard such regimes in favor of others which come to appear as less "dangerous."

The tendency, therefore, must be for an *ensemble* of agents who are BAR-users to be propelled (although the nature of the process would, perhaps, be conveyed more precisely by the phrase "jiggled and jostled") toward the subset of *comparatively anti-natal* regimes by the reactions of individual agents to contraceptive failures. Being "functionally adaptive" with reference to the individual agents' goals, the members of the subset of relatively "safe" regimes also possess the property that their selection will cause the agent's behavior to stabilize – thereby incidentally fulfilling the behavioral psychologists' minimalist criterion for the "completion of learning." As a larger and larger proportion of the ensemble becomes thus stabilized in relatively safe regimes, the average monthly probability of a conception must be reduced.

At the macro level that diminution gives rise to the impression of a process of continuous learning on the part of a "representative (contracepting) agent." The insights imparted by the evolutionary metaphor are not inaptly invoked at just this point: we were to think of the collection of regimes that were in use in each month by the ensemble of agents as constituting a population (of "memes"), the BAR routines followed by the agents could be viewed as a mechanism which drives the "regime population" to evolve in the (desired) anti-natal direction by differentially selecting and retaining for use those regimes that were relatively "safe." It is important to stress that in this evolutionary formulation the population, but not necessarily any of its constituent members, is doing the "learning."

To see that this evolutionary mechanism works much more swiftly, and therefore more effectively in controlling fertility within a finite time-span, when the level of coital frequency is low, we may now turn to consider the statistics presented in Table 5. The proportion of women who remain childless at the end of a continuous 264-month span is shown there as a function of the invariant monthly frequency of coitus. Each of the three columns of the table does this for a different population, but fundamentally they all make the same point: the lower the coital frequency rate, the more likely it is that one will be able, purely by chance, to avoid unprotected sexual intercourse on those days (in a month chosen at random) on which the probability of a conception is relatively high. The column at the extreme right shows the theoretically calculated proportion of cases in which a random distribution of coitus within the intermenstruum would avoid hitting one (or more) of the six possible susceptible days in an infinite life-time of independent monthly trials. Supposing these proportions to describe the expected frequency of randomly landing in a "safe" regime in the first month of the woman's married life, we see that for monthly coital frequencies below six there is an appreciably high chance of her becoming "locked in" to a perfect anti-natal regime by subsequent BAR-driven revisions of her initially diffuse priors.

The simulation results for the proportion of childless women found in runs of 150 lives with BAR, at each of the invariant coital frequencies indicated, are shown in the lefthand column of the table. They closely match the theoretical calculations, with some deviations due to sampling errors arising from the stochastic workings of the model. In the middle column we report the corresponding proportions, as calculated from the respective simulation runs that yielded the first 50 *mothers* for each parametric level of τ.[38] It is seen that even with the greater possibilities of divergences due to sampling errors, the agreement with the theoretical probabilities remains quite close. One observation which should be made in connection with the picture emerging from Table 5, bears on the reading of the results reported earlier on the basis of the statistics for the mothers in our simulation samples. Inasmuch as the latter ignore the impact on childlessness, strictly speaking, they *understate* the efficacy of combining BAR with lower coital frequency as a means of achieving lower levels of completed fertility; the understatement entailed is particularly pronounced when coital frequency is in the range $\tau \leq 6$. For example, it is found from Table 5.1 that the average number of births to mothers who consistently had used BAR at coital frequency $\tau = 4$, was 2.12, whereas we now can see that after correcting for the theoretical probability of childlessness, the average figure can be put at 1.63 for all *women* (because the corresponding expected fraction of mothers among all women is 0.772). A corollary implication, however, is that expected numbers of births averted *per woman*, due to "learning with BAR," are somewhat lower than those shown by Table 5.1 and Figure 5.2 for the low end of the range of coital frequencies.[39]

Coming now to the nub of the present question, Table 5.5 tells us that the "stick with a winner" rule which BAR embeds within it will be likely to come into operation more rapidly at lower coital frequencies, especially when the routine starts from a position in which the woman's priors are diffuse. To grasp the reason

Table 5.5 Proportion of women remaining childless at end of 264-month reproductive life

Invariant monthly frequency of coitus (τ)	*Simulations with BAR* ($\theta = 0.06$): *Random sample of 150 lives: simulated with BAR* ($\theta = 0.06$)	*In sample of lives containing first 50 mothers, simulated with BAR* ($\theta = 0.06$)	*Expected frequency of safe regime being chosen initially* $\Pi_{k=0}^{\tau}\left\{\begin{matrix}(24-6)-k\\(28-4)-k\end{matrix}\right\}$
0	1.000	1.000	1.000
2	.600	.515	.554
4	.293	.342	.228
6	.113	.123	.138
8	.060	.038	.022
10	.030	.019	.013
12	.000	.000	.007

for this intuitively, consider that in the event that an unlucky choice at the beginning of the process produced a quick pregnancy, the ensuing updating of the woman's beliefs will lead her, when intercourse is resumed, to select a regime that previously had not been tried. And then, as coital frequency is *ex hypothesis* held to the same low level as before, the odds of choosing a "safe" regime out of the hitherto untried days must be even better than before, on average. This is so because, in the first instance, the odds would have been those shown in the righthand column of Table 5.5 as being determined purely by chance when coition on the days that gave rise to the first conception had not been excluded.

To be sure, the inertial tendencies of the "stick with a winner" kernel of Bayesian adaptation can become a drawback in certain circumstances, making it something of a two-edged sword for the individuals who seize upon this mode of learning. Suppose that a woman, who by chance had selected a potentially quite dangerous regime, was favored by a succession of rare contingencies and so escaped conceiving a child. In the course of the associated sequential updating of her priors, she would be led to believe quite firmly that her past regime was a comparatively safe one, compared to the others that had remained untried; and so, would regard persisting in the selection of that previous regime to be the best way (myopically) to minimize the monthly expectation of a pregnancy. It could then require the experience of repeated unwanted conceptions (and time-consuming pregnancies) before her subjective evaluations of the relative "dangerousness" of the days associated with that regime were raised sufficiently to eradicate the erroneous beliefs that had been acquired in the course of her early experience. Only at that point would she be "cognitively liberated" to select a different regime. As unhappy a tale as this is for the individuals involved, instances in which a woman's family limiting efforts will be largely vitiated by her accidental imprisonment in the grip of her early history, must themselves be very much the exception when coital frequency is low. For that serves to reduce the probability of randomly selecting an initial regime so as to include coitus on a day of peak susceptibility.

The mystery is now thoroughly dispelled: BAR "works" at low coital frequency because, under those conditions, the odds favor the formation of functionally adapted behaviors that stabilize as "rationalized habits." This is so, even though we have seen that an individual's persistence in such goal-satisfying behaviors is not only quite compatible with the holding of cognitive convictions that are objectively false, but that it also may cause such myths and fantasies to become more and more deeply entrenched in the minds of those who are guided by them.

5.4 Conclusions and provocations

Cognitive evolution that proceeds within a Bayesian decision-theoretic framework is a path-dependent process, and so, when coupled to myopic optimizing behaviors, it will generate perceptible hysteresis effects in actions and observed consequences. At each stage in the process those acting under the instruction of their *a priori* views have made themselves, in effect, creatures of a potentially tenacious past – a past that will have been distilled down and incorporated into their prevailing subjective evaluations of alternative hypotheses about the nature of the world with which they have to contend. In this way, historical experiences – whether in the form of belief-structures instilled in them by others, or acquired unconsciously, or consciously formed from personal observation of the temporal association between particular actions and sequelae – are able to lay down a (boundedly) rational basis for behaviors that come to resemble habits. Whether the resulting transiently, or permanently stabilized patterns of behavior truly qualify as "habits" is beside the point here; what matters is that they are "habit-like," even to the extent that the actions entailed are conditioned on beliefs that grow more and more difficult to cast off quickly. Thus they are able to persist even after they have revealed themselves to be responsible for the recurrence of unwanted consequences. This is "sunk cost hysteresis" – in the realm of cognitive evolution. That functional habits, rather than dysfunctional ones, will emerge from such a process is not, however, merely a matter of luck. Good fortune in trial-and-error learning can be systematically favored more strongly by some "learning environments" than by others, as the preceding analysis of the effect of parametric changes in the frequency of unprotected coitus has demonstrated.

The general terms in which the foregoing conclusions are formulated are meant to suggest that their relevance is not confined to the particular problem in the history of contraceptive knowledge and practices. What has been brought to light by that inquiry seems to have a much wider validity, pertaining to many other contexts involving a reciprocal and mutually-reinforcing interplay between cognitive evolution and behavioral adaptation. It may be thought that this is enough, and that it is not really warranted to go beyond the quantitatively grounded and analytically straightforward summary propositions which we have just set out. But, there are several still larger issues that already have been touched upon in the preceding pages, and to which it seems worth devoting some concluding reflections of a more speculative nature.

5.4.1 Instructionist versus selectionist mechanisms in evolution

The intertwined cognitive changes and behavioral adaptations that we have examined here appear unambiguously to be classifiable as evolutionary mechanisms of the Lamarckian *instructionist* rather than of the strict neo-Darwinian variety. New regime configurations in our simulation model cannot be represented (after the first month) as having emerged through "blind variation," which is what the Darwinian paradigm of evolution strictly requires. Instead, these regimes (considered now as "memes") emerge, and are available to be replicated in subsequent use, through a process that is definitely Larmarckian in spirit. They are reshaped by the responses of the goal-seeking individual agent to the outcomes of interactions between her past choices of behavior and the objective (stochastic) environment represented by her rhythm of susceptibility. In view of the intentional manner in which it operates, however, this process qualifies as Larmarckian in spirit but not as "natural instructionism." Indeed, a *rational* course of cognitive evolution is the purpose behind the calculation of likelihoods and the revision of priors in the Bayesian process; just as the selection of regimes follows from the intention to minimize the expectation of an unwanted conception.

All that seems very clear, and it may be found helpful thus to locate our simulation model with reference to the crisp taxonomic boundaries that separate Larmarckian from Darwinian evolution. In actuality, however, the character of the underlying evolutionary process responsible for the adaptive performance of the BAR algorithm is considerably fuzzier than this exercise in classification would suggest. We already have pointed out that it is the "stay-with-a-winner" rule buried in the Bayesian routine that enables BAR to manage so successfully to avert births for the representative woman in the population. It remains now to observe that with one simple modification we can effect what may seem to be a profound alteration in the character of the learning model, transforming Larmarckian BAR into a purely Darwinian evolutionary process, and yet not substantially change its adaptive properties.

It is easy enough to replace the sub-routines for the monthly revision of priors and the regime optimization in the model (see Figure 5.1), substituting an altogether simpler routine that, similarly, responds to successes and failures in the avoidance of conceptions. This routine is based upon the rule: "Win, Stay – Lose, Start Again" (WSLSA). Beginning, as before, from a regime chosen at random, it will retain the initial selection so long as a conception does not occur, but when coition is resumed following a birth the new regime will be, again, chosen randomly. This would be a ruthless policy in labor relations, discarding faithful servants who have had a long record of success as soon as they revealed themselves to be fallible – even if it does permit the possibility of being reinstated by random draw. In the context of our rather different application it might be supposed that the failure of control, by initiating a condition of pregnancy, would effect the erasure of all memory of the woman's antecedant priors – a form of "maternal amnesia" that returned her beliefs to their original, "diffuse" state. Evaluating the performance of WSLSA by

Table 5.6 Effect of pure Darwinian (WSLSA) adaptive strategy: number of births per mother during reproductive life of 264 months in simulation samples of 50 mothers

Invariant monthly frequency of coitus	*Randomized monthly regime:*		WSLSA[1]		*Incremental births averted per mother due to* WSLSA	
	Mean	*Std. dev.*	*Mean*	*Std. dev.*	*Mean difference*	*Pooled Std. Error of estimate*
2	5 62	1.38	2 20	1.39	3.42	0.28
4	8 22	1.57	2 58	1.83	5.64	0.34
6	10 18	1.62	4 36	2.83	5.82	0.46
8	11 28	1.54	8 20	3.55	3.08	0.54
10	12 70	1.23	10 34	3.45	2.36	0.52
12	12 90	1.04	11 56	2.68	1.34	0.40

Note:

1 The WSLSA strategy re-randomizes after each birth, but thereafter remains invariant (up until the next birth). Hence: :'**W**in **S**tay, **L**ose **S**tart **A**gain'.

simulations comparable with those we have examined for BAR shows us what can be achieved in this context with a purely Darwinian process of adaptation based on "blind variation and selective retention" of regimes.

By comparing the performance of WSLSA against a perfectly random process of regime choice, as we have done in Table 5.6, one can see how powerful is the fertility reducing effect that comes just from the selective retention feature of BAR – furnished by its mimicry of a "stay-with-a-winner" policy. The average numbers of births averted among mothers using WSLSA exhibit the same sensitivity to parametric variations in coital frequency as that found in the simulations of BAR. To determine how important the non-Darwinian, cognitive adaptation component of BAR is for its adaptive performance (in the same transversal measures corresponding to Learning Definition 2), we may examine Table 5.7, and Figure 5.3, wherein the expected number of births averted with WSLSA are matched against the figures for BAR (from Table 5.1). *Mirabile dictu*, even though it had been found that something approaching half of the population of BAR practitioners were undergoing a significant cognitive evolution of some sort, the intentional, cognitively guided component of this algorithm is seen not to be making much of a difference at all in the behavioral domain. At the very lowest coital frequency level, it is true, turning on the information processing and optimization sub-routines that make WSLSA into BAR improves performance by 20 percent in terms of expected births averted per mother (i.e., that is the proportional gain recorded relative to the performance of WSLSA). But, when coital frequency is moved into the range between 4 and 6 times per month, this differential vanishes completely; indeed, within the range between 6 and 8, BAR does slightly, although not significantly worse, than its Darwinian counterpart.

Two morals might be drawn from these revelations. The first is that advances in knowledge, empirically grounded upon inferences from trial-and-error in a myopic control process, cannot be a big help when you are restricted in both the number

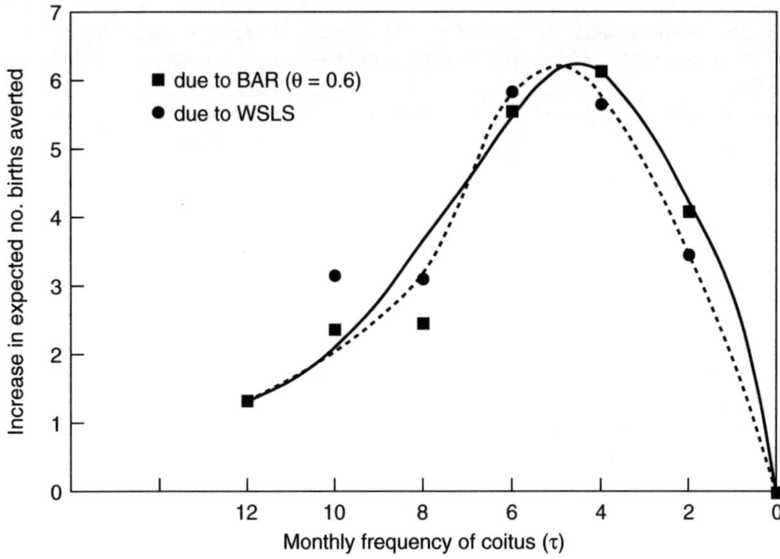

Figure 5.3 Bounded Bayesian learning versus Darwinian adaptive (WSLS) behavior: comparison of simulation results for expected number of births averted (runs of 50 sample lives, each of 264 months in duration)

Note: Data plotted in the figure are averages of births averted per mother: in simulation results for regimes of randomly-timed coition, the number of mothers always equaled the number of women (50). The curves are hand-drawn, disregarding deviations caused by "sampling errors" in simulations for coital frequencies 8 and 10.

Source: Table 5.6

of trials you can undertake, and the states of the world you can imagine as worth considering. This, then, is not a new point, but one that serves to underscore the propositions advanced in the preceding section. The second, and perhaps more contentious, lesson would seem to be that in social science invocations of evolutionary metaphors, the effort spent in carefully distinguishing non-biological processes that are Lamarckian from those which are properly Darwinian, may be misplaced and reflective of analogical rather than analytical reasoning. What appears here, at least outwardly, to be a classically instructionist mechanism of a thoroughly intentional sort, has turned out to be effectual only to the extent that its operation mimics the workings of Darwinian selectionism. At least it is worth bearing in mind that there can be contexts where the instructionist-selectionist distinction is operationally less important than would be suggested by the amount of paper and ink that has been devoted to it in the literature of evolutionary epistemology. It is a distinction that is likely to be worth insisting upon when cognitive evolution must undergird behavioral adaptation, but that is something to be demonstrated rather than presumed.

Table 5.7 Incremental effect of Bayesian vs. Darwinian (WSLSA) strategy upon mean number of births averted during reproductive life of 264 months: simulation samples of 50 mothers

Invariant monthly frequency of coitus	*Difference in means between BAR* ($\theta = 0.06$) *and WSLSA*	*Pooled standard error of the difference*
2	0.66	0.277
4	0.46	0.324
6	−0.30	0.615
8	−0.52	0.716
10	0.82	0.706
12	0.02	0.524

Source: Computed from Tables 1 and 6.

5.4.2 Advances in knowledge and improvements of learning in history

For students of the past, the domain of our findings' relevance would seem to be especially broad. Throughout much of human history, and, indeed, until very recent times in a number of important fields of human endeavor – the control of disease, and other biological processes being especially notable, but scarcely unique among these – the quest for practical knowledge has been heavily dependent upon trial-and-error learning in situations resembling those stylized by our stochastic simulation model. That is to say, people have of necessity engaged in processes of causal inference from their observations, and have been obliged to do so in situations that left them handicapped by one or more of a variety of constraints: (i) where pure experimentation was limited or denied to them by perceptions that such a strategy would conflict with their other purposes, or normative values; (ii) where the possibilities of discovering the true state of the world though such procedures were closely circumscribed by maintained, *a priori* suppositions about seemingly secondary aspects of the phenomenon under examination; and (iii) where much of the motivation for seeking knowledge about the natural world rested upon the hope of acquiring it and being able to benefit from its application within a time-span that was comparatively short. Of course, the point in the foregoing formulation is to emphasize the limitations upon myopic learning-by-doing of the kind which Arrow (1962) first brought to the attention of economists seeking insight into endogenous mechanisms of technological change. This less rosy perspective on the large role that cognitively and materially bounded trial-and-error adaptation had to play in permitting people in the past to improve their ability to control their natural and social environments, grows still darker when one focuses upon the severe and "costly" constraints that needed to be accepted, in certain features of "the learning environment" (here represented most notably by the parameter), in order that significant gains in discretionary control of fertility might be achieved by adapting the timing of coitus. Even so, it must be acknowledged, what was learned in a behavioralsense would not seem safely transferable to situations that appeared superficially the same but might be critically different in some respects that had remained very imperfectly understood.

To be sure, the Bayesian adaptive procedure has been found to permit remarkably effective adaptations in behavior, and fertility, even under constraining conditions which cause cognitive evolution to remain quite tightly circumscribed. Hence it is possible to read our findings as support to those behaviorists, many economists included, who generally are skeptical about the value of modeling "learning" explicitly as a cognitive activity. But, quite the opposite conclusion actually is warranted. It should be clearly understood that to be obliged to act myopically on what you have just "learned" through your previous action, is a strategy that is dominated by one of learning first, through implementing an experimental design, and only then, after a period devoted to gathering data, trying to infer and select the best course for actual implementation. The possibility of making a switch to that superior learning mode, from hand-to-mouth adaptive modes of the sort with which our analysis has been concerned, represents an important transition in the historical emergence of the knowledge-based economy.

Such transitions, which doubtless have occurred in different areas of human endeavor at different times in the past, would repay closer investigation than they have received hitherto. Indeed, it is through developing a better understanding of what could, and what could not, be "learned" in the behavioral domain (via myopic learning-by-doing) that economic historians may be able to evaluate the magnitude of the economic gains, and the improvements of human well-being in other dimensions – that are properly attributable to the ascendance of organized R&D as the modern mode of knowledge-based innovation and endogenous economic growth.

One cannot help but come away from an analysis of constrained trial-and-error learning, such as the one essayed here, without a sharpened appreciation for the repercussions in the sphere of cognitive evolution that were permitted by historical changes in certain of the conditions of material culture. Among the sorts of developments that spring readily to mind in connection with the secular relaxation of the constraints on "learning-while-doing" are those which shortened the real-time duration of the learning cycle; which multiplied the opportunities to conduct, and increased the ability of individuals and organizations to finance learning-by-controlled-experimentation. All manner of institutional innovations can be seen to have had significant and inadequately appreciated side-consequences in encouraging the de-coupling of experimentation from the restrictions of simultaneously having to meet pressing, day-to-day material need. No less noteworthy in this connection would have been the growing importance of forms of economic activity that provided "learning environments" that were more and more amenable to standardization. The latter must have greatly increased the scope for beneficial application of the behaviorial rules upon which individual learning sequences had (successfully) stabilized. In short, one unexpectedly arrives via this somewhat roundabout route at a renewed awareness of much that remains to be studied about the linkages between secular economic change and the systematic application of the emerging methods that have come to be associated with the pursuit of knowledge by means of "modern science."

5.4.3 Cognitive limitations, information processing and the origins of heuristics

It is reasonable enough to suppose that "heuristic procedures" fundamentally originate in the cognitive limitations of human agents. We have been concerned with the limitations of the sorts of heuristics that are resorted to in processing data and analyzing decision problems, whether they are consciously employed by the individual problem-solver, or have been embedded in the routines followed by human organizations for collecting, filtering and analyzing data to extract information on which discretionary control will be conditioned. Those limitations, indeed, may be at the root of perceptual distortions of the sort that have been identified by behavioral psychologists as "framing biases," "salient aspect" comparisons in multidimensional choice situations, and suchlike. Certainly, one may justifiably label as cognitive deficiencies the manifold difficulties that ordinary people display in grasping elementary concepts of probability, and in applying such notions to everyday decision problems. The latter they nonetheless proceed to answer by some means or other, often incorrectly, as Kahneman and Tversky (1983) have shown.

One troublesome aspect of the view that heuristics arise through cognitive errors is that it leads to just the same conundrum that causes many economists to hang back from embracing the implications of the concept of bounded rationality. It allows them to go on modeling individuals and firms as if they behaved as thoroughly informed rational maximizers, even when they accept the psychological evidence that, more often than not, when people are set decision problems they do not get the concepts or the sums right. There are just too many ways to make mistakes, and no *a priori* principle seems available on which to justify selecting one rather than another flawed heuristic as the standard model. A theory of bounded rationality that could offer more guidance in characterizing how people and organizations proceed when confronted with complex problems, surely, would be of use in breaking this methodological log-jam. The modeling exercise described in the preceding pages does not constitute such a theory. But, it may have stumbled upon a useful way to think about the formation of heuristic procedures, one that is close to the spirit of Henry Simon's original observations about rationality being bounded by cognitive constraints on decision analysis. Limitations on computational capability, as well as on information collection, storage and retrieval, may preclude attempting to base decisions upon representations of the world that reflect the full range of its perceived complexities. As mathematical theorists in the natural sciences know well, and as practising engineers publicly profess, there is an art of simplifying that enables people to use manageable quantities of data to extract information upon which to base real-time predictions and action. Rules of thumb that are inexact, but nonetheless have practical utility in that way, might then arise from the effort to simplify the problem to the point of ready computability. In our simulation model, by grossly simplifying the representation that the decision agents give to the time-pattern of fecundability within the intermenstruum, the updating of priors in strict Bayesian fashion is rendered equivalent to an easily implemented heuristic procedure.

Of course, as we have seen, to have mis-specified the models of the world (in the way that Appendix A details) is likely to be a serious handicap when it comes to making progress in understanding the processes that one is trying (with success) to manage. Furthermore, an outside observer who had an inkling of the true complexity of the underlying process could justifiably scoff at the lack of statistical sophistication manifested in the reduced form algorithm. Such an observer might not even perceive the strict Bayesian properties of a routine that was described as nothing more than ranking the days of the intermenstruum according to a subjective evaluation of their inherent "dangerousness," and then mechanically modifying those rankings, depending on the outcomes. Nevertheless, the feasible Bayesian heuristic to which those simplifications led turned out to be usable to very good effect, on average, in attaining the agent's family limitation goals. It therefore would fulfill a minimal consistency requirement for its continuation in practical usage. Venturing to extrapolate from this particular case, I will baldly state the following general hypothesis: At any point in the history of an organization or a culture, rational economic agents needing to manage complex technical and social processes (the underlying structure of which is incompletely known to them) will as a rule be found to be relying upon heuristics and decision-rules that had been formed by framing some model of the world so as to render feasible the necessary "calculations."

Implementable rules of this kind may far outlive the conditions under which they were formed, especially when they become embedded in the ritualized operating procedures of social organizations. Codes and information channels are notably durable, become easier to work with more frequent usage, and represent large sunk costs for the organizations in question. That alone may enable the organization to withstand for some time the competitive pressures from new entrants, as David (1994) suggests, even when the latter possess superior capabilities in gathering and processing information to support their internal decision processes. By proceeding a little further along this line of speculation, one arrives at a potentially fruitful research approach in the study of cognitive evolution – namely, to examine "computability and tractability" of information management requirements, as an attribute for which theories are selected for implementation in a given, technologically constrained environment. Under this hypothesis one would consider major technical and organizational advances that relaxed the constraints imposed on information processing as having potentially profound cognitive repercussions, analogous to those of catastrophic shifts in the natural environments of biological species. Such "environmental" transformations affecting the costs of acquisition and analysis of relevant data could render totally obsolete large portions of the existing array of computational routines, thereby causing the associated scientific theories, management heuristics – along with the people adept in implementing these – to be dislodged from the cultural, economic and political niches into which they had been selected.

The foregoing is at least one way in which we might begin to think more analytically, rather than metaphorically, about the long-run evolutionary implications of the "information revolution" that is taking place around us.

Appendix A

A.1 Model Notation

t	: index of days in the intermenstruum.
T	: number of days in the intermenstruum.
τ	: number of events (days) of coitus in the intermenstruum, a parameter.
n	: coital frequency rate $n = \tau / T$; $(1 - n)$ is the rate of periodic abstinence.
θ_t	: hazard for conception when coitus occurs on the i-th day.
$\tilde{\theta}^i$	: the i-th inherent rhythm of susceptibility, a $1 \times T$ vector representing the inherent probabilities of conception for each of the T days in the intermenstruum.
$A^\circ(\tilde{\theta}^i)$	: *a priori* subjective probability of the i-th rhythm of susceptibility $\tilde{\theta}^i$.
$A\prime(\tilde{\theta}^i)$	: *a posteriori* subjective probability of the i-th rhythm of susceptibility $\tilde{\theta}^i$.
ϕ_t	: binary variable defined on the days, which takes the value 0 if there is no coitus on the t-th day of the month ; and 1 if coitus occurs on the t-th day.
$\tilde{\phi}^j$	: the j-th regime of intercourse, a $(1 \times T)$ vector comprised of the elements ϕ_t.
$\tilde{\phi}^\tau_*$	: an element of the set of regimes characterized by τ, which also satisfies the condition: min $E(c_j)$.
l_{ij}	: the conditional likelihood of a pregnancy, given the i-th rhythm of susceptibility and j-th configuration.
$E(c_j)$	: the *a priori* expectation of a pregancy conditional on the j-th regime being selected.

A.2 Maintained restrictions on the "admissible" rhythms of susceptibility

The vector(s) describing an i-th "rhythm of susceptibility", $\bar{\theta}^i$, must satisfy certain general restrictions:

(1) In $\tilde{\theta}^i = (\theta_1, \theta_2, \ldots, \theta_T), 0 \leq \theta_t \leq 1$ for $t = (1, \ldots, T)$. Defining θ to be the set of all vectors formed by all permutations of the possible values of θ_t over the days $(1, \ldots, T)$, and letting $S \in \theta$ denote the "admissible rhythms of susceptibility" a subset comprising the θ^i's for which the transformation $A^\circ(\tilde{\theta}) > 0$, then we impose

(2) The prior general restriction on rhythms of susceptibility: $\tilde{\theta}^i \in S$.

Our rules for forming S are simple. We interpret θ_t as a discrete random variable and impose a further restriction that admissible rhythms be generated by canonical permutation of a symmetric unimodal rhythm of susceptibility.

(i) First, we formally define $S = \bar{S}$ where $\bar{S} \in \theta$ s.t. if $\tilde{\theta}^i \in \bar{S}$ then $\exists$ is a canonical permutation of $\tilde{\theta}^i$, say $\tilde{\theta}^v$, s.t. $\tilde{\theta}^v \in \bar{S}$.

(ii) Since for computational ease it is desirable that $\bar{S}$ take the form of limiting the (discrete) values which θ_t may assume, we impose the most extreme nontrivial restriction:

(3) Only two values of the day-specific inherent hazards of a conception are considered

$$\theta_t \in ({}_1\theta, {}_2\theta) \text{ for } t = (1, \ldots, T),$$

in which case $\bar{S}$ contains as many as $T(T-1)$ admissible rhythms (vectors $\tilde{\theta}^i \in \bar{S}$).

(iii) A final restriction on S that proves computationally useful is to limit the number of days of the month on which $\theta \neq_1 \theta$ may occur. Note that if this number lies anywhere in the set $(1, \ldots, T-1)$, and the restrictions described in (i) and (ii) also hold, then $\bar{S} \in \theta$ has only $s = T$ vector-elements.

These restrictions on the "admissible rhythms of susceptibility" really amount to maintained "priors" about the pattern of inter-menstrual variation in susceptibility. We shall say that the distributions of θ_t through the month must be

(1) symmetrical and unimodal: they are generated by a phase-shift of some standard distribution in which there is a single day of maximum inherent risk of conception, and (2) of the form in which $\theta_t = \bar{\theta}$ for the vector's i-th element, and ϵ for all others.

This says that the woman firmly believes there is one "day" of peak conception-risk ($\bar{\theta}$) within the intermenstruum that remains the same from "month-to-month" – save for the months in which she is pregnant, of course, but is uncertain as to where exactly it falls within her "month."

A.3 Subjective probabilities on admissible rhythms

Being uncertain, she nonetheless can form subjective probability evaluations of each of the admissible rhythms that might be her actual rhythm:

$$A^{\circ}\begin{pmatrix} \mu & \\ \theta & \iota \end{pmatrix} = A^{\iota}_{\circ}$$

is defined formally as a transformation that expresses the *a priori* (subjective) probability over the states described by $\bar{\theta}i \in \bar{S}$ whose size is s.

Thus $A^{i}_{\circ} \in A_{\circ}$ whose size is s, and the transformations must satisfy the conditions:

$$A^{i}_{\circ} \leq 1 \text{ and } \sum_{i}^{s} A^{i}_{\circ} = 1.$$

A.4 Regimes of coitus and regime optimization

A.4.1 Regimes

A "regime" of coitus is represented as a $1 \times T$ vector whose ordered elements signify whether or not coitus is held on the given day of the month. Thus, in j-th regime, the time-pattern of unprotected coitus is described by a permutation of 0 and 1 elements forming the vector $\bar{\phi}_j = (\phi_1, \phi_2, \ldots \phi_t, \ldots \phi_T)$ where 1 = coition,

0 = no coition. The regime index is $j = \left(1, \ldots K\left(\begin{smallmatrix} T \\ \tau \end{smallmatrix}\right)\right)$, where T, the number of days on which intercourse is held , is simply:

$$\tau = nT = \sum_{t}^{T} \phi_t.$$

(Note that in discrete simulation applications of the model, the parameter *n is* restricted to regular fractions in the interval (0,1); it is assumed that effectively only one act of coitus can occur on any day, and the maximum number is limited to T.)

A.4.2 Regime optimization criterion

Given the *a priori* probability, A_i°, and any j-th regime of coition, it is possible to ascertain the corresponding subjective probability of a conception, P_{ij}:

$$P_{ij} = [l_{ij}]A_{\circ}^{i} = Pr[c|\tilde{\theta}^{i}, \bar{\phi}_{j}]A^{\circ}(\tilde{\theta}^{i}).$$

Then, the monthly expectation of a conception conditional on the selection of the j-th "regime" can be calculated as:

$$E(c_j) = 1 - \sum_{i=1}^{T}\left[\prod_{t=1}^{T}(1 - \phi_{jt}\tilde{\theta}_t)\right]A^{\circ}(\tilde{\theta}^{i}),$$

since

$$\sum_{i=1}^{T} A_{\circ}^{i} = 1.$$

By evaluating these expectations for every possible regime, the hypothetical woman can choose the regime that minimizes her monthly subjective expectation of a pregnancy.

A.5 Bayesian revision of priors

For each regime chosen, it can be observed whether or not a conception has ensued. The conditional likelihoods $l_{ij} \in L_{ij}$ may then be used to compute the *a posteriori* probabilities of the rhythms of susceptibility – by Bayesian revision, or updating the priors A°, to obtain

A'. Formally, invoking Bayes' Rule, the *a posteriori* probability of the i-th rhythm is found from the expression:

$$A'(\tilde{\theta}^{i}) = \frac{(l_i)A^{\circ}(\tilde{\theta}_i)}{\sum_{i=1}^{s}(l_i)A^{\circ}(\tilde{\theta}^{i})} \quad \text{when a conception has occurred;}$$

and from the expression:

$$A'(\tilde{\theta}^i) = \frac{(1 - l_{ij})A^\circ(\tilde{\theta}^i)}{\sum_{i=1}^{s}(1 - l_{ij})A^\circ(\tilde{\theta}^i)}$$

when no conception has occurred in the month past.

Given the restrictions specified in A.2, subjective probabilities A° correspond to subjective evaluations of the relative "dangerousness" of unprotected coitus on the respective days (of hypothesized peak-susceptibility). To implement a Bayes Exact heuristic algorithm it is therefore sufficient to rank-order all the days of the intermenstruum according to the woman's subjective estimate of their "dangerousness."

A proof of this is omitted here, but can be found in David, Sanderson and Steinmueller (1988). The key is to consider first the subjective likelihood function under the foregoing restrictions $S = \bar{S}$, s.t.

$$\theta_t \in ({}_1\theta = \epsilon, {}_2\theta = \bar{\theta}),$$

and $\theta_t \neq 1\theta$ on only one day of T possible days , where $0 < \epsilon < \bar{\theta}, 1$. Only two values of l_{ij} need then be considered:

$$l_{ij} = \begin{cases} l_+ = 1 - (1 - \bar{\theta})(1 - \epsilon)^{\tau - 1} \\ l_\circ = 1 - (1 - \epsilon)^\tau \end{cases} .$$

The first option applies if regime j entails coitus on the i-th day, and the second if not. It then follows that $E(c_j)$ can be expressed as a weighted sum of the A^{circ} for the days on which coitus occurs, from which the minimization rule derives directly.

Bayesian updating of the priors, using these likelihoods, can be achieved by proportional rescaling of the initial index of "dangerousness" for the month in question, using a pair of constant multipliers. Concretely: denote by (ρ_c^v), the multiplier that proportionally *raises* the "dangerousness rating" of coition-days *relative* to days on which coitus was omitted, in the event of a pregnancy; and by (ρ_N^{v*}) the dual multiplier, which *lowers* the relative dangerousness rating of the coition days when no pregnancy occurs. Then, following David, Sanderson and Steinmueller (1988: para.10) it can be proved that the relevant pair of multipliers for the present model must be given by:

$$\rho_c^{v*} = \frac{1 - (1 - \theta)(1 - \epsilon)^{\tau - 1}}{1 - (1 - \epsilon)^\tau}$$

$$\rho_N^{v*} = \frac{(1 - \tilde{\theta})}{(1 - \epsilon)}$$

Appendix B: The objective biological component of the simulation model

B.1 Structural specifications

The structural component of the simulation model (see Figure 1) that governs the fecundability states of the hypothetical woman is based upon the following specifications:

Specification 1. In any given month fertilization leading to a conception may result from coitus on any one of three consecutive days, the day of ovulation and the two days preceding.

Specification 2. A menstrual cycle is always 28 days long and the menstrual flow's duration always lasts for 4 days. These are assumptions made for the sake of simplicity, not realism. In actuality, the length of menstrual cycles varies from cycle to cycle, and the position of the day of ovulation, and the duration of menstruation itself may also vary within a cycle to some extent.

Specification 3. The day of ovulation varies month by month, but always remains within a given consecutive range of days. In order to take the latter variations into account while keeping the cycle a fixed length, we describe the behavior of the day of ovulation with four parameters, a, b, c, and d. Let v_t be the day in the month in which ovulation occurs. We assume that v_t is in the closed interval $[a, b]$. Further, we assume that v_t and v_{t+1} are not serially independent of one another, and posit the following stochastic motion: Letting $R(c, d)$ be an observation randomly drawn from a uniform distribution defined over the closed set of integers from c to d, then

$$v_{t+1} = v_t + R(c, d) \text{ if } v_{t+1} \leq b$$

$$v_{t+1} = a + (v_t + R(c, d) - b) \text{ otherwise.}$$

Letting the first day of the menses be counted as day 1, our simulations are generated using the parameter values $a = 13, b = 16, c = 0$, and $d = 1$.

Specification 4. In the female reproductive tract, sperms gradually lose their ability to fertilize an ovum. For our simulations we assume that the probability of conception from a single act of intercourse on the day preceding ovulation is 0.5 times the probability of

- conception from a single coitus on the day of ovulation. Similarly coition two days before ovulation produces 0.25 times the probability of a conception for a coitus on the day of ovulation. These assumptions are roughly in accord with the biological literature, e.g., Hartman (1962).

B.2 Parameter values: mean daily hazards for "fecundability"

The "true" day-specific probabilities of conception from a single act of intercourse to which these specifications will give rise, *on the average*, are set out in tabular form below.

Table 5.8 Objective probabilities of conception from isolated coitus on various days of the menstrual cycle*

	Possible ovulation days							
	1–10	11	12	13	14	15	16	17–28
Probability of a conception	0.00	0.01	0.04	0.09	0.08	0.05	0.00	

**Note:* These probabilities are not independent from month to month, because of the auto-correlation in the location of the day of ovulation.

Source for Table 5.8:

We let Ψ_t be the probability of a conception resulting from intercourse on day t:

$$\Psi_t = \theta_\circ \sum_{k=0}^{2} q_{t+k}\lambda(k)$$

where q_{t+k} is the probability that day $t+k$ is the day of ovulation. The numbers in the table above are generated with this formula and the following specifications:

$$\lambda_0 = 1; \lambda_1 - 0.5; \lambda_2 = 0.25;$$
$$\theta_0 = 0.2;$$
$$q_1 = \ldots = q_{12} = q_{17} = \ldots = q_{28} = 0.0;$$
$$q_{13} = q_{14} = q_{15} = q_{16} = 0.25.$$

Acknowledgments

This paper makes free and extensive use of material co-authored with W.C. Sanderson: "Making Use of Treacherous Advice: Cognitive Learning, Bayesian Adaptation and the Tenacity of Unreliable Knowledge," in *The Frontiers of Institutional Economics*, (eds.) J. V.C. Nye and J. N. Drobak, Academic Press: San Diego, CA, 1997. Among the many people who are thanked for their help in connection with the latter publication, W. Edward Steinmueller deserves especial, repeated mention here. I have benefited also from the comments received on an earlier version of this paper presented to the CESPRI Seminar convened by Franco Malerba at the University of Bocconi, Milan, 5 December 1996; and also from the comments of Joel Mokyr, Richard Nelson, John Ziman, and other participants in The Epistemology Group Conference on "Technological Innovation as an Evolutionary Process," held Wallingford, Oxon., 8–11 January 1997. I have benefited particularly from Frank Hahn's discussion of the paper, on the occasion of its presentation to the University of Siena International School of Economic Research Summer Workshop (X) on Evolution and Economics, held 27 June – 5 July 1997 at Certosa di Pontignano, Siena, Italy.

Notes

1 This follows the distinction drawn by Bradie (1986) in an illuminating review of the literature on evolutionary epistemology. The most fully worked out account of conceptual change in modern science as an evolutionary process is that provided by Hull (1988).

2 Waters (1990) refers to the view that the growth of knowledge should be modeled as an evolutionary process as the "model version" of evolutionary epistemology, and contrasts it with the "implications version," the latter he associates particularly with the suggestions advanced by epistemologists such as Quine (1969), and Kornblith (1985), to the effect that natural selection has given us cognitive mechanisms that have a tendency to produce true beliefs. Waters (1990: 80–81) makes a persuasive case for "naturalizing" epistemology by pursuing cognitive science, and then working out "the philosophical implications of discoveries to be made in psychology, linguistics, artificial intelligence and neurology," rather than by pondering "the evolutionary origins of mechanisms we do not yet understand."

3 See David and Sanderson (1997) for the background to that research and full acknowledgements.

4 Commencing with the formation of the Stanford Project on the History of Fertility Control, in 1976, this larger program of research was conducted by the authors and several generations of graduate students in the Stanford University Department of Economics. The studies of particular relevance here are discussed in David and Sanderson (1978a, 1978b, 1986); David, Sanderson and Steinmueller (1988).

5 Cf. Himes (1970), index references to 'Sterile Period'; Hopkins (1965), esp. p. 134, gives an alternative translation of the references made by Soranus to the period "suitable for conception".

6 For decades after the startling late seventeenth-century discovery of the viviparous ovum, by Reinier de Graff (1641–1673), and the reports of microscopic observations of the spermatozoa by his fellow Hollander, Antoine van Leeuwenhoek (1632–1723), ancient beliefs, such as the one which held that the human fetus was the product of "semen" contributed by the two sexes, continued to be affirmed in theses submitted to the Faculty of Medicine in Paris. Pierre Darmon (1981) has entertainingly described the flourishing of such fables during the seventeenth and eighteenth centuries, and the profusion of prescriptions compounded from them, as how best to conceive boys or girls as needs might be. These baroque fantasies Darmon attributes to escapist reactions on the part of medical professionals and lay people alike, reflecting their frustrating and persisting bafflement concerning the details of the procreative process. On the question of whether generation was a "secret of nature" that man some day would be able to uncover, even Voltaire and *L'Encyclopédie* of Diderot, remained pessimistic.

7 Cf. Knowlton (1841:16), cited by Hopkins (1965:134). Knowlton was the first modern proponent of douche as a contraceptive and did not advocate continence during the susceptible period (as he delimited it). Bergues *et al.*, (1960: 116–119), discusses the writings of Pouchet (1847) on the safe period, and the eighteenth-century European medical literature upon which he drew – both of which are slighted in Himes (1970).

8 Cf. e.g. Ashton (1865: 14–15), and, more influentially, Stockham (1887: 29, 324–326).

9 Cf. *American Physician* (1855: 59–61), among American writers on birth prevention, and the earlier influential work of the Frenchman Pouchet (1847). Still other theories led to equivalently anti-natal recommendations. The rather unorthodox views of Drysdale (1854: 348), who described the sterile period as an interval commencing two

or three days before the menses and ending on the eighth day following, continued to claim some adherents among respectable purveyors of birth prevention advice in England. Cf. Himes (1970: 234–235) on Drysdale, and H.A. Albutt's *The Wife's Handbook* (London, 1878). On the other hand, opposing suppositions about the coincidence of ovulation with menstruation were so widely held that it is not difficult to understand why Drysdale's message was garbled by some other writers, who relabeled as the susceptible period the exact interval he described as "sterile." Cf. Himes (1970: 23, n71), on the inversion of Drysdale by "M.G.H.," the anonymous author of *Poverty: Its Causes and Cure* (London, c. 1854–61).

10 Cf. Hartman (1962) for extensive discussion and references on the actual location of the period of susceptibility within the normal menstrual cycle.

11 Cf. the references to Himes' (1970) treatment of the safe period, above. When Himes' monumental work was first published (1936), however, the discovery of the rhythm of ovulation was a recent thing, and his discussion of the historical literature in regard to the safe period – unlike his approach to other contraceptive practices – was dominated by a concern for the scientific accuracy of the various authors' views on the time of ovulation, rather than the differing contraceptive value of each of the several major brands of advice that were offered. Himes' (1970: 182–185) survey of the "effective" methods of contraception found in European folk medicine and folk beliefs also rather pointedly excludes all forms of the safe period.

12 In the survey responses dating from the 1890s, the "safe period" was the second most frequently mentioned method of contraception, after "douche." Cf. David and Sanderson (1978a, and 1986: 317ff) for further details relating to demographic aspects and the statistical representativeness of the so-called Mosher Survey sample – the latter being a collection of some 48 interviews (involving 44 individual women) conducted by Clelia Duel Mosher during 1892–96, 1913, and 1920 at Stanford University, and during 1897–1900 at The Johns Hopkins University. The contents of Mosher Papers were first described by Degler (1974) and a reasonably accurate transcription of the manuscript interview records is available in MaHood and Wenburg (1980).

13 Various implications of importance, which economic theorists concerned with evolutionary processes might absorb from this simple observation, are to be found in Gould (1980: Ch.1) and Crick (1988: 137–142). Although insufficiently appreciated by many economists who employ the evolutionary metaphor in modeling technological change, this point holds even in regard to genetic mutations; for, at every point in time, the overwhelming number of mutant genes are those already latent in the gene pool.

14 In the views on evolution held by the French botanist Jean-Baptiste Pierre Antoine de Monet, le Chavalier de Lamarck (1744–1829), the motive forces for evolutionary change are the needs of living organisms and the activities they engage in to satisfy them, which results in the acquisition of characteristics that are heritable by the next generation, and so leads to the development of more complex organisms. See, e.g., Hull (1988: 86–88). Whereas in *Darwinism* heritable variations that are the subject of natural selection arise spontaneously, produced by mechanisms that are "blind" in regard to the processes of selection, *Lamarckian* evolutionary theory would accommodate processes of "instruction" by experience (subsuming imaginative perception, cognitive learning, memory and purposive alteration of design) as sources of variations that can be propagated from one generation to the next. Of course, Larmarckism contravenes the "central dogma" of molecular biology, according to which genetic information is transmitted only from nucleic acid to protein or other products, and never passes in the opposite direction.

15 See, e.g., Suppes and Atkinson (1960); Atkinson, Bower and Crothers (1965).

16 On the mathematics of Markov learning models particularly, see Suppes and Atkinson (1960). Dynamical systems with non-Markovian transition probabilities, and their relationship to "strongly historical" processes are discussed in David (1988); the special significance of advances in computational methods for the study of path-dependent

economic phenomena is noticed in David (1993).

17 Indeed, for reasons shortly to be indicated, the admissible rhythms in our implementation are greatly simplified and so exclude the more complex biological reality. The important formal implication, of thus setting the *a priori* probability of the true state to zero, is that there is then nothing in our model which guarantees that the Bayesian algorithm will converge on any one among the set of admissible states of the world.

18 In our implementation of the model, the assumption that there is a taboo on sexual intercourse during a 4-day interval of menstruation (at the end of the 28-day month) reduces T' to 24 days. This assumption is consistent with the evidence of the Mosher Survey, and with the diary of Mary Pierce Poor discussed by Brodie (1993: Ch. 1).

19 For further discussion of contemporary findings from the National Fertility Surveys on coital frequency within marriage, and comparisons with historical sample data, see David and Sanderson (1986).

20 See the Appendix for the restrictions that satisfy these conditions. A proof built upon these formal specifications of the model is available in David, Sanderson and Steinmueller (1988), but, in consideration of space limitation, its analogue has been omitted here.

21 The former of the two branches must concern itself with the interactions of egg life, sperm life, ejaculate volume, sperm mobility, and the like.

22 A further consideration was our impression that among the latter investigations there was less consensus in conclusions than modern reproductive biology has managed to obtain. The persisting difficulties of drawing sharp inferences from epidemiological data, of course, are a part of the story of the unreliability of many of the pre-modern safe-period prescriptions.

23 To capture the possibility of the spermatozoa staying motile in the female's reproductive tract for periods as long as 60 hours following ejaculation, whereas the released ovum remains in a "fresh" state for fertilization for approximately 12 hours, we attach positive (albeit reduced) probability of conception occurring as a result of isolated coitus preceding the ovulation day by 48 hours. See Appendix B, Table 5.8. This accords roughly with the physiological data summarized by Hartman (1962). "Fecundability", as used in the text and Appendix B, refers to the conditional *daily* probability of a conception resulting from unprotected coitus held on the specified day, and on no other day of the month, for a randomly chosen month in the life of a woman who is ovulating (i.e., not pregnant, and not undergoing lactational amenorrhea).

24 The modest amount of algebra required to state this rigorously is, along with the other propositions in this paragraph, relegated to Appendix A. Proofs have been omitted here in the interest of brevity, but are given in David, Sanderson and Steinmueller (1988).

25 Were one to ask what is the "objective" magnitude that would represent a "correct" guess at the value of the parameter $\bar{\theta}$ in this *a priori* specification of $\tilde{\theta}^i$, an approximate answer can be obtained by computing the probability that a single act of coitus on the susceptible day would result in a conception. The six possible susceptible days, for which the respective "susceptibility" or fecundability levels are indicated by the table in Appendix B, would be selected with equal likelihood if the woman's priors on the admissible rhythms were "diffuse," which is what will be the assumed initial condition of a learning sequence. We thus can use those parameter values (from Appendix B, section B.2) to obtain the following estimate:

$$\bar{\theta} = \sum_{t=11}^{16} \phi_t / 6 = 0.006$$

The direction and magnitude of discrepancies between maintained beliefs about the mean level of fecundability and the object level can influence the effectiveness of BAR, as it affects the speed of response to unwanted outcomes. But this is a more complicated matter that must be left for treatment on another occasion

26 Another feature of the model's specifications will contribute further to such confusions. After a child is conceived we assume that a woman enters a period of sub-fecundity lasting for 3 months, during which time the schedule describing the objective conditional probabilities of a conception is reduced by 75 percent. Although we make this reduction ostensibly to allow for the effects of lactational amenorrhea, we assume that the woman remains unaware of the possibility that her susceptibility to impregnation would be lowered in that way by breast-feeding her newborn, and that the couple's return to a normal regime in conjugal relations was not inhibited by any taboo on sexual intercourse during lactation. The model further augments the element of confusion that "safe-period" practitioners would have had to cope with, by allowing a woman to begin revising her priors on the rhythm of susceptibility in the months immediately following the birth of a child as if her normal level of fecundability had been immediately re-established – even though that is inconsistent with the actual suppositions made by many women in the past.

27 See Suppes and Atkinson (1960) for discussion of the approach of Bush, and Mosteller, among other pioneers of mathematical learning theory.

28 In the simplified specifications detailed in the Appendix, each of the admissible rhythms is characterized by the placement of the (single) spike of susceptibility on a different day of the month. The subjective evaluation placed on the *i*-th rhythm being the true state of the world thus becomes, in effect, the probability that she assigns to the truth of the hypothesis that *i*-th day is her (single) day of non-negligible susceptibility. The current state of her subjective assessment of the risks of conceiving, for each day in her month, can then be found by taking the convolution of the distribution of her "priors" on the set of admissible rhythms, with her maintained beliefs as to the inherent peak and non-peak levels of the conception-hazard rate characteristic of every "rhythm" in the admissible set.

29 In this model every conception translates into a live birth: no allowance has been made for the possibility of the conceptus being aborted spontancously and still-births, likewise, are excluded outcomes.

30 The monthly probability of 0.06 compounds the monthly probabilities of conception resulting from coitus on a given "susceptible" day, with the probability that the given day is a fertile day for the month in question. See the discussion in Section 5.2.1 and Table 5.8 in Section B.2 of Appendix B. It may be recalled that we specified there that a woman may conceive as a result of having unprotected coitus at any time within a 3-day interval which terminates with the day of ovulation. As our simulation allows the day of ovulation to range randomly within a 4-day interval (from one month to the next), over the course of the woman's life there are 6 days in her standard month(s) on which conception is possible, even though in any given month of our simulated life-spans there will be only 3 "fertile" days.

31 To be sure, we recognize that the reduction in coital frequency required to achieve this may be viewed as a "cost" of a different kind. The relationship between the middle class Victorian ideology of marital sexual continence and successful family limitation employing rudimentary contraceptive techniques is explicitly discussed in David and Sanderson (1986: esp 359ff).

32 It may be noted, however, that coital frequency averaging around 4 times per month is reported by the married middle-class women (aged 25–34) who were included in the pre-1913 Mosher Survey interviews. See David and Sanderson (1986) for further discussion.

33 This measure is defined as follows:

$$IRS_m = \sum_{i=l}^{T} \phi_{mi}\theta_i^*,$$

where ϕ_{mi} is an element of the intercourse regime vector ϕ_m; θ_i^* is an element of the vector of objective "susceptibilities" probability of becoming pregnant from a single act of intercourse on day i standardized so that the ϕ_i^* sum to unity; T is the length of the month in days (= 28).

34 Consulting table 5.8 in Section B.2 of Appendix B, above, it will be seen that among all possible regimes in which $\tau = 6$, the one that assigns days 11 through 16 as coitus days would generate the maximum average probability of a conception (in a randomly chosen month). This conception probability is $0.36 = (0.06 \times 6)$ and is the normalization constant that sets the maximal regime score to unity, corresponding to the index value 100 in Table 5.2. Although no higher maximum than this is attainable with regimes in which τ exceeds 6, the highest "relative dangerousness" index possible with $\tau = 4$ is $86[= (0.31/0.36) \times 100]$; with $\tau = 2$, it is $50[= (0.18/0.36) \times 100]$. The likelihoods of hitting the bound at 86 by random assignment (at the start of the BAR process) of 4 days of coitus out of the 24 days "available is sufficiently small that a unique normalization, rather than a t-specific normalization, was used to present the results in Table 5.2.

35 Notice that the statistically significant differences indicated (by *) in Table 5.2 between the mean level of the dangerousness index attained towards the end of the reproductive life-span, i.e.,averaging the values for months 217, 241 and 264, applies also to the difference between the scores for month 169 and scores at earlier months. This is the case for regime selection when coital frequency is 8, as well when it is 4. In the latter case, however, by month 169 the absolute monthly probability of a conception has been reduced to a quite small magnitude – [.005 x (0.36) =] .0018, implying that the probability of having an unwanted conception in the course of a year is 0.02. With coital frequency at 8, the corresponding mean probability of a conception occurring during the 14th year (month 169 being the first month of that year) is more than twenty times larger than the latter magnitude; i.e.,as high as 0.40.

36 Similarly, sampling errors result in small deviations between the theoretically expected proportions found for significant beginning-of-life correlations at the 30 percent and 50 percent error levels of significance, namely 24 percent and 44 percent, respectively.

37 It sometimes is said that such an attitude toward sufficiency in "knowledge" distinguishes the stance of the professional engineer from that of the scientist. But, for us to characterize our hypothetical BAR-using women as "family limitation engineers" would be to venture into territory that is likely to prove to be doubly hazardous.

38 Thus, to be concrete, at coital frequency 4 it was necessary to perform simulation runs for 76 lives in order to accumulate 50 women who did not remain childless after the 264th month: the proportion childless is therefore 26/76 = .342.

39 The proportional reduction of the average completed fertility rate for all women decreases as coital frequency increases, so that it is only .987 at $\tau = 8$. The effect of these adjustments, starting at coital frequency 2, therefore, yields the following figures for the average numbers of children born to all women using BAR: 0.991, 1.63, 4.01, 8.53. To obtain the corresponding figures for the expected number of births averted, similar adjustments can be made to the data for mothers in Table 5.1. The resulting estimates for births averted due to BAR are, for $\tau = 2, \ldots, 8: 1.82, 4.71, 4.75, 2.50$. Note that, with this in mind, when discussing the coital frequencies that were optimal for "learning" with BAR, we were careful to place these in the range between 4 and 6 times per month, rather than literally following the figures computed for the case of *mothers* in Table 5.1.

References

Albutt, H.A. (1878) *The Wife's Handbook* (3rd edn). London: W.J. Ramsay.

American Physician (1855) *Reproductive Control, Or a Rational Guide to Matrimonial Happiness . . ., by an American Physician.* Cincinnati.

Arrow, K.J. (1962) The economic implication of learning by doing. *Review of Economic Studies* 29: 155–173.

Ashton, J. (1865) *The Book of Nature.* New York.

Atkinson, R.C., G. Bower and E.J. Crothers (1965) *Introduction to Mathematical Learning.* New York: Wiley and Sons.

Bergues, H. *et al.* (1960) *La prévention des naissances dans la famille* (Institut national d'études demographiques, cahier no 35), Paris: INED.

Bradie, M. (1986) Assessing evolutionary epistemology. *Biology and Philosophy* 1: 401–459.

Brodie, Janet Farrell (1994) *Contraception and Abortion in 19th-Century America.* Ithaca: Cornell University Press.

Campbell, Donald T. (1959) Methodological suggestions from a comparative psychology of knowledge processes. *Inquiry* 2: 152–182.

—— (1960) Blind variation and selective retention in creative thought as in other knowledge processes. *Psychological Review* 67: 380–400.

Crick, F. (1988) *What Mad Pursuit: A Personal View of Scientific Discovery.* New York: Basic Books.

Darmon, Pierre (1981) *Le mythe de la procr(e)eation? L'age baroque.* Paris: Editions du Seuil.

David, P.A. (1975) *Technical Choice, Innovation and Economic Growth.* Cambridge: Cambridge University Press.

—— (1988) *Path-Dependence: Putting the Past into the Future of Economics.* Technical Report 533. Institute for Mathematical Studies in the Social Sciences, Stanford University.

—— (1993) Historical economics in the long run: some implications of path-dependence. In G.D. Snooks (ed.) *Historical Analysis in Economics.* London: Routledge.

—— (1994) Why are institutions the "carriers of history"? *Structural Change and Economic Dynamics* 5(2): 205–220.

David, P.A. and W.C. Sanderson (1978a) The effectiveness of nineteenth-century contraceptive practices: an application of microdemographic modelling approaches. *International Economic History Association, Seventh International Economic History Congress: Edinburgh, 1978.* Edinburgh: University of Edinburgh Press.

—— (1978b) *The Role of Experience and Adaptive Behavior in Contracepive Efficiency.* Stanford Project on the History of Fertility Control, Working Paper 1. Department of Economics, Stanford University.

—— (1986) Rudimentary contraceptive methods and the American transition to fertility control, 1855–1915. In S.L. Engerman and R.E. Gallman (eds) *Long-Term Factors in American Economic Growth* (NBER Studies in Income and Wealth, vol. 51), Chicago: University of Chicago Press.

—— (1997) Making use of treacherous advice: cognitive learning, Bayesian adaptation and the tenacity of unreliable knowledge. In J.V.C. Nye and J.N. Drobak (eds) *The Frontiers of Institutional Economics.* San Diego: Academic Press.

David, P.A., W.C. Sanderson and W.E. Steinmueller (1988) *Bounded Bayesian Learning and Performance Improvement in Complex Production Processes: A Stochastic Simulation Approach.* Stanford University Center for Economic Policy Research – IOIP Project Research Memorandum, March. (Original draft 1978.)

Degler, C.N. (1974) What ought to be and what was: women's sexuality in the nineteenth century. *American Historical Review* 79 (December): 1467–1490.

Drysdale, G.R. (1854) *Physical, Sexual and Natural Religion: By a Student of Medicine.* London: E. Truelove.

Gould, S.J. (1980) *The Panda's Thumb.* New York: W.W. Norton.

Hartman, C.G. (1962) *Science and the Safe Period.* Baltimore: Williams and Wilkins Co.

Himes, N.E. (1970) *Medical History of Contraception.* (Shocken paperback edition, with a new preface by C. Tietze), New York: Shocken.

Hopkins, K. (1965) Contraception in the Roman Empire. *Comparative Studies in Society and Science* 8 (October): 124–151.

Hull, D.L. (1988) *Science as a Process: An Evolutionary Account of the Social and Conceptual Development of Science.* Chicago: University of Chicago Press.

Kahneman D., P. Slovic and A. Tversky (1982) (eds) *Judgment under Uncertainty: Heuristics and Biases.* Cambridge: Cambridge University Press.

Knowlton, C. (1841) *Fruits of Philosophy or the Private Companion of Young Married People.* (Reprinted from the American edition.) London: J.Watson.

Kornblith, H. (1985) What is naturalized epistemology? In H. Kornblith (ed.) *Naturalizing Epistemology.* Cambridge, MA: MIT/Bradford.

Lewis-Fanning, E. (1949) *Report on an Enquiry into Family Limitation and Its Influence on Human Fertility During the Past Fifty Years* (Papers of the Royal Commission on Population, Vol. 1), London.

MaHood, J. and K. Wenburg (1980) *The Mosher Survey: Sexual Attitudes of 45 Victorian Women.* New York: Arno.

"M.G.H." (c. 1854–61) *Poverty: Its Causes and Cure.* London.

Pouchet, F.A. (1847) *Théorie positive de l'ovulation spontané, et de la fécundation des mammifées et de l'espèce humaine.* Paris: J.B. Baillière.

Quine, W.V.O. (1969) Natural kinds. In W.V.O Quine (ed.) *Ontological Relativity and Other Essays.* New York: Columbia University Press.

Rothschild, M.W. (1974) Searching for the lowest price when the distribution of prices is unknown. *Journal of Political Economy* 82 (July/August): 689–711.

Stockham, A.B. (1887) *Tokology.* Chicago: Sanitary Publishing Co.

Suppes, P. and R.C. Atkinson (1960) *Markovian Learning Theory* (Stanford Mathematical Studies in the Social Science), Stanford, CA: Stanford University Press.

Tversky, A. and D. Kanneman (1974) Judgment under uncertainty: heuristics and biases. *Science* 185: 1124–1131.

Waters, C.K. (1990) Confessions of a creationist. In N. Rescher (ed.) *Evolution, Cognition and Realism: Studies in Evolutionary Epistemology.* Lanham: University Press of America.

6 Learning dynamics, lock-in, and equilibrium selection in experimental coordination games

Vincent Crawford

6.1 Introduction

Coordination and equilibrium selection are central to many questions in economics, from the determination of bargaining outcomes to the design of incentive schemes, the efficacy of implicit contracts, the influence of expectations in macroeconomics, and the nature of competition in markets.[1] Such questions are usually modeled as noncooperative games with multiple *Nash equilibria* – combinations of strategies such that each player's strategy maximizes his expected payoff, given the others' strategies. The analysis of such games must address the issue of *equilibrium selection*, the determination of which, if any, equilibrium should be taken to represent the model's implications. This issue is particularly acute in games with multiple *strict* equilibria – those in which players strictly prefer playing their equilibrium strategies to deviating. In applications involving such games, equilibrium selection is often done by introspection, goodness of fit, custom, or convenience. Yet this begs the questions of how players come to expect a particular equilibrium and what they do when their expectations are less sharply focused, limiting the insight the analysis can give into how the environment influences coordination outcomes.

Theorists have now begun to study equilibrium selection more systematically. Several leading approaches can now be distinguished: traditional equilibrium analyses and refinements, including Harsanyi and Selten's (1988) general theory of equilibrium selection and its underlying notions of risk- and payoff-dominance; equilibrium analyses of perturbed games; rational learning models that extend equilibrium analysis to the repeated game that describes the learning process; deterministic evolutionary dynamics; analyses of the long-run equilibria of stochastic evolutionary dynamics; and adaptive learning models.

These approaches sharpen the predictions of equilibrium analysis in different ways, emphasizing different aspects of the process by which players choose their strategies or form the expectations or *beliefs* about others' strategies on which their choices are based. They differ in the amount of *strategic sophistication* they attribute to players – the extent to which their beliefs and behavior reflect their analysis of the environment as a game rather than a decision problem, taking its structure and other players' incentives into account – and the amount of *strategic uncertainty* (players' uncertainty about each other's strategy choices) they allow. Traditional equilibrium analyses and rational learning models take a deductive view of behavior, attributing perfect rationality and a very high degree of sophistication to players, in effect assuming that they have complete models of each other's decisions and thereby ruling out all strategic uncertainty. Models of evolutionary or adaptive dynamics, by contrast, take an inductive view of behavior that attributes far less sophistication to players and usually allows unlimited strategic uncertainty.

The leading approaches also differ in the extent to which they follow the game-theoretic custom of striving to predict behavior as much as possible by theory, without recourse to empirical information. The general theory of equilibrium selection and the analysis of long-run equilibria are the most ambitious in this regard, determining behavior entirely by theory even in games with multiple strict equilibria. Equilibrium refinements and deterministic evolutionary dynamics do not discriminate *a priori* among strict equilibria, and implicitly admit some empirical information by taking players' initial beliefs as determined partly or wholly outside the model. Adaptive learning models have exogenous behavioral parameters that also create a role for empirical information.

Recent theoretical analyses have the potential to make game theory more useful in applications, but the persistence of approaches with such diverse behavioral assumptions and conclusions suggests that the issue of equilibrium selection will not be resolved by theory alone. Confronting theory with empirical evidence provides useful discipline by highlighting unrealistic behavioral assumptions, and should help to fill in the gaps in our understanding. Experiments are a particularly useful source of such evidence, because they have the tight control of preferences and information needed to test game-theoretic predictions and they make it possible to observe the entire coordination process. Crawford (1997) surveys a number of studies whose subjects repeatedly played games with multiple equilibria, uncertain only about each other's strategies. The typical result was convergence to equilibrium, often with a systematic pattern of equilibrium selection in the limit. Explaining such patterns and the dynamics that led to them promises to shed considerable light on coordination and equilibrium selection, in the field as well as the laboratory.

In this chapter I assess the leading approaches to equilibrium selection in the light of some of the clearest and most intriguing experimental evidence of which I am aware, that reported in Van Huyck, Battalio, and Beil (henceforth "VHBB")(1990, 1991, 1993), following the analyses in Crawford (1995), Broseta (1993, 2000), and Crawford and Broseta (1998). VHBB's (1990, 1991) designs are of unusual economic interest, with subjects repeatedly playing symmetric coordination games in which their payoffs each period were determined by their own strategies, called "efforts," and an order statistic of their own and other subjects' efforts. VHBB's (1993) subjects repeatedly played one such game preceded by an auction in which a larger group of subjects bid for the right to play it. In each case, with minor exceptions, subjects were uncertain only about each other's strategies, and usually converged to an equilibrium of the stage game that was repeated each period – VHBB's (1990, 1991) coordination games or VHBB's (1993) auction-cum-coordination game. However, the large strategy spaces and variety of interaction patterns yielded rich dynamics, with large, systematic differences in equilibrium selection for different values of the *treatment variables* that define the environment, the order statistic and the number of players in the coordination game and the auction.

Crawford's and Broseta's models are based on a flexible characterization of individual behavior, which allows for strategic uncertainty in the form of idiosyncratic random shocks to players' initial responses and their adjustments to new observations. They include representatives of the leading theoretical approaches, distinguished by different values of empirical behavioral parameters that represent certain aspects of players' adjustments, including variances that represent the level of strategic uncertainty as it varies over time as players learn to predict each other's responses. These variances play a crucial role in equilibrium selection, but cannot be reliably explained by theory alone because they reflect differences in the beliefs of players who have identical roles, preferences, and information. The need for empirical parameters will come as no surprise to anyone who recalls Schelling's (1960) comparison of purely theoretical analyses of coordination to attempts to "prove, by purely formal deduction, that a particular joke is bound to be funny."

Crawford's and Broseta's models provide a framework within which to estimate the behavioral parameters econometrically using data from the experiments, and permit an informative analysis of the dynamics, which shows with considerable generality how the parameters interact with the treatment variables to determine the outcome. Both the estimates and the dynamics they imply discriminate sharply among the leading approaches, favoring an adaptive learning model with strategic uncertainty declining gradually to zero.

The resulting model is a Markov process with nonstationary transition probabilities and history-dependent dynamics, which lock in on behavior consistent with equilibrium in the stage game in the limit. The model's implications for equilibrium selection can be summarized by the prior probability distribution of the limiting outcome, which is normally nondegenerate due to persistent effects of strategic uncertainty. The analysis shows that strategic uncertainty imparts a drift to the learning dynamics, whose magnitude and direction are determined by the environment and the behavioral parameters, and whose effects persist long after strategic uncertainty has been eliminated by learning. This drift makes the distribution of the limiting outcome vary across treatments much as its empirical frequency distribution varied in the experiments. Thus, studying how strategic uncertainty interacts with the learning dynamics allows a simple, unified explanation of VHBB's results. The mechanism of equilibrium selection in VHBB's experiments seems typical of other experiments of this type, and presumably also of field environments.

The chapter is organized as follows. Section 6.2 describes VHBB's (1990, 1991, 1993) experimental designs and results. Section 6.3 describes a class of environments that generalizes VHBB's designs and introduces a portmanteau model of behavior that includes representatives of the leading approaches to equilibrium selection. The next three sections compare VHBB's results with the implications of the leading approaches. Section 6.4 considers traditional equilibrium analyses and refinements, Harsanyi and Selten's general theory of equilibrium selection, equilibrium analyses of perturbed games, and rational learning models. Section 6.5 considers deterministic and stochastic evolutionary dynamics. Section 6.6 considers adaptive learning models. Section 6.7 is the conclusion.

6.2 VHBB's experimental designs and results

In VHBB's (1990, 1991) experiments, populations of indistinguishable subjects played symmetric coordination games in which they chose among seven strategies called "efforts," 1, . . . ,7, with payoffs determined by their own efforts and an order statistic of their own and other subjects' efforts. Effort had a commonly-understood scale, which makes it meaningful to say that a subject chose the same effort in different periods or that different subjects chose the same effort, and which made it possible to define the order statistic. Subjects played these coordination games repeatedly, usually for 10 periods. Explicit communication was prohibited throughout; the relevant order statistic was publicly announced after each play; and with minor exceptions the structure was publicly announced at the start, so subjects were uncertain only about each other's efforts. Subjects seemed to understand the rules and were paid enough to induce the desired preferences.

I introduce the structures of VHBB's games by considering a simplified version, in which each of n players choose between two efforts, 1 and 2, with the minimum of their efforts determining total output, which they share equally. Effort is costly, but is productive enough that if all n players choose the same effort their output shares more than repay their costs. If anyone shirks, however, the balance of the others' efforts is wasted.

This game has a long history in economics, which can be traced to the stag hunt example Rousseau (1973 [1755]: 78) used to discuss the origins of the social contract. To see the connection, imagine (adding some game-theoretic detail to Rousseau's discussion) that each of a number of hunters must independently decide whether to join in a stag hunt (effort 2) or hunt rabbits by himself (effort 1). Hunting a stag yields each hunter a payoff of 2 when successful, but success requires the cooperation of every hunter and failure yields 0. Hunting rabbits yields each hunter a payoff of 1 with or without cooperation, and thereby determines the opportunity cost of effort devoted to the stag hunt.

Figure 6.1 gives the payoffs when output per capita is twice the minimum effort and the unit cost of effort is 1. For any n, Stag Hunt has two pure-strategy Nash equilibria, "all-2" and "all-1." All-2 is the best feasible outcome for all players, better for all than all-1. This rationale for playing effort 2 does not depend on game-theoretic subtleties; it is clearly the "correct" coordinating principle. However, effort 2's higher payoff when all players choose it must be traded off against its risk of a lower payoff when someone does not.

For a player to prefer effort 2, treating the influence of his choice on future developments as negligible, he must believe that the correctness of this choice is sufficiently clear that it is more likely than not that all of the other players will believe that its correctness is sufficiently clear to all. People are often uncertain

		Minimum effort	
		2	1
Player's effort	2	2	0
	1	1	1

Figure 6.1 Stag Hunt

about whether other people will believe this, and most choose effort 2 in small groups but not in large groups.[2]

In VHBB's (1990, 1991) experiments there were five leading treatments with seven efforts per subject, which varied the order statistic and the size of the groups playing the game. In VHBB's (1990) "minimum" treatments, populations of 14-16 subjects repeatedly played games like Stag Hunt, first in large groups with the population minimum effort determining payoffs, and then in random pairs (with new partners each period) in which each subject's payoff was determined by his current pair's minimum. Denoting subjects' efforts and the relevant minimum at time t by $x_{1t}, \ldots, x_{nt}$ and N_t respectively, subject i's period t payoff in dollars was $0.2N_t - 0.1x_{it} + 0.6$. In VHBB's (1991) "median" treatments, populations of nine subjects repeatedly played games like stag hunt in large groups, with the population median effort determining payoffs, and variations in the payoff function across three treatments. In the leading median treatment, Γ, subject i's period t payoff in dollars, denoting the median by M_t, was $0.1M_t - 0.05(M_t - x_{it})^2 + 0.6$. There were two other median treatments, Ω and Φ. Ω retained Γ's premium for equilibria with higher efforts but replaced its quadratic penalty for efforts away from the median with a uniform payoff, and Φ eliminated the premium but retained the quadratic penalty.

Each treatment's strategic structure was qualitatively similar to stag hunt. Subjects' payoffs were highest, other things equal, when their efforts equaled the relevant order statistic. Because a subject's effort can influence the minimum only by lowering it, which is never advantageous, and no subject's effort can influence the median when all other players are choosing the same effort, any symmetric configuration of efforts, with $x_{it} = N_t$ or M_t for all i, is an equilibrium. These seven symmetric equilibria are the only pure-strategy equilibria. These equilibria are strict and Pareto-ranked, with equilibria with higher efforts better for all subjects than those with lower efforts. The efficient equilibrium is plainly the "correct" coordinating principle, but it is best for a subject to play his part of that equilibrium only if he thinks it likely that enough other subjects will do so. This creates a tension between the higher payoff of the efficient equilibrium and its fragility due to strategic uncertainty. (These features extend to the random-pairing minimum treatment, with the stage game describing the interactions of the entire population each period, and payoffs evaluated taking into account uncertainty about how they interact. It is shown in Crawford (1995: 110 n10) that players' best responses in this treatment are given by an order statistic of the population effort distribution, the median for VHBB's payoffs.)

VHBB's (1990, 1991) designs are among the simplest models of the emergence of conventions to solve coordination problems, with a range of possible outcomes and a natural measure of efficiency. They pose central questions about how the difficulty of coordination depends on the number of players and the robustness of the efficient equilibrium, which is greater the farther the order statistic is from the minimum. Their structures are mirrored in important economic models, from the Stag Hunt to Keynes's beauty contest analogy and the more prosaic macroeconomic models surveyed in Cooper and John (1988) and Bryant (1994). To bring them closer to home, they have the structure of a faculty meeting that cannot start until a given quorum is achieved (100% in the large-group minimum game, 50% in the large-group median games). All would prefer that the meeting start on time, but waiting is costly, so each member prefers to arrive just when he expects the quorum to be achieved. Thus there is a range of Pareto-ranked equilibrium, one in which all members come on time, one in which all are one minute late, and so on.

In VHBB's (1993) experiment subjects played the nine-person median coordination game of VHBB's (1991) treatment Γ for 10–15 periods, with the right to play auctioned each period in a population of 18 subjects. The auction was a multiple-unit ascending-bid English clock auction, as in McCabe, Rassenti, and Smith (1990), in which subjects indicated their willingness to pay the current asking price by holding up bid cards, with subjects who dropped out not allowed to re-enter the bidding. The market-clearing price was determined as follows. If the lowest price at which nine or fewer subjects remained in the auction left exactly nine subjects, all nine were awarded the right to play at that price. If that price left fewer than nine subjects, they were all awarded the right to play, with the remainder of the nine slots filled randomly from those who dropped out at the last increase, and all nine subjects paying the price before the last increase.[3] As in VHBB's (1990, 1991) experiments, explicit communication was prohibited; the median was publicly announced after each play; the structure was publicly announced at the start; and the market-clearing price was publicly announced after each auction, before the median game was played.

VHBB's (1993) auctions are an interesting form of preplay communication, in which subjects' willingnesses to pay may signal how they expect to play, and thereby alleviate the tension due to strategic uncertainty.[4] They also capture important aspects of "general equilibrium" analogs of VHBB's (1990, 1991) environments, in which players choose among coordination games with the market-clearing price analogous to opportunity costs determined by their best alternatives. The models in Cooper and John (1988) and Bryant (1994), for instance, view the entire economy as a single coordination game, but it may be more realistic to view it as composed of sectors, regions, or firms, each of which is a coordination game.

Because participants must often choose among these, such an economy may be closer to VHBB's (1993) design than to their 1990 and 1991 designs.

The strategic structures of VHBB's (1990, 1991, 1993) designs and their tight control of preferences and information make them of considerable game-theoretic interest, and the experiments yielded striking results, which allow powerful tests of alternative approaches to equilibrium selection.[5] Their treatments elicited roughly similar initial effort distributions, with high to moderate variances and inefficiently low efforts. With minor exceptions subjects quickly converged to behavior consistent with equilibrium in the stage game. However, the large strategy spaces and variety of interaction patterns yielded rich dynamics, in which subjects' subsequent behavior differed strikingly and systematically across treatments, with persistent differences in equilibrium selection.

In the large-group minimum treatment subjects' choices gravitated toward the lowest effort, even though this led to the least efficient equilibrium. In the random-pairing minimum treatment, by contrast, subjects' efforts converged very slowly with little or no trend. And in the median treatments subjects invariably converged to the equilibrium determined by the initial median, even though it varied across runs in each treatment and was usually inefficient. Thus, the dynamics were sensitive to the size of the groups playing the coordination game, with very different drifts, rates of convergence, and limiting equilibria in the large-group and random-pairing minimum treatments. They were also sensitive to the order statistic that determined payoffs, with strong drift and no history-dependence in the large-group minimum treatment but no drift and strong history-dependence in the median treatments.

Auctioning the right to play the median game in VHBB's (1993) experiment yielded even more striking results. When that game was played without auctions in VHBB's (1991) experiment, most subjects initially chose inefficiently low efforts, and six out of six subject groups converged to inefficient equilibria. Auctions might be expected to yield more efficient outcomes simply because subjects have diverse beliefs about each other's efforts, auctions select the most optimistic subjects to play, and optimism favors efficiency in the median game. But VHBB's (1993) subjects did much better than this argument suggests: In eight out of eight groups, they bid the market-clearing price to a level recoverable only in the efficient equilibrium and then converged to that equilibrium within 3–5 periods. Their limiting behavior was consistent with subgame-perfect equilibrium in the stage game, and their beliefs appeared to be focused as in the intuition for forward induction refinements, in which players infer from their partners' willingnesses to pay to play a game that they expect their payoffs to repay their costs, and intend to play accordingly (Ben-Porath and Dekel (1992)). The efficiency-enhancing effect of auctions suggests a novel and potentially important way in which competition might promote efficiency.

6.3 A portmanteau model

Although VHBB's results convey a powerful impression by themselves, they raise more questions than they answer. Were the outcomes VHBB observed inevitable in their environments? How would they vary with changes in the environment? Would they extend to environments beyond those that directly generalize VHBB's designs? What guidance can they offer about equilibrium selection? Only an analysis that identifies the mechanism behind VHBB's results can provide a firm basis for generalization beyond the environments they studied, and realize the full power of their experiments to inform analysis.

Because learning models easily explain the rapid convergence to equilibrium in the stage game observed in almost all treatments, the main difficulty the analysis must address is explaining the differences in equilibrium selection across VHBB's treatments. The similarity across treatments of subjects' initial responses suggests that the differences in their limiting behavior cannot be understood without analyzing the dynamics. I begin by describing a class of environments that generalizes VHBB's designs. I then introduce a portmanteau model of behavior that nests representatives of the leading approaches to equilibrium selection, both static and dynamic, so that the analysis can use the experimental evidence to distinguish among them. I apply all but rational learning to the stage game rather than the repeated game, which is less plausible, and does no better. In its most general form, the model is an adaptive learning model, based on a flexible characterization of individual behavior that allows for strategic uncertainty in the form of idiosyncratic shocks to players' initial responses and their adjustments to new observations. The leading approaches are distinguished by different values of behavioral parameters, including variances that represent the level of strategic uncertainty as it varies over time.

I assume complete information because the structures of VHBB's designs were publicly announced. For simplicity I focus on VHBB's (1990, 1991) experiments, and consider VHBB's (1993) extensive-form auction environment only when it yields additional insight; and I take effort to be continuously variable.[6]

6.3.1 Strategic environments

I begin by describing a class of environments that generalizes VHBB's designs by allowing arbitrary values of their treatment variables and more general payoff structures.

A finite population of n indistinguishable players play an n-person coordination game each period. The coordination game has symmetric player roles and one-dimensional strategy spaces, with strategies called "efforts." Effort has a commonly understood scale, the same for all players.[7] Any symmetric effort combination is an equilibrium; such combinations are the only pure-strategy equilibria; and, by symmetry, those equilibria are Pareto-ranked. Each player's best responses are given by an order statistic of all players' efforts whenever it is unaffected by his own effort. I write this order statistic, y_t, as a function of the x_{it}, players' continuous efforts at time t:

$$y_t \equiv f(x_{it}, \ldots, x_{nt}), \tag{6.1}$$

where $f(\cdot)$ is continuous, and for any $x_{1t}, \ldots x_{nt}$ and constants and $b \geq 0$,

$$f(a+bx_{1t}, \ldots, a+bx_{nt} \equiv a+bf(x_{1t}, \ldots, x_{nt})). \tag{6.2}$$

These assumptions are satisfied for the coordination games in VHBB's (1990, 1991, 1993) environments, including the random-pairing minimum treatment when players' expected payoffs are evaluated before the uncertainty of pairing is resolved (the relevant order statistic is then the population median effort; see Crawford (1995: 110 n10)).

The structure is made public before play begins. Players then choose their efforts, and the resulting value of y_t is publicly announced.[8] Players then choose new efforts, and so on. Throughout this process, players face uncertainty only about each other's decisions, and the effects of those decisions on their payoffs are filtered through the order statistic.

6.3.2 Behavior

The model of behavior must be flexible enough to include representatives of the leading approaches to equilibrium selection, so that the empirical analysis can identify the essential features of an explanation of VHBB's results. It must, in particular, capture the idea that even if players form their beliefs and choose their efforts sensibly, they may differ in unpredictable ways. It must also describe the dynamics of beliefs and efforts realistically, in terms of observable variables, in a way that permits an informative analysis.

With these desiderata in mind, I assume that players are rational in the standard sense that their decisions maximize expected payoffs given their beliefs. I also assume that players treat their individual influences on y_t as negligible, which is plausible given the large subject populations in VHBB's experiments. This implies that players' optimal efforts each period are determined by their current payoff implications, and thus by their beliefs about the current y_t. I further imagine that in forming their beliefs, players focus on the stage game, beginning with prior beliefs about the process that generates y_t, using standard statistical procedures to revise their beliefs each period in response to new observations, and then choosing the efforts that maximize expected payoffs. Players whose priors differ may then have different beliefs even if they have always observed the same history and used the same procedures to interpret it.

I now describe a simplified version of the model in Crawford (1995), which exploits the "evolutionary" structure of VHBB's designs to give a simple statistical characterization of the dynamics in the style of the adaptive control literature, in a way that allows a more informative analysis of the effects of strategic uncertainty than now seems possible for games in general.[9] The key insight of the control literature is that describing how beliefs respond to new information does not require representing them as probability distributions or their moments. It is enough to model the dynamics of the optimal decisions they imply, which are the only aspects of beliefs that directly affect the outcome.

I represent players' beliefs by their optimal efforts, x_{it}, which when continuously variable preserve enough information to realistically describe beliefs.[10] The x_{it} adjust toward the value suggested by the latest observation of y_t according to simple linear rules:

$$x_{i0} = \alpha_0 + \zeta_{i0} \tag{6.3}$$

and

$$x_{it} = \alpha_t + \beta_t y_{t-1} + (1 - \beta_t) x_{it-1} + \zeta_{it}, \tag{6.4}$$

where the α_t and β_t are exogenous behavioral parameters, with $0 < \beta_t \leq 1$ and $a_t \to 0$ as $t \to \infty$. These assumptions imply that players quickly and reliably learn to predict y_t if it converges and choose the x_{it} that are optimal given their predictions, and that the long-run steady states of the dynamics coincide with the pure-strategy equilibria of the stage game. The ζ_{it} are independently and identically distributed (henceforth, "i.i.d.") random shocks with zero means and given variances, $\sigma^2_{\zeta t}$, which represent the level of strategic uncertainty. In effect each player has his own theory of others' behavior, which gives his initial beliefs and his interpretations of new observations an unpredictable component. The independence of the ζ_{it} means that any correlation in players' beliefs or efforts that emerges, does so in response to their common observations of y_t rather than as an artifact of the distributional assumptions.

Although the form of (6.4) suggests partial adjustment, it is best thought of as full adjustment to players' current estimates of their optimal efforts, which respond less than fully to new observations because they are only part of players' information about the process.

Suppose, for instance, that player i's decisions are certainty-equivalent, so that his optimal effort equals his current estimate of the mean of y_t. Then if he thinks that the y_t are independent draws from a fixed distribution, and puts as much weight on his prior as he would on τ such draws, he will set $\alpha_t = 0$ and $\beta_t = 1/(\tau + t + 1)$, as in "fictitious play." If he believes instead that the y_t are generated by a driftless random walk, he will set $\alpha_t = 0$ and $\beta_t = 1$, as in a "best-response" process. Thus (6.4) includes as special cases two of the learning rules most often studied in the game theory literature, while allowing a wide class of values for parameters that represent the initial levels, trends, and inertia in beliefs. Learning rules of this kind have been shown in the control literature to be a robust approach to the estimation problems faced by agents who understand their environments but are unwilling to make the specific assumptions about it or unable to store and process the large amounts of information an explicitly Bayesian approach would require.

In general (6.4) is not fully "rational" in the game-theoretic sense, because players' priors need not be correct and linearity may be inconsistent with the rules that are optimal given their priors. However, (6.4) also includes representatives of traditional equilibrium analysis and the other leading approaches to equilibrium selection, as explained below.

Eq. (6.4) differs from the "reinforcement learning" model of Roth and Erev (1995), which is its leading competitor in the adaptive learning literature, in that in the Roth–Erev model players adjust the probabilities with which they play their strategies directly in response to their realized payoffs, without reference to their best responses. The models are otherwise similar; both allow the variances of players' responses to decline over time with experience. Although reinforcement learning describes observed behavior in experiments with matrix games quite well, as explained in Crawford (1997: Section 6.3), VHBB's subjects seemed to understand the best-response structures of the games they played, and taking this into account yields a better description of their behavior. Roth (1995: 39, Figure 1.2), for instance, found that the Roth-Erev model tracks the dynamics in VHBB's large-group minimum treatment much better if it is modified to allow "common learning," in which players adjust as if they had played the most successful strategy in the population. When the population is diverse, this approximates the situation when players' learning rules incorporate the best-response structure, as in (6.4). In these environments, reinforcement learning also yields adjustments an order of magnitude too slow; this discrepancy cannot be corrected simply by adjusting the behavioral parameters because this disturbs the balance between the stochastic and deterministic parts of the learning dynamics.

6.4 Traditional equilibrium analyses

In traditional equilibrium analyses, players are assumed to be rational in the decision-theoretic sense that their strategies are best responses to their beliefs, and this assumption is supplemented with the hypothesis that players share common beliefs, so that there is no strategic uncertainty (Aumann and Brandenburger (1995)). In Section 6.3's portmanteau model, equilibrium analyses are distinguished by the restrictions $\zeta_{it} \equiv \sigma^2_{\zeta t} \equiv 0$ for all i and t. When they are applied to the stage game, it is natural also to require $\alpha_t \equiv 0$ for all $t = 1, \ldots$ because there is no reason to predict different equilibria in different periods. Different approaches are distinguished by different assumptions about α_0. When equilibrium analyses are applied to the repeated game, as in rational learning models, α_t may vary over time. (Since $x_{it} \equiv y_t$ when $\zeta_{it} \equiv \sigma^2_{\zeta t} \equiv 0, \beta_t$ is irrelevant in each case.)

Even though in most of VHBB's (1990, 1991, 1993) treatments subjects converged to an equilibrium in the stage game, equilibrium analyses stop well short of what is needed to understand the observed patterns of equilibrium selection. It is nevertheless instructive to consider their implications in VHBB's environments. I now discuss the implications of traditional refinements; the general theory of equilibrium selection, including risk- and payoff-dominance; equilibrium analyses of perturbed games; and rational learning models.

6.4.1 Traditional refinements

Traditional refinements such as trembling-hand perfectness and strategic stability refine equilibrium analyses by requiring that a given equilibrium is "self-enforcing" in some stronger sense. Because they take beliefs as given, they do not discriminate among the strict equilibria in any of VHBB's (1990, 1991) treatments. Traditional refinements simply do not address the strategic issues raised by these games, which all pose essentially the same question in the absence of strategic uncertainty.

The situation is a bit different in VHBB's (1993) stage game, where extensive-form refinements such as subgame-perfectness and forward induction do address some of the issues it raises. In this experiment subjects' bids and efforts were almost always consistent with the intuition for forward induction, in that they seldom bid more than their efforts made it possible to recoup, and never after the first few periods; and their limiting behavior was consistent with subgame-perfect equilibrium in the stage game (VHBB (1993: Tables V–VI)). However, both refinements are consistent with any of the seven symmetric pure-strategy equilibria of the coordination game, with players bidding their equilibrium payoffs. They are therefore too unrestrictive to help in explaining VHBB's (1993) results.

6.4.2 The general theory of equilibrium selection

Harsanyi and Selten's (1988) general theory of equilibrium selection is the most ambitious attempt to define a comprehensive theory of equilibrium selection to date. Its main building blocks are their notions of risk- and payoff-dominance, which discriminate among strict equilibria and thereby (along with *ad hoc* devices that come into play in special cases) yield unique predictions in a wide class of games, including VHBB's.

Payoff-dominance is defined as Pareto-superiority within the set of equilibria, with certain qualifications involving dominated strategies and symmetry. *Risk-dominance* is defined via a mental tâtonnement called the "tracing procedure," in which players begin with naive priors and then mentally simulate each other's best responses and adjust their priors accordingly, until they converge to identical (and therefore equilibrium) beliefs. These simulations are independent across players but the same for all. Roughly speaking, risk-dominance selects an equilibrium whose *basin of attraction* – the set of beliefs that make its efforts best responses – is larger than those of other equilibria, in a certain sense.

Harsanyi and Selten's theory gives priority to payoff-dominance, so that where one equilibrium is Pareto-superior to all others, as in all but one of VHBB's treatments, risk-dominance has no influence. However, their theory is coherent without this priority; and risk-dominance is of particular interest here because it embodies most of their ideas about the effects of strategic uncertainty, and it captures some of the variations in behavior across VHBB's (1990, 1991) treatments. I therefore consider the implications of Harsanyi and Selten's theory both with and without the priority they give payoff-dominance.

The logic of Harsanyi and Selten's theory suggests comparing its predictions with subjects' initial efforts in each stage game. Payoff-dominance selects the all-7 equilibrium in all but VHBB's median treatment Φ, where payoff-dominance is neutral and the theory selects all-4 in response to symmetry. This yields success rates of 31% and 37% in the large-group and random-pairing minimum treatments and 15%, 52%, and 41% in median treatments Γ, Ω, and Φ (VHBB (1991, Table II)). Without priority to payoff-dominance, Harsanyi and Selten's theory selects all-1 in the large-group minimum treatment in response to risk-dominance; all-4 in the random-pairing minimum treatment, where risk-dominance is neutral and the theory applies the tracing procedure to a uniform prior over undominated strategies; all-7 in median treatments Γ and Ω in response to risk-dominance; and all-4 in median treatment Φ in response to risk-dominance, after imposing symmetry. This lowers the success rates to 2% and 17% in the large-group and random-pairing minimum treatments and leaves it unchanged in the median treatments.

Although it is impressive that any purely theoretical principle can pick up this much of the variation in subjects' responses to VHBB's treatments, these success rates – though mostly better than random, which with seven efforts would imply a success rate of 14% – fall far short of the perfect prediction the logic of the theory requires. And this cannot be attributed to the dispersion of subjects' responses: The theory predicts the modal outcome in three out of five or two out of five treatments respectively with or without payoff-dominance, missing a large part of the central tendency of initial responses.

The theory's overall success rates are no higher for subjects' limiting behavior. This comparison leaves them unchanged for median treatments; roughly unchanged for the random-pairing minimum treatment; and significantly lower or higher, respectively with and without payoff-dominance, for the large-group minimum treatment. Without priority to payoff-dominance, Harsanyi and Selten's theory essentially reduces to the tracing procedure, so the latter comparison amounts to using the tracing procedure as a model of the learning process. Section 6.6's analysis shows that there were significant interactions between strategic uncertainty and the learning dynamics. Perhaps it is unsurprising that a model in which players mentally simulate each other's responses does not adequately capture these, so that learning from actual observations of behavior is different from mental tâtonnements. However, describing the central tendency of initial responses is also important in predicting equilibrium selection via history-dependent learning dynamics, which may create an important role for theories like Harsanyi and Selten's.

6.4.3 An aside on equilibrium analyses of perturbed games

I now discuss equilibrium analyses of randomly perturbed versions of VHBB's stage games that do not fit neatly into the portmanteau model, but are potentially relevant.

Anderson, Goeree, and Holt (1996) adapt McKelvey and Palfrey's (1995) notion of *quantal response equilibrium* to analyze a continuous-effort version of the large-group minimum game. A quantal response equilibrium is an equilibrium in a perturbed game in which players' payoffs are subject to privately observed, i.i.d. mean-zero shocks with a commonly known distribution, whose variance is treated as a behavioral parameter. Thus it roughly resembles a snapshot of behavior at some point (depending on the variance) during the tracing procedure. Anderson, Goeree, and Holt show that for a given variance their minimum game has a unique, symmetric quantal response equilibrium. Its effort distributions stochastically decrease with the number of players and the cost of effort, capturing some of the sensitivity to changes in treatment variables suggested by VHBB's results.[11] However, the mechanism that yields this sensitivity is very different from the one suggested by the analysis below, where all random variation is eliminated in the limit and the learning dynamics can lock in on equilibria far from the quantal response equilibrium.

Carlsson and van Damme (1993) study a class of n-person, two-effort games against the field that includes Section 6.2's Stag Hunt example and other order-statistic games, in which the payoff of high effort is a nondecreasing function of the number of players who play it. However, there is incomplete information, with each player's payoff for low effort perturbed by a privately observed, i.i.d. mean-zero shock with a commonly known, uniform distribution. They show that when this distribution is sufficiently concentrated around zero, the only strategies that survive iterative elimination of strictly dominated strategies are those in which each player plays low effort: Inferences about these arbitrarily small payoff perturbations turn the unperturbed game (which has two strict equilibria) into a dominance-solvable game with a unique equilibrium. For more dispersed distributions, low efforts are more likely the more players there are and the closer the order statistic is to the minimum, and the equilibrium displays a sensitivity to treatment variables qualitatively similar to VHBB's results. Then, however, each player plays both efforts with nonnegligible probabilities, so that there is a significant probability of disequilibrium even in the limit. Thus, the model can capture either the sensitivity of equilibrium selection to VHBB's treatment variables or their subjects' tendency to lock in on an equilibrium, but not both at once. In any case, the inferences required to identify the equilibrium by iterated dominance go far beyond the degree of strategic sophistication usually exhibited by experimental subjects, and are presumably beyond the sophistication of players in the field.

6.4.4 Rational learning

Most rational learning models extend equilibrium analyses to the repeated game that describes players' entire interaction. They are dynamic in the sense that they allow nontrivial interactions between periods; but like equilibrium analyses of the stage game they rule out all strategic uncertainty. Just as any configuration in which all players choose the same effort is an equilibrium in any of the stage games of VHBB's (1990, 1991) experiments, any deterministic pattern of jumping among such configurations over time is an equilibrium in their repeated games. Rational learning models therefore add little to the power of equilibrium analyses to explain behavior in these environments.

6.5 Evolutionary Dynamics

Evolutionary analyses study environments in which games are played repeatedly in populations, characterizing the dynamics of the population strategy frequencies under simple assumptions about how they respond to current expected payoffs. In the simplest evolutionary models, a large population of indistinguishable players repeatedly play a symmetric stage game with undistinguished roles. Players' stage-game strategies are one-dimensional and have a fixed common scale, as in VHBB's (1990, 1991) experiments. Individual players play only pure strategies, with payoffs determined by their own strategies and the population frequencies of others' strategies, often by a simple summary statistic such as the mean, minimum, or median.

Most discussions of evolutionary games treat them as synonymous with random pairing to play a two-person game, as in VHBB's random-pairing minimum treatment. However, many applications are better modeled by assuming that the entire population simultaneously plays a single symmetric n-person game, known in biology as a *game against the field*.[12] The above description allows both interaction patterns, and it is often convenient to view random pairing as a special case of games against the field, with payoffs evaluated before the uncertainty of pairing is resolved. "Stage game" refers to the game that describes the simultaneous interaction of the entire population, rather than the two-person game played by matched pairs.

Evolutionary models attribute little or no rationality or sophistication to players and allow unlimited strategic uncertainty, and thus occupy the opposite end of the behavioral spectrum from equilibrium analyses. Instead behavior is summarized by the law of motion of the population strategy frequencies, which in biology is derived (usually in a form known as the "replicator dynamics") from the assumption that players inherit their actions from their parents, who reproduce at rates proportional to their payoffs; and in economics from plausible assumptions about individual adjustment (Schelling (1978)).

In each case the goal is to identify the locally stable steady states of the dynamics. A remarkable conclusion emerges: If the dynamics converge, they converge to a steady state in which strategies that persist are optimal in the stage game, given the limiting strategy frequencies. Thus the limiting strategy frequencies (viewed as a mixed strategy) are in Nash equilibrium in the stage game. Although strategies are not rationally chosen (in biology, not even chosen) the population collectively "learns" the equilibrium as its frequencies evolve, with selection doing the work of rationality and strategic sophistication.

Although evolution, taken literally, has little direct influence on behavior in experiments, most experimental designs are similar in structure to evolutionary models. Crawford (1991) showed that VHBB's (1990, 1991) designs satisfy the structural assumptions of evolutionary game theory, in most cases as games against the field. This fact and an imperfect but informative analogy between evolutionary and learning dynamics make an "evolutionary" analysis helpful in understanding VHBB' results. Here I discuss two leading evolutionary approaches, deterministic evolutionary dynamics and analyses of the long-run equilibria of stochastic evolutionary dynamics.

6.5.1 Deterministic evolutionary dynamics

In the portmanteau model, deterministic evolutionary dynamics are represented by the parameter restrictions $\sigma^2_{\zeta 0} > 0$ but $\zeta_{it} \equiv \sigma^2_{\zeta t} \equiv \alpha_t \equiv 0$ for all i and $t = 1, \ldots,$ which allow initial heterogeneity but rule out subsequent differences in players' adjustment rules. Crawford (1991) considered the extent to which VHBB's (1990, 1991) results could be explained by finite-population variants of deterministic evolutionary dynamics or (equivalently here) static refinements such as evolutionary stability. The flavor of the analysis and the relationship between random pairing and games against the field are well illustrated by an evolutionary analysis of Section 6.2's two-effort Stag Hunt example, whose conclusions extend immediately to VHBB's seven-effort games.

Recall that for any number of players, stag hunt has two symmetric pure-strategy equilibria, all-2 and all-1, both of which correspond to steady states of the dynamics. The same conclusions hold when n players are randomly paired to play two-person versions of Stag Hunt. In each case there is also a symmetric mixed-strategy equilibrium, which also corresponds to a steady state.

Figure 6.2 (Crawford 1991: Figure 1) graphs the expected payoffs of efforts 1 and 2 against the population frequency of effort 1 for Stag Hunt with random pairing and against the field. Effort 1's payoff is constant at 1 in each case. With random pairing effort 2's payoff is a population frequency-weighted average of its payoffs when the other player chooses efforts 1 and 2, hence linear in those frequencies; while against the field, effort 2's payoff drops discontinuously from 2 to 0 as the frequency of effort 1 rises above 0. The mixed-strategy equilibrium frequency is always unstable in this game. With random pairing both all-2 and all-1 are locally stable, and their basins of attraction are equally large. Against the field only all-1 is locally stable (even though all-2 is strict in the stage game, as explained in Crawford (1991)) and its basin of attraction is almost the entire state space. Moving the order statistic above the minimum moves the discontinuity in effort 2's payoff to the right, making all-2 locally stable, but with small basins of attraction for order statistics near the minimum. These conclusions extend to finite populations.

Similarly, in VHBB's large-group minimum game with seven efforts only the all-1 equilibrium is locally stable. But in VHBB's median treatments, or in any such game with an order statistic other than the minimum (including the random-pairing minimum treatment, which is equivalent to a large-group median treatment as explained in Crawford (1995)), all seven symmetric pure-strategy equilibria are locally stable.

Deterministic evolutionary dynamics have two advantages over equilibrium analyses for the purpose of explaining results like VHBB's. Together with the dispersion of initial responses, the effect of the order statistic on the sizes of the basins of attraction begins to capture the interaction between strategic uncertainty and learning dynamics. And the dynamics give a rudimentary account of history-dependent equilibrium selection, in which the population always converges to the equilibrium whose basin of attraction includes its initial state. I now record a

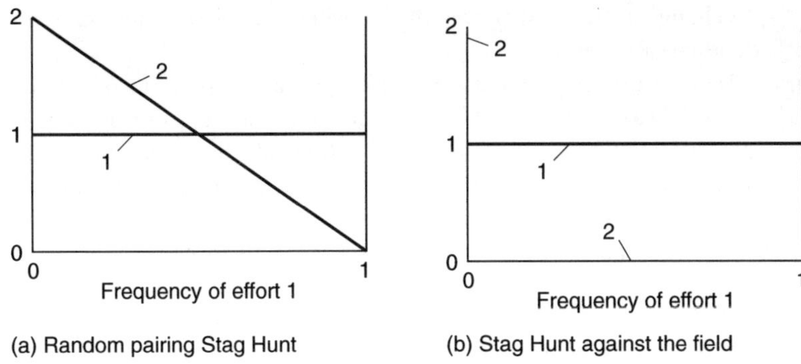

Figure 6.2 a) Random pairing Stag Hunt. b) Stag Hunt against the field

result (stated informally in Crawford (1995)) that gives a more general account of this history-dependence, and thereby shows how to use the model as a kind of accounting system for keeping track of the probabilities of possible changes in y_t.

Proposition 6.1 *Suppose that* $\alpha_t = 0$ *and* $\beta_t \in (0, 1]$ *for all* $t = 1, \ldots,$ *and that there exists an integer* $T \geq 1$ *such that* $\zeta_{it} \equiv \sigma^2_{\zeta t} \equiv 0$ *for all* $t = T, \ldots$. *Then for all* $i, x_{it} \to y_{T-1}$ *monotonically, without overshooting, and* $y_t = y_T$ *for all* $t = T, \ldots,$ *independent of the number of players n and the order statistic* $f(\cdot)$.

Proof: (6.4) with $\alpha_t = 0$ and $\beta_t \in (0, 1]$ for all $t = 1, \ldots,$ and $\zeta_{it} = 0$ for $t = T, \ldots,$ implies that $x_{iT} - y_{T-1}$ always has the same sign as $x_{iT-1} - y_{T-1}$, with x_{iT} closer to y_{T-1} than x_{iT-1} was. Because $f(\cdot)$ is an order statistic, it follows that $y_T = y_{T-1}$, and so on.

The proof exploits the fact that, by the definition of an order statistic, y_t can change only if more players overshoot it in one direction than in the other. When players' adjustments follow (6.4), on average they do not overshoot, because $\beta_t \in (0, 1]$. Thus, unless their responses to new observations continue to differ, their efforts collapse mechanically on the current y_t, and continued change in y_t depends on *persistent* strategic uncertainty. In particular, if players differ in their initial responses but interpret new observations in the same way, y_t remains forever at y_0, independent of the treatment variables.

This perfect history-dependence is consistent with the results for VHBB's median treatments, but not for their large-group minimum treatment. There, the average subject with effort above the minimum adjusted only part of the way toward the minimum, and if subjects did not differ in their responses to new observations, the minimum could never have fallen. In fact there was enough variation in subjects' responses to make the minimum fall in 9 out of the 13 instances in which it was not already at the lowest possible level. The model of adaptive learning dynamics discussed below captures this variation by allowing moderate values of $\sigma^2_{\zeta 0}$, with $\sigma^2_{\zeta t} \to 0$ steadily over time as one would expect as subjects learn from their common observations of y_t. This yields enough overshooting to explain the dynamics of y_t in the large-group minimum treatment, while also reproducing the failure of y_t to change in the median treatments, where the median smoothes the effects of individual dispersion.

Overall, deterministic evolutionary dynamics hint at the patterns of equilibrium selection in VHBB's (1990, 1991) experiments, but are too unrestrictive to explain them. They have two main drawbacks: (i) they take the initial state of the population as a datum, even though it is the principal determinant of the limiting outcome; and (ii) they give little guidance on how the sizes of basins of attractions affect equilibrium selection, beyond the intuition that the initial state is more likely to fall into a larger basin. Section 6.6's adaptive learning model responds to these drawbacks by estimating the distribution of subjects' initial responses and using an explicit, stochastic model of learning at the individual level, which allows "tunneling" across basins of attraction with positive probability and the more subtle forms of history-dependence found in the experiments.

6.5.2 Stochastic evolutionary dynamics and long-run equilibria

Analyses of long-run equilibria of stochastic evolutionary dynamics (Kandori, Mailath, and Rob (1993) and Young (1993)) assume population interaction patterns like those in simple evolutionary game theory. The state of the population is characterized by its current mix of strategies, and players' adjustments are assumed to move their strategies to or toward their best responses to the current state. The main difference from deterministic evolutionary dynamics is that players' adjustments are subject to random "mutations," whose probability is constant over time and independent of the state.

In the portmanteau model, the required assumptions correspond to the parameter restrictions $\sigma^2_{\zeta t} \equiv \varepsilon > 0$ (or $\sigma^2_{\zeta t} \to \varepsilon > 0$) and $\alpha_t \equiv 0$ and $\beta_t \equiv \beta$ for all $t = 1, \ldots$. The resulting dynamics are a Markov process with (at least eventually) stationary transition probabilities. The analysis allows strategic uncertainty, in that the population need not be in equilibrium from the start, and assumes little or no strategic sophistication.

When $\varepsilon = 0$ the dynamics may have many steady states, which normally include the game's symmetric pure-strategy equilibria, and in games like VHBB's coincide with them. Which one, if any, the population converges to depends on the initial state, as in deterministic evolutionary models, and is difficult to predict. But when $\varepsilon > 0$ the limiting outcome paradoxically becomes more predictable. The dynamics are then ergodic, so that they converge to a distribution over states that is independent of history. In the long run the process cycles perpetually among those states, with their prior probabilities at any given time determined by the ergodic distribution. This distribution depends on ε, and is difficult to characterize in general. But when $\varepsilon \to 0$ the ergodic distribution is concentrated around the steady states of the dynamics without mutations (in VHBB's games, the symmetric pure-strategy equilibria) and approaches a limit that can be characterized by estimating the relative likelihoods of entering and exiting the steady states from the number of simultaneous mutations such changes require. The *long-run equilibrium* is defined as the support of the ergodic distribution as $\varepsilon \to 0$. This distribution usually puts probability one on a single steady state, which in sufficiently simple random-pairing environments is determined by risk-dominance, and more generally by the relative difficulty of entering and leaving the various steady states.[13]

Although analyses of long-run equilibria usually assume random pairing, VHBB's games against the field are no harder to analyze this way. Transitions between equilibria occur if and only if more players cross the order statistic from below than above, or vice versa. Consider Figure 6.2b's Stag Hunt game. When the order statistic is below the median, the discontinuous drop in effort 2's expected payoff occurs in the left half of the horizontal axis, so that the basin of attraction of the low-effort equilibrium at the right end of the horizontal axis is larger than the basin of attraction of the high-effort equilibrium at the left end, and fewer simultaneous mutations are required to go from the high-effort equilibrium to the edge of the basin of attraction of the low-effort equilibrium than from the low-effort equilibrium to the edge of the basin of attraction of the high-effort equilibrium. A noninfinitesimal mutation probability therefore makes the probability of tunneling leftward across the boundary lower than the probability of tunneling rightward, so that the ergodic distribution assigns higher probability to the low-effort equilibrium. As the mutation probability approaches zero, the ratio of the two tunneling probabilities approaches infinity and the probability the ergodic distribution assigns to the low-effort equilibrium approaches one. Robles (1997) gives a complete characterization of long-run equilibria in these environments. Here I give the result for the portmanteau model, whose proof formalizes the intuitive argument just given.

Proposition 6.2 *In VHBB's (1990, 1991) games, the long-run equilibrium assigns probability one to the equilibrium with lowest (highest) effort whenever the order statistic is below (above) the median, and positive probability to every equilibrium when the order statistic is the median. In each case the long-run equilibrium is independent of the number of players and the order statistic, as long as it remains below (or above) the median.*

Proposition 6.2 shows that analyses of long-run equilibria discriminate among strict equilibria and obtain unique predictions in most of VHBB's (1990, 1991) environments. These predictions are appealing in their simplicity. They are obtained without modeling players' initial responses or using empirical information about behavior, by studying ergodic dynamics and passing to the limit as the mutation probability approaches zero. However, although they distinguish between VHBB's large-group minimum treatment and their median and random-pairing minimum treatments in a way that is qualitatively consistent with the variations in observed outcomes, they are otherwise undiscriminating. By limiting the effects of history, such analyses eliminate much of the information about the effects of changes in treatment variables an analysis of VHBB's results can provide.

An analysis of long-run equilibria also seems possible in VHBB's (1993) environment, as in Kim's (1996) analysis of stochastic evolutionary dynamics. This would likely reproduce Kim's conclusion that limiting outcomes assure efficient coordination for any numbers of players in the auction and the coordination game, and any order statistic. Although this was the case in VHBB's experiment, Cachon and Camerer's (1996) and Weber's (1994) closely related experiments suggest that efficiency is not inevitable for all such treatments. Once again, the long-run equilibrium appears to lose some information that is important in understanding the full implications of VHBB's results.

6.6 Adaptive learning

In the portmanteau model, adaptive learning models are distinguished by the parameter restrictions $\sigma^2_{\zeta 0} > 0, \sigma^2_{\zeta t} \to 0$ and $\alpha_t \to 0$ (or $\alpha_t \equiv 0$) for all $t = 1, \ldots$. The crucial difference between adaptive learning as defined here and stochastic evolutionary dynamics is that $\sigma^2_{\zeta t} \to 0$ gradually, rather than $\sigma^2_{\zeta t} \equiv \varepsilon > 0$ or $\sigma^2_{\zeta t} \to \varepsilon > 0$, so that learning dynamics are inherently nonstationary. This reflects the belief that players in an environment that approaches stationarity sufficiently rapidly will learn to predict each other's behavior accurately enough to lock in on a particular equilibrium. Only if there is new uncertainty each period, or if players continually enter and leave the population, will the process have the kind of perpetual randomness that allows an analysis of ergodic dynamics.

Although this may seem like a fine point, adaptive learning and stochastic evolutionary dynamics have quite different implications. The choice is still a subtle one, because predictions based on long-run equilibria are qualitatively consistent with the patterns of equilibrium selection in VHBB's experiments, and no amount of real data can refute a long-run prediction. The real issue is whether a model in which $\sigma^2_{\zeta t} \to 0$ gradually, but quickly enough to allow the dynamics to lock in on a particular equilibrium, is a more useful description of behavior. As I will show, such a model makes patterns of equilibrium selection like those VHBB observed a long-run phenomenon, and is a better language in which to express and generalize the lessons to be learned from their experiments.

6.6.1 Convergence

Once the distributions of the ζ_{it} are specified, (6.3) and (6.4) define a Markov process with time-varying transition probabilities and state vector x_t, in which players' beliefs and strategy choices are identically distributed *ex ante* (but not in general otherwise). The model's dynamics are driven by strategic uncertainty, as represented by the ζ_{it} or the $\sigma^2_{\zeta t}$. Its recursive structure and the conditional independence of players' deviations from the average learning rule capture the requirement that players must form their beliefs and choose their strategies independently which is the essence of the coordination problem.

Proposition 6.3 shows that, unless the level of strategic uncertainty declines to 0 very slowly, the learning dynamics converge, with probability 1, to one of the symmetric equilibria of the coordination game.[14] In this proposition, for technical reasons, I bound players' strategies by increasing x_{it} to its lower bound, denoted $\underline{x}$, or reducing it to its upper bound, denoted $\overline{x}$, whenever it would otherwise fall outside the interval $[\underline{x}, \overline{x}]$.

Proposition 6.3 *Assume that the distributions of the ζ_{it} are truncated so that the x remain in the interval $[\underline{x}, \overline{x}]$. Then if $0 < \beta \leq 1$ and $\sum_{s=0}^{\infty} \sigma_{\zeta s}^2$ is finite, y_t and the x_{it} converge, with probability 1, to a common, finite limit, which is an equilibrium of the stage game.*

The proof follows the martingale convergence arguments of Nevel'son and Has'minskii (1973, Theorem 2.7.3), using the stochastic Lyapunov function $V_t \equiv \sum_{i,j}(x_{it} - x_{jt})^2$. Clearly $V_t \geq 0$, with $V_t = 0$ if and only if $x_{it} = x_{jt}$ for all i and j. It can be shown that the expected motion of the Lyapunov function is downward out of equilibrium. With the stated variance conditions, which are what would be needed to establish the strong law of large numbers in the absence of interactions between the stochastic and deterministic parts of the dynamics, this assures convergence with probability 1.

6.6.2 Closed-form solution

Given Proposition 6.3, the model's implications for equilibrium selection can be summarized by the prior probability distribution of the limiting equilibrium, which is normally nondegenerate due to the persistent effects of strategic uncertainty by Proposition 6.4 below. The probabilistic nature of the model's predictions follows naturally from its statistical characterization of players' beliefs, and is fully consistent with the variation across runs within treatments that are commonly observed in experiments.

The distribution of the limiting equilibrium is influenced by interactions between strategic uncertainty and the learning dynamics. To build intuition about the interactions, reconsider Section 6.2's analogy between VHBB's (1990) large-group minimum game and a faculty meeting with a 100% quorum. Members who can perfectly predict when others will arrive might coordinate on an inefficient equilibrium, but with perfect prediction there is no reason for them to favor such an equilibrium. On the contrary, one would expect such sagacious beings to coordinate on the efficient equilibrium in which everyone arrives on time. There is then also no reason to expect the outcome to vary with the quorum or the size of the faculty. But as anyone who has attended a series of such meetings can testify, such perfect prediction is unlikely, and the resulting dispersion of arrival times creates incentives for members to arrive later and later as they try to avoid having to wait for their colleagues. The meetings begin progressively later until the members gain enough experience to predict each other's arrival times, but by then they have converged to a common arrival time later than all would have preferred. Further, it is intuitively clear that this problem is less severe the smaller the faculty, or the more moderate the quorum.

I now show how the portmanteau model, with $\sigma_{\zeta t}^2 \to 0$ gradually, captures this intuition. Note first that with no restrictions on the a_t, the portmanteau model is formally consistent with any history of the y_t for any n and $f(\cdot)$, with $\zeta_{it} \equiv \sigma_{\zeta t}^2 \equiv 0$ for all i and t and a_t varying over time so that $\sum_0^t \alpha_s = y_t = x_{it}$. Such solutions, in which players jump from one stage-game equilibrium to the next following some commonly understood pattern, are not inconsistent with game-theoretic ideas of rationality. But they are empirically bizarre because the *ad hoc* variation in a_t they require violates the hypothesis that past behavior in an environment is directly indicative of current behavior, which most people take for granted, and which is the foundation of adaptive learning models. I therefore rule out such *ad hoc* variation by imposing the restrictions $\alpha_t = 0$ and $\beta_t \equiv \beta$ for all $t = 1, \ldots$. In most of the analysis I leave $\sigma^2_{\zeta t}$ free to vary, although the model's dynamics are closest to those observed in the experiments when $\sigma^2_{\zeta t}$ declines steadily toward zero as players learn to predict each other's responses, and it is sometimes useful to impose intertemporal restrictions of the form $\sigma^2_{\zeta t} = \sigma^2_{\zeta t}/t^{\lambda}$ for $t = 1, \ldots,$ where $\lambda \geq 0$.

The resulting model is nonlinear, with nonstationary transition probabilities and nonergodic, history-dependent dynamics that would normally be difficult to analyze. The key to the analysis is the evolutionary structure of VHBB's designs and the scaling properties of order statistics noted in (6.2), which Proposition 6.4 exploits to obtain a closed-form solution for y_t and the x_{it} as functions of the behavioral parameters, the treatment variables, and the shocks that represent strategic uncertainty. This allows an informative analysis of the dynamics, whether or not $\sigma^2_{\zeta t} \to 0$. In what follows, sums with no terms (like $\sum_{s=0}^{t-1} \beta_{s+1} f_s$ for $t = 0$) equal 0 and products with no terms equal 1.

Proposition 6.4 *The unique solution of (6.3) and (6.4) is given, for all i and t, by*

$$x_{it} = \alpha_0 + \sum_{s=0}^{t-1} \beta f_s + z_{it} \tag{6.5}$$

and

$$y_t = \alpha_0 + \sum_{s=0}^{t-1} \beta f_s + f_t, \tag{6.6}$$

where

$$z_{it} \equiv \sum_{s=0}^{t} (1-\beta)^{t-s} \zeta_{is} \text{ and } f_t \equiv f(z_{1t}, \ldots, z_{nt}). \tag{6.7}$$

Proof: As in Crawford (1995, Proposition 1), the proof is immediate by induction on t once the solution has been found. The solution is constructed by using (6.2) to pass the common elements of the x_{it} through $f(\cdot)$. Combining (6.1) and (6.4) and using (6.2) to simplify,

$$\begin{aligned}
y_t - y_{t-1} &\equiv f(x_{1t}, \ldots, x_{nt}) - f(x_{1t-1}, \ldots, x_{nt-1}) \\
&\equiv f(\beta y_{t-1} + (1-\beta)x_{1t-1} + \zeta_{1t}, \ldots, \beta y_{t-1} + (1-\beta)x_{nt-1} + \zeta_{nt}) \\
&\quad - f(x_{1t-1}, \ldots, x_{nt-1}) \\
&\equiv \beta(x_{1t-1}, \ldots, x_{nt-1}) + f((1-\beta)x_{1t-1} + \zeta_{1t}, \ldots, (1-\beta)x_{nt-1} + \zeta_{nt}) \\
&\quad - f(x_{1t-1}, \ldots, x_{nt-1})
\end{aligned}$$

$$\begin{aligned} &\equiv f((1-\beta)x_{1t-1}+\zeta_{1t},\ldots,(1-\beta)x_{nt-1}+\zeta_{nt}) \\ &\quad -f((1-\beta)x_{1t-1},\ldots,(1-\beta)x_{nt-1}). \end{aligned} \tag{6.8}$$

Using (6.2) to remove the common elements of the x_{it-1} from both parts of the last expression, noting that $z_{it}=(1-\beta)z_{it-1}+x_{it-1}$, and using (6.2) and (6.7) yields

$$\begin{aligned} y_t-y_{t-1} &\equiv f((1-\beta)z_{1t-1}+\zeta_{1t},\ldots,(1-\beta)z_{nt-1}+\zeta_{nt}) \\ &\quad -f((1-\beta)z_{1t-1},\ldots,(1-\beta)z_{nt-1}) \\ &\equiv f_t-(1-\beta)f_{t-1} \end{aligned} \tag{6.9}$$

Given y_0, this yields (6.6) by successive substitution. To derive (6.5) from (6.6), note that

$$\begin{aligned} x_{it}-y_t &\equiv x_{it}-f(x_{1t},\ldots,x_{nt}) \\ &\equiv \beta y_{t-1}+(1-\beta)x_{it-1}+\zeta_{it}-f(\beta y_{t-1}+(1-\beta)x_{1t-1} \\ &\quad +\zeta_{1t},\ldots,\beta y_{t-1}+(1-\beta)x_{nt-1}+\zeta_{nt}) \\ &\equiv (\beta)x_{it-1}+\zeta_{it}-f((1-\beta)x_{1t-1}+\zeta_{1t},\ldots,(1-\beta)x_{nt-1}+\zeta_{nt}) \\ &\equiv (1-\beta)z_{it-1}+\zeta_{it}-f((1-\beta)z_{1t-1}+\zeta_{1t},\ldots,(1-\beta)z_{nt-1}+\zeta_{nt} \\ &\equiv z_{it}-f_t, \end{aligned} \tag{6.10}$$

which immediately yields (6.5).

Proposition 6.4 shows how the outcome is built up period by period from the shocks that represent strategic uncertainty, each of whose effects persist indefinitely. The persistence of the shock terms makes the learning process resemble a random walk in the aggregate, but with declining variances and nonzero drift. Thus, equilibrium selection via adaptive learning is an inherently dynamic phenomenon: The limiting equilibrium is the cumulative result of interactions between strategic uncertainty and the learning process, and depends on the entire history; a shock that affects y_t in some period will persist in the limiting outcome. This persistence (and the fact that the extent of strategic uncertainty cannot be explained by theory alone) makes the analysis inherently partly empirical.

6.6.3 Comparative dynamics

The form of Proposition 6.4's solution indicates that unless the behavioral parameters vary sharply with changes in the treatment variables – which econometric estimates suggest is unlikely – outcomes will vary across treatments in stable, predictable ways. Changes in treatment variables have a direct effect, holding the behavioral parameters constant, and an indirect effect via induced changes in behavioral parameters. As I will show, theory has a lot to say about the direct effect, which shows up in the drift of the process. It is important to note, however, that theory by itself has little to say about the indirect effect: if sunspots that do not affect payoffs can focus players' expectations, then so can changes in treatment variables, however small. It is not irrational for players to expect all to choose effort 7 when n is even and effort 1 when n is odd, in which case their expectations will be confirmed; it is just inconsistent with sound empirical judgment.

The point is that any analysis of the effects of changes in treatment variables will inevitably be based in part on empirical knowledge about induced changes in behavioral parameters. This reliance on empirical knowledge is unusual in game theory, though accepted without question elsewhere in economics. What is needed is a theory that indicates what empirical knowledge is needed to predict the outcome, and that provides a framework within which to gather it. Making strong assumptions that yield conclusions independent of behavioral parameters can give a misleading view of important strategic phenomena. This problem is dealt with in Crawford (1995), Broseta (1993, 2000), and Crawford and Broseta (1998) by conducting as much of the theoretical analysis as possible contingent on behavioral parameters, closing the model when necessary by using it to estimate the parameters, separately for each treatment, from the experimental data, taking the discreteness of efforts into account. The estimated parameters generally satisfy the restrictions suggested by theory, but differ significantly from the values needed to justify an equilibrium analysis or an analysis of long-run equilibria. Instead they show the characteristic pattern of adaptive learning analyses: large initial levels of strategic uncertainty, declining to zero gradually, though with one exception quickly enough to assure lock-in on an equilibrium of the stage game. The estimated model gives an adequate statistical summary of individual subjects' behavior, and the model generates dynamics and limiting outcomes whose prior probability distributions (estimated by repeated simulation) closely resemble their empirical frequency distributions in the experiments.

Proposition 6.5 uses the closed-form solution of Proposition 6.4 to characterize the direct effect of changes in the treatment variables, expressing the mean outcome as a function of behavioral parameters, statistical parameters, and treatment variables. Let σ_{zt}^2 denote the common variance of the z_{it}. (6.7) implies that $\sigma_{zt}^2 \equiv \sum_{s-0}^{t}[(1-\beta)^{t-s}]^2\sigma_{zs}^2$ Define $\mu_t \equiv Ef(z_{1t}/\sigma_{zt}, \ldots, z_{nt}/\sigma_{zt})$. Because the random variables z_{it}/σ_{zt} are standardized, with common mean 0 and common variance 1, μ_t is completely determined by n, $f(\cdot)$, and the joint distribution of the z_{it}/σ_{zt}. μ_t is subscripted only because the distribution of the z_{it}/σ_{zt} is generally time-dependent; its dependence on n and $f(\cdot)$ is suppressed for clarity.

Proposition 6.5 *The* ex ante *means of* y_t *and the* x_{it} *are given, for all* i *and* t, *by*

$$Ex_{it} = \alpha_0 + \beta\sum_{s-0}^{t-1}\sigma_{zs}\mu_s \tag{6.11}$$

and

$$Ey_t = \alpha_0 + \beta\sum_{s-0}^{t-1}\sigma_{zs}\mu_s + \sigma_{zt}\mu_t. \tag{6.12}$$

Proof: The proof uses the fact that although the x_{it} become correlated as players respond to their common observations of y_t, adopting an *ex ante* point of view makes it possible to express their means as simple functions of the behavioral parameters, statistical parameters, and treatment variables. The shock terms in (6.5) and (6.6) are known functions of the z_{it}, which are *ex ante* i.i.d. across i with zero means for any given t. Taking expectations in (6.5) and (6.6), using (6.7), and noting that

$$EF(z_{1s}, \ldots, z_{ns}) \equiv E[\sigma_{zs} f(z_{1s}/\sigma_{zs}, \ldots, z_{ns}/\sigma_{zs})] \equiv \sigma_{zs}\mu_s \qquad (6.13)$$

immediately yields (6.11) and (6.12).

Proposition 6.5 expresses the mean coordination outcome as the sum of the initial mean level of players' beliefs and the cumulative drift of the process. (The remaining term, $\sigma_{zt}\mu_t$ in (6.12), is subsumed in the sum after the period in which it first appears.) The drift in period s is the product of the behavioral parameter β which measures the extent to which players' beliefs respond to new observations of y_t, on average; the behavioral parameter σ_{zs} (determined by β and the $\sigma^2_{\zeta t}$ as indicated above), which measures the cumulative dispersion of players' beliefs; and the statistical parameter μ_s, which is completely determined by n, $f(\cdot)$, and the distribution of the z_{is}.

Using the properties of order statistics, μ_s is easily shown to be decreasing in n and increasing in $f(\cdot)$, as required for qualitative consistency with the variations across VHBB's treatments. Crawford (1995) and Broseta (1993, 2000) conduct more detailed qualitative comparative dynamics analyses, making precise the common intuitions that coordination tends to be less efficient, the less robust desirable equilibria are to disruption by subgroups (here, the closer the order statistic is to the minimum) and less efficient in larger groups because it requires coherence among a larger number of independent decisions.

To say more than this, values must be assigned to α_0, β, the σ_{zs}, and the μ_s. The behavioral parameters α_0, β, and the σ_{zs} can be estimated from the experimental data, as described above. The statistical parameters μ_s are difficult to evaluate due to the complexity of their dependence on the distribution of the z_{is}. This problem can be sidestepped by estimating the probability distributions the model implies directly by repeated simulation, as in Crawford (1995, Section 7); but it is informative to approximate the outcome distributions analytically. The approximations are based on the simplifying assumption that the z_{is} are jointly normally distributed for any given s. Normality is a reasonable approximation because the z_{is} are weighted sums of the ζ_{it}, which are weakly dependent and likely to be approximately conditionally normal, for familiar reasons. This makes the common distribution of the z_{is}/σ_{zs} independent of s, so that $\mu_s \equiv \mu$. Given that the z_{is}/σ_{zs} are uncorrelated for any given s, the parameter μ is tabulated in Teichroew (1956) for any order statistic of the normal distribution and any $n \leq 20$.

An explanation for the dynamics in VHBB's experiments can now be discerned. Suppose, for simplicity, that $\sum_{s-0}^{t} \sigma_{zs} \to S$ as $t \to \infty$. Propositions 6.3 and 6.5 then imply that Ey_t and Ex_{it} approach the approximate common limit $\alpha_0 + \mu\beta S$. This formula shows how the mean coordination outcome is determined by the behavioral parameters α_0 and β; the number of players and the order statistic, via μ; and the initial dispersion of beliefs and the rate at which it is eliminated by learning, via S.

By symmetry, $\mu = 0$ for VHBB's median treatments and their random-pairing minimum treatment (viewed as a median treatment, as in Crawford (1995)), so there is no drift in those treatments and the approximate common limit of Ey_t and Ex_{it} is α_0. The estimates of α_0 were 4.30 in the random-pairing minimum treatment; 4.71 and 4.75 in median treatments Φ and Γ; and 6.26 in median treatment Ω, whose structure made the all-7 equilibrium more prominent.[15] μ is negative (positive) for order statistics below (above) the median and, as suggested by the faculty meeting example above, strongly negative for the large-group minimum treatment, where, setting $n = 15$ for simplicity, $\mu = -1.74$ (Teichroew (1956, Table I). There the estimates of α_0 and β were 5.45 and 0.25 respectively, and S (which is difficult to estimate for this treatment) appeared highly unlikely to be less than 10. Thus, the approximate common limit of Ey_t, and Ex_{it} in the large-group minimum treatment, $\alpha_0 + \mu\beta S$, is at most 1.10.

Comparing these approximations with VHBB's results shows that for large initial levels of strategic uncertainty, declining gradually to zero over time, differences in drift across treatments make the prior probability distribution of the limiting outcome vary with the number of players and the order statistic in a way that yields patterns of equilibrium selection like those in the experiments. The most important changes across treatments were between the random-pairing and large-group minimum treatments, and between the median treatments and the large-group minimum treatment. Viewing the random-pairing minimum treatment as a median treatment, the model treats the differences between these treatments primarily as changes in the order statistic (even though the former difference is "really" a change in group size and the latter also involves a change in group size, from 9 to 14–16). The above estimates suggest that each of these changes altered the drift of the process much more than the changes in behavioral parameters they induced.

6.6.4 Extension to VHBB's (1993) auction environment

Crawford and Broseta (1998) generalized the analysis just summarized to the extensive-form stage game of VHBB's (1993) auction environment, in which subjects played one of the nine-person median coordination games of VHBB's (1991) experiments with the right to play auctioned each period in a population of 18. Recall that when that game was played without auctions subjects always converged to inefficient equilibria, but that in eight out of eight trials with auctions subjects bid the market-clearing price to a level recoverable only in the efficient equilibrium and then converged to that equilibrium.

The model combines a learning rule like (6.4) with a bidding equation in the same style, and a stochastic structure that allows for the diversity of subjects' initial beliefs and inferences from their observations of the market-clearing price and the order statistic. If players treat their individual influences on the market-clearing price and the order statistic as negligible, their optimal bids and efforts each period are determined by their beliefs about the current value of the order statistic. This makes it possible to summarize their decisions throughout the extensive-form stage game by a single beliefs variable for each player, as in our earlier analyses. This and the fact that the market-clearing price is also an order statistic makes it possible to generalize Propositions 6.1 and 6.3–6.5 to VHBB's auction environments, including a closed-form solution for the dynamics as in Proposition 6.4. The solution shows that the coordination process resembles that in environments without auctions, and that interactions between strategic uncertainty and the learning dynamics generate an order statistic effect like the one that drives the dynamics without auctions, plus optimistic subjects and forward induction effects that are large enough together to explain the efficiency-enhancing effect of auctions in VHBB's experiment.

These effects can be approximated as functions of the treatment variables, behavioral parameters, and tabulated statistical parameters. The optimistic subjects and order statistic effects together have approximately the same magnitude in VHBB's environment (where the right to play a nine-person median game was auctioned in a group of 18) as the order statistic effect in an 18-person coordination game without auctions in which payoffs and best responses are determined by the fifth highest (the median of the nine highest) of all 18 players' efforts. In this respect the auctions transformed VHBB's median game, whose order statistic effect without auctions would contribute zero drift to the dynamics, into a 75th percentile game (0.75 = 13.5/18) whose order statistic effect contributes a large upward drift. Our estimates suggest that this drift is responsible for roughly half of the efficiency-enhancing effect of auctions in VHBB's environment, and that the other half is due to a strong forward induction effect. A qualitative comparative dynamics analysis generalizes to auction environments our earlier results that coordination tends to be less efficient, the less robust desirable equilibria are to disruption by subsets of the population, and less efficient in larger groups. It also establishes a new result for auction environments, that increased competition for the right to play favors efficiency because it tends to yield higher market-clearing prices and intensifies the optimistic-subjects effect.

6.7 Conclusion

This chapter outlines a model to explain the results of recent experiments by VHBB (1990, 1991, 1993), in which subjects repeatedly played coordination games, uncertain only about each other's strategy choices, with striking patterns of equilibrium selection across treatments. Theoretical and econometric analyses suggest that these outcomes were governed by history-dependent learning dynamics, which lock in on a particular equilibrium with high probability. The model's implications can be summarized by the prior probability distribution of this limiting equilibrium, which is normally nondegenerate due to the persistent effects of interactions between strategic uncertainty and the learning dynamics. The analysis shows that taking these effects into account yields a unified explanation of VHBB's results.

The need for an analysis of history-dependent learning dynamics stands out especially clearly in VHBB's experiments because their structure permits a closed-form solution of the dynamics and an informative analysis. But the mechanism suggests that similar patterns of equilibrium selection will be found in a variety of related laboratory or field environments. This has already been confirmed by the results of other experiments, such as Brandts and Holt (1992, 1993) and Roth and Erev (1995).

In environments like VHBB's – as in many other environments – equilibrium selection is an inherently dynamic phenomenon: a shock that affects the outcome early on persists in the limiting outcome. This persistence and the fact that the extent of strategic uncertainty and other aspects of behavior cannot usefully be explained by theory alone make the analysis inherently partly empirical. Approaches like Harsanyi and Selten's general theory of equilibrium selection and analyses of long-run equilibria reach precise conclusions about equilibrium selection, independent of behavioral parameters, only by making unrealistic assumptions that rule out either strategic uncertainty or the history-dependence that allows it to affect the limiting outcome. Such approaches can capture the outcomes of history-dependent dynamics only by coincidence, and lose much of the information results like VHBB's can provide about how the structure of the environment affects coordination outcomes. The same criticism applies to equilibrium analyses of perturbed versions of VHBB's stage games, as in Carlsson and van Damme (1993) and Anderson, Goeree, and Holt (1996). Finally, it applies for different reasons to analyses of deterministic evolutionary dynamics as in Crawford (1991), which yield history-dependence too mechanical to describe VHBB's results.

Results like VHBB's, properly understood, have the power to change the way we think about models with multiple equilibria, even in field environments where one is confident that equilibrium has long since been reached. In Cooper and John (1988), for instance, all pure-strategy equilibria are treated as equal. VHBB's results show that this kind of agnosticism about equilibrium selection is no longer supportable. We should ask of any explanation based on a model that has an equilibrium – or a risk- or payoff-dominant equilibrium, or an evolutionarily stable or long-run equilibrium – that seems to fit the data, whether that equilibrium is likely to be reached by a realistic learning process.

Acknowledgments

This chapter is based on Crawford (1995), Broseta (1993, 2000), and Crawford and Broseta (1998). It was prepared for Workshop X, "Evolution and Economics," International School of Economic Research, University of Siena. I gratefully acknowledge the advice of many friends and colleagues and the support of the US National Science Foundation.

Notes

1 Coordination failure models have considerable unrealized potential in macroeconomics because they yield Keynesian conclusions about the importance of expectations and the nonneutrality of policy without relying on irrationality, uncertainty, or frictions; see for example Bryant (1994) and Hahn and Solow (1995: 138–139 and 150–152).

2 Note that these beliefs are self-confirming. They are plausible because if players choose independently, with probabilities independent of the number of players, the clarity of the principle is less likely to be sufficient the larger the group. Because this intuition concerns a choice between strict equilibria, however, it is not captured by traditional refinements like trembling-hand perfectness or strategic stability.

3 Thus subjects never pay more than they have indicated they are willing to, and they are never excluded involuntarily unless they have indicated approximate indifference.

4 The auction is an unusual form of preplay communication in that players' messages can directly influence their payoffs, hence are not "cheap talk"; and they are communicated only through an aggregate, the market-clearing price.

5 VHBB's results are replicable, with similar results reported for many related designs.

6 Crawford and Broseta (1998) models VHBB's (1993) experiment formally. Like Crawford (1995) and Broseta (1993, 2000), it allows for the discrete efforts of VHBB's (1990, 1991, 1993) experiments by viewing players' continuous efforts as the latent variables in an ordered probit model of discrete choice, in which players' efforts are determined by rounding the latent variables to the nearest feasible integer.

7 The scale concerns the labeling of strategies, and would thus be assumed irrelevant in a traditional analysis. Here it plays an important role in defining the order statistic and players' learning rules, as the language in which they interpret their experience.

8 Although a subject was told only his pair minimum in the random-pairing minimum treatment, this can be viewed as a noisy estimate of the population median that determined his best response, which causes an increase in the dispersion of beliefs.

9 See Nevel'son and Has'minskii (1973) or Woodford (1990: Section 2).

10 The model with discrete efforts, by contrast, describes beliefs and efforts separately.

11 They do not consider changes in the order statistic, and their uniqueness result appears not to hold for all order statistics other than the minimum.

12 The founding analysis of evolutionary game theory, Fisher's (1930) explanation of the tendency of the ratio of male to female births to remain near 1, is a game against the field (Maynard Smith 1982: 23–27). This problem – one of the most beautiful in science – requires a game-theoretic explanation because a ratio of 1 equalizes the fitnesses of having male and female offspring, and does not maximize the growth rate of the entire population. The model is a game against the field because the fitnesses depend (nonlinearly) on the population frequencies of male and female offspring.

13 Bergin and Lipman (1996) have shown that these predictions have an element of arbitrariness, in that if one allows state-dependent mutation probabilities and defines long-run equilibria using the limit of the ergodic distribution as they approach zero together, remaining in fixed proportions, the long-run equilibria vary with the proportions, and for some proportions put probability one on any given steady state.

14 For random-pairing environments, Robles (1995) shows that if $\sigma^2_{\zeta t} \to 0$ there are only two possibilities: (i) the model is ergodic, and the result is the same as the long-run equilibrium when $\sigma^2_{\zeta t} \equiv \epsilon \to 0$; or (ii) the dynamics lock in on a particular equilibrium as in Proposition 6.3. (Robles's result continues to hold with state-dependent mutation probabilities as in Bergin and Lipman (1996), and ergodic dynamics yield their generalized long-run equilibrium.) Thus with random pairing at least, the key issue is whether $\sigma^2_{\zeta t} \to 0$ fast enough to make the dynamics nonergodic.

15 The estimated model also makes it possible to allocate the variance of the limiting outcome among periods. This suggests that in VHBB's median treatments Γ, Ψ, and Ω, the initial median y_0 "explains" 46%, 58%, and 81% of the respective variances

of the limiting medians, and that the contributions of subsequent periods decline very rapidly over time. In VHBB's twelve trials with treatments Γ, Ψ, and Ω, subjects always converged to the initial median. Thus, the model suggests that VHBB's sample somewhat overstated the history-dependence of the dynamics.

References

Anderson, Simon, Jacob Goeree and Charles Holt (1996) Minimum-effort coordination games: an equilibrium analysis of bounded rationality. Manuscript, University of Virginia.

Aumann, Robert and Adam Brandenburger (1995) Epistemic conditions for Nash equilibrium. *Econometrica* 63: 1161–1180.

Ben-Porath, Elchanen and Eddie Dekel (1992) Signaling future actions and the potential for sacrifice. *Journal of Economic Theory* 57: 36–51.

Bergin, James and Barton Lipman (1996) Evolution with state-dependent mutations. *Econometrica* 64: 943–956.

Brandts, Jordi and Charles Holt (1992) An experimental test of equilibrium dominance in signaling games. *American Economic Review* 82: 1350–1365.

Brandts, Jordi and Charles Holt (1993) Adjustment patterns and equilibrium selection in experimental signaling games. *International Journal of Game Theory* 22: 279–302.

Bray, Margaret and David Kreps (1987) Rational learning and rational expectations. In George Feiwel (ed.) *Arrow and the Ascent of Modern Economic Theory*. New York: New York University Press.

Broseta, Bruno (1993) Strategic uncertainty and learning in coordination games. Discussion Paper 93–34, University of California, San Diego.

—— (2000) Adaptive learning and equilibrium selection in experimental coordination games: An ARCH(1) approach. *Games and Economic Behavior* 32: 25-50.

Bryant, John (1994) Coordination theory, the stag hunt, and macroeconomics. In James Friedman (ed) *Problems of Coordination in Economic Activity*. Boston: Kluwer Academic Publishers.

Cachon, Gerard and Colin Camerer (1996) Loss avoidance and forward induction in experimental coordination games. *Quarterly Journal of Economics* 111: 165–194.

Carlsson, Hans and Eric van Damme (1993) Equilibrium selection in stag hunt games. In Ken Binmore, Alan Kirman and Piero Tani (eds) *Frontiers of Game Theory*. Cambridge, MA: The MIT Press.

Cooper, Russell, and Andrew John (1988) Coordinating coordination failures in Keynesian models. *Quarterly Journal of Economics* 103: 441–463.

Crawford, Vincent P. (1991) An "evolutionary" interpretation of Van Huyck, Battalio, and Beil's experimental results on coordination. *Games and Economic Behavior* 3: 25–59.

—— (1995) Adaptive dynamics in coordination games. *Econometrica* 63: 103–143.

—— (1997) Theory and experiment in the analysis of strategic interaction. In David Kreps and Ken Wallis (eds) *Advances in Economics and Econometrics: Theory and Applications*, Volume I. Cambridge: Cambridge University Press.

Crawford, Vincent and Bruno Broseta (1998) What price coordination?: the efficiency-enhancing effect of auctioning the right to play. *American Economic Review* 88: 198–225.

Crawford, Vincent and Hans Haller (1990) Learning how to cooperate: optimal play in repeated coordination games. *Econometrica* 58: 571–595.

Fisher, R. A. (1930) *The Genetical Theory of Natural Selection*. Oxford: Clarendon Press.

Hahn, Frank and Robert Solow (1995) *A Critical Essay on Modern Macroeconomic Theory*. Oxford: Blackwell.

Harsanyi, John and Reinhard Selten (1988) *A General Theory of Equilibrium Selection in Games*. Cambridge, MA: MIT Press

Kandori, Michihiro, George Mailath, and Rafael Rob (1993) Learning, mutation, and long run equilibria in games. *Econometrica* 61: 29–56.

Kim, Yong-Gwan (1996) Evolutionary analyses of tacit communication in Van Huyck, Battalio, and Beil's game experiments. *Games and Economic Behavior* 16: 218–237.

Maynard Smith, John (1982) *Evolution and the Theory of Games.* Cambridge: Cambridge University Press.

McCabe, Kevin, Stephen Rassenti and Vernon Smith (1990): Auction institutional design: theory and behavior of simultaneous multiple-unit generalizations of the Dutch and English auctions. *American Economic Review* 80: 1276–1283.

McKelvey, Richard, and Thomas Palfrey (1995) Quantal response equilibria for normal-form games. *Games and Economic Behavior* 10: 6–38.

Nevel'son, M. B., and R. Z. Has'minskii (1973) *Stochastic Approximation and Recursive Estimation.* Volume 47, Translations of Mathematical Monographs. Providence, RI: American Mathematical Society.

—— (1997): Evolution and long run equilibria in coordination games with summary statistic payoff technologies. *Journal of Economic Theory* 75: 180–193.

Robles, Jack (1998) Evolution with changing mutation rates. *Journal of Economic Theory* 79: 207-223.

Roth, Alvin (1995) Introduction to experimental economics. In John Kagel and Alvin Roth (eds) *Handbook of Experimental Economics.* Princeton, NJ: Princeton University Press.

Roth, Alvin and Ido Erev (1995) Learning in extensive-form games: experimental data and simple dynamic models in the intermediate term. *Games and Economic Behavior* 8: 164–212.

Rousseau, Jean-Jacques (1973 [1775]) A discourse on the origin of inequality. In *The Social Contract and Discourses* (translated by G.D.H. Cole) 27–113. London: J. M. Dent & Sons

Schelling, Thomas (1960) *The Strategy of Conflict.* First Edition: Cambridge, MA: Harvard University Press.

—— (1978) *Micromotives and Macrobehavior.* New York: W. W. Norton.

Teichroew, D. (1956) Tables of expected values of order statistics and products of order statistics for samples of size twenty and less from the normal distribution. *Annals of Mathematical Statistics* 27: 410–426.

Van Huyck, John, Ray Battalio and Richard Beil (1990) Tacit coordination games, strategic uncertainty, and coordination failure. *American Economic Review* 80: 234–248.

—— (1991) Strategic uncertainty, equilibrium selection principles, and coordination failure in average opinion games. *Quarterly Journal of Economics* 106: 885–910.

—— (1993) Asset markets as an equilibrium selection mechanism: coordination failure, game form auctions, and tacit communication. *Games and Economic Behavior* 5: 485–504.

Weber, Roberto (1994) The role of alternative market institutions on equilibrium selection in coordination games. B.A. honors thesis, Texas A&M University

Woodford, Michael (1990) Learning to believe in sunspots. *Econometrica* 58: 277–307.

Young, H. Peyton (1993) The evolution of conventions. *Econometrica* 61: 57–84.

7 On the dynamics of cognition and actions

An assessment of some models of learning and evolution

Giovanni Dosi, Giorgio Fagiolo and Luigi Marengo

7.1 Introduction

The purpose of this brief work (drawing on the much more detailed companion paper Dosi, Marengo and Fagiolo (1996)) is to provide a sort of selective guide to the enormous and diverse literature on learning processes in economics.

Other critical reviews of a partly overlapping literature have recently been produced: see for example Marimon (1995). However, in the latter the "yardstick" of comparison of learning models is almost exclusively their ability to yield convergence to those equilibrium behaviors often assumed by economic theory. Here we take a quite different perspective, and try to assess: a) the extent to which models have been able to account for learning in evolutionary environments – which we shall define shortly; and b) the consistency of such modeling endeavors with the empirical evidence stemming from cognitive and social sciences.

In the most generic terms, learning may occur in all circumstances whereby agents have an imperfect understanding of the world in which they operate. Basically, most of economic theory has, either explicitly or implicitly, confined such imperfect understanding to the realm of lack of information about the environment. But, more fundamentally, imperfect understanding of the world can arise from an imprecise knowledge of its structure; or, whenever agents master only a limited repertoire of actions in order to cope with whatever problem they face – as compared to the set of actions that an omniscient observer would be able to conceive; or, finally, when agents have only a blurred and changing understanding of what their goals and preferences are.

Learning – broadly defined as the dynamic process governing the transformation of such an imperfect understanding – is of course an ubiquitous feature of economic decisions and it acquires an even greater importance in truly *evolutionary* environments (cf. Nelson and Winter (1982), Dosi and Nelson (1994), Nelson (1995), Coriat and Dosi (1995)), where: (i) heterogeneous agents systematically display various forms of bounded rationality; (ii) there is non-stationarity in the fundamentals, mainly due to a persistent appearance of novelty, both as exogenous shocks and, in particular, as the result of innovations introduced by the agents themselves; (iii) markets and other institutions perform as selection mechanisms;

(iv) aggregate regularities are primarily emergent properties stemming from out-of-equilibrium interactions among economic entities. As a consequence, note that agents behaving in evolutionary environments would typically hold only a partial and imperfect understanding of the structure of their environment and, therefore, they would not be able either to give an exhaustive description of all the states of the world or to attribute them some probability measure.

As argued at some greater length in Dosi, Marengo and Fagiolo (1996), any positive theory of economic behavior, when faced with *evolutionary* issues as those briefly outlined above, has to account for the potential appearance of systematic mistakes, cognitive biases and persistently sub-optimal decision processes. In this respect, the empirical evidence stemming from cognitive and social sciences is quite robust.[1]

For our purposes here, let us just telegraphically recall what we consider to be some "stylized facts" on cognitive and behavioral learning pointed out by this massive literature:

1. one of the fundamental features of learning processes is the dynamics governing *categories* and *mental models*. In turn these dynamics are definitely not amenable to any procedure that simply updates either the parameters of a pre-formed model or the weights – e.g. probabilities – with which alternative ex-ante exogenously given models are chosen or selected;

2. judgments, action/choices and learning are often based on *heuristics*, which may well lead to systematic biases as compared to the predictions of "rational" decision theoretic models;

3. mental models and heuristics are strongly context-dependent, in the sense that the same information about the environment, when collected in contexts that are perceived as qualitatively different from one another, could trigger different categorizations and behaviors;

4. preferences – as well as all other criteria allowing one to make judgements about patterns of actions – are *endogenous*; moreover, different and possibly contradicting systems of preferences tend to survive over time "inside the head," so to speak, of a given economic agent;

5. All the foregoing regularities refer to some generic properties of cognition, action-choice and learning of both individuals and collections of them and, of course, find their validation or rejection in the evidence stemming to a good extent also from disciplines outside economics, such as cognitive and social psychology.

Conversely, at a more phenomenological level, many authors have begun to single out some historical regularities in collective learning processes, with particular regard to technical change and organizational learning (see among others the analyses on the nature of technological paradigms, *routines*, organizational competencies, etc.).[2]

As an introductory device, some taxonomies of learning processes will be presented in Section 7.2, where different learning models will be grouped with respect to the *object of learning* (action or strategies, representations, performance of behavioral patterns, preferences) and to both the *domains of learning* and the *constraints* one imposes on learning processes themselves. Next, a basic model which allows to characterize more precisely the *loci* of learning will be set forth in Section 7.3. In Section 7.4, we shall begin to examine some different classes of learning models, primarily concerned with adaptive dynamics on the grounds of a fixed menu of behavioral patterns. Section 7.5 will enlarge the analysis to these models employing artificially adaptive agents (AAA), allowing some formal account also for "open-ended" dynamics whereby cognitive and behavioral novelties are allowed to emerge along the evolutionary learning path. Together we shall discuss some properties of more history- grounded, "open-ended" models of technological learning (Section 7.6). Finally, in Section 7.7, some open questions will be pointed out by way of a conclusion.

7.2 Some taxonomies of learning processes

The simplest representation of learning is in terms of some search process in some appropriately defined space. As a consequence, one should be primarily interested in identifying: (a) its *dimensions* (whose precise meaning is given below); (b) the *constraints* one imposes on the domains of learning processes; (c) the *mechanisms* of learning (e.g. the algorithms implemented in such a search). Once answers are provided to the above questions, one obviously should hold useful criteria to build taxonomies of diverse learning models.

Concerning (a), basically four *classes of objects of learning* can be singled out: 1) "states of the world" (as in games against nature); 2) other agents' behaviors (as in strategic games); 3) problem-solving algorithms (where the object of learning is not forecasting but designing algorithms); 4) some features of the learner itself (e.g. preferences).

In turn, this categorization of the *objects of learning* partially maps into different formal representations of the *dimensions of the state-space* in which learning occurs namely: 1) the space of environment representations (ER) or models of the world, 2) the space of parameters within a given model, 3) the space of actions and 4) the space of realized performance outcomes.

Learning in the space of representations is a search for "better" ERs. Agents are supposed to hold ER either explicitly (as in rule-based models) or implicitly (as in connectionist models) and learning is defined as a structural modification (and not just as a tuning of parameters) of the ER themselves. Note that in the expression "better environment representations," *better* can have two very different meanings: it can either indicate better performing ER (e.g. supporting actions with higher payoffs) or epistemologically more "correct" ones (i.e. producing better predictions of the state of the environment).[3] Moreover, the very perception of what is a good prediction depends on the model itself (for instance a change in the state of the world form s_i to s_j might not be perceived as such by the agent whose information partition has s_i and s_j in the same equivalence class, and, thus, the agent is led to think that its model has not decreased its predictive power . . .).

Learning in the space of parameters assumes that the ER is given in its functional structure and is equal – or at least isomorphic – to the "real" one. Learning is thus just a refinement of the estimation of some unknown parameters. A typical example is Bayesian learning, where the learning agent updates its probability estimates within a given and immutable set of categories which constitute a partition of the real world (whatever that means).

Learning in the space of actions assumes instead that either the ER is constant or that it does not exist at all. As we shall see in Section 4, this is typically the case of simple stimulus-response models and of most of *evolutionary games*, where learning is simply a selection process in the space of alternative actions.

Learning can be finally formalized as a dynamic process in the *space of modeling performance outcomes*, whereby the actual (micro-) processes of learning are not described, but one just considers their results in terms of some dynamics in the space of performance parameters. Typical examples can be found among models of technological innovation and imitation, whereby learning is modeled as a stochastic process in the space of some productivity coefficients.

Given the underlying objects of learning – or, more formally, the dimensions of the state space of learning dynamics – an additional classification is useful according to the *constraints* one assumes on the *domains of learning processes* themselves. Here a crude distinction might be made between: 1) *search/adaptation over a fixed menu of possibilities* – which are all accessible from the start to all agents – and 2) *open-ended dynamics*, where the discovery of genuine novelties is always possible. Notice that this latter classification is actually closely related to the previous one. If all notional elements of the spaces in which learning must take place are known from the start, agents might be indeed assumed to attach probabilities to each of them, as well as their consequences, thus possibly using some inferential procedure to adjust their behaviors (e.g. as in Bayesian models). Conversely, whenever novelties persistently appear, probability updating turns out to be a rather clumsy learning procedure, since the state space can no longer be usefully partitioned, due to the emergence of surprises and unforeseen (indeed, unforeseeable) events.

Finally, concerning the *mechanisms of learning* leading the dynamics of search, a distinction can be made among models in which learning is: 1) a shorthand characterization of a population-level selection mechanism involving differential reproduction of entities (e.g., in economics, business firms); 2) an adaptation process driven by stimulus-response adjustments, without any explicit underlying cognitive process; 3) an agent-specific mechanism which is able to generate, update and modify expectations, mental models, decision rules, etc.

On the grounds of the different conceivable taxonomies discussed so far, Table 1 presents an impressionistic (albeit not exhaustive) classification of examples of each *genre* in the current realized literature. However, differences in learning processes can also be formally accounted as variations and restrictions on the grounds of a unified basic representation. This is what we shall attempt to do in the next section.

Table 7.1 Dimensions of learning and constraints on learning process: a guide to some examples from modeling literature

Domains and contraints on learing processes		*Learning spaces*			
		Actions / strategies	*Representation / "Models of the world"*	*Realized performance*	*Preferences*
	"Fixed menus"	• Learning in game-theoretic setups • "Evolutionary" games • Adaptive learning in multi-arm bandit problems (e.g. Arthur (1993) • Self-organization models à la Lesourner (1991) • Urn models and other types of innovation-adoption models (cf. Arthur *et al.* (1991), Arthur and Lane (1993), Kirman (1993) etc.) • Special cases of evolutionary models (cf. Winter (1971)) (implicitly) adaptive models in stationary environments (e.g. Arifovic (1994), Marimon *et al* (1990).	Bayesian reduction of information incompleteness in games	Learning by doing and by using for given best-practise technologies (e.g. Silverberg *et al.* (1988), Eliason (1985))	Socially shaped preferences (e.g. Duran (1987), Brock and Durlauf 1995), Akerlog and Dickens (1982)
	"Open-ended" sets of learning objects	Behavioral search in Lindgren (1991), Silverberg and Verspagen (1995), Andersen (1994), Marengo and Tordjman (1996), Dosi *et al.* (1994), Aversi *et al* (1997).		Open-ended technological search as in Nelson and Winter (1982), Silverberg and Verspagen (1995), Chairomonte *et al* (1993), Dosi *et al* (1995)	

7.3 A basic model and various specifications

Let us consider a standard decision problem whereby an agent faces an environment which can be in one out of an enumerable set of elementary outcomes (or "states-of-the-world," s.o.w. in the following):

$$S = \{s_1, s_2, \ldots, s_i, \ldots\}$$

At some time t, the agent does not know the whole set S, but it will possess only an imprecise and partial representation thereof:

$$\Theta^t = \{\vartheta_1^t, \vartheta_2^t, \ldots, \vartheta_j^t, \ldots\} \text{ where } \vartheta_j^t \subseteq S \text{ and } \Theta^t \subseteq 2^S.$$

Each set ϑ_i includes all the s.o.w. which the agent considers as possible (or cannot discriminate) when one or more elementary outcomes $s_k \in \vartheta_i$ occurs. Note that in most economic models it is either assumed that: (i) $\Theta^t = S$, meaning that the agent "knows" the structure of the world; or that (ii) Θ^t is a partition of S. The latter assumption implies, on the one hand, that the agent holds an ER which is isomorphic to the world itself and, on the other, that both total and partial ignorance about some s.o.w., as well as genuine surprises, are definitely excluded (i.e. the cases when $\bigcup_i \vartheta_i^t \subset S$; cf. also Shackle (1969)). Moreover, it rules out hierarchies of hypotheses and/or partially overlapping hypotheses (i.e. when $\vartheta_i \cap \vartheta_j \neq \emptyset$ and $\vartheta_i \neq \vartheta_j$), and systematic mistakes (i.e. an outcome is believed to occur when it does not and it is not thought as possible when it actually does occur).

Conversely, by assuming, more generally, that $\Theta^t \subseteq 2^S$, one can easily account for the above mentioned phenomena of ignorance, incoherence and/or substantial uncertainty, which, in our view, are inevitable and customary in any human representation of the world. It seems indeed to us that the prominent issue in learning realized is precisely to account for the very processes by which economic agents try to reduce the unavoidable gap between the "ontological" structure of the world and their (necessarily limited and faulty) representation thereof.

Let then assume that the agent is notionally endowed with an enumerable set of possible actions $A = \{Q_1, Q_2, \ldots, Q_j, \ldots\}$ and that, at any point in time, it holds a finite formalized repertoire built upon the basic "atomic" actions in A, subject to revision, modification and recombination. Let us denote the known repertoire at time t by:

$$\Xi^t = \{\xi_1^t, \xi_2^t, \ldots, \xi_j^t, \ldots\} \text{ where } \xi_j^t \subseteq A \text{ and } \Xi^t \subseteq 2^A.$$

Notice that Θ^t and Ξ^t entail some sort of *grammar* determining the "legal" cognitive representations and formalized repertoires that can be notionally generated.[4] Hence, genuinely constructive models of cognition and problem-solving ought to start from the very process generating different grammars and consider the sets ϑ_i and ξ_i themselves as the outcome of a search in some functional space (see Fontana and Buss (1996) for a fascinating attempt in this direction).

The set of "perceived" histories at time t contains some finite-length histories of perceived states of the world and perceived actions which have occurred up to time t:

$$H^t = \{h_k^t\}, k = 1, 2, \ldots, t \text{ where } h_k^t \in \Theta^k \times \Theta^{k+1} \ldots \times \Theta^t \times \Xi^k \times \Xi^{k+1} \ldots \Xi^t.$$

In this formal setting, an *interpretation* or *mental model* can be seen as an algorithm attributing a causal sense to perceived histories or to a subset of them. Let us call such *mental models*:

$$\Phi^t = \{\phi^t(h), h \in H\}.$$

Accordingly, a *decision rule* will be a mapping between *interpretations*, so defined, and action repertoires:

$$r_i^t : \Phi^t \to \Xi^t.$$

An agent's decision-making capabilities at time t can then be represented by the (finite) set of decision rules it holds:

$$\Re^t = \{r_1^t, r_2^t, \ldots, r_q^t\}.$$

When an agent acts upon the environment, it receives a "response" (or an *outcome*) out of a set P of possible "responses":

$$p^t : S \times A \to P.$$

However, in general, the agent will only know an imprecise and partial representation of such outcomes. Moreover, it might well change over time its evaluation criteria (i.e., in standard language, its "preferences"). Let us call *payoffs* such evaluations in terms of some desirability criterion (being it utility, peace of mind, problem-solving achievements, etc.):

$$U^t = \Psi^t(p^t),$$

and accordingly define a payoff function as:

$$\pi^t : \Theta^t \times \Xi^t \to U^t.$$

On the grounds of this very general sketch of a decision-making model, we can perform some re-classification exercises of the notional learning processes we have discussed so far.

1. *Learning about the states of the world*: This implies changing the representation Θ^t. Obviously, the ways in which learning takes place will strongly depend on the causal relation between the environment and the learner itself. In particular, we can distinguish among: a) interactions with nature without *feed back*; b) interactions with nature with *feed back*; c) multi-agent strategic interactions (including standard game-theoretic ones).[5]

2. *Learning about the actions space*: This entails changing the action repertoires Ξ^t.

3. *Learning about the payoff function*: If the agent does not know S and A but holds only imprecise and partial representations thereof, it will have *a fortiori* an imprecise and partial knowledge of the payoff function. Hence, learning about the payoff function entails changing those representations.[6]

4. *Learning about decision rules*: As mentioned above, a basic (but still largely unresolved) issue concerns the dimensions of the state space of rule search.[7]

In following section we shall briefly discuss some classes of learning models, that, in a sense, depart from the most restrictive assumptions required in the Bayesian tradition.[8] We shall focus, in particular, on *evolutionary* learning models, that is on those formalizations which explicitly take on board learning and adjustments dynamics of some kind.

7.4 Learning as adaptation and selection

Without any doubt, the state of the art in the formal realized literature still falls quite far from any satisfactory account of the whole foregoing dynamics (and admittedly, also "appreciative theorizing" grounded on empirically robust patterns is well short of what one would like to have in order to make more precise statements on the nature of learning processes).

This notwithstanding, a rapidly growing literature in economics has addressed the formal representation of adaptation/learning of some kind in populations of diverse agents. Let us consider some of them.

7.4.1 Selection-based learning models

Models belonging to this class involve one of the least demanding ways of introducing learning, in particular with respect to the prior knowledge agents are assumed to possess from the start. In many versions of *evolutionary games*, for instance, each agent is often identified with one action and carries no cognitive capabilities.[9] Learning entirely occurs at the population-level by means of a selection mechanism that rewards larger payoffs actions by letting them to reproduce in the population at an higher diffusion rate.

In their standard formulation, evolutionary game models (cf. Maynard Smith (1982), Friedman (1991), Kandori, Mailath and Rob (1993), Weibull (1995)), consider agents having basically two roles, namely that of carrying the memory of the system (by replicating actions from time t to time $t+1$) and that of introducing some exploration (via random mutations). For example, given N agents and a finite set of actions $A = \{a_1, a_2, \ldots, a_k\}$ and denoting by $n_i(t)$ the number of agents adopting action a_i, the basic selection principle states that:

$$\frac{n_i(t+1) - n_i(t)}{n_i(t)} > \frac{n_j(t+1) - n_j(t)}{n_j(t)} \text{ if and only if } \pi^t(a_i, s^t) > \pi^t(a_j, s^t), \qquad (7.1)$$

implying that actions getting relatively higher payoff are increasingly sampled in the population.

It is often the case that the selection principle takes the special form of a *replicator dynamics* equation, originally suggested by biological arguments (cf. Maynard Smith (1982)), but widely used also in economic models,[10] of the kind:

$$n_i(t+1) = g\left(\pi^t(a_i, s_t) - \bar{\pi}^t\right) n_i(t), \qquad (7.2)$$

where $\bar{\pi}^t$ is the average payoff across the population and g is some real function. Learning is then driven by the joint action of the selection principle and random mutations (e.g. agents mutate their actions with a small probability). Originally, mutation was conceived as a pointly and isolated phenomenon, introduced as a device for studying the evolutionary stability of equilibria. More recent developments (cf. Kandori, Mailath and Rob (1993), Foster and Young (1990), Fudenberg and Harris (1992)) have incorporated mutation as a continuous process, so that equilibria could emerge as limit distributions of some stochastic (possibly non ergodic) process.

7.4.2 Stochastic models with self-reinforcement

In evolutionary games it is generally assumed that actions having better performed in the past will tend to diffuse at an higher speed across the population. The selection mechanism either acts on some statistics of the global fitness of the system (e.g. average payoffs) or stems from adaptation driven by infinitely frequent interactions among agents at each iteration (as in Kandori, Mailath and Rob (1993)). Other kinds of models consider instead mechanisms of diffusion in which agents choose an action according to some simple algorithm, such a *majority rule* (e.g. choose the action which is adopted by the majority of some observed sample of the population).

If one considers a finite population of N agents, the actual frequency $x_i(t) = n_i(t)/N$ of players selecting action a_i at time t defines a Markov chain whose transition probabilities depend on actual frequencies themselves. In the simplest case where only two actions are available, i.e. $A = \{a_1, a_2\}$, one could assume that agent i, who has selected action a_1 at time $t-1$, will switch to action a_2 at time t with probability:

$$P_i^t(a_1 \to a_2) = \alpha \frac{n_2(t)}{N} + \varepsilon \qquad (7.3)$$

where $n_2(t) = N - n_1(t)$ is the number of agents selecting action a_2. The α parameter measures the weight of the self-reinforcing component, while ε captures components which are independent from the choices of other agents. In simplest cases, it is possible to show that the time spent by the system in each state (i.e. the number of time periods t in which actual frequencies $x_i(t), i = 1, 2$, assume values in the support $\{0, 1/N, \ldots, (N-1)/N, 1\}$) has a limit distribution depending on α and ε. For instance, if the imitative component (α) is large enough relatively to the "idiosyncratic" one (ε), the limit distribution will tend to be a linear combination of two δ-Dirac on 0 and 1, implying that the population will oscillate between the two macro states "all agents choose action a_1" and "all agents choose action a_2."

A second realized strategy assumes an infinitely growing population, where at each time period a new entrant makes a once-and-forever choice among the finite set of actions $\{a_1, \ldots, a_k\}$, with probabilities proportional to the relative frequencies of past choices. In these models (cf. among others, Arthur, Ermoliev and Kaniovski (1984), Dosi and Kaniovski (1994)), learning takes place by means of a population dynamics described by an equation such as:

$$x_k(t+1) = x_k(t) + \frac{1}{N_t}\{[f_k(\underline{x}(t))] + \varepsilon(\underline{x}(t), t)\} \tag{7.4}$$

where N_t is the size of the population at time t (usually, $N_t = N_{t-1} + 1$), $x_k(t)$ is the share of the population which has chosen a_k and $\varepsilon(\underline{x}(t), t)$ is a zero-mean stochastic term, independent on t. The map f_k embeds possible self-reinforcing mechanisms, while its functional form defines the number and the attainability properties of fixed points. In case of multiple equilibria, the process is generally non ergodic (i.e. it displays path-dependence), and equilibrium selection depends on both initial conditions and the finite sequence of "early" choices (Arthur, Ermoliev and Kaniovski (1984); Dosi, Ermoliev and Kaniovski (1994)).

A theoretical issue which is crucial in self-reinforcement models is the interaction between, so to speak, "the weight of history" and agents' ability of extracting information from it. For instance, Arthur and Lane (1993) consider a model of choice between two competing technologies A and B. The states of the world $S = \{s_A, s_B\}$ represent the properties of such technologies and are unknown to the agents, who only hold prior normal distributions on them, denoted by $N(\mu_A, \sigma_A)$ and $N(\mu_B, \sigma_B)$. At each time period t, an agent adopts the technology which maximizes its expected utility (with constant risk-aversion). The expectation is made with respect to a posterior distribution computed (via the Bayes rule) using a likelihood function which captures the information coming from a sample of τ agents who have already adopted a technology. Arthur and Lane show that, notwithstanding the procedural "rationality" of the agents, the dynamics might lead to a collective lock-in into the intrinsically "inferior" option. Moreover, Lane and Vescovini (1996) find that apparently "less rational" decision rules turn out to be dynamically more efficient from a collective point of view.

7.4.3 Local learning

The class of models illustrated above assumes that agents base their actions on some global observation of (or feedback from) the population or a sample thereof. Another perspective describes instead economies where agents respond to some *local* observation of the characteristic of a given subset of the population.[11] Agents only observe their "neighbors" (Kirman (1994), David (1992), Dalle (1993, 1994), Jonard (1997)), defined according to some spatial or socio-economic measure of "distance." Denoting by $d(i,j)$ the "distance" between agent i and j and letting d^*

to be a given threshold, the set of neighbors of agent i is defined as:

$$V_i = \{j \in I : d(i,j) \leq d^*\}$$

If the set V_i are not mutually disjoint, local phenomena of learning and adaptation (i.e. inside a given neighborhood) can eventually spread in the entire population. An agent's neighborhood represents a sort of window through which it can only observe a part of the world: thus agents try to adaptively infer the state of the entire graph from such partial observation.

One way of endeavors this kind of processes is based on Markov fields (e.g. Allen (1982), An and Kiefer (1995), Dalle (1994), Durlauf (1994), Orléan (1990), Jonard (1997)), in which it is assumed that agents are distributed on the nodes of an integer lattice and stochastically select their actions depending on the actions or "states" of their neighbors. If payoffs increase in the degrees of coordination with the neighborhood, collective outcomes will depend upon the strength of the incentives (as compared to some "internal" motivation of each agent). When incentives are not strong enough, high levels of heterogeneity will persist. Conversely, if the premium on coordination is high enough, the system will spend most of its time in states of maximal coordination (though it might keep oscillating between them, cf. Kirman (1993)).

Another class of models assumes, on the contrary, that agents choose their action (almost completely) in deterministic way (cf. Blume (1995), Berninghaus and Schwalbe (1996), Nowak and May (1993), Nowak, Bonnhoefer and May (1994)), in ways that are basically isomorphic to simple cellular automata, whereby the state of each agent depends, according to some deterministic rule, on the states of its neighborhood.

Finally, it is worth stressing that an important limitations of most local learning models discussed so far is the total absence of a dynamics in the so-called *interaction structure.*[12] However, Kirman, Oddou and Weber (1986), Ioannides (1990), Bala and Goyal (1993) and Guriev and Shakova (1995) begin to provide a more general formulation, in which the very structure of the graph (and, accordingly, neighborhoods) is modified stochastically. In these models learning might involve, so to speak, an "enlargement of the window" so that agents could achieve a more complete picture of the world, or in any case endogenous modifications of the window itself.

7.4.4 Population-level vs. agent-level learning

We have already remarked that, at least in their early versions, evolutionary games assume agents carrying no explicit cognitive capability. They are simply "replicators" of actions and learning occurs at a population level. More sophisticated formalizations, as in Young (1993), are instead meant to explore some (boundedly rational) cognitive capability of the agents, such as the memory of the previous events and some simple decision-making algorithms.

In general, note that (under some implicit restrictions on the nature of environmental feed-backs) quite a few simple evolutionary games allow a symmetry between a population-based interpretation and an agent-based one. In the latter, a population of (quasi-pure-strategy) individuals is replaced by a single agent who adaptively learns by selecting among a set of feasible actions (i.e., so to speak, the "ecology of strategies" in its head). Stochastic approximation models of adaptive beliefs hold a similar perspective.

Assume an agent choosing among a fixed and finite menu of actions $A = \{a_1, \ldots, a_n\}$. Though it ignores the current realization of the state of the world $s^t \in S$, it can only perceives a modeling payoff π^t. An adaptive learning process[13] requires that the agent randomly chooses an element out of A according to some *strength* it attaches to the actions. Let us call F_k^t the *strength* of the action a_k at time t and assume that the strength is updated according, say, to the recursive rule:

$$F_k^{t+1} = F_k^t \frac{f^k(\pi^t(s^t, a_k))}{\sum_i f^i(\pi^t(s^t, a_k))}. \tag{7.5}$$

Actions will then be randomly selected at time t with probability:

$$P^t(a_k) = \frac{F_k^t}{\sum_i F_i^t}, \quad k = 1, 2, \ldots, n \tag{7.6}$$

and the stochastic process induced by the selection mechanism on the strength assigned to competing rules can be studied (see among others Arthur (1993), Easley and Rustichini (1995), Fudenberg and Levine (1995)). Easley and Rustichini's model, in particular, provides a neat connection between population-level and individual-level evolutionary arguments. They consider an individual decision-maker facing an unknown environment represented by a stochastic variable. Instead of forming beliefs on the set of possible processes and updating them according to the Bayesian approach, any agent adaptively selects among a set of theorizing rules R (of the same kind of our basic model) according to a strength updating rule of the kind of expression (7.5) and a random selection rule of the kind of expression (7.6). This enables them to study the stochastic process induced on the strengths of rule r_i, which is given by the expression:

$$F_k^{t+1} = \prod_{z=0}^{t} F_k^z \frac{f^k(\pi^z(a_k))}{\sum_k f^k(\pi^z(a_k))}. \tag{7.7}$$

With some further assumptions on the characteristics of the underlying stochastic process on the states of the world (e.g. stationarity and ergodicity) and on the selection dynamics (e.g. monotonicity, symmetry and independence) they are able to prove that: (i) an individual using this kind of adaptive selection dynamics eventually acts as if it was an objective expected utility maximizer; and, moreover, that (ii) the set of rules which are selected by such dynamics corresponds to the set of rules which would be selected by a replicator dynamics.

Some comments on the importance and limitations of this kind of models are in order.

First, note that these approaches are pure adaptation/selection models. While it is indeed an encouraging result that the outcome of such simple learning algorithms could often mimic optimizing behavior prescribed by normative theories, it is of course a necessary (and highly demanding) condition for such behaviors to be selected that they are there in the first place. In other words, the population must contain individuals holding decision rules that imply optimal actions (given the environment in which they operate) in order for them to be selected by whatever selection mechanism. Hence, moving from standard models of optimizing behavior to stochastic models of adaptive learning, one moves from a world where agents are assumed to be naturally endowed with the correct model of the world, to a world where agents are still endowed with the correct theorizing rules (which define an implicit model of the world), but these are mixed together with "incorrect" ones and have to be adaptively selected. It is clear that this amounts to assuming away the cognitive problem of how such rules are formed and modified. In complex and changing environments, in particular, it seems a rather far-fetched assumption to start with (see also below).

Second, it is often assumed, as in Easley and Rustichini (1995), that, at each stage of the adaptive learning process, the strength of all rules is updated according to the payoff they would have received in that modeling state of the world. This assumption is justified if and only if the actual actions of the agent do not determine any feed-back on the environment and if and only if the agent knows all that.[14] When this is not the case, only the strength of the actually employed rule can be updated and therefore lock-in phenomena and non-ergodicity may well emerge: exploitation vs. exploration and multi-armed-bandit type dilemmas are unavoidable. In an essential sense, whenever one faces evolutionary environments, the very dynamics of the learning process determines also the features of the environment one wants to learn about.

7.5 Open-ended dynamics and artificially adaptive agents

If we drop the assumption that agents are naturally endowed with the correct ER, the fundamental topic of the inquiry becomes how necessarily imprecise and partial ER are generated, stored and modified by economic agents. On the one hand, as we have already argued, this consideration carries the requirement for some form of cognitive and psychological grounding. On the other hand, it opens up new possibilities for applications to economics of families of models developed in Artificial Intelligence (AI), and especially in that branch of AI which considers selection and variation mechanisms as basic driving forces for learning. This kind of challenge are indeed taken up by most of the so-called "Artificially Adaptive Agents" models (AAA in the following).[15]

7.5.1 Learning with AAA: genetic algorithms

The main points of interest in AAA models are, firstly, that they are not restricted to simple selection dynamics, but, together, consider the introduction of novelty, innovation, generation of new patterns of behavior, as the basic forces driving learning and adaptation, and, secondly, that they naturally put a greater emphasis on the heterogeneity among agents and the complexity of interaction patterns as crucial aspects of the endeavors exercise.[16] These two features imply together that the dynamics in AAA models is a truly "open-ended" one: dynamic processes never really settles into equilibrium states and, typically, seemingly persistent equilibria tend to be, in fact, transient states of temporary "ecological" stability, where small variations can trigger non-linear self-reinforcing effects.

The above features are clearly illustrated by two prototypical examples of AAA learning models, both using *genetic algorithms* (GA) in order to depict innovation in theorizing rules.

In a GA (see Goldberg, 1989) information is coded in strings of a finite length (in analogy with DNA coding, think of a sequentially ordered set of genes) and such strings undergo an evolutionary process of selection, reproduction and modification. Each element of a string can take two or more alternative forms (or "alleles"). For instance, in case of binary strings of length n, denoted by $a_1 a_2 \ldots a_n$, we normally assume for simplicity $a_i \in \{0, 1\}$. GA evolve through time by means of *genetic operators, as*: (i) *crossover*, which entails a recombination over two strings, once a cutting point has been chosen at random (e.g. if $n = 5$ and the cutting point is $k = 3$, the two strings 01010 and 10011 become 01011 and 10010); (ii) *mutation*, which involves the change of state of any one random element of the string (e.g. if the third element has been chosen, the string 10010 becomes 10110); (iii) *duplication*, that entails a generation of a 2n-string by a copy/attach operation (e.g. the 5-string 10110 becomes the 10-string 1011010110); (iv) *splitting*, when a string is copied by discarding at random its k last (of first) elements (e.g. if $k = 2$, the string 00110 could either be copied as 001 or 110).[17] Since each string usually encodes (directly or indirectly) some theorizing patterns, one might superimpose some selection mechanisms in order to study how different families of strings are born, reproduce themselves and survive in changing environments.

Lindgren (1991) considers a classical repeated prisoner's dilemma played by a given population of players. Each agent is completely characterized by a strategy, which deterministically maps finite-lengths histories of the game (here represented by binary strings of Defeat or Cooperate actions performed by the player itself and his opponent) into an action (Defeat or Cooperate). This population is then processed via genetic operators allowing for variable length genomes. Strings are then selected over time with respect to the payoffs obtained in a repeated interactions setting. Simply allowing for strategies based on variable length histories makes the number of possible species in the population practically infinite and the search space unlimited. Hence, evolution is no longer a selection path in a finite and closed space of alternatives, but "[. . .] can then be viewed as a transient phenomenon in a potentially infinite-dimensional dynamical system. If the transients continue forever, we have *open-ended evolution*" (Lindgren (1991), p. 296, emphasis in original).

Aversi *et al.* (1997) explore instead some aggregate dynamic properties of demand patterns, when preferences, encoded in binary strings, are shaped by the cognitive structures of consumers and evolve in socially embedded fashions. At any time t, each consumer j is characterized by its income level, together with a binary string $L_j(t)$ of length l (i.e. the number of actual and eventually possible goods, metaphorically ordered from "basic necessities" to "luxury" commodities). Each element of the string takes the value 1 if and only if the corresponding good appears in the consumption pattern of consumer j. Monetary incomes of individual consumers evolve as random walks, while commodities prices fall as a function of cumulated sales. Moreover, new goods are randomly introduced in the system. At each time period, consumers face – and solve by means of quasi *routinized* behavior – the non-trivial problem of distributing their income among the currently preferred existing goods and carefully adjusting their choices whenever they do not fulfill the budget constraint. Moreover, agents have always a positive probability to change part of the consumption pattern via innovation (i.e. buy a newly introduced commodity) or imitation (i.e. adopt part of other agents' consumption pattern). Crossover and mutation are used here to model imitation and innovation, so that these two *genetic operators* solely drive the evolution of consumption patterns[18] in ways that are *path-dependent* (with respect to both individual consumption patterns and collective history of past preferences and consumption acts) and *socially embedded* (i.e. preferences and revealed purchasing patterns emerge from collective mechanisms of social imitation). Notwithstanding totally uniform initial conditions, and despite the very simple algorithm implemented by consumers, the model is able to generate, as sorts of *emergent properties* (see Lane, 1993a), those aggregate regularities that one generally detects in empirically observed consumption patterns (i.e. s-shaped diffusion patterns, Wald axiom, law of demand, etc.).

In the two above examples, the dimension and complexity of strategies become themselves elements subject to evolutionary selection, adaptation and variation, enriching in this way the concept of strategy implicit in the standard evolutionary game framework. While, in the latter, "strategy" is most often squeezed down to an action taken from a given set of possibilities, in AAA models it is easy to account for evolving "strategies" made up by changing combinations of a set of basic operators, categories, and/or variables.

This distinction is even clearer in more explicitly *rule-based* AAA models. They consider learning as the joint outcome of the processes of generation, replication, selection and modification of theorizing rules, that typically takes place as a search in both spaces of representations of the world and action repertoires. As those spaces are, in general, potentially infinite, ill-defined and subject to change, rule-based AAA models are not likely to generate – except in very simple problems nested in stationary environments – a single theorizing rule. Rather, they typically exhibits, as the outcome of the learning process, a whole "ecological" system of rules which together form a distributed representation of the environment.[19] Behavioral patterns which emerge in AAA models therefore are likely to be much richer than those predicted by pure selection models. Straightforward examples of rule-based AAA models are Classifier Systems and Genetic Programming.

7.5.2 Classifier systems

A typical class of rule-based learning models is represented by the so-called Classifier Systems[20] (CS in the following). Learning in CS presents three general features. First, it takes place in the space of representations of the world. When faced with complex and ever-changing environments, agents must indeed define sets of states (i.e. models of the world) which they consider as equivalent for purpose of action, or, in other words, they must build pragmatic representations, contingent upon the particular purpose the routine is serving, in order to discover regularities exploitable by their actions. Second, learning is driven by the search for better performance (i.e. agents use some system of performance assessment). Third, there must exist a procedure for the evaluation of the usefulness of behavioral rules that allows agents to select, add, modify or discard theorizing rules.[21]

In its most basic formulation, a CS is a set $R = \{R_1, R_2, \ldots, R_q\}$ of condition-action parallel-processed rules making the execution of a certain action conditional upon the agent's perception of a certain state of the world. Usually, each decision-maker is modeled as a CS by initially endowing it with a set of rules R.

At any given time, a message (or signal) is received from the environment informing the CS about the last state of the world. Each rule R_h is made up by a *condition part*, which encodes a subset of states of nature and is activated when the last message falls into such a subset; and an *action part* which encodes the actions to be taken up when the rule is activated.

More formally, assume that the signal is represented by a binary string $m_1 m_2 \ldots m_n$, where $m_i \in S = \{0,1\}$ and that the condition part consists in a string of the same length $c_1 c_2 \ldots c_n$ where $c_i \in \{0, 1, \#\}$ and the symbol "#" acts as a "don't care" operator (i.e. it does not pose any constraint on the corresponding element of the environmental signal[22]). The condition is satisfied - and the action part is accordingly prepared to be activated – whenever $c_i = m_i$ or $c_i =$ "#". Let the action part be a binary string of length p, denoted as $a_1 a_2 \ldots a_p, a_i \in A = \{0,1\}$. A CS (or equivalently a decision-maker) is then represented as a set R of rules, i.e. mappings of the kind $R_i : c_1 c_2 \ldots c_n \to a_1 a_2 \ldots a_p$. In addition, to each rule is then assigned a *Strength*, measuring the past usefulness of the rule, and a *Specificity*, assessing the strictness of its condition part.[23]

The dynamics of learning in CS typically works as follows. At the beginning of each simulation the decision maker is usually supposed to be absolutely ignorant about the characteristics of the environment and to have limited computational capabilities. Thus all the rules are initially randomly generated and the number of rules stored in the system at each moment is kept constant and relatively "small" in comparison to the complexity of the problem which is being tackled.

At each time period, all the rules whose condition satisfies the environmental message enter a competition in order to designate the one which is allowed to execute its encoded action $a_1 \ldots a_p$. The winning rule is randomly chosen according to a probability proportional to a synthetic measure of the current performance of each rule (called "bid"). Usually it is assumed that:

$$\text{Bid}(R_i, t) = k_1 [k_2 + k_3 \textit{Specificity}\ (R_i)] \textit{Strength}\ (R_i, t) \tag{7.8}$$

where k_1, k_2, k_3 are constant coefficients. When rule R_j is implemented, its *strength* is updated according to the received payoff and the bid "paid" for having been selected in the following way:

$$\textit{Strength}\ (R_j, t+1) = \textit{Strength}\ (R_j, t) + \text{Payoff}(t) - \text{Bid}\ (R_j, t). \tag{7.9}$$

However, a CS is not only able to select the most successful rules, but also to discover new ones. This is ensured by applying genetic operators (basically *mutation* and *crossover*) which, by recombining and switching elements of the already existing and most successful rules, introduce new ones which could improve the overall performance of the system. *Mutation* acts in opposite directions by simply generating switches in the condition part of a rule, either increasing or decreasing its specificity. *Crossover* generates new rules by recombining useful elements of the condition parts of two selected rules. New rules so generated substitute the weakest ones, so that the total number of existing rules is kept constant.

In order to give a flavor of how CS are implemented in actual models, let us consider two applications to economic problems. Marengo and Tordjman (1996) examine a population of speculators in an artificial centralized financial market where only two assets exist and agents trade on the basis of the exchange rate market. Agents can observe up to three variables in any time period, encoded in three binary strings of length n, namely: the last-period exchange rate, its moving average in the last k periods and the ratio between the numbers of buyers and the number of sellers. The condition part of each rule is made up of three binary strings (one for each variable), defining sets of intervals on the real axis of the corresponding variable that can be roughly interpreted as "categories" containing all the states of the world which are indistinguishable to the agent. To each condition will correspond an action, which is simply a ternary bit encoding the three actions at disposal, namely Buy, Sell or Hold, i.e. not engaging in any trade (formally, set $p = 1$ and $A = \{\text{Buy, Sell, Hold}\}$).

Vriend (1995) builds instead a model of decentralized trade where consumers "shop around" among existing firms in order to buy units of an homogeneous commodity. The CS governing each consumer is even simpler. In shopping around, consumers could face up to 6 different environmental states, depending whether they find a shop or not, manage to buy the good or not, receive some information signals from firms or not. Accordingly, they can choose among up to three possible actions, namely return to the last visited shop, go to one out of the shops already identified during the day or draw at random one of the existing shops. Shops' behavior is similarly governed by a CS that selects a point in the production/signalling space according to a stochastic function of the correspondent predicted payoffs.

Let us briefly assess the power and limitations of this formal instrument for representing learning processes. First, CS and genetic operators allows the study of learning dynamics in truly evolutionary environments, where selection acts in an environment in which agents endogenously introduce a never ending element of exploration of new possibilities: this guarantees some – albeit necessarily imperfect – adaptation to an ever changing world. Second, CS capture a very important feature of learning in evolutionary environments, namely its local and adaptive nature. By acting with higher probability on the most successful rules and by exploring other possibilities in neighborhoods of their condition parts, *genetic operators* tend to exploit more thoroughly what has already been discovered (i.e. introduce incremental innovations) rather than generating totally new theorizing patterns (i.e. radical innovations). Hence, search is not completely random, but it is influenced by the system's past history.

Rule-based AAA learning models employing CS for the analysis of multi-agent interactions in economics study the emergence of "ecologies of representations," that is, they are suited in principle to address the following questions: a) Given a population of decision-makers – characterized by heterogeneous initial endowments of theorizing rules – and an unknown complex and changing environment, what are the properties of the long-run system behavior? b) Does the system settle down into a long-run equilibria based on stable distributed representations of the environment or does one observe only transient states of "ecological" stability, which tend to temporarily emerge, as meta-stable point outcomes of selection pressure and innovation mechanisms? 3) What are the relationships between the *ex-post* emerging long-run patterns of representation and action and the degree of inter agents heterogeneity of the initial set of rules? Or, conversely, can *ex-ante* homogeneity result in an *ex-post* diversity of representations? 4) Finally, can one say something about the specificity vs. generality of the theorizing rules that tend to be selected ?

For what concerns long-run behavior of CS-based systems, one usually observes that environments which are stable in their "fundamentals" tend to generate relatively stable "ecological" equilibria. Agents seem to learn, on average, very fast about the overall environment. For instance, Vriend (1995) shows that the market self-organizes in a macroeconomic steady state where production, signaling and consumers' behaviors entail relatively ordered patterns of aggregate coordination. Similarly, in Marengo and Tordjman (1996) the market reaches a quasi market-clearing condition almost all the time.

However, in general, agents will not converge to homogeneous models, but only to patterns which are somehow "compatible" for the particular states of the world which actually occur. Moreover, learning never actually stops and the application of the genetic algorithm always introduce an element of exploration of new possibilities which might disrupt the temporary ecological equilibrium. The same environment can in fact support very diverse non-partitional representations: stochastic elements in the learning process, combined with the high degree of path-dependency of the systems, will very likely produce a high degree of diversity of representations even when one begins with perfectly homogeneous agents. In Vriend (1995), for instance, systematic and significant differences among firms (in sales, production, etc.) tend to emerge from an initial homogeneity. In general, both Marengo and Tordjman (1996) and Vriend (1995)[24] are able to show that the market can sustain high and persistent degrees of diversity between the models of the world that agents holds.

7.5.3 Genetic programming

A slightly different endeavors strategy, albeit very much in the spirit of GA, employs *Genetic Programming* (GP).[25] Unlike standard CS and GA, search does not take place in the space of string representations, but in the space of all *variable length functions* which can be generated out of a primitive set of *operators* and *operands*.

In GP, the learner is indeed endowed with a set of basic "primitive" operations (such as the four arithmetic operations, Boolean operators, if-then operators, etc.) and combine them in order to build complex procedures (functions) which map environmental variables into actions. Each agent is represented by a set of such procedures and learns to adapt to the environment through an evolutionary process which involves both fitness-driven selection among existing procedures and generation of new ones through *genetic operators*. More formally, symbolic functions are represented by trees, whose nodes contain either operators or variables. Operators have connections (as many as the number of operands they need) to other operators and/or variables, while if they are variables they do not have, of course, any further connection and constitute therefore the leaves of the tree. Every node can be chosen in a set of operators and operands:

$$BF = \{+, -, *, +, \ldots, \text{OR, AND, NOT}, >, <, =, \ldots, \underline{\mathbf{v}}, \underline{\mathbf{c}}, \ldots\} \quad (7.10)$$

where $\underline{\mathbf{v}}$ is a vector of variables and $\underline{\mathbf{c}}$ is a vector of given constants.

The execution cycle of a GP system proceeds along the following steps: (i) an initial set of function/trees is randomly generated. Each tree is created by randomly selecting a basic function; if the latter needs parameters, other basic functions are randomly selected for each connection. The operation continues until variables (which can be considered as zero-parameter functions) close every branch of the tree. (ii) Once a population of trees is so created, the relative strength of each function is determined by calculating its own fitness in the given environment. (iii) A new generation of functions/trees is generated by means of *selection* and *genetic operators*. Selection consists in preserving the fittest rules and discarding the less fit ones. Moreover, genetic operators generate new rules by modifying and recombining as in CS the fittest among the existing ones.[26] Dosi *et al.* (1994) apply this methodology to study pricing decisions by n firms selling an homogeneous good in a characterized oligopolistic market where: (a) customers are imperfectly informed about the prices of other suppliers and exhibit some inertia in their purchasing behaviors due to non-zero search costs; (b) there exists an exogenous linear demand function $p = a - b \cdot q$, whose parameters are unknown to suppliers; (c) firms are supposed to start-up with equal market shares, $s_i^0 = 1/n$; (d) at time t, firms incur in a unitary production cost c_i^t; and, finally, (e) individual prices $p_i^t, i = 1, \ldots, n$, are simultaneously and independently fixed by all firms at discrete time intervals $t = 1, 2, \ldots,$ but each supplier does not know individual prices currently set by its competitors. The focus being on the evolution of pricing rules by suppliers, it is supposed that, once price and quantities decisions have been taken, individual market shares evolve according to a discrete-time (quasi) replicator dynamics such as: $s_i^t = [p_i^t/p^t]s_i^{t-1}, i = 1, \ldots, n$, where the market price p^t is computed as a weighted average of all individual prices.[27] Firms are modeled as GP systems, endowed by a set of operators and operands as in (7.10), where the vector of feasible variables contains all information about the past behavior of the economy the supplier could take into account in order to build its pricing rules (e.g. market price, aggregate demanded quantity, individual prices, unitary costs, etc.). At any time period, each firm holds a portfolio of pricing rules and it selects (in probability) the one which has received the highest payoff in the past. Moreover, new rules are created by means of genetic operators that replace the weakest one in the portfolio. Finally, new firms enter in the market whenever some of the existing ones disappear (cf. previous footnote).

Given this setting, Dosi *et al.* (1994) show the endogenous emergence of pricing routines as an evolutionary robust form of adaptation to complex and possibly non-stationary environments. In particular, in the case with constant costs and stable demand curve, pricing rules which "look like" optimization rules emerge and market price rapidly converge to the optimal one (at least in a single-agent set-up). However, beyond a certain threshold of environmental complexity (e.g. oligopolistic interactions with aggregate stochastic shocks upon both demand and costs and also idiosyncratic ones on the latter), firms tend to develop simple robust rules that behave "as if" they were either mark-up pricing schemes or "follower" strategies (i.e. set the price equal to the last observed value of the "leader"). Hence, robustness and simplicity seem to turn out to be the most frequent and the most efficient response of boundedly rational agents to environmental complexity.

7.5.4 Neural networks

One of the main drawbacks of rule-based learning devices as Classifier Systems and Genetic Algorithms is that they generally process discrete (mostly binary) variables and often their implementation in a real-valued search space turns out to be a very difficult task.[28] Conversely, a neural network (NN) is a biological-inspired, parallel-distributed, sub-symbolic computational device which *learns* to (non- linearly) associate real-valued outputs in response to real-valued inputs.[29]

In its most general definition,[30] a NN is composed of: (i) a finite set N of entities, called *neurons*; (ii) a finite set of connections between pairs of neurons $i \neq j : (i,j) \in NxN$; (iii) an external environment E. To each connection is attached a real-valued non-negative strength w_{ij} called *weight*. Each neurons $i \in N$ is in principle able to receive a real-valued vector of inputs $\underline{x}_i$ from the other neurons in the net, as well as from the external environment E, process it according to some non-linear mapping $f_i(\underline{x}_i)$ and deliver in response a vector of real-valued outputs $\underline{y}_i = f_i(\underline{x}_i)$.

Usually, a well-defined fixed architecture of neurons and weights is assumed. The most commonly employed ones in the literature are three-layers, fully interconnected, feed-forward network. In this setting, neurons are organized in three subsequent layers (input, hidden and output) through which the information flows unidirectionally.[31] Each neuron of a given layer is interconnected with all neurons of the subsequent layer, while no connections are assumed between neurons of the same layer. *Input neurons* (labeled, say, as $i = 1, \ldots, I$) receive inputs $x_1, \ldots, x_I$ from E (and possibly from some other neurons in the net) and process no information, but only deliver outputs to the *hidden layer* neurons. Each hidden neuron $h = 1, \ldots, H$ computes a weighted sum of inputs :

$$x'_h = \sum_{i=1}^{I} w_{ih} x_i$$

(where $w_{ih} \geq 0$ is the weight attached to the connection between the input neuron i and the hidden neuron h) and it transmits to the *output layer* a non-linear transformation of this weighted input, say $y_h = f_h(x'_h)$ (the function f_h is usually a logistic one, but also simpler threshold functions might be employed). Finally, each output neuron $o = 1, \ldots, O$, only performs a non-linear transformation f_o of a weighted sum of its inputs $y_1, \ldots, y_H$, submitting a final output real-valued vector to the external environment E.

Learning in a NN occurs by an updating process on the weights w_{ij}, the aim being to tune weights (i.e. the "memory" of the system) in order to teach the net to properly associate inputs coming from the environment to desired output targets.[32] The standard learning algorithm employed in the NN literature is a Back-Propagation (BP) one, see Rumelhart and McClelland (1986). Given a *loss function* L imposing a metric in the output space, the BP method simply requires an initial learning (or training) phase, in which a given set of inputs and outputs (i.e. targets) is presented to the net and weights are dynamically updated in order to minimize the overall loss computed through L.[33] Then, once the net has been trained and weights have relaxed to their loss-minimizing values, it may be employed in order to efficiently associate inputs to "correct" outputs (Baum (1991)).

In the spirit of this short assessment of the state of the art, let us again telegraphically suggest some evaluating remarks. First, because of both the global pattern of connections between neurons and the implicit way in which knowledge is stored across weights, learning occurs in a parallel-distributed, content-addressable way (cf. Marris (1992) for an appraisal from the point of view of an economist). Second, thanks to hidden layers, NN are able to build internal representations of the environment, which however are hardly interpretable even *ex-post* in terms of semantic categories. Moreover, since associations between classes of inputs and outputs can overlap, a NN might link a "correct" input pattern to a "wrong" output, and likewise a "correct" output may be delivered in response to "incorrect" or "incomplete" inputs. This is a consequence (in our view empirically sound) of the fact that learning in a NN occurs in an inductive form, and a related property is also that the emerging patterns of information detection and theorizing response are robust to slight modifications in the structure of the network.[34] Third, a distinction must be drawn between models employing *supervised learning* (in which the net is fed by a training pattern defining targets) and network assuming an *unsupervised* one, where weights (and possibly the architecture of the net itself) self-organize without being fed by exogenous targets (Kohonen, 1984).[35]

Interesting and successful applications of the NN paradigm in artificial-intelligence have been successfully developed concerning, e.g. generalization tasks, such as pattern recognition (i.e. learning by examples or pattern overlapping), specialization tasks, which involve reduction in the number of conditions which place an object into a category, feature extraction, e.g. symmetry identification, and so on (see *inter alios* Serra and Zanarini (1990), Baum (1991)).

Neural networks have also been recently employed in endeavors learning in economic environments. First of all, as long as supervised learning is assumed, NN might be used as a time-series predictor (see for instance Sargent (1993), Salmon (1994) and Beltratti *et al.* (1996)). As no assumption about the true data generation process' structure is required – only input conditioning variables and output targets are needed – economic agents could be assumed to hold NN-like learning mechanisms in order to predict future values of relevant economic variables in evolutionary environments (with no feedback with other agents). Indeed, NN have been shown to perform rather well in generating non parametric estimates of the unknown quantities, such as conditional expectations functions, even in the case of "intrinsically hard" predictable chaotic time-series (Hornik *et al.*, 1989). For instance, White (1991) and (1992) shows that a multi-layer feed-forward network can learn any arbitrary real-valued mapping. Hence, "attributing a NN to agents learning does not give agents the knowledge of the true model of the economy but at the same time does not restrict them to forecast with an inefficient model such a linear one" (Beltratti *et al.*, 1996: 181). Moreover, even when one keeps the net structure as fixed and allows only weights to be learned, the NN is capable of self-modeling its representation of the world in response to an environment which is changing through time (e.g. when structural changes occur in the time-series data generation process).

However, as one turns to model more complicated economies populated by heterogeneous interacting agents who try to learn in a truly evolutionary environment, the NN paradigm apparently displays some significant shortcomings. First, most intuitively, with reference to fully fledged evolutionary environments, one is bound to assume some form of unsupervised learning (after all, it would be somewhat bizarre to assume that whatever entity is trained to handle any type of novelty before the very appearance of the latter). Second, and more generally, the downside of non-symbolic parallel-distributed NN learning, as already mentioned, is a sort of semantic black-boxing of learning outcomes. We leave the assessment of its relative worth in terms of Artificial Intelligence philosophy to the much more competent judgement of the practitioners of the field. However, for social scientists trying to utilize NN as a device for formally representing learning processes, this is certainly a reason of concern in that, short of any Friedmanian type of methodology (. . . any assumption goes provided it delivers a seemingly correct answer . . .), one has to trust a lot the empirical robustness of the postulated learning procedure.

7.6 Learning as a dynamic in the space of the outcomes

Some of the typologies of learning models reviewed in the last section attempt, to different degrees, to open up the "black-box" of cognitive processes. They do so in ways which allow some dialogue, in different modes, with appreciative theories and models stemming from other social sciences such as cognitive psychology, sociology and a few branches of artificial sciences. As we argued, it is a highly promising development, notwithstanding major challenges still to be faced. Among others, they concern a) the structures which one should inbuild ex-ante into the postulated learning processes;[36] and b) the nature of selection mechanisms which drive learning itself (Is it simple payoff reinforcement? Does one need an additional explicit representation of how agents endogenously evolve their reinforcement perceptions? Etc.). In these respects, many of the diverse classes of learning models discussed so far address decision- and learning-theoretic issues at a level of abstraction similar to that, say, of standard "rational" decision theory. In that vein, we tried to evaluate achievements and limitations of various endeavors efforts against some "socio-cognitive" yardsticks stemming from whatever we know from the discipline naturally addressing these issues.[37]

There are, however, other streams of endeavors efforts of evolutionary dynamics which look at learning processes in economics at a different level of abstraction. Further away from decision-theoretic "primitives," one typically builds upon empirically grounded generalizations on the ways collections of individuals and organizations learn especially in the domain of technological innovation and imitation, and, based on that, one tries to explore the aggregate outcomes of such processes in decentralized market economies. Most models in the spirit of evolutionary economics over the last twenty years or so have been built indeed in this spirit. There one normally finds some black- boxing in the explicit formalization of agent-level learning (together with a rich qualitative "appreciative formalized": cf. Nelson and Winter (1982)). In that vein, within models of growth and industrial change driven by technological advances, learning dynamics is typically represented in terms of changes in the space of some technological coefficient.

Possibly, the simplest formal ancestor of a whole mode of "stylizing" learning patterns is the early account by Arrow (1962) of learning-by-doing, since then corroborated by a few empirical studies, showing a "quasi-law" of falling costs (or increasing productivity) as a function of cumulated production.

At a similar level of abstraction, Silverberg, Dosi and Orsenigo (1993) model a process by which firms learn to efficiently use a new capital-embodied technology, as a function of firm specific skills and of both actual and cumulated output.

In fact, most evolutionary models starting from the seminal work of Nelson and Winter (1982), explicitly account for uncertain processes of technical search, and often, also for the dependence of future discoveries upon the knowledge already achieved in the past. In the last resort, endeavors learning in the technology space comes down to a specification of the stochastic process driving agents from one technique to the next (cf. also Silverberg and Lehnart (1994), Chiaromonte and Dosi (1993), Chiaromonte *et al.* (1993), Dosi *et al.* (1995), Kwasnicki (1996)).

Moreover, a few evolutionary models account also for learning *via imitation*, that is by the stochastic access of each firm to the best practice available at each time or to the set of combinations between best practice and the technique currently known by any generic incumbent (cf. Nelson and Winter (1982), Chiaromonte *et al.* (1993), Silverberg and Verspagen (1995), Kwasnicki (1996), among others).

It is worth noting that the spirit of most formalizations of learning processes in a technology space, however defined, has an essential "phenomenological" feature: formal representations are meant to capture stylized facts, basic dynamic regularities, etc., generally placed at a much "higher" (and more aggregate) level of description than the "foundational" processes of cognition, problem-solving, etc. discussed earlier. Given this more phenomenological level, however, a requirement far from being fulfilled in the current state-of-the-art concerns the *empirical robustness* of the purported dynamics.[38]

The requirement of empirical robustness is even more pressing if one acknowledges that one of the main concerns of evolutionary models ought to be the discovery of *transient* (finite-time) properties rather than limit ones.[39] More generally, a major research puzzle ahead concerns the links between, so to speak, "nano-descriptions" of learning processes building upon constructive formal stories in the domain of cognitive and theorizing evolution, on the one hand, and more parsimonious phenomenologically richer but more "black-boxed" and aggregate representations on the other.

7.7 Some open questions by way of a conclusion

One of the purposes of this survey was to provide a broad map of diverse lines of inquiry which, different ways, take the analysis of cognition, action and learning in economics beyond the boundaries of the canonical model of rational decision and rational learning. Let us conclude by flagging some issues that, in our view, are still left unresolved, but that, notwithstanding, we consider very high on the research agenda.

7.7.1 Learning and Selection

In evolutionary theorizing, learning and selection are the two basic mechanisms driving the dynamics of every economy. Although almost all existing models fall in the classes of "pure learning" (as in canonical decision-theoretic models) or "pure selection" (as in standard evolutionary games), we suggest that all actual dynamics of socio-economic change are somewhere in between. However, learning and selection may act in opposite directions: for instance, a quite weak selective pressure might prevent inefficient behaviors from disappearing, but it might also allow a more effective exploration of new opportunities and a more extensive "trial-and-error" learning (cf. the so-called *exploration-exploitation* trade-off, March (1991)). Note that this dilemma can be also seen as a time-scale issue: learning and selection might well proceed at different paces and even the tightest selection environment can leave room for individual learning, provided that selection is a low frequency event as compared to the rates of search/learning. Conversely, institutions – such as markets – are not only fundamental selection mechanisms, but also an essential source for feedbacks which stirs learning processes.

Another related issue concerns the possible tension between individual and collective learning: for example, it might well happen that persistent individual mistakes (e.g. decision biases) turn out to have a positive collective role (cf. Dosi and Lovallo (1995), Lane and Vescovini (1996)).

7.7.2 Learning, path-dependency and co-evolution

We have already pointed out that a quite general property of learning processes is their *path-dependent* nature, since new knowledge is typically accumulated on existing knowledge bases. However, a more complicated and fascinating question concerns path-dependent outcomes driven by the correlation across (cognitive, theorizing, organizational) *traits*, which in biology comes under the heading of *epistatic correlation*[40]. The intuition is simple. Consider again the basic formal framework presented in Section 7.3 and assume that learning, as typically does, generates a system of closely interrelated theorizing rules, representations of the world and preferences. In general, one is not able to say whether a rule is absolutely "good" or "bad," since its "value" could be assessed only in a relative way, with respect to another given set of rules, representations and preferences. Hence, any learning process would typically entail mutual adaptation and *co-evolution* of existing *traits*. In this respect, Kauffman (1993) shows that, as correlation among traits increases, learning is no longer likely to entail a smooth path-dependent process of incremental overall changes. Rather, it is more likely that an improvement on the fitness of a single "trait" will dramatically lower the global fitness of the system.

7.7.3 Expectations formation and endogenous preferences

If some tentative insights toward the formalization of the co-evolution between mental models and action repertoires have already been taken up, two other domains, however, have been so far neglected, namely *expectation formation* and *endogenous preferences*.

Concerning expectations, the state-of-the-art offers two largely dissatisfying alternatives. On the one hand, the rational expectation paradigm basically assumes agents who already know what they are supposed to learn. On the other hand, various *ad hoc* extrapolative expectations mechanism are suggested. A major step forward would be, in our view, the development of models whereby search in the space of expectations on the states of the world and search in the space of actions is partly de- coupled. A consequence would also be the possibility of handling the coexistence of partly conflicting systems of beliefs and action patterns. This, in turn, would allow an explicit account of phenomena like cognitive dissonance (Festinger (1957), Hirschman (1965) and Akerlof and Dickens (1982) for some economic applications).

Finally, some progress has been recently made toward endeavors preferences as influenced by social interactions (cf. e.g. Kuran (1987)), Brock and Durlauf (1995), Aversi *et al.* (1997)). The time is possibly ripe to take the issue further, right into the foundational model of agency, and account for the endogeneity of the criteria by which representations, actions and payoffs are evaluated, certainly as a result of social imitation, but also driven by attempts to adjust desires to organize outcomes.

A short assessment over vast and diverse fields of interrelated research is bound to be highly biased and idiosyncratic. Given all that, some implications are quite straightforward. First, if our interpretative perspective is not too far off the mark, time is ripe for formal explorations of (individual and collective) learning processes which relax the most restrictive assumptions well summarized by e.g. Savage's "small world" assumption which indeed turned out to be the natural frame of analysis for most scholars thereafter. Evolutionary, open-ended dynamics might begin to be within the reach of an improved formal endeavors toolbox.

Second, "stylized facts" stemming from cognitive and social sciences are likely to be precious guiding constraints for any endeavors efforts of learning in general and also concerning economic behaviors.

Third, admittedly, the models that one has been able to develop so far, as compared to all the challenges mentioned above are still rather rudimentary and clumsy. But, possibly for the first time, one may envisage the development of sound microfoundations of learning processes grounded upon highly imperfect but notionally unlimited abilities of individuals to adapt but also to experiment and discover in open-ended environments, whereby novelties can always endogenously emerge.

Notes

1 For a more detailed review of the literature on this field, see again Dosi, Marengo and Fagiolo (1996) and the references therein.

2 Cf. for instance Nelson and Winter (1982), Dosi (1988), Freeman (1994), March (1994), Cohen *et al.* (1996), Montgomery (1995), Teece *et al.* (1994). Some of these issues are quite similar to those one could find in the so-called post-Keynesian models of learning; see, among others, Davidson (1996), Katzner (1990), Neal (1996).

3 Notice that, if agents simply adjust to received payoffs, a completely wrong ER which, by chance, produces effective actions (given some states of the world) will always be preferred to an "almost" correct one producing less rewarding actions (in some of the same state of the world). Similarly, bad ER producing good predictions must generally be preferred to good ER which produce worse predictions.

4 By *grammar* here we mean, loosely speaking, some basic rules specifying and binding any combinatorial exercise involving re-arrangements of "elementary bits" of cognition or elementary actions. Intuitive examples are, of course, grammars in natural languages whereby sets of rules prescribe, say, the constraints which any combination of the words of the English dictionary should obey in order to yield "meaningful" sentences. Somewhat similarly, combinatorial exercise on e.g. actions or organizational routines may be thought as subject to specific grammars (more on this in Dosi and Egidi (1991)).

5 A similar distinction is made in Marimon (1995).

6 Incidentally, it is worth pointing out that most current learning algorithms simply assume that the learner adaptively develops its representations of the world and action repertoires toward pay-off *quasi-equivalence* classes (i.e. classes reflecting regularities of the payoff function rather than those underlying sets of states of the world and actions).

Thus, under some conditions, adaptive learning algorithms tend to produce a better knowledge of the payoff function than of the sets S and/or A.

7 Note that most of the existing learning models avoid the problem by postulating that learning results in a simple selection of the best rule among a known, fixed (finite), menu of notional rules.

8 For some discussion on Bayesian learning in the spirit of the paper, see Dosi, Marengo and Fagiolo (1996). Cf. also Kalai and Lehrer (1993), Blackwell and Dubins (1962), Feldman (1991).

9 Coherently with the terminology introduced in the basic model above, we prefer to use the term *action* rather than the more common *strategy* for this kind of models.

10 Many recent models have worked with broader classes of selection rules (cf. Kandori, Mailath and Rob (1993), Kaniovski and Young (1994)). See also below.

11 For a more thorough discussion of models with locally interactive agents in economics, see Fagiolo (1999).

12 Typically, decision rules and neighborhood sets are time-independent. Moreover, agents are completely homogeneous in their decision rules, endowments, etc.

13 For a general overview of adaptive processes in economics, see the pioneering work of Day (1975).

14 Note also that given the overwhelming "adaptationist" emphasis, it seems somewhat awkward to suppose that agents are always able to undertake the thought experiment concerning what it would have gained had it undertaken a different course of action.

15 For a general overview on the AAA perspective in economics see, for instance, Arthur (1993) and Lane (1993a, 1993b).

16 For instance, the AAA approach has been recently applied to model interactions in spatial-distributed decentralized economies. Cf. among others Axtell and Epstein (1994); Dosi and Fagiolo (1999).

17 Notice that the first two operators leave unchanged the length of the strings, while the last two allow for strings of different length.

18 No selection mechanism of consumption patterns is in fact assumed in the model. There is indeed no reason to think that some consumption pattern may be intrinsically *better* than another one, as well as there is no collective mechanism to check it.

19 On the so-called "computational ecologies" see also Huberman and Hogg (1995).

20 Cf. Holland *et al.* (1986) for the basic model. See also Arthur (1993) and Lane (1993b) for general overviews. Marengo (1996), Marengo and Tordjman (1996), Palmer *et al.* (1994), Marimon *et al.* (1990), Vriend (1995) present specific applications to diverse economic learning problems.

21 Note that this problem might not have a clear solution when the performance of the system may be assessed only as a result of a long and complex sequence of interdependent rules (such as in the game of chess).

22 Thus, consistently with the basic model presented above, a set of conditions defines a subset of the power set of S. In turn, each condition defines a subjective state of the world – as perceived by the agent – and its relationship with the objective states of the world. This relationship remains anyway unknown to the decision-maker, who only "knows" the subjective states.

23 Basically, any specificity measure is time-invariant and it is increasing in the number of "#" symbols appearing in the string $c_1 \ldots c_n$. Two extremes condition rules are: (i) highest specificity, $c_i \neq$ "#," all i, i.e. the rule is activated only when the particular state encoded in $c_1 c_2 \ldots c_n$ occurs; (ii) lowest specificity (highest generality), $c_1 =$ "#," all i, the rule is activated no matter what the state of the world is. General rules are robust ones and in this sense they can be thought as *routines*, in that general rules provide the same automatic response (i.e. the same action) to a range of different signals (i.e. different states of the world). However, general rules might also mean that agents are simply ignorant and that they cannot decode their environment successfully.

24 For similar results, see also Palmer *et al.* (1994). Marengo (1996), furthermore, applies CS to the emergence of a commonly shared knowledge basis in team decision making processes, and shows that different types of environment can generate very different balances between homogeneity and heterogeneity of knowledge.
25 See Koza (1993). For applications see also Dosi *et al.* (1994), Moss and Edmonds (1994), Edmonds *et al.* (1996), Edmonds (1997).
26 Genetic operators – mainly crossover – act here on the nodes of the tree representation of symbolic functions by selecting at random two nodes of the parents' trees and swapping the sub-trees having such nodes as roots.
27 Note that such replicator function may yield negative shares, in which case the firm is declared "dead" and shares of other firms are accordingly adjusted.
28 See e.g. Belew *et al.* (1991), Beltratti *et al.* (1996: 29–40).
29 For a comparison between CS and NN see Davis (1989) and Belew and Gherrity (1989). Note that Genetic Programming overcome the mentioned drawbacks of CS and GA, but at the price, alike NN, of rendering any semantic interpretation of what the algorithm actually does overwhelmingly difficult.
30 Neural networks have recently given birth to a very large body of literature, mostly in artificial-intelligence related fields. Space constraints prevent us from providing a survey of the main issues and applications of the NN paradigm. Hence, we will limit ourselves to some considerations on the realm of applicability of NN to economic endeavors (for a more detailed treatment from an economic point of view, see *inter alios* Beltratti *et al.* (1996), Baum (1991), Salmon (1994) and the references therein).
31 Notice that, in this setting, both the number of input, hidden and output neurons, as well as the number of hidden layers, are fixed by the modeler (see above) and will depend on problem-specific issues, such as the nature of the processed information, the precision of the learning process, computational constraints, etc.
32 Obviously, this is a very restricting assumption. In principle, learning in a NN may also occur in: (a) the number of layers; (b) the number of neurons in each layer; (c) the way neurons are connected. See also Schaffer (1989) and Kohonen (1984).
33 Obviously, a trade-off arises between the representativeness/accuracy of the training set and the computational constraints, on the one hand, and the accuracy of the subsequent performances of the net, on the other.
34 Some of the above features of learning in a NN are striking in that they replicate similar properties of the biological counterpart a NN would like to mimic (i.e. the brain), see Caudill and Butler (1992).
35 An additional class of learning is called *quasi-supervised.* In that kind of NN, the structure of the net is fixed, but targets are not provided during the learning phase. Indeed, a GA is employed in order to rule out the case in which the net becomes stuck in a local-maximum and to allow the NN to perform a search in the whole output space (Belew *et al.* 1991).
36 The point closely relates to the issue of grammars briefly mentioned above. Of course it related also to the broader divide between those schools who prefer explicitly symbolic representations of learning mechanisms (such as most classic AI models, but also e.g. CS models) vs. sub-symbolic models (such as NN). And it links also with the issue of context-dependence of models-of-the-world mentioned earlier (more in Dosi, Marengo and Fagiolo (1996))
37 A noticeable exception to this perspective on "microfoundations" of theorizing patterns stems from that long tradition of formal models in psychology building on stimulus-response processes (i.e. the so-called "reinforcement learning") dating back to at least Estes (1950) and Bush and Mosteller (1955) (see also Suppes (1995)). Interestingly, this is the psychological tradition nearest in spirit to the evolutionary game models discussed in section 7.4 above.
38 For example, on which empirical grounds does one justify e.g. the assumption of Poisson arrival processes in innovation endeavors? Why not another distribution function? On

what criteria does one choose the (often used) Markov process specifications driving search?, etc.

39 *A fortiori*, all this applies to learning dynamics which are *open ended* according to the above definition.

40 Cf. the so-called NK-model in Kauffman (1993); see also Levinthal (1996) for a suggestive exploratory application to the analysis of organizational inertia.

References

Akerlof, G.A. and W.T. Dickens (1982) The economic consequences of cognitive dissonance. *American Economic Review* 72: 307–19.

Allen, B. (1982) Some stochastic processes of interdependent demand and technological diffusion of an innovation exhibiting externalities among adopters. *International Economic Review* 23: 595–608.

An, M. and N. Kiefer (1995) Local externalities and societal adoption of technologies. *Journal of Evolutionary Economics* 5: 103–117.

Andersen, E.S. (1994) *Evolutionary Economics – Post-Schumpeterian Contribution.* London: Frances Pinter; New York: St. Martin's Press.

Arifovic, J. (1994) Genetic algorithm learning and the cobweb model. *Journal of Economic Dynamics and Control* 18: 3–28.

Arrow, K. (1962) Economic welfare and allocation of resources for invention. In N. Rosenberg (ed.) *The Economics of Technological Change.* Harmondsworth: Penguin.

Arthur, B.W. (1993) On designing artificial agents that behave like human agents. *Journal of Evolutionary Economics* 3: 1–22.

Arthur, B.W. and D. Lane (1993) Information contagion. *Structural Change and Economic Dynamics* 4: 81–104.

Arthur, B.W., Y. Ermoliev and Y. Kaniovski (1984) Strong laws for a class of path-dependent stochastic processes with applications. In S. Argin and P. Shiryayev (eds) *Proceedings of Conference on Stochastic Optimization.* Lecture Notes in Control and Information Sciences. Berlin: Springer-Verlag.

Aversi, R., G. Dosi, G. Fagiolo, M. Meacci and C. Olivetti (1997) *Demand Dynamics With Socially Evolving Preferences.* Interim Report. Laxenburg: IIASA.

Axtell, R. and J. Epstein (1994) *Modelling Artificial Economies Of Adaptive Agents.* Colloquium on Evolutionary Economics. Laxenburg: IIASA.

Bala, V. and S. Goyal (1993) *Learning from neighbors.* Mimeo.

Baum, E.B. (1991) Neural nets for economists. In P.W. Anderson, K.J. Arrow and D. Pines (eds) *The Economy as an Evolving Complex System.* Redwood City, CA: Addison-Wesley.

Belew, R.K. and M. Gherrity (1989)'Back propagation for the classifier system." In J.D. Schaffer (ed.) *Proc. of the 3rd Intl. Conf. on Genetic Algorithms.* San Mateo, CA: Morgan Kauffman.

Belew, K.R., J. McInerney and N.N. Schraudolph (1991) Evolving Networks: using the genetic algorithm with connectionist learning. In C.G. Langton and C. Taylor (eds) *Artificial Life II.* Santa Fe: Santa Fe Institute.

Beltratti, A., S. Margarita and P. Terna (1996) *Neural Networks for Economic and Financial Modelling.* London: Thomson Computer Press.

Berninghaus, S.K. and U.G. Schwalbe (1996) Evolution, interaction and Nash equilibria. *Journal of Economic Behavior and Organization* 29(1): 297–312.

Blackwell, D. and L. Dubins (1962) Merging of opinions with increasing information. *Annals of Mathematical Statistics.* 33: 882–886.

Blume, L.E. (1995) The statistical mechanics of best-response strategy revision. *Games and Economic Behavior* 11: 111–145.

Brock, W., and S. Durlauf (1995) *Discrete Choices with Social Interactions I: Theory.* WP 95-10-084. Santa Fe: Santa Fe Institute.

Bush, R.R. and F. Mosteller (1955) *Stochastic Models for Learning.* New York: Wiley.

Caudill, M. and C. Butler (1992) *Understanding Neural Networks*, vols 1 and 2. Cambridge, MA: MIT Press.

Chiaromonte, F. and G. Dosi (1993) Heterogeneity, competition and macroeconomic dynamics." *Structural Change and Economic Dynamics* 4: 39–63.

Chiaromonte, F., G. Dosi and L. Orsenigo (1993), Innovative learning and institutions in the process of development: on the microfoundations of growth regimes. In R. Thomson (ed.), *Learning and Technological Change.* London: Macmillan.

Cohen, M., R. Burkhart, G. Dosi, M. Egidi, L. Marengo, M. Warglien, S. Winter, and B. Coriat (1996) Routines and other recurring action patterns of organisations: contemporary research issues. *Industrial and Corporate Change* 5: 653–698.

Coriat, B. and G. Dosi (1995) *The Institutional Embeddedness Of Economic Change. An Appraisal Of The "Evolutionary" And "Regulationist" Research Programmes*, Working Paper WP 95–117. Laxeburg: IIASA.

Dalle, J.M. (1993) *Dynamiques d'adoption, coordination et diversité: le cas des standard technologiques* Mimeo.

Dalle, J.M. (1994) *Decisions autonomes et coexistence des technologies.* IEPE Working Paper 9401.

David, P.A. (1992), Path-dependence and predictability in dynamic systems with local externalities: a paradigm for historical economics. In D. Foray and C. Freeman (eds) *Technology and the Wealth of Nations* London: Frances Pinter.

Davidson, P. (1996) Reality and economic theory. *Journal of Post-Keynesian Economics* 18.

Davis, L. (1989), Mapping neural networks into classifier systems. In J.D. Schaffer (ed.) *Proc. of the 3rd Intl. Conf. on Genetic Algorithms* San Mateo, CA: Morgan Kauffman.

Day, R.H. (1975), Adaptive processes and economic theory. In R.H. Day and T. Groves (eds) *Adaptive Economic Models.* New York: Academic Press.

Dosi, G. (1988) Sources, procedures and microeconomic effects of innovation. *Journal of Economic Literature* 26: 1120–1171.

Dosi, G. and M. Egidi (1991) Substantive and procedural uncertainty. An exploration of economic behaviours in complex and changing environments. *Journal of Evolutionary Economics.* 1: 145–168.

Dosi, G. and G. Fagiolo (1999) *Exploring The Unknown: On Entrepreneurship, Coordination And Innovation-driven Growth* In: Lesourne, J. and A. Orléan (eds) (1999) Advances in Self-Organization and Evolutionary Economics. Paris: Economica.

Dosi, G. and Y. Kaniovski (1994) On "badly behaved" dynamics, *Journal of Evolutionary Economics* 4

Dosi, G and D. Lovallo (1995) Rational entrepreneurs or optimistic martyrs? Some considerations on technological regimes, corporate entries and the evolutionary role of decision biases. WP 95–77. Laxenburg: IIASA. Also in R. Garud, P. Nayyar and Z. Shapiro (eds) (1996) *Technological Foresights and Oversights* Cambridge: Cambridge University Press.

Dosi, G., Y. Ermoliev and Y. Kaniovski (1994). Generalized urn schemes and technological dynamics. *Journal of Mathematical Economics* 23: 1–19.

Dosi, G., C. Freeman, R. Nelson, G. Silverberg and L. Soete (eds) (1988) *Technical Change and Economic Theory.* London: F. Pinter; New York: Columbia University Press.

Dosi, G., L. Marengo, A. Bassanini and M. Valente (1994) *Norms as Emergent Properties of Adaptive Learning. The Case of Economic Routines.* WP 94–73. Laxenburg: IIASA.

Dosi, G., L. Marengo and G. Fagiolo (1996) *Learning in Evolutionary Environments.* WP. Laxenburg: IIASA.

Dosi, G., O. Marsili, L. Orsenigo, and R. Salvatore (1995) Learning, market selection and the evolution of industrial structure, *Small Business Economics* 7: 411-436.

Dosi, G. and R. Nelson (1994) An introduction to evolutionary theories in economics. *Journal of Evolutionary Economics* 4.

Durlauf, S.N. (1994) Path-dependence in aggregate output. *Industrial and Corporate Change.* 3: 149-171.

Easley, D. and A. Rustichini (1995)*Choice Without Beliefs*. Working paper. Louvain-la-Neuve: CORE, Catholic University of Louvain.

Edmonds, B. (1997) *The Introduction Of Learning Into The Modelling Of Boundedly Rational Economic Agents Using The Genetic Programming Paradigm*. Manchester: Centre for Policy Modelling, Manchester Metropolitan University.

Edmonds, B., S. Moss and S. Wallis (1996) *Logic, reasoning and a programming language for simulating economic and business processes with artificially intelligent agents*, AIEM96, Tel Aviv.

Eliasson, G. (1985) *The Firm And Financial Markets In The Swedish Micro-To-Macro Model*. Working paper. Stockholm: IUI.

Estes, W.K. (1950) Toward a statistical theory of learning, *Psychological Review* 57: 94-107.

Fagiolo, G. (1999) Spatial Interactions in Dynamic Decentralised Economies, in: Cohendet, P., P. Llerena, H. Stahn, and G. Umbhaver (eds) (1999) The Economics of Networks: Interaction and Behaviours. Berlin-Heidelberg: Springer-Verlag.

Feldman, M. (1991) On the generic nonconvergence of Bayesian actions and beliefs. *Economic Theory*. 1: 301-321.

Festinger, L. (1957) *A Theory of Cognitive Dissonance*. Stanford: Stanford University Press.

Fontana, W. and Buss, L. (1996) *The Barrier of Objects: From Dynamical Systems to Bounded Organizations*. WP 96–27. Laxenburg: IIASA.

Foster, D. and P.H. Young (1990) Stochastic evolutionary game dynamics. *Theoretical Population Biology*. 38: 219-232.

Freeman, C. (1994) *The Economics of Industrial Innovation*. 2nd edn. London: Frances Pinter.

Friedman, D. (1991) Evolutionary games in economics, *Econometrica*. 59: 637-66.

Fudenberg, D. and C. Harris (1992). Evolutionary dynamics with aggregate shocks, *Journal of Economic Theory* 57: 420-441.

Fudenberg, D. and D.K. Levine (1995) Consistency and cautious fictitious play. *Journal of Economic Dynamics and Control* 19: 1065-89.

Goldberg, D. (1989) *Genetic Algorithms in Search, Optimization and Learning*. Reading, MA: Addison-Wesley.

Guriev, S. and M. Shakhova (1995). *Self-organization of trade networks in an economy with imperfect infrastructure*. Working paper. Moscow: Computing Centre of the Russian Academy of Sciences.

Hirschman, A. (1965) Obstacles to development: A classification and a quasi-vanishing act. *Economic Development and Cultural Change* 13: 385–393.

Holland, J.H., K.J. Holyoak, R.E. Nisbett and P.R. Thagard (1986) *Induction*. Cambridge, MA: MIT Press.

Hornik, K., M. Stinchcombe and H. White (1989) Multilayer feed-forward networks are universal approximators. *Neural Networks* 2: 359–66.

Huberman, B. and T. Hogg (1995) Distributed computation as an economic system. *Journal of Economic Perspectives* 9: 141–52.

Ioannides, Y.M. (1990) Trading uncertainty and market form. *International Economic Review* 31(3): 619–638.

Jonard, N. (1997) *Heterogeneité et structure d'interactions: la diffusion des standard technologiques*. PhD thesis. Strasbourg: BETA, Université Louis Pasteur.

Kalai, E. and E. Lehrer (1994) Weak and strong merging of opinions. *Journal of Mathematical Economics* 23: 73–86.

Kandori, M., G.J. Mailath and R. Rob (1993) Learning, mutation and long run equilibria in games. *Econometrica* 61: 29-56.

Kaniovski, Y. and P.H. Young (1994) Learning dynamics in games with stochastic perturbations. *Games and Economic Behavior* 11: 330-363.

Katzner, D.W. (1990) The firm under conditions of ignorance and historical time. *Journal of Post-Keynesian Economics* 13: 124–156.

Kauffman, S. (1993) *The Origins of Order*. Oxford: Oxford University Press.

Kirman, A.P. (1993) Ants, rationality and recruitment. *Quarterly Journal of Economics* 108.

Kirman, A.P. (1994), *Economies with interacting agents*. Mimeo.

Kirman, A.P., C. Oddou and S. Weber (1986) Stochastic communication and coalition formation. *Econometrica* 54: 129–138.

Kohonen, T. (1984) *Self-Organization and Associative Memory*. Berlin: Springer-Verlag.

Koza, J. (1993) *Genetic Programming*. Cambridge, MA: MIT Press.

Kuran, T. (1987) Preference falsification, policy continuity and collective conservatism. *Economic Journal* 97: 642–655.

Kwasnicki, W. (1996) *Knowledge, Innovation and Economy*. Cheltenham: Edward Elgar.

Lane, D. (1993a) Artificial worlds in economics: Part I. *Journal of Evolutionary Economics* 3: 89–107.

Lane, D. (1993b) Artificial worlds in economics: Part II. *Journal of Evolutionary Economics* 3: 177–197.

Lane, D. and R. Vescovini (1996) Decision rules and market share: aggregation in an information contagion model. *Industrial and Corporate Change* 5: 127–146.

Langton, C. (ed.) (1989) *Artificial Life*. Redwood City, CA: Addison-Wesley.

Lesourne, J. (1991) *Economie de l'ordre et du désordre*. Paris: Economica.

Levinthal, D. (1996) Adaptation in rugged landscapes.*Management Science*.

Lindgren, K. (1991) Evolutionary phenomena in simple dynamics. In C.G. Langton *et al.* (eds) *Artificial Life II*. Addison-Wesley.

March, J.G. (1991) Exploration and exploitation in organizational learning. *Organization Science* 2: 71–87.

March, J.G. (1994) *A Primer on Decision Making. How Decisions Happen*. New York: Free Press.

March, J.G., L.S Sproull and M. Tamuz (1991) *Learning from samples of one or fewer Organization Science* 2: 1–13.

Marengo, L. (1996) Structure, competences and learning in an adaptive model of the firm. In G. Dosi and F. Malerba (1996).

Marengo, L., and H. Tordjman (1996) Speculation, heterogeneity and learning: A model of exchange rate dynamics. *Kyklos* 47: 407–38.

Marimon, R. (1995) *Learning from learning in economics (Towards a theory of the learnable in economics)*. Mimeo. Florence: European University Institute.

Marimon, R., E. McGrattan and T.J. Sargent (1990) Money as a medium of exchange in an economy with artificially intelligent agents. *Journal of Economic Dynamics and Control* 14: 329–373.

Marris, R. (1992) Economics and intelligence. In S. Moss and J. Rae (eds) *Artificial Intelligence and Economic Analysis. Prospect and Problems*. Cheltenham: Edward Elgar.

Maynard Smith, J. (1982) *Evolution and theory of games*. Cambridge: Cambridge University Press.

Montgomery, C.A. (ed.) (1995) *Resource-based and Evolutionary Theories of the Firm*. Dordrecht: Kluwer.

Moss, S. and B. Edmonds (1994) *Modelling learning as modelling*. Manchester: Centre for Policy Modelling, Manchester Metropolitan University.

Neal, P. (1996) Keynesian uncertainty in credit markets. *Journal of Post-Keynesian Economics* 18: 45–67.

Nelson, R.R. (1995) Recent evolutionary theorizing about economic change. *Journal of Economic Literature* 33: 48–90.

Nelson, R.R. and S.G. Winter (1982) *An Evolutionary Theory of Economic Change*. Cambridge, MA: The Belknap Press of Harvard University Press.

Nowak, M.A., S. Bonnhoefer and R.M. May (1994) More spatial games. *International Journal of Bifurcation and Chaos* 4(1): 33–56.

Nowak, M.A.and R.M. May (1993) The spatial dilemmas of evolution. *International Journal of Bifurcation and Chaos* 3(1): 35–78.

Orléan, A. (1990) Le rôle des influences interpersonnelles dans la détermination des cours boursiers. *Revue Economiques* 41: 839–868.

Palmer, R.G., W.B. Arthur, J.H. Holland, B. LeBaron and P. Tayler (1994) Artificial economic life: a simple model of a stock market, *Physica D* 75.

Rumelhart, D.E. and J.L. McClelland (1986) *Parallel Distributed Processing: Exploration in the Microstructure of Cognition, Vol.1: Foundations.* Cambridge, MA: MIT Press.

Salmon, M. (1994) *Bounded Rationality And Learning: Procedural Learning.* Working Paper. Florence: European University Institute.

Sargent T. (1993) *Bounded Rationality in Macroeconomics* Oxford: Oxford University Press.

Schaffer, J.D. (1989) (ed) *Proceedings of the 3rd International Conference on Genetic Algorithms.* San Mateo, CA: Morgan Kauffman.

Shackle, G.L.S. (1969) *Decision, Order and Time in Human Affairs.* 2nd edn. Cambridge: Cambridge University Press.

Serra, R. and G. Zanarini (1990) *Complex Systems and Cognitive Processes.* Berlin: Springer-Verlag.

Silverberg, G., G. Dosi and L. Orsenigo (1988) Innovation, diversity and diffusion: a self-organization model. *Economic Journal* 98 1032–1054.

Silverberg, G. and D. Lenhart (1994) Growth fluctuation in an evolutionary model of creative destruction. In G. Silverberg and L. Soete (eds) *The Economics of Growth and Technical Change.* Aldershot: Edward Elgar.

Silverberg, G. and B. Verspagen (1995) *From The Artificial To The Endogenous: Modelling Evolutionary Adaptation And Economic Growth.* WP 95-08. Laxenburg: IIASA.

Suppes, P. (1995) *A Survey Of Mathematical Learning Theory 1950–1995.* Mimeo. Stanford University.

Teece, D., R. Rumelt, G. Dosi and S. Winter (1994), Understanding corporate coherence: theory and evidence, *Journal of Economic Behavior and Organization* 23: 1–30.

Vriend, N. (1995) Self-organized markets in a decentralized economy. *Journal of Computational Economics* 8: 205–231.

Weibull, J.W. (1995) *Evolutionary Game Theory.* Cambridge, MA: MIT Press.

White, H. (1991) Learning in artificial neural networks: a statistical perspective. *Neural Computation* 1: 425–464.

White, H. (1992) *Artificial Neural Networks: Approximation and Learning Theory.* Oxford: Blackwell.

Winter, S.G. (1971) Satisficing, selection and the innovative remnant. *Quarterly Journal of Economics* 85: 237–261.

Young, P.H. (1993) The evolution of conventions, *Econometrica* 61: 57–84.

Part III

Technical change in organizations and economic growth

8 Evolutionary theories of economic change

Richard R. Nelson

8.1 Introduction: strands of evolutionary theory impinging on economics

This volume, and the workshop on which it draws, reflects the fact that evolutionary economics, or at least bodies of thought and writing that are associated with that term, have become increasingly fashionable. In this chapter, I will discuss the kind of evolutionary theory Sidney Winter and I, and kindred souls both in economics and in other fields of social science, have been trying to develop. However, our particular orientation toward evolutionary theory is only one of several that are impinging on economic analysis. While the different strands have certain things in common, there also are some major differences. It is useful, therefore, to begin by laying out some of the differences as well as the similarities.

One important strand of evolutionary analysis bearing on economics, represented in this volume by the chapters by Boyd, and by Feldman, has roots in biology, and sociobiology, and is becoming a significant influence in anthropology. It is focused on the factors influencing the evolution of various social practices and beliefs – aspects of culture – including prominently kinds of economic organization and behavior. Here its interests are broadly in common with those of the economic evolutionary theory which I will discuss, but its origins and focal topics are different.

The early work of this genre, especially that of Lumsden and Wilson (1981), saw social behavior and cultural traits as very closely tied to, and limited by, biological ones. Subsequent work, as by Boyd and Richerson (1985), and further writings as described by Boyd in this volume, and by Cavalli-Sforza and Feldman (1981), discussed and extended by Feldman in this volume, developed perspectives in which the evolution of culture came to stand, as it were, on its own. However, in all of these treatments, cultural evolution is viewed as, in some fundamental sense, an extension of biological evolution. In most of this writing the focus is on cultural traits in relatively primitive societies. And the human social structures carrying and developing the cultural elements in question are treated as rather simple. Institutions like universities, or the corporate M form (multidivisional), or Government regulation of pharmaceuticals, are not in the picture.

In contrast, the body of evolutionary analytic writing I will focus on here is strictly focused on "cultural" evolution, with no connections with biological evolution assumed at all. The focus tends to be on aspects of modern industrial economies and societies, as contrasted with more primitive ones. And the institutional structures involved in evolution are understood, implicitly or explicitly, to be very complex.

Another important strand of "evolutionary analysis" in economics is evolutionary game theory. That strand is represented in this volume in the chapters by Mailath, Bowles and Gintis, Crawford, and Vannucci. In turn, evolutionary game theory would appear to have two distinct sources. One is from evolutionary biology, and especially the work of Maynard Smith (1982). Maynard Smith was interested in formalizing, and formally analyzing, the notion of an "evolutionarily stable" set of genetically programmed (if perhaps environmentally conditioned) "strategies" or behavior patterns. One important consequence of this work was the sharpening of understanding that there could be several different kinds of evolutionary equilibria in this sense, and that which equilibrium obtained could be strongly influenced by initial conditions and "out of equilibrium" behavior.

Much of the work by economists on evolutionary game theory has proceeded independently. That work has been motivated by the awareness that many repeated games, or multiple-period games with long time horizons and uncertain end points more generally, can have a number of different equilibria. Here, as with the analysis of biological equilibria, which (if any) equilibrium ultimately is reached in an economic game is determined by initial conditions, and by the dynamic "out of equilibrium" evolutionary processes built into the model.

The kind of evolutionary analysis that Winter and I, and colleagues working along a similar path, have been espousing also stresses the historical path dependency of economic processes. However, as the above discussion indicates, most of the analysts using evolutionary game theory, whether they come from biology or economics, basically are interested in the equilibria. Analysis of out of equilibrium behavior, or processes of change more generally, mainly are vehicles for trying to understand equilibrium configurations.

In contrast,most of the evolutionary analysis of the kind I will be focusing on is centrally concerned with processes of change. In some cases the subject of analysis is an observed body of practice, or mode of organization, that prevails at a particular moment of time, and which may seem relatively durable. Examples are the pricing policies of firms, or their mode of organizing R & D. However, even here the presumption is that these variables are not likely to stay constant for very long, and that it is important, therefore, to understand the dynamic processes that have molded them as they are, and which will mold their evolution in the future.

More generally, the central concern is understanding the dynamics. In many cases, it is recognized, indeed highlighted, that the phenomena under study are almost always in flux. Indeed, much of the body of such evolutionary theorizing is focused expressly on variables that seem to be undergoing continuing change, like technology, or fashions of business strategy and organization. This is why, for many of its practitioners, this kind of evolutionary theory is viewed as a way of understanding economic growth.

The by now rather extensive body of writing by economists, who have developed complex, nonlinear dynamic models that purport to represent in abstract form certain classes of economic process, seems to me to be still another strand. While not represented in this volume, such analysis is becoming very fashionable. The art form is self-consciously interdisciplinary. The basic intellectual faith is that there are common properties of complex dynamic processes, whether they be in physics, biology, or economics.

Unlike most evolutionary game theory, the central interest in such modeling endeavors is exactly in the dynamics. In many cases, simulation is the vehicle for modeling. The key theoretical arguments draw from what has come to be understood about the mathematics of nonlinear dynamic systems more generally. Bifurcation points, chaos, and emergent properties, are often part of the language used. The models tend to be very abstract. Explaining with any precision particular bodies of empirical phenomena is not generally part of the agenda.

In contrast, understanding observed empirical dynamic patterns is the central focus of the kind of evolutionary theorizing I will discuss here. The theoretical part of the analysis generally is presented verbally, at least at the start, with the theorizing intertwined with reference to the empirical phenomena to be analyzed. The formal modeling is often simulation, because the analyst's understanding of the processes driving the phenomena under study suggests sharp limits as to what can be learned by building and running a more simple model. However, the latter may be brought into play to depict special cases of the more complex model, or to help explore its logic.

Let me pull strands together and focus the discussion. The body of evolutionary writing I will discuss here has the following hallmarks:

First, it has no connections whatsoever with evolutionary biology, save in the sense that the processes of change being proposed, and evolutionary processes in biology, are both regarded as members of a general class of dynamic processes. The key features of those processes are these: at any time there usually exist some variety regarding the variables under interest; selection mechanisms operate to winnow down that variety, and there are relatively strong inertial forces bearing on what survives selection; but at the same time, there are mechanisms that generate new variety.

Second, the central interest is in the dynamic processes *per se*. In general, there is no special interest in any "steady states" that those processes might have, and in general the presumption is that the phenomena in question are always undergoing change. This is so even when the variables under study seem to be relatively constant, when not looked at closely or over a long time period, like the way firms organize R & D. And "disequilibrium dynamics" is the strong presumption when the analysis is focused on topics like technological change, and the competition and industry structure associated with technological innovation, which have been of central interest to this brand of evolutionary economists, and a central reason why we have sought to develop an economic evolutionary theory.

Third, the analyses are motivated by empirical phenomena of interest, and the analysts in many cases are very knowledgeable about the empirical phenomena in question. In addition to being targeted to explain empirical phenomena, in many cases such evolutionary analyses also are molded and constrained by a desire for what might be called "process realism." That is, explanations which "fit the data" are not regarded as satisfactory unless the key processes that go into that explanation also are regarded as consistent with what is known about what really is going on in the arena in question.

There are a large number of analyses of cultural, social, and economic change, that fit the above bill. While up to now I have written as if the class was quite unified, in fact one can discern two but related subbranches, which I discuss respectively in Sections 8.2 and 8.3.

The first is a body of writing concerned with particular aspects of culture or social structure. The scholars doing this work include some economists, but many come from other disciplines. For the most part the theorizing is verbal, not mathematical, but explicitly evolutionary. The evolutionary perspective is motivated by the analyst's detailed understanding of the subject matter.

The second body of evolutionary theorizing I will consider is more formal. The practitioners are mostly economists. And the express evolutionary theorizing often is put forth as an alternative to neo-classical theory of the same phenomena, motivated by the author's belief that the dynamics require evolutionary modeling.

Finally, in Section 8.4, I focus on two key analytical and epistemological questions that evolutionary economic theorizing brings to the fore. The first is the role of human understanding and foresight in determining individual and organizational behavior. Much of economic evolutionary theory treats human action as to a considerable extent rule driven, with the rules themselves "evolving." Within such a conception of human behavior, what is the role of the kind of human "rationality" that occupies central place in standard economic analysis? Second, most of the theorizing described in Section 8.2, and some discussed in Section 8.3, is presented verbally. But some of it has been developed mathematically, sometimes in analytic form, but often in the form of simulation models. What are the relationships between verbal, and more formal, theorizing in the social sciences?

8.2 Evolution of particular aspects of culture

The collection of theories discussed in this section are concerned with particular facets of human culture and practice. Evolutionary theory of the sort I have been describing has proved attractive to many scholars studying aspects of cultural and social change. By and large the groups studying different facets, and proposing evolutionary theories of how they change, have had little intellectual contact with each other. The theories discussed in this section are all qualitative, and expressed verbally, rather than being laid out mathematically. But each is an explicit evolutionary theory along the lines I marked out above.

Each of the bodies of evolutionary theorizing discussed is very large, and quite varied. My treatment of each, therefore, must be highly selective. My particular selection is designed not to be representative of the literatures involved, but rather to bring out the particular analytic flavor of evolutionary theorizing, and to highlight the kind of theoretical arguments one can find within the camp of cultural evolutionary theorists. The following discussion follows along the lines of Nelson (1995)

8.2.1 Science

The proposition that science "evolves" has been around for some time, and there has been and continues to be a lively discussion about just how that evolutionary process works. (For overviews see Henry Plotkin 1982; and David Hull 1988.)

Of recent writers in this vein, Donald Campbell (1960, 1974) probably is the most cited. Using Campbell's term, the development of new scientific hypotheses, or theories, is to some extent "blind," in that their originators cannot know for sure how they will fare when they are first put forth. Thus new scientific theories are like "mutations" in that some will succeed and be incorporated into the body of science, perhaps replacing older theories, or correcting them in some respects, or adding to them, and some will sink beneath the waves.

Campbell relies largely on the ideas of Karl Popper (1968) for his "selection mechanism." Under Popper's argument scientific theories never can be proved true, but they can be falsified. New theories that solve scientific problems and are not falsified are added to the body of science. That is, employed and "not falsified" is the characterization of fitness in this theory of science. For the most part Campbell treats science as a relatively unified body of doctrine, and his language implies a scientific community together searching after truth. On the other hand, his theory is compatible with the notion of individual scientists putting forth their particular theories in hope of winning a Nobel prize. A good case can be made that both images of science – cooperative and competitive – are partly correct (see Hull 1988).

In any case this theory of selection leaves open two questions. The first is what determines which theories are to be rigorously tested, and what is the standing of theories that have not been. "Theories" that have not (as of yet) been subject to rigorous testing do not necessarily have the same standing. Some may never be brought to a serious test simply because they are regarded as irrelevant, or, taken at face value, absurd. Others may fit so well with prevailing understanding that they are absorbed without direct testing. The second question is what falsification means; in many cases the conclusions of a test may be ambiguous, or there may be reason to question the way it was run, or whether it was appropriate. Often a theory which seems to fail a test can be patched up with a well-crafted modification or amendment. These issues open the door to a much more complicated theory of the evolution of science than at least the simple interpretation of Campbell's.

The "social constructionists" recognize and revel in these complications (see e.g., Bruno Latour 1986). They propose that very few theories, or scientific arguments more generally, are ever completely falsified, or even put to a test that all would regard *ex ante* as conclusive. Thus scientific opinion is what matters and, in a context where different individuals and groups have different opinions, what is considered scientific fact and is published in reputed journals, taught to graduate students, etc., is largely a matter of scientific politics.

Thomas Kuhn (1970) presents a view somewhat between Campbell and the social constructionists. On the one hand Kuhn proposes that most "normal science" proceeds in almost unthinking acceptance of prevailing theory, and that there is strong built-in disbelief of results that challenge that theory. On the other hand, also central to Kuhn's theory of the evolution of science is that unanswered questions or anomalies tend to accumulate and, as they do, questions increasingly are asked about the adequacy of prevailing theory. A standard response of the scientific community is to propose modest modifications or additions to prevailing theory. However these may not succeed or the developing theoretical structure may come to be seen as rococo. The seeds then are planted for a scientific revolution.

Neither Campbell nor Kuhn (in their earlier versions) address the issue of competing theories. However, such competition is the heart of scientific revolutions. Imre Lakatos (1970) proposes that broad theories should be regarded as defining research programs. These programs can be judged by the community as proceeding effectively – that is as making good progress – or as more or less stuck. Lakatos proposes that there are almost always competing theories around. The one that defines the more effective research program tends to win out. But again, one can ask what defines "effective." A particular theory almost always points to a number of predicted implications, and exploring these defines a variety of puzzles and problems and tasks. A research program may be good in dealing with some of these, and not so effective on others. What counts?

Note that several different "theories" of the evolution of science have been described above. Some are in conflict. In particular the social constructionists would seem at odds with scholars, like Campbell, who believe that new scientific hypotheses, or at least those taken seriously, are subject to test, and that enough of the tests are sufficiently objective and unambiguous to monitor the enterprise. (This also clearly is Hull's view.) Some of the theories are compatible, and can be joined. Thus Kuhn might be regarded as providing an evolutionary theory of science within a given research program, and Lakatos a theory which explains selection among competing programs. Regarding what criteria are used to weigh program effectiveness, I shall shortly suggest that part of the answer may reside in the connections between science and technology.

Does science make progress? While the social constructionists seem strongly reserved about this, I think it fair to say that most of the theorists who propose that science evolves believe that the process does generate progress, at least along the lines of research pursued. (This clearly is Hull's view.) While occasionally we delude ourselves that we have understood something when we do not, and often the going toward better understanding is hard, by and large through science we have come to know more and more about nature and hot it works. Or at least this is the flavor of most of this body of theorizing.

8.2.2 Technology

A number of analysts have proposed that technology evolves. The analyses of Nathan Rosenberg (1976, 1982), Christopher Freeman (1974), George Basalla (1988), Joel Mokyr (1990), Nelson and Winter (1977), Dosi (1988), and Walter Vincenti (1990) are strikingly similar in many respects. To keep the discussion below simple, I will follow the discussion of Vincenti.

In Vincenti's theory, the community of technologists at any time faces a number of problems, challenges, and opportunities. He draws most of his examples from aircraft technology. Thus, in a recent paper (Vincenti 1994) he observes that in the late 1920s and early 1930s, aircraft designers knew well that the standard pattern of hooking wheels to fuselage or wings could be improved upon, given the higher speeds planes were then capable of with the new body and wing designs and more powerful engines that had come into existence. They were aware of several different possibilities for incorporating wheels into a more streamlined design. Vincenti argues that trials of these different alternatives were, in the same sense put forth by Campbell, somewhat blind. This is not to say that the engineers thinking about and experimenting with solutions were ignorant either of the technical constraints and possibilities or of what was required of a successful design. Rather, his proposition that, while professional knowledge and appreciation of the goals greatly focused efforts at solution, there still were a number of different possibilities, and engineers were uncertain about which would prove best, and disagreed among themselves as to where to place bets.

This kind of uncertainty, together with the proposition that uncertainty is resolved only through *ex post* competition, is the hallmark of evolutionary theories. In this case it turned out that having the wheel be retractable solved the problem better than did the other alternatives explored at that time. Thus, "fitness" here is defined in terms of solving particular technological problems better.

One might propose that identification of this criterion only pushes the analytic problem back a stage. What determines whether one solution is better than another? At times Vincenti writes as if the criteria were innate in the technological problem, or determined by consensus of a technological community who are, like Campbell's community of scientists, cooperatively involved in advancing the art.

However, Vincenti also recognized that the aircraft designers are largely employed in a number of competing aircraft companies, whose profitability may be affected by the relative quality and cost of the aircraft designs they are employing, compared with those employed by their competitors. But then what is better or worse in a problem solution is determined at least partially by the "market," the properties of an aircraft customers are willing to pay for, the costs associated with different design solutions, etc. In the case of aircraft, the military is an important customer, as well as the airlines. Thus the evolution of aircraft at least partially reflects military demands and budgets, as well as civilian.

As with the case of science, some authors dispute that the evolution of technology follows a path that might be considered as "progress," or even that there are any objective criteria for technological fitness. The book by Wiebe Bijker, Thomas

Hughes, and Trevor Pinch (1989) surveys various theories of "social construction" of technology. (See also Bijker 1995.) Michael Tushman and Lori Rosenkopf (1992) develop a more nuanced view of social determinism, but one which also implicitly denies the importance of economic efficiency, save as a gross screen. On the other hand, evolutionary theorists of the development of technology of the Vincenti camp believe strongly that there is technological progress, and ask the doubting reader to compare modern aircraft with those of fifty years ago, modern pharmaceuticals with those available before World War II, etc.

In recent years a particular insight or argument has somewhat complicated this discussion. While those that profess that science "progresses" generally seem to have in mind a unitary concept of "truth" toward which science is going, recent scholarship on the evolution of technology has proposed that there may be a number of different directions, and that movement down one may block movement down another. Thus the rapid evolution of gasoline-powered automobiles may have improved these, but at the same time may have scotched progress toward battery-powered cars.

8.2.3 Business organization

Alfred Chandler's research (1962, 1990) has been concerned with understanding how the complex structures that characterize modern multi-product firms came into existence. For our purposes his story is especially interesting, in that it is a story of co-evolution of technology and business organization. He argues that a variety of technological developments occurred during the mid- and late-19th century which opened up the possibility for business firms to be highly productive and profitable if they could organize to operate at large scales of output, and with a relatively wide if connected range of products. He describes various organizational innovations that were tried, and while his central focus is on those that "succeeded," it is clear from his account that not all did.

Arguing in a manner similar to Vincenti, Chandler's "fitness criterion" is that the new organizational form solved an organizational problem. Presumably the solution to that problem enabled a firm to operate at lower costs, or with greater scale and scope, in either case, with greater profitability. Like Campbell and Vincenti, Chandler clearly sees a community, in this case of managers. But he also sees companies competing with each. His argument is that companies which found and adopted efficient managerial styles and structural forms early won out over their competitors who did not, or who lagged in doing so. Oliver Williamson (1985), drawing from Chandler, but putting forth a much more explicit formal theory, proposes that a relatively sharp "fitness" criterion determined which organizational forms survived and which ones did not – economic efficiency.

Chandler's and Williamson's accounts of the development of the large multi-dimensional corporation stress the need of senior managers concerned with market-defined efficiency somehow to decentralize, and yet still control large and diversified bureaucracies. Marxians highlight a different aspect of the organizational forms that evolved – that they sharply reduced the importance of workers with special skills, and hence shifted power toward capital. Neil Fligstein (1990) presents a still different view on corporate fitness, which emphasizes responsiveness to changed legal regimes, public policies, and the climate of political opinion more generally toward what corporate action and form ought to be.

Note that the theories discussed above are similar in certain respects, but differ in others. They are similar in that they all are concerned with a particular aspect of cultural and focus on its evolution. They are similar in proposing that the processes that generate new cultural elements or modify old ones are to some extend blind, although the details of these mechanisms differ from case to case, and in some the mutation or innovation mechanisms have strongly directed elements as well as random. However, in each of these theories the "selection mechanism" provides a large share of the explanatory power. That is, the power of these theories depends on their ability to specify "fitness" plausibly.

Both neo-classical economists and economists inclined to evolutionary theorizing are prone to look to a market or a market analogue as the mechanism which defines what will "sell," and to "profit" or its analogue as the reward to actors that meet the market test. The theories above clearly differ in the extent to which they can be forced into that mold.

There certainly is no real "market" out there in Campbell's or Kuhn's or Lakatos' theory of science as an evolutionary process, save for the metaphorical "market of scientific judgment." In the cases of technology and the organization of enterprises, a moderately persuasive case can be made that, in many sectors at least, real, not metaphorical, markets have a powerful influence on what is "fit" and what is not, and that profit is an important measure of fitness. However, as we have seen there are dissenters, mainly from outside economics. One important issue is the extent to which competition provides a sharp fitness test in sectors where markets are operative. If it does not there is room for a variety of nonmarket forces to influence what "survives."

Also, there are serious questions about the range of sectors – kinds of technologies and organizations – where markets are strongly operative. In the case of military or medical technologies, or military bases or hospitals, it can be argued that market forces are weak, and that the "selection environment" is determined largely by professional judgments, and by political processes that regulate how much professionals in the sector have to spend. The analytic problem, then is to identify how these forces define "fitness."

8.3 Evolutionary theories of economic growth fueled by technical advance

The body of evolutionary theorizing considered in this section differs from that discussed above in at least three respects.

First, the theorizing is more complex in the sense that it involves a number of different variables, and the focus is on their co-evolution.

Second, the theory is expressed mathematically; in some cases the logical connections are developed as theorems, while in others they are explored through simulation methods.

Third, while motivated by empirical understanding of certain key processes and phenomena, and a desire to build the essence of that understanding into a theory, the theorizing discussed here has been motivated, as well, by the presence of, and the authors' strong dissatisfaction with, a widely-recognized and accepted theory that, in the authors' view, did not square with that empirical understanding. In the case that will be examined in some detail, the theory is neo-classical growth theory. And the phenomena that theory allegedly misspecifies is technological advance.

Virtually all economists studying economic growth recognize technological advance as the key driving factor. And, as I have noted, virtually all serious scholars of technical advance have stressed the uncertainty, the differences of opinion among experts, the surprises, that mark the process. Most knowledgeable scholars agree with Vincenti that the process must be understood as an evolutionary one. However, neo-classical growth theory, while recognizing the centrality of technological advance, represses its evolutionary nature. This tension has been the primary motivation of the scholars whose work is described in this section.

On the other hand, neo-classical growth theory does a reasonably good job of explaining, or at least in being consistent with, a number of the macroeconomic patterns of experienced economic growth; in particular the correlated rise of *per capita* incomes and worker productivity, growing capital intensity, and rising wage rates, along with a relatively constant rate of return on capital. The challenge faced by the authors considered here has been to devise a theory of growth which is capable of explaining the observed macroeconomic patterns, but on the basis of an evolutionary theory of technical change rather than one that presumes continuing equilibrium.

Without any exception I know, the evolutionary theories of economic growth that have been developed all draw inspiration from Joseph Schumpeter's *Capitalism, Socialism and Democracy* (1976, first published 1942). In that work, Schumpeter developed a theory of endogenous technological advance, resulting from the investments made by business firms to better or stay level with their rivals. The earliest class of formal evolutionary growth models based on these ideas was developed by myself and Winter (1974, 1982), and because it has provided much of the base for subsequent work, I shall concentrate on it. However, I also will consider variants or extensions that have been developed by others.

In these models, firms are the key actors. Firms are, from one point of view, the entities that are more or less fit, in this case more or less profitable. But from another point of view firms can be regarded as merely the incubators and carriers of "technologies" and other practices that determine "what they do" and "how productively" in particular circumstances. Winter and I have used the term "routines" to denote these. The concept of routines is analytically similar to the genes in biological theory, or the memes or culturgens in sociobiology.

The term "routine" connotes, deliberately, behavior that is conducted without much explicit thinking about it, as habits or customs. On the other hand, within these models routines can be understood as the behaviors deemed appropriate and effective in the settings where they are invoked. Indeed they are the product of processes that involve profit-oriented learning and selection. Metaphorically, the routines employed by a firm at any time can be regarded as the best it "knows and can do." To employ them is rational in that sense, even though the firm did not go through any attempt to compare its prevailing routines with all possible alternative ones. Whether that translates into "optimizing" behavior depends on what one means by that term. (For a fine discussion of this issue in biology and in economics, see Paul Schoemaker 1991.)

These models generally involve three different kinds of firm "routines." First, there are those that might be called "standard operating procedures," those that determine how and how much a firm produces under various circumstances, given its capital stock and other constraints on its actions that are fixed in the short run. Prominent among these are technologies. Second, there are routines that determine the investment behavior of the firm, the equations that govern its growth or decline (measured in terms of its capital stock) as a function of its profits, and perhaps other variables. Third, the deliberative processes of the firm, those that involve searching for better ways of doing things, also are viewed as guided by routines. While in principle within these models search behavior could be focused on, any one of the firms prevailing routines – its technologies, or other standard operating procedures, its investment rule, or even its prevailing search procedures – in practice, in all of them search is assumed to be oriented to uncover new production techniques or to improve prevailing ones. Winter and I have found it convenient to call such search R & D.

Firm search processes provide the source of differential fitness; firms whose R & D turn up better technologies will earn profits and grow relative to their competitors. But R & D also tends to bind firms together as a community because in these models a firm's R & D partly attends to what its competitors are doing, and profitable innovations are, with a lag, imitated by other firms in the industry.

The firm, or rather the collection of firms in the industry, perhaps involving new firms coming into the industry and old ones exiting, is viewed as operating within an exogenously-determined environment. The profitability of any firm is determined by what it is doing, and what its competitors do, given the environment. Generally the environment can be interpreted as a "market," or set of markets.

Note that in the theory that has been sketched above, just as routines are analogous to genes, firms are analogous to phenotypes, or particular organisms, in biological evolutionary theory, but there are profound differences. First, firms do not have a natural life span, and not all ultimately die. Neither can they be regarded as having a natural size. Some may be big, some small. Thus in assessing the relative importance of a particular routine in the industry mix, or analyzing whether it is expanding or contracting in relative use, it is not sufficient to "count" the firms employing it. One must consider their size, or whether they are growing or contracting. Second, unlike phenotypes (living organisms) that are stuck with their genes, firms are not stuck with their routines. Indeed they have built in mechanisms for changing them.

The logic of these models defines a dynamic stochastic system. It can be modeled as a complex Markov process. A standard iteration can be described as follows.

At any moment of time all firms can be characterized by their capital stocks and prevailing routines. Decision rules keyed to market conditions look to those conditions "last period." Inputs employed and outputs produced by all firms then are determined. The market then determines prices. Given the technology and other routines used by each firm, each firm's profitability then is determined, and the investment rule then determines how much each firm expands or contracts. Search routines focus on one or another aspect of the firm's behavior and capabilities, and (stochastically) come up with proposed modifications which may or may not be adopted. The system is now ready for next period's iteration.

Within this class of models, "profitability" determines the "fitness" of technology, and of firms, and firms are the only organizational actors. These observations call attention to the fact that this theory would seem to apply only to economic sectors where the market provides the (or the dominant) selection mechanism winnowing on technologies and firms. It is not well-suited for dealing with sectors like medical care, or defense, where professional judgments, or political process, determine what is fit and what is not. Selection environments clearly differ from sector to sector, and it would seem that these differences need to be understood and built into sectoral level analyses. (For an elaboration of this point, see Nelson and Winter 1974, 1982.)

However, the central purpose of the models considered in this section is to explain economic growth at a macroeconomic level. Thus a fundamental question about them is this. Can they generate, and hence in a sense explain, the rising output per worker, growing capital intensity, rising real wages, and a relatively constant rate of return on capital, that have been the standard pattern in advanced industrial nations and that neo-classical growth theory seems to explain? The answer is that they can, and in ways that to many economists seems a much more plausible story than the neo-classical account.

Within these models a successful technological innovation generates profits for the firm making it, and leads to capital formation and growth of the firm. Firm growth generally is sufficient to outweigh any decline in employment per unit of output associated with productivity growth, and hence results in an increase in the demand for labor, which pulls up the real wage rate. This latter consequence means that capital using but labor-saving innovations now become more profitable, and when by chance they appear as a result of a "search," they will be adopted, thus pulling up the level of capital intensity in the economy. At the same time that labor productivity, real wages, and capital intensity are rising, the same mechanisms hold down the rate of return on capital. If the profit rate rises, say because of the creation of especially productive new technology, the high profits will induce an investment boom, which will pull up wages, and drive capital returns back down.

These deductions of evolutionary growth theory would not surprise an advocate of neo-classical theory. On the surface they appear similar to those of neo-classical growth theory. However, if one looks beneath the surface one can see that the mechanisms in fact are very different. In particular, one theory is based on the conception of a moving equilibrium, and the other most emphatically is not.

And if one takes a closer look, it becomes clear that evolutionary theory enables one to see, to expect, phenomena to which neo-classical theory is blind, or denies. At the same time that the model generates "macro" time series that resemble the actual data, beneath the aggregate at any time there is considerable variation among firms in the technologies they are using, their productivity, and their profitability. Within this model more productive and profitable techniques tend to replace less productive ones, through two mechanisms. Firms using more profitable technologies grow. And more profitable technologies tend to be imitated and adopted by firms who had been using less profitable ones. Thus the theory is consistent with both the large body of empirical work that has documented considerable and persistent intra-industry inter-firm dispersion (e.g. Richard Rumelt 1991 and Mueller 1989) and with what is known empirically about the diffusion of new techniques (see e.g., Stanley Metcalfe 1988). Neo-classical growth theories have trouble being consistent with these elements of economic growth as we have experienced it.

Metcalfe (1988, 1992) and Metcalfe and Gibbons (1989) have developed evolutionary growth models focusing on diffusion of techniques. These authors repress the stochastic element in the introduction of new technologies that was prominent in the models described above and, in effect, work with a given and fixed set of technologies. However, within these models each of the individual technologies may be improving over time, possibly at different rates. At the same time, firms are tending to allocate their investment portfolios more heavily toward the more profitable technologies than toward the less. As a result, rising productivity in the industry as a whole, and measured aggregate "technical advance," is the consequence of two different kinds of forces. One is the improvement of the individual technologies. The other is the expansion of use of the more productive technologies relative to the less productive ones.

Both groups of authors point out that the latter phenomenon is likely to be a more potent source of productivity growth when there is prevailing large variation in the productivity of technologies in wide use, than when the best technology already dominates in use. Thus the aggregate growth performance of the economy is strongly related to the prevailing variation beneath the aggregate.

The model by Gerald Silverberg, Giovanni Dosi, and Luigi Orsenigo (1988) develops the basic theoretical notions introduced in this section in another direction. In their model there are only two technologies. One is potentially better than the other, but that potential will not be achieved unless effort is put into improving prevailing practice. Rather than incorporating a separate "search" activity, in Silverberg *et al.* a firm improves its prevailing procedures (technologies) through learning associated with operation. What a firm learns is reflected in its increased productivity in using that technology, but some of the learning "leaks out" and enables others using that technology to improve their productivity for free, as it were.

In contrast with the other models considered in this section where firms do not "look forward" to anticipate future developments, in the model of Silverberg *et al.*, firms, or at least some of them, recognize that the technology that initially is behind in productivity is potentially the better technology, and also that they can gain advantage over their competitors if they invest in using and learning with it. In contrast with the Nelson–Winter model, a firm may employ some of both technologies, and hence may use some of its profits from using the prevailing best technology to invest in experience with presently inferior technology that is potentially the best. If no firm does this, then of course the potential of the potentially better technology never will be realized.

An early "innovator" may come out a winner, if it learns rapidly, and little of its learning "spills out,' or its competitors are sluggish in getting into the new technology themselves. On the other hand, it may come out a loser, if its learning is slow and hence the cost of operating the new technology remains high, or most of its learning "spills out," and its competitors get in a timely manner, taking advantage for free of the spillover.

Several other evolutionary growth models have been developed. Gunnar Eliasson and colleagues have been constructing over the years a very detailed evolutionary model calibration of the Swedish economy. (See Eliasson's chapter in Day and Eliasson 1986.) Francesca Chiaramonte and Dosi (1993) have recently blended into the Silverberg–Dosi–Orsenigo model elements of the Nelson–Winter assumptions about stochastic search for new techniques. Katsuhito Iwai (1984) and John Conlisk (1989) also have published models in this class.

8.4 Some methodological issues

The structure of the evolutionary theorizing I have described in the last two sections obviously represents a sharp break from that which has become standard in modern economics. The analyses play down the role of informed human foresight in determining what happens. Rather, without denying that human knowledge and purpose play a role, the stress is on the variety of different actions that individuals and organizations take at any time, often in response to the same basic stimuli. The processes of change involve, in an essential way, feedback from the consequences of those actions which, in some cases, cause change in behavior on the part of the individual actors, and in some cases involve the expansion or decline in the organization associated with particular actions. The rationality of the actors is most emphatically "bounded."

The divergence from the assumptions of standard economic theory perhaps can be rationalized through recognizing that the emphasis in the evolutionary theories considered here is on processes of change, and the change processes assumed involve disequilibrium in a fundamental way. Thus the assumptions about human behavior are similar to those in evolutionary game theory when the focus in on "out of equilibrium" context. However, it should be recognized that when and if the evolutionary processes described earlier reach a steady state or equilibrium, the interpretation of that equilibrium here is much more akin to the biologist's conception of an "evolutionarily stable strategy" than to an economist's concept of "profit- or utility-maximizing behavior," at least if the latter presumes that the actors are consciously contemplating a wide range of alternative actions.

The kind of evolutionary economic theory I described shares a general perspective with the branch of evolutionary economic theory coming from biology. There is by now an extensive body of evolutionary writing concerned with the development of the human brain, the human "mind," language and other attributes that enable humans to communicate with each other on a much richer basis than do other animals, and which permit culture to evolve. Human consciousness and ability to reason are highlighted in these writings. The power of these attributes to enhance human learning capacity is stressed. But nowhere is it proposed that human mind, and socially acquired and developed understanding, are sufficient to enable humans to understand fully the world in which they reside. Rather, the emphasis is on how they enhance human ability to adapt to the parts of the world with which they become familiar through accumulated experience, and to learn relatively rapidly to cope with new circumstances, and new situations. The biological argument is most emphatically about the evolution of a human rationality that is "bounded."

Another difference in the models described above and the contemporary standard in economics, but also with much of evolutionary game theory, and with many of the new models that exploit non-linear mathematics, is the strong proclivity to address complex empirical phenomena, and to keep the empirical complexity in mind throughout the analysis. This does not mean that the analyst eschews simple models focused on "special cases" or designed to explore highly simplified abstractions of the real phenomena in question. However, these tend to be viewed as thinking aids, and ways of exploring various logical connections, and more generally as scaffolding that will fall or be pulled away when the analyst tries to express what he or she thinks "really is going on."

Winter and I feel strongly regarding the merits of this philosophy for doing economic theory. We have couched our argument in terms of the relationship between formal theory, and appreciative theory.

We have proposed that most of the solid understanding economists possess is in the form of what we have called "appreciative theory," which is causal analysis quite close to the empirical phenomena and policy issues in focus. Appreciative theory represents what the economist studying an issue believes is "really going on." In contrast, formal theory is more abstract, and laid out with a certain distance from the empirical phenomena under study. Formal theory encompasses only a small portion of what economists know about economic phenomena, and even that portion is a highly stylized version of what really is known. This position has led us to the argument that, to be really useful in advancing economic understanding, formal theory must be able to engage in dialogue, as it were, with the appreciative theory, which is where most of our understanding really resides.

Recently, Winter and I, in collaboration with Franco Malerba and Luigi Orsenigo, have developed these arguments further in the context of what we have called "history-friendly evolutionary models." The basic philosophy we have articulated there is to use the appreciative theoretic arguments put forth by empirical scholars of certain phenomena to explain the patterns they describe as the target for formal modeling. From this perspective, the task of formal modeling is to characterize those appreciative theoretic arguments in abstract form, that is true to the gist of those arguments, but to formalize them so that their logic can be checked out. Thus formal theorizing is viewed, explicitly, as a handmaiden to appreciative theorizing.

I realize very well that this view of the role of formal modeling, or more generally of the nature of productive theorizing in economics, and in social science more generally, is strongly at odds with much of contemporary thought. That is good reason for stating, and highlighting, it here.

References

Basalla, George (1988) *The Evolution of Technology*. Cambridge: Cambridge University Press.

Bijker, Wiebe E. (1995) *Bicycles, Bakelites, and Bulbs: Towards a Theory of Sociotechnical Change*. Cambridge, MA: MIT Press.

Bijker, Wiebe E., Thomas P. Hughes and Trevor J. Pinch (1987) *The Social Construction of Technological Systems*. Cambridge, MA: MIT Press.

Boyd, Robert and Peter J. Richerson (1985) *Culture and the Evolutionary Process*. Chicago: The University of Chicago Press.

Campbell, Donald (1960) Blind variation and selective retention in creative thought as in other knowledge processes. *Psychological Rev.* 67: 380–400.

—— (1974) Evolutionary epistemology. In Paul A Schilpp (ed) *The Philosophy of Karl Popper*. La Salle, IL: Open Court.

Cavalli-Sforza, Luigi L. and Marcus W. Feldman (1981) *Cultural Transmission and Evolution: A Quantitative Approach*. Princeton: Princeton University Press.

Chandler, Alfred D. (1962) *Strategy and Structure: Chapters in the History of Industrial Enterprise*. Cambridge, MA: Harvard University Press.

—— (1990) *Scale and Scope: The Dynamics of Industrial Capitalism*. Cambridge, MA: Harvard University Press.

Chiaromonte, Francesca and Giovanni Dosi (1993) Heterogeneity, Competition, and macroeconomic dynamics. *Structural Change and Economic Dynamics* 4: 39–63.

Conlisk, John (1989) An aggregate model of technical change. *Quart. J. Econ* 104(4): 787–821.

Day, Richard H. and Gunnar Eliasson (1986) *The Dynamics of Market Economies*. Amsterdam: North Holland.

Dosi, Giovanni *et al.* (eds) (1988) *Technical Change and Economic Theory*. London: Pinter

Fligstein, Neil (1990) *The Transformation of Corporate Control*. Cambridge, MA: Harvard University Press.

Freeman, Christopher (1974) *The Economics of Industrial Innovation*. London: Penguin.

Hull, David (1988) *Science as a Process*. Chicago: The University of Chicago Press.

Iwai, Katsuhito (1984) Schumpeterian dynamics. Part I." *J. Econ. Behav. Organ* 5(2): 159–90.

Kuhn, Thomas S. (1970) *The Structure of Scientific Revolutions*. Chicago: The University of Chicago Press.

Lakatos, Imre (1970) Falsification and the methodology of scientific research programmes. In Imre Lakatos and Alan Musgrave (eds) *Criticism and the Growth of Knowledge*. New York: Cambridge University Press.

Latour, Bruno (1986) *Science in Action*. London: Milton Keynes Press.

Lumsden, Charles J. and Edward O. Wilson (1981) *Genes, Mind, and Culture*. Cambridge, MA: Harvard University Press

Maynard Smith, John (1982) *Evolution and the Theory of Games*. Cambridge: Cambridge University Press.

Metcalfe, Stanley (1988) The diffusion of innovation: an interpretative survey. In Giovanni Dosi *et al. Technical Change and Economic Theory*. London: Pinter.

—— (1992) Variety, structure, and change: an evolutionary perspective on the competitive process. *Revue d'Economie Industrielle* 59: 46–61.

Metcalfe, Stanley and Michael Gibbons (1989) Technology, variety and organization. In Richard S. Rosenbloom and Robert A. Burgelman (eds) *Research on Technological Innovations, Management and Policy*. JAI Press

Mokyr, Joel (1990) *The Lever of Riches*. New York: Oxford University Press.

Mueller, Dennis (1989) *Public Choice II*. Cambridge: Cambridge University Press.

Nelson, Richard R. (1995) Recent evolutionary theorizing about economic change. *Journal of Economic Literature* March: 48–90.

Nelson, Richard R. and Sidney Winter (1974) Neoclassical vs. Evolutionary theories of economic growth: critique and prospectus. *Econ. J* 84(336): 886–905.

—— *An Evolutionary Theory of Economic Change*, Cambridge, MA: Harvard University Press.

Plotkin, Henry C. (1982) *Learning, Development, and Culture: Essays in Evolutionary Epistemology*. New York: John Wiley.

Popper, Karl R. (1968) *Conjectures and Refutation: The Growth of Scientific Knowledge*. New York: Harper Torchbooks.

Rosenberg, Nathan (1976) *Perspectives on Technology*. Cambridge: Cambridge University Press.

Rumelt, Richard P. (1991) How much does industry matter? *Strategic Management Journal* 12(3): 167–85.

Schoemaker, Paul J. (1991) The quest for optimality: a positive heuristic of science? *Behavioral and Brain Sciences* 14(2): 205–45.

Schumpeter, Joseph A. (1976[1942]) *Capitalism, Socialism, and Democracy*. 5th edn. London: George Allen & Unwin

Silverberg, Gerald, Giovanni, Dosi and Luigi Orsenigo (1988) Innovation, diversity and diffusion: a self organizing model. *Econ. J* 98(393): 1032–54.

Tushman, Michael and Lori Rosenkopf (1992) Organizational determinants of technological change: toward a sociology of technological evolution. *Research in Organizational Behavior* 14: 311–47.

Vincenti, Walter (1990) *What Engineers Know and How They Know It?*. Baltimore: Johns Hopkins Press.

—— (1994) The retractable airplane landing gear and the Northrup anomaly: variation-selection and the shaping of technology. *Technology and Culture*. 35: 1–33.

Williamson, Oliver E. (1985) *The Economic Institutions of Capitalism*. New York: Free Press.

9 Variety and irreversibility in scientific and technological systems

The evolution of an industry network

Fabio Pammolli, Luigi Orsenigo and Massimo Riccaboni

9.1 Introduction

Networks of collaborative relationships among firms have attracted a great deal of attention in recent times among sociologists, organizational theorists and industrial economists.

In particular, it is now widely recognized that collaborative relationships are an important form of organization of innovative activities.

However, one can find in the literature widely different interpretations of the nature, motivations, structure and functions of these networks, ranging from more sociologically oriented approaches to economic explanations based on (various mixes of) alternative theoretical backgrounds, e.g. transaction costs, contract theories, game theory and competence-based accounts of firms' organization.

In turn, these interpretations generate widely different predictions about the evolution of collaborative relationships over time.

For example, with reference to the case of biotechnology, collaborative relations are often considered as a transient phenomenon, bound to decrease in scale and scope as the technology matures and as higher degrees of vertical integration are established in the industry (Pisano, 1991).

In a rather different perspective, the role played by scientific knowledge in pharmaceutical research is stressed and the nature and properties of the learning processes fuel the emergence and evolution of networks. In this vein, collaborations represent a new form of organization of innovative activities, which are emerging in response to the increasingly codified and abstract nature of the knowledge bases on which innovations draw (Arora and Gambardella,1994; Gambardella, 1995). To be sure, substantial market failures exist in the exchange of a commodity like information. However, the abstract and codified nature of science makes it possible, in principle, to separate the innovative process in different vertical stages. Thus, the innovative process can be adequately represented as a sequence going downstream from science to marketing, in which division of labor can occur at any stage of the process. Different types of institutions tend to specialize in the stage of the innovative process in which they are more efficient: universities in the first stage, small firms in the second, big established firms in the third. In this view, then, a network of ties between these actors can provide the necessary coordination of the innovative process. Collaborations are likely to be a permanent feature of the industry, with a large (and possibly continuously expanding) number of entities interacting with an equally large number of other entities, generating an intricate network within which each subject specializes in particular technological areas or stages of the innovative process getting benefits from an increasing division of innovative labor.

Finally, according to some more radical interpretations, the complex and interdisciplinary nature of relevant knowledge bases in pharmaceutical R&D tends to make technological innovations the outcome of interactions and cooperation among different types of agents commanding complementary resources and competencies (Orsenigo, 1989; Pisano, 1991; Pammolli, 1996). In this perspective, it has also been suggested that the locus of innovation (and the proper unit of analysis) is no longer a firm, but a network of differentiated agents (see Powell, Koput, Smith-Doerr, 1996). In this case, the direction of causation is reversed: it is the structure of the network and the position of agents within it that fundamentally determine agents' access to relevant sources of scientific and technological knowledge and therefore innovative activities and performances (see also Walker *et al.* 1997).

However, albeit with some notable exceptions (see Powell, Doput and Smith-Doerr, 1996; Walker, Kogut and Shan, 1997), it has proved very difficult to provide strong empirical evidence in support or against these different accounts. In fact, while the natural test bed of these different interpretations should be based on the observation of network dynamics over time, most of the analyses are static in nature or perform comparative statics exercises. On the contrary, very little has been done, at the empirical level, on the dynamics of collaborative relationships, i.e. how are they formed, how do they change over time, to which sort of configuration do they converge at, if any.

Moreover, the theory of the dynamics of networks is still in its infancy and does not yet provide robust conclusions (see Suitor, Wellman and Morgan, 1997).

We do not review here this rapidly expanding and complex literature. However, it is possible to observe that despite their differences, most of these approaches and explanations seem to agree in principle that, particularly in high growth, technology intensive industries, networks of collaborative relationships have to be analyzed as organizational devices for the coordination of heterogeneous learning processes by agents endowed by different skills, competencies, access to information and assets.

Thus, learning ought to be a central concern in the analysis of collaborative relationships. Beyond a rather generic agreement, though, available empirical analyses do not address the specific nature and properties of the underlying knowledge bases and search activities that should be used as explanatory constructs. Consequently, it becomes hard to understand clearly what are the implied relationships (if any) between the structure and functions of the network and its evolution on the one hand and the fundamental features of the relevant learning processes on the other.

Starting from this state of affairs, we try to move a step forward in the direction of establishing a closer connection between the structure and evolution of knowledge and the structure and evolution of organizational forms in innovative activities.

We focus on the case of the pharmaceutical industry after the "molecular biology revolution" (Henderson, Orsenigo and Pisano, 1997; Pammolli, 1996).

The fundamental role of technological innovation and the development of a dense network of collaborative relationships among a variety of different actors have been a distinctive feature of the structural evolution of this industry and, in fact, several studies have provided sound analyses of the determinants of collaboration as well as of the basic structural features of the network (Barley, Freeman and Hybels, 1992; Kogut, Shan and Walker, 1992; Arora and Gambardella, 1994; Gambardella 1995; Zucker and Darby, 1995; Powell, Doput and Smith-Doerr, 1996; Pammolli, 1996; Orsenigo, Pammolli and Riccaboni, 1996).

As compared to the existing literature, this paper is characterized by its explicit focus on the dynamics of the network. On one hand, we specify some fundamental properties of search activities and learning processes that drive the evolution of the relevant knowledge bases in pharmaceutical R&D after the "molecular biology revolution" (see Henderson, Orsenigo and Pisano, 1997). On the other hand, we analyze the relevant features of the structure and the evolution of the industry network. We use a comprehensive dataset, built by integrating several well reputed sources in the industry, covering the most important R&D collaborations in place between established pharmaceutical and new biotechnology firms, worldwide. For each collaborative agreement, the dataset traces the identity and age of constituent firms. Therefore, it is possible to analyze the structure of the network at different points in time, and investigate the structure of collaborations opened by firms of different generations. For the analysis of the dynamics of the network over time we follow a strategy which is original in at least two respects. First, we define the relevant time intervals by following the inner dynamics of change in the industry, according to a descriptor which is causally related to the dynamics itself. In fact, during the last twenty years the pace of change in the industry has been determined by clearly detectable waves of entry of new firms, which in turn reflect the timing of generation of new hypotheses following progress in science. By looking at entry rates of new firms in the period under analysis, we identify three main subperiods, separated by peaks of entry. Second, we analyze the relational behavior of firms according to the period in which they were born: by looking at the propensity of each firm to enter into relation with firms that were born in the same or in a different period, we are able to identify some deep determinants of change of network structure. With regards to network structure, we find that, while the size of the network increases over time due to net flows of entry, its topological properties remain relatively unchanged. In fact, the evolution of the network has occurred without relevant deformations in the core- periphery profile. With regards to age-dependent propensity to collaborate, we find that the extent of inter-generational collaboration is much more significant than intra-generational collaboration. In addition, the propensity of firms of a given generation to enter into collaboration with firms of a different generation increases with the distance between the two, while the total number of intra-generational collaborations decreases over time and, moreover, tends to decrease for most recent generations. In the paper we offer a unitary and coherent explanation for both bodies of evidence. We claim that a striking isomorphism can be found between the cognitive structure underlying the dynamics of knowledge and the structure generated by the evolution of the network. After the "Molecular Biology Revolution" pharmaceutical research has witnessed a spectacular increase in the number of research projects originated by ex-ante plausible scientific hypotheses. The impact of science has been one of proliferation of increasingly more specialized hypotheses, following a tree-like structure, with an open-ended dynamics. In some cases, new hypotheses have generated totally new sub-disciplines, requiring new sets of search techniques, testing procedures, and skills. Due to the nature of search activities in pharmaceutical R&D after the Molecular Biology Revolution, over time entrants tend to be more and more specialized in terms of the scientific hypotheses they try to test, and the search techniques they employ. As it will be argued in the paper, these intrinsic characteristics of search activities and patterns of learning in pharmaceutical R&D may explain simultaneously why the network expands over time, why it remains nevertheless relatively stable in the core-periphery profile, and why entrants make agreements with incumbents or older NBFs, rather than with firms of the same generation.

Whilst these results are to be considered as preliminary, they are consistent with the suggestions of the "competence-based" theory of the firm (Nelson and Winter, 1982) and – at a different level of analysis – of the notion of "technological regimes" (Winter, 1984; Malerba and Orsenigo, 1996). Moreover, by claiming explicitly that there is a mapping that goes from the evolution of knowledge to the evolution of the network, the paper has the merit to offer some falsifiable propositions and, at the same time, generates further questions that are worth to be placed in the research agenda.

The paper is organized as follows.

Section 9.2 provides some background information on the history and scope of the "molecular biology revolution" and highlights the key features of discovery and development activities in the pharmaceutical industry after the emergence of biotechnology.

In Section 9.3, the fundamental features of the growth of knowledge in molecular biology are mapped into the evolution of the industry and the aggregate dynamics of the structure of the network. Standard algebraic network analysis techniques – which are intrinsically static in nature – are used in such a way to produce some information on the dynamics of the network over time.

The presentation of the main findings of the analysis and the discussion of the implications for the study of organization and industrial dynamics close the paper.

9.2 The essentials of drug discovery after the "molecular biology revolution"

The last twenty-five years witnessed a revolution in the biological sciences, with significant basic advances in molecular biology, cell biology, biochemistry, protein and peptide chemistry, physiology, pharmacology and other relevant scientific disciplines. In general, the application of molecular biology to pharmaceutical industry has had an enormous impact on the nature of pharmaceutical R&D, on the organizational capabilities required to introduce new drugs and on the patterns of industry evolution.

The case of the molecular biology revolution lends itself to a study of the detailed mechanisms of industrial transformation and of the co- evolution between scientific knowledge and organizational capabilities, industry structure and institutional settings (Henderson, Orsenigo, Pisano, 1997; Pammolli, 1996).

On one hand, the extent of the molecular biology revolution and the rise of biotechnology have been deeply affected by a set of country- specific and institutional factors (Orsenigo, 1989). These include characteristics such as industry structure, firms' diversification strategies, degrees of industrial concentration and patterns of competition, etc., as well as the public policies that are placed to support innovative activities. Moreover, other institutional dimensions have played an important role: the quality and structure of the scientific and financial systems, patent laws, regulation concerning research, product approval and prices, and public reactions towards genetic engineering.

On the other hand, the evolution of the institutional arrangements that govern research activities in pharmaceutical research after the "molecular biology revolution" can be explained with reference to the fundamental features of the relevant knowledge bases and learning processes in this field. It is our contention that a detailed, fine-grained analysis of the process of discovery in pharmaceutical research after the molecular biology revolution is of invaluable importance for building a rich explanation of the evolution of the industry.

In this perspective, it is possible to say that the application of molecular biology to drug research has followed the success, in the biomedical sciences, of a scientific paradigm according to which the achievement of deeper knowledge on the nature of biological processes that are going on into the human organism can lead to the development of powerful and selective therapeutic solutions.

As a consequence, the short-term objective of drug research, i.e. the creation of new medicinal agents to meet current therapeutic needs, has started to be strongly connected with a long-term objective of biomedical research, that is the generation of knowledge to help us to understand some of the phenomena associated with the complex systems that confront drug researchers (electrons, atoms, molecules, macromolecules, cells, organisms) (see Testa, Meyer, 1995: 37).

In fact, the so-called "molecularization" of physiology, of pathology and of pharmacology corresponds to a principle according to which for the development of new powerful and selective drugs search has to penetrate deeply into the human organism to unravel the biochemical interactions at the cellular, infra-cellular and, most, important, at the molecular level (see Vos, 1991).

On this, it is important to observe that according to the molecular biology paradigm the route to understanding of human organism (nature) is through the dissection of the system to its parts, followed by the study of these parts. This dissection is also performed in time, which is broken and sampled in a number of snapshots. "In general, then, according to this view, the properties of the whole – and hence its behavior – are the sum of the properties of the parts. This philosophy has had profound effect on the methods of inquiry (. . .). It has guided scientist to pursue the pattern of study: dissect, identify, classify, and dissect further. The logical extension of this approach is to search for the ultimate, ahistoric particle as the fountainhead of creation (. . .)" (Testa, Meyer, 1995: 6).

In other words, according to the molecular biology paradigm, pathologies can be analyzed in terms of specific alterations of the molecules that constitute the human organism. In this perspective, for the development of new powerful and selective drugs it is necessary to evolve theories which give a continually "deeper" explanation of the processes which take place at higher levels of the organization of matter into the organism.

Without doubt, fundamental theories like the oncogen theory in cancer research or the antibody-antigen theory in immunology can lead to deeper knowledge and better explanation of the processes in the human organism, revealing deeper lying structures which are the basis for the observed symptoms of a certain disease.

Nevertheless, the effects on the research of new drugs of these advances on the scientific knowledge bases need to be analyzed in depth.

In general, a theory T_2 is "more fundamental" than a theory T_1 if it explains a sequence of causal events longer and "more complex" than the one explained by T_1.

In terms of Figure 9.1, T_1 explains the events chain B-C-D-(E/F), while T_2 poses on the discovery of the mechanism A, and then it explains both the chains A-G-H-I-(E) and A-B-C-D-(E/F).

In other words, the discovery of A, that involves a physiological mechanism at a deeper level of organization of the matter, allows to collapse into a common explanation two physiological processes that were previously regarded as independent.

According to theory T_1, the pathology E depends on (is influenced by) a sequence of biological mechanisms localized in B-C-D. Theory T_1 then identifies a causal sequence and indicates some possible points of intervention in the treatment of E.

Theory T_2 is more general and claims that the A is at the root both of the sequence B-C-D-E and a new sequence, before considered independent, G-H-I (E). If T_2 is true, then the explanation of two different causal chains, B-D-C-E (F) and G-H-I-E (F) is unified by a deeper unitary principle, identified in A.

Hence, from the point of view of scientific explanation, the transition from T_1 to T_2 and the discovery of A can be considered a manifestation of a process of convergence.

If T_2 holds, moreover, in order to treat E(F) it is possible to search, besides A, for

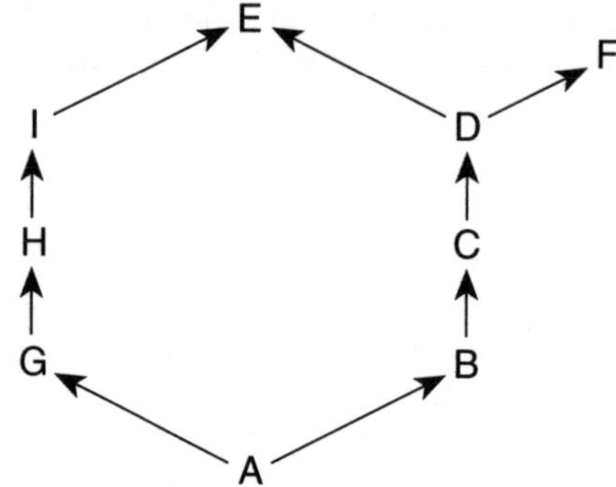

Figure 9.1

molecules which interfere with both the mechanisms B-C-D and the mechanisms G-H-I. If T_2 is more fundamental than T_1, then T_2 contains a longer and more complex chain of causal events.

As a consequence, with reference to the range of possibilities for therapeutic intervention, the *convergence* at the level of scientific explanation guaranteed by the progress of theoretical knowledge corresponds to the identification of a longer and more complex chain of causal events. This achievement can lead to a process of *divergence*, with an increase in the number of possibilities to intervene in the disease process.

At the same time, the progress of theoretical knowledge towards more fundamental explanations allows to identify a certain number of search trajectories that will not lead to the production of new drugs in the treatment of given pathologies (see also David, Mowery, Steinmuller, 1992; Arora, Gambardella, 1994). For example, T_2 permits to predict the failure of a possible program aiming to intervene in E through the physiological chain of events B-C-D.

In short, as knowledge – at the molecular and inframolecular level – on both the pathogenesis and the diseases mechanisms make progress (through the individuation of the structure and of some of the functions of genes and proteins), there is an increase of information on what it should not to be done. At the same time, a proliferation of the drug/receptor pairs to be explored is reported.

Over time, for every complex pathology such as viral infections, neurological disorders, autoimmune diseases and most solid cancers, at increasing levels of resolution, several mechanisms on which it turns out to be plausible to intervene are singled out (Pammolli, 1996).

In general, for every theoretical hypothesis on the etiology of a given pathology, the advances of knowledge and the development of new therapeutic treatments occur through the identification of specific objects, mechanisms, and objectives, embedded in a long and uncertain complex of experimental activities.

In turn, for every mechanism, several possible ways of intervention are usually identified, each of them associated to specific technical problems, heuristics, research tools and tests. Moreover, due to the high cospecialization between research techniques and targets, one observes a proliferation also in the number of trajectories, techniques and ex ante conceivable exploration strategies.

In sum, for most of the complex pathologies with the greatest unmet medical need, the inner dynamics of knowledge leads, at least in a first stage of indeterminate length, to a branching of a priori hypotheses on plausible research trajectories.

This dynamics creates *a dilemma*: by definition, "more fundamental theories explain more but, simultaneously, they multiply the number of points of entry for the discovery and the development of new therapeutic treatments" (Vos, 1991: 272), opening up new opportunities for specialization.

And, in fact, looking at the normal state of affairs at the forefront of drug research, one would almost invariably find individuals and groups with widely divergent opinions and research hypotheses, which determine strong irreversibilities, path dependencies and the possibility of ex post errors.

At the same time, the dynamics of knowledge in the field has an intrinsic hierarchical nature: starting from general hypotheses, more specific hypotheses come up and proliferate at lower and lower levels of a tree- like belief structure. Each new hypothesis poses on the validity of higher levels of the hierarchy. Findings of search activities carried out at lower levels can or cannot "corroborate" the more general hypotheses from which they were generated. However, individually, as they are unable to achieve ultimate results, they cannot falsify higher level beliefs. Whilst new scientific explanations and discoveries can lead to deeper knowledge and, moreover, more fundamental explanations of the nature of processes that happen in the human organism can focus search at a given level of resolution, the very same achievements generate new hierarchies of sub-hypotheses.

This structure of the evolution of knowledge can be seen as the result of the dominance, within the scientific community, of a reductionist stance according to which complex problem solving under conditions of strong substantive and procedural uncertainty calls for hierarchy and logical depth (Simon, 1969). At the same time, it reflects an "open ended" dynamics in which learning opportunities are continually generated, but what each agent can achieve at any level of the hierarchy is constrained by what he has previously learned at different levels of abstraction.

9.3 The evolution of interfirm network in biotechnology

In this section, the transformations in the organization of innovative activities following the evolution of the scientific and technological knowledge bases in the pharmaceutical industry after the "molecular biology revolution" have been studied starting from an analysis of license contracts and partnerships in R&D drawn up on a worldwide base in the period between 1978 and 1993.

Graph theory and numerical representations of networks are used to analyze the evolution of the relational structure that characterizes the development of innovative activities in pharmaceutical industry following the "molecular biology revolution" and the emergence of new biotechnology.

The analysis has been carried out using UCINET IV (Borgatti, Everett and Freeman) and MatLab software packages. The data base has been built integrating, for the years between 1978 and 1993, the information drawn from Bioscan, a yearly directory published six times a year by Oryx Press, with data provided by Arthur D. Little Inc. (*Spectrum*) and data recovered on annual reports and specialized press.

Bioscan lists information on a firm's ownership, its current products, and its research in progress. All information about agreements and the characteristics of organizations reported here are drawn from the 1988 and 1993 volumes. Our focus on research-driven companies in human therapeutics resulted in a sample of 223 independently owned companies. Afterwards, we identified the core of the network, eliminating 36 firms borne after January 1st 1991 and analyzing the trend of the 174 firms occupying more central positions among those alive in the final year of the monitored period. This solution allowed to take into account the total intensity of the relational activity of each firm and, in particular, the different potentialities of "control" of communication flows internal to the network in function of the occupied *position.*

The analysis has been focused on the network of collaborative agreements in R&D and on license contracts relating to molecules under development drawn up among the firms of the sample still alive at the end of the period. On the contrary, direct reference to the numerous informal relationships with single researchers, to collaborations with Universities, research centers and other firms, and to formal agreements referring only to the production and/or marketing areas, has been omitted.

Analyzing the patterns of entry by *NBF*s in pharmaceutical industry, three peaks have been identified, on 1981, 1984, and 1987 (see also Barley *et.al.*, 1992). Evidence indicates that after every founding peak the number of firms not stipulating collaborative agreements with other firms (*freestanding* firms) increased, while the number of relationships with universities and research centers did not decrease. After this initial period, the number of *freestanding* starts to decrease and, correspondingly, the number of interfirm collaborative agreements increases.

After this preliminary analysis, firms have been divided according to the year they were founded, to split the units in existence before the emergence of molecular biology from subsequent generations of *NBF*s That, in particular, in order to analyze the role played, in the structuring of the network, by firms that entered the industry in different moments of the process of proliferation and specification of research trajectories described in the previous paragraph.

Firms founded before 1973 have been classified as *incumbents* (*INC*s); firms founded between 1973 and 1980, before the entry peak registered in 1981, have been classified as *first generation biotechnology firms* (NBF_1); firms founded between 1981 and 1986, before the new entry peak of 1987, have been classified as *second generation biotechnology firms* (NBF_2); firms borne after 1987 have been classified as (NBF_3).

Moreover, firms have been grouped according to the periods in which they engaged in cooperative agreements. In this perspective, three different groups of agreements have been identified (C_1, C_2, C_3). C_1 indicates cooperative agreements drawn up before January 1st 1987: in this period (T_1) the network was composed of a relatively small number of incumbents and *NBFs*$_1$; C_2 indicates cooperative agreements drawn up between January 1st 1987 and January 1st 1991: in this second period (T_2) a relevant increasing of the number of agreements has been detected, following the entry pattern started from the 1987 peak; a high number of firms, in particular a lot of pharmaceutical incumbents and *NBFs*$_2$, formed their first agreements in this period; C_3 indicates cooperative agreements drawn up between January 1st 1991 and August 1st 1993.

The identification of four different generations of firms and of three periods in which they engaged in cooperative agreements allowed to use in a "dynamic settlement" some well-established techniques for the analysis of *positions* and *roles* within a graph (see Scott, 1991; Pattison, 1993; Wasserman, Faust, 1994).

The use of a *k-core* technique allowed to analyze the dynamics of positions occupied by firms and the structural evolution of the interfirm network. In a non-oriented graph, a *k-core* is a subgraph in which each node is adjacent to at least a minimum number *k* of the other nodes in the subgraph. In other words, a *k-core* analysis permits to distinguish the principal component (the maximally connected subgraph) from the secondary ones (the other connected subgraphs) in the graph.

By the stratification produced by the analysis of the k levels of decomposition one can identify the nodes that within the network play a function of *connectors* and, in particular, the areas of the graph containing *clique* structures. Therefore, the identified components define disconnected subgroups and capture the degree of fragmentation in the structure of the network.

For each of the three periods, the networks $G_i(n, r)$ have been reconstructed, where n indicates the number of firms which were alive in the period i, and r is the number of agreements drawn up among them during the same period.

The use of a *k-core* technique, which focus on nodal degree and requires all members of a cohesive subgroup to be adjacent to some minimum number of other subgroup members, allowed to partition firms into five mutually exclusive subgroups.

For the different periods considered, has been indicated with:

- *2A*: firms in the principal component of the network with at least two agreements;
- *A*: firms in the principal component of the network with only one agreement;
- *B*: firms in secondary components of the network;
- *F*: freestanding: firms alive in the considered period, but not present in the internal network of agreements;
- -: firms not yet alive.

The role played in the network by different types of firms has been reconstructed by organizing the overall structure into homogeneous groups through a *role equivalence* analysis.

Table 9.1 Descriptive statistics of network structure

	T_1	T_2	T_3
Centrality	5,59	5,70	5,17
Average	1,02	1,77	2,16
StandDev	1,04	2,12	2,19
Sum	112	292	376
Var	1,96	4,50	4,81
Min	0	0	0
Max	7	7	11
Number of firms	110	161	174
Number of firms with at least one agreement	46	98	136

The role equivalence analysis has been carried out through the following steps: at a first stage, all the firms have been put in the same group; afterwards, firms have been classified according to three relational periods, distinguishing the units that drew up new collaborative agreements in every one of the three periods (*role* 123), from those that drew up new agreements only in the second and third periods (*role* 23), from those that drew up new agreements only in the second period, and so on for the six possible combinations; finally, firms partitioned in the different groups have been further classified according to the role of the nodes with which they were related to (firms that in the third period drew up agreements only with units of *role* 23 have been collected in the same group and so on for every further typology).

Comprehensively, the analysis of the structure and the evolution of the network of collaborative agreements and the role equivalence analysis lead to the following considerations:

1. As shown in Table 9.1, *the dimension of the network has increased over time*, due to the entry of new firms and the increase in the average number of agreements per firm. This process reflects the opening of new technological opportunities driven by the evolution of scientific knowledge bases in the industry and the concurrent expansion of the startup set following the branching of research trajectories and techniques that has been discussed in Section 9.2. In fact, the number of firms in the network increased overtime, from 110 in the period before January 1st 1987 to 161 in the second period (until December 1990 included), to 174 in the third period (starting from January 1991).

2. *The evolution of the network has occurred without relevant deformations in the core-periphery profile.* In the three periods considered, the principal component of the network widened both in absolute and in relative values, from 46 firms (42% = 46/110) to 136 (78% = 136/174). Data shows an increasingly crowding process of the principal component by firms that play a role of connectors in it: 16 firms, equal to 15% (16/110) in period one; 57, equal to 35% (57/161) in period two; 86 firms, equal to 49% (86/174) in period three. Confirming the relative stability of the core-periphery profile over time, the

analysis of Table 9.2 allows to detect that the expansion of the principal component of the network has been coupled by the expansion of a relatively "turbulent" periphery, with several small secondary components, usually populated by NBFs. The centrality of the network remained relatively stable, with variations explicable in the light of the intensity and of the temporal sequence of entry patterns.

3. The evolution of the network has been characterized by a relatively *high structural stability* caused, among other things, by the absolute prevalence of long term agreements associated with the length of the process of discovering, developing, testing and commercializing biotechnology products (see Walker, Kogut and Shan, 1997). Data in Table 9.2 and the results of the *role equivalence* analysis relative to the first twenty-five firms for number of connections (Table 9.3), allow to observe that the firms that entered into the principal component in the first period (2*A*, *A*) drew up new agreements in all the three considered periods (I_{123}-type firms) and maintained their position until the end of the last period. In particular, it is possible to detect the structuring role carried out, starting from period 2, by a relatively small number of pharmaceutical incumbents that lagged the first *NBFs* in adopting the new drug discovery technologies. On the contrary, startups have much higher variability than established firms in number of relationships over time. More precisely, for *NBFs* of new generations, in spite of the high propensity to draw up collaborative agreements, *the entry in the principal component has become progressively more difficult* and, anyway, it did not happen on a permanent way. In fact, among the firms that stay in the principal component in T_3 and are included in the top 25 relation-intensive list, almost two thirds were in the core of the network since period T_1. At the same time, of the 58 firms that were freestanding at T_1, 41 entered the principal component at T_2. However, only 31 remained in the principal component, while 10 went back in a freestanding position. On the contrary, of the 46 firms that were in the principal component at T_1, only 6 exited and entered secondary components or went back in a freestanding position.

4. The analysis of Table 9.4 brings forth some further points. *Firms that drew up agreements in all the three periods considered* (I_{123}) *played an important role in the structuring of the network.* The average number of agreements per year, referring to the different classes of firms defined by local role equivalence (LRE) analysis, decreases significantly moving from the group of (I_{123}) to that of (I_{23}) and, finally, to that of (I_3). More precisely, moving from the group of (I_{123}), to that of (I_{23}), to that of (I_3), it is possible to observe, on the one side, an increase of the number of firms ($(I_{123}) = 21$; $(I_{23}) = 46$; $(I_3) = 63$) and, on the other side, a decrease of the average value of both the degree index and, especially, the normalized betweeness index (*nbetweeness*). Even accounting for the differences in terms of length of the relational period, (I_3) firms would have drawn, on average, 10 and 3 connections short, respectively, than (I_{123}) and (I_{23}). The average number of connections, as well as the minimum and

Table 9.2 Transition matrix across structural roles within the network

T_1	T_2		T_3			
			2*A*	*A*	*B*	*F*
2*A*16	2*A*	11	9	2	–	–
	A	3	2	1	–	–
	B	1	1	–	–	–
	F	1	–	1	–	–
*A*30	2*A*	18	12	2	2	2
	A	8	3	3	–	2
	B	1	1	–	–	–
	F	3	–	2	–	1
*B*6	2*A*	3	2	1	–	–
	A	1	–	–	–	1
	B	1	1	–	–	–
	F	1	1	–	–	–
*F*58	2*A*	21	12	5	–	4
	A	20	7	7	–	6
	B	4	3	–	–	1
	F	13	2	3	1	7
–64	2*A*	4	2	2	–	–
	A	9	4	1	1	3
	B	4	1	2	–	1
	F	34	18	12	–	4
	–	13	5	6	–	2

the maximum, are decreasing, with a contraction of the variance intervals, moving from (I_{123}), to (I_{23}), to (I_3). *New nodes tend to enter the network via "non redundant" connections with preexisting nodes.* This evidence is much more relevant as the increase of the average value of the n- betweenwess index has occurred in spite of a constant expansion of the network.

5. Data presented in Table 9.5 and the curves reported in Figure 9.2 allow to catch a low propensity to draw up R&D agreements among firms of the same generation. Table 9.5 shows the total number of agreements made in the period under observation. Each column shows the distribution of the number of agreements made by each generation of firms with firms of the same and different generations. Table 9.5 highlights three important findings of our analysis. First, it is possible to observe a low propensity to draw up agreements among firms of the same generation. In fact, intra-generational collaboration is evidently much less important than inter-generational collaboration. The proportion of agreements made between firms of the same generation is much less than the proportion that would result from a matching proportional to the number of firms of that generation out of the total. As an example, incumbent firms represent 31.6% of the total number of firms in the sample; however, agreements between incumbents account for only 13.2% of the total number of agreements made by incumbents (n =

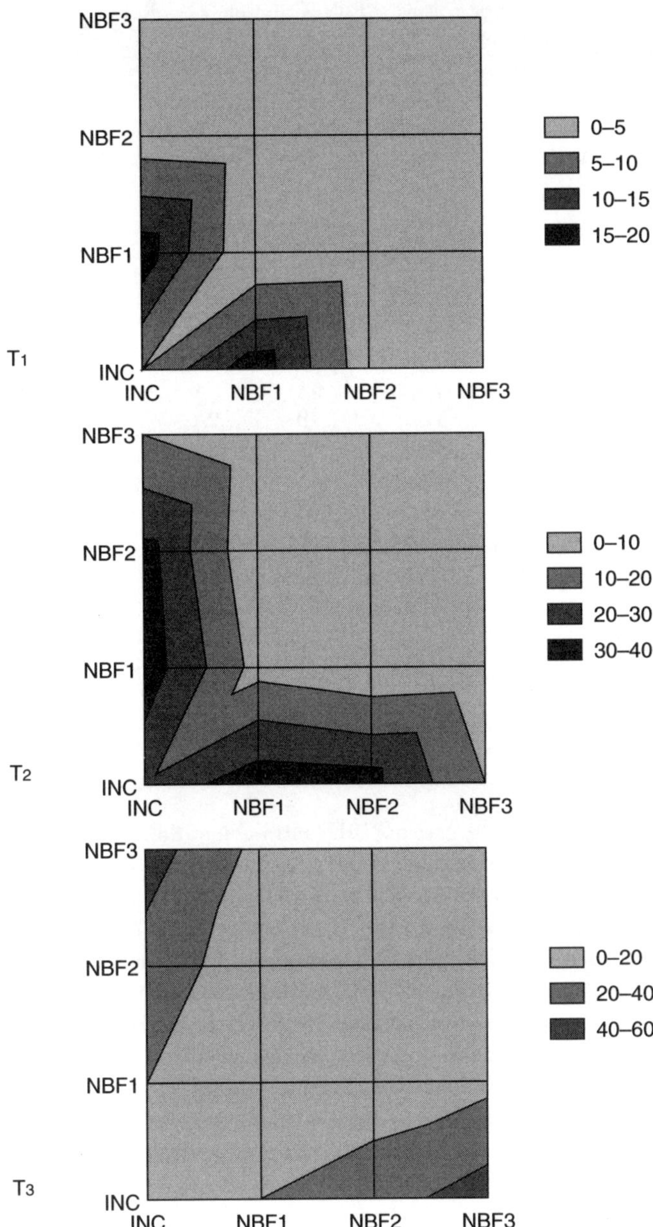

Figure 9.2 Intensity of intergeneration and intrageneration agreements

Table 9.3 Top 25 relation-intensive firms

Firms	Number of agreements	Role	Role T_1	Role T_2	Role T_3
Genentech	60	I_{123}	2A	2A	2A
Centocor	44	I_{123}	2A	2A	2A
EliLilly	44	I_{123}	2A	A	2A
Cambr.Bio.	43	I_{23}	F	2A	2A
Merck	40	I_{123}	A	2A	2A
Chiron	35	I_{123}	A	2A	2A
Abbott	33	I_{123}	2A	2A	2A
Enzon	33	I_{123}	A	2A	2A
Upjohn	30	I_{123}	B	2A	2A
Bri-Myers	30	I_{123}	A	2A	2A
Roche	28	I_{123}	2A	2A	2A
Green Cross	28	I_{123}	2A	A	A
Scios Nova	26	I_{23}	B	2A	2A
Pfizer	26	I_{123}	A	2A	2A
Sandoz	26	I_{123}	A	A	2A
E I DuPont	25	I_{123}	A	2A	2A
Am. Cy.	24	I_{23}	F	2A	2A
Biogen	24	I_{123}	2A	2A	2A
Sch-Plough	24	I_{123}	2A	A	2A
GenPhInt.	23	I_3	-	F	2A
War.-Lamb.	23	I_{123}	2A	2A	2A
Ciba	23	I_{123}	2A	2A	2A
J&J	21	I_{123}	B	2A	2A
Yamanouchi	21	I_{123}	2A	2A	A
AHP	20	I_{23}	F	2A	2A

235). Similarly, in the case of NBF_3, intra-generational agreements are only 5 (5.6% of the total number of agreements made by NBF_3), while the proportion of NBF3 is equal to 33.9% of total number of firms in the sample. In general, the proportion of agreements located in the diagonal of the matrix is much less than it would be if each firm of age i would make an agreement with a firm of the same generation according to the proportion of firms in that class out of the total. Second, the probability that two firms of the same generation enter into a collaborative agreement tends to decrease across generations. For example, while 12.1% of agreements made by NBF_1 is directed towards firms of the same generation, the figure drops to 1.3% and 5.6% for NBF_2 and NBF_3, respectively. As far as NBF_1 are concerned, it should be reminded that a relatively high proportion of intra-generational agreements are made between the few firms that have been able to become structurally similar to INCs into the network (Amgen, Biogen, Chiron, Genentech, Genzyme) and other firms of the same generation. Third, data presented in Table 9.5 confirm the structuring role played by INCs in that for the three generations of NBFs, 63.2% of agreements are

Table 9.4 Centrality indexes, according to the periods of relational activity

	I_{123}		I_{23}		I_3	
	Deg	*nBet*	*Deg*	*nBet*	*Deg*	*nBet*
Aver	26	3,8	13,8	1,41	5,6	0,2
StDev	12,89	2,60	8,62	1,62	4,04	0,41
Tot.	546	79,8	635	64,6	438	15,3
Min	6	0,10	2	0,01	2	0
Max	60	9,4	43	6,5	20	1,8
Md		1,81		1,27		0,80
n		21		46		63

Table 9.5 Intra-generational and inter-generational agreements

	INC	NBF_1	NBF_2	NBF_3	
INC (55)	31 (13.2%)	101 (64.3%)	51 (66.2%)	52 (58.5%)	235
NBF_1 (24)	101 (43%)	19 (12.1%)	15 (19.5%)	22 (24.7%)	157
NBF_2 (36)	51 (21.7%)	15 (9.6%)	1 (1.3%)	10 (11.2%)	77
NBF_3 (59)	52 (22.1%)	22 (14%)	10 (13%)	5 (5.6%)	89
(174)	235	157	77	89	

drawn with INCs (204/323). This finding is even more robust and significant taking into consideration that the available data sources tend inevitably to underestimate the number of agreements drawn by INCs as compared to the number of agreements made by NBFs.

6. So far, the discussed evidence is consistent with the hypothesis that posits a correspondence between the structure and evolution of relevant knowledge bases and the structure and evolution of the network of R&D agreements. In fact, the opening up of new opportunities generated by the growth of scientific knowledge in molecular biology fuels the entry of progressively more specialized firms. This increase in the degree of specialization across generations can be inferred by the observed asymmetry, in terms of propensity to enter into agreements with firms of the same or different generations, together with the increasing propensity to draw agreements with more "distant" firms. The mentioned correspondence gives origin to a peculiar dynamics, whose outcome can be captured by looking at Figure 9.2. Figure 9.2 is built by spreading the total number of agreements in each of the three periods according to generations, originating a landscape marked by level curves. Areas in dark show the location of peaks of relational intensity, while the proportion of the landscape covered by level curves gives an insight on the directions of the expansion of the network over time. As it is evident, areas with higher relational intensity always involve INCs. Moreover, the location of dark areas in the three periods moves following the sequence of waves of entry. After a first period in which INCs concentrated their relational activity mostly with NBF_1, one can observe a spread of agreements drawn with NBF_2 in T_2, and, finally, in T_3, a marked concentration towards

the corner of the landscape occupied by NBF_3. Moreover, the area close to the principal diagonal tends to be less and less populated by agreements as time goes by; that is, the probability that two firms of the same generation enter into a collaborative agreement is decreasing in time.

7. The above findings show both the central role played by *INCs* in the structuring of the network and the high cumulativeness that characterized the evolution of the relational structure over time. Starting from these results, the analysis of the degree of structural stability of relationships internal to the group of INCs and among these and the different generations of *NBFs* is used to estimate how much the relational structure has been altered by network growth through entry. Four matrix have been constructed, describing, respectively, relationships of incumbents among themselves and with the three different generations of*NBFs*. For every matrix, an analysis of structural equivalence has been carried out using a divisive hierarchical clustering method based on the convergence of iterated correlation (*CONCOR*), which permits to partition actors into positions based on structural equivalence. In this way, it has been possible to detect the groups of pharmaceutical firms structurally equivalent in the way they connect to the different generations of firms.

Formally, given k pharmaceutical incumbents and given Graphs $(G = (1, \ldots g, \ldots, 4))$ that represent their internal relationships and the relationships with the three generations of *NBFs*, we have that:

If $i = j$, then $\Phi(i) = \Phi(j) =_g \beta_p$; if $i \neq j$, then $\Phi(i)_g\beta - z, \Phi(j) =_g \beta_h, \forall g \in G, z \neq h$, where Φ is a law of assignment of the units (i,j) to the position $_g\beta_x$.

Once obtained the decomposition by applying the assignation law to every single couple (i, j), it is possible to build a matrix in which:

The upward left cell presents $\sum_g (i,j)_{\mathrm{SE}} \xrightarrow{\text{and}} \sum_{g+i} (i,j)_{\mathrm{SE}}$;

The upward right cell presents $\sum_g (i,j)_{SE} \xrightarrow{\text{and}} \sum_{g+i} (i,j)_{\mathrm{NSE}}$;

The downward left cell presents $\sum_g (i,j)_{\mathrm{NSE}} \xrightarrow{\text{and}} \sum_{g+i} (i,j)_{\mathrm{SE}}$;

The downward right cell presents $\sum_g (i,j)_{\mathrm{NSE}} \xrightarrow{\text{and}} \sum_{g+i} (i,j)_{\mathrm{NSE}}$;

For every pair of INCs, the three matrix presented in Table 9.6 map the transitions from structural equivalent (non equivalent) groups in respect to the relationships with the firms of the I_{t-1} generation, to groups of structural equivalence (non equivalence) in respect to the relationships with firms of the I_t generation.

In each matrix, entries on the main diagonal indicate persistence. To assess whether these entries are larger than the off-diagonal entries, the cross-product ratio has been calculated for each matrix. The cross-product ratio is a commonly used statistics for estimating the degree of association between two variables (see Agresti, 1990). A cross-product ratio of zero indicates no association between the variables, and values of the ratio greater than one imply a positive relationship. Because the logarithm of the cross-product ratio is less skewed than the ratio itself, we use the log of the ratio to test for structural persistence (see also Walker, Kogut and

Table 9.6 Waves of entry and the dynamics of structural stability within the network

I: INC/INC (row), INC/NBF_1 (column)		
	SE	*NSE*
SE	144	238
NSE	366	737
log c.p.ratio = 0,20		
II: INC/NBF_1 (row), INC/NBF_2 (column)		
	SE	*NSE*
SE	186 (+42)	348 (+110)
NSE	303 (−63)	648 (−89)
log c.p.ratio = 0,13		
III: INC/NBF_2 (row), INC/NBF_3 (column)		
	SE	*NSE*
SE	223 (+37)	266 (−82)
NSE	351 (+48)	645 (−3)
log c.p.ratio = 0,43		

Shan, 1997). Data indicate, in the first place, a significant persistence of structural dissimilarity, with a high number of pairs of firms that start being structurally non equivalent and continue to be so (*NSE*→*NSE*). Values along the off-diagonal of matrix II show, moreover, the significant alteration that followed the entry into the network by NBF_2. In particular, the high number of *SE*→*NSE* (a high number of *INC*s that were structurally equivalent in respect to the relationships with NBF_1 have become non equivalent in respect to the relationships with NBF_2) reflects both the number of new agreements and the delay with which some of the *INC*s entered the network. In sum, the structure of the network has been continually reshaped by the entry of new generations of firms. Nevertheless, the analysis of matrix II and III allows to detect an increase of the level of structural stability and similarity in the course of time, with an increasing number of pairs that continue to be structurally equivalent (*SE*→*SE*).

The stabilization of the entry flow in the transition from NBF_2 to NBF_3 allows to interpret the increase in the number of pairs *SE*→*SE* and the relevant decrease in the number of pairs *SE*→*NSE*, *SE*→*NSE*, and *NSE*→*SE* as sufficiently accurate indicators of a significant reduction over time of the entity of the perturbation introduced into the structure of the network by the entry of new generations of *NBF*s. Briefly, the undertaken analysis evidences the progressive decrease of the alteration of the structure of the network determined by the entry of new generations of firms. The analysis allows to precise, among other things, that new firms that entered the principal component of the network, did that through the definition of collaborative relationships with firms already present in the principal component, rather than deforming its profile.

9.4 Conclusions

This paper has carried out an inductive exercise on industrial structure and its evolution over time, looking at the micro-dynamics of network formation and evolution in the pharmaceutical industry after the "molecular biology revolution" in drug research.

More precisely, we argue that an isomorphism between features of problem solving activities carried out by individual agents and firms and patterns of industry dynamics can be identified, and we analyze it in detail.

From the above results the following points can be highlighted.

1. Discovery and development of new effective drugs can be considered a case in which exploration and search activities are subject to strong substantive and procedural uncertainty (Dosi, Egidi, 1991; Dosi *et.al.*, 1996). More precisely, the emergence of the molecular biology paradigm has corresponded to a search for more fundamental explanations, at lower levels of organization of matter, of phenomena occurring at higher level of organization into the human organism. Given the inherent complexity and hierarchical structure of the human organism, the growth of scientific knowledge in this field has entailed both an explosion of conceivable targets and the transfer of information collected at one level through to theory/concept forming at another level and back again, together with a pressure towards the development of more specific and powerful procedures and techniques.

2. As it has been shown in Section 9.2, given the complexity of the human organism, the process of convergence at the level of scientific theories has been paralleled by an explosive divergence at the level of specific hypotheses and opportunities for exploration. Even once ex ante substantive and procedural uncertainty over the structural properties of matter has been dealt with until the characterization of a new molecule, there is still strong ex post uncertainty over the mapping between the structure of the artifact (i.e. the molecule) and its functions (Bonaccorsi, Pammolli, 1997). In order to deal with this uncertainty, firms are forced to implement cycles of testing activities aimed at improving their understanding, using drugs as experimental tools. In this process, the artifact act as reference point, because judgment about effects and side-effects drives the identification of new plausible mechanisms of action and the characterization of new theoretical hypotheses.

3. As in any problem solving within complex search spaces, the structure of knowledge in pharmaceutical research tends to differentiate in a hierarchical way (Simon, 1969). This hierarchical structure actually reflects the adoption, under conditions of strong uncertainty, of a research strategy based on the dissection of the system and on the decomposition of the search space into sub-spaces. Moreover, the search for explanations at more fundamental levels of organization of matter, which is the essence of the molecular biology paradigm, naturally makes the dynamics of knowledge similar to a branching

process in which each fundamental hypothesis on the properties of matter gives origin to a variety of sub-hypotheses, each of which in turn develops other sub-hypotheses at lower levels of generality. The process is highly cumulative, since it is based on a dynamics which generates progressive specifications of hypotheses at each level of the hierarchy. The inherent dynamics of growth of knowledge imposes a structure of the selection of hypotheses: at higher levels of the hierarchy, theoretical hypotheses tend to stay relatively stable, since their falsification occurs over a long time scale, being based on the falsification/selection of all hypotheses at lower levels of generality.

4. Moreover, in addition to this hierarchical structure, one can observe that in the period of observation considered in this study, the exploration process has not been characterized by the availability of powerful general-purpose search technologies, i.e. technologies for experimentation and testing that apply equally well to widely different domains. On the contrary, search technologies have tended to be strongly co-specialized with research objects, so that each family of research hypotheses is explored through a set of tools which are often adapted, if not invented and developed, by researchers themselves. This situation is in marked contrast with the paradigm of chemical synthesis, which prevailed in pharmaceutical research before the molecular biology revolution, which was based on large scale experimentation using generic search rules (Schwartzman, 1976). In fact, the ways through which biological-molecular and pharmaceutical research has developed has led, in a short time, to the generation of a wide variety of approaches and specific lines of research. Just ten years ago, the biopharmaceutical discovery and development armamentarium contained only two fundamental tools: recombinant DNA and monoclonal antibody technologies. Paradoxically, although these techniques have yielded a slower-than expected flow of new products and financial returns, they have spawned hundreds of derivative technologies and techniques, which in turn have transformed the process of discovering, developing and manufacturing pharmaceuticals. And, in fact, over time pharmaceuticals and biotechnology have experienced an explosive growth in the number of drug discovery approaches that a company can pursue and in the number of technological issues with which it must grapple.

5. The combination of variety, irreversibility of investment and co-specialization between search technologies and objects that characterize pharmaceutical R&D after the molecular biology revolution has strong economic and organizational implications. The huge variety of search hypotheses and investment trajectories generated by the progress of science produces two fundamental consequences. On one hand, learning new search technologies involves some fixed costs, which makes extremely costly to explore the whole tree of relevant hypotheses, or even large portions of it. The high level of co-specialization between objects and procedures of search, the nature of the dominant scientific paradigm and, finally, the presence of strong com-

plementarities and feedbacks between theories and experimental practices in the process of search jointly induce high path dependency and strong irreversibilities in the exploration activities carried out by firms in the industry. On the other hand, the required degree of structural differentiation is much higher than the one that hierarchy can handle, if it has to maintain internal consistency and identity (Levinthal, 1996). By its very nature, hierarchy tends to impose tight constraints to the process of generation of new competing hypotheses, and therefore tends to naturally limit the degree of cognitive diversity. To explore a search space which is characterized by large variety of plausible *a priori*, then, it is necessary to use a mix of alternative coordination principles, including large integrated multi-technology corporations (Granstrand, Patel, Pavitt, 1997), different types of market institutions, and network of ties between firms and between firms and institutions. In sum, the very nature of search and learning in pharmaceutical research after the molecular biology revolution seems to require some kind of organizational form which realize a better compromise between flexibility and irreversibility than either complete integration of R&D opportunities by large established firms or postponement of investment at later stages of the innovative process (Pammolli, 1996; Bonaccorsi and Pammolli, 1997).

6. In this perspective, it is illuminating to put attention to the dynamics of the network of agreements, seen as an adaptive response to the structural features of the dynamics of search activities. To start with, one can observe that the hierarchical nature of the growth of knowledge helps to explain the relative stability of the network that has been clearly demonstrated by our data. Entry of new firms does not change significantly the core-periphery profile of the network, and the level of structural stability and similarity tends to increase over time. This means that incumbent firms and *NBF*s of the first generation are not crowded out by new generations of biotech firms. After the biotechnology revolution, pharmaceutical incumbents have heavily invested into fundamental research and high order capabilities (Gambardella, 1995; Galambos, Sturchio, 1996) and are in the position to observe the evolution of knowledge from a higher position in the belief tree. Therefore, although it is still impossible to scan exhaustively the research hypotheses and investment opportunities generated by the growth of scientific knowledge, incumbents can avoid the competence-destroying effect of innovation. Companies that are able to locate themselves higher on the hierarchy of beliefs enjoy higher degrees of strategic flexibility. By means of cooperative agreements incumbents get access to research opportunities at lower levels of the belief tree without committing heavy financial resources. This cumulativeness of knowledge and innovation seems to be an important source for the dynamic increasing returns observed in the evolution of the network over time. The hierarchical nature of knowledge evolution can also explain why, even although the core of the network stabilizes, the total number of agreements initiated by core firms and the average number of agreements

per firm still increases over time. For the same reason, new entrants enter the industry pursuing hypotheses that become more and more specific as time goes by and specializing in a small subset of the overall search space. It could be said that each generation of *NBF*s enter at a given level in the tree of beliefs, although the levels are arguably differentiated across therapeutic areas. This can explain why the growth of scientific knowledge and the proliferation of scientific hypotheses in molecular biology and related fields does not translate into an accumulation of projects within large established companies, but rather into an expansion of the network over time. The hierarchical nature of the growth of knowledge, coupled with the increasing co-specialization of search technologies and research objects, can explain the expanding dynamics of the network of cooperative relationships. This can also explain one of the most relevant results of our analysis, that is that inter-generational collaborations are more frequent than intra- generational collaborations. In this context, the network appears to be the emergent product of an adaptive process by which agents try to cope with the underlying tight exploitation-exploration trade-off (March, 1991). In fact, it can be considered as an organizational form that permits profitable opportunities to be exploited through the integration of downstream stages in the innovation chain, but also extremely uncertain prospects to be explored with adequate investment. Moreover, in an evolutionary perspective, the network seems to be a powerful selection device, one that feeds new species until they are sufficiently strong and then leaves capital markets to allocate resources to them according to their strength.

References

Agresti, F. (1990) *Categorical Data Analysis*. New York: John Wiley.

Arora, A. and A. Gambardella (1994) Evaluating technological information and utilizing it: scientific knowledge, technological capability and external linkages in biotechnology. *Journal of Economic Behavior and Organization* 24: 91–114.

Barley, S.R., J. Freeman and R. C. Hybels (1992) Strategic alliances in commercial biotechnology. In N. Nohria and R.G. Eccles (eds) *Networks and Organizations*. Cambridge MA: Harvard Business School Press.

Bioscan (1988–1993) The biotechnology corporate directory service, Phoenix, AR.

Bonaccorsi, A. and F. Pammolli (1997) Technical development, design, and the division of innovative labour. *International Journal of Technology Management*. Special issue on "Structural change, institutional change and models of capitalism". Forthcoming.

David, P.A., D. Mowery and W.E. Steinmuller (1992) Analysing the economic payoffs from basic research. *Economics of Innovation and New Technology* 2: 73–90.

Dosi, G. (1988) Sources, procedures and microeconomic effects of innovation. *Journal of Economic Literature* 26: 1120–1171.

Dosi, G. and M. Egidi (1991) Substantive and procedural uncertainty. *Journal of Evolutionary Economics* 1: 145–168.

Dosi, G., L. Marengo and G. Fagiolo (1996) *Learning in Evolutionary Environments*. WP 96–124. Laxenburg: IIASA.

Galambos, L. and J. Sturchio (1996) The pharmaceutical industry in the twentieth century: a reappraisal of the sources of innovation. *History and Technology* 13(2): 83–100.

Gambardella, A. (1995) *Science and Innovation: The US Pharmaceutical Industry During the 1980s*. Cambridge: Cambridge University Press.

Granstrand, O., P. Patel and K. Pavitt (1997) Why they have “distributed” rather than “distinctive core” competencies. *California Management Review* 39(4): 8–25.

Henderson, R., L. Orsenigo and G. Pisano (1997) *The Pharmaceutical Industry and the Revolution in Molecular Biology: Exploring the Interactions Between Scientific, Institutional and Organizational Change*. Mimeo. CCC Matrix.

Kogut, B., W. Shan and G. Walker (1992) The make-or-cooperate decision in the context of an industry network. In N. Nohria and R.G. Eccles (eds) *Networks and Organizations*. Cambridge, MA: Harvard Business School Press.

Levinthal, D. (1996) *Organizations and Capabilities: The Role of Decompositions and Units of Selection*. Mimeo. Wharton School, University of Pennsylvania.

Malerba, F. and L. Orsenigo (1996) The dynamics and evolution of industries. *Industrial and Corporate Change* 5(1): 51–88.

March, J.G. (1991) Exploration and exploitation in organizational learning. *Organization Science* 2(1): 71–87.

Nelson, R.R. (1961) Uncertainty, learning and economics of parallel research and development efforts. *Review of Economics and Statistics*. 43: 351–364.

Nelson, R.R. and S.G. Winter (1982) *An Evolutionary Theory of Economic Change*. Cambridge, MA: Harvard University Press.

Orsenigo, L. (1989) *The Emergence of Biotechnology*. New York: St. Martins Press.

Orsenigo, L., F. Pammolli and M. Riccaboni (1996) *A Model of Network Evolution in Biotechnology*. Mimeo.

Pammolli, F. (1996) *Innovazione, concorrenza e strategie di sviluppo nell’industria farmaceutica*. Milan: Guerini.

Pattison, P. (1993) *Algebraic Models for Social Networks*. Cambridge: Cambridge University Press.

Pisano, G.P. (1991) The governance of innovation: vertical integration and collaborative arrangements in the biotechnology industry. *Research Policy* 20: 237–249.

Powell, W.W. (1996) Interorganizational collaboration in the biotechnology industry, *Journal of Institutional and Theoretical Economics* 152(1): 197–215.

Powell, W.W., K.W. Doput and L. Smith-Doerr (1996) Interorganizational collaboration and the locus of innovation: networks of learning in biotechnology. *Administrative Science Quarterly* 41: 116–145.

Schaffner, K.F. (1986) Exemplar reasoning about biological models and diseases: a relation between the philosophy of medicine and philosophy of science. *The Journal of Medicine and Philosophy* 11: 63–80.

Schwartzman, D. (1976) *Innovation in the Pharmaceutical Industry*. Baltimore: Johns Hopkins University Press.

Scott, J. (1991) *Social Network Analysis: A Handbook*. London: Sage.

Simon, H.A. (1969) The architecture of complexity. In *The Sciences of the Artificial*. Cambridge, MA: MIT Press.

Suitor, J.J., B. Wellman and D. L. Morgan (1997) It’s about time: how, why, and when networks change. *Social Networks* 19: 1–7.

Testa, B. and U.A. Meyer (1995) *Advances in Drug Research*. New York: Academic Press.

Vos, R. (1991) *Drugs Looking for Diseases*. Dordrecht: Kluwer Academic Publishers.

Walker, G., B. Kogut and W. Shan (1997) Social capital, structural holes and the formation of an industry network. *Organization Science* 8(2): 109–125.

Wasserman, S. and K. Faust (1994) *Social Network Analysis: Methods and Applications*. Cambridge: Cambridge University Press.

Winter, S.G. (1984). Schumpeterian competition in alternative technological regimes. *Journal of Economic Behavior and Organization* 287–320.

Zucker, L.G. and M.R. Darby (1995) Present at the revolution: transformation of technical identity for a large incumbent pharmaceutical firm after the biotechnological breakthrough. *NBER*. WP 5243, August. Cambridge, MA.

10 The firm as an evolutionary enforcement device

Antonio Nicita

10.1 Introduction

According to Williamson (1985), in order to prevent post-contractual opportunism in an incomplete contract framework, economic agents have to design endogenous enforcement devices. The purpose of this chapter is to explain the firm as an evolutionary enforcement device emerging in an institutional context characterized by incomplete contracts and *cross competition.* Here, "cross competition" identifies the strategic context which emerges when, in order to enforce a bilateral incomplete contract, the agents involved try to reach a monopolistic position, *vis-à-vis* their counterparts, by "destroying" their competitors and/or by "encouraging" counterpart's competitors. Such a framework is here studied by assuming that a party's outside option is affected by the investment made by the other contractual party. Given that the outside option of an agent identifies the potential competitors of the contractual counterpart, with such endogenous outside options, a party is induced to invest strategically in order to encourage counterpart's competitors and/or to deter own competitors, raising the exit costs of the other contractual party.

The framework proposed is aimed at understanding how agents' investment decisions, in an incomplete contract, are affected by the degree of competition faced by each agent in the outside market. Most of the theories on incomplete contracts are generally based on the assumption that agents' outside options (i.e. the degree of market competition) are exogenous, focusing mainly on bilateral relationships.[1] The analysis of incomplete contracts characterized by specific investments has thus been confined to the Williamsonian "fundamental transformation,"[2] for which an *ex-ante* competitive transaction is *ex-post* transformed into a monopolistic one. According to this perspective, the level of *ex-ante* parties' outside options acts as a default point in the *ex-ante* contracting and as a threat point in the *ex-post* bargaining over the joint surplus. In both cases, according to the related literature, outside options are never affected by the investments made by parties. In other words, investment decisions are affected by the *ex-ante* market configuration, but they do not affect each agent's *ex-post* competitors. The "market" is implicitly supposed to be an *equilibrium market* and hence for contractual parties it is not possible to affect (and to be affected by) competitors' strategies. Thus, in most of these analyses, "fundamental transformation" acts only in one way: from market exchange to bilateral monopoly, whereas the opposite direction of causality is almost neglected.

In this work it is argued that if parties face multidimensional investments (specific or general-purpose) and these investments affect parties' *ex-post* outside options, at least one agent in the contract might be induced to select the type of investment which increases the counterpart's competitors and/or reduces own competitors in the outside market.

The rationale for such a behavior relies upon the circumstance that affecting parties' outside options may alter parties' threat point[3] in the *ex-post* bargaining over surplus sharing, neutralizing counterpart's potential hold up. Under the assumption of endogenous outside options, each contractual party is thus induced to switch from the selection of *ex-ante* efficient investment in the attempt to lock the counterpart into the contract by reducing endogenously his/her *ex-post* contractual power.

In other words, when contracts are incomplete agents may use the outside market as a discipline device in order to sanction (and prevent) post-contractual opportunism. A great part of everyday transactions seem to accord to such a view: economic agents normally face a set of multiple investment types (or multidimensional investments[4]) and in an uncertain world they are induced to select those investments which may enhance their future contractual power *vis-à-vis* the potential counterparts. Thus, the number of expected potential sellers and buyers play a crucial role in the choice of the investment type in an incomplete contract framework.

The main results of the paper are as follows. First, depending on the degree of *ex-post* market competition, the investment choice might regard not only the dychotomic choice between *ex-ante* efficient investment and underinvestment, but it may be extended in order to consider other investment types which may enhance agents' post-contractual power. Second, the introduction of the choice of investment type (specific or general-purpose) in a endogenous outside options framework reverses, in the model proposed, some of the main conclusions of the related literature: (i) contractors may have strong incentives to make a over-investment (specific or general purpose); (ii) over-investment may act as an endogenous enforcement device. Here, the over-investment result is related to the extra-costs involved by the investment selected with respect to the *ex-ante* efficient one. Third, it is shown – in sharp contrast with the main contributions of the relevant literature[5] – that specific investments may in some cases constitute an optimal enforcement strategy, rather the failure of incomplete contracts. Fourth, the framework proposed by the introduction of endogenous outside options may help to provide an explanation of the nature of the firm, which explicitly takes into account (i) firm-market interactions in a dynamic perspective along the original intuitions of J.R. Commons and R. Coase; (ii) the diversity of institutional arrangements observed in different economic systems (mainly the capitalistic firm, the Japanese firm and the German industrial system), and (iii) their co-existence and co-evolution.

We suggest that the organization of production within the firm (in all its different structures) introduces appropriate forms of pre-commitment in the agents' behaviors so as to introduce some form of outside options' rigidity and to transform multilateral market cross competition into a network of bilateral cross competition relationships within the firm between management and the workers.

10.1.1 An example

It is useful to illustrate the *cross competition* framework by a simple (fictitious) example. Let us imagine a contractual relationship between two firms, say Microsoft and Netscape, where Netscape is the seller, supplying a widget called "internet facility," and Microsoft is the buyer, who needs the widget to sell a complete bundle of software products to its clients and customers. Suppose that, in order to adapt its software to the internet facility provided by Netscape,[6] Microsoft has to make a specific investment. In a constant world, Microsoft and Netscape may find it easy to write a long-term contract specifying the quantity, the quality, and the price of "internet facility" provided by Netscape. However, the world of computer operating systems changes very fast, as technological innovation takes place. In this world the optimal number of "internet facility" to be provided, as their quality and price, depends on a variety of factors: the demand for Microsoft computers, technological innovation in software systems, Netscape's costs, the innovations introduced by competitors, and so on. As a consequence it may be impossible for the parties involved in the above contractual relationship to write a binding contract, specifying all the relevant conditions in every possible contingency. Thus, parties are likely to write a (short-term) incomplete contract that will be revised or renegotiated over time. Therefore, as the incomplete contract is renegotiated, Microsoft might be deterred from making the relationship-specific investment that would be optimal in a first-best world, given its fear that Netscape will "hold-up" it at the renegotiation stage.

Assume that Microsoft has two investment options: efficient specific investment, say m^*, and a generic investment, say m°. Efficient specific investment m^* has a cost of 10 monetary units and gives Microsoft a gain of 100 and a net payoff of 90, whereas Netscape obtains a quasi-rent greater than zero; generic investment m° has a cost of 5 units and gives Microsoft a gain of 30 units (a net payoff of 25), whereas Netscape has no quasi-rent. The quasi-rent of Microsoft in the case of m^* amounts to 65 (90 – 25) monetary units, because in the case of generic investment m°, i.e. without "internet facility," Microsoft software systems are sold at a lower price. In an incomplete contract world, however, the choice of m^* is hindered by Netscape's hold up. After m^* is selected, Netscape is induced to renegotiate surplus sharing, giving Microsoft a payment just sufficient to cover its costs (10 monetary units) and appropriating thus all the expected quasi-rent of Microsoft. In the absence of *ex-post* sanctions on Netscape opportunistic behavior, Microsoft will thus be induced to select m° instead of m^*. The standard literature on incomplete contracts would probably stops here, describing m° as an "underinvestment" choice. However, the story might be more complex than this.

It should be noticed that, in the case of Microsoft's under-investment, Netscape will lose the chance to receive its positive expected gains. As a consequence, the threat of hold-up might not be credible, since Netscape would be damaged by Microsoft's under-investment choice. Hence, the only case in which underinvestment by Microsoft has not adverse effects on Netscape's *ex-post* payoff is given by the possibility for Netscape to bargain with a Microsoft's competitor, say Sun. Under

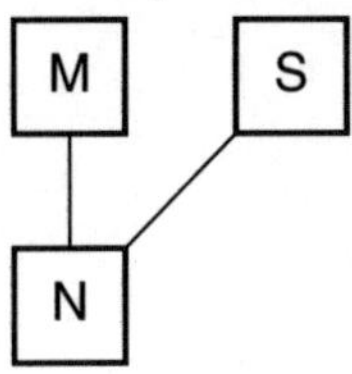

Figure 10.1

this assumption, the underinvestment choice by Microsoft increases the probability of Netscape contracting with Sun. Under the assumption of exclusive dealing (the investor may reasonably require such verifiable clause in order to fully appropriate the expected gains from trade[7]), this means that, under m°, Microsoft sells its software without "internet facility" and faces downstream competition by Sun-Netscape. As a consequence, underinvestment choice might not be rational for Microsoft in the presence of efficient competitors.

Therefore, (i) it is the existence of a competitor of Microsoft which makes it credible for Netscape to hold-up; (ii) *ex-post* competition affects Microsoft's *ex-ante* investment choice.

In order to take into account the impact of *ex-post* competition on Microsoft's investment incentives – a case generally neglected by standard literature on hold-up – let us assume now that it is possible for Microsoft to select another investment type, say m^1, which costs 20 units (10 more than m^*) and represents a specific *and* sunk investment, i.e. an investment which generates positive quasi-rent for Microsoft and also acts as a deterrence variable on Microsoft's competitors,[8] or as a raising rival's cost variable, according to the standard literature on sunk investments. Under m^1 investment, the expected net payoff for Microsoft is now 80, and the expected quasi-rent is 55 (80 – 25). The m^1 choice, by reducing *ex-post* competition by Sun, minimizes also the probability of hold-up by Netscape. In particular, we assume that Sun has not incentives to induce Netscape to switch to Sun, starting a price war with Microsoft. The bargaining over the *ex-post* surplus will thus be a bilateral monopoly bargaining, where the breakdown of renegotiation penalizes both Microsoft and Netscape. Compared to the efficient investment choice m^*, the selection of m^1 reduces Microsoft's quasi-rent ($55 < 65$) while minimizes the probability of Netscape hold-up. The economic loss incurred by Microsoft represents here a kind of "enforcement cost" sustained by the investor to deter counterpart's hold-up (see Figure 10.1).

Let us assume now that Microsoft may select a fourth investment level, say m^2, which costs 50 monetary units and represents a general purpose investment which enables Microsoft to trade indifferently for acquiring "internet facility" with Netscape or with a Netscape's competitor, say Explorer. This investment gives Microsoft an expected net payoff of 50 units in every *ex-post* trade and a quasi-rent of 25 (50 – 25). The rationale for selecting m^2 is that it increases Microsoft's outside options and decreases Netscape's post-contractual power (as well as that of Explorer), improving thus Microsoft's *ex-post* contractual power. However, the choice of m^2 by Microsoft depends in turn on the expected reactions of actual and

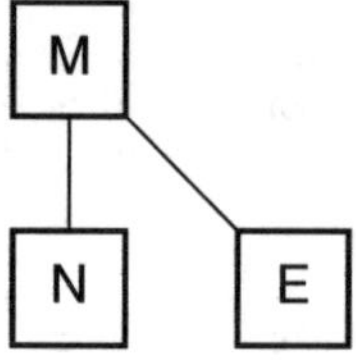

Figure 10.2

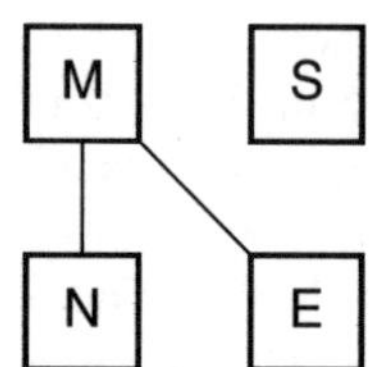

Figure 10.3

potential Microsoft's competitors. In other words, Netscape's post-contractual power *vis-à-vis* Microsoft is affected not only by Netscape's competitors, but also by the expected reaction by Microsoft's competitors to m^2 (see Figure 10.2).

The following case takes thus into account the complex interactions among Microsoft, Netscape, Sun and Explorer.

Let us consider the choice by Microsoft of a fifth investment type, say m^3, which merges the characteristics of m^1 and m^2, acting as a deterrence variable on Microsoft's competitors and increasing Microsoft's outside options, i.e. Netscape's competitors. The cost of m^3 investment type is 65 units, giving a net payoff of 35 units and a quasi rent of 10 (35 – 25). The rationale for m^3 investment type is that it allows Microsoft to reach a monopolistic configuration. As long as quasi-rent generated by m^3 is greater than that obtained under the underinvestment choice ($35 - 25 = 10$), Microsoft is induced to select m^3.

In other words, in a multiple investment settings, with many buyers and/or many sellers, investment decisions are made according to their expected impact on *ex-post* parties outside options (see Figure 10.3).

This example is a one-sided investment case. It is worthy to imagine a two-sided investment case (in which both parties have to make specific investments in order to generate positive quasi-rents) where Microsoft chooses the investment type from the set $M = [m^*, m^\circ, m^1, m^2, m^3]$ and Netscape chooses the investment type from the set $N = [n^*, n^\circ, n^1, n^2, n^3]$, with symmetric payoffs and quasi-rents. The complex interaction among four agents [M (Microsoft), N (Netscape), S (Sun), E (Explorer)] is represented in Figure 10.4.

If we disregard underinvestment and efficient investment choices, the interesting outcomes of Microsoft–Netscape strategic interactions might be: a bilateral monopoly (m^1, n^1), a competitive market (m^2, n^2), a bilateral monopoly or a competitive market (m^3, n^3). In this last case, as in all other cases, the ultimate outcome depends on the relative market power of each contractual agent, as Table 10.1

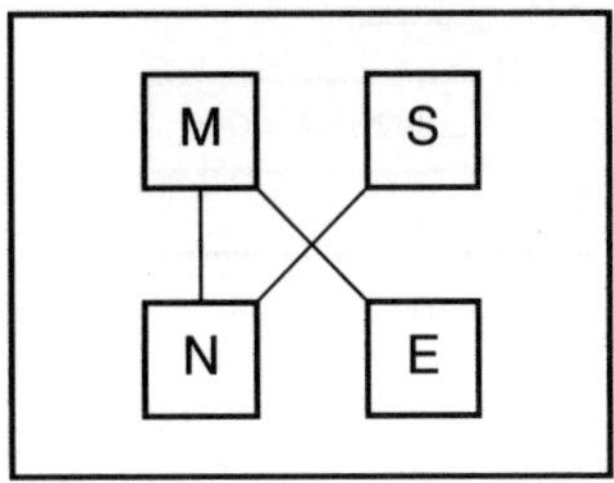

Figure 10.4

Table 10.1 M–N example: some *ex-post* market configurations

		Firm M		
		m^1	m^2	m^3
Firm N	n^1	Bilateral monopoly	Bilateral monopoly or M's dual sourcing	Bilateral monopoly or M's dual sourcing
	n^2	Bilateral monopoly or N's dual sourcing	Competitive market	Competitive market or M's dual sourcing
	n^3	Bilateral monopoly or N's dual sourcing	Competitive market or N's dual sourcing	Bilateral monopoly or Competitive markets

shows.[9]

The example above illustrates how the introduction of endogenous outside options in the standard incomplete contract framework, identifies market conditions characterizing under-investment results and efficient specific investments choice in incomplete contracts. When outside options are affected by the investments made, each agent is induced to reach a monopolistic position by deterring its competitors and/or by "encouraging" counterpart competitors.

10.2 Transactions and "cross competition"

As J. R. Commons (1924, 1934, 1950) has emphasized, economic exchanges which take place in the real world economy are characterized by positive transaction costs. In order to properly assess the nature and the extent of transaction costs it is necessary to investigate in more detail the notion of transaction.

According to Commons (1950: 50),

> when we reduce all prospective buyers and sellers upon a given market to those who participate in one bargaining transaction as our smallest unit of investigation, then they are the "best" two buyers and the "best" two sellers, meaning the two buyers who offer the highest prices and the two sellers who offer to accept the lowest prices, in consideration of transfers of ownership.[10] [. . .] The best two sellers are those able to sell at the lowest price. They

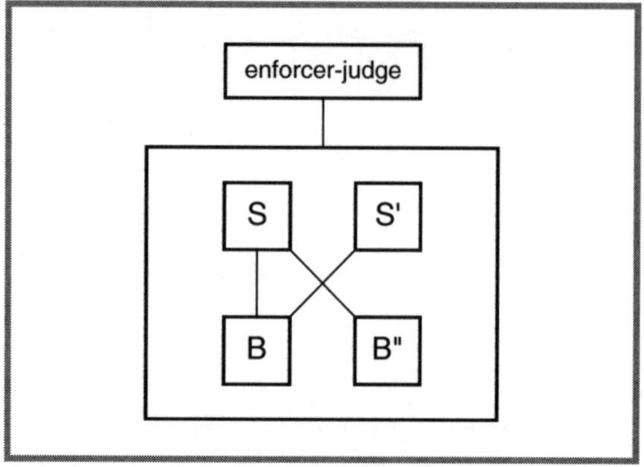

Figure 10.5 Five parties transaction (Commons, 1924, 1950)

compete for choice of alternatives offered by the best two buyers, those able to buy at the highest prices, while, in turn, the best two buyers are competing for choice of alternatives offered by the best two sellers. As a consequence, under a transaction, "instead of the 'exchange' of physical things between two parties, as contemplated in the former physical economics, there are five parties, all of whom are 'potential' and then they are successively 'actual' participants in the lawful alienation and acquisition of ownership.

These five parties are four competitors (two buyers and two sellers) and the 'enforcer' or judge who is "ready to issue commands to any of the buyers and sellers in the name of sovereignty, if any dispute arises." Given a transaction among these five agents, a contract regards at least three agents: the "actual" buyer and seller (those who agree upon the terms of the transaction) and the judge or third party. Figure 10.5 outlines a transaction *à la* Commons.

Once we refer to a five parties transaction, transaction costs have to include:

1. "competition costs," i.e. the costs sustained by each economic agent (S, B) to exclude the best competitor (S', B') from contracting with the counterpart;

2. "contractual costs," i.e. the costs sustained by "actual" contractual parties to design contractual terms;

3. "enforcement costs," i.e. the costs sustained by the enforcer (judge) and the parties to enforce the contract and solve the disputes (public and private legal orderings).

Under this framework, when contracts are incomplete, transaction costs sustained to enforce the contract and solve disputes are infinite or prohibitive.[11] The question to be solved is thus how to enforce an incomplete contract when the costs sustained to enforce the contract and solve disputes are infinite or prohibitive. The New Institutional Economics has been concerned mainly with the design of second best "private orderings" in order to enforce incomplete contracts characterized by specific investments. However, the analysis of private orderings seems to be conducted only at a bilateral level, between the two contracting parties, neglecting the role played by the best competitor of each agent in shaping the transaction. This means that a relevant component of transaction costs, i.e. the costs sustained by each economic agent (S, B) to exclude the best competitor (S', B'), is not properly taken into account. These "competition costs" may even modify the nature and the extent of transactions, since the best competitor of each contractual party might induce a potential counterpart to breach the contract and switch to a counterpart's competitor agreement when there are gains from contractual switch. Moreover, since market competition acts as a discipline device[12] on parties' contractual power, excluding competitors might be an efficient enforcement strategy given that it affects parties' surplus sharing.

Once "competition costs" are taken into account under an incomplete contract framework, transaction costs have to include not only all the "internal" costs (contractual and enforcement costs between parties S and B) necessary to allow contractual exchanges (what Williamson (1988) calls *incentive alignment* or *agency* costs), but also all the "external" costs necessary to make the institutions "work well."

Several meanings of transaction costs are commonly used and need to be distinguished. Given an incomplete contract we define transaction costs the sum of *enforcement costs* and *competition costs*. Enforcement Costs ("EC") are generally defined as all *ex-ante* incentive alignment costs and post-contractual enforcement costs associated with the transaction and hence with the contractual relationship (Williamson, 1988). These costs normally include also the wide range of legal and political costs necessary to set up an enforcement system. Competition Costs ("CC") are all those extra-costs sustained by agents when they seek to exclude their competitors from contracting with counterpart. *EC* and *CC* are here defined as extra-costs because they constitute an amount of economic resources in excess with respect to the level required in a neo-classical ideal-type.

Given a complex transaction among agents S, B, S', B', each economic agent has to sustain the extra-costs associated with two different types of economic rivalry: (i) *contractual rivalry* against a contractual counterpart, which derives from the position assumed in the contract *vis-à-vis* the counterpart and (ii) *market rivalry* which in turn describes competitors rivalry in the market. Table 10.2 shows the market configurations and the kind of rivalry associated with alternative levels of EC and CC. We assume only two levels of extra-costs (zero and greater than zero).

10.2.1 Perfect competition

In Table 10.2, when both EC and CC are zero, the resulting market configuration is perfect competition. According to the neo-classical ideal-type, economic exchanges are achieved with zero enforcement and competition extra-costs. Since each agent is always substitutable contractual performance is ensured by market discipline. At the same time, every opportunistic behavior is always sanctioned by judicial or public ordering or hindered by agents' morality. In such a perfect neo-platonic world, the only competition costs to be sustained by economic agents

Table 10.2 Market configurations and economic rivalry

		Enforcement Costs, EC	
		$EC = 0$	$EC > 0$
Competition Costs, CC	$CC = 0$	i Perfect competition	ii Contractual rivalry
	$CC > 0$	iii Strategic competition	iv Cross competition

are those necessary to take part to market exchanges (access market costs). These competition costs are therefore determined by market dimension rather then by strategic actions. As Bowles and Gintis (1999) have pointed out (p.13),

> in competitive equilibrium [. . .] conditions of unimpeded entry and exit ensure that for each commodity (including such factors of production as labor and capital) there is a selling price such that each buyer faces a large number of sellers offering this commodity at this price, and no seller offers the commodity at a lower price; similarly there is an offer price such that each seller faces a large number of buyers offering to buy at this price, and no buyer offering to buy at a higher price.

In a perfect competition configuration CC are then zero in the sense that it is useless for agents to employ economic resources to exclude *efficient* competitors from market participation.

10.2.2 Contractual rivalry

Starting from the neo-classical ideal-type, and relaxing the assumption that the enforcement structure is exogenously given by *public orderings*, the enforcement costs become non-negative[13] as pointed out by the new institutional literature on incomplete contracts. Under this assumption, in order to enforce transactions, especially those characterized by specific assets, agents have to incur in complex negotiations to build effective *private orderings* (Williamson, 1985). We define this configuration as *contractual rivalry* to indicate an institutional order in which contractual parties, in order to ensure contractual performance, have to spend an amount of economic resources (enforcement costs) which exceed those required under perfect competition configuration. Contractual rivalry arises particularly when incomplete contracts require specific investments. In this case, the quasi-rent generated by specific investments is greater than zero only if the underlying transaction takes place. Once made, a specific investment locks the investors into the contractual relationship, by raising their *ex-post* exit costs. As a result, the economic resources spent to make specific investments will be fully dissipated in the case of counterpart's hold up.

When agents make specific investments, they are thus vulnerable to counterpart's post-contractual opportunism and may require *ex-ante* appropriate safeguards. Endogenous enforcement arrangements, defined by Williamson as "private orderings," should then be built by agents in order to align parties' incentives and thus maximize their joint rent. As it is normally assumed by the New Institutional literature, incomplete contracts characterized by specific investments, cause. at least for one party in a contract, the Williamsonian "fundamental transformation," for which an *ex-ante* competitive transaction is *ex-post* transformed into a monopolistic one. Thus, contractual rivalry is mainly directed to the analysis of *ex-post* surplus sharing between contractual parties S and B, neglecting rent sharing "outside" the contract, among contractual parties and their competitors (S', B'). In this respect, the standard literature assume exogenous outside options and the agents involved in incomplete contracts, do not bear competition costs (CC) in excess with respect to those sustained by agents in the case of perfect competition.

10.2.3 Strategic competition

On the opposite side, when we have $CC > 0$ and $EC = 0$, some agents will sustain positive extra-costs of competition to deter competitors. Given the efficiency of the external enforcement structure $(EC = 0)$, contractual enforcement is guaranteed by efficient breach penalties. However, economic agents (S, B) have to face competition extra-costs $(CC > 0)$ to exclude competitors (S', B') and enhance their contractual power or market share. The resulting institutional context will thus be characterized by positive "competition costs," as it is generally assumed in the *strategic competition* literature and in the analyses of strategic sunk costs to deter rivals' entry or raise rivals' costs. Here, we refer to the wide range of deterrence actions outlined by a huge scholarly literature (the commitment effect of sunk costs, the inducement of exit, product-differentiation advantages, limit pricing behaviors, most-favored-customer clause, target rebates, tying arrangements, systems and product compatibility and so on). Under such a configuration, competition induces economic agents to make actions or investments which deter the competitors' entry, by sustaining positive competition costs (CC), in excess with respect to those sustained by agents in the case of perfect competition, whereas they do not bear any enforcement cost (EC).

10.2.4 Cross competition

Departing from "perfect competition' configuration and removing both the assumptions of zero competition and enforcement costs, agents involved in market transactions have to spend a greater amount of economic resources with respect to the neoclassical ideal-type in order (a) to enforce contractual performance and/or (b) to preserve their contractual power or market share. Under such a framework, in order to enforce a bilateral incomplete contract, contractual parties are induced to reach a monopolistic position, *vis-à-vis* their counterpart, by "destroying" their competitors and/or by "encouraging" counterpart competitors. As we have shown in the above example, agents may select a sunk *and* specific investment in order to improve their *ex-post* contractual power and to minimize the probability of counterpart's hold-up. As a consequence, parties may even overinvest in specific or sunk assets in order to raise rivals' costs in the market. Bilateral enforcement mechanisms are thus affected by the actions selected by agents in order to deter a competitor's entry, and vice versa, competition strategies are affected by the economic incentives promoted by parties for the enforcement of contractual obligations. We define such a complex institutional context as *cross competition* to indicate an institutional order in which the outcome of a transaction – even when specific assets are involved – is always a complex interaction among four representative agents, the two parties involved in a transactional exchange and the best competitor of each.

According to the original notion of transaction provided by Commons, cross competition occurs, when, absent an efficient external enforcement structure, i.e. absent the "enforcer" in Figure 10.5, economic agents try to enforce a transactional exchange (i) by reducing the *ex-post* outside options of the counterpart in the contract (which in turn requires to minimize a competitor's threat) and/or (ii) by increasing his own *ex-post* outside options (which requires to maximize the potential competitors of the counterpart from a competitor). When both agents in a contract try to make endogenous enforcement strategies by sustaining extra-costs of competition (CC) and enforcement (EC) they could promote competition on the opposite side of the market, i.e. the side of counterpart's competitors. This joint mechanism may, in turn, promote a bilateral monopoly, in which, a portion of the expected joint rent will be dissipated by cross competition strategies; alternatively, contractual parties may enhance market competition by raising the number of *ex-post* competitors of each party in a contract. When an agent in an incomplete contract wins the cross competition challenge *vis-à-vis* the transactional counterpart, he/she will gain a monopolistic position. Thus, in a cross competition context, rent dissipation represents the amount of endogenous enforcement costs – in terms of competition and enforcement costs – sustained by economic agents to make contractual performance effective. Therefore, with respect to Contractual Rivalry configuration, Cross Competition rejects the implicit assumption of perfect competition markets, stressing the role of enforcement strategies acting on parties' outside options, i.e. the role of market-contract interactions along the original notion of transaction provided by Commons.

A formalization of cross competition equilibria is shown in Nicita (1999) where under the assumption of endogenous outside options, (i) contractors maintain strong incentives to make a specific over-investment; (ii) specific over-investment acts as an enforcement device against post-contractual opportunism; (iii) general over-investment, by increasing post-contractual outside options, could even destroy the initial agreement.

10.3 Contractual rivalry and the ideal-type of perfect competition in Coasian and post-Coasian theories of the firm

Contractual rivalry (i.e. the ideal-type of perfect competition with positive transaction costs) has been implicitly assumed by R. Coase (1937) in his pioneering paper on the nature of the firm. The idea of competitive markets seems crucial for a theory of the firm based on the comparison between the efficiency of the firm and the efficiency of the market. According to the Coasian perspective, the existence of market and firms is explained in terms of their relative transaction costs, which means in terms of the relative efficiency of firm's performance with respect to market performance for given transactions. As Coase (1937) explains:

> It can, I think, be assumed that the distinguishing mark of the firm is the supersession of the price mechanism [. . .]; there is a cost of using the price mechanism [. . .]; the operation of a market costs something and by forming an organization and allowing some authority (an "entrepreneur") to direct the resources, certain marketing costs are saved.

And again:

> Naturally, a point must be reached where the costs of organizing an extra transaction within the firm are equal to the costs involved in carrying out the transaction in the open market, or, to the costs of organizing by another entrepreneur.

Coase recurs to the "marginal cost" argument to mark the boundaries of the efficient internalization of market transactions within the firm with respect to the market. According to Coase, firms exist to the extent that they organize transactions at a lower cost with respect to market exchanges. It is the entrepreneur's direction of resources inside the firm which make the firm efficient respect to the market. At the same time, not all the production observed in an economic system can be carried on by only one big firm: as firms get larger, there may be decreasing returns to the entrepreneur function. There are thus two possible explanations for the internalization of a transaction within the firm: the relative efficiency of the production within the firm with respect to market out-sourcing and the firm's dimension. Thus, the boundaries of the firm depend on market efficiency and vice versa.

However, a theory of the firm based on the relative efficiency of make or buy policies raises a problem about the informational role of market prices and the type of market configuration which is assumed. Since the comparison of make or buy choices for a given transaction should be drawn on an efficiency basis, managers have to share perfect information about the cost of producing a given transaction within the firm and about the price of acquiring the same through the open market. However, how to compare prices when there are no market exchanges and how to select market prices equilibrium when there are too many exchanges?

If the "market configuration" is a monopolistic one, the internalization of market transactions could result in an inefficient make-or-buy choice. On the opposite side, if the market is a perfect competition market, no transactions at all will occur inside the firm. Under the assumption that each entrepreneur has the same informational endowments, when the internalization of market transactions within the firm is more efficient than market exchange, we should expect no market exchange at all and hence no market prices for transactions internally produced by firms. By contrast, when the internalization of a given transaction within the firm is costly with respect to the outsourcing choice, we should expect only market exchanges. One possible way to avoid this vicious circle of logic is to imagine virtual exchanges in a virtual market where price equilibrium is unaffected by agents' choices, sharing the characteristics of a perfect competition market. However, this means reproducing the neo-classical ideal-type of perfect competition market. As a consequence, the Coasian perspective shows a crucial weakness in analyzing contract-market interactions, in non-equilibrium markets.

Following the Coasian perspective, Alchian and Demsetz (1972) have developed a theory of the firm as an institution characterized by a nexus of contracts which do not possess any special characteristic with respect to market contracts. According to Alchian and Demsetz, the main purpose of the firm is to provide the coordination and control function of entrepreneurs when team production is required. In a team production organization workers' effort is not observable by third parties (entrepreneurs). Hence, opportunistic behavior by workers – as *free-riding* or *shirking* – may arise inside the firm. In other words, agents whose effort is not observable by the principal (entrepreneurs) might select a level of effort which is lower than the efficient one. In team production organization it may be very difficult to detect opportunism and, consequently, to impose sanctions on free-riders. Given the failure of monitoring and sanctioning each agent might be induced to provide a sub-optimal effort level. According to Alchian and Demsetz, such a dilemma is solved – in the economic system – by the existence of the firm. Inside the firm, some agents – the entrepreneurs – are induced to monitor the workers and to direct all the resources involved in the production process toward the maximization of the joint surplus.

Beyond the monitoring function there is nothing else, according to Alchian and Demsetz, which makes any difference between transactions occurring inside the firm respect to those exchanged in the open market. At the same time, for Alchian and Demsetz,[14] the open market is a competitive market in which each agent can impose sanctions on the opportunistic behavior of any contractual counterpart by exiting the relationships previously started. This means that, even if Alchian and Demsetz stress the role of the manager for the monitoring of team production firm, their theory seems to be built – as in Coase – on the idea of a competitive market configuration. The idea of competitive markets seems to be implicitly assumed also by the New institutional economics (NIE), mainly based on the contributions given by Oliver Williamson.

NIE's economists have provided an explanation of the firm based on the enforcement role of internal hierarchy. As Williamson has pointed out, there are two components of enforcement costs: the first one relies on *ex-ante* agency costs, while the second is determined by the governance of post-contractual opportunism.

Agency costs refer to the *ex-ante* enforcement costs necessary to ensure an optimal *ex-ante* incentives alignment, and are given by:[15]

> (i)the monitoring expenditures of the principal, (ii) the bonding expenditures by the agent, and (iii) the residual loss

while the *ex-post* enforcement costs are given by:[16]

> (i) the maladaptation costs incurred when transactions drift out of alignment, (ii) the haggling costs incurred if bilateral efforts are made to correct ex post misalignments, (iii) the set-up and running costs associated with the governance structures to which disputes are referred and (iv) bonding costs of effecting secure commitments.

Ex-post enforcement costs, according to Williamson, are thus stronger when specific investment and/or specific assets are involved in incomplete contracts relationships. In such an institutional context the emergence of *ex-ante* and *ex-post* enforcement costs requires a sort of unified governance structure which minimizes overall enforcement costs. According to Williamson the firm represents the efficient governance structure which emerges as an endogenous optimal response to the problem of the minimization of the enforcement costs which characterize recurrent incomplete contracts sustained by asset specificity. This theory provides not only an explanation of the existence of the firm but it also suggests a theory of firm's boundaries: according to Williamson, not every transaction should be organized within the firm but only those transactions which present a high degree of uncertainty and specificity, while generic and standardized transactions should be directed to the market exchange. Hence, the Williamsonian firm is composed by a bundle of internal (long term and specific) and external (generic and spot) contracts. As Klein, Crawford and Alchian (1978) have pointed out (p. 249):

> Firms are formed and revised in markets and the conventional sharp distinction between markets and firms may have little general analytical importance. The pertinent economic question we are faced with is "what kind of contracts are used for what kinds of activities, and why."

The answer is given by Reve (1988: 136), who stresses that

> the nexus of contracts view of organizations then reduces to conceiving the firm as a bundle of *skills* and incentives. The *skills* are needed to realize economic opportunities, and the incentives make sure that the *skills* are kept in place.

The explanation of the nature of the firm as a bundle of *skills* and incentives was also the starting point of the New Property Rights School – associated with the contributions by Grossman, Hart and Moore (GHM). The resulting theory of the firm was based on the efficient governance structure provided by the firm for the enforcement of incomplete contracts sustained by assets specificity. According to GHM, inside the firm, the costs necessary to enforce contractual obligations are minimized by an appropriate allocation of property rights, in the form of residual control right and/or in the form of rights to residual income. The firm constitutes thus an efficient governance structure which allocates contractual safeguards in the most appropriate way. In order to maximize joint surplus within the firm, property rights should be given to those agents who own specific assets or make specific investments. The assignment of property rights on assets will induce contractual parties to participate in the firm's organization. For investors in specific assets, having property rights over them will further increase their incentives to invest. The resulting path-dependent technology will affect the growth of the firm and its economic performance.

The evolution of an explanation of the nature of the firm based on "bundle of skills" theories has been founded on the pioneering works by Nelson and Winter (1982). According to their theory, firms are organizational structures in which skills and information are combined in a rather different way than markets would do, providing the opportunity to improve the joint surplus generated by the members involved. Within the firm, indeed, skills and information are strictly interconnected in *routines* (defined as a complex set of rules and action/reaction programmes) which are not "verifiable" in the sense that underlying behaviors and complimentarities are governed by personal and tacit knowledge (Polanyi, 1958). Nelson and Winter implicitly assume that the emergence – and stabilization – of routines in a firm occur at zero-transaction costs. However, as NIE's economists have stressed, when agents' behaviors require specific investment, in order to ensure optimal incentive alignments, it is necessary to assign and/or exchange property rights on assets. In a dynamic perspective, property rights assignments may raise further distributional conflicts among members. To deter potential post-contractual opportunism when tacit knowledge is present, the resolution of distributional conflicts requires, however, positive enforcement extra-costs. As tacit knowledge increases within the firm, asymmetric distribution of knowledge, information and skills will take place, shaping opportunistic behavior and distributional conflicts among firm's members.

Only if property rights on assets and/or residual control rights are instantaneously transferred (with zero transaction and coordination costs) to the most informed members and/or to those who posses the most essential skills for the organization, the endogenous emergence of knowledge and skills will be fixed in a stable routine. Otherwise, some part of organizational rents will be dissipated by member conflicts and by their opportunistic behavior. However, some property rights configurations could even enhance the evolution of knowledge and skills in a particular direction (routine) without causing any distributional conflicts among asset owners and the members of the firm. In these cases, as Pagano and Rowthorn (1996) have pointed out, the emergence of particular routines in organizations may be explained as *organizational equilibria* between property rights distribution and technological organization: property rights endowments encourage thus the development of a particular technological organization within the firm, and vice versa, a given technological organization induces a particular property rights endowment inside the firm. However even organizational equilibria require positive costs and cumulative effects induced by organizational equilibria are not *per se* irreversible.

Let us consider human capital investments. According to GHM's analysis, developing idiosyncratic skills could be a rational strategy in order to gain residual control rights over some level of the organization. If all members belonging to a given organization invest in human capital, the selection of a particular organizational equilibrium and/or routine will be undermined. As a consequence, it will be very difficult to assess the relative efficiency of firms and routines with respect to any market exchange.

Even if all post-Coasian contributions recalled above explicitly recognize the existence of a reciprocal dependency between the market and the firm, most of them are mainly concerned with the analysis of the structure of the firm, taking for granted the functioning of market institutions and implicitly assuming that "the market" is always an equilibrium market. NIE's approach is mainly concerned with the analysis of an institutional order in which economic agents make their choices alternatively in "the market" or in "the contract." "The market" (the efficiency branch[17]) is characterized by zero extra-costs of competition and zero extra-costs of enforcement – as mentioned above – given that agents are price-taker and there is no room for strategic competition. "The contract" refers to a bilateral monopoly configuration (the monopoly branch) where specific/idiosyncratic economic agents receive appropriate safeguards (extra-costs of enforcement are positive) in order to make the investments which maximize the expected joint surplus. Hence, in the monopoly branch, an *ex-ante* market relationship is transformed into an *ex-post* bilateral monopoly (fundamental transformation[18]).

Now, for this transformation to be "fundamental," it is necessary to assume that future variations of agents' outside options and/or of market configuration will not generate any dissipation of contractual quasi-rents. In other terms, post-Coasian theories of the firm implicitly assume that once the parties are "locked-in" to the contract, both the parties become definitely *co-specific*. The cross competition configuration reverses this conclusion, by stressing the effects of potential changes in parties' outside options for contractual enforcement.

10.4 From contractual rivalry to cross competition

According to the standard literature on incomplete contracts, for a contract to lock-in the parties involved, every change affecting parties' outside options should not be "binding."[19] In order to guarantee that this outcome occurs, the *ex-post* division of surplus between the parties should always give them a payoff greater than that associated with their next best alternative. Moreover, if the type of investment selected by agents affects their outside options – and therefore their degree of co-specificity – at least one agent in the contract might be induced to select the investment type which increases counterpart's competitors and/or reduces own competitors. Thus, each contractor may be induced to switch from the selection of efficient investments in the attempt to lock the counterpart into the contract by reducing endogenously his/her *ex-post* contractual power. This means that *ex-post* variation in parties' outside options could occur not only in response to exogenous contingencies, but also as a reaction to agents' strategic behavior. According to NIE's economists, in an incomplete contract framework characterized by assets' specificity, the fundamental transformation acts only in one way: from a spot contract to a bilateral monopoly. There is no room, in such an approach, for the opposite "transformation" occurring from a bilateral monopoly to a spot contract. In other words, once made – and enforced by private orderings – a bilateral monopoly will be always "protected" from any *ex-post* change in parties' outside options.

Moreover, as Williamson (1985) has argued, fundamental transformation has some dynamic consequence. In the case of the adoption of a specific technology, there will be a tendency to develop safeguards to protect this specific investment. The new property rights school (mainly based on the"GHM approach") shares the same view, stressing that an appropriate allocation of property rights on assets constitutes a sufficient condition to induce parties in a contract to make specific investments and hence to ensure the enforcement of incomplete contracts. Assigning property rights on assets will induce efficient investments as long as the technology adopted is coherent with the initial distribution of property rights. Thus, the nature of the resources belonging to the firm depends upon the property rights assigned and/or the governance system adopted.

As Hart (1995) has argued (p.29):

> Why does ownership of physical and non-human assets matter? The answer is that ownership is a source of power when contracts are incomplete.

The GHM approach shows however two main limits. The first one, is that it implicitly assumes that, for a given contract, any *ex-post* changes in the market will not have a remarkable impact on parties' outside options (assumption 1: variations of exogenous outside options are never binding). A second weakness is given by the assumption that agent's skills and capabilities will not be affected by any investment made in human capital. This means that the original substitutability or complementarities between agents will not change in response to the investments made by the parties, preserving the original incentive alignments from any *ex-post* distributional conflict (assumption 2: parties' outside options are not affected by the investment made).

Assumption 1 is simply unrealistic. Exogenous shocks on the form of the market could destroy the gains associated with the initial agreement when, for at least one of them, the outside option becomes binding (for example a new potential counterpart enters in the market and makes an offer). As a consequence, exogenous variations in parties' outside options could modify parties incentives to perform contractual obligation.

Assumption 2 is controversial as well. The circumstance that the original substitutability and/or complementarities between agents are not affected by the investments made implies that agents' skills and capabilities are not affected by human capital investments. This requires, in turn, the absence of learning processes, which represent an essential characteristic of any investments in human capital. However, if human capital investments involve agents' learning processes then their original substitutability or complementarities relationships are inevitably affected by the investments made. As a consequence, original agents' heterogeneity could be destroyed and agents could substitute each other in the organization process. In other terms, when human capital investments involve learning process, parties' outside options will be endogenously modified by the investments made (Barca, 1994).

If assumptions 1 and 2 in the GHM model are removed, the efficient device given by property rights assignment collapses, and we are forced to look for alternative enforcement devices.

The removal of assumption 2 implies that investors could use the endogenous variation of parties' outside options as a strategic tool for the enforcement of the contract. Given that a party's outside option represents its next best alternative, the removal of assumption 2 implies that the parties involved in a bilateral contract face a complex interaction among four representative agents, the two parties involved in the transactional exchange and the best competitor of each, according to the transaction *à la* Commons.

10.4.1 A graphical illustration

The graph in Figure 10.6, represents the joint surplus S^* generated by a buyer b and a seller s when they make optimal specific investments (m^*, n^* in the example in Section 10.1). Given *ex-ante* parties' contractual power (α represents buyer's contractual power), a point like A determines expected surplus sharing (U_{s^*}, U_{b_*}) after optimal investments have been selected by parties, whereas D represents the *ex-ante* default or disagreement point. Here, D is determined by parties' *ex-ante* outside options $[v_{s^\circ}, v_{b^\circ}]$. In the case of first-best investments, the triangle BDC identifies parties' quasi-rents. However, as we have stressed in previous sections, when contract is incomplete, parties are induced to delay investment decisions in the attempt to hold up contractual counterpart. As a consequence, parties cannot commit themselves not to renegotiate, and bilateral underinvestment will be the dominant strategy for both. Let us assume now, for instance, that the buyer selects the optimal investment whereas the seller may select an investment which reduces seller's competitors but requires a higher cost with respect to the first-best investment. Given that the outside option of an agent identifies the potential competitors of the contractual counterpart, such an investment allows the seller to reduce buyer's outside option from v_b° to $v_b^{\circ\circ}$, shifting in Figure 10.6 the default point from D to D'. Since D' acts as a threat point at post-contractual renegotiation stage, the seller will improve its bargaining position *vis-à-vis* the buyer. In particular, if the buyer maintains the *ex-ante* contractual power (we can assume an exogenous surplus sharing rule as in the case of Nash generalized bargaining solution), the new surplus sharing point will be determined by A' on the $S^{*\circ}$ line [where the difference $(S^* - S^{*\circ})$ is due to the extra-costs sustained by the seller]. However, if we assume a take-it-or-leave-it renegotiation, the seller may even obtain an *ex-post* payoff given by $(S^{\circ *} - v_{b^{\circ\circ}})$, by extracting all the buyer's quasi-rent, in point B'.

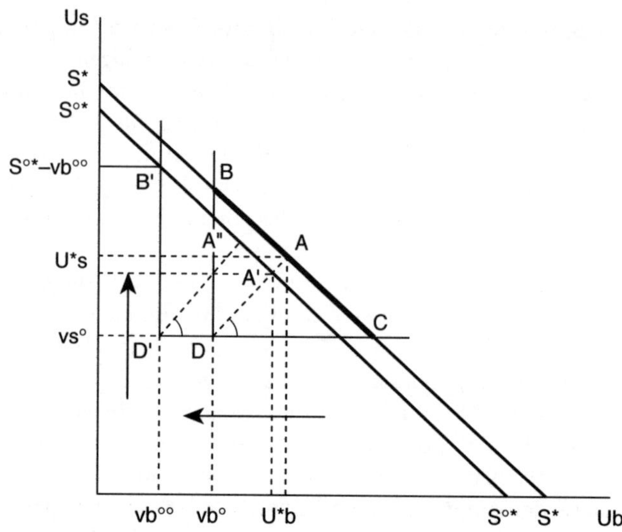

Figure 10.6

Now, suppose that the buyer also may select an investment which decreases seller's outside option, shifting the default point from D to D'' as in Figure 10.7. If both the agents "overinvest', their combined actions may generate a default point as D''', leaving unaffected parties' surplus sharing, whereas increasing their co-specificity and decreasing their joint surplus l [the difference $(S^* - S^{\circ\circ})$ is due to the extra-costs sustained by the parties]. The bilateral over-investment equilibrium is reached in K, and the segment $A''K$ represents the quasi-rent loss sustained by the seller for the enforcement of the contract (similar loss is incurred by the buyer). If the extra-costs sustained by agents are such that the joint surplus is given by S°, then parties dissipate all the expected rent in order to improve their post-contractual power and deter counterpart's hold-up.

In Figure 10.8, we assume that the seller may select a (over)investment $\hat{i}_s$ (a general purpose investment), increasing his own outside option until the new default point is reached in d' which increases counterpart's competitor, improving seller's outside option. The triangle $B'D'A''$ which represents the new joint surplus.

If the default option is greater than D' (on the segment $D'B''$) then the new bargaining area will be given by the triangle $B''D'A''$. If the seller makes a take-it-or-leave-it offer to the buyer then the new surplus sharing point will be given by B'', which transfers to the seller all the *ex-post* joint surplus given by the triangle $B''D'A''$, which corresponds to a seller post-contractual power equal to 1.

However, if the buyer selects a specific over-investment (which reduces the outside option of the seller), then the expected increase in seller's outside option will be fully compensated by buyer's investment. In this case, the joint rent generated will be equal to $S^{\circ\wedge}$ which is lower than $S^{*\wedge}$, given the extra-costs sustained by agents in the case of over-investment.

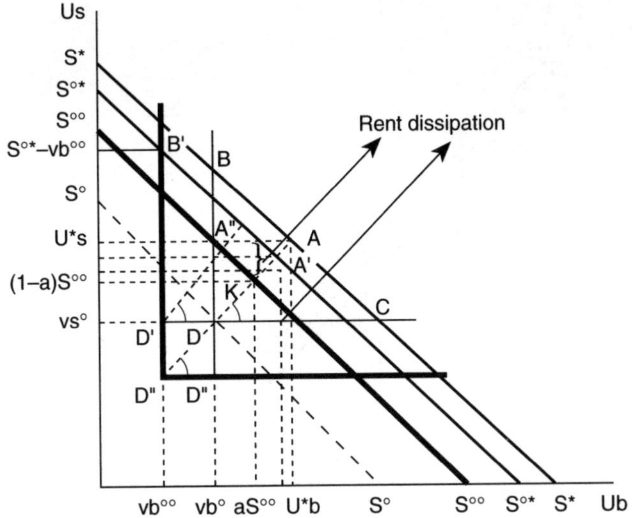

Figure 10.7

If we assume that the variation induced by an agent on his own outside option is fully compensated by the opposite variation induced by the other agent's specific over-investment, then the default option will not be affected by the investments made by contractual parties. The joint rent dissipation – as the case shown above – represents then the costs require to endogenously enforce the contract. In this case the surplus sharing will be given by the point G in Figure 10.9.

However, if the buyer and seller both select a general over-investment, the *ex-post* default point, will be given by H in Figure 10.9 with a negative joint surplus. In such a case "market exchanges" assign to the agents a payoff which is greater than the one obtained within the contractual relationship, so that agents select their outside options (escape).

The incentives alignment process which gives safeguards to the investor is always the result of a complex interaction among the agents involved. In a multilateral setting, like the nexus of contracts characterizing the organization of the firm, the degree of assets specificity is thus endogenous, depending on the strategies made by other agents within the firm.

In a cross competition configuration, the degree of assets specificity affects parties' outside options and the only two possible equilibria are i) bilateral over-investment; ii) bilateral under-investment. For a formal proof see Nicita (1999).

10.5 Cross competition and the co-evolution of skills and routines

The preceding section shows how difficult it is to enforce an efficient configuration that would correspond to efficient bilateral investments: in an incomplete con-

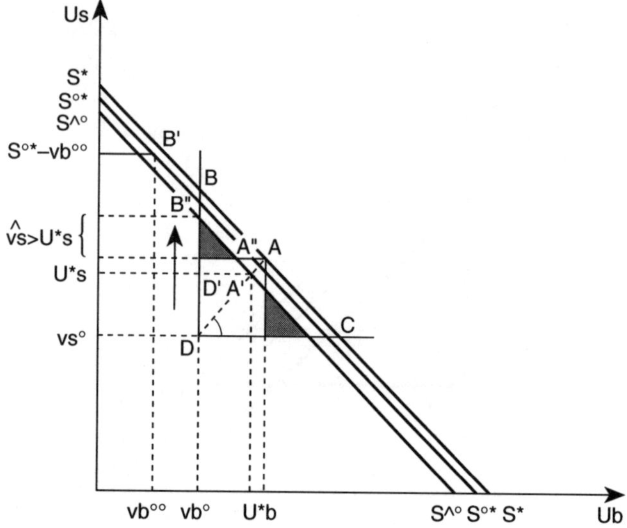

Figure 10.8

tract framework, a bilateral under-investment or even a bilateral over-investment represent the most probable outcomes, in the absence of any form of third party verifiability or coercion (Nicita, 1999). This means that the efficient harmonized routines inside the firm do not easily evolve in a cross competition context. According to the perspective originated by Nelson and Winter (1982), agents involved in firm organizational routines will decide to invest in human capital, despite the fact that by doing so they reduce their *ex-post* outside options, becoming firm specific and then a potential victim of post-contractual opportunism.

The absence of any potential conflict among the agents involved in organizational routines implicitly implies in turn (i) the assumption of a continuous instantaneous redistribution device constantly redirecting property rights on assets assigning them to the most specific agents, or (ii) the assumption of "agent morality" in the sense that agents involved in organizational routines are not opportunist. In the first case, even if we assume an initial efficient redistribution of property rights on assets, human learning and human capital investments will change assets specificity over time. As we have shown above, agents could over-invest in order to become the most specific resource and gain the right to residual control over organizational assets, or they could under-invest and then act as opportunists making take-or-leave-it offers. Unless one assumes that whatever is the investment made in human capital, it will not modify agents' substitutability or complementarity – which is the assumption made by GHM – nothing will ensure that the initial attribution of property rights will continue to be the optimal response to agents skills profiles: skills will compete with one another to gain rights to residual income or to residual control. Nelson and Winter seem to neglect the internal evolution of routines. Departing from agents' skills, Nelson and Winter define organizational routine as organic rationality, emphasizing the problem of competition among rou-

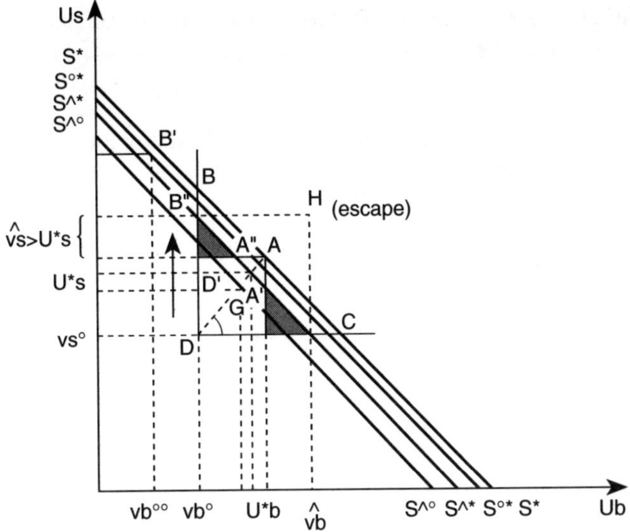

Figure 10.9

tines, whereas neglecting the question of competition among skills. According to their analysis, they focus on the case of "a firm imitating the routine of another," disregarding all the potential conflicts that can raise within organizations when competition among skills involve a process of imitation (and then of substitution) among skills. This is somehow paradoxical since internal skills' competition affects a single routine and its relationship with other routines. As a consequence, not only competition among routines affects their internal skills, but also internal competition among skills within a routine can modify routines and affect competition among routines. The result of such a complex interaction is a co-evolution process of skills and routines dynamics.

For a routine to be preserved by internal competition among skills it is necessary to inhibit the endogenous variability of agents' outside options.

In the following sub-sections we show thus how alternative institutional arrangements in recent economic history, like the Tayloristic firm, the Japanese firm and the German industrial organization system, might be explained in terms of alternative organizational "rigidities" of parties' outside options.

10.5.1 The Tayloristic firm

In his famous contribution "What do bosses do?" S. Marglin (1973) asserts that the emergence of hierarchical organizations in the capitalistic society was not the result of their technical efficiency. Rather, it represents the immediate outcome of the capitalistic accumulation process. According to Marglin, the division of labor inside the capitalistic firm was not the optimal response to an efficient maximization process, rather, it was essential in order to give the "boss" an essential role in the production process.

As Braverman points out, the Tayloristic firm provides such a "scientific" organization of work. The main characteristics of the Tayloristic firm are (Pagano, 1990):

1. the dissociation of the labor process from the skills of the workers;
2. the separation of conception from execution;
3. the use of this monopoly over knowledge to control each step of the labor process and its mode of execution.

In terms of the cross competition framework, these characteristics imply that:

(a) in order to be employed in a wide range of different tasks within the firm, human capital should possess a high degree of malleability (workers' outside options must be affected by management's investments);
(b) having control over human capital, gives the capitalist the power to direct such assets to the desired specialization (i.e. the capitalist has control over workers' outside options);
(c) as human capital specializes, it loses its potential generality, becoming specific to a particular task (or to a particular division of labor); as human capital becomes specific to the Tayloristic firm, the capitalist becomes *essential* for the worker (asymmetry in the variations of outside options gives the capitalist the chance to defeat workers' cross competition);
(d) if the distribution of knowledge inside the firm is not affected by exogenous changes, then the "scientific" division of labor – within the Tayloristic firm – minimizes workers' outside options and maximizes capitalists' outside options.

As Braverman (1974) has stressed (p. 180),

> the capitalist mode of production systematically destroys all-around skills where they exist, and brings into being skills and occupations that correspond to its needs. (. . .) The generalized distribution of knowledge of the productive process among all its participants becomes, from this point on, not merely "unnecessary," but a positive barrier to the functioning of the capitalist mode of production.

This process of work degradation may be hence represented as a process of workers' outside options minimization. As Edwards (1979: 286) has pointed out, the capitalist mode of production is based on three elements:

> (1) Direction, or a mechanism or method by which the employer directs work tasks, specifying what needs to be done, in what order, with what degree of precision or accuracy, and in what period of time; (2) Evaluation, or a procedure whereby the employer supervises and evaluates to correct mistakes or other failures in production, to assess each worker's performance, and to identify workers or groups of workers who are not performing work tasks

adequately; (3) Discipline, or an apparatus that the employer uses to discipline and reward workers, in order to elicit cooperation and enforce compliance with the capitalist's direction of the labor process.

According to Taylor, in order to induce workers to reveal their knowledge the direction has to give them the appropriate incentives: workers should be encouraged to suggest any possible improvement in the production process. Besides, inducing workers to reveal their knowledge is a way of monitoring them and extracting from them any new information they are able to capture. Once the information is acquired by the capitalist manager it is possible to communicate that information to a new worker. This means that (i) a growing number of workers will share the same information and (ii) any worker could be replaced by another. In other words, the three elements characterizing the Tayloristic firm – *Direction, Evaluation, Discipline* – allow the capitalistic manager to modify capitalists' and workers' outside options: capitalists are essential for each worker, while capitalists could instantly replace any worker.[20] Thus, the role of capitalists relies upon their ability to extract diffused knowledge from workers and to increase the asymmetric information between capitalists and workers with the purpose: (1) to make workers' knowledge specific to the capitalist mode of production, selecting and reinforcing the division of labor and the technical combination of assets which minimize workers' outside options; (2) to make capitalists able to replace workers instantly; (3) to make capitalists essential for the firm given their ability to direct and control human and physical assets, selecting and reinforcing the division of labor and the technical combination of assets which maximize capitalists' outside options.

The "degradation of work" (Wood, 1982) thus requires the degradation of workers' knowledge and skills. As Braverman (1974: 406) refers:

> (the capitalist division of labor) shapes not only work, but populations as well, because over the long run it creates that mass of simple labor which is the primary feature of population in developed capitalist countries.

The process of knowledge appropriation by capitalists implies then that the only possible organization of work is the capitalistic one. Since the process of the degradation of work is extended to the market, the capitalist can use the market (capitalists' outside options) as a workers' discipline device. In Braverman's view, the combined action of each capitalist will polarize social classes, causing the formation of two opposite social classes: capitalist and worker classes. However, while collective action it is difficult to be sustained by workers (especially of the unemployment rate is positive), capitalists successfully collude to minimize workers' outside options. As S. Bowles (1985) has stressed (p. 346),

> [. . .]the concept of capitalist technology is based on the proposition that cost minimization by competitive employers implies the selection of profitable but inefficient technologies even in the absence of market failures arising from collusion, externalities, extended time horizon and the like. [. . .] The capitalist has chosen an inefficient technology when there exist some other method of

> production that, per unit of output, uses less of at least some input and not more of any. The logic of the concept of capitalist technology is that a technology that is inefficient in the above sense may nonetheless be cost minimizing if it allows the capitalist to lower the cost of some input. This is possible in the Marxian model because the firm is not a price taker with respect to the price of labor, but rather may alter this cost through the selection of various labor extraction strategies.

In other terms, the selection of inefficient technologies by the capitalist, could nonetheless be cost-minimizing if the technologies which are selected are able to minimize workers' outside options and/or to maximize capitalists' outside options. Hence, what the *cross competition* framework suggests is that the strategic use of the degree of assets specificity is sufficient to modify endogenously agents' outside options, and capitalists do not need to recur to the unemployment rate as a worker discipline device (Shapiro and Stiglitz, 1984). The capitalistic firm is thus shaped as a bundle of technical interdependencies which make the capitalist able to defeat workers' cross competition.

10.5.2 The Japanese firm and the German industrial system

In the cross competition framework, agents in an incomplete contract might be induced to under-invest or to over-invest in assets specificity when specific investments affect parties' outside options (Nicita, 1999). When the economic resources spent to sustain bilateral over-investments exceed the expected joint surplus, the interactions between contractual parties will lead to a full rent dissipation equilibrium. In the case of symmetric agents, assuming endogenous outside options may even destroy any expected joint rent. In order to avoid joint rent dissipation it may be useful to introduce some external "rigidities" over parties' outside options variability, as in the graphical example in Section 10.4. Such rigidities can be introduced at the market level (market rigidities) or at the level of the firm (organizational rigidities). The introduction of "market rigidities" means that a given task – within a firm operating in a given industrial sector – is not specific to that firm in a specific routine, but corresponds to a standardized task. This means that firm's organization is the result of a combination of standardized tasks with different degrees of specialization. The possessor of a standardized task skill will be able to offer his human capital in different firms over industrial sectors: his outside options do not vary across different market opportunities. On the opposite side, "firm rigidity" refer to firm specific human capital. The possessor of a firm specific skill will not be able to sell his human capital over different firms and industrial sectors: his outside options will vary across different market opportunities but they do not vary across different tasks inside the firm.

The introduction of such rigidities, by reducing the endogenous variability of agents' outside options (across market opportunities or across firms tasks), also decreases the possibility of rent dissipation induced by over-investment.

Looking at the historical evolution of firms in alternative institutional settings, it is possible to select two historical examples of market and firm rigidity, showing how they represent alternative institutional solutions to cross competition conflicts within the firm and in the market: the first one is represented by the German industrial structure, the second is given by the organization of the Japanese firm. Between these two opposite cases it is possible then to classify the socialist organization and the Tayloristic organization as alternative institutional arrangements.

In the case of German industrial system, the standardization of tasks enables workers with different degree of specialization to exit at negligible costs (in the absence of unemployment). Salary levels and tasks are negotiated by labor unions and industrial associations. Though it takes place in firms, worker's performance is already pre-arranged and defined at the market level. This means that due to market rigidity, managers may not reduce workers' outside options. The task is "fixed" and "defined" but there is a high degree of worker flexibility among different firms. In other terms, in the German industrial system workers' outside options are rigid downward. Thus, in such an institutional setting, workers receive appropriate safeguards to develop skills which are specific to standardized tasks.

On the opposite side, the traditional Japanese firm provides tenure to workers. Once locked into the firm, workers provide a high degree of mobility among different tasks and the tenure acts as an appropriate safeguard in order to induce workers to make specific investments in human capital. This means that in the Japanese firm workers' outside options result relatively unaffected by investments which increase the opportunities for workers outside the firm. The worker task is not defined inside the firm and as a consequence the worker may perform different tasks; however, there is a low degree of worker flexibility among different firms. In other terms, in the Japanese firm workers' outside options are rigid upward. Thus, in this institutional setting, workers receive appropriate safeguards to develop firm specific skills.

Between the German industrial system and the Japanese firm, workers' organization in classical socialism constitutes another different example of institutional equilibrium, where workers' outside options are perfectly rigid: in order to develop firm and task specific skills workers receive appropriate safeguards (firm and market rigidities ensure tenure and market opportunities across firms). Finally, the Tayloristic firm corresponds to the case of perfect elastic workers' outside options. The absence of any firm or market rigidity implies that workers can be employed in different tasks in different firms and the capitalists may affect workers' outside options with the purpose of extracting them all contractual power.

The co-existence of alternative governance structures of the firm may be explained thus as a second best response to the market failures which would arise in a "cross competition" context. The evolution of such alternative organizational arrangements may represent thus multiple "second best" configurations in an incomplete contract framework. In this sense, the framework of cross competition may offer some sort of "microfoundations" for the explanation of (i) the emergence of occupational markets rigidities (which ensure an easy switch of workers from one firm to another) and (ii) the structuring of internal labor markets within the firm which isolate workers from external competition.

Table 10.3 Workers' outside options elasticity in alternative institutional settings

		Market structure	
		Market rigidity	*Market flexibility*
Firm organizations	Firm rigidity	Socialism *Outside options* Rigid	Japanese firm *Outside options* Rigid upward
	Firm flexibility	German industrial system *Outside options* Rigid downwards	Taylorism *Outside options* Elastic

10.6 Revisiting the Coasian firm

The cross competition framework provides some interesting implications in terms of the theory of the firm. In a bilateral incomplete contract with positive extra-costs of competition (CC), each agent selects the degree of assets' specificity which maximizes his/her own outside options and/or minimizes the counterpart's outside options.

Since such an endogenous enforcement device is founded on the variation of parties' outside options, in order to determine the correct function of outside options, agents involved in market transactions have to acquire a very high level of information. In particular, they have to know not only the prices of market exchanges, as in the original Coasian formulation, but they also have to know the set of possible investments each potential counterpart faces and the expected impacts of such investments on the outside options of every party involved in transactions (agents S, S', B, B' in the transaction *à la* Commons). Given these complex contract-market interactions, one should expect that in a cross competition context characterized by a high number of economic agents, it will be impossible to realize endogenous enforcement devices "in the market." This means that the only equilibrium configuration that will characterize cross competition markets will be the inefficient one associated with under-investment by agents. Even if we assume perfect knowledge, one possible outcome might be that of multilateral over-investment with a total dissipation of the expected joint surplus.

In recent economic history, as in the case of the Japanese firm and the German industrial organization, economic agents seem having built over time, complex institutional arrangements with the purpose of introducing some form of outside options' rigidity, minimizing the possibility of uncontrolled cross competition among economic agents. Such complex institutional arrangements characterize the modern firm in its different forms, as we have seen above. The organization of economic activity in firms introduces thus appropriate forms of pre-commitment in the agents' behaviors which mitigate the incentives to cross competition. The decision to delegate to managerial direction the function of control over the actions realized by each economic agent involved in a given transaction, helps in inhibiting the multilateral cross competition among economic agents, even if it cannot eliminate bilateral cross competition between each single agent and the direction.

Such principal-agent relationship may thus be shaped as an authority relationship in which the direction (the managers) holds the residual control rights over actions undertaken by agents belonging to the same economic organization. In order to save the amount of extra-costs of competition and enforcement otherwise necessary to make the economic transaction effective, each agent will thus accept to be monitored by the direction. Moreover, given that each agent belonging to the same economic organization, shares the same direction, each agent is involved in a single bilateral cross competition challenge with the direction. Internal multilateral competition is thus mitigated by a network of bilateral cross competition challenges within the firm.

The notion of cross competition provides hence an alternative explanation for the emergence of the firm, in its different forms, as an evolutionary enforcement device which allows economic agents to save the extra-costs of competition (*CC*) and enforcement (*EC*) otherwise unavoidable in a cross competition market.

The circumstance that multilateral cross competition is transformed – within the firm – into a network of bilateral cross competition relationships between each agent and the direction, shows how firm organization may perform only a second best configuration (over-investment or under-investment) as in the standard literature on incomplete contracts.

We may thus re-formulate the main points of the Coasian theory of the firm in a context of cross competition (i.e. when competition and enforcement costs are positive):

1. The firm constitutes a complex institutional structure for the governance of all the economic transactions which the market is not able to govern.

2. The firm is aimed at transforming the multilateral cross competition occurring within the market into a network of bilateral cross competition relationships, minimizing the extra-costs of competition and enforcement occurring in the market. While in the Coasian formulation the impossibility of coordinating economic transactions through market exchanges was given by agents' difficulty of knowing the market prices, in a cross competition context the economic agents share the difficulty of knowing the slope of the functions of relevant agents' outside options.

3. The organization of economic activity within the firm introduces some rigidities on the endogenous variations of agents' outside options, minimizing social rent dissipation resulting from over-investments. While in a Coasian perspective the dimension of the firm was given by the limits of coordination of the entrepreneur-manager, here the dimension of the firm is determined by the endogenous variation of agents' outside options.

4. Endogenous changes in agents' outside options might even result in a full dissipation of expected social rent and thus in a "destruction" of the firm.

10.7 Conclusions

When incomplete contract relationships occur in an institutional context characterized by positive extra costs of competition and enforcement, the emergence of institutional arrangements which introduce some form of rigidity on the variations of agents' outside options constitutes a second best enforcement device which transforms multilateral cross competition into a network of bilateral cross competition relationships.

When both agents in a contract try to make endogenous enforcement strategies they could promote competition on the opposite side of the market, i.e. the side of the counterpart's competitors. This joint mechanism could, in turn, promote a bilateral monopoly, in which, a positive amount of the expected joint rent will be dissipated by cross competition strategies, or it could enhance market competition by raising the number of *ex-post* competitors of each party in a contract. The latter strategy will reduce *ex-post* contractual power of each contractual party, causing a full rent dissipation equal to the amount of competition and enforcement costs spent by each party. Alternatively, when an agent in an incomplete contract wins the cross competition challenge *vis-à-vis* the transactional counterpart, he/she will gain a monopolistic position. Thus, in a cross competition context, rent dissipation represents the amount of endogenous enforcement costs – in terms of competition and enforcement costs – sustained by agents to make the contractual performance effective.

The framework proposed shows – in sharp contrast with the main contributions in standard literature on incomplete contracts and the nature of the firm – that in order to enforce incomplete contracts in a cross competition context, the agents involved might even overinvest when their outside options are affected by the investment selected.

When parties' outside options are endogenous, the nature and the extent of the variation of agents' outside options will shape firms and markets in a co-evolutionary way. The diversity which characterizes alternative models of the firm could thus be explained on the basis of the multiplicity of second best solutions emerging as efficient responses to the complex interactions occurring between the firm and the market.

Acknowledgments

Author is grateful for useful comments to U. Pagano and S. Bowles, F. Cafaggi, S. Chiu, V. Crawford, N. Dimitri, M. Franzini, F. Hahn, R. Pardolesi and O. Williamson. The usual disclaimers apply.

Notes

1 Only some recent papers are explicitly concerned with investment decisions in a market environment, as K. Chatterjee and Y.S. Chiu (1999) and de Meza and Lockwood (1998). The analysis of contractual enforcement in a market context is also studied by MacLeod and Malcomson (1993) and Bolton and Whinston (1993).

2 See Williamson (1985).
3 On this, see also Edlin and Hermalin (1998) and Osborne and Rubinstein (1990).
4 See Hölmstrom and Milgrom (1991).
5 See Williamson, 1975, 1985; Klein, Crawford and Alchian, 1978; Grossman and Hart, 1986; Hart and Moore, 1990.
6 This is just an extension of the well-known case of General Motors and Fisher Body. See Klein, Crawford and Alchian (1978) and Hart (1995) for a survey.
7 We can also assume that Netscape is not able to cover entirely the whole market demand for widgets.
8 For instance, a specific and sunk investment which is a "signal" of future predatory behavior by Microsoft in downstream markets; a multiple investment which is specific to Netscape and increases Microsoft advertising expenses, or realizes targets rebates policies towards Microsoft's retailers, and so on.
9 A crucial point here regards the assumption made on the existence of symmetric information between the two contractual parties, as it is usual done in the standard literature.
10 According to Commons every economic exchange implies alienation and acquisition of property rights in a commodity, whereas the word "commodity" identifies not only the merely possession of a physical thing but also a "lawful ownership" (1950: 48–49).
11 As Commons (1950: 51) points out: "[e]ventually there is a future Supreme Court to which appeal may be made on any alleged act of injustice by the trial court, or by the legislature or executive which has given directions to the trial court.
12 See also Shapiro and Stiglitz (1984).
13 According to Hart (1995) a contract is incomplete when it involves at least one of the following transactions costs: (1) the cost to each party of anticipating the various eventualities that may occur during the life of the relationship; (2) the cost of deciding, and reaching an agreement about, how to deal with such eventualities; (3) the cost of writing the contract in a sufficiently clear and unambiguous way that the terms of the contract can be enforced; and (4) the legal cost of enforcement.
14 Alchian and Demsetz (1972) have stressed that the main characterization of modern organization of firms is the organization of team production rather than contracts' length.
15 See Jensen and Meckling (1976), p. 309.
16 See Williamson (1988).
17 See O. Williamson (1985), p. 26
18 See O. Williamson (1985).
19 See MacLeod and Malcomson (1993).
20 The underlying assumption is that (i) it is not possible to co-ordinate workers collective action and/or (ii) a positive unemployment rate acts as a worker discipline device (see Shapiro and Stiglitz, 1984).

References

Alchian, A. and H. Demsetz (1972) Production, information costs and economic organization. *American Economic Review* 62: 777–95.

Barca, F. (1994) *Imprese in cerca di padrone*. Laterza

Bolton P. and M.D. Whinston (1993) Incomplete contracts, vertical integration and supply assurance. *Review of Economic Studies* 60(1): 121–148.

Bowles, S. (1985) The production process in a competitive economy: Walrasian, neo-Hobbesian, and Marxian models. In L. Putterman (ed.) (1986) *The Economic Nature of the Firm. A Reader*. Cambridge: Cambridge University Press.

Bowles, S. and H. Gintis (1999) Power in competitive exchange. In S. Bowles, M. Franzini and U. Pagano (eds) *The Politics and Economics of Power*. London: Routledge.

Braverman, H. (1974) *Labour and Monopoly Capital.* New York: Monthly Review Press.
Chatterjee, K. and Y.S. Chiu (1999) *When Does Competition Lead to Efficient Investments?* Mimeo.
Coase, R. (1937) The nature of the firm. *Economica.* 4: 386–405.
Commons, J.R. (1924) *Legal Foundations of Capitalism*, Translated in *I Fondamenti Giuridici del Capitalismo.* (1981). Bolgona: Il Mulino.
Commons, J.R. (1934) *Institutional Economics.* Madison: University of Wisconsin Press.
Commons, J.R. (1950) *The Economics of Collective Action.* Madison: University of Wisconsin Press.
de Meza and Lockwood (1998) Does asset ownership always motivate managers? Outside options and the property rights theory of the firm. *Quarterly Journal of Economics* 113(2): 361–86.
Edlin, A. and Hermalin (1998) *Contract Renegotiation and Options in Agency Problems.* Mimeo.
Grossman, S. and O. Hart (1986) The costs and the benefits of ownership: a theory of vertical and lateral integration. *Journal of Political Economy* 94: 691–719.
Hart, O. (1995) *Firms, contracts and Financial Structure.* Oxford: Oxford University Press.
Hart, O. and J. Moore (1990) Property rights and the nature of the firm. *Journal of Political Economy* 98: 1119–1158.
Hölmstrom, B. and P. Milgrom (1991) Multitask principal agent analyses: incentive contracts, asset ownership, and job design. *Journal of Law, Economics and Organization* 7: 24–52.
Jensen, M.C. and W. Meckling (1976) Theory of the firm: managerial behaviour, agency costs and ownership structure. *Journal of Financial Economics* 3: 305–60
Klein, B., R. Crawford and A. Alchian (1978) Vertical integration, appropriable rents, and the competitive contracting process. *Journal of Law and Economics* 21: 297–326. Reprinted in L. Putterman (ed.) (1986) *The Economic Nature of the Firm.* Cambridge: Cambridge University Press.
MacLeod, B. and J. Malcomson (1993) Investments, hold-up, and the form of market contracts. *American Economic Review* 83: 811–837.
Marglin, S. (1973) What do bosses do? the origins and functions of hierarchy in capitalist production. In A. Gorz (ed.) *The Division of Labour: The Labour Process and Class Struggle in Modern Capitalism.* Paris: Seuil.
Nelson, R. and S.G. Winter (1982) *An Evolutionary Theory of Economic Change.* Cambridge, MA: Harvard University Pres.
Nicita, A. (1999) Incomplete contracts, assets' specificity and overinvestment. *Quaderni del Dipartimento* 249, Università di Siena.
Osborne, M.J. and A. Rubinstein (1990), *Bargaining and Markets.* San Diego, CA: Academic Press.
Pagano, U. (1990) Braverman, Harry. *Quaderni del Diparimento di Economia Politica* 108: 3, Università di Siena.
Pagano, U. and R. Rowthorn (1996) *Democracy and Efficiency in the Economic Enterprise.* London: Routledge.
Polanyi, M. (1958) *Personal Knowledge.* Chicago: The University of Chicago Press.
Reve, T. (1990) The firm as a nexus of internal and external contracts. In M. Aoki, B. Gustafsson and O. Williamson (eds) *The Firm as a Nexus of Treaties.* London: Sage.
Williamson, O. (1975) *Markets and Hierarchies.* New York: Free Press.
Williamson, O. (1985) *The Economic Institutions of Capitalism: Firms, Markets, Relational Contracting.* New York: The Free Press.
Williamson, O. (1988) Corporate finance and corporate governance. *Journal of Finance* 43. Reprinted in O. Williamson (1996) *The Mechanisms of Governance.* Oxford: Oxford University Press.
Wood, S. (1982) *The Degradation of Work?* London: Hutchison.

Part IV
The evolution of norms

11 Equilibrium selection and the evolution of norms

Robert Boyd

11.1 Introduction

In this lecture, I want to bring together two bodies of evolutionary theory and then apply the resulting amalgam to a very interesting problem, the evolution of norms in human societies. The two bodies of theory are:

- *Evolutionary game theory* provides simple, analytically tractable models of the evolution of social behavior. Originally developed by biologists, it has recently been adopted by economists dissatisfied with "traditional" game theory which assumes perfectly rational agents.
- *The theory of evolution in structured populations* provides models of evolution in populations that are subdivided so that mating, social and ecological interactions are not uniform throughout the population. It has been developed by population geneticists interested in more basic problems such as the evolution of sets of co-adapted genes.

While these two bodies of theory have developed almost independently, I believe that they are relevant to each other in the following important way: evolutionary game theory is mainly about equilibrium behavior. The existence of a particular observed behavior or social pattern is explained by demonstrating that such behavior is a evolutionarily stable. This explanatory strategy works fine if there is only one equilibrium outcome, or if you can convincingly argue that only one of a small number equilibria is the likely outcome. The problem is that a broad class of important games have vast numbers of alternative stable equilibria. Different equilibria often support radically different behavioral outcomes, so, in effect, evolutionary game theory predicts that anything can happen.

I believe that one empirically plausible way out of this problem is to embed evolutionary game theory in a structured population. In real human societies no-one interacts with anyone at random. Instead, human populations are structured in various ways. In simple societies that interest anthropologists like me, people interact more often with people in their own village, their own lineage or moiety, or their own ethnic group. In modern societies population structure is created by neighborhoods, unions, firms, and a variety of other institutions. In structured populations, under the right conditions, different subpopulations may arrive at different, persistent quasi-equilibrium states, and then the interaction between different subpopulations can eventually lead to the predictable evolution of the entire population to a single equilibrium state.

Combining these two bodies of evolutionary theory is relevant to the evolution of norms in human societies because such a combination can provide an explanation for why the norms are often group beneficial that is consistent with the idea that much human behavior is driven by self-interest. Many social scientists are convinced that societies show evidence of design – societies are structured for the good of the whole. Functionalism, an old and still influential school in anthropology and sociology, holds that beliefs, behaviors and institutions exist because they promote the healthy functioning of social groups. (Spencer, 1891; Radcliffe-Brown, 1952; Malinowski, 1922; Aberle *et al.*, 1950). The conviction that people are selfish drives others to argue that the appearance of design is an illusion – the complex structure merely reflects a standoff in a struggle among selfish individuals. Such rational individualists, mainly economists, political scientists and philosophers, hold that human choices must be explained in terms of individual benefits; any group benefits are an accidental side effect of selfish individual choices. I believe that the properties of evolutionary games in structured populations can provide a body of theory in which the behavior of selfish individuals sometimes leads to group beneficial behavior.

First, I will motivate the theoretical exercise by briefly reviewing some relevant facts about norms in human societies. Then, I will briefly discuss evolutionary game theory and why we should take it seriously as a model of human behavior. Finally I will review the work of population geneticists who have studied the properties of evolution in structured populations, and show how these results can be usefully applied to evolutionary game theory.

11.2 Stylized facts about norms in human societies

11.2.1 Human behavior is strongly influenced by culturally-transmitted norms

Much evidence indicates that behavior in human societies is strongly affected by norms – culturally-acquired beliefs and values that specify what is good and bad, valuable and shameful in any particular society. The best evidence for the importance of norms comes from what biologists would call a "common garden" experiment. Suppose a botanist notices that individuals of a particular plant species are larger in high altitude environments than at sea level. To determine whether this size difference is due to genetic differences between high and low altitude populations, or the result a phenotypic response to the different environments, the botanist plants seeds collected from the two populations in the same carefully-controlled greenhouse environment. If the plants differ, then it can be inferred that the two populations are genetically different. In the same way, the best evidence for the importance of culturally-transmitted norms on behavior is data which shows that groups of people who have different cultural histories behave differently in the same environment. Here, the fact that such differences in behavior are correlated with other culturally-transmitted behaviors, such as language or dialect, and the fact that differences in behavior often correspond to stated beliefs indicates that differences in behavior are caused by cultural differences in beliefs and values.

Of course, conducting such an experiment with people would be both impractical and immoral. Fortunately, the history of human migrations provides us with some natural experiments that provide strong evidence for the importance of norms.

11.2.2 The Nuer and the Dinka

The differences between the Nuer and the Dinka, two ethnic groups of the southern Sudan provide a classic anthropological example. Both groups lived a migratory existence in the vast marshes of the southern Sudan, living in villages and growing millet and corn in the wet season and then spreading out to graze their cattle on pastures uncovered by the subsiding flood the dry season. While The Nuer and the Dinka both numbered more than 100,000 of people, each was subdivided into many politically and militarily independent tribes numbering between 3,000 and 10,000 people.

Despite living in the same environment, utilizing the same technology the Nuer and the Dinka differed in many important ways. For example, their subsistence economies were quite different. The Nuer maintained larger herds with about two cows for each bull, while the Dinka kept smaller herds with about nine cows per bull. The Nuer rarely slaughtered cattle, subsisting mainly on milk, corn, and millet. In contrast the Dinka frequently ate meat. As a result, Nuer population densities were significantly lower than that of the Dinka. The smaller human populations and larger cow populations of the Nuer led to a number of differences between their yearly subsistence round and that of the Dinka. Most importantly the dry season settlements of the Nuer were much larger than those of the Dinka.

The political systems of the two groups also differed. Among the Dinka, a tribe was the group of people who lived together in a wet season encampment. In contrast, membership in Nuer tribes was based on kinship through the male line. As a result, the growth of Dinka tribes was constrained by geography, while Nuer tribes could in theory grow indefinitely. In fact, Nuer tribes averaged about 10,000 people while Dinka tribes averaged only about 3,000.

Kelly (1985) argues that the differences in subsistence practice and political organization were caused by the differences in bride price customs. Among both the Nuer and the Dinka, the families of the bride and groom made exchanges of livestock at the time of a wedding. Custom specified the number of cows and goats that various classes of kin were expected to give and receive. Among both the Nuer and the Dinka there was a net transfer of livestock from the groom's family to the bride's family, and thus anthropologists classify the payments as bride price (rather than dowry). The details of such payments differed substantially between the Nuer and the Dinka. Among the Nuer there was a minimum payment. The groom's family had to come up with about 20 head of cattle (the exact number varied among Nuer tribes) or no wedding. Credit was not accepted. There was also an ideal payment of about 36 head. Between the minimum and the ideal payments, the groom's family had to pay all that it could, keeping only enough for subsistence. In contrast, Dinka had no minimum payment and readily allowed credit so when times were tough, for example during the rinderpest epidemic weddings proceeded even though the bride's family might not receive any cows for a generation. The the ideal and the minimum payments were substantially lower among the Dinka than among the Nuer, and Dinka payments often included goats. Accordingly, Kelly argues, the Nuer kept larger herds to accommodate their larger and more inflexible bride wealth payments. There were also differences in the pattern of distribution of the livestock. The Dinka distributed livestock to groom's paternal and maternal relatives while the among the Nuer only the groom's paternal relatives benefited. This difference, Kelly argues, caused alliances to form among patrilateral kin among the Nuer and more diffusely among the Dinka. This difference in turn caused the Nuer to develop a political system based on patrilineal clans, while the Dinka evolved a system based on co-residence.

Such differences cannot be attributed to environmental differences because when Nuer tribes occupied Dinka land, they continued to behave like Nuer. Originally the Nuer and the Dinka lived in any case in very similar habitats in the same seasonally flooded swamp that covers much of the southern Sudan. Thus, it seems unlikely that the striking differences between the two groups are the result of environmental differences. Of course, there are small environmental differences between the original Nuer homeland and the areas originally occupied by the Dinka, and people committed to strict environmental determination have argued that these small differences are responsible for the differences between the Nuer and the Dinka. For example, Glickman (1972) argues that the drier Nuer homeland allowed larger encampments during both the wet and dry seasons which gave rise to the other differences. Arguments of this kind all fail because, as the Nuer expanded, they came to occupy exactly the same environment as the departed and conquered Dinka. If environment determines culture then the Nuer should have adopted Dinka bride wealth and cattle-keeping behaviors, but this did not happen. The Nuer continue to keep larger herds, manage them differently, have different political systems and marriage customs, despite occupying these territories for over a hundred years. In fact tens of thousands of Dinka who remained in the conquered territories adopted the Nuer customs surrounding bride price, subsistence practice and political organization. Instead of the Nuer becoming Dinka, the Dinka became Nuer.

Nor are the differences between the Nuer and the Dinka trivial; they led to the Nuer military superiority which allowed them to expand at the expense of the Dinka. Beginning in about 1820 one of the Nuer tribes, the Jikany Nuer, migrated about 200 miles to the east of their homeland invading land occupied by several Dinka tribes. The Jikany Nuer defeated the Dinka, killing many of them and incorporating the rest into Nuer society. Over the next 60 years the Nuer expansion continued as other Nuer tribes expanded south and west conquering

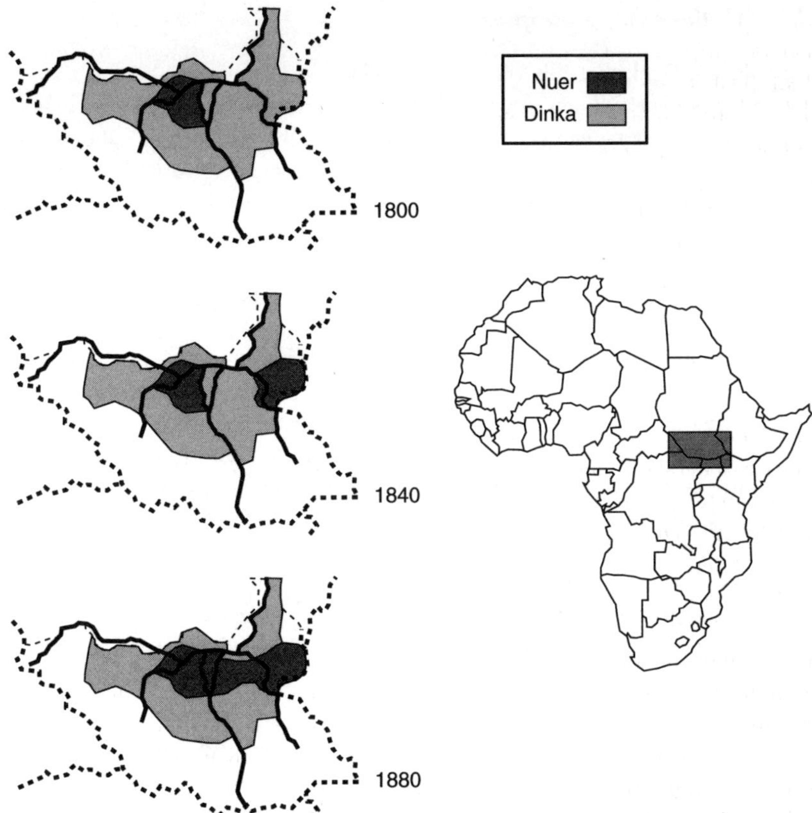

Figure 11.1 Nuer tribes expanded into the territories that had been occupied by their Dinka neighbors during most of the nineteenth century. The Nuer did not adopt Dinka subsistence practices, marriage customs or political organization

Dinka. As is shown in Figure 11.1 in this sixty year period the land occupied by the Nuer increased from a small area to more than half of the swampland of the southern Sudan. Kelly (1985: 36) estimates that about more than 180,000 people, mostly Dinka, lived in the area conquered by the Nuer. There is every reason to believe that the Dinka would have eventually been eliminated had not the British acted in early 1900s to suppress the conflict.

It is important to keep in mind that among both the Nuer and the Dinka, tribes were the units which conducted warfare. The Nuer did not conquer the Dinka, rather various Nuer tribes, the Jikany, the Lou, and so on, conquered various Dinka tribes. A Dinka tribe never conquered a Nuer tribe, despite the fact that the military technology and tactics of the two groups were very similar. Nuer tribes were always victorious because they were larger. Nuer armies of 1500 men easily defeated Dinka armies numbering around 600. The Nuer were able to recruit larger armies because their tribes were larger and because warfare typically occurred during the dry season and Nuer dry season encampments were larger than those of the Dinka.

11.2.3 Modern day examples

You should not think that this kind of data is limited to the exotic societies studied by anthropologists. There is good evidence that norms have important affects on behavior in modern western industrialized societies. Important cultural differences exist in the United States today – farmers descended from German and British immigrants exhibit strongly different economic behavior (Salomon 1985). Sonya Salomon studied two farming communities in southern Illinois: "Freiburg" (a pseudonym) was settled by German immigrants during the 1840s, while "Libertyville" was settled by Yankees (British-descended people from Kentucky, Ohio, and Indiana) in 1870. These two communities are only about 30 km apart and have been carefully matched for similar soil types. Nonetheless, the people in these two communities have different values about family, property and farm practice, and these differences seem consistent with their ethnic origins. People in Freiburg tend to value farming as a way of life, and they want at least one son or daughters continue as a farmers. As a result, they are very reluctant to sell land, and parents put considerable pressure on children to become farmers, but place little importance on education. In contrast, the "Yankee" farmers regard their farms as profit-making businesses. They buy, or rent land depending on economic conditions, and if the price is right, they sell. Many Yankee farmers would like it if their children were to continue farming, but they see it as an individual decision. Some families help their children enter farming, but many do not, and they generally place a strong value on education.

The difference in norms between Freiburg and Libertyville lead to different farm practices despite proximity of the two towns and the similarity of their soils. Farms are substantially larger in Libertyville – the mean size of farm operations is 518 acres compared to 276 acres in Freiburg. The Libertyville farms are larger because Yankee farmers rent more land. German operators are conservative, mainly farming the land they own, while Yankee farmers aggressively expand their operations by renting. The two communities also show striking differences in farm operations. In Libertyville, as in most of Southern Illinois, farmers specialize in grain production – it is the primary source of income for 77 percent of the farmers in Libertyville. In Freiburg grain production is the most important source of income for 44 percent. Many Germans mix grain production with dairying or livestock raising, activities that are almost absent in Libertyville. Because animal operations are labor intensive, they allow Germans to accommodate their larger families on limited acreage consistent with the German farming goals. Yankee farmers decided against dairying and stock raising because ". . . we could make more money from the land without all that work. (Salomon 1984: 334)."

The differing values of German and Yankee farmers lead to differing patterns of land ownership in the two communities. In Freiburg land rarely comes up for sale, and when it does, the price is high compared to neighboring areas. Salomon argues that Germans are willing to pay more for land because they are not solely maximizing profit – their goal is to provide land for their children. As a result, land is virtually never sold to non-Germans; In 1899 90 percent of the land in Freiburg was owned by Germans, and by 1982 it was 97 percent. Moreover, 1953 Germans began purchasing land in an area about 14 miles to the south, and by 1982 2,074 in this area were owned by Freiburg families an almost 40 percent increase in the land owned by members of the Freiburg community. In Libertyville land comes up for sale more often and at a lower price. The proportion of land owned by Yankee farmer has fluctuated from about 80 percent to 63 percent and back to 79 percent in the period 1899–1982. Moreover, consistent with the fact that Yankees view land as a commodity, absentee land ownership is more common in Libertyville – 56 percent of the land is owned by local people compared with 79 percent in Freiburg.

There are many other modern examples of this kind. Richard Nisbet and Dov Cohen (1996) have shown that people who grow up in the rural south have a stronger sense of personal honor than other Americans, a fact which may explain why the certain kinds of homicide are more common in the South. Economists such as Richard Nelson and Sidney Winter have argued that persistent differences between firms are in part due to differences in norms that are culturally transmitted within firms.

11.2.4 Norms are sometimes group beneficial

Norms seem to be group beneficial in a wide variety of cultures. Sober and Wilson (1998) surveyed the norms from 25 societies randomly selected from the more than 700 societies whose ethnographies have been cataloged in the Human Relationship Area Files. This survey shows that in most societies "individuals are expected to avoid conflict and practice benevolence and generosity toward members of a socially defined group (Sober and Wilson 1998: 5–14). In society after society, bravery, honesty, and sexual propriety are valued, while cowardice, avarice, and incest are punished. Thus, norms seem to encourage people to behave in ways that solve public goods problems such as group defense, regulation of economic activity, and sexual activity The survey also suggests that norms typically reward mutual monitoring and punishment of norm violators. However, there are also many norms that seem arbitrary, or even frankly stupid (see Edgerton 1992).

11.3 Evolutionary game theory

I will now look at the structure and assumptions of evolutionary game theory. I will then argue that this body of theory is a useful model for human behavior because it provides is a simple tractable approximation to more realistic models of cultural evolution. Finally I will argue that evolutionary games also give us a useful way to think about norms.

11.3.1 A simple example of evolutionary game theory

Rather than deal with game theory in the abstract, I will begin with a particularly simple example. Consider a very large population of agents. Pairs of agents are sampled at random from the population and interact in a simple coordination. There are two behaviors in this game; I'll label them P and Q. The social interaction results in a payoff that depends on an individual's own behavior and the behavior of the individual with who he interacts – hereafter "ego" and "other." The payoffs are given in the following game matrix.

		Other's Behavior	
		P	Q
Ego's Behaviors	P	$1+x$	$1-y$
	Q	$1-y$	1

So far this will all seem pretty familiar to economists because it's a lot like traditional von Neumann–Morgenstern descended game theory. (The similarity is not an accident: when Maynard Smith first formulated evolutionary game theoretic models, he borrowed the game matrix formalism from traditional game theory. However, he did not borrow much else, because, he told me once, he didn't know much about traditional game theory.)

Now comes the big difference. The payoffs in the matrix are not utilities that represent the preferences of the agents for different states of the world. Instead, they are a related to the rate of replication of the different strategies. In evolutionary game theory agents don't choose their behavior, they inherit a strategy that specifies how they will behave. In this game the possible strategies are the pure strategies always play P and always play Q, and a range of mixed strategies. To keep things simple, however, lets assume that only pure strategies are possible. This means that we can specify the state of the population at any given time by the fraction of the population who are characterized by one of the strategies. Let p represent the fraction (or frequency) of the population with strategy P, and q represent the frequency of Q (that is $1-p$).

Since the population is assumed to be very large, the average payoff of P strategists will be:

$$W(P) = (1+x)p + (1-y)q$$

The first term is the payoff that a P individual interacts with another P individual multiplied by the probability that such an interaction occurs given random interaction. The second term gives the payoff of a P individual who interacts with a Q individual multiplied by the probability that such and interaction occurs.

Similarly, the average payoff of Q strategists will be:

$$W(Q) = (1-y)p + (1)q$$

Now assume that after all interactions take place, all of the agents die and are replaced by a new generation of agents. The new agents acquire their strategies by copying the previous generation. However, they don't copy at random – instead the likelihood that individual are copied is proportional to their payoff relative to others in the population. Since the population is large this means that he frequency of P in the next generation, p', will be given by:

$$p' = p\left(\frac{W(p)}{\bar{W}}\right) \tag{11.1}$$

where $\bar{W} = pW(P) + qW(Q)$ is the average payoff in the population as a whole. (In economics I've noticed it is more common to write this recursion as a difference equation.)

$$\Delta p = p\left(\frac{W(P) - \bar{W}}{\bar{W}}\right)$$

Thus the consequences of social behavior will cause the frequency of different strategies, and therefore the behavior, to change through time. To determine the behavior of the population we solve the recursion or difference equation that describe this change.

In this example, the dynamics of the population are very simple as long as x and y are not too big. If the initial frequency of the population, p_0, is less than a threshold frequency

$$\tilde{p} = \frac{y}{y + 2x}$$

the population eventually reaches a stable equilibrium in which only Q individuals are present. If $p_0 > \tilde{p}$, the population evolves toward a stable equilibrium at which only P is present.

In more complicated models, however, it is usually not practical to actually solve the equations describing the dynamic system, and instead we just determine which equilibria are stable. The idea is that in most well behaved systems, the population will eventually come to rest at one of the stable equilibria. (Of course if x and y are large enough, the system could oscillate or behave chaotically in which case it will never settle down anywhere.)

11.3.2 *The structure of evolutionary game theory*

Evolutionary game theory ends up looking deceptively like more traditional game theory: We start out with a some behaviors and associated payoffs, and we end up determining which behavioral strategies are "stable" according to their payoffs. Underneath, however, the differences are profound. Here's a short list:

- *Every individual has a type.* Traditional game theory assume agents have "free will" – they may choose any strategy. In evolutionary game theory individuals are characterized by an inherited strategy. This strategy may be very complex, and allow very sophisticated play in multi-stage game, but underneath there is a fixed strategy. This means that it is possible, in principle at least, to determine individuals' strategy by observing their behavior, a fact that can have profound effects on some kinds of games.

- *The outcome depends on the way that individuals are sampled from the population to interact.* In the simple example given above, pairs of individuals are sampled at random, and this generates outcomes very similar to the traditional Nash equilibrium concept. In many cases individuals may be sample non-randomly. For example, in genetic applications this can occur when genetically related individuals interact. One simple way to model such non-random interaction is to assume that there is a constant probability r of interacting with individuals like yourself, and a probability $1-r$ interacting at random. With this model, the probabilities of interacting with a P individual, for example, are:

$$\Pr(P|P) = r + (1-r)p$$
$$\Pr(Q|P) = (1-r)q$$

  Different patterns of sampling can completely change the evolution of alternative strategies in the population. For example, if $rx - (1-r)y > 0$, the only stable equilibrium in the game given above is $p = 1$, the game is no longer a coordination game, despite the payoffs! Population structure is another process that can give rise to non-random interaction, and a we will see it can have equally important effects.

- *Evolutionary game theory is about dynamics.* Much evolutionary game is about finding stable equilibria, so-called ESS's, and so looks like standard game theory. At the core, however it is a theory about dynamics, and as we will see this will make a big difference in structured populations.

11.3.3 Evolutionary models of culture

So why should we take evolutionary game theory seriously as a model of human behavior? The answer, I think, is that evolutionary game theory is useful because it provides a simple, analytically-tractable version of more realistic models of cultural change. Over the past two decades, a number of scholars have modeled culture and cultural change using ideas from population and evolutionary biology (Cavalli-Sforza and Feldman, 1981; Lumsden and Wilson, 1981; Boyd and Richerson, 1985; Durham 1992). The idea that unifies this body of work is that culture constitutes a system of inheritance. People acquire beliefs, attitudes, and values both by teaching and by observing the behavior of others. Culture is not behavior; culture is information stored in human brains that, together with individuals' genes and their environments, determines their behavior. Norms, on this view, are culturally-transmitted ideas about appropriate behavior. Since culture is communicated from one person to another, individuals sample from and contribute to a evolving cultural pool, much as they do an evolving gene pool.

This view of culture implies that cultural evolution should be modeled as a population dynamic process. To understand why people behave as they do in a particular environment, we must know the nature of the skills, beliefs, attitudes, and values that they have acquired from others by cultural inheritance. To do this we must account for the processes that affect cultural variation as individuals acquire beliefs, use the acquired information to guide behavior, and act as models for others. What processes increase or decrease the proportion of people in a society who hold particular ideas about how to behave? We thus seek to understand the cultural analogs of the forces of natural selection, mutation, and drift that drive genetic evolution.

Some of the forces of cultural evolution derive from the goal directed, albeit myopic, choices of individuals. For example, individuals evaluate alternative behaviors and tend to adopt the behaviors that serve their ends, or individuals may observe the success of others and copy the successful. Other cultural evolutionary forces arise from what happens to people who have adopted different ideas. For example, individuals with some ideas may be more likely to achieve social positions in which they will be imitated, or firms characterized by some norms may be more likely to go bankrupt. Finally some cultural evolutionary forces may result from random, entropic processes. Some ideas may be lost because, by chance, none of the individuals carrying them survive.

This approach to modeling cultural change has much in common with evolutionary game theory. The main difference is that the replicator dynamics focuses almost exclusively on evolutionary forces that arise from while we have considered a broader range of evolutionary processes including those that arise from population structure. As we will see below, such non-adaptive processes may be crucial for understanding the evolution of norms and many other forms of adaptive behavior.

11.3.4 Norms and evolutionary game theory

Evolutionary game theory and traditional game theory share, what at first sight seems, like an unfortunate property: There are lots of interesting games with plausible payoff structures that have many, many equilibria. Here are a few examples:

- Bargaining games with incomplete information admit essentially every possible kind of subgame perfect equilibrium because there are lots of alternative sets of beliefs that lead to self-confirming behavior during the game. As far as I know, such games have not been extensively studied in an evolutionary context but there is every reason to believe that they will have many evolutionary equilibria as well.

- Asymmetric contests have many equilibria in which different uncorrelated asymmetries (for example, ownership) may be used to resolve contests.

- Iterated games without a known end point and the possibility of punishment allow, according to the famous folk-theorem, any behavior to be a subgame perfect equilibrium. The essential idea here is that the threat of future punishment can induce any present behavior. Similar, although more limited results have been proved for evolutionary game theory.

If you look at evolutionary game theory purely formally, then the existence of multiple equilibria means that the outcome depends on the initial state of the population. Each equilibrium will be associated with some basin of attraction. The only way of determining which equilibrium will be reached is to know the which basin of attraction the population began in. Since we typically know little or nothing about the actual history of the systems we are interested in, the fact that outcomes depend on initial conditions means that game theory predicts that only that all equilibria are possible. Since feasible equilibria support very wide ranges of behavior in lots of interesting games this seems like an unfortunate situation.

However, I think that this is the wrong way to think about the problem. I think that game theory is telling us something about the world. The same social situations do have many possible outcomes, and, in fact, this is one of the processes that maintains differences among societies. Think about the Nuer and the Dinka. They live in the same environment using the same technology. Nonetheless, they have very different rules about social life: among the Nuer political loyalty and military fealty is owed to members of a man's patriclan. Among the Dinka, it is owed to a group defined by both descent through the male and female lines and geography as well. How are these differences maintained? Among the Nuer, people who behave inappropriately are punished; ditto for the Dinka. But the rules are different. This is just a very complex repeated game in which different behaviors can be maintained by monitoring and punishment.

Thus, game theory provides a natural explanation for the vast diversity of culturally-transmitted norms we observe in human societies. However, it does not explain why norms should be group beneficial. To do that we have to turn to the theory of evolution in structured populations.

11.4 Evolution in structured populations

Most evolutionary game theory assumes that everybody in a population is equally likely to interact with everybody else. However, in virtually all real situations, people don't interact at random. Instead, human populations are structured in various ways. In simple societies that interest anthropologists like me, people interact more often with people in their own village, their own lineage or moiety, or their own ethnic group. Nuer people were much more likely to interact with people in their own tribe, than people belonging to other Nuer tribes or Dinka tribes. In modern societies population structure is created by neighborhoods, unions, firms, and a variety of other institutions. You interact with people in your own university much more than people at institutions. Of course, social groups are rarely completely isolated, even in small scale societies. Nonetheless, the outcomes of interactions with other group members will have far greater effect on your welfare than interactions with others.

11.4.1 Structured populations and maintenance of variation between groups

In structured populations, under the right conditions, different subpopulations may arrive at different, persistent quasi-equilibrium states. To see how this works, let embed the coordination game I sketched above in a very simple structured population called a "island" model. Imagine that there is a very large population made up of a very large number of subpopulations. People randomly pair with other members of their own population to play the coordination game I already described. On a particular focal island the island the frequency of strategy P is p, while on all the rest of the islands the frequency of P is zero. Then the change in p due to social interaction in each time period is given by (1) above. If we assume that the population changes relatively slowly so that x and y are small enough to ignore terms of order x^2, y^2, and xy, then (1) becomes approximately:

$$p' = p + sp(1-p)(p-\tilde{p})$$

where $s = x + 2y$ measures the overall rate of change and $\tilde{p} = y/s$ is the threshold frequency of P necessary for P to have a higher payoff, and therefore increase in frequency.

Each time period, each subpopulation receives migrants drawn at random from all other subpopulation. You can think of these migrants as people who actually physically move from place to place, or you can think of them ideas or beliefs that flow from one subpopulation to another as a result of social contact. The focal island also contributes migrants to other subpopulations, but the effect is negligible because there are so many other subpopulations. Suppose that there are N individuals on the island, and each time period that M immigrants arrive from the continent. Then the frequency after migration, p'', is

$$\begin{aligned} p'' &= \frac{p'}{1+\frac{M}{N}} \\ &= \frac{p + sp(1-p)(p-\tilde{p})}{1+m} \end{aligned}$$

where $m = M/N$ is the number of immigrants as a fraction of the island population. The equilibria, $\hat{p}$,of this recursion satisfy:

$$m\hat{p} = s\hat{p}(1-\hat{p})(\hat{p}-\tilde{p})$$

The left hand side is proportional to the decrease in the frequency of P due to migration from the continent, and the right hand side is proportional to the change due to social interaction. Notice that $\hat{p} = 0$ is always an equilibrium – when the continent and the island are the same, they stay that way. If the rate of migration is high enough, this is the only equilibrium (see Figure 11.2a). However, if the rate of migration is not too high, then there is another stable arrangement at which P is common on the island (see 11.2b).

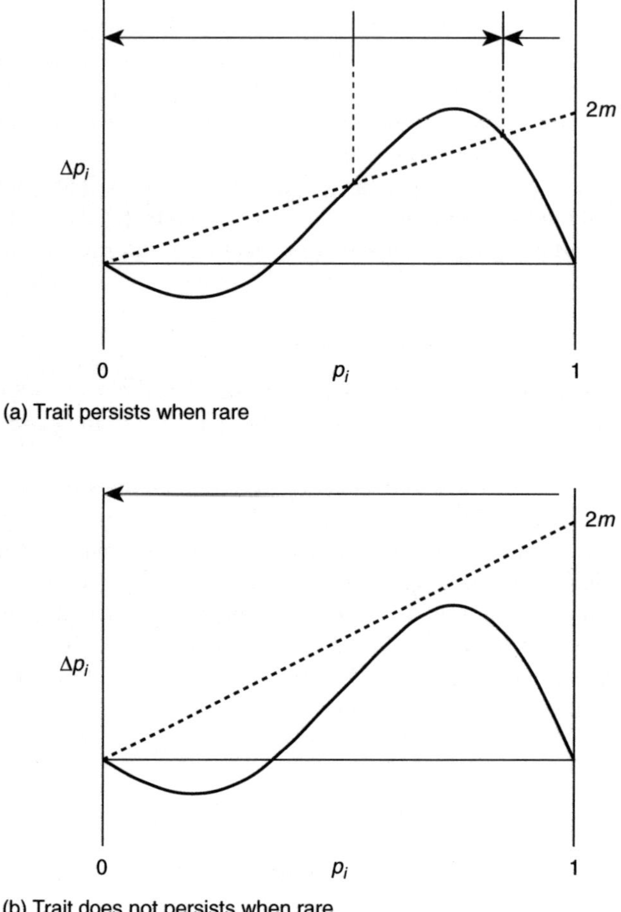

Figure 11.2 Shows the change in the frequency of the focal trait in subpopulation $i, \Delta p_i$, as a function of the frequency of that trait in a single subpopulation, p_i. The S-shaped line gives the change due to adaptive processes within population i. The dashed line gives the change due to migration in a subpopulation i when all immigrants have the alternative strategy. In a), selection is strong compared to migration and the subpopulation can exist in one or two stable equilibria. At one of these equilibria the focal strategy persists at substantial frequency. In b), selection is weak compared to migration, and at the only equilibrium state, the other strategy is identical to all other subpopulations.

11.4.2 Group selection among alternative equilibria

This model illustrates how evolutionary game theory can be embedded in a structured population model. In this very simple island model every population was equally connected to every other population. This is not very realistic for either biological or cultural evolution. In more realistic models, each population has more contact with some populations than others. In the most extreme case, called "stepping stone" models, each population exchanges migrants only with its immediate neighbors. However, the island model may be an adequate approximation to more realistic models, when rates of migration are high.

Notice that the average welfare of a subpopulation depends on the frequency of P. Subpopulations in P is common have a higher average payoff than subpopulations in which the frequency is zero. This suggests the possibility that competition between subpopulations might lead to the spread of P. This process, called group selection by biologists, would provide an explanation for why norms are sometimes group beneficial. Namely, differences between societies are maintained because there are multiple equilibria, and those societies with group-beneficial norms survive and proliferate and those with disadvantageous norms become extinct. This is an old idea in anthropology and sociology, but one that has received little explicit theoretical treatment. A similar idea is implicit in many economic models – even if managers are not optimizers, firms will be profit maximizing because only such firms will survive over the long run. However, explicit treatment is also rare (see Nelson and Winter 1982).

In biology, however, there has been a good deal of analysis of group selection models. Much of it has been devoted deducing the conditions under which group selection can lead to the evolution of altruistic behaviors, such as giving predator alarms, in non-human animal populations. Extensive modeling by biologists suggests group selection of this kind has little effect on the prevalence of altruistic behavior (Eshel, 1972; Levin and Kilmer, 1973; Wade, 1978; Slatkin and Wade, 1978; Boorman and Levitt, 1980; Wilson, 1983; Aoki, 1982; Rogers 1990). The situation is quite different when selection is strong enough to maintain subpopulations at different equilibria. As we shall see, group selection can be very important in this case.

To see why, we will use a useful formula derived by Price (1970) that expresses the response to natural selection into two components: the average change in the frequency of alternative traits *within* groups, and the change in the frequency *between* groups. To see how this works lets work through a simple example: Once again suppose that there are two strategies P and Q in a population structured into a large number of groups. Let p_i be the frequency of P in group i, p_{ij} be the "frequency" of P in the jth individual in group i – that is, if individual j is P, then $p_{ij} = 1$; that is, if individual j is Q, then $p_{ij} = 0$. Let w_{ij} be the payoff earned by individual j in group i, and w_i be the average payoff of individuals in group i.

Then we can use Price's formula;

$$W\Delta p = \text{cov}(w_i, p_i) + E(\Delta p_i w_i)$$

where as before w_i is the average fitness of individuals in group i. Then Price showed that the change in the frequency of P due to selection alone is:

$$W\Delta p = \text{var}(p_i)\beta(w_i, p_i) + E\{\text{var}(p_{ij})\beta(p_{ij}, w_{ij})\} \quad (11.2)$$

Each of these terms has an interesting and important interpretation:

$\text{var}(p_i)$	=	variation among groups
$\beta(w_i, p_i)$	=	the effect of P on average payoff of group i
$\text{var}(p_{ij})$	=	variation within group i
$\beta(w_{ij}, p_{ij})$	=	the effect of P on payoff relative to others in group i
$E\{\}$	=	average over all groups

Thus the effect of selection can be partitioned into two components: one measures the effect of P on the average payoff of groups, and a second that measures the payoff of P relative to others in the same group. (Its important to understand that this formula gives only the change due to adaptive processes, not migration, drift, or any other process that may effect the population.

Suppose P is an altruistic trait. By definition, altruists have lower payoff than other group members in every group, but groups with more altruists have higher payoff. Thus the first term is always positive, and the second term is always negative. The relative magnitude of the two terms depends on the relative amount of variation within and among groups. If groups are formed at random, drift is the only important process increasing variation between groups, and thus the second term is usually very small. Contrast this situation with the case in which both P and Q are equilibria in isolated populations, and adaptive processes are strong enough relative to drift so that the population is a mosaic of subpopulations some with P common and some with Q common. Then P will have a higher payoff relative to Q in some subpopulations and a lower payoff in others. Then, assuming that the population as a whole is near equilibrium, the second term is approximately zero because the two processes balance out. Now if (and this is a big if) the higher average group payoff of high P subpopulations translates into some kind of group advantage, the group-beneficial trait will spread.

At this juncture, two different kinds of models are possible. First, if adaptive processes are so strong that subpopulations can persist at a high frequency of either strategy, groups become like asexual individuals. Groups can then compete either through differential extinction. There is no doubt that this kind of "quasi-individual" group selection can occur, and there is substantial evidence that it does occur. However, there is also reason to believe that it is typically to slow to explain many kinds of cultural change. Second, if adaptive processes of intermediate strength, then the group-beneficial trait may spread to neighboring subpopulations by differential diffusion. Models of this type have been recently analyzed by biologists interested in Sewall Wright's shifting balance theory. They have concluded that the fact that a trait is group beneficial has little impact on whether it will spread, and thus that this type of group selection is unlikely to be important. We will see, however, that these conclusions may not hold when models of the shifting balance are modified so that they represent selection among multiple equilibria.

11.4.3 Groups as quasi-individuals

Pete Richerson and I have built a simple model of this kind of group selection (Boyd and Richerson 1990). We assume that there is a cultural trait with two variants – labeled P and Q. Within each group, adaptive processes lead to the increase of P if its frequency is greater than a threshold value. Otherwise Q increases in frequency. These assumptions are meant to capture the effects of multiple equilibria. Migration between groups in an island model or stepping stone model spreads beliefs from one group to another. To represent group selection, we assume that groups in which P is common are less likely to go extinct and more likely to grow and fission. Cultural extinctions need not involve actual deaths as would be required in biological models; only the break up and dispersal of the group is required. Habitats vacated by group extinction are recolonized by people drawn from the surviving group or groups. If you assume that the rate of extinction is very low compared to the rate of within group change, it is easy to derive the following conditions for the group-beneficial trait to spread:

- The rate of within group adaptation must be greater than the rate of change due to migration between groups. Otherwise groups in which P is common, cannot persist when P is rare in the population as a whole.
- There must be a substantial probability that new groups are formed by the fissioning of existing groups. Otherwise, when P is rare in the population as a whole, groups in which P is common cannot reproduce themselves. Beneficial group properties cannot be transmitted.

Extensive simulations indicate that this is approximately correct even when extinction is much more common.

There is no doubt that this kind of process occurs in human populations. The spread of the Nuer at the expense of their Dinka neighbors is one clear example. The norms regulating marriage transactions and political obligations differed between Nuer and Dinka tribes. These differences persisted despite considerable cultural contact between these language groups. Then Nuer norms caused them to be less likely to be defeated in military contests over land and cattle, and as a consequence the Nuer norms spread over a good part of the southern Sudan between about 1820 and 1880. There are many other examples in the ethnographic record. Linguistic and genetic evidence suggests that agriculture spread in Europe and Austronesia in many parts of the world, as a result of the spread of farmers, not farming techniques. One way to understand this is to assume that the transition from foraging to farming require many change in norms about property, sharing, kinship, etc. Because farmers maintain higher population densities they can exclude foragers by depressing game densities if nothing else. Evolutionary models in economics can also be interpreted in this way. Firms differ in culturally-transmitted practices, and these effect profitability. Less profitable firms go bankrupt leaving only the more profitable ones.

The problem with this model is that it is too slow to explain many observed episodes of cultural change. The basic problem is that the rate of evolution is limited by the rate of group proliferation and extinction. While data on extinction rates and modes of new group formation gleaned from ethnographic accounts of New Guinea societies suggests that while the model generally applies to the small scale social groupings that have characterized much of human history, it also suggests that this form of group selection is a relatively slow process – 500 to 1000 years is required for a group level adaptation to spread through a population of groups (Soltis *et al*,. 1995). This observation suggests that the group selection process modeled is not fast enough to account for many observed cases of the evolution of norms. This problem is greatly exacerbated if social systems depend on the assembly of a number of different norms because group replication does not allow recombination – analogous to asexual replication. The same within-group dynamics which preserve variation in norms among groups will prevent beneficial norms arising in different groups from recombining within a single group. Experience with genetic models suggests that the lack of recombination greatly slows the evolution of adaptations involving more than one trait.

11.4.4 Sewall Wright's shifting balance theory

Group selection could proceed more rapidly if group competition was driven by individual learning – if norms spread from successful to less successful groups because individuals in the less successful group imitate individuals in the more successful group, not because less successful groups go extinct. It turns out that with a little modification, models of Sewall Wright's "shifting balance" can be applied to this problem.

Wright was one of the triumvirate of theoretical population geneticists who in first half of this century showed Mendelian genetics could be reconciled with Darwin's theory of adaptation by natural selection (the others were J. B. S. Haldane, and R. A. Fisher). Wright's experimental work had convinced him that understanding how co-adapted complexes of genes evolved was crucial for understanding the evolution of complex adaptations. The basic idea is sets of genes work well together, and mixing genes from different sets is bad for the organism. This means that natural selection alone can't cause a population to shift from one coadapted set of genes to a second, superior set of genes.

The simplest example is what geneticists call "underdominance." Consider a single genetic locus with two alleles labeled *P* and *Q*. The fitnesses of the three genotypes are given in Table 11.1 where x and y are positive numbers. Thus, the two homozygous genotypes, *PP* and *QQ* have higher fitness than the heterozygote, *PQ*. Let p be the frequency of the *P* allele in the population. Then, if mating occurs at random (which means that alleles are combined at random to form individuals), then the recursion for change in p due to natural selection is identical to (1) above. There are stable equilibria at $p = 1$ and $p = 0$, and thus if a population begins

Table 11.1

Genotype	*PP*	*PQ*	*QQ*
Relative fitness	$1+x$	$1-y$	1

with all *QQ* individuals, natural selection alone cannot lead to the evolution of the superior *PP* genotype.

Wright argued that favorable gene combinations evolved through a combination of genetic drift and natural selection in structured populations. He envisioned three stages in this "shifting balance" process:

1. In one subpopulation, genetic drift causes the frequency of *P* to exceed the threshold frequency necessary for *P* to be favored by natural selection. Genetic drift refers to changes in gene frequency due to sampling variation in finite populations. The rate of genetic drift is much greater in small populations than in larger ones. Wright imagined that natural populations were subdivided into many subpopulations small enough that genetic drift could be important even when opposed by natural selection.

2. Natural selection increases the frequency of *P* to near one within this subpopulation.

3. Because the average fitness of this subpopulation is higher than that of neighboring subpopulations, the high p subpopulation produces more emigrants than neighboring subpopulations. As a result, the favorable gene combination (*PP*) spreads through group selection.

Wright devoted a great deal of work to the study of genetic drift, but never really modeled all three stages of the shifting balance. Recently, however, a number of theorists have tackled the problem (Rouhani and Barton, 1987; Crow *et al.*, 1990; Barton, 1992; Rouhani and Barton, 1993a, 1993b; Gavrilets, 1996), and we can use their efforts to help us understand how group selection among alternative game theoretic equilibria can occur through the differential diffusion of strategies.

All the stages of the shifting balance process are relevant to cultural group selection. There needs to be some process that causes at least one group to shift from one equilibria to the other (the analog of mutation at the group level), and there needs to be some processes that causes groups at superior equilibria to spread at the expense of other groups (the analog of selection at the group level). I am going to focus mainly on the latter processes because I think that there are good reasons to think that the processes that lead to group level mutations may be very different in cultural evolution than they are in genetic evolution. In contrast, I think that we can get useful insight about the group selection process from the genetic models.

Models of the third stage of the shifting balance can usefully be divided into two classes: models in which the group selection occurs by deterministic spread, and those in which it occurs by biased drift. I will first briefly sketch the differential drift process and result, and then turn to the models of deterministic spread.

Biased drift

Consider the following model drawn from Rouhani and Barton (1993a, 1993b). Suppose that there is an underdominant genetic locus with two alleles P and Q with the fitnesses given above. The population is structured into an infinite number of subpopulations each of size N. Each time period a fraction m of each subpopulation is replaced by immigrants drawn from all other subpopulations at random. There is symmetric mutation at a rate μ?

With these assumptions Wright showed the population will eventually reach a stationary distribution in which the probability density of the frequency of P in each subpopulation, $\Psi(p,\bar{p})$ is given by:

$$\Psi(p,\bar{p}) = Cp^{4N(\mu+m\bar{p})+1}(1-p)^{4N(\mu+m(1-\bar{p}))-1}\bar{W}^{2N}$$

where C is a constant such that the density integrates to one. Notice that the density depends on the mean value of p over all subpopulations, $\bar{p}$. To find $\bar{p}$ we need to solve:

$$\bar{p} = \int p\Psi(p,\bar{p})dp$$

which must be done numerically.

The results are shown in Figure 11.3 which plots $\bar{p}$ as a function of the Nm. Notice that as migration rate increase the $\bar{p}$ also increases, until a threshold is reached (around 0.2) and the solution bifurcates and either the group-beneficial trait is either at high or low frequency. These results can be interpreted as follows: Because selection within subpopulations favoring the group-beneficial allele is stronger than selection favoring the other allele, the stationary distribution is asymmetric even when there is no migration, and as a result, the mean in the population is greater than one half. Because immigrants are biased toward P, allowing a some migration further increases $\bar{p}$ which in turn increases the probability mass at higher values of p. Increasing migration continues to have this effect up to the point that there is so much migration that the entire population evolves as a single unit either toward a high or low value of $\bar{p}$ depending on initial conditions. Thus, intermediate levels of migration in a structured population can lead to a substantial increase in the frequency of the group-beneficial trait.

The interesting thing about these results though is that group selection has nothing to do with the spread of the group-beneficial trait. Each subpopulation was assumed to contribute the same number of migrants to the population as a whole. The group-beneficial trait spreads, but because it is more strongly favored by *individual* selection. Moreover, adding group selection so that subpopulations with higher average fitness contribute more to the pool of migrants has only a very small effect on the outcome. The side effect of individual selection is much greater than the direct effect of group selection. We will see a similar phenomenon in the next model which deals with deterministic spread.

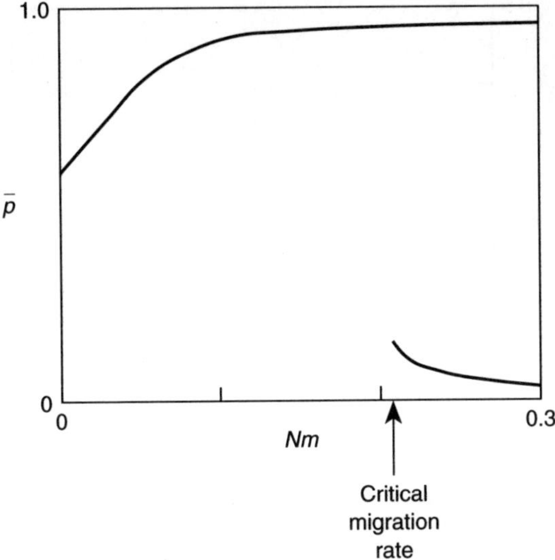

Figure 11.3 The mean value of the group-beneficial trait in the metapopulation at equilibrium as a function of the scaled migration rate (m). As migration increases, the equilibrium mean frequency of the group-beneficial trait also increases. At the critical migration rate, however, there are two stable values of the mean frequency of the group-beneficial strategy. One of these values is very low.

Deterministic spread

A number of authors have analyzed models in which the group-beneficial trait spreads deterministically after reaching a high frequency in a single subpopulation (Rouhani and Barton 1987, Crow *et al.* 1990, Barton 1992, Gavrilets 1996). These models vary in the population structure assumed (two populations, one and two dimensional stepping stones and continuously distributed population). To see how these models work consider a one dimensional stepping stone model. There are a large number of large subpopulations arranged in one dimension. The frequency of the group-beneficial trait in subpopulation i is P_i. Each time period two processes affect the frequency of the trait. First, social interaction in the simple game above leads to a change given by:

$$p_i' = p_i + sp_i(1 - p_i)(p_i - \tilde{p})$$

Then, each subpopulation exchanges migrants only with its two neighbors in the chain of populations. The frequency of the group-beneficial variant in population i after migration, p'', is:

$$p_i'' = \frac{p_i' + p_{i-1}' M\left(p_{i-1}'\right) + p_{i+1}' M\left(p_{i+1}'\right)}{1 + M\left(p_{i-1}'\right) + M\left(p_{i+1}'\right)}$$

Thus, M gives the rate of flow of traits from neighboring populations, and is a function of the frequency of the group beneficial trait in those populations to

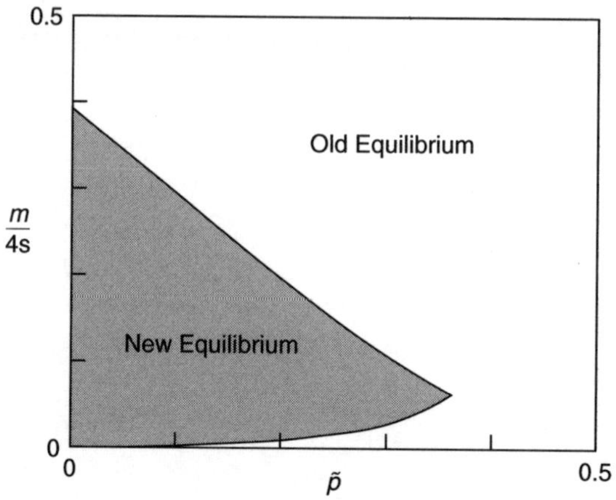

Figure 11.4 A phase diagram for a one locus genetic model with underdominance showing the conditions under which the higher fitness allele will spread in a stepping stone population structure, the horizontal axis is the frequency of the higher fitness allele at the unstable equilibrium separating the two basins of attraction, and the vertical axis gives the relative strength of migration and selection.

represent the effects of group selection. If $M(p) = m$, there is no group selection. If there is group selection we expect that $M(0) < M(1)$. M will not always be monotonically increasing – the initial deleterious effects of a few P individuals may lead to a decrease in group welfare for small values of p. For the moment lets ignore the effects of group selection and assume that $M(p) = m$. If N is large enough, this model is deterministic, and with dynamics that depend only on initial conditions and two parameters m/s and $\tilde{p}$.

To model the third stage of the shifting balance, Gavrilets performed computer simulations of this model over a wide range of combinations of these two parameters. In each simulation, he set the initial frequency of the group-beneficial trait to 1 in one subpopulation, and set it to zero in the remaining subpopulation. There are three possible outcomes: the group-beneficial trait spreads from the initial subpopulation to all other subpopulations, the other trait replaces the group-beneficial trait in all subpopulations, or the group-beneficial trait remains common in one subpopulation and is present in neighboring subpopulations because of diffusion, but does not spread through the whole population. Figure 11.4 shows the results. If, the group beneficial trait disappears. If m/s is small, and $\tilde{p}$ is not too large, the group-beneficial trait persists but does not spread. The group-beneficial trait spreads only if m/s takes on an intermediate value, and or $\tilde{p}$ is not too large.

To get some insight into what's going on here, consider the following approximate models.

1. For a single population to persist at a high frequency, must satisfy (2) above. If migration is too strong relative to adaptive processes, there is no equilibrium in which the group-beneficial trait persists at high frequency. The threshold amount of migration decreases as $\tilde{p}$ increases because the selective advantage

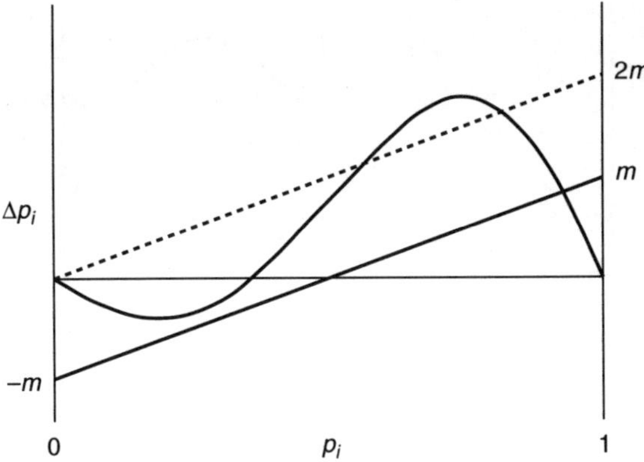

Figure 11.5 Shows the change in the frequency of the group-beneficial trait in subpopulation $i, \Delta p_i$, as a function of the frequency of that trait in that subpopulation p_i. The S-shaped line gives the change due to adaptive processes within population i. The dashed line gives the change due to migration in a subpopulation i when all immigrants have the alternative strategy. When the migration rate is m, as shown, the group-beneficial trait can persist in subpopulation i at high frequency even when it is absent in all other subpopulations. The solid line that intersects the y-axis at $-m$ give the rate of change of p_i, when half the immigrants have the group-beneficial trait, and the other half are characterized by alternative trait, the migration rate is m, and there is no group selection. If, as is shown, subpopulation i cannot persist at a low frequency of the group-beneficial train then the group-beneficial trait will spread once it is established even though it does not cause groups to produce more immigrants.

of the group-beneficial trait relative to the other trait also decreases. Thus the combinations of m/s and $\tilde{p}$ that satisfy (2) are shown in figure 11.5.

2. We can understand the conditions that allow the spread of the group-beneficial trait by the analyzing a stepping stone model with three subpopulations. Fix the frequency of the group-beneficial trait in population 1 at one, and the frequency of the group-beneficial trait in population 3 at zero. Depending on the values of m/s and $\tilde{p}$, the intermediate population will have either have one stable equilibrium at which the frequency of P is high, or two stable equilibria, one with a high value of p and one with a low value of p. It seems plausible that the group-beneficial trait will spread only if the former condition holds, and computer simulations confirm that it provides an excellent approximation to the complete stepping stone model. As can be seen in Figure 11.5, this condition then provides a lower bound on the amount of migration. If migration rates fall below this threshold, the trait cannot spread because adaptive forces favoring the more common trait are stronger than migration. However, if migration rates are higher, but not so high to violate (2) then adaptive forces are strong enough to stabilize the group-beneficial trait, but not the other trait, and thus it spreads deterministically once established in a single subpopulation.

Notice that the group-beneficial trait spreads here without any group selection. It spreads because in the simple coordination game described above (and in the

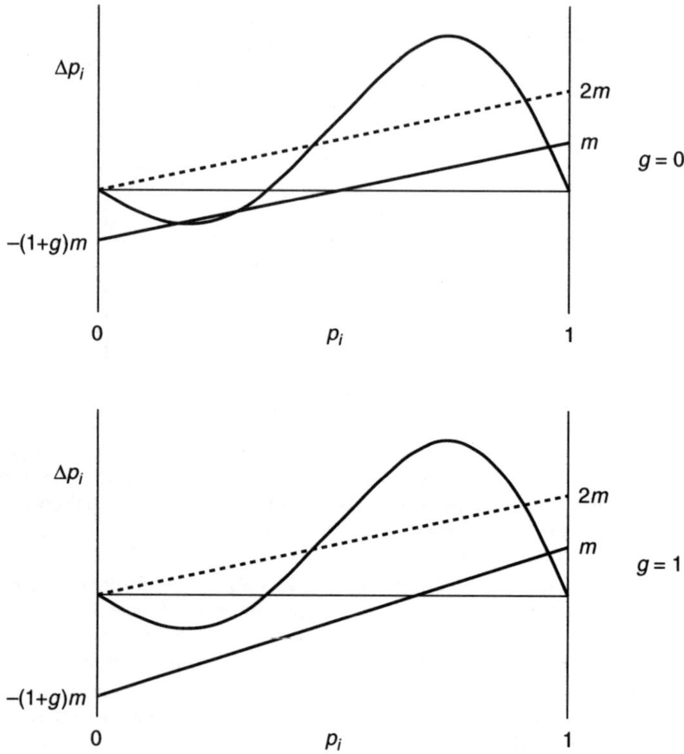

Figure 11.6 Shows the change in the frequency of the group-beneficial trait in subpopulation $i, \Delta p_i$, as a function of the frequency of that trait in a single subpopulation, p_i. As in Figure 11.5, the S-shaped line gives the change due to adaptive processes within populations i, and the dashed line give the change due to migration in a subpopulation i when all immigrants have the alternative strategy. The solid line that intersects the y-axis at $-m$ gives the rate of change of p_i when the immigration rate of the group-beneficial trait is $(1 + g)m$ while the immigration rate of the other trait is m. For the values of m and s shown, the group-beneficial trait cannot spread without group selection (top) but can if $g = 1$ (bottom).

formally identical one locus underdominant model) because the group-beneficial trait is more strongly favored by individual adaptive processes within each subpopulation.

Interestingly, a number of geneticists like Barton and Gavrilets have concluded that adding group selection has little effect on the conditions under which the group-beneficial trait can spread. It is easy to understand why they have reached this conclusion, and why it may not apply to the evolution of norms by considering the simple three population stepping stone model we just analyzed. As is shown in Figure 11.6, adding group selection increases the range of conditions under which the group-beneficial trait can spread. However, this effect will be very small in genetic models because it is usually assumed that the effect on migration is proportional to average fitness. But in the simple genetic models that have been

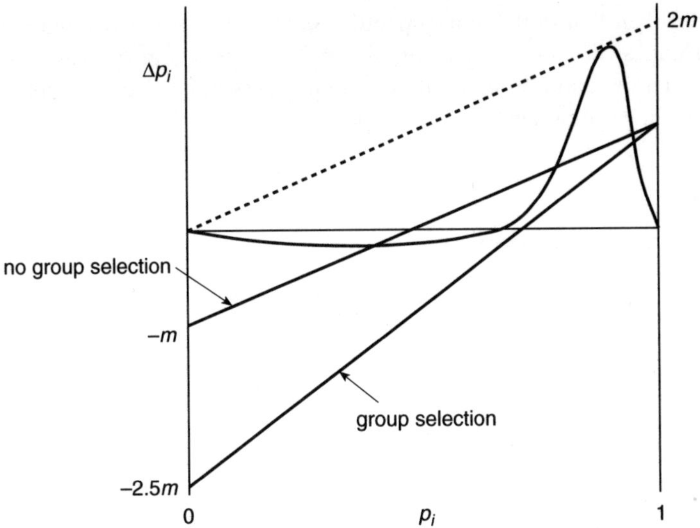

Figure 11.7 Shows the change in the frequency of the group-beneficial trait in subpopulation i, Δp_i, as a function of the frequency of that trait in a single subpopulation, p_i. The dashed line gives the change due to migration in a subpopulation i when all immigrants have the alternative strategy. The maximum migration rate that allows the group-beneficial trait to persist is given by m. The solid line that intersects the y-axis at $-m$ gives the rate of change of p_i when half the immigrants have the group-beneficial trait and the other half are characterized by the alternative trait, the migration rate is m, and there is no group selection. When threshold frequency for the group-beneficial trait to increase when there is no migration is greater than 0.5, the group-beneficial trait cannot spread. However, if there is group selection as shown in the lower solid line, then the group-beneficial trait can spread.

analyzed, the change of gene frequency due to natural selection is proportional to the derivative of average fitness with respect to frequency. That is:

$$\Delta p = p(1-p)\frac{\partial \bar{W}}{\partial p}$$

Thus, the basin of attraction of the group-beneficial trait is always larger than the domain of attraction of the other trait (i.e. $\tilde{p} < 1/2$) and the strength of selection in favor of the group-beneficial trait with in populations is proportional to the magnitude of the effect of the trait on average fitness. Thus the range of conditions under which there is a very large group effect, and at the same time, the group-beneficial trait wouldn't spread in any case is very limited.

This is definitively not the case in the more general payoff structures than can result from social interactions. For example, the iterated n person prisoner's dilemma leads to payoff structures like those shown in Figure 11.7. A trigger strategy that cooperates only if all others in the group cooperate can be evolutionarily stable, and once common enough can achieve very high payoffs if groups persist over long time periods. However, the basin of attraction of the trigger strategy is much smaller than that of the noncooperative strategy because cooperation is not sustained until it becomes very common. It is easy to see in this case, the group-beneficial trait cannot spread without group selection, but even a factor of three advantage in migration guarantees its spread.

References

Aberle, D.F., A.K. Cohen, A.K. Davis, M.J. Levy, and F.X. Sutton (1950) The functional prerequisites of a society. *Ethics* 60: 100–111.

Aoki, K. (1982) A condition for group selection to prevail over counteracting individual selection. *Evolution* 36: 832–842.

Barton, N.H. (1992) On the spread of a new gene combination in the third phase of Wright's shifting balance. *Evolution* 46: 551–557.

Boorman, S. and P. Levitt (1980) *The Genetics of Altruism.* New York: Academic Press.

Boyd, R. and P.J. Richerson (1985) *Culture and the Evolutionary Process* Chicago: University of Chicago Press, Chicago.

Boyd, R. and P.J. Richerson (1990) Group selection among alternative evolutionarily stable strategies. *Journal of Theoretical Biology* 145: 331–342

Cavalli-Sforza, L.L. and M.W. Feldman (1981) *Cultural Transmission and Evolution: A Quantitative Approach.* Princeton: Princeton University Press.

Crow, J.F., W.R. Engels and C. Denniston (1990) Phase three of Wright's shifting-balance theory. *Evolution* 46: 551–557.

Durham, W.H. (1992) *Coevolution* Stanford: Stanford University Press.

Edgerton, R.B. (1992) *Sick societies: challenging the myth of primitive harmony.* New York: Free Press.

Eshel, I. (1972) On the neighborhood effect and the evolution of altruistic traits *Theoretical Population Biology* 3: 258–277.

Glickman, M. (1972) The Nuer and the Dinka, a further note. *Man* 7: 587–594.

Gavrilets, S. (1972) On phase three of the shifting balance theory. *Evolution* 50: 1034–1041.

Kelly, R. (1985) *The Nuer Conquest.* Ann Arbor: University of Michigan Press.

Levin, B.R. and W.L. Kilmer (1974) Interdemic selection and the evolution of altruism: A computer simulation study. *Evolution* 28: 527–45.

Lumsden, C.J. and E.O. Wilson (1981) *Genes, Mind, and Culture: The Coevolutionary Process.* Cambridge, MA: Harvard University Press.

Malinowski, B. (1922) *Argonauts of the Western Pacific* (reissued 1984). Prospect Heights, IL: Waveland Press.

Nelson, R. and S. Winter (1982) *An Evolutionary model of Economic Change.* Cambridge, MA: Harvard University Press.

Nisbett, R.E. and D. Cohen (1996) *Culture of honor: the psychology of violence in the South.* Boulder: Westview Press.

Price. G.R. (1970) Selection and covariance. *Nature* 227: 520–521.

Radcliffe-Brown, A.R. (1952) *Structure and Function in Primitive Society.* London: Cohen & West.

Rogers, A.R. (1990) Group selection by selective emigration: the effects of migration and kin structure. *American Naturalist* 135: 398–413.

Rouhani, S. and N. Barton (1987) Speciation and the "shifting balance" in a continuous population. *Theoretical Population Biology* 31: 465–492.

Rouhani, S. and N. Barton (1993a) Adaptation and the shifting balance. *Genetical Research*

Rouhani, S. and N. Barton (1993b) Group selection and the shifting balance. *Genetical Research* 61: 127–135.

Salomon, S. (1985) Ethnic communities and the structure of agriculture. *Rural Sociology* 50: 323–340.

Slatkin, M. and M.J. Wade (1978) Group selection on a quantitative character. *Proceedings of National Academy of Sciences* 75: 3531–3534.

Sober, E. and D.S. Wilson (1998) *Unto Others: The Evolution and Psychology of Unselfish Behavior.* Cambridge, MA: Harvard University Press.

Soltis, J., R. Boyd and P.J. Richerson (1995) Can group functional behaviors evolve by cultural group selection? An empirical test. *Current Anthropology* 36: 473–494.

Wade, M.J. (1978) A critical review of group selection models. *Quarterly Review of Biology* 53: 101–114.

Wilson, D.S. (1983) The group selection controversy: history and current status. *Annual Review of Ecology and Systematics* 14: 159–187.

12 Endogenous interactions

George J. Mailath, Larry Samuelson and Avner Shaked

12.1 Introduction

"It's not what you know, it's who you know that counts." We have all encountered assertions of this type, stressing the importance of interacting with the right people. In a similar vein, how does one explain the tremendous premium prospective MBAs put on attending a top business school if one is unconvinced that such schools differ greatly in their value-added or in the ability of their students? A common response is that the real reason for obtaining an MBA from the right school is the chance to "network" with future captains of industry.

In this paper, we examine groups or populations of players who interact in pairs to play a game. However, a player may not be equally likely to meet each member of the opposing population. Instead, patterns can arise in which some pairs of agents are more likely to interact than others. In addition, players may have both the desire and the ability to affect the pattern of such interactions. Hence, the game involves choosing a strategy that one plays whenever matched with an opponent and also choosing an *activity* that will affect which opponents one is matched with to play the game.

The existence of large populations of players who are matched to play the game suggests an evolutionary model. We follow conventional models in assuming that a player is characterized by a single pure strategy that is played against all opponents the player happens to meet, and in allowing that strategy to be adjusted via an evolutionary process. We depart from conventional models both in assuming that agents are more likely to meet some opponents than others and in assuming the activities that affect these meeting patterns are themselves subject to evolutionary pressures. We say that an evolutionary process exhibiting the first characteristic has *local interactions* and a process that also has the second characteristics exhibits endogenous local interactions or simply *endogenous interactions*.

We are interested in local interactions because we believe such interactions to be the rule rather than the exception, and also because such interactions can have important stability implications in an evolutionary model. In particular, local interactions may cause a mutant to face a local environment that differs considerably from the aggregate population. By supplying "bridgeheads" for invasion, primarily by allowing mutants to initially face a relatively high concentration of other mutants, local interactions may allow mutants to succeed that would otherwise be doomed to extinction.[1] If local interactions are important, however, then our attention is naturally directed to the forces that determine these interactions, and hence to endogenous interactions.

We are interested in three questions. What can we say about the rest points of an evolutionary process with local interactions? Can an evolutionary process with endogenous interactions lead to heterogeneous outcomes, in which different groups of agents play different strategies and receive different payoffs? Under what conditions will an evolutionary process with endogenous interactions yield efficient outcomes?

We first review Mailath, Samuelson, and Shaked (1997), which examines the case where interactions are local but agents' activities are fixed, so that agents cannot alter the opponents with whom they play. That paper also restricts attention to Nash equilibria in strategy choices given the local interaction pattern. We found there that the Nash equilibria with fixed (local) interactions correspond to correlated equilibria of the underlying game. Conversely, for any correlated equilibrium of the underlying game, there is a pattern of local interactions such that, fixing this pattern, there is a Nash equilibrium in strategy choices that gives the correlated equilibrium outcome.

Since we want to describe the evolution of a population with local interactions, we need an appropriate notion of state for such a population. A complete description of such a state involves listing the strategy chosen by each agent as well as his pattern of interactions. This is a complicated object, and it is helpful to have a simpler statistic that captures the important features of a state. In conventional evolutionary models, this simple statistic is the mixed strategy profile played by the total population. In our model with local interactions, the simple statistic is the correlated equilibrium induced by the state.

Our interest then turns to the case in which interactions are endogenous, with both strategies and activities adjusted by an evolutionary process. What properties will stable equilibria of the evolutionary process have, and in particular will they be homogeneous or efficient? The answers to these questions depend upon the extent to which agents can control their interactions. The key factor here is whether agents can ensure that they do *not* meet certain opponents. If agents do not have the ability to seclude themselves, then heterogeneous stable outcomes are possible, including outcomes in which agents are separated into groups, some of which play a "good" equilibrium and others of which play an inefficient, Pareto inferior "bad" equilibrium. If agents have the ability to seclude themselves without meeting undesired opponents, then stable outcomes must be efficient as well as homogeneous.[2]

These results may initially appear to be counterintuitive. Heterogeneity would appear to be most likely when secluded groups can form; while the coexistence of good and bad equilibrium outcomes would appear to be problematic when those playing the bad outcome cannot be excluded from interacting with those players enjoying the good outcome. However, heterogeneity persists in the latter case, even though agents playing the bad equilibrium can seek interactions with agents playing the good outcome, because the former cannot avoid other agents playing the bad equilibrium. Because some agents cannot avoid others playing the bad equilibrium, it can be a best response to acquiesce in playing the bad equilibrium, rather than seeking other partners with whom to play the good equilibrium and in the process miscoordinating with those who play the bad one. Conversely, efficient outcomes are ensured if groups of agents have the ability to segregate themselves from others. An outcome that is not efficient can be displaced by a small group of agents who seclude themselves and play an efficient outcome. This group will attract other agents who then find it optimal to switch to the efficient outcome because they are ensured of meeting only opponents playing that outcome.

These results depend heavily on the assumption that each agent must play the same strategy against all opponents he happens to meet. In particular, an agent could always (at least weakly) improve his outcome by making his strategy contingent on the strategy played by the opponent he meets.[3] In many cases, however, such discrimination is impossible, either because it is impossible to discern the opponent's strategy before choosing one's own or because the technology of choosing strategies allows only one choice. This inability to make strategies contingent on opponents is the essence of the local interaction problem. If contingent strategies could be played, then each interaction could be treated as a separate game and local interaction issues would be uninteresting.

To help in interpreting the process by which agents affect their interactions, we use the analogy of economists at the annual winter meetings of the Allied Social Sciences Associations in North America.[4] Interactions or networking are the heart of these meetings. Those who attend the meetings often devote great attention to arranging their activities so as to achieve desired contacts. Participants interact in many different ways, including interviews, paper sessions, cocktail parties and encounters in hotel lobbies. These activities provide quite different opportunities to control one's pattern of meetings.

The following section considers fixed interaction patterns. Our analogy here is with interviews at the winter meetings, where there is very little ability, once the meetings have started, to control one's interactions. Nash equilibrium strategy choices with fixed local interactions correspond to correlated equilibria of the underlying game. Section 12.3 introduces the dynamics by which interactions evolve. Sections 12.4 and 12.5 examine endogenous interactions. Section 12.4 shows that stable, heterogeneous outcomes can arise if agents do not have the ability to avoid other agents. Our analogy here is with paper sessions at the meetings, where one can choose which sessions to attend but cannot help but interact with those who attend one's own sessions. Section 12.5 shows that stable outcomes must be efficient if agents have the ability to interact in isolated groups. Our analogy here is with cocktail parties and hotel lobbies at the winter meetings, where groups can always steal off into seclusion. Indeed, the number of societies and associations (and corresponding cocktail parties) at the meetings has been growing steadily over the years, presumably reflecting a desire for like-minded participants to interact with each other (though we would hesitate to claim that the meetings are efficient).

12.2 Fixed interactions and correlated equilibria: interviews

In this section, we explore the implications of equilibrium strategy choices in the presence of local interactions. The pattern of interactions between agents is fixed, so that agents have no freedom to affect the distribution of their opponents.

In terms of the winter meetings, our analogy here is with the interviewing process. Agents interact according to a fixed interview schedule, with very little ability to affect this pattern by arranging interviews at the meetings. The interaction pattern is local, however, with some pairs of agents much more likely to meet than others. In addition, certain aspects of one's strategy are constrained to be the same against all opponents. For example, graduate students typically have only a single paper to present to all interviewers.

The interaction between a pair of agents is described by a finite, two-player normal form game, denoted $G = (S, \pi)$, where $S = S_1 \times S_2$ is the joint action set and $\pi = (\pi_1, \pi_2)$ is the reward function for the pairwise interaction. We assume that there is a finite population $\mathcal{N}_1$ of player 1's and a finite population $\mathcal{N}_2$ of player 2's. We think of these populations as being large, and require each population to have at least as many members as there are pure strategies for that player, i.e., $|\mathcal{N}_1| \geq |S_1|$ and $|\mathcal{N}_2| \geq |S_2|$. Each member of each population is associated with a pure strategy, so that $s_1 : \mathcal{N}_1 \rightarrow S_1$ and $s_2 : \mathcal{N}_2 \rightarrow S_2$ are functions specifying the strategies of the members of populations 1 and 2, with player $i \in \mathcal{N}_1$ playing $s_1(i)$ and player $j \in \mathcal{N}_2$ playing $s_2(j)$. Players from these populations are drawn in pairs, one from each population, to "meet" and play the game.[5] These meetings are described by a list of the number of times that each pair of agents meets. Without loss of generality, we normalize the total number of meetings to one. The proportion of meetings between players i and j can then also be described as the probability that, given a meeting, it involves players i and j. The interactions between the two populations are thus described by a probability distribution μ on the finite space $\mathcal{N}_1 \times \mathcal{N}_2$, with $\mu(i,j)$ interpreted as either the proportion of all matches that are matches between i and j or as the probability that, given a match, it involves player i from population 1 and player j from population 2.

Definition 1 *A triple $(s_1, s_2; \mu)$, consisting of an assignment of strategies to agents (s_1, s_2) and an interaction pattern μ, is an* equilibrium with fixed interactions *if, for all $i \in \mathcal{N}_1$,*

$$\sum_{j \in \mathcal{N}_2} \pi_1(s_1(i), s_2(j))\mu(i,j) \geq \sum_{j \in \mathcal{N}_2} \pi_1(\hat{s}_1, s_2(j))\mu(i,j) \quad \forall \hat{s}_1 \in S_1, \tag{12.1}$$

and for all $j \in \mathcal{N}_2$,

$$\sum_{i \in \mathcal{N}_1} \pi_2(s_1(i), s_2(j))\mu(i,j) \geq \sum_{i \in \mathcal{N}_1} \pi_2(s_1(i), \hat{s}_2)\mu(i,j) \quad \forall \hat{s}_2 \in S_2. \tag{12.2}$$

In equilibrium, different members of a population may face different opponents, and hence find different strategies optimal. This has the flavor of a correlated equilibrium, where different signals from a referee also result in different

		2	
		L	R
1	T	4,4	1,5
	B	5,1	0,0

Figure 12.1 The hawk-dove game

	Player 2_a (L)	Player 2_b (L)	Player 2_c (R)
Player 1_a (T)	1/6	0	1/6
Player 1_b (T)	0	1/6	1/6
Player 1_c (B)	1/6	1/6	0

Figure 12.2 A distribution of meetings

actions being optimal. To illustrate this notion, consider the Hawk-Dove game in Figure 12.1. Suppose there are three members each of player 1's and player 2's populations, so that $\mathcal{N}_1 = \{1_a, 1_b, 1_c\}$ and $\mathcal{N}_2 = \{2_a, 2_b, 2_c\}$. The interactions between the two populations are represented by the matrix in Figure 12.2. It is easy to verify that the local interactions with the assignment of strategies indicated in parentheses in Figure 12.2 describes an equilibrium with fixed interactions.

We now compare the notion of an equilibrium with fixed activities with correlated equilibrium. The definition of correlated equilibrium we use is motivated by the following interpretation.[6] A referee randomly determines an action profile (s_1, s_2) according to some distribution ξ, and then privately recommends the action s_k to player k. The distribution ξ is a correlated equilibrium if it is a best reply for each player to follow the recommendation:

Definition 2 *A correlated equilibrium is a probability distribution ξ on $S_1 \times S_2$, such that, for $i = 1, 2, i \neq k = 1, 2,$ if $\xi(s_i) > 0$, where $\xi(s_i)$ is the probability that the referee recommends action s_i to player i, then*

$$\sum_{s_k \in S_k} \pi_i(s_i, s_k)\xi(s_k|s_i) \geq \sum_{s_k \in S_k} \pi_i(\hat{s}_i, s_k)\xi(s_k|s_i) \quad \forall \hat{s}_i \in S_i. \tag{12.3}$$

The distribution in Figure 12.3 is a correlated equilibrium of the Hawk-Dove game in Figure 12.1.

A correlated equilibrium allows a player to contemplate changing his strategy (and requires such a change to be suboptimal), but does not allow the player to alter the information that is conveyed by the recommendation received by the referee. This is important, because different recommendations may give different

		2	
		L	R
1	T	1/3	1/3
	B	1/3	0

Figure 12.3 A correlated equilibrium for the Hawk-Dove game

equilibrium payoffs.[7] The counterpart of this in the model with fixed interactions is that the player can choose a strategy, but cannot affect the mix of opponents with whom he plays the game. This is again important, as the player may well prefer some different mix of opponents.

Let strategies be given by (s_1, s_2) and the pattern of interactions by μ. Then the probability that the strategy pair (s_1^*, s_2^*) is played in a meeting between two agents is denoted $\xi_{(s_1,s_2,\mu)}(s_1^*, s_2^*)$ and is given by:

Definition 3 *The distribution over strategy pairs generated by* $(s_1, s_2; \mu)$ *is*

$$\xi_{(s_1,s_2;\mu)}(s_1^*, s_2^*) = \sum_{\{i:s_1(i)=s_1^*\}} \sum_{\{j:s_2(j)=s_2^*\}} \mu(i,j). \tag{12.4}$$

It is straightforward to support some outcomes that are correlated but not Nash equilibria as equilibria with fixed interactions: Suppose each population has two players (or two groups of players), called α and α' in population 1 and β and β' in population 2. Let the matching be such that players α and β meet and players α' and β' meet. Moreover, suppose the game G is a battle of the sexes. One equilibrium in fixed activities is then for agents α and β to play one of the pure strategy equilibria of the game and for agents α' and β' to play the other. This equilibrium coincides with a correlated, non-Nash equilibrium of the game G. Moreover, the correlated equilibrium of Figure 12.3 is generated by the equilibrium with fixed interactions in Figure 12.2.

Mailath, Samuelson, and Shaked (1997) show that any correlated equilibrium can be supported as an equilibrium with fixed activities:

Theorem 1 *(1.1) If a triple* $(s_1, s_2; \mu)$ *is an equilibrium with fixed interactions, then* $\xi_{(s_1,s_2;\mu)}$ *is a correlated equilibrium.*

(2.2) If ξ *is a correlated equilibrium, then there exists an equilibrium with fixed interactions* $(s_1, s_2; \mu)$ *such that* $\xi_{(s_1,s_2;\mu)} = \xi$.

What is the intuition behind this result? Beginning with an equilibrium with fixed interactions, we construct a correlated equilibrium by recommending the pure strategy combination (s_1, s_2) with the same probability that the equilibrium with fixed interactions produces a match in which (s_1, s_2) is played. Now suppose player 1 receives a recommendation to play strategy s_1^*. The distribution over S_2, describing the opponent's strategy conditional on receiving a recommendation to play s_1^*, is a weighted average of the distributions over opponent strategies faced by all of the population-1 agents in the equilibrium-with-fixed-interactions who play s_1^*. But if s_1^* is a best reply to the distribution over opponent strategies facing each of these agents, then it is a best reply to the weighted average of these distributions. Hence, it is a best reply to play s_1^* when it is recommended, ensuring that we have a correlated equilibrium. The converse is demonstrated by noting that, given a correlated equilibrium, we can simply assign each pure strategy to a single player and then construct interactions between these players so that the probabilities with which any two players meet matches the probability with which the correlated equilibrium pairs the strategies played by these players. This construction potentially leaves large numbers of players with no possibility for meeting others and playing the game. It is straightforward to bring these players into the game by replacing the individual players in our construction with groups of players. In some cases, the pattern of interactions may be fixed by restrictions inherent in the environment. For example, population 1 may be buyers and population 2 sellers of a durable good. Population 1 includes dealers who buy for later resale as well as consumers who buy for private use. Population 2 also includes dealers and private consumers. Examples are the markets for antiques, works of art, used cars, or financial assets. Dealers buy from and sell to both consumers and dealers, but consumers typically interact only with dealers, yielding a local interaction pattern. In other cases, the interaction pattern may arise endogenously out of the actions taken by agents. We turn to this in the next section.

12.3 Evolution

The equivalence between equilibria with fixed activities and correlated equilibria depends upon the assumption that the pattern of interactions is indeed *fixed*, so that agents cannot choose or affect the distribution of their opponents. This restriction is important, because some opponents may provide higher payoffs than others, so that switching between opponents would occur if it were possible. We now expand the model to allow agents to affect their pattern of interactions.

We are interested in two types of questions. First, what patterns of interactions evolve? Second, we know from Theorem 1 that correlated equilibria are likely candidates for rest points of the evolutionary process. Which correlated equilibria will be selected?

We now find it convenient to assume that the players are drawn from infinite populations, so that there is an infinite population of row players (population 1) and a population of column players (population 2), each of which has measure 1. We allow population 1 to consist of $\mathcal{J}_1$ distinct subpopulations or groups. Similarly, population 2 consists of $\mathcal{J}_2$ distinct subpopulations. We think of these groups as being observable labels that are irrelevant to the payoffs of the game and are exogenously attached to players. For example, the groups may be characterized by ethnicity or culture. At the winter meetings, these groups may be fields of specialization among economists or may be departmental affiliations. The role played in the analysis by these groups will depend upon the details of the process by which interactions evolve.

We assume that interactions are determined by some features, characteristics, or choices of the players, which we refer to as *activities*. At the winter meetings, these activities may include attending particular paper sessions or cocktail parties. The finite set of activities for group $j \in \mathcal{J}_i$ in population $i (i = 1, 2)$ is denoted by A_i^j, and the set of available activities that could be chosen by some member of population i is $A_i \equiv \cup_j A_i^j$. To simplify notation, we assume that the activities of different groups have different "names," so that $A_i^j \cap A_i^{j'} = \emptyset$ for all $j \neq j'$ and $i = 1, 2$.[8] This includes the case in which different groups can choose the same activity, since we can simply give these activities different names.

For any activity $\alpha_i \in A_i$ and action $s_i \in S_i$, the proportion of agents of population i with activity α_i and action s_i is denoted $q_{\alpha_i s_i}$. A specification of $q_{\alpha_i s_i}$ for each activity, action, and population comprises a *state* of the system. We denote a state by θ and the state space by Θ. It is also convenient to define

$$Q_{\alpha_i} \equiv \sum_{s_i \in S_i} q_{\alpha_i s_i},$$

so that Q_{α_i} is the proportion of population i with activity α_i.

The activities of players affect the identities of their opponents. In particular, interactions between players are described by a function $\zeta : \Theta \times A_1 \times A_2 \to [0, 1]$. We interpret $\zeta(\theta, \alpha_1, \alpha_2)$ as the probability that, given state θ, a match occurs and is between agents with activities α_1 and α_2. Hence, for all θ,

$$\sum_{(\alpha_1, \alpha_2) \in A_1 \times A_2} \zeta(\theta, \alpha_1, \alpha_2) \leq 1.$$

We assume that the matching configuration ζ depends only on the proportion of agents with each *activity*, and not on their actions.[9] Finally, we assume that agents choosing a given activity are randomly selected to participate in matches, so that the probability that an agent of activity α_i is matched is $\sum_{\alpha_k \in A_k} \zeta(\theta, \alpha_i, \alpha_k)/Q_{\alpha_i}$.[10]

We view $\zeta(\theta, \alpha_1, \alpha_2)$ as a technological phenomenon, determined by the society or environment in which the agents interact. The function $\zeta(\theta, \alpha_1, \alpha_2)$ is thus fixed. However, agents can potentially alter the opponents with whom they interact by altering their choice of activity, and the pattern of interactions may evolve as agents' choices of activities evolve.

The evolutionary process by which agents change both actions and activities is described by the time path $\theta(t, \theta_0)$ which gives the state at time t if the state at time zero is θ_0. Time is continuous and the path is a differentiable function of both time and initial state. We often write $\theta(t, \theta_0)$ as $\theta(t)$.

We assume that action/activity pairs that currently earn higher payoffs grow proportionately faster than those that earn lower payoffs. Let $\pi_{\alpha_i s_i}$ be the expected payoff to an agent who chooses action s_i and activity α_i (we suppress the dependence of this payoff on the state). More specifically, we assume that $\theta(t, \theta_0)$ is *monotonic*, by which we mean:

$$\pi_{\alpha_i s_i}(\theta(t)) > (=) \pi_{\hat{\alpha}_i \hat{s}_i}(\theta(t)) \Rightarrow \frac{dq_{\alpha_i s_i}(\theta(t))}{dt} \frac{1}{q_{\alpha_i s_i}} > (=) \frac{dq_{\hat{\alpha}_i \hat{s}_i}(\theta(t))}{dt} \frac{1}{q_{\hat{\alpha}_i \hat{s}_i}} \qquad (12.5)$$

for all $\alpha_i, \hat{\alpha}_i \in A_i^j$, $s_i, \hat{s}_i \in S_i$, $j \in \mathcal{J}_i$, $i = 1, 2$.[11] The best-known dynamic satisfying this condition is the replicator dynamics.

There are several possible interpretations of these dynamics. It may be that individual agents play the game only once, with new agents constantly replacing old ones, but with new agents choosing their strategies on the basis of the payoffs in the previous generation. This may be especially appropriate if the matches are taken to be choices of mates. Alternatively, it may be that agents play the game repeatedly, adjusting their payoffs over time in response to their experience. This may be the appropriate model if the matchings represent social interactions. For more discussion of the various justifications of this type of dynamic analysis, see Mailath (1992, 1998), Samuelson (1997), and Selten (1991).

We define an *evolutionary rest point* to be a state θ with $d\theta(t)/dt = 0$. This definition leads immediately to a straightforward but important observation concerning evolutionary rest points:

Remark 1. If all agents in a population have access to the same set of activities, then in an evolutionary rest point, all agents (of the same population) must receive the same payoff (otherwise at least one agent would change activity or action).

If activities are fixed, then every equilibrium with fixed activities is an evolutionary rest point. The converse need not hold. Every pure state, meaning every state in which all of the agents in a given population play the same strategy, is an evolutionary rest point for the replicator dynamics for example, but not all of these will be equilibria with fixed activities. The difficulty is that there are pure states in which some agents are not playing best replies (because not all pure strategy combinations are Nash equilibria of the underlying game). These states are not equilibria with fixed activities, but they are stationary points and hence evolutionary rest points under the replicator dynamics. In particular, the replicator dynamics induces no movement toward best replies as long as these best replies are currently played by a zero proportion of the population. One suspects that these evolutionary rest points will have poor stability properties, with a small perturbation in the direction of a best reply prompting dynamics that lead away from the evolutionary rest points.

We accordingly require that rest points be asymptotically stable. An asymptotically stable state is a state with the property that if the process starts nearby, then it stays nearby (so that the state is Liapunov stable) and the process converges to the state in question. There may be many states that are stable, meaning simply that if the system starts nearby, then it stays nearby (though it may not converge to the state in question). *Asymptotically stable* states are unlikely to exist because the multitude of activities allows ample opportunity for the system to drift between states. We therefore consider a set-valued notion, which is that a set of states, each of which is individually Liapunov stable, be collectively asymptotically stable:[12]

Definition 4 *The set* $\Theta' \subseteq \Theta$ *is* asymptotically stable *if* Θ' *is closed and connected, and if*

(4.1) for every $\theta \in \Theta'$, $d\theta/dt = 0$;

(4.2) for every $\theta \in \Theta'$ *and every open set* V *containing* θ, *there exists an open set* U *with* $\theta \in U$ *such that* $\theta_0 \in U \Rightarrow \theta(t, \theta_0) \in V \forall t$; *and*

(4.3) there exists an open set U' *with* $\Theta' \subset U'$ *such that* $\theta_0 \in U' \Rightarrow \theta(t, \theta_0) \rightarrow \Theta'$ *as* $t \rightarrow \infty$.

A stable set is thus a collection of states with the property that each of the states is an evolutionary equilibrium (4.1), the dynamics surrounding each state in the set cannot lead the system too far away from that state (4.2), the dynamics take states near the set to the set (4.3), and points within the set can be viewed as connected via a drift process (the latter is the connectedness assumption). It is the possibility of drift to move the system along a connected set of states, without creating any dynamic forces, that forces us to use a set-valued rather than singleton valued stability notion. A number of papers have recently used similar stability conditions, including Kim and Sobel (1992), Matsui (1991), Nöldeke and Samuelson (1993), Sobel (1993), and Swinkels (1992a, 1992b, 1993).[13]

12.4 Endogenous interactions: paper sessions

12.4.1 Interactions

We now examine a model with endogenous interactions. Our first model of interactions is based on the idea that agents may have preferences over the groups from which their opponents are drawn, prompting us to refer to this as the "preferences" model. These preferences are induced by the possibility that agents in different groups may choose different actions.

There are many ways that a person's actions may affect the set of opponents with whom the person is likely to interact. We examine a particularly simple model of such activities: Each activity for an agent designates one group from the opposing population with whom the agent seeks to interact. This choice will make it more likely that one's opponents are drawn from the preferred group. However, each agent i belongs to a group that opponents may be seeking, and agent i cannot be assured of avoiding meetings with opponents who are seeking i's group, even if i prefers to avoid such meetings.

Continuing with our analogy, we think of discussions held at paper sessions at the winter meetings. The groups consist of those working in the various fields of economics, such as game theory, macroeconomics, labor economics, and so on. Activities consist of choices of paper sessions. Hence, a game theorist may prefer to talk with other game theorists. This objective can be advanced by attending and asking questions at game theory sessions. However, the game theorist must present a paper at his own session, and cannot preclude the possibility of questions from macroeconomists at that session.

To model this type of interaction, we associate with each group of agents a distinct "location." We will often speak of these as if they are physical locations, though other interpretations are possible. An activity consists of an attempt to visit a location in order to meet members of the group associated with that location. However, there is a positive probability that any agent will be matched at his "home" location with agents from the other population who have chosen to visit that location.

More formally, each agent in group j of population 1 has available $\mathcal{J}_2$ activities (corresponding to the locations or sessions of the other population). We can then denote an activity for population 1 agents by $\alpha_{j\ell}$, where $\alpha_{j\ell}$ represents an attempt by a member of group j to be matched with a member of group ℓ. Similarly, each member of group ℓ in population 2 has available $\mathcal{J}_1$ activities, denoted $\beta_{\ell j}$, where $\beta_{\ell j}$ represents an attempt by a member of group ℓ in population 2 to meet an opponent from group j in population 1. We let $|\mathcal{J}_j|$ denote the size of the jth group in population 1 and $|\mathcal{J}_\ell|$ the size of the ℓth group in population 2.

We assume that $\alpha_{j\ell}$ causes an agent from group j in population 1 to be assigned to location j in with probability 1/2, and to location ℓ with probability 1/2. The agent then interacts with the agents from the other population who are also assigned to the location to which he has been assigned. This specification is designed to capture the fact that agents can pursue their preferences for matching partners, but cannot completely escape potential matches who are seeking them. Hence, the rich may prefer to meet the rich, but cannot completely escape any poor trying to meet them. The probability 1/2 that a population 1 agent from group j is assigned to location j is then interpreted as stating that with probability 1/2, the agent is matched as a result of a population 2 agent seeking a match with group j. The 1/2 probability of being assigned to a population 2 group represents the probability of being matched as a result of one's own efforts to meet a certain opponent.[14]

Notice that we *force* agents to seek a match with some group from the opposing population, i.e. we do not allow players the option of endeavoring to not play the game at all. In some cases, this restriction may be undesirable from the player's point of view, because every possible match may yield a lower payoff than not playing. Our opinion is that if players are to have the choice of hiding from the world and not playing the game, then this should be modeled as one of the choices in the game. We return to the importance of the payoff of not playing the game below.

Given a particular pattern of activities, each location has a collection of population 1 agents, of size H_1, and of population 2 agents, of size H_2. The probability that an agent from population i is matched is given by the function $\rho^i(H_1, H_2)$, $i = 1, 2$. One important example is the *proportional matching rule*, which has the property that all agents on the "short side" of the market are matched:

$$\rho^i(H_1, H_2) = \min\{1, H_k/H_i\}. \tag{12.6}$$

Note that the same matching function is used at all locations, with the matching probabilities at a location determined only by the relative sizes of the collections of population 1 agents and population 2 agents at that location.

We assume that matching is anonymous within groups. Hence, an agent in population 1 can attempt to meet a member of group ℓ in population 2, but has no control over which member of that group he will meet. Hence, the distribution of the strategies of the opponents he meets is given by the distribution of opponents' strategies in the group to which he is assigned. This reflects our assumption that groups represent observable labels, so that agents can readily seek certain groups from the opposing population, but that agents cannot distinguish between different members of a group and cannot observe their opponents' strategies before play. This is important because the members of that group may play different actions. The formulas for the matching probabilities are in Section 12.7.1.

12.4.2 Heterogeneous outcomes

In this section, we discuss three examples showing that given the matching technology described in the previous section, asymptotically stable states can give heterogeneous outcomes.

Example 1 Consider the following game:

	L	R
T	4,4	$-1,-1$
B	$-1,-1$	2,2

Let the matching rule be proportional. Each population is divided into two groups of equal sizes, denoted groups a and b. Suppose group a agents play T (in population 1) and L (in population 2), and they seek each other. Suppose group b agents play B (in population 1) and R (in population 2) and they seek each other.[15] We can represent this schematically as:

$$1_a\,(T) \Leftrightarrow 2_a\,(L)$$

$$1_b\,(B) \Leftrightarrow 2_b\,(R)$$

As a result, half of the agents earn a payoff of 4 (the "rich," or group-a agents from both populations), while half earn a payoff of 2 (the "poor," or group-b agents from both populations). Rich agents meet other rich agents (and play the good equilibrium – this is why they are "rich"), while poor agents meet other poor agents (who, in turn, play the bad equilibrium). This state, considered as a singleton, is asymptotically stable.

How can the equilibrium in Example 1 be stable when poor agents receive an inferior payoff? Given that poor agents are most likely to meet other poor agents, it is in their best interests to continue to play the bad equilibrium. But why do the poor agents not simply seek rich agents with which to play the good equilibrium of the game? Equivalently, why isn't the movement in the direction of some group b agents in population 1 choosing $\alpha_{ba}T$ rather than $\alpha_{bb}B$ destabilizing? The rich agents are indifferent between playing against group a agents who choose T and group b agents who choose T, and hence are happy to meet the poor. The difficulty, however, is that the rich are not seeking the poor, and other poor *are* seeking the poor. No matter how much a poor agent desires to play the game with rich agents, he cannot escape the fact that nearly half of his matches are going to be with poor agents who play the bad equilibrium, and it is then not a best response to switch to seeking rich agents and playing the good equilibrium.

In particular, the payoff to a poor agent i in population 1 from playing T and seeking rich agents is $\frac{1}{2}4 + \frac{1}{2}(-1)$, which falls short of the payoff of 2 garnered from playing B and seeking other poor agents. The key here is that agent i can be identified as belonging to group b. Other agents expect group b agents to play B. Hence, population 2 agents who play R attempt to meet the agent i, and i cannot avoid such meetings. These meetings occur often enough that i's best response is to surrender to playing B and receiving the bad-equilibrium payoff.

This example also illustrates the importance of the assumption that agents cannot make their strategy depend on their opponent's group. While a strong assumption, there are situations where "code switching" is difficult if not impossible. Anderson (1994), for example, describes the "code of the street," behavior in some inner city neighborhoods of the US that many residents find difficult to switch from when interacting with nonresidents of these neighborhoods.

This example provides some insight into the questions of equality and income distribution. Attention has recently been devoted to the question of how an economy consisting of agents who are *ex ante* identical can give rise to persistent income inequality.[16] Existing theories have shown that as long as economic outcomes are stochastic, different outcome realizations can lead initially identical agents to different incomes. But why do these differences persist rather than being eliminated by the propensity of independent random processes to regress to the mean? The conventional explanation invokes externalities to create a link between current income and future prospects (e.g. Durlauf, 1992). For example, low incomes can lead to low investment in children's education which leads to low future incomes. If there is also a link between community income levels and the effectiveness of education (perhaps because different income levels lead to different academic habits and norms of achievement), then this cycle can be reinforced and can create an absorbing "poverty trap."

Our example suggests that a poverty trap can arise without externalities (or, depending upon one's interpretation, from externalities in the matching process). Poor agents are poor, and will remain poor, simply because most of their interactions are with other poor people who happen to have coordinated on a low-payoff equilibrium; and because one's wealth or social status is sufficiently correlated with observable characteristics that one cannot simply decide to hereafter be taken for a rich person and interact only with other rich people. This example illustrates the argument that a poverty program serving only a few of the poor and leaving them in their current environment ignores potentially important factors. In particular, to the extent that our example is capturing a crucial feature, it suggests that breaking the "cycle of poverty" will require either a massive intervention to switch the poor groups to the good equilibrium or will require removing poor agents from their environments and putting them into environments where they will be sought by (as well as being able to seek) rich agents.

We need only attach labels such as "black" and "white" to the groups in Example 1 to obtain an outcome in which one group appears to be the victim of discrimination. "Statistical" theories of discrimination have produced models with equilibria in which blacks fare less well then whites even though the latter entertain no antipathy for the former.[17] Example 1 suggests yet another such theory, with the statistical discrimination taking the form of white agents not seeking interactions with blacks because the latter play the bad equilibria, while blacks play the bad equilibria because whites do not seek interactions with them. Once again, the key is that certain behaviors have come to be associated with the labels black and white. For a black agent i, switching behavior does not alter the fact that others still observe simply that i is black, and play against i as they would against other blacks.

One's first impression is that affirmative action policies, by vitiating the statistical profile of the oppressed group, should be able to eliminate such discrimination. Coate and Loury (1993) show that the effectiveness of affirmative actions in such situations, and especially the question of whether a temporary affirmative action policy can have permanent effects, depends critically upon how the policy affects whites' beliefs about blacks. They find that in some cases only permanent affirmative action policies will be effective. In our case, the affirmative action would have to involve ensuring blacks sufficient access to interactions with whites to allow the good equilibrium to become a best reply for the former. Once blacks were induced to play the good equilibrium, the policy would be unnecessary.

Example 2 Consider the Hawk-Dove game of Figure 12.1. Again we suppose that the each populations is divided into two groups, denoted groups a and b. Consider the state in which group a agents play T (population 1) and L (population 2) and seek each other, while group b agents play B (population 1) and R (population 2) and seek group a from the opposing population. This is described schematically by:

$$\begin{array}{ccc} 1_a\,(T) & \Leftrightarrow & 2_a\,(L) \\ \Uparrow & & \Uparrow \\ 2_b\,(R) & & 1_b\,(B) \end{array}$$

Assume, however, that group a in each population is of size x while group b is of size $1-x$.[18] It is straightforward to verify that if $1/4 < x < 1/3$, then each agent's activity-action choice is a strict best reply, and so the state is asymptotically stable. *Conditional* on being matched, a group a agent in population 1 is matched with a population 2 agent choosing L with probability $2x/(1+x)$. Also, conditional on being matched, a group b agent in population 1 is matched with a population 2 agent choosing L with probability 1. Thus, for x close to (but less than) 1/3, the conditional distributions are close to those in the correlated distribution that places equal probabilities on the three profiles TL, TR, and BL.

In contrast to the fixed activities case of Example 1, there is a positive probability that an agent will not be matched in the equilibrium described in Example 2. For example, group-b agents are not matched when the matching process allocates them to their own location (which occurs with probability 1/2). In addition, the entire population is attempting to match with group-a agents of the opposing population, but only a fraction x can succeed at that location. Thus, group b agents in each population are not matched with a probability of $1/2+(1-x)/2 = 1-x/2$. An analogous calculation shows that group a agents are not matched with probability $(1-x)/2$.

As long as interactions are endogenous, so that agents have some ability to affect the identity of their opponents, then we must take seriously the possibility that some agents are not matched or, equivalently, that some agents are matched more often than others. The desired matching plans of all agents may not be compatible or feasible, and the result may be that some agents are frustrated in their efforts to meet others. In calculating the payoff to an activity, agents must then include the possibility that they are not matched, with its attendant payoff.

As a result, the payoffs in a game do not provide a complete description of the strategic situation until the payoff to not being matched is specified. While it is tempting to set this payoff to zero, this is not the only possibility. The following example shows how the magnitude of this payoff can affect the outcome of the evolutionary process:

Example 3 Suppose that we alter the payoff to not being matched in the Hawk-Dove game of Figure 12.1 to be 1 rather than 0. We can then normalize the payoffs in the new game by subtracting 1 from each payoff, *including* the payoff of not being matched, to obtain a game in which the payoff to not being matched is zero and the other payoffs are:[19]

		2	
		L	R
1	T	3,3	0,4
	B	4,0	$-1,-1$

As in Example 2, suppose population 1 is divided into two groups, as is population 2. Let x denote the size of the first group (assume that it is the same size for each population). Again suppose all groups wish to meet the opposing group a's; and the row group a's choose T and group b's choose B; the column group a's choose L and the group b's choose R.

Is this an asymptotically stable state when $1/4 < x < 1/3$, as it was in Example 2? Consider a group a player from population 1. Choosing $\alpha_{aa}T$ yields payoffs:[20]

$$\frac{1}{2}(x \times \pi_1(T,L) + (1-x) \times \pi_1(T,R)) + \frac{1}{2}(x \times \pi_1(T,L))$$

$$= \frac{1}{2}(x \times 3 + (1-x) \times 0) + \frac{1}{2}(x \times 3) = 3x.$$

The pair $\alpha_{aa}B$ yields:

$$\frac{1}{2}(x \times 4 + (1-x) \times (-1)) + \frac{1}{2}(x \times 4) = \frac{1}{2}(9x-1).$$

The pair $\alpha_{ab}T$ yields (note that the player is now never rationed):

$$\frac{1}{2}(x \times 3 + (1-x) \times 0) + \frac{1}{2}(0) = \frac{3}{2}x.$$

Finally, $\alpha_{ab}B$ yields:

$$\frac{1}{2}(x \times 4 + (1-x) \times (-1)) + \frac{1}{2}(-1) = \frac{1}{2}(5x-2).$$

The pair $\alpha_{aa}T$ yields a strictly higher payoff than the other choices if $x < 1/3$. It is also straightforward to verify that the group b's strictly prefer $\alpha_{ba}B$ to the other choices (and similarly for population 2) if $x < 1/3$. We thus have an equilibrium that resembles that of Example 2, but this equilibrium is an asymptotically stable state as long as $x < 1/3$ (rather than also requiring $1/4 < x$, as in Example 2). The difference is that the value of not being matched is higher here than in Example

2. This makes it more attractive to endure the rationing associated with $\alpha_{aa}T$ in quest of the relatively high payoff $\pi_1(T,L)$ (rather than avoiding rationing by choosing $\alpha_{ab}T$ and settling for the relatively low payoff $\pi_1(T,R)$). As a result, the constraint $1/4 < x$, needed in Example 2 to ensure that agents choosing $\alpha_{aa}T$ are not too severely rationed, is not needed here.[21]

12.5 Endogenous interactions: cocktail parties and hotel lobbies

12.5.1 Interactions

In the preferences model of the previous section, agents could express preferences over desired matches but could not avoid undesired matches. We now examine a model in which agents can sometimes be assured of avoiding certain other agents. We will find it convenient to again describe the interaction technology in terms of locations, and will refer to this as the "location" model.

In our winter meetings parable, the locations are cocktail parties and hotel lobbies. Agents frequent a location in an attempt to meet other agents, and interact with others who appear at that location. By finding a suitably secluded corner or hotel suite, agents can always ensure that they are not found by those they prefer not to meet. However, this ability to avoid others carries with it a lessened ability to ensure any meeting. There is now no guarantee that any agents of the other population will be at any particular location. One need not attend even the cocktail party of one's own department if one prefers not to, unlike paper sessions.

More formally, suppose there are a finite number of locations, denoted $\lambda \equiv \{\ell_1, \ldots, \ell_L\}$. In its simplest form, a choice of an activity consists of a choice of location. In general, however, this choice of location may be random, with an activity inducing a probability distribution over locations rather than corresponding to a single location. For example, an activity might be a decision to frequent one of the convention hotels on a certain day. Once there, this may induce a distribution concerning the likelihood that one is to be found in various locations, including cocktail parties, book displays, bars and the hotel lobby. At each location, other agents are likely to be encountered. Finally, notice that a location need not be a physical location in the usual sense of the word, though the latter provides a convenient interpretation that we shall adopt when describing the model. A formal description is contained in Section 12.7.2.

12.5.2 Efficient outcomes

We now derive conditions under which the outcome in the location model is not only homogeneous, but also satisfies an efficiency condition. The sufficient conditions for efficiency come in three parts. First, we need the matching technology to be unrestricted, meaning that all agents have access to the same set of activities. Second, we need it to be possible that an isolated group of agents can form. Third, we require that neither large nor small groups are penalized in terms of matching probabilities, which holds if the matching technology exhibits constant returns to scale (see Section 12.7.2 for the precise definition).[22]

Isolated groups of agents will be able to form if the matching technology contains pure activities, where:

Definition 5 *An activity α is* pure *if there exists a location ℓ with the property that the activity guarantees that the location is reached.*

We then have:

Theorem 2 *Let all agents (of both populations) have access to the same set of activities in the location model. Suppose that game G has a Nash equilibrium whose payoffs strictly dominate the payoffs of all other correlated equilibria. Suppose that the matching process exhibits constant returns. Let there be at least three locations, with a pure activity for each population associated with each location. Then in every state in an asymptotically stable set, every agent is choosing the efficient equilibrium action.*

The proof appears in Section 12.8. To see why the result holds, consider first a state in which there is a "free" location, meaning that there is a location at which no agents appear. Suppose further that there is a pure activity corresponding to this location for each population, and that agents are currently earning less than the efficient payoff. Then the existing state is not part of an asymptotically stable set. Instead, consider a perturbation that attaches a small number of agents from both populations to the pure activity corresponding to the vacant location, with these agents playing the actions of the efficient equilibrium. This activity/action pair will earn a higher payoff than any other activity/action pair, attracting agents to the previously vacant location and the efficient equilibrium and thus destabilizing the existing state and precluding its membership in an asymptotically stable set.

The potential difficulty is that the current state may entail agents visiting every location, so that there is no free location with which to work. However, we show that every candidate for an asymptotically stable set of states includes states with unused locations. Intuitively, the system can drift among the states in the stable set, until a state is reached with an unused location. We refer to this process as "freeing a location." The assumption of constant returns to scale is used in this demonstration, as it allows agents to drift between locations without creating congestion affects at these locations. Once a state with a free location is reached, the perturbation described in the previous paragraph prompts dynamics that lead away from the state, precluding its stability.

In order to conclude that asymptotically stable sets are efficient, Theorem 2 assumes the existence of an equilibrium that *strictly* dominates all other equilibrium payoffs. We cannot reduce this requirement to weak domination. Suppose, for example, that the stage game is given by:

	L	R
T	1,1	2,1
B	1,2	2,2

Then evolution puts no pressure on strategy choices and the only candidate for an asymptotically stable set is the entire state space, not all of which is efficient.

The forces ruling out inefficient behavior are analogous to those appearing in cheap talk games, including Kim and Sobel (1992), Matsui (1991), and Sobel (1993). Consider a model in which a round of communication is allowed before a game is played. Consider an equilibrium that is not efficient, and suppose a state yielding this equilibrium belongs to a stable set. If the message space is rich enough to ensure that some messages are not sent, then the stable set contains a state featuring the same play of the game, but in which all agents would respond to the unsent message by playing their part of the Pareto dominating equilibrium. A perturbation that causes that message to be sent now creates dynamics that lead away from the allegedly stable set, which is a contradiction.

A similar mechanism is at work in our model. The place of the unsent message is taken by an unused location with a matching pair of pure activities. The condition that the message space be sufficiently rich to ensure that there is an unsent message is replaced by the condition that there exists at least three locations with pure activities, which we show is sufficient for drift to be able to free a location.[23]

The assumption of constant returns to scale in the matching technology plays two roles in the argument. It ensures that a location can be freed and that agents can be relocated to the freed location. If ρ^i_ℓ exhibits decreasing returns to scale, so that locations suffer from congestion, it may be difficult to free a location by adding agents to other, populated locations.[24] If ρ^i_ℓ exhibits increasing returns to scale, then it may be difficult to attract agents to playing the efficient outcome at a freed location.[25]

Our result says nothing about the *existence* of asymptotically stable sets. General sufficient conditions for existence of an asymptotically stable set in evolutionary models are severe. In particular, evolutionary models readily yield characterization results but only grudgingly offer general existence results. A trade-off then arises. Existence can be ensured under mild conditions by appealing to a solution concept that places little structure on the resulting "stable" sets, allowing these sets to be large and placing little structure on the states that appear in such sets. Alternatively, one can ask for well-behaved stable sets, such as asking that each state in such a set be a rest point of the dynamics (our condition (4.1)), but existence can then be ensured only under strong assumptions. For example, Kim and Sobel (1992) (in a model of cheap talk games) and Nöldeke and Samuelson (1993) (in a model of extensive form games) find that demanding conditions, involving essentially the existence of an outcome whose payoffs strictly dominate the payoffs of every other outcome, are needed to establish the existence of well-behaved stable sets.[26] In the presence of endogenous interactions, where there are activities that affect payoffs only indirectly through their effect on the matching process, additional strong assumptions on the matching technology would be required, such as assumptions that the matching scheme is proportional and all activities are pure.

12.6 Conclusion

Our results provide two main insights into local interactions. First, they give rise to correlated equilibria, providing a new interpretation for the latter. Second, outcomes can depend crucially on the ability of agents to affect their interactions. We have seen that the ability to avoid undesired matches can make the difference between efficient outcomes and outcomes that doom some agents to inferior payoffs. This suggests that more attention might usefully be devoted to the process by which agents are matched to play games; a topic we hope to pursue further.

12.7 The matching process

12.7.1 Probabilities when there are group specific locations

Consider an agent of population 1 who chooses activity $\alpha_{j\ell}$, meaning that the agent belongs to group j and would like to meet an opponent from group ℓ. The probability that this agent is matched is given by:

$$\frac{1}{2}\left(\rho^1\left(\frac{1}{2}\sum_{\kappa=1}^{\mathcal{J}_1} Q_{\alpha_{\kappa\ell}}, \frac{1}{2}|\mathcal{J}_\ell|\right)\right) + \frac{1}{2}\left(\rho^1\left(\frac{1}{2}|\mathcal{J}_j|, \frac{1}{2}\sum_{\kappa=1}^{\mathcal{J}_2} Q_{\beta_{\kappa j}}\right)\right).$$

The first term represents the probability of being matched as a result of being assigned to location ℓ in population 2; the second term as a result of being assigned to location j in population 1. The arguments of ρ^1 in the first term are the measure of the population-1 agents who are assigned to location ℓ, which is 1/2 of all the agents who attempt to meet members of group ℓ (which is given by $\sum_{\kappa=1}^{\mathcal{J}_1} Q_{\alpha_{\kappa\ell}}$; and the number of population-2 agents assigned to that location, which is 1/2 of the population-2 agents who are members of group ℓ (which is $|\mathcal{J}_\ell|$). The arguments of ρ^1 in the second term are analogous.

The probability that a match with an opponent from the desired group ℓ of population 2 occurs is given by:

$$\frac{1}{2}\left(\rho^1\left(\frac{1}{2}\sum_{\kappa=1}^{\mathcal{J}_1} Q_{\alpha_{\kappa\ell}}, \frac{1}{2}|\mathcal{J}_\ell|\right)\right) + \frac{1}{2}\left(\rho^1\left(\frac{1}{2}|\mathcal{J}_j|, \frac{1}{2}\sum_{\kappa=1}^{\mathcal{J}_2} Q_{\beta_{\kappa j}}\right)\right)\frac{Q_{\beta_{\ell j}}}{\sum_{\kappa=1}^{\mathcal{J}_2} Q_{\beta_{\kappa j}}}. \tag{12.7}$$

The probability that a match with an opponent from group $h \neq \ell$ occurs is:

$$\frac{1}{2}\left(\rho^1\left(\frac{1}{2}|\mathcal{J}_j|, \frac{1}{2}\sum_{\kappa=1}^{\mathcal{J}_2} Q_{\beta_{\kappa j}}\right)\right)\frac{Q_{\beta_{hj}}}{\sum_{\kappa=1}^{\mathcal{J}_2} Q_{\beta_{\kappa j}}}. \tag{12.8}$$

An extra term appears in (7) that does not appear in (8) because the population-1 agent in question is seeking a meeting with an opponent from group ℓ, and hence has two possibilities for such a meeting, arising out of his attempt to meet a member of group ℓ or an attempt by a group-ℓ member to meet the population-1 agent. In contrast, the population-1 agent does not seek a meeting with group $h \neq \ell$, and such a meeting potentially occurs only out of the efforts of the group h agent.

12.7.2 The general location model

The meeting technology is specified by a collection of probabilities of the form $\gamma_{\alpha\ell} \in [0,1]$, where $\gamma_{\alpha\ell}$ is the probability that an agent choosing activity α arrives at location ℓ, so that $\sum_{\ell\in\lambda}\gamma_{\alpha\ell} = 1$. Let $H_{\ell s_1}$ denote the proportion of population 1 agents who play action s_1 and arrive at location ℓ:

$$H_{\ell s_1} = \sum_{\alpha\in A_1} q^1_{\alpha s_1}\gamma_{\alpha\ell}.$$

The measure of population 1 agents arriving at location ℓ is $\sum_{s_1\in S_1} H_{\ell s_1}$. Normalizing to obtain a probability distribution, we have $h_{\ell s_1}$ as the proportion of player 1 agents at location ℓ who play action s_1:

$$h_{\ell s_1} = \frac{H_{\ell s_1'}}{\sum_{s'1\in s_1} H_{\ell s_1'}}$$

The agents at each location are randomly matched to play, with the possibility arising that not all agents are matched. We let ρ^i_ℓ be the probability that an agent from population i who arrives at location ℓ is matched. We assume, as in Section 12.4, that this probability is a function only of the total numbers of agents from populations 1 and 2 who arrive at location ℓ:

$$\rho^i_\ell = \rho^i\left(\sum_{s_1\in S_1} H_{\ell s_1}, \sum_{s_2\in S_2} H_{\ell s_2}\right),$$

where $\rho^i : [0,1]^2 \to [0,1]$. We require ρ^i to be continuous on $[0,1]^2\backslash\{(0,0)\}$,[27] and that the number of matches by population 1 agents equal the number of population 2 matches:

$$\rho^1\left(\sum_{s_1\in S_1} H_{\ell s_1}, \sum_{s_2\in S_2} H_{\ell s_2}\right)\sum_{s_1\in S_1} H_{\ell s_1} = \rho^2\left(\sum_{s_1\in S_1} H_{\ell s_1}, \sum_{s_2\in S_2} H_{\ell s_2}\right)\sum_{s_2\in S_2} H_{\ell s_2}.$$

We also assume that ρ^1 is increasing in its first argument and decreasing in its second, while ρ^2 is decreasing in its first argument and increasing in its second. This implies that an agent is more likely to be matched the fewer agents from his own population at the location and the more agents from the other population at the location.

We restrict attention to the case in which ρ^i is homogeneous of degree zero, so that there are no congestion effects at locations. We refer to this as the case of *constant returns to scale*, in the sense that increasing the number of agents at a location yields a like increase in the expected number of matches at that location. The proportional matching rule used in Section 12.4 is an example of a constant returns to scale rule. Other interesting possibilities are *increasing returns to scale*: $\rho^i(an_1, an_2) > \rho^i(n_1, n_2)$ $\forall a > 1$; and *decreasing returns to scale*: $\rho^i(an_1, an_2) < \rho^i(n_1, n_2)$ $\forall a > 1$. Increasing returns to scale capture the idea that more agents at a location make it more likely that agents will "meet" each other (such as in search models), while decreasing returns to scale capture congestion effects – more agents at a location make it less likely that agents will "meet" each other.

The preference model of Section 12.4 is a special case of the location model. To obtain the preference model we let $\mathcal{J}_1$ be the set of locations associated with population 1, $\mathcal{J}_2$ the set of locations associated with population 2, $\mathcal{J}_1 \cap \mathcal{J}_2 = \emptyset$, and for $i \in \mathcal{J}_1, j \in \mathcal{J}_2$, $\gamma_{\alpha_{ij}\ell} = 1/2$ if $\ell = i, j$, and 0 otherwise. More generally, the matching function ζ implied by the location model is given by:[28]

$$\zeta(\theta, \alpha_1, \alpha_2) = \sum_{\ell \in \lambda} \frac{\rho_\ell^1 \gamma_{\alpha_1 \ell} Q_{\alpha_1} \gamma_{\alpha_2 \ell} Q_{\alpha_2}}{\sum_{\alpha_2' \in A_2} \gamma_{\alpha_2' \ell} Q_{\alpha_2'}} = \sum_{\ell \in \lambda} \frac{\rho_\ell^2 \gamma_{\alpha_1 \ell} Q_{\alpha_1} \gamma_{\alpha_2 \ell} Q_{\alpha_2}}{\sum_{\alpha_1' \in a_1} \gamma_{\alpha_1' \ell} Q_{\alpha_1'}}$$

12.8 Proof of Theorem 2

Let s^* be the strategy profile of the strict Nash equilibrium identified in the Theorem. Suppose Θ' is an asymptotically stable set and $\theta \in \Theta'$. Because all agents have access to the same activities, all agents of population i must receive the same payoff in state θ (otherwise it cannot be that $d\theta/dt = 0$); let $\hat{\pi}_i$ denote this payoff. Let s^* be the efficient Nash equilibrium. We now suppose that $\hat{\pi}_i < \pi_i(s^*)$ and derive a contradiction.

By hypothesis, there are three locations associated with pure activities; label them as 1, 2, and 3. Let $H_\ell^i \equiv \sum_{s_i \in S_i} H_{\ell s_i}$, the size of the population of player i agents at location ℓ.

Suppose that at one of the locations, say 1, $H_1^i = 0$, for $i = 1, 2$, so that no agents arrive at that location under θ. Then consider the following perturbation of state θ. Reduce by a factor δ the proportions of agents at every activity/action combination for each population. (Since the ratio of the population of player 1 agents to the size of the population of player 2 agents at each location is unchanged by this, the payoffs to the activity/action choices in θ have not changed.) Place these agents at the pure activity associated with location 1, and have them play s^*. This yields a payoff at location 1 that is strictly higher than the payoff under θ. As a result, the dynamics will converge to a state in which all agents are choosing the pure activity associated with location 1 and playing s_i^*. This ensures that θ is not stable (i.e., fails condition (4.2)) and hence that Θ' is not asymptotically stable.[29]

It remains to show that Θ' contains a state in which $H_\ell^i = 0$, for $i = 1, 2$, and some $\ell \in \{1, 2, 3\}$. Suppose, first, that Θ' contains a state θ' in which $H_\ell^1 = H_\ell^2$ for some $\ell \in \{1, 2, 3\}$. Without loss of generality, suppose this is location 1. Let f_i^1 denote the distribution of actions faced by a player j ($j \neq i$) agent at location 1. Now consider the following perturbation. Reduce by δ the proportions of agents at every activity/action combination for each population. (As before, since H_ℓ^1/H_ℓ^2 for all ℓ is unchanged by this, the payoffs to the activity/action choices in θ' have not changed.) Place these agents at the pure activity associated with location 1, and have the agents of player i play choose actions in accordance with f_i^1. Since

$H_1^1 = H_1^2$, the payoffs at this pure activity have not changed. This perturbed vector is thus also an element of Θ'. Continuing in this way will eventually result in a state, contained in Θ', in which all agents choose the pure activity associated with location 1, ensuring that no agents choose the pure activities associated with locations 2 and 3.

Finally, suppose, $H_\ell^1 \neq H_\ell^2$ for all $\ell \in \{1, 2, 3\}$. Without loss of generality, suppose H_ℓ^1/H_ℓ^2 is maximized at location 1 and minimized at location 2. Note in particular that $\eta_1 \equiv H_1^1/H_1^2 > 1$ and $\eta_2 \equiv H_2^1/H_2^2 < 1$, so that $\tau \equiv (1-\eta_2)/(\eta_1 - \eta_2) \in (0,1)$. Let f_i^ℓ denote the distribution of actions faced by a player j ($j \neq i$) agent at location ℓ. Consider the following perturbation. Reduce by δ the proportions of agents at every activity/action combination for each population. (As before, since H_ℓ^1/H_ℓ^2 for all ℓ is unchanged by this, the payoffs to the activity/action choices in θ' have not changed.) Assign a fraction $\tau\eta_1$ of the player 1 population and a fraction τ of the player 2 population to location 1, and a fraction $1-\tau\eta_1 = (1-\tau)\eta_2$ of the player 1 population and a fraction $(1-\tau)$ of the player 2 population to location 2. Specify that the agents of player i at location ℓ play in accordance with f_i^ℓ. By construction, the ratio of the size of the population of player 1 agents to the size of the population of player 2 agents at locations 1 and 2 have not changed, and so the payoffs at these locations have not changed. Thus the perturbed vector is an element of Θ'. The argument is now completed as in the previous paragraph.

Acknowledgments

Presented at the Tenth Workshop of the International School of Economic Research on "Evolution and Economics" held at the Certosa di Pontignano, Siena (Italy), June 27 – July 5, 1997. George Mailath thanks Professor Ugo Pagano and Dr. Giovanni Forconi for organizing the workshop. This is a revision of "Evolution and Endogenous Interactions," first draft, December 10, 1992. Part of this work was done while George Mailath and Larry Samuelson were visiting the University of Bonn and while all three authors were visiting the Institute for Advanced Studies at the Hebrew University of Jerusalem. We are grateful for the hospitality of both. We thank Ken Binmore for helpful discussions. This work has been presented under the titles "The Evolution of Heterogeneity," "Evolution with Endogenous Interactions," and "Evolution and Correlated Equilibria." Financial support from the National Science Foundation and the Deutsche Forschungsgemeinschaft, SFB 303, at the University of Bonn, is gratefully acknowledged.

Notes

1 The viscosity model of Myerson, Pollock and Swinkels (1991) is in this vein.

2 As we will discuss, there is a similar result in cheap talk games. Ely (1996) has obtained a similar result for a related model.

3 See Banerjee and Weibull (1993) for a model of "discriminating" players.

4 Any large conference will serve as an analogy, as long as there are interviews associated with the conference. At the ASSA winter meetings, graduate students soon to receive their PhDs are interviewed by potential employers.

5 Notice that we explicitly assume asymmetric interactions, i.e. there is role identification. We can allow for no role identification at the cost of additional notational complexity.

6 There are several equivalent definitions of correlated equilibrium. An alternative involves specifying an information structure for the players and action choices as functions of signals received. The equilibrium condition is that prescribed choices are optimal given beliefs conditional on the players' information (i.e. signals).

7 Different recommendations may correspond to different conditional distributions of the opponent's recommendations and hence to different behavior.

8 We now use the index i and k for populations and j for groups.

9 That is, if $Q_{\alpha_1}(\theta) = Q_{\alpha_1}(\theta')$ and $Q_{\alpha_2}(\theta) = Q_{\alpha_2}(\theta')$, then $\zeta(\theta,\alpha_1,\alpha_2) = \zeta(\theta',\alpha_1,\alpha_2)$, for all $(\alpha_1,\alpha_2) \in A_1 \times A_2$.

10 Hence, for $k \neq i$ we must have $\sum_{\alpha_k \in A_k} \zeta(\theta,\alpha_i,\alpha_k) \leq Q_{\alpha_i}$.

11 Notice that α_i and $\hat{\alpha}_i$ are both taken to be elements of A_i^j in (5). Hence, we are explicitly restricting each group of agents to playing only activities that are available to that group.

12 An alternative formulation would be to replace (4.2) with a minimality requirement.

13 Gilboa and Matsui (1991) consider a stability concept that shares a similar spirit of being set-valued, but allows movements between members of the set to arise out of forces other than genetic drift.

14 The 1/2s are motivated by the equal population sizes. A number of alternatives readily suggest themselves. For example, agents may be able to identify a number of groups from the opposing population with whom they would like to play the game, possibly with weights. Agents might also be able to choose the mix of probabilities between being assigned to one's own location and being assigned to a location in the other population. A higher probability of being assigned to the other population would be interpreted as an increased ability to avoid matches with unsought partners.

15 Formally, $q_{\alpha_{aa}T} = q_{\beta_{aa}L} = q_{\alpha_{bb}B} = q_{\beta_{bb}R} = 1/2$.

16 See Durlauf (1992) for a discussion and references.

17 See Coate and Loury (1993) for a discussion and references.

18 Formally, $q_{\alpha_{aa}T} = q_{\beta_{aa}L} = x$, and $q_{\alpha_{ba}B} = q_{\beta_{ba}R} = 1 - x$.

19 This example is thus equivalent to the game in Figure 12.1 with the payoff to not being matched set at 1.

20 Since with probability 1/2, the player is at his own location, is not rationed and faces the distribution x of group a and $1 - x$ of group b; and with probability 1/2, the player is at the opponent group a's location and only matches with probability$x$.

21 Notice that the payoff to not playing the game does not affect the relative payoffs to strategies $\alpha_{aa}T$ and $\alpha_{aa}B$, since these involved identical rationing frequencies, so that the equilibria in Examples 2 and 3 share the constraint $x < 1/3$, needed to ensure that the payoff of $\alpha_{aa}T$ exceeds that of $\alpha_{aa}B$.

22 We assume throughout that equilibria exist that give all agents higher payoffs than not being matched, so that efficiency requires that the game be played.

23 The destabilizing perturbation in cheap talk models requires agents from a single population to adopt an unused message, even if both populations have the opportunity to send messages before play. In contrast, our destabilizing perturbation sends agents of *both* populations to the free location. If our dynamics allowed the population proportion playing a strategy to grow whenever that strategy is a best reply, even if it is currently played by a zero proportion of the population, then it would suffice for members of a single population to switch to a vacant location (at which point members of the other population would be drawn to the new location). Notice that because actions in a cheap talk model are contingent on messages, the sending of a new message is equivalent to switching *both* agents to a new location. Moreover, if a population-1 agent deviates to the new message in a cheap talk model, then it is possible that drift within the equilibrium component has already endowed population-2 agents with the behavior at this new message that is needed to destabilize the current component.

24 While the payoff conditional on matching is unchanged as agents are added to a location, the payoff from the corresponding activity falls since the probability of matching has fallen.

25 The payoff conditional on matching is high at this location, but the payoff from the corresponding activity is low because the probability of matching is low.

26 To see the difficulties that can arise, notice that Ritzberger and Weibull (1995) present an example (Figure 3) of a game with a unique Nash equilibrium component that satisfies condition (4.3) from our definition of stability but not (4.2). In a normal form game, this type of outcome could be excluded by requiring the Nash equilibrium to be strict. In the presence of cheap talk or in an extensive form game, strict equilibria generally do not exist, so that a very strong condition on payoffs, such as an outcome producing payoffs strictly higher than any other, is needed.

27 It is necessary to exclude (0,0) from the domain where continuity is required: Suppose $\rho^i(n_1, n_2)$ is given by the proportional matching rule of Section 4. Then, as n_i and $n_k \to 0$, $\rho^i(n_1, n_2) \to 0$ if $n_k/n_i \to 0$ while $\rho^i(n_1, n_2) = 0$ if $n_k > n_i$.

28 Note that number of matches by population 1 agents choosing α_1 at ℓ is $\rho^1_\ell \cdot \gamma_{\alpha_1 \ell} Q_{\alpha_1}$, the total number of matches at ℓ is $\rho^1_\ell \cdot \sum_{\alpha'_1 \in A_1} \gamma_{\alpha'_1 \ell} Q_{\alpha 1'}$, and the number of matches at ℓ between a population 1 agent choosing $\alpha 1$ and an opponent choosing α_2 is $\rho^1_\ell \cdot \gamma_{\alpha_1 \ell} Q_{\alpha_1} \cdot \gamma_{\alpha_2 \ell} Q_{\alpha_2} / \left(\sum_{\alpha'_2 \in A_2} \gamma_{\alpha'_2 \ell} Q_{\alpha'_2} \right)$.

29 Note that the rate of inflow to location 1 may be different for the two populations, and hence rationing at location 1 may occur. However, the non- rationed population will still have an inflow, eventually relieving the rationing of the other population at location 1.

References

Anderson, E. (1994) The code of the streets. *The Atlantic Monthly*. May: 81–94.

Banerjee, A. and J. Weibull (1993) *Evolutionary selection with discriminating players*. Research paper in economics, University of Stockholm.

Coate, S. and G.C. Loury (1993) Will affirmative-action policies eliminate negative stereotypes? *American Economic Review* 83: 1220–1240.

Durlauf, S.N. (1992) *A theory of persistent income inequality*. Mimeo. University of Wisconsin.

Ely, J. (1996) *Local conventions*. Mimeo. Berkeley: University of California.

Gilboa, I. and A. Matsui (1991) Social stability and equilibrium *Econometrica* 59: 859–867.

Kim, Y.-G. and J. Sobel (1992) An evolutionary approach to pre-play communication. Mimeo.

Mailath, G.J. (1992) Introduction: Symposium on evolutionary game theory. *Journal of Economic Theory* 57: 259–277.

Mailath, G.J. (1997) *Do people play Nash equilibrium? Lessons from evolutionary game theory*. *Journal of Economic Literature* 36:1347–1374.

Mailath, G.J., L. Samuelson and A. Shaked (1997) Correlated equilibrium and local interactions. *Economic Theory*. 9: 551–556.

Matsui, A. (1991) Cheap-talk and cooperation in society' *Journal of Economic Theory* 54: 245–258.

Myerson, R.B., G.B. Pollock and J.M. Swinkels (1991) Viscous population equilibria. *Games and Economic Behavior* 3: 101–109.

Nöldeke, G. and L. Samuelson (1993) An evolutionary analysis of backward and forward induction. *Games and Economic Behavior* 5: 425–454.

Ritzberger, K. and J.W. Weibull (1995) Evolutionary selection in normal-form games. *Econometrica* 63: 1371–1399.

Samuelson, L. (1997) *Evolutionary Games and Equilibrium Selection*. Cambridge, MA: MIT Press.

Selten, R. (1991) Evolution, learning, and economic behavior. *Games and Economic Behavior* 3: 3–24.
Sobel, J. (1993) Evolutionary stability and efficiency. *Economics Letters* 42: 301– 312.
Swinkels, J.M. (1992a) Evolutionary stability with equilibrium entrants. *Journal of Economic Theory* 57: 306–332.
Swinkels, J.M. (1992b) Evolution and strategic stability: From Maynard Smith to Kohlberg and Mertens. *Journal of Economic Theory* 57: 333–342.
Swinkels, J.M. (1993) Adjustment dynamics and rational play in games. *Games and Economic Behavior* 5: 455–484.

13 Social networks and efficient evolutionary outcomes in recurrent common interest games

Stefano Vannucci

13.1 Introduction

The relevance of "social capital" – or, more generally, of social networks – for explaining the performance of different economic and political institutions has been recently very often alluded to and is now in principle widely recognized (see e.g. Coleman (1990), Putnam (1993), Ostrom, Gardner and Walker (1994), Van Dijk (1997), Bowles and Gintis (1998) among many others). Moreover, such a widespread interest in social networks and their political-economic effects has arguably serious theoretical grounds that are related to the intuitive connection one can immediately and plausibly establish between "social capital," trust, and incomplete contracts. Thus, it can be safely predicted that social networks are here to stay – along with incomplete contracts – in mainstream literature.

However, it is still less than clear by what mechanisms the putative role of social networks might be exerted to the effect of influencing (indeed, enhancing) the efficiency of institutions. In order to tentatively address this issue, the present chapter focuses on a highly stylized problem, namely the selection of efficient outcomes in recurrent common interest (CI) games. This sort of model has indeed two main advantages to offer: a well-defined target (the efficient outcome being by definition unique) and a serious challenge (i.e allowing the existence of both efficient and inefficient evolutionarily stable states, with no obvious grounds for selecting the efficient outcome, and even several theoretical approaches favoring selection of the inefficient one when risk-dominant: see e.g. Weibull (1995), and Kim (1996), respectively).

In the following, the emphasis will be mostly, if not solely, on evolutionary game-theoretic models, reflecting the now widespread view that evolutionary reasoning is by far the most promising approach to equilibrium selection problems. The potential role of social networks in solving such selection problems is assessed by means of the following basic modeling choice: the relevant social network is taken to result in a set of repeated pure coordination (PC) games (to be possibly interpreted as the activities of a set of civic associations). Such games are meant to represent social interactions that involve coordination efforts but no relevant conflicts of interest. In that setting our problem concerning the possible role of social networks in improving the performance of economic and political institutions specializes to a simpler reverse comparative statics issue, namely: by what means players engaged in a set of repeated PC games could be plausibly more successful than their "socially disconnected" counterparts in coordinating on the efficient solution of a recurrent CI game?

Two different simple mechanisms (by no means an exhaustive list) are singled out and shown to provide the required explanation for social-network-based "efficient selection" in recurrent CI games. The first one relies – very unsurprisingly – on opponent-discriminating behavior: strategies evolve which selectively cooperate with their own copies while defecting against "others." Here, thick social networks operate as reliable information transmission channels that effectively help a large population of farsighted players to tell "cooperators" from "defectors." The second mechanism is based upon the hypothesis that under certain conditions – involving a population of boundedly rational agents that play simultaneously many similar and hardly distinguishable games – playing schemas (i.e. families of strategy-types, as opposed to strategies) are the relevant replicating units. Whenever this is the case, it is easily shown that in a noisy context a social network resulting in a suitably large set of repeated PC games can provide a favorable environment for the evolution of "cooperative" playing schemas within recurrent CI games. This effect works by lowering the threshold-frequency of "cooperators" that ensures fixation of cooperation in the long run.

13.2 Selecting efficient outcomes in common interest games: overview

As mentioned in the Introduction, the aim of this chapter is to provide a tentative analysis of the possible role of social networks in explaining the emergence of cooperation at large. The evolution of cooperation – a major theme in game theory, in economics, and in evolutionary biology – has been typically studied with reference to repeated and/or recurrent (that is, repeatedly played with varying opponents) prisoner dilemma games (see e.g. Axelrod (1984), Bowles and Gintis (1998), Sober and Wilson (1998)). However, it is now widely held that coordination games – i.e. symmetric games with two or more equilibrium states – might be better suited to that aim (see e.g. Maynard Smith and Szathmàry (1995) for a recent authoritative suggestion to that effect). Within the class of coordination games several options can be considered: here we shall be mainly focused on common interest (CI) games, namely games with a single unanimously preferred outcome. In particular, we shall consider the Stag Hunt game G° (namely, a CI coordination game in strategic form with a conflict of interest and two or more Pareto-ranked symmetric strict Nash – hence evolutionarily stable – equilibria) as determined – in the 2×2 case – by the following payoff matrix

$$\prod(G^\circ) = \begin{bmatrix} a & c \\ b & d \end{bmatrix} \text{ where } a > b > d > c.$$

The basic intuition underlying the main selection dilemma for G° is the following: while the "cooperating" equilibrium outcome (a, a) is uniquely Pareto-efficient, the "defecting" equilibrium outcome (d, d) is less risky or risk-dominant whenever $(d - c) > (a - b)$.

The old-fashioned "equilibrium refinements" have obviously no bite here, since by definition even strict Nash equilibrium, which goes far beyond their conventional boundaries, has not. Moreover, standard evolutionary solution concepts – both static (e.g. evolutionarily stable strategies) and dynamic (e.g. suitably stable states of the classic replicator dynamics) – are also clearly unable to select one equilibrium of G° (see for example Weibull(1995)).

In that connection, one may well wonder whether and how social networks could possibly be of any help in selecting the efficient outcome of G° within the framework of simple evolutionary models (it should be remarked here that, for the aims of our analysis a social network can be conveniently modeled as an hypergraph having players as nodes and associations or coalitions of players as hyperedges). As a matter of fact, a strong case for a positive correlation between the existence of "civic" social networks and the comparative efficiency of local political institutions has been persuasively put forth by Putnam (1993) relying on evidence from Italy's contemporary history. Indeed, such a positive correlation may strike some of us as perfectly plausible, perhaps even commonsensical. Furthermore, the available historical evidence can be matched with arguments coming from a rich if sparse, heterogeneous, and largely informal literature. The bulk of that literature suggests that "civic" social networks can foster reciprocity and cooperative norms in the following ways (see again Putnam 1993: 173–4):

1. by producing a template for the relevant cooperative behavior;
2. by establishing a favorable environment for the evolution of cooperative behavior;
3. by providing a reliable information transmission system;
4. by increasing the scope for repeated interactions and strategic interdependence.

Arguably, each of those statements – by itself – enshrines some highly suggestive if somehow vague intuitions. We shall devote the bulk of this chapter to probing their strength within some standard evolutionary game-theoretic models.

As mentioned in the Introduction, the question we want to ask is the following: by what means, if any, could the existence of a social network of "civic" associations amongst the players conceivably favor the evolution of cooperation as modeled in the setting of recurrent common interest games of the Stag Hunt variety?

The most obvious source of inspiration to look at closely is the large and fast growing literature on equilibrium selection models. Indeed, lack of simple and indisputable criteria for predicting one of the strict Nash equilibria of a Stag Hunt game as its unique outcome has significantly contributed to trigger a rich flow of game-theoretic literature on equilibrium selection problems, which adds to the already imposing body of work on the evolution of cooperation and altruism (a representative sample of the many proposed approaches should include at the very least works as diverse as those contributed by – or surveyed in – Boyd and Richerson (1985), Harsanyi and Selten (1988), Kim (1996), Vega-Redondo (1996), Samuelson (1997), Sober and Wilson (1998)). Selection results in the game-theoretical literature rely mostly on the introduction of some stochastic perturbations or "trembles" within the relevant model. As it happens, such "trembles" can be motivated and introduced in several different ways to the effect of obtaining sharply different results. Indeed, several proposed approaches (both evolutionary and not) concur in selecting the risk-dominant equilibrium (see e.g. Carlsson and Van Damme (1993a, 1993b), Kandori, Mailath and Rob (1993), Young (1993), Ellison (1993), Harsanyi (1995), Matsui and Matsuyama (1995), Crawford (1995), Kim (1996)). But here, of course, we are mainly interested in those approaches that either definitely favor or are at least consistent with selection of the efficient outcome. In fact, a most convenient distinction is to be made between

- unconditional efficient selections based upon general principles (e.g. via suitable adjustments of the solution concept) and
- parameter-dependent efficient selections.

Apparently, all those approaches that select the efficient outcome tend to rely on one or more of the following principles:

- Discriminating behavior within interactions (i.e. cooperating with cooperators and defecting with defectors) as made possible by lack of total anonymity of the matching process or more generally by the ability to establish a successful preliminary communication phase. This most typically amounts to the "secret handshake" principle or equivalently – as far as we are concerned – to its public counterpart, the "green beard" effect (see e.g. Dawkins (1982), Robson (1990), Binmore and Samuelson (1992). See also Aumann and Sorin (1989), Fudenberg and Maskin (1990), Anderlini (1990), Matsui (1991), Sobel (1993), Kim and Sobel (1995), Anderlini and Sabourian (1995), Vega-Redondo (1996) for some different versions of this broad signaling principle).
- Non-random interactions as engendered by the availability of exogenous signals, by viscosity of the population structure, or by drift in small populations: by making interactions between efficient cooperators more likely this non-random-interacting approach can also be interpreted as implicitly enacting a sort of "intrademic" group selection effect with possibly high mobility but virtually zero random migration between behaviorally insulated subpopulations (see e.g. Eshel and Cavalli-Sforza (1982) and Kitcher (1993), where the availability of exogenous signals enabling players to selectively avoid interactions after matching is simply postulated; Ely (1996), Dieckmann (1997), and Mailath (1997), which use different solution concepts but share a common basic scenario where several interaction-loci exist, and players are able to choose their locus and to observe – with a positive probability-strategy

profiles at every locus; Myerson, Pollock and Swinkels (1991) where viscosity of the population structure is invoked in order to propose a new equilibrium solution concept; see also Robson and Vega-Redondo (1996), where the role of matching-noise or drift when encounters are comparatively rare is emphasized).

- Dominance of efficiency-enforcing group selection of the "interdemic" variety, possibly supported by "conformist" cultural transmission and/or by viscosity of the population structure: under this approach the basic requirements are the existence of several interaction-loci with associated subpopulations or "demes," and a persistent group-selection-sustaining variation among them. The latter is maintained by the local intrademic "conforming" pressure – possibly enhanced by "conformist" cultural transmission – provided that such pressure is strong enough to overcome random migration effects. Efficiency of the outcomes of group selection is then ensured whenever a large enough fraction of the founders of newly formed "demes" come from a single "deme" (see e.g. Boyd and Richerson (1990), and Sober and Wilson (1998) for an attempt at extending this approach to the evolution of altruism; see also Simon(1990) for a somewhat related approach to the evolution of altruism that disregards group selection but emphasizes both "bounded rationality" and "conformist" social learning). Clearly enough, viscosity of the population structure may have a significant causal role in establishing the foregoing scenario (see again Myerson, Pollock and Swinkels (1991) on the role of population viscosity).

It is at least conceivable that the efficiency-enhancing effects of social networks, if any, should sometimes operate thanks to some of the foregoing "principles." In what follows, however, models relying on group selection processes – that is on the existence of many distinct interaction loci with associated "demes" exhibiting possibly different behaviors but sharing the same interaction structure among their members – will be consistently ignored. The main reasons for that choice are the following. First, the emphasis of the present chapter will be on the simplest and least controversial evolutionary concepts and models, while the relevance and strength of group selection processes are indeed hotly debated issues (see e.g. Dawkins (1982) and Sober and Wilson (1998) for two virtually opposite views on that matter). Second, in our setting group selection models are in a sense subsidiary since they apparently require either smallness of "demes" in order to leave a suitably large causal role to drift (a very restrictive and unsatisfactory postulate), or some degree of neutrality of social networks with respect to equilibrium outcomes of CI games, if variation among possibly large "demes" is to be persistent enough (a clearly preposterous assumption, given our aims). Third, if a suitable degree of outcome-neutrality of social networks for CI games is conceded, then – at least for some group selection models – the pro-efficient causal role of social networks turns out to be self-evident (for instance, social networks might plausibly enhance exit costs from "demes" thereby *ceteris paribus* limiting "random" migration, and thus affect in a pro-efficient way the parameters of the highly reputed cultural group selection model proposed by Boyd and Richerson (1990), which indeed requires migration effects to be dominated by the differential evolutionary benefits induced by the efficient trait). Therefore, while leaving completely open the possible significance of group selection processes, the discussion to follow will be largely confined to evolutionary models that do not rely on group selection.

13.3 Selecting efficient outcomes in common interest games: two simple evolutionary models with social networks

This section is devoted to describing two simple mechanisms which both suffice to explain a social-network-driven efficient outcome selection in recurrent CI games of the Stag Hunt variety within two different and very well known evolutionary game-theoretic models. No special prominence (let alone exhaustiveness) is claimed for such proposals: indeed, other examples and models are expected to follow in due course. As mentioned in the Introduction, we model social networks by means of hypergraphs. An hypergraph ($\mathcal{N}$, $\mathbf{E}$) consists of a set of nodes $\mathcal{N}$ and a set $\mathbf{E} \subseteq P(\mathcal{N})$ of hyperedges. Under the suggested interpretation nodes represent players, and hyperedges associations of players, or coalitions. Players can be sorted into types according to their memberships: player-types amount to subsets of $\mathbf{E}$. The population of players is endowed with a measure μ, and can be small (i.e. $\mathcal{N}$ is finite and μ is the counting measure), or large (i.e. $\mathcal{N}$ is infinite). Moreover, the social network ($\mathcal{N}$, $\mathbf{E}$) is thick with respect to μ if for any player $i \in \mathcal{N}$ the set $\cup_i \mathbf{E}\ (i)$ of i's associates has positive measure (i.e. $\mu(\cup_i\ \mathbf{E}\ (i)) > 0$). In what follows, the associative activities of players may be explicitly described by means of certain repeated 2-person 2-valued pure coordination games in a given class Γ. In that case the relevant social networks – and their hypergraphs – are said to be Γ-labeled. The two models to be presented below share reliance on social networks thus modeled, but are otherwise very different from each other.

13.3.1 First model. Evolutionary stability and "handshakes" between perfectly farsighted players: social networks as reliable information transmission channels

The first mechanism we propose requires that the relevant social network – and the "civic" associations it represents – be regarded as a set of loci where participants (*inter alia*) freely exchange reliable information concerning their previous interactions. In fact, we take as part of the definition of "civic" associations that the participants freely release such information. Thus, the players take part in several associations (i.e. play "successfully" the efficient equilibria of several repeated pure coordination games) and are randomly matched to play a recurrent Stag Hunt game G°. Playing recurrently such a game in discrete time amounts to choosing a list of routines or (initial, deterministic, Mealy) automata (we recall here that an initial deterministic Mealy automaton is a sextuple consisting of a set of states, a set of possible inputs, a set of possible outputs, an initial state, a next-state function mapping state-input pairs into states, and an output function mapping state-input pairs into outputs). An initial deterministic Mealy automaton A in turn defines a strategy for recurrent play of G° in discrete time. Strategies can be of course conditioned on some statistic of past performances (in particular on performances at some fixed period). Hence, the actions chosen at some past period (e.g. at the initial period) can be used as signals concerning the types of the automata that perform them. Such signals as produced by a certain player are assumed to be made available to all of her associates. Therefore, a player i virtually recalls the action chosen by another player j at a given previous date t° whenever i and j happen to share membership in some association of the given social network. This key postulate can be conveniently summarized by assuming the existence of a social-network-induced profile $\rho = \rho(\mathcal{N}, \mathbf{E})$ of recall functions which specify the portion of opponents' previous output histories that each player has access to. Moreover, we envisage perfectly farsighted players, namely players that are only interested in persistent long run outcomes. The stability of population states is assessed using semi-neutral evolutionary stability (SNES) as a solution concept (see e.g. Binmore and Samuelson (1992)). A strategy or automaton A for recurrent play of G° is semi-neutrally evolutionarily stable if for any other automaton B for recurrent play of G° – and for all but a finite number of periods – one of the following conditions holds true:

1. A is a strictly better reply to itself than B;
2. B is as good a reply to A as A itself, but A is a strictly better reply to B than B itself;
3. A and B are equivalent replies both to A and to B, and the number of A's states is not larger than the number of B's states.

Thus, SNES amounts to a version of evolutionary stability which takes into account the complexity-cost of implementing strategies as measured by the number of states of the associated automata, while implicitly assuming that such cost is always negligible as compared with prospective positive payoff gains. Of course, SNES is a solution concept of the equilibrium-variety.

Suppose now that the prevailing automata play inefficiently the recurrent Stag Hunt game under consideration. Then, "mutant" automata can invade this incumbent "inefficient" population, provided they can somehow – with a non-negligible probability – gather information on the previous (e.g. initial) behavior of other players. Indeed, "mutant" automata may release a distinctive signal at the initial period and then "imitate" the incumbents' behavior while selectively cooperating (the "handshake") to bring about the efficient outcome in interactions with their likes. The key issue here is the following: assuming as we do both non-anonymous matching and perfect recall of personal encounters, under what conditions the "non-negligible probability" of information transmission mentioned above obtains? Clearly enough, in a small population the answer is "always," since at any time and for any player the probability of meeting again the player already met at a given previous period is positive. In a large population, however, the probability of being matched again to the same opponent already met at a given previous period is – at any time and for any player – negligible. Thus, if the social network of "civic" associations is thick then information transmission by means of social networks – as represented by the resulting recall function profile – plays here a decisive role by making possible an effective discriminating behavior on the part of the efficient cooperating "mutants." All this is summarized by the following proposition (Vannucci (1998)):

Proposition 1 *Let* (N, μ) *be a large population of perfectly farsighted players that are embedded in a* μ*-thick social network* $(N, \mathbf{E})$*. Then, the strategy* $\sigma(A)$ *induced by an (initial, deterministic, Mealy) automaton* A *for recurrent play of* G° *at recall function profile* $\rho(N, \mathbf{E})$ *induces a semi-neutral evolutionarily stable strategy only if* $(\sigma(A), \sigma(A))$ *is a Pareto-efficient strategy profile.*

Sketch of proof. Let A be a Pareto-inefficient incumbent automaton for recurrent play of G°. Then, a "mutant" automaton A^* can be defined such that: (i) the action a^* chosen by A^* at the first period is different from A's initial action; (ii) at any subsequent period A^* replicates A's behavior unless it is able to recall that the opponent has played a^* at the initial period: in the latter case A^* chooses the efficient "cooperating" action (i.e. the efficient "cooperating" strategy of G°). Thus, the first round is the only one at which the payoff of A^* may be less than A's own payoff (because G° is a CI game). Since players are by hypothesis perfectly farsighted, such a temporary loss is totally irrelevant. This makes the signaling activity of A^* de facto free, in the hypothesized A-dominated environment (i.e. the relevant long run payoff accruing to A^* when playing against A is the same as that gained by A when playing against itself). Also, whenever two "mutants" are matched and happen to be able to recall each other's initial action, they can enjoy the payoff gains resulting from efficient cooperation. Now, by our definition of a recall function, a player i can recall j's initial action if and only if the reverse is also true. Hence, at any non-initial period the payoff gained by when matching another A^* is strictly larger than the payoff gained by A against A^* provided that the probability of such (mutual) recall is positive, which is indeed the case since the social network $(N, \mathbf{E})$ is by hypothesis μ-thick. Therefore the A-population can be "invaded" by A^*-"mutants." It follows that the strategy $\sigma(A)$ induced by A is not a semi-neutrally evolutionarily stable strategy. ••

Therefore, the efficient selection result established by this model is independent of payoff-parameters and rests upon the role of social networks as reliable information transmission channels that enable the players to enact a discriminating behavior within interactions. The main subsidiary assumptions are: (i) a large population, which is required in order to make sense of semi-neutral evolutionary stability as a solution concept, and to provide thick social networks with a significant role; (ii) perfect farsightedness of the players, that makes such opponent-discriminating behavior cost-free; (iii) virtual irrelevance of implementation-complexity costs of strategies as compared to prospective payoff-benefits (a requirement embodied in semi-neutral evolutionary stability).

13.3.2 Second model. Stochastic stability and the power of successful examples for busy boundedly rational players: social networks as a pro-efficient environment

The second mechanism we propose provides a parameter-dependent efficient selection process, and relies on the detailed structure of Γ-labeled social networks as described above. Here, we envisage a finite population of players that play simultaneously many games while being generally unable to distinguish the exact structure of the latter, or even the identity of the opponents. Therefore, the players are supposed to rely on a shared repertoire T of strategy-types i.e. equivalence-classes of strategies of games of the given population, such as "cooperate," "defect," and so on (we assume $\#T \geq 2$ in order to avoid trivialities). Two symmetric games G, G' are said to be T-similar whenever they share the same set of strategy-types (in T) in such a way that payoff orderings induced by "symmetric" profiles of strategy-types in G and G' are also the same. Moreover, a game is said to be T-non-degenerate if it has at least two strategy-types from T. The players choose (T-supported) playing schemas, namely functions mapping each class of similar games into a strategy-type in T. Thus, playing schemas are to be considered as routines that apply to "similar" games, and amount indeed to a variety of "memes" or cultural replicators (just as strategies or automata implicitly were in the first model as described above). Of course, a player might conceivably opt for a "fine tuning" approach when choosing strategies for different games, by trying hard on each occasion to figure out the exact nature of the game at hand and consequently selecting an apt strategy for it. However, we suppose here that this is not a feasible option due both to the exceedingly high costs attached to such information gathering activities and to persistent change of the population of relevant games. Thus, we are going to model an environment where choosing a certain playing schema is the only practically available course of action open to the players. Moreover, in order to assess the possible impact of the given Γ-labeled social network on the outcomes of G°, we also assume that players regard as T-similar (as well as T-non-degenerate) the Stag Hunt game G° and all the games in Γ (perhaps they perceive Common Interest as their focal property). Hence, T-supported playing schemas for $\Gamma^* = \Gamma \cup \{G^{\circ}\}$ have a singleton-domain and reduce therefore to a single strategy-type $t \in T$. It follows that the set T^* of playing schemas for Γ^* is (modulo bijections) a certain subset of T such that $\#T^* = 2$ (in view of T-non-degeneracy of games in Γ^*): its members may be aptly denoted by "cooperating" and "defecting." All this allows the population state of playing schemas for Γ^* to be represented by a single non-negative integer $x \in X \equiv \{0, 1 \ldots, n\}$ denoting the number of players that are currently using, say, the efficient "cooperating" playing schema t^*. In that setting, the nature of the "right" playing schema to be chosen will obviously depend on the environment i.e. essentially on the current population of playing schemas and, ultimately, on the population of games that are being played. Therefore, it is fairly plausible that an existing social network of "civic" repeated PC games should help the evolution of the "cooperating" playing schemas by establishing, quite literally, a more favorable environment for the latter. Plainly, the more games are being played where individual cooperative behavior pays in terms of valuable resources, the better "cooperating" playing schemas thrive. The present model probes this general idea within the "boundedly rational" setting outlined above, using stochastic stability of population states as a solution concept (following Foster and Young (1990), and Kandori, Mailath and Rob (1993)). In the present framework stochastically stable states are defined as follows. To begin with, population states are to be regarded as (discrete-)time-varying realizations x_t of the random variable X. The evolution of the population state x_t is affected both by a certain monotonic selection dynamics $f : X \to X$ (i.e. according to f the strategy-type or playing schema with the highest payoff either stays put or increases its frequency at the next period) and by noise (a small, positive, and constant-across-states probability of mutation or error ε). In order to scrutinize the possible effects of a Γ-labeled social network ($\mathcal{N}$, **E**, L) in that connection we consider the ($\mathcal{N}$, **E**, L)-situated monotonic selection dynamics $f^* = f^*(\mathcal{N}, \mathbf{E}, L)$: $X \to X$ for the set T^* of playing schemas as defined below. The selection dynamics f^* summarizes the evolution of playing schemas as determined by the global expected payoff they gain within both the recurrent Stag Hunt game G° and the repeated ("civic") Pure Coordination games in Γ, namely

$$f^*(x_t) \gtreqless xt \text{ if}$$

$$(a\cdot(x_t-1)+c\cdot(n-x_t))\cdot(n-1)^{-1}+\sum_{\tau}\rho(\tau)\cdot \sum_{G\in\{L(E):\tau(E)=1\}} \alpha_G\cdot(\#L^{-1}(G)-1)\gtrless$$

$$\gtrless(b\cdot x_t+d\cdot(n-x_t-1))\cdot(n-1)^{-1}$$

where $\rho(\tau)$ denotes the relative frequency of τ-type players in ($\mathcal{N}$, **E**), α_G denotes the positive efficient expected payoff of game $G \in \Gamma$, and the inefficient payoffs of G are 0-normalized for the sake of convenience. The terms above are meant to refer to expected payoffs, which makes sense because players are indeed assumed to be involved in a large number of interactions at any time.

Now, take the transition probability matrix $M(f^*, \varepsilon)$ induced by selection dynamics f^* and mutation probability ε. Positiveness of ε implies that the ensuing stochastic process $\{X_t\}_{t\in\mathcal{Z}}$ is an irreducible aperiodic Markov chain on the finite state space X. Hence, by a well-known basic result on Markov chains, it follows that the long-run behavior of this process can be represented by a unique stationary probability distribution $p(f^*, \varepsilon)$, which does not depend on the initial population statc. It can also be shown that – under general conditions – a (unique) limit distribution $p^*(f^*) = \lim_{\varepsilon\to 0} p(f^*, \varepsilon)$ for a vanishing mutation probability exists (see e.g. Kandori, Mailath, Rob (1993), Vega-Redondo (1996)). A population state $x \in X$ is a stochastically stable state of selection dynamics f^* if it belongs to the support of such a limit probability distribution (i.e. if $(p^*(f^*))(x) > 0$). It can be shown that a stochastically stable state of f^* must also belong to some absorbing set of the zero-noise transition probability matrix $M(f^*,0)$ of f^*, and is entirely determined by the basins of attraction of such absorbing sets (an absorbing set of $M(f^*,0)$ is a set of states that cannot be left after being entered, and such that any two states in it are mutually reachable in a finite number of f^*-steps; the basin of attraction of an absorbing set of $M(f^*,0)$ is the set of states from which such an absorbing set is reachable in a finite number of f^*-steps). Thus, while evolutionary stability embodies the idea of resistance to any particular single small mutation, stochastic stability is meant to capture the long run (stable) behavior of a dynamical system that is persistently subjected to many small – and possibly cumulating – random perturbations i.e. to a persistent, if vanishing, noise (see Foster and Young (1990)).

It is easily shown in the present framework that – for a given set Γ of "civic" games – the larger the social network the larger the basin of attraction of the absorbing set consisting of the efficient fully cooperative state. This is so because the Pure Coordination games of the social network enhance the expected payoff resulting from the efficient "cooperating" playing schema: the social network simply changes the relevant parameters in a way that can only favor the latter schema. Thus, for certain configurations of parameters (population size, payoffs, ...) the fully cooperative state may well be uniquely stochastically stable for the situated monotonic selection dynamics f^*, when f^* is embedded in a suitably large social network, and not stochastically stable at all if f^* is embedded in some smaller ones. Most remarkably, unique stochastic stability of the fully cooperative state may also obtain when the efficient outcome of the Stag Hunt game G° is risk-dominated. This is summarized by the following proposition (Vannucci (1998)):

Proposition 2 *Let N be a finite population of players, $(N, \mathbf{E}, L)$ a Γ- labeled social network, $\Gamma^* = \Gamma \cup \{G^\circ\}$, and f^* an $(N, \mathbf{E}, L)$-situated monotonic selection dynamics for the shared set T^* of playing schemas for Γ^* as defined above. Then, the efficient fully "cooperative" population state $n \in X$ is the unique stochastically stable state of f^* if and only if*

$$2 \cdot (n-1) \cdot \sum_{\tau} \rho(\tau) \cdot \sum_{G \in \{L(E):\tau(E)=1\}} \alpha_G \cdot (\#L^{-1}(G) - 1) > n \cdot (d - c - a + b) + 2 \cdot (a - d).$$

Hence, in particular, $n \in X$ may be the unique stochastically stable state of f^* even if the efficient outcome of the Stag Hunt game G° is risk-dominated: this is indeed the case whenever $(d-c) > (a-b)$ and

$$\sum_{\tau} \rho(\tau) \cdot \sum_{G \in \{L(E):\tau(E)=1\}} \alpha_G \cdot (\#L^{-1}(G) - 1) > \left[(d - c - a + b) + (a - d) \cdot \tfrac{2}{n} \right] \cdot \tfrac{n}{2 \cdot (n-1)}.$$

Sketch of proof. The fully "cooperative" state is clearly an absorbing (singleton) set (because its payoffs are global maxima and the selection dynamics f^* is monotonic, by definition). Its basin of attraction is made up of all those states $x \in X$ such that – at x – the expected payoff of the efficient "cooperating" playing schema is larger than the inefficient one's. Also, using well-known methods developed by Freidlin and Wentzell as presented by Kandori, Mailath and Rob (1993) or Vega-Redondo (1996), it can be shown that the stochastically stable states are those states which require the minimum number of mutations in order to become reachable from all other states according to f^*. Hence, a state is stochastically stable for f^* if its basin of attraction is largest, which in the present setting amounts to having more than $(n+1)/2$ states in it. Now, the given social network enlarges the basin of attraction of the "cooperating" playing schema by enhancing its expected payoff. Hence, the social network makes it easier for the fully "cooperative" state to become stochastically stable. In particular, an otherwise prevailing inefficient risk-dominance effect may be overcome. ••

The efficient selection result embodied in this second model is in a sense weaker than the one established by means of the first model in that it amounts to a parameter-dependent selection. It relies heavily on "bounded rationality" considerations, including the assumption that all the players be engaged in a large class of games, and endowed with the same classification of strategy-types across such games. Implicitly, it is also assumed that information gathering and processing costs – and, ultimately, strategy-design costs – may well dominate over prospective payoff-gains to be possibly extracted by taking part into the games of the relevant population. It should also be mentioned here that the same efficient selection result through stochastic stability can be easily extended to a related but distinct scenario. Namely, efficient selection obtains if busy boundedly rational players adjust their strategies in a suitable – non-monotonic – manner according to aspiration levels which are determined by the underlying labeled social network and the degree of players' participation in it (see Vannucci (1998)). On the other hand, the argument outlined above in the (sketch of) proof of Proposition 2 is not readily extendable beyond the class of 2×2 games.

13.4 Related literature

No explicit attempt at modeling the possible role of social networks as efficient selection devices in an evolutionary game-theoretic setting is known to the present author. There certainly exist, however, (i) some work that can be immediately related to our game-theoretic analysis of the possible effects of social networks, and (ii) a significant literature on efficient equilibrium selection in common interest games.

Concerning point i), it should be mentioned that Kandori (1992) has two ideas that are somehow related to certain aspects of the first model presented above. Indeed, Kandori explicitly states that "observability in the community is a substitute for having a long-term frequent relationship with a fixed partner" (Kandori (1992), p. 68); moreover, he emphasizes the focal contribution of certain reliable information transmission mechanisms (including social memberships) in sustaining any feasible individually rational outcome in recurrent games from a quite large class. However, in Kandori's paper, the role of (universal) observability in the community is mainly connected to collective enforcement of norms; also, and crucially, the focus of that work is on extensions of folk theorems, hence on multiplicity of equilibria as opposed to selection among them.

Conversely, Simon's proposal to explain altruism as a bounded-rationality-induced by-product of "docility" i.e. a certain propensity towards social learning (see Simon (1990)) bears a certain similarity to our second model as presented above. However, apart from other significant differences in scope, detail, and concern (e.g. altruism versus efficient selection), Simon's insistence on "docility" seems to evoke a special role for "conformist" cultural transmission, which is not implied at all by the general monotony requirement for the selection dynamics of our model. It should also be mentioned that the basic scenario underlying the model proposed in Carlsson and Van Damme (1993a) involves boundedly rational players that play simultaneously many different games without being able to distinguish them from each other. Such a model – which is not phrased in evolutionary terms and relies on iterated strict dominance as a solution concept-provides a sharp selection result favoring the risk-dominant equilibrium outcome in Stag Hunt games. This should be contrasted with the opposite result provided by our second model, that also relies on a somehow related scenario. Indeed, apart from other significant technical differences, this sharp contrast between the respective predictions of Carlsson–Van Damme's and our own model can be largely traced to the fact that in the former model the class of indistinguishable 2×2 games is definitely larger than in the latter. This is so because the class of indistinguishable games in the Carlsson–Van Damme equilibrium selection model must include both games where a strategy – or rather strategy-type – s is strictly dominant and games where the other strategy t is strictly dominant. In a sense, Carlsson–Van Damme's players are "busier" or "less rational" than the busy boundedly rational players of our second social-network-based model.

Concerning point (ii), it has been already mentioned that a few efficient selection results for CI games – with no role at all for social networks – are available and well known. Indeed, many unconditional efficient selection results have been obtained by focusing on repeated CI games, where earlier interactions can be somehow used as effective communication devices (see Aumann and Sorin (1989), Fudenberg and Maskin (1990), Binmore and Samuelson (1992), Anderlini and Sabourian (1995); Tadelis (1995) has an efficient selection result for certain repeated extensive CI games using "nondiscriminating optimistically stable standards of behavior" – a notion related to Von Neumann–Morgenstern stable sets – as a solution concept).

In the non-repeated case, unconditional efficient selection has been typically obtained by adapting the solution concept itself in a more or less radical manner and/or by embedding the relevant CI game in a larger two-stage game with a preliminary communication phase. Thus, Harsanyi and Selten (1988) plainly advocate priority of payoff-dominance over risk-dominance as an equilibrium selection criterion. Anderlini (1990) retains perfect equilibrium as a solution concept but adds a preliminary communication stage between computationally specified players. Myerson, Pollock and Swinkels (1991) rely on ecological considerations to motivate "fluid equilibria" as limits of suitable "viscous equilibria" which provide an efficient selection in CI games. The notion of an invasion-resistant set (a version of neutral evolutionary stability) as introduced by Basu (1995) for so-called "human evolutionary games" – i.e. essentially evolutionary games endowed with a Nash equilibrium selection for their reduced games – can also be used to establish an efficient selection result for 2×2 CI games. In order to obtain an efficient selection result for general CI games Sobel (1993) and Vega-Redondo (1996) both add a pre-play communication stage and propose a new non-equilibrium (static) notion of evolutionary stability that is meant to capture the role of drift. Matsui (1991) adds a pre-play communication phase and relies on "cyclically stable sets" i.e. essentially the absorbing sets of the best-reply dynamics (another non-equilibrium solution concept). Kim and Sobel (1995) also add a pre-play communication stage and focus on a class of payoff- monotonic adjustment dynamics using (nonempty, minimal) absorbing sets as a solution concept.

In that connection, our first model shows how social networks can be instrumental in extending "handshake"-driven unconditional efficient selection results to recurrent one-shot CI games (under farsightedness) without appending to them a communication phase, invoking group selection effects, or embarking on major reforms of the solution concept (either in a pro-efficient manner or in a disequilibrium vein).

The potential role of social networks seems to be even more transparent when it comes to those models that provide parameter-dependent selections. A most typical result established by means of such models – whenever cultural group selection processes are not invoked as in Boyd and Richerson (1985,1990) – is that the efficient outcome of a CI game can be possibly selected only if it happens to be risk-dominant as well. Indeed, this result is consistently obtained in several models that use quite different solution concepts, including stochastic stability and iterated strict dominance (see e.g. Kandori, Mailath, Rob (1993), Young (1993), Ellison (1993), Carlsson and Van Damme (1993a), Harsanyi (1995), Matsui and Matsuyama (1995), Kim (1996)). Two notable exceptions are Binmore, Samuelson and Vaughan (1995), and Robson and Vega-Redondo (1996) which provide models wherein the population state corresponding to the efficient outcome of a 2×2 Stag Hunt game can be uniquely stochastically stable even if it fails to be risk-dominant. The Binmore–Samuelson–Vaughan selection theory is based upon a "muddling" model where even the selection component of the evolutionary dynamics is randomized (and non-monotonic): while switching to more successful strategies is more likely than the opposite, as long as a strategy is used by some player there is a significant probability that it will attract more players, however poor its comparative performance in terms of current payoffs (see Binmore, Samuelson and Vaughan (1995), and Samuelson (1997)). A major feature of such a randomized non-monotonic adjustment dynamics is that all states except the boundary or monomorphic ones belong to the basins of attraction of both the monomorphic states themselves: mutations are only required to escape boundary states.

Moreover, a single mutation is needed for that – as opposed to the entire combination of simultaneous mutations which is typically required in order to escape the basin of attraction of an equilibrium state under a monotonic selection dynamics of the Kandori–Mailath–Rob type. Incidentally, this also implies that, for small mutation rates, long-run convergence (or rather ultralong, in Binmore, Samuelson, Vaughan's terminology) to the unique stochastically stable state may well be considerably faster in the "muddling" model than under a monotonic selection dynamics of the Kandori–Mailath–Rob type. In the Binmore–Samuelson–Vaughan model, the efficient outcome of a 2×2 CI game is uniquely stochastically stable if the population is large enough and the ratio between the probabilities of switching away from the "efficient" and the "inefficient" equilibrium strategies, respectively, is suitably small (see Samuelson (1997)). A similar result obtains if the selection dynamics is a convex mixture of the "muddling" adjustment dynamics described above and an entirely random i.e. payoff-independent imitation dynamics. When the weight of such a random imitation dynamics is large enough, the latter result may be interpreted in terms of background payoffs. Namely, it can be said that the efficient outcome turns out to be selected whenever the background payoff is low enough to confer adequate payoff-prominence to the CI game under consideration. On the other hand, if the selection dynamics consists of a convex mixture of the "muddling" adjustment dynamics and the best-reply dynamics – with a suitably large weight on the latter – then the risk-dominant equilibrium re-emerges as uniquely stochastically stable (see again Binmore, Samuelson and Vaughan (1995), and Samuelson (1997)). Clearly enough, the Binmore–Samuelson–Vaughan efficient selection result is indeed driven by reliance on a "muddling" selection dynamics as opposed to a monotonic one. By contrast, the model proposed by Robson and Vega-Redondo (1996) sticks to a monotonic selection dynamics of the Kandori–Mailath–Rob type. In that model the population is allowed to grow indefinitely large and the mutation probability is taken to be vanishing. However, it is assumed that a possibly large but fixed finite number of rounds is to be played with the same arbitrarily chosen strategy by each player at each period. Thus, whenever the population is large enough at each period every player necessarily interacts with a small sample of the entire population of players. As a result, matching-noise (hence the prevailing, nonuniform matching structure) is allowed to gain prominence over mutation-noise, and a small-"deme"-effect of sorts is produced enabling the efficient outcome to emerge as uniquely stochastically stable given a large enough overall population. Thus, the Robson–Vega-Redondo selection model apparently shares some key general features of certain group selection models (see Robson and Vega-Redondo (1996), and Vega-Redondo (1996)).

The foregoing parameter-dependent selection models can be fruitfully contrasted with the second social-network-based model for busy boundedly rational players as presented above. Indeed, it should be recalled that such a model provides a parameter-dependent efficient selection result for 2×2 CI games which is consistent with lack of risk-dominance of the efficient outcome, relies on a standard monotonic selection dynamics, and does not invoke group selection arguments of any sort. This is not the place to dwell on the respective merits and drawbacks of these general properties of our second model, and of alternative assumptions. My point here is rather to emphasize again that, arguably, social networks as modeled above may have after all a distinct contribution to offer for a solution of the equilibrium selection problem in CI games.

13.5 Concluding remarks

This last section is devoted to a discussion of the significance, scope and limitations of the models and results proposed in the present chapter. To begin with, a few comments are in order on the basic modeling choice of the paper, which relates social networks, civic associations and repeated pure coordination games. Unfortunately enough, if understandably, to many minds social networks evoke "mafia"-like relationships as well as (or even rather than) civic associations. Now, civic associations and "mafia"-like relationships are generally regarded by social analysts as more or less polar opposites in all relevant respects (and rightly so, in my view): for instance civic associations are typically connected to the existence and production or diffusion of trust, while "mafia"-like relationships are deemed to thrive under conditions of public distrust, and further reinforce them (see e.g. Gambetta (1988) for a lucid discussion and defense of those propositions). Therefore, to the minds mentioned above – whom I met among several seminar audiences – the interpretation (and motivation) I propose for the models presented above is bound to look like preposterous or arbitrary at best. A first objection to such a (any)-social-network-as-"mafia" view is that "mafia" denotes – or should denote – a (typically criminal) organization or set of organizations that provide private protection as a substitute for public protection (see again Gambetta (1988) on this point). Hence, models that lack (as ours do) the minimum structure needed to describe private as opposed to public protection cannot possibly produce any meaningful statement about "mafia"-like organizations. On the other hand, since presumably some similar "lack-of-structure" claim might be made with reference to some relevant definition of "civic associations," that objection could admittedly be regarded as unfair and thus inconclusive. However, a more general and stronger argument is available. Indeed, under a strict definition of a "mafia"-like organization, membership must be confined to a proper (and presumably small) subset of the entire population. To be sure, since "mafia"-like relationships tend unfortunately to become pervasive by involving the "customers" of a "mafia"-like organization in many and sometimes subtle ways, one may also opt for a weaker definition of participation in "mafia"-like relationships. In that case, universal participation of a community into such relationships becomes at least conceivable. But then, a minimum requirement should be that the relevant interactions be modeled as distinctly asymmetric (except at most for members in a strict sense, or a suitable subset of them). Summing up, one can advance a plausible criterion that makes it possible to discriminate between civic-like associations and "mafia"-like relationships when regarding them as game-labeled social networks or even social networks with no further structure. Namely, a game-labeled social network arising from a model of "mafia"-like relationships should either be disconnected or involve asymmetric games among its labels. Accordingly, a social network arising from such a model should be disconnected (and, arguably, with a totally disconnected component). Now, it is easily checked that the social network attached to the "handshake" model presented above may well be connected, and – due to its thickness-definitely lacks a totally disconnected component, while the game-labeled social network that is part of the "busy-boundedly-rational-players" model includes by definition only symmetric games among its labels. Whatever their merits as models of civic associations, the social networks employed in the present paper are apparently detailed enough to rule out any interpretation in terms of "mafia"-like relationships.

An obvious limitation of the models presented in this paper is that social networks are entirely exogenous. No attempt whatsoever is made at modeling their origins or evolution (see e.g. Mailath (1997), and Barberà, Maschler and Shalev (1998) for two interesting approaches to those issues). This stance can certainly be justified on practical grounds, given the specific aims of the present analysis. However, it should be remarked here that by taking social networks as parameters our models implicitly assume that evolutionary processes involving civic structures are orders of magnitude slower than the evolutionary dynamics of the interactions to be analyzed. This may or may not be a wise postulate. It is in any case far from being an indisputable assumption since the selection processes which constitute the focus of our models are themselves long-run (or perhaps ultralong-run) evolutionary episodes.

The time horizon required by our models in order to deliver their efficient selections involves another crucial issue. Indeed, a general implication of the results established in this paper is that – if given time to operate – social networks of "civic" associations might really embody a significant positive externality, and bring about considerable benefits for both members and non-members. This in turn suggests the obvious policy implication that, ceteris paribus, social networks of "civic" horizontal associations should be encouraged and promoted in any suitable way by governments and public institutions. However, the foregoing argument loses much of its practical appeal if the putative beneficial long-run outcome of such social networks takes too long to materialize. It may be observed that the cultural nature of the "replicators" involved could arguably speed-up the entire selection process. In any case, it should be admitted that the long-run character of the selection processes studied in our models might well result in a major limitation of their practical significance.

In a more positive vein, it is most instructive to compare our results to the informal explanations of the efficiency-enhancing effect of social networks listed by Putnam as quoted in section 13.2. Quite remarkably, all of them have a well-defined counterpart in at least one of the (two) evolutionary selection models presented in section 13.3 above. In particular, the relationship between social networks and repeated interactions is a basic assumption of both models, and the role of social networks as reliable information transmission channels is a key feature of the "handshake" model. Moreover, the "busy- boundedly-rational-players" model provides a mechanism through which both the pro-cooperative-environment idea and the cooperative-template hypothesis can effectively operate in a pro-efficient manner. It should also be emphasized again that the two models presented in this paper provide qualifications concerning the validity of the proposed explanations (e.g. a large population of farsighted players and "low" complexity-costs for the first model, a possibly small population of busy boundedly rational players and "high" complexity-costs for the second model). Since such qualifications point to quite different conditions, the results established in the present paper suggest that some of the intuitive reasons usually offered to explain the beneficial role of "civic" social networks might well apply to mutually exclusive sets of circumstances. All in all, the feasibility of comparatively simple models that deliver social-networks-driven efficient selection in recurrent CI games under widely diverse environments – while being confined to the most standard evolutionary concepts – is perhaps to be considered as an encouraging testimony to the robustness and significance of the efficiency-enhancing potential of certain social networks.

References

Anderlini, L. (1990) *Communication, Computability and Common Interest Games.* Economic Theory Discussion Paper No. 159, University of Cambridge.

Anderlini, L. and H. Sabourian (1995) Cooperation and effective computability. *Econometrica* 63: 1337–1369.

Aumann, R.J. and S. Sorin (1989) Cooperation and bounded recall. *Games and Economic Behavior* 1: 5–39.

Axelrod, R. (1984) *The Evolution of Cooperation.* New York: Basic Books.

Barberà S., M. Maschler and J. Shalev (1998) *Voting for Voters: A Model of Electoral Evolution.* Discussion Paper #170. Center for Rationality and Interactive Decision Theory, Hebrew University of Jerusalem.

Basu, K. (1995) Civil institutions and evolution: concepts, critique and models. *Journal of Development Economics* 46: 19–33.

Binmore, K.G. and L. Samuelson (1992) Evolutionary stability in repeated games played by finite automata. *Journal of Economic Theory* 57: 278–305.

Binmore, K.G., L. Samuelson and R. Vaughan (1995) Musical chairs: modeling noisy evolution. *Games and Economic Behavior* 11: 1–35.

Bowles, S. and H. Gintis (1998) How communities govern: the structural basis of prosocial norms. In A. Ben-Ner and L. Putterman (eds) *Economics, Values, and Organization.* Cambridge: Cambridge University Press.

Boyd, R. and P.J. Richerson (1985) *Culture and the Evolutionary Process.* Chicago: Chicago University Press.

Boyd, R. and P.J. Richerson (1990) Group selection among alternative evolutionarily stable strategies. *Journal of Theoretical Biology* 145: 331– 342.

Carlsson, H. and E. Van Damme (1993a) Global games and equilibrium selection. *Econometrica* 61: 989–1018.

Carlsson, H. and E. Van Damme (1993b) Equilibrium selection in stag hunt games. In K.G. Binmore, A. Kirman and P. Tani (eds) *Frontiers of Game Theory.* Cambridge, MA: MIT Press.

Coleman, J.S. (1990) *Foundations of Social Theory.* Cambridge, MA: Harvard University Press.

Crawford, V.P. (1995) Adaptive dynamics in coordination games. *Econometrica* 63: 103–143.

Dawkins, R. (1982) *The Extended Phenotype.* New York: Freeman.

Dieckmann, T. (1997) *The Evolution of Conventions with Endogenous Interactions.* Mimeo. Center Tilburg.

Ellison, G. (1993) Learning, local interaction, and coordination. *Econometrica* 61: 1047–1071.

Ely, J. (1996) *Local Conventions.* Mimeo. University of California at Berkeley.

Eshel, I. and L.L. Cavalli-Sforza (1982) Assortment of encounters and evolution of cooperativeness. *Proceedings of the National Academy of Science* 79: 1331–1335.

Foster, D. and H.P. Young (1990) Stochastic evolutionary game dynamics. *Theoretical Population Biology* 38: 219–232.

Fudenberg, D. and E. Maskin (1990) Evolution and cooperation in noisy repeated games. *American Economic Review (Papers and Proceedings)* 80: 274–279.

Gambetta, D. (1988) Mafia: the price of distrust. In D. Gambetta (ed.) *Trust: Making and Breaking Cooperative Relations*. Oxford: Blackwell.

Harsanyi, J. (1995) A new theory of equilibrium selection for games with complete information. *Games and Economic Behavior* 8: 91–122.

Harsanyi, J. and R. Selten (1988) *A General Theory of Equilibrium Selection in Games*. Cambridge, MA: MIT Press.

Kandori, M. (1992) Social norms and community enforcement. *Review of Economic Studies* 59: 63–80.

Kandori, M., G. Mailath and R. Rob (1993) Learning, mutation, and long run equilibria in games. *Econometrica* 61: 29–56.

Kim, Y. (1996): Equilibrium selection in *n*-person coordination games. *Games and Economic Behavior* 15: 203–227.

Kim, Y. and J. Sobel (1995) An evolutionary approach to pre-play communication. *Econometrica* 63: 1181–1193.

Kitcher, P. (1993) The evolution of human altruism. *Journal of Philosophy* 90: 497–516.

Mailath, G. (1997) Endogenous relationships. In *Evolution and Economics: Proceedings of the Siena International School of Economic Research 10th Workshop*.

Matsui, A. (1991) Cheap talk and cooperation in a society. *Journal of Economic Theory* 54: 245–258.

Matsui, A. and K. Matsuyama (1995) An approach to equilibrium selection. *Journal of Economic Theory* 65: 414–435.

Maynard Smith, J. and E. Szathmàry (1995) *The Major Transitions in Evolution*. New York: Freeman.

Myerson, R.B., G.B. Pollock and J. Swinkels (1991) Viscous population equilibria. *Games and Economic Behavior* 3: 101–109.

Ostrom, E., R. Gardner and J. Walker (1994) *Rules, Games, and Common-Pool Resources*. Ann Arbor: University of Michigan Press.

Putnam, R.D. (1993) *Making Democracy Work: Civic Traditions in Modern Italy*. Princeton: Princeton University Press.

Robson, A. (1990) Efficiency in evolutionary games: Darwin, Nash and the secret handshake. *Journal of Theoretical Biology* 144: 379–396.

Robson, A. and F. Vega-Redondo (1996) Efficient equilibrium selection in evolutionary games with random matching. *Journal of Economic Theory* 70: 65–92.

Samuelson, L. (1997) *Evolutionary Games and Equilibrium Selection*. Cambridge, MA: MIT Press.

Simon, H.A. (1990) A mechanism for social selection and successful altruism. *Science* 250: 1665–1668.

Sobel, J. (1993) Evolutionary stability and efficiency. *Economics Letters* 42: 301–312.

Sober, E. and D.S. Wilson (1998) *Unto Others. The Evolution and Psychology of Unselfish Behavior*. Cambridge, MA: Harvard University Press.

Tadelis, S. (1995) *Pareto Optimality and Optimistic Stability in Repeated Extensive Form Games*. Mimeo. Department of Economics, Harvard University.

Van Dijk, F. (1997) *Social Ties and Economic Performance*. Dordrecht: Kluwer.

Vannucci, S. (1998) *Social Networks and Efficient Evolutionary Selection*. Mimeo. Department of Political Economy, University of Siena.

Vega-Redondo, F. (1996) *Evolution, Games, and Economic Behavior*. Oxford: Oxford University Press.

Weibull, J. (1995) *Evolutionary Game Theory*. Cambridge, MA: MIT Press.

Young, H.P. (1993) The evolution of conventions. *Econometrica* 61: 57–84.

14 Community governance

An evolutionary analysis

Samuel Bowles and Herbert Gintis

14.1 Introduction

The age of commerce and the dawn of democracy were universally thought to mark the eclipse of community. Writers of all persuasions believed that markets, the state, or simply "modernization," would extinguish the values and traditions that for millennia had sustained forms of governance based on intimate and traditional relationships. According to the romantic conservative Edmund Burke (1955: 86–88),

> But the age of chivalry is gone. That of Sophisters, economists, and calculators has succeeded . . . The unbought grace of life . . . is gone! . . . Nothing is left which engages the affection on the part of the commonwealth . . . so as to create in us love, veneration, admiration or attachment. But that sort of reason which banishes the affections is incapable of filling their place.

The liberal Alexis de Tocqueville echoes Burke's fears in this comment on democratic culture in America during the 1830s:

> Each . . . living apart is a stranger to the fate of all the rest, . . . his children and his private friends constitute to him the whole of mankind; as for the rest of his fellow citizens, he is close to them but he sees them not, . . . he touches them but he feels them not; he exists but in himself and for himself alone . . .
>
> de Tocqueville [1958: 336]

For the socialist Karl Marx, commerce itself was the corrosive element destroying the bonds of community:

> Finally, there came a time when everything that men had considered as inalienable became an object of exchange, of traffic, and could be alienated. This is the time when the very things which till then had been communicated but never exchanged; given, but never sold; acquired, but never bought – virtue, love, conviction, knowledge, conscience, etc. – when everything in short passed into commerce. It is the time of general corruption, of universal venality.

These writers were mistaken. Communities have survived. Associations of non-kin have not disappeared. Some have even proliferated: nations, clubs, political parties, trade unions, neighborhoods, ethnic groupings, recreational and educational associations are still with us.

Burke, Marx and de Tocqueville were mistaken because they believed that communities owe their existence to a distinct set of values – which Talcott Parsons labeled "particularistic" as opposed to "universalistic" – and that these values were bound to be extinguished by economic and political competition in markets and democratic states, or as Marx put it by "the icy waters of egotistical calculation."

We do not doubt that markets and democratic states represent cultural environments in which some values flourish and others wither. Indeed, the dismay concerning their effects, expressed so long ago by Burke, Marx and de Tocqueville, may have been prescient. But the basis for the rise, fall, and transformation of communities, if we are correct, is to be sought not in the survival of vestigial values of an earlier age, but in the capacity of communities, like that of markets and states, to govern social interactions and provide valued solutions to social problems people confront in their daily lives.

We will represent communities, then, as structures of economic governance, by which we mean rules of ownership, forms of social interaction, and patterns of information exchange that regulate the incentives and constraints faced by social actors and hence that determine the nature of the coordination problems that arise and set the limits for their feasible solutions. States, markets, and communities are each structures of governance, distinguished from one another not by the individual values or motives they draw upon, but by their distinctive rules of social interaction. By a community we mean a group of individual whose interactions are long-term, frequent, personal, and structure by shared social norms. Families, residential neighborhood, and workplaces are communities in this sense.

Our argument is that communities play a central role in the governance of modern economies and that this role is likely to grow, given the evolving structure of our economies. To identify the governance niche occupied by communities, we must first explore the distinctive governance characteristics of markets and states, for it is the deficiencies of these that has left ample room for the flourishing of communities in modern society.

14.2 Communities and the maintenance of pro-social norms

By "norms" we mean cultural traits governing actions that affect the well-being of others but that cannot be regulated by costlessly enforceable contracts. Other usages of the term norms have been proposed. Ours highlights the problem that norms pose, namely how social interactions might be structured to foster pro-social norm-governed behaviors. Pro-social norms are those whose increased frequency in a population enhances the average level of well-being. Examples of pro-social norms are truth telling, a predisposition to cooperate (either unilaterally or conditionally) in prisoner's dilemma situations, "dove-like" behaviors in hawk-dove interactions, and a predisposition to retaliate against others pursuing anti-social behaviors.

The importance of pro-social norms arises in interactions structured such that the uncoordinated (technically "non-cooperative") actions of individuals lead to outcomes inferior to those that would have been attainable had coordination of the individual actions been possible. Examples are prisoner's dilemmas, hawk-dove games, and interactions with multiple equilibria some of which are unambiguously superior to others. These interactions are generically called *coordination problems* and the associated inferior results are termed *coordination failures*. The generic source of coordination failures is that the benefits and costs motivating individual action do not take appropriate account of the related beneficial or costly consequences of the action on others.

Communities overcome free-rider problems and punish "anti-social" actions, by supporting behaviors consistent with such pro-social norms as truth telling, reciprocity, and a predisposition to cooperate towards common ends. These norms are often considered to be the historical legacy of a traditional culture supported by intentional indoctrination and virtually universally adhered to in a population. But this account of community-based norms is uncompelling. First, groups appear to be quite internally heterogeneous with respect to many important norms and the theory of "deviance" from universal norms does not provide an adequate understanding of the distribution of normative orientations in members of a group (Gintis 1975). Second, the implied power of intentional inculcation of norms is belied by many failed experiments in the social engineering of the psyche, the attempted construction of the "new socialist man," in the former Soviet Union and elsewhere, being the most notable. Third, value orientations appear to be subject to quite rapid shifts, as witnessed by such events as the precipitous unraveling of indigenous cultures and the meteoric rise of modern feminism in the Twentieth century, suggesting that while history matters, particular norms are sustained by contemporary processes.

We suggest that the contemporary structure of social interactions that characterize communities account for the viability of the pro-social norms we have indicated. By the "structure of social interactions" we mean the rules governing how members of the population meet, what actions they may take in their common activities, and what are the outcomes of these actions. We will later formalize the structure of social interaction by a set of rules pairing members of the population and describing the game structures of their paired interactions.

Our argument may be summarized as follows. First, communities influence the evolution of norms because they structure social interactions in ways that affect the benefits and costs of norm governed actions, and the acquisition and retention of norms is influenced by the associated payoffs. Second, communities support equilibria with substantial frequencies of pro-social norms. We conclude that communities persist because they attenuate coordination failures not easily addressed by markets, states, and other competing institutions.[1]

Our reasoning thus centrally concerns norms and the manner in which people come to have the norms they do. Because many of the traits in question are moral rules or behavioral regularities that, like one's accent, may not have been actively and purposefully chosen by the people in question, we require an approach more general than the standard economic view, whereby actions, or the rules governing actions, are instrumentally chosen to maximize an objective function. Instead, we adopt the evolutionary view that key to the understanding of behaviors in the kinds of social interactions we are studying is *differential replication*: durable aspects of behavior, including norms, may be accounted for by the fact that they have been copied, retained, diffused, and hence replicated, while other traits have not.[2]

Differential replication may result from individuals seeking to acquire and retain traits that have proven successful to others. Differential replication may also take place through less instrumental means: those with "successful traits" may become privileged cultural models, such as parents or teachers. The process of differential replication also may work through the exercise of power by nations, classes, or other collectivities, as when those who lose wars adopt the culture, constitutions and the like of winners (Kelly 1985, Weber 1976).

14.3 Community governance

> Most if not all economic acts [among the Trobriand Islanders] are found to belong to some chain of reciprocal gifts and counter gifts, which in the long run balance . . . The real reason why all these economic obligations are normally kept, and kept very scrupulously, is that failure to comply places a man in an intolerable position . . . The honorable citizen is bound to carry out his duties, though his submission is not due to any instinct or intuitive impulse or mysterious "group sentiment," but to the detailed and elaborate working of a system, in which every act has its own place and must be performed without fail. Though no native however intelligent can formulate this state of affairs in a general abstract manner . . . every one is well aware of its existence and in each concrete case he can foresee the consequences.
>
> (Malinowski 1926: 40)

Communities as we have defined them structure social interaction in ways that foster (a) frequent interaction among the same agents; (b) partly as a result, low cost access to information about other community members; (c) a tendency to favor interactions with members of one's own community over outsiders; and (d) restricted migration to and from other communities. These structural characteristics, we will show, contribute to the ability of communities to promote pro-social behavior.

The structure of interactions in communities contrasts with that of markets and states, at least in their idealized forms. Market interactions are characterized by ephemerality of contact and anonymity among interacting agents while idealized state bureaucracies are characterized by long-term anonymous relationships. The relevant contrasts appear in Figure 14.1. States and markets have distinctive capacities and shortcomings as governance structures, but our concern here is with communities.[3]

	Ephemeral	Enduring
Anonymous	Markets	States
Personal	—	Communities

Figure 14.1 The structure of interactions in different institutions

	Cooperate	Defect
Cooperate	b, b	d, a
Defect	a, d	c, c

Figure 14.2 The prisoner's dilemma: payoffs (row, column)

Note: $a > b > c > d$, $a + d < 2b$

Consider, for concreteness, a particular community facing a coordination problem of the prisoner's dilemma type. Suppose the community is composed of a large number of people who interact in pairs, with available actions and payoffs as indicated in Figure 14.2, with the familiar payoffs[4]

$$a > b > c > d \quad \text{and } a + d < 2b. \tag{14.1}$$

The actions taken by each are not subject to enforceable contracts. Universal defect is the dominant strategy equilibrium for this interaction.

If the players could contract to play cooperate, they would surely do so. But the assumption that the behaviors in question are non-contractible, namely that the interaction is non-cooperative, precludes this. How might the structure of the community nonetheless induce universal cooperation? We have identified three ways in which communities solve coordination problems. Each is based on familiar game-theoretic models.

First, a high frequency of interaction among community members lowers the cost of gathering information, and raises the benefits associated with discovering the characteristics of those with whom one interacts. The more easily acquired and widely dispersed this information, the more will community members have an incentive to act in ways beneficial to their neighbors. Thus when agents engage in repeated interaction, they have an incentive to act in ways that build their "reputation" for cooperative behavior (Shapiro 1983, Gintis 1989, Kreps 1990). This is the *reputation effect* of community.

Second, since in a community the probability is high that members who interact today will interact in the future, there is an incentive to act favorably towards one's partners to avoid future repercussions (Axelrod and Hamilton 1981, Axelrod 1984, Taylor 1987, Fudenberg and Maskin 1986). The more multifaceted is the relationship among people involved in the interaction, the more opportunities there

	Effect favoring the solution of coordination problems	Characteristic of community necessary for this effect	Variable in model to follow
Reputation	Enhanced value of reputations for pro-social behaviors	Low cost of information about other agents	δ
Retaliation	Punishment of anti-social behaviors	Frequent or long-lasting interactions	ρ
Segmentation	Disadvantageous pairing of anti-social agents	Non-random pairing of agents	σ
Parochialism	Enhanced pressures favoring pro-social traits	Limited migration among groups	μ

Figure 14.3 How communities solve coordination problems

are for the later redress of opportunistic treatment. We refer to this as the *retaliation effect.*

Third, pro-social and anti-social behaviors typically involve conferring benefits and inflicting costs on others, in a situation where the costs and benefits in question are not subject to cost effective contracting. In a large population of many communities, the greater likelihood of interacting with a member of one's own community than with a randomly selected member of the population enhances the frequency of likes interacting. A result is that pro-social behaviors are more likely to be rewarded, those with pro-social norms being more likely to interact with other pro-social agents, and conversely for anti-social behaviors (Grafen 1979, Axelrod and Hamilton 1981, Bowles 1996). This is the *segmentation effect.*

The retaliation, reputation, and segmentation effects above allow communities to support higher equilibrium frequencies of pro-social traits. These effects may be enhanced by the limited mobility among groups entailed by the high entry and exit costs characteristic of communities. We call this the *parochialism effect.* The parochialism effect operates not by inducing pro-social behaviors directly, but by enhancing reputation, retaliation, and segmentation effects under the appropriate conditions (Bowles and Gintis 1997). Note that the parochialism effect is distinct from group selection mechanisms, which depend upon inter-group differences in frequencies of traits. Reputation, retaliation, and segmentation effects are supported by Nash equilibria within groups, and hence are viable in the absence of inter-group competition.[5]

Figure 14.3 summarizes these causal links between the structure of communities and the attenuation of coordination problems. In subsequent sections we will investigate the workings of each of these four effects, but first we will need to be more precise about how the payoffs associated with traits affect their differential replication, as this relationship is the key to understanding the effect of institutions on cultural evolution.

14.4 Economic institutions and cultural evolution

> . . . the (Salem) "witch hunters" of 1692. . . were (not) simple peasants clinging blindly to the imagined security of a receding medieval culture, . . . (they were) trying to expunge the lure of a new order from their own souls by doing battle with it in the real world.
>
> (The accused were). . . a group of people who were on the advancing edge of profound historical change. If from one angle they were diverging from an accepted norm of behavior, from another angle their values represented the "norm" of the future. In an age about to pass, the assertion of private will pose the direst possible threat to the stability of the community; in the age about to arrive it would form a central pillar on which that stability rested.
>
> (Boyer and Nissenbaum 1974: 180, 109)

Economic institutions and other rules of the game governing social life influence the structure of social interactions in a population, which in turn affects the payoffs associated with distinct behaviors governed by norms and other cultural traits. Because these payoffs influence the differential adoption, retention and abandonment of cultural traits, institutions affect the equilibrium distribution of cultural traits in a population. It follows that changes in the mix of institutions affect cultural evolution by altering the structure of social interactions and hence altering the process of cultural transmission.

By a *culture* we mean a set of cultural traits. A cultural trait is a belief, value, or other acquired aspect of an individual that influences the individual's behavior in some durable fashion.[6] A predisposition to help others, or to have large families, or generally to skip breakfast, are cultural traits, as are the practices of reciprocating social invitations and always selling to the highest bidder. Cultural evolution is the process of change over time in the distribution of cultural traits in a population. A cultural equilibrium is a distribution of cultural traits not subject to endogenous sources of change. A cultural environment is any social situation affecting the propensity of existing cultural traits to be adopted and retained by others (whether willingly, consciously, or not) and new cultural traits to be introduced.

Communities, like markets and states, are environments in which cultural traits develop and change. These different cultural environments may be distinguished by the way they favor the copying and hence growth of distinct cultural traits.[7]

Suppose cultural evolution takes place under the influence of the differential replication of traits that are perceived to be successful by members of the population.[8] Emulation of the cultural traits of individuals perceived to be socially successful is analogous to the reproductive success of biologically fit organisms. Emulation may be very rapid if the cultural traits correlated with success have no moral force, and are embraced only because of their expected consequences. Even where there is a conflict between deeply a held moral value and the perceived success of individuals and groups who reject that value, there is a tendency for the moral value to be abandoned. This may happen through group selection, since groups that espouse the more successful value may simply displace groups that espouse the less (Soltis *et al.* 1995). In addition, individuals themselves may abandon inopportune values (Festinger 1957), or a new generation may simply refuse to embrace the inopportune values of the previous (Fromm and Maccoby 1970). Moreover, values found useful in one social setting (e.g., the workplace) may be unconsciously "transported" to another, where they threaten and possibly displace more traditional values (Kohn 1969, Bowles and Gintis 1976). Finally, successful individuals may obtain positions, as governmental leaders, media figures, and teachers for example, in which they have privileged access to the population as cultural models and thus may be copied disproportionately for reasons associated with their location in the social structure rather than success *per se*, others deemed equally successful being less replicated (LeVine 1966).

Notice a rough learning rule underlying differential replication has replaced the role usually assigned to conscious optimization. We do not specify why traits are copied. The previous paragraph leaves this issue open. Rather, we simply posit that successful traits are more likely to be copied.

Cultural transmission based on the favored replication of successful traits may be modeled as follows. Let there be one of two mutually exclusive traits (x and y) present in each member of a large population (y may be considered to be the absence of x). Let p_x be the fraction of members of the population that has trait x, and let r_x be the rate of growth of p_x over time.[9] The structure of the transmission process is this: in a large population with a given distribution of traits, agents implement the strategy dictated by their trait in a game that assigns benefits to each, following which the traits are replicated, generating a new population distribution. Equilibrium is defined as stationarity of the frequency of traits.

Suppose members of the population are randomly paired to interact in a two person game, the payoffs of which are denoted $\pi(i,j)$, the payoff to playing trait i against a j-playing partner. Thus the probability of an individual meeting an x-type is p_x, and the probability of meeting a y-type is $(1-p_x)$. The expected payoffs are given by

$$\begin{aligned} b_x(p_x) &= p_x\pi(x,x)+(1-p_x)\pi(x,y) \\ b_y(p_x) &= p_x\pi(y,x)+(1-p_x)\pi(y,y). \end{aligned} \tag{14.2}$$

Read the first equation: "with probability p an x-person is paired with another x-person with payoff $\pi(x,x)$, and with probability $(1-p)$ is paired with a y-person with payoff $\pi(x,y)$."

Suppose at the end of each period each agent A, with probability $\gamma_1 > 0$, decides to reassess the value of his "type" by comparing his b_i with that of a randomly chosen person B. If B has a lower payoff than A, we assume A does not change his cultural trait. But if B has a higher payoff than A, and if B is not of the same type as A, A shifts to B's type with a probability that is proportional to the difference in the payoffs to A and B, with a proportionality factor $\gamma_2 > 0$. Then we can show that (Gintis 1997)

$$r_x = \gamma_1\gamma_2[b_x(p_x) - \bar{b}(p_x)], \tag{14.3}$$

where $\bar{b}(p)$ is the average payoff in the population:

$$\bar{b}(p_x) = p_x b_x(p_x) + (1 - p_x) b_y(p_x). \tag{14.4}$$

It is obvious that the population distribution p_x will be unchanging if and only if $r_x = 0$. Rewriting (14.3) as

$$r_x = \gamma_1\gamma_2(1 - p_x)[b_x(p_x) - b_y(p_x)], \tag{14.5}$$

we see that population is in equilibrium if and only if

$$b_y(p_x) = b_x(p_x). \tag{14.6}$$

Thus a condition for an interior equilibrium (unchanging p_x) is that payoffs be equal. For a solution to (14.6), which we will call p_x^*, to be stable (i.e. to return to p_x^* when perturbed) a small increase in p_x (the fraction of those with trait x) must increase the replication propensity of the y trait more than the x trait, thereby favoring the y trait in replication and lowering p_x. This can be written:

$$\frac{dr_x}{dp_x} < 0, \tag{14.7}$$

requiring that

$$\pi(y, x) - \pi(x, x) > \pi(y, y) - \pi(x, y) \tag{14.8}$$

We turn now to a consideration of each of the four effects of community governance.

14.5 Reputation

> Honesty comes much more easily in a tiny community than it does in a great city, where misconduct always hopes that the multitude of alien tracks will cover up its own footprints.
>
> Diamond Jenness, pp. 128–9, commenting on the Eskimo lack of fear of stealing.

Suppose now each agent is one of two types of players, which we call "nice" and "nasty." An agent can determine whether a partner is "nice" by paying an inspection cost $\delta > 0$.[10] A nice agent is one who either cooperates unconditionally, or who inspects and responds to a nice partner by cooperating and to a nasty partner by defecting. Otherwise an agent is nasty. There are clearly six pure strategies, as shown in Figure 14.4. We have named only three of these strategies, since the others are strictly dominated, and hence cannot appear in a Nash equilibrium: (a) and (c) are strictly dominated by Defect and (b) is strictly dominated by Trust.

The payoff matrix for a pair of agents who agree to interact is now given by the normal form matrix shown in Figure 14.5.

Strategy	*Inspect*	*Action*	*Frequency*
Defect	no	defect	$1-\alpha-\beta$
Trust	no	cooperate	β
(a)	yes	defect	—
(b)	yes	cooperate	—
Inspect	yes	defect if partner nasty	α
		cooperate if partner nice	—
(c)	yes	defect if partner nice	—
		cooperate if partner nasty	—

Figure 14.4 Strategies in the inspect variant of the prisoner's dilemma

	Inspect	Trust	Defect
Inspect	$b-\delta, b-\delta$	$b-\delta, b$	$c-\delta, c$
Trust	$b, b-\delta$	b, b	d, a
Defect	$c, c-\delta$	a, d	c, c

Figure 14.5 Payoffs for the inspect variant of the prisoner's dilemma

We call a Nash equilibrium a *universal defect equilibrium* if all agents Defect, a *nontrust equilibrium* if some agents Inspect but no agent Trusts, and a *trust equilibrium* if at least one agent Trusts. There are no other types of Nash equilibria in this game.[11] Not surprisingly, a universal defect equilibrium exists and is locally stable, so Defect is an evolutionarily stable strategy.

To investigate the possibility of a trust equilibrium, let $\alpha \geq 0$, $\beta > 0$, and $(1-\alpha-\beta) \geq 0$ be the probability that strategies Inspect, Trust, and Defect are used, respectively. If there were no defection, then Inspect would be dominated by Trust because inspectors pay a cost without ever locating a defector, so all agents would Trust. But then Defect dominates Trust, which is a contradiction. Thus there is a positive level of Defect. If there were no Inspect, then again Defect would dominate Trust, which is impossible in equilibrium. Thus there must be positive levels of all three strategies if there are any trusters (i.e. $\beta > 0$) in equilibrium.

We now determine the population frequencies of Trust, Inspect, and Defect in a trust equilibrium. Let $\pi^i(\alpha,\beta)$ be the expected payoff to adopting strategy i in a population whose composition is described by α,β. Then by (14.6), the payoffs to each must be equal in equilibrium. Thus we have $\pi^I(\alpha,\beta) = \pi^T(\alpha,\beta) = \pi^D(\alpha,\beta)$, or

$$\begin{aligned} \alpha(b-\delta) \;+\; \beta(b-\delta) \;+\; & (1-\alpha-\beta)(c-\delta) \\ = \; & (\alpha+\beta)b + (1-\alpha-\beta)d. \qquad (14.9) \\ = \; & \alpha c + \beta a + (1-\alpha-\beta)c. \qquad (14.10) \end{aligned}$$

These equations imply (using an asterisk* to indicate an equilibrium value)

$$\alpha^* + \beta^* = 1 - \frac{\delta}{c-d}, \tag{14.11}$$

from which it is clear that the fraction adopting pro-social strategies (Inspect or Trust) varies inversely with the cost of information δ, attaining a value of unity when $\delta = 0$. Further, solving (14.9) and (14.10) for α and β, we get

$$\alpha^* = \frac{1}{a-c}\left[(a-b)\left(1-\frac{\delta}{c-d}\right)+\delta\right], \tag{14.12}$$

$$\beta^* = \frac{1}{a-c}\left[(b-c)-(b-d)\frac{\delta}{c-d}\right]. \tag{14.13}$$

For such a solution to exist with $\alpha^*, \beta^* > 0$, equation (14.11) shows that we must have $\delta < c-d$. Then from (14.13), $\beta^* > 0$ requires

$$\delta < (c-d)\frac{b-c}{b-d}. \tag{14.14}$$

Notice that the right hand side of equation (14.14) is strictly positive, so such a $\delta > 0$ exists. Now $\alpha > 0$ follows trivially. Since equation (14.14) also implies $\delta < c-d$, given the prisoner's dilemma structure (14.1) of the payoffs, we see that (14.14) is necessary and sufficient for a mixed strategy Nash equilibrium with a positive level of Trust. In this case the frequency $1-\alpha^*-\beta^*$ of Defect is $\delta/(c-d)$, which is an increasing function of the cost of inspection. Also, the frequency β^* of Trust is a decreasing function of δ, since from (14.13)

$$\frac{d\beta}{d\delta} = -\frac{b-d}{(c-d)(a-c)} < 0. \tag{14.15}$$

Since the payoffs to all strategies are equal in equilibrium, the expected payoff to all the players is the same as to Trust which, from (14.9), is $(\alpha^*+\beta^*)(b-d)+d$. Using (14.11), this gives

$$d+(b-d)(\alpha^*+\beta^*) = b - \frac{b-d}{c-d}\delta, \tag{14.16}$$

which decreases as the cost of inspection δ increases.[12]

In sum, we have four distinct reputation effects based on the capacity of community to provide low-cost information on the types of those with whom one interacts. First, reduced cost of information may make possible an equilibrium in which trusting behaviors occur (14.14). Second, in such an equilibrium the amount of trusting behavior will be greater the lower is the cost of information (14.15). Third, if trusting occurs in equilibrium, the average payoff to all members of the population will vary inversely with the cost of information (14.16). Finally, the fraction of the population defecting will vary directly with the cost of information (14.11).

14.6 Retaliation

> Antonia did not speak to Juan for 15 years. He had offended her in public while she was mourning for her husband . . . through gossiping and chatting, the community of women [in Oroel, a Spanish town of 150 inhabitants] evolves a fund of information, impressions and understandings . . . which they draw on and interpret in order to make decisions about their daily interactions.
>
> (Harding 1978: 16)

We will show that if the prisoner's dilemma in Figure 14.2 is repeated with some probability, cooperation may be supported by the threat of retaliation against defectors, the threat being more effective the more likely is the repetition. If repetition is sufficiently likely, and if the time elapsing between repetition is sufficiently brief, the payoff structure is transformed so as to have two equilibria: universal defect, as before, and universal cooperate.

The transformed payoff matrix is called an assurance game (Sen 1967), because each player does best by cooperating as long as each can be assured that the other cooperate as well.[13]

Unlike the underlying prisoner's dilemma, for which defection is the dominant strategy (i.e., affords a player a superior payoffs whatever the action of the other player), the assurance game merely supports the socially optimal outcome (mutual cooperation) as an equilibrium that is sustained if each participant believes the others will play the cooperative strategy. We will see that the high exit and entry costs defining communities, and the consequent frequent and repeated interactions among community members, may in this manner transform an intractable coordination problem into one more amenable to solution. We will also see that communities may enlarge the basin of attraction of the mutual cooperation equilibrium and reduce the size of the mutual defection equilibrium, thus making cooperative outcomes more robust in the presence of stochastic disturbances.

Thus to the extent that the high exit and entry costs that characterize communities entail frequent and repeated interaction with the same individuals, they may support a cooperative outcome unattainable under more ephemeral conditions.

Repetition changes the interaction in two ways. It allows more complicated strategies, ones that take account of one's partner's prior actions, and it requires that payoffs be accounted for as expected gains over the entire interaction. Players might now want to adopt the so called nice Tit-for-Tat strategy: cooperate on the first round and on all subsequent rounds do what your partner did on the previous round. To keep things simple let us confine the choice of strategies to just Tit-for-Tat (T) and unconditional defect (D). The expected payoffs may now be calculated.

Suppose that after each play the above interaction is to be terminated with a given probability ρ, and repetitions occur over a brief enough period to justify ignoring the players' rates of time preference (an assumption of no consequence in what follows). When two Tit-for-Tatters meet, for example, they will both cooperate, and then continue to do so until the interaction is terminated (that is for

	Tit-for-Tat	Defect
Tit-for-Tat	b/ρ b/ρ	$d+(1-\rho)c/\rho$ $a+(1-\rho)c/\rho$
Defect	$a+(1-\rho)c/\rho$ $d+(1-\rho)c/\rho$	c/ρ c/ρ

Figure 14.6 The payoffs in the repeated prisoner's dilemma game(ρ is the probability of termination).

an expected duration of $1/\rho$ iterations) giving expected benefits of b/ρ. When a Tit-for-Tatter meets a defector, the former will get d on the first iteration, and then both will defect until the game terminates, the expected number of iterations after the first iteration being $1/\rho-1=(1-\rho)/\rho$, and the resulting expected payoffs thus being $d+(1-\rho)c/\rho$. The resulting payoff matrix for the iterated game appears in Figure 14.6.

If the fraction of the population adopting Tit-for-Tat is τ (the remainder adopting unconditional Defect) and if members of the population are paired randomly to interact so that the probability of being paired with a Tit-for-Tatter is τ, expected returns to Tit-for-Tat and Defect, respectively, π^T and π^D are

$$\pi^T(\tau) = \tau b/\rho+(1-\tau)\{d+(1-\rho)c/\rho\} \tag{14.17}$$

$$\pi^D(\tau) = \tau\{a+(1-\rho)c/\rho\}+(1-\tau)c/\rho, \tag{14.18}$$

which, when equated to determine the equilibrium population fraction τ^*, yields

$$\tau^* = \frac{c-d}{2c-a-d+(b-c)/\rho}. \tag{14.19}$$

For payoffs and termination probability such that

$$\rho < \frac{b-c}{a-c} \tag{14.20}$$

and for $c > d$, we have $\tau^* \in (0,1)$, giving an interior equilibrium. Note that (14.20) also ensures that the denominator of (14.19) is positive. The second condition must be true because the single period payoffs describe a prisoner's dilemma. The first will be true when the gains to universal cooperation relative to the gains to single period defection are great relative to the termination probability. The payoffs above and an interior equilibrium τ^* are illustrated in Figure 14.7.

But unlike the equilibria in the reputation game considered above, τ^* is unstable, small deviations from τ^* do not result in a convergence back to τ^*. This is because

$$\frac{d\pi^D(\tau^*)}{d\tau} < \frac{d\pi^T(\tau^*)}{d\tau},$$

violating the stability condition (14.7). We may see this as follows. For values of τ greater than τ^* the expected return to D relative to T is diminished, but as the

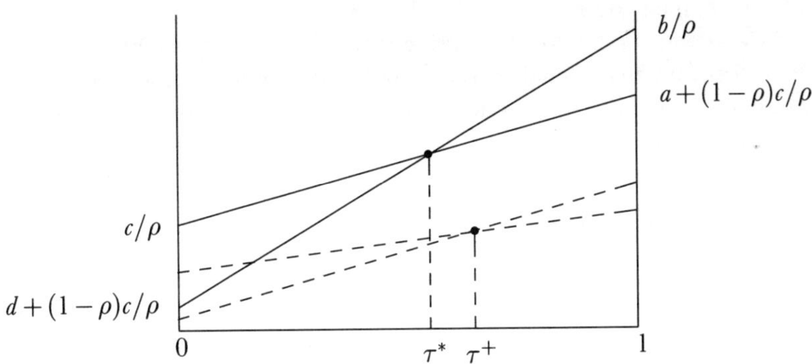

Figure 14.7 The retaliation effect: an increase in the probability of termination (dashed lines) diminishes, and may eliminate, the basin of attraction of the Universal Cooperate equilibrium.

payoffs were equal at τ^* the returns to D must therefore be inferior to T, which by the dynamic process described in Section 14.4 will lead to further increase in T rather than a return to τ^*. As a result there are three equilibrium population frequencies, namely 0, τ^*, and 1. The first and third are stable. The unstable equilibrium τ^* defines the boundary between the basin of attraction of the two stable equilibria.

It is readily confirmed that equation (14.20) implies that the payoff to Tit-for-Tat in a population with no defectors exceeds the payoff to Defect in that population or $b/\rho > a+(1-\rho)c/\rho$ making Tit-for-Tat a best response to itself. We say that Tit-for-Tat is an *evolutionarily stable strategy* if there exists some positive frequency of defection in this population ϵ such that if the population share of Defect is below ϵ, the process of differential replication of traits will lead to its elimination (Weibull 1995). Thus invasion by a group of defectors comprising less than a fraction ϵ of the population will fail. Where (14.20) holds, Tit-for-Tat is thus an evolutionarily stable strategy, and the critical value of ϵ in the above definition is $1-\tau^*$.

Two results concerning the governance effects of community follow. First the interaction will have an equilibrium of universal cooperation if the probability of termination is sufficiently low (universal defect will remain an equilibrium). This follows directly from condition (14.20) above: if an interior equilibrium exists and is unstable, $\tau = 0$ must be a stable equilibrium. Second, an increase in the probability of termination will reduce the basin of attraction of the cooperative equilibrium. This is because

$$\frac{d\tau^*}{d\rho} = \frac{(\tau^*)^2(b-c)}{\rho^2(c-d)}$$

which must be positive if the initial payoffs are a prisoner's dilemma and if $\tau^* \in (0,1)$. Thus as the expected duration of interactions is reduced (an increase in ρ), the dividing line between the basin of attraction of universal defect and universal cooperation shifts toward the latter, widening the range of initial conditions yielding

$\tau^* = 0$ as an outcome.

Condition (14.20) does not ensure that universal cooperation will take place. It ensures only that should universal cooperation occur, such cooperation would not unravel by the process of unilateral defection. This is the sense in which that continuity of interactions (low ρ) characteristic of communities favors cooperation.

14.7 Segmentation

> Like ethnic businesses generally, [Korean rotating credit associations] encourage the ethnic solidarity they require. . . . bureaucratized financial institutions accelerated the atomization of the population rather than having, as previously thought, served the otherwise intractable needs of an already atomized population.
>
> (Light, Kwuon and Zhong 1990: 48)

The high entry and exit costs that characterize communities result in populations being segmented, members of the communities making up the larger population interacting with outsiders less frequently than with insiders. Examples include members of a population residing in villages who engage in frequent exchanges with co-residents and occasionally exchange goods at a single market serving the entire population.

Suppose individuals are either defectors or cooperators in a single period prisoner's dilemma, and as before they periodically update their type in response to the relative success of the two strategies. By contrast to the reputation and retaliation models, in which members of the population are randomly paired to interact, the segmentation model is based on nonrandom pairing. The communities into which the population is segmented are more homogeneous with respect to type than is the larger population, either because they share a common ancestry and parents have privileged roles as cultural models, or because of a sorting process based on some characteristic correlated with the cultural traits under study.[14]

The clustering of likes attenuates coordination problems because pro-social behaviors such as cooperating in a prisoner's dilemma situation confer advantages to those with whom one interacts, while defecting inflicts costs. Thus a biased pairing process that disproportionately pairs likes with likes raises the payoffs to those exhibiting the pro-social traits. The segmentation associated with community allows those exhibiting pro-social behaviors to capture more of the benefits of the pro-sociality of others than would be the case under random pairing, and thus supports a greater frequency of these traits in a population.

We define the degree of segmentation as follows. If the fraction of the population who are cooperators is α, the probability that a cooperator will meet a fellow cooperator is no longer α but $\sigma + (1 - \sigma)\alpha$ where $\sigma \in (0, 1)$ is the degree of segmentation of the population. Correspondingly the probability of a defector meeting a fellow defector is now $\sigma + (1 - \alpha)(1 - \sigma)$. Note that $\sigma = 1$ implies pairing of likes with likes whatever the population composition, and $\sigma = 0$ implying random assignment. The degree of segmentation is thus identical to the degree

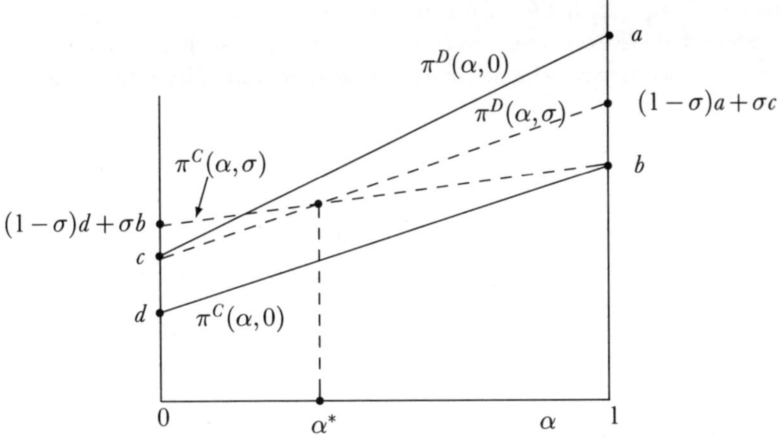

Figure 14.8 The segmentation effect: stable interior equilibrium case

of relatedness in Hamilton's rule governing the evolution of altruistic behaviors (Grafen 1979, Grafen 1984, Axelrod and Hamilton 1981). A particularly simple (if implausible) case arises if groups are entirely homogeneous, in which case σ is the probability that one's partner for an interaction will be drawn from the group rather than from the entire population, or in the example above, the fraction of exchanges at the village level rather than in the general market. The expected returns to each are then

$$\begin{aligned}\pi^C(\alpha,\sigma) &= \sigma b+(1-\sigma)(\alpha b+(1-\alpha)d)\\ \pi^D(\alpha,\sigma) &= \sigma c+(1-\sigma)(\alpha a+(1-\alpha)c).\end{aligned}$$

We take the pairing rule and the degree of segmentation as an exogenously given characteristic of the clustering of types supported by community and now consider its effect on the equilibrium level of cooperation.[15] To find this effect, we find the value of α equating the two above expected payoffs, or

$$\alpha^* = \frac{\sigma(d-b)+c-d}{(1-\sigma)(b-d-a+c)}$$

Depending on the payoffs this equilibrium may be stable or unstable. In the latter case α^* marks the boundary between the basin of attraction of stable equilibria at $\alpha=1$ and $\alpha=0$. Figure 14.8 illustrates the case of a stable interior equilibrium.[16]

Four results support our interpretation of the segmentation effect of community. First, there exists some value of $\sigma<1$ such that universal cooperation is an equilibrium, even where the interaction is a single shot prisoner's dilemma. Call this critical value of the degree of segmentation σ', which is simply the value for which $\alpha^*=1$. Thus

$$\sigma' = \frac{a-b}{a-c} < 1,$$

where the inequality holds because the prisoner's dilemma payoffs specify $b > c$.

Second, there exists some value of $\sigma < 1$, call it σ'', such that for $\sigma > \sigma''$ some level of cooperation may be sustained as an equilibrium. This is the value of σ for which $\alpha = 0$, or

$$\sigma'' = \frac{c-d}{b-d},$$

which is less than one because $c < b$.

Third, if α^* is stable, an increase in segmentation will increase the frequency of cooperation in the population. This is because $d\alpha^*/d\sigma$ has the sign of $(c-b)(b-d-a+c)$, which is positive for a stable equilibrium.

Fourth, if α^* is unstable, then α^* separates the basins of attraction of the all defect and the all cooperate stable equilibria, and an increase in segmentation will enlarge the basin of attraction of the universal cooperation equilibrium because, for the reasons supplied just above, $d\alpha^*/d\sigma < 0$ in this case.

14.8 Parochialism

> . . . the advantages of widespread generosity [among llama herders in the Peruvian highlands] outweigh the advantages of cheating or ignoring those who are not one's kin . . . the custom of [reciprocal generosity] once adopted, might have been strongly selected for at the group level. In our models, herd systems that practice it have larger and far more stable herds after 100 years than systems without it . . . universal adherence . . . – even if it includes giving good breeding stock to non-kin – can make it possible for one's children to pass on more animals to one's grandchildren. It does that by ensuring that there will be lots of other herds around from which the children and grandchildren can get (help) when they need it.
>
> (Flannery, Marcus and Reynolds 1989: 202)

If subgroups in a population exhibit differing levels of pro-social norms, and hence experience coordination failures of differing extent, a high rate of migration into a relatively pro-social group may render the cooperative equilibrium unattainable. "Parochial" cultural values that reduce the rate of migration may thus interact synergystically with the pro-social norms themselves to help maintain stable cooperative interactions in communities. We show this by adapting a model of Boyd and Richerson (1990) to the prisoner's dilemma interaction we have used to illustrate our three previous community effects.

To illustrate, we return to our model of the retaliation effect, but we now embed the group studied in Section 14.6 in a population composed of many groups. Interactions take place only within groups, but in each period some migration among groups takes place, with a fraction μ of each group relocating each period.

The migration process is the following. As before, individuals interact for an indeterminate number of periods with termination probability ρ, and following termination of the interaction they update their behaviors through inspection of the payoffs of others. Following this updating, a fraction $\mu \in (0,1)$ of the group leaves and is replaced by new community members drawn randomly from the larger population. More complicated and more realistic models of migration – those taking account of the probability that migrants will choose successful groups as their destinations, for example – would not alter the results that follow (Bowles and Gintis 1997). The higher the entry and exit costs the lower will be μ.

Suppose the frequency of those playing Tit-for-Tat in a particular group is τ, and its change over time due to updating of behaviors is governed by

$$\tau' = \tau + \dot{\tau}\, dt$$

Migration alters the composition of the updated population, converting the post updating, pre-migration frequency τ' to the post-migration frequency τ'' according to

$$\tau'' = (1 - \mu\, dt)\tau' + \mu\bar{\tau}\, dt,$$

where $\bar{\tau}$ is the frequency of Tit-for-Tat players in the larger population.[17]

The equilibrium frequency of Tit-for-Tatters in the group must satisfy $\tau = \tau''$ (the frequency must be stationary) or

$$\frac{\dot{\tau}}{\tau} = \frac{\mu}{1-\mu}\left(1 - \frac{\bar{\tau}}{\tau}\right), \tag{14.21}$$

which may be read: the effects of trait switching due to updating (the left hand term) must just be offset by the effects of migration. As one would expect, where the trait frequency in the group is equal to the population average, migration has no effect on within group frequency and so (14.21) requires that $\dot{\tau} = 0$, or equivalently that condition (14.6) obtain.

We know from (14.5) that the rate of growth of the population frequency $\dot{\tau}/\tau$ can be expressed

$$\begin{aligned}\frac{\dot{\tau}}{\tau} &= \gamma_1\gamma_2[\pi^T(\tau) - \bar{\pi}(\tau)] \\ &= \gamma_1\gamma_2(1-\tau)[\pi^T(\tau) - \pi^D(\tau)]\end{aligned}$$

Using the payoffs for the retaliation game (14.17) and (14.18), this may be expressed:

$$\frac{\dot{\tau}}{\tau} = \gamma_1\gamma_2(1-\tau)\left[\tau\left\{2c - a - d + \frac{b-c}{\rho}\right\} - c + d\right].$$

Using this expression and the equilibrium condition above we define an equilibrium population frequency, τ_μ as is shown in Figure 14.9 for a population in which $\tau_\mu > \bar{\tau}$. To see if τ_μ is stable, suppose $\tau > \tau_\mu$. The effects of migration on the population composition more than offset the effects of behavioral updating in light of the payoffs in the previous interaction, and hence $d\tau/dt < 0$. The opposite is true for $\tau < \tau_\mu$, so by (14.7), τ_μ is stable.

Recall that in the retaliation model universal cooperation (by use of the Tit-for-Tat strategy) was a stable equilibrium for sufficiently low termination probabilities,

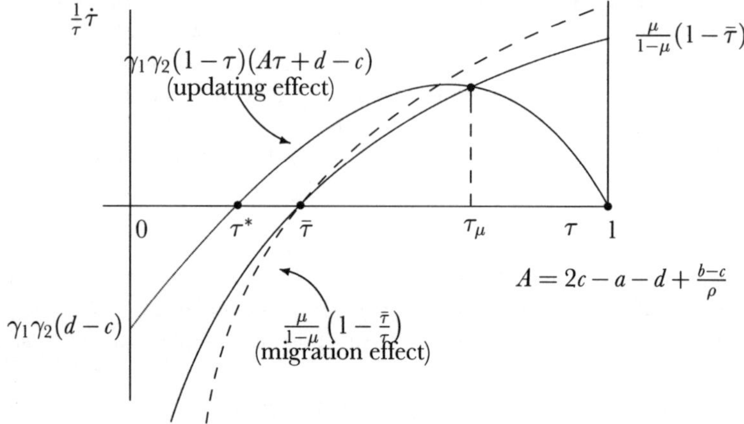

Figure 14.9 The retaliation effect with migration: increased immigration (dashed lines) reduces equilibrium frequency of cooperative behavior.

and this being the case, the higher payoffs to members of this group could have fostered the proliferation of the trait through differential growth of the favored population. The presence of intergroup migration alters this result in the following way.

First, if the frequency of Tit-for-Tat players at τ^* is lower than that of the larger population, $\bar{\tau}$, as is shown in Figure 14.9, then

$$\frac{d\tau_\mu}{d\mu} < 0.$$

This means that an increase in the rate of migration will reduce the frequency of Tit-for-Tat players and increase the frequency of defectors in equilibrium, as is indicated by the dashed line in Figure 14.9.

Second, if $\bar{\tau} < \tau^*$ (not shown) there will exist either one equilibrium with a low level of cooperation (below τ^*) or three equilibria, two being stable equilibria, one with a high and one with a low level of cooperation, and an unstable equilibrium intermediate between these two.[18] In this case an increase in the rate of migration will decrease the level of cooperation at the upper stable equilibrium and increase it at the lower, and there exists some rate of migration sufficiently high as to eliminate the high cooperation equilibrium altogether.

14.9 Conclusion

> What the entrepreneurial group of Islamic small businessmen most lacks is not capital, for . . . their resources are not inadequate, not drive, for they display the typically "Protestant" virtues of industry, frugality, independence and determination in almost excessive abundance; certainly not a sufficient market. What they lack is . . . the capacity to form efficient economic institutions . . . Despite the advantages of such bold and rugged, not to say ruthless, individualism in stimulating creativity and destroying customary constraints on enterprise in a traditional society, it seems that . . . it also involves very important limitations on the capacity to grow . . . by limiting the effective range of collective organization.
>
> (Geertz 1963: 23, 126)

Personal interactions among agents are structured by communities, markets, states, and families, as well as other institutions. The importance of communities in this nexus of governance will evolve at least in part in response to the balance of benefits conferred by the community effects just identified relative to the opportunity costs of community governance and the corresponding benefits of alternative institutional structures. Though we will not model the process here, we think it reasonable to suppose that populations whose interactions are regulated by a balance of community and other governance structures that successfully address coordination failures will tend to grow and to occupy new territories, to absorb other populations, and thus to replace other less successful governance structures. The selective pressures operating in these cases may include military and economic competition as well as people replacing unsuccessful governance structures by successful ones observed in other societies.

Communities have properties allowing them to persist in a world of market exchanges and modern states despite their inability to exploit the efficiency-enhancing properties of markets and the advantages of universal enforcement of rules provided by states. Among these properties, and the one explored in this chapter, is the capacity of communities to foster cooperative behavior among community members and thus to avert or attenuate costly coordination problems of the prisoner's dilemma type. Similar results hold for more general payoff structures (Bowles 1996). By inducing pro-social behaviors, communities may also support the norms and values that regularize and justify these behaviors, given that people typically seek consistency between their actions and their valuations.

We have not shown that communities have persisted for these reasons. We have shown only that they might have. Other reasons are commonly suggested, prominent among which is the view that communities and their associated values have persisted by virtue of the conformist and other inertial tendencies of the process of cultural transmission. We do not doubt that these tendencies are present and are sometimes decisive. But for reasons indicated at the outset, we do not believe that any purely inertial or backward-looking approach can provide an adequate explanation of the emergence and persistence of either community-based social interactions or their associated social norms.

Rather our strategy has been to depict communities, like states and markets, as modern governance structures whose patterns of proliferation, diffusion, decline and extinction are regulated by contemporary processes. Far from being vestigial anachronisms, we think communities may become more rather than less important in the nexus of governance structures in the years to come, since communities may claim some success in addressing governance problems not amenable to market or state solution.

Many have argued that as production shifts from goods to services, and within services to information-related services (Quah 1996), and as team-based production methods increase in importance, the gains from cooperation will increase as well. The reason is that monitoring such activities by those not directly involved is generally costly or impossible and hence neither the complete contracts required by well-functioning markets nor the centralized information required by state regulation are feasible. If, as we suspect, this is the case, we may expect the viability of communities to increase rather than to ebb. On the other hand the kinds of social exclusion often associated with community-based social interactions often violate strongly held universalistic norms and may motivate either legal prohibition or other evolutionary disabilities not considered in this model.

Acknowledgments

We would like to thank Avner Ben-Ner, Robert Boyd, Minisk Choi, Vincent Crawford, Martin Daly, Paul David, Daniel Dennett, Marcus Feldman, Geoff Heal, Karla Hoff, Bruno Micone, Ugo Pagano, Louis Putterman, David Sloan Wilson, Elisabeth Wood, seminar participants at the University of Siena, the Centre d'Études Prospectives d'Économie Mathématique Appliquées à la Planification (CEPREMAP) and Stanford University, for comments on an earlier draft, Eric Verhoogen and Jeff Carpenter for research assistance, and the MacArthur Foundation for financial support.

Notes

1 Of course communities as we have defined them may obstruct efficiency-enhancing economic arrangements and can persist nonetheless. See for example Platteau (1996).

2 The cultural transmission process may also be "conformist," whereby individuals copy cultural forms that have high frequency in the population. Key sources on cultural evolution are Cavalli-Sforza and Feldman (1981), and Boyd and Richerson (1985).

3 We provide an information theoretic account of the capacities and shortcomings of markets, states, and communities in Bowles and Gintis (1999). See also Farrell (1987).

4 The second requirement simply precludes the social optimality of alternating roles of defector and cooperator. Cooperation is universally pro-social only if we also have $a+d > 2c$, though we will not need this fact.

5 Note that our support equilibria with positive frequencies of pro-social traits in the absence of conformist cultural transmission. There is good reason to think that both conformism and group selection may contribute to the evolution of pro-social traits (Wilson 1980, Boyd and Richerson 1990, Soltis, Boyd and Richerson 1995, Wilson and Sober 1994). Our models investigate cases where these forces are not operative.

Our model of parochialism is thus in the spirit of a suggestion by Hamilton (1975) that altruistic traits may proliferate in a single group due to the tendency for genetic relatedness to increase over time in the absence of significant in-migration.

6 This framework draws on the sources mentioned in note 2. Others defining culture often stress aspects absent here, such as the functional or legitimating role of culture, its integrated nature and its grounding in historical tradition.

7 Of course the structure of cultural transmission under which human societies acquire cultural traits is itself the result of both genetic and cultural evolutionary processes. For this reason the transmission processes postulated must be capable of reproducing themselves. We do not explore this question here.

8 This framework is derived from the models of cultural evolution cited above, but it is also consistent with a variety of other approaches. See, for instance, Bandura (1977).

9 We assume the population is sufficiently large that we can treat p_x and r_x as real numbers.

10 This treatment of inspection and trust is adapted from Güth and Kliemt (1994). The dynamics of this model are more fully explored in Bowles and Gintis (1997).

11 We will assume that number x of players is sufficiently large that we can treat x as a continuous real variable. In particular, we assume any Nash equilibrium can be supported by all players choosing the appropriate pure strategies, and we will allow functions of x to be continuous over the positive real numbers.

12 For completeness we should also deal with the case where only Inspect and Defect strategies are used with positive probability. If Inspect is used with probability $\alpha^* > 0$ then Defect must be used with the strictly positive probability $1 - \alpha^*$ in equilibrium. Since the payoff to Defect is c, the expected payoff to Inspect must also be c. Thus this equilibrium produces no social benefits over the universal Defect equilibrium. Such an equilibrium can be shown to be unstable under a replicator dynamic, so it will not be observed in practice (Bowles and Gintis 1997). We will not consider this equilibrium further.

13 This game is also called a "stag hunt," after a parable given by J.-J. Rousseau (1987[1755]).

14 For example, if a group is the "offspring" of those sharing a trait, and if vertical transmission of cultural traits from parents is substantial, the groups will be relatively homogeneous by comparison to the larger population.

15 The pairing rule and σ might evolve under group selection pressures, because group-average benefits will covary with σ, though not necessarily monotonically for plausible cases. We do not explore this possibility here.

16 The condition for stability given in Section 14.4 requires that the denominator of the above expression be negative, requiring for $\alpha > 0$ that the numerator be also negative, the intuition behind this result being clear from the vertical intercepts of the payoff functions in Figure 14.8. Stability obtains when the reward from unilateral defection $(a - b)$ is larger than the penalty of cooperating against a defector $(d - c)$.

17 For simplicity of exposition, we assume the general population is sufficiently larger than the community in question that we can consider $\bar{\tau}$ to be unaffected by migration.

18 It may occur that the equilibria coincide.

References

Axelrod, Robert (1984) *The Evolution of Cooperation*. New York: Basic Books.

—— and William D. Hamilton (1981) The evolution of cooperation. *Science* 211: 1390–1396.

Bandura, Albert (1977) *Social Learning Theory*. Englewood Cliffs, NJ: Prentice Hall.

Bowles, Samuel (1996) *Markets as cultural institutions: equilibrium norms in competitive economies*. University of Massachusetts Discussion Paper.

—— and Herbert Gintis (1976) *Schooling in Capitalist America: Educational Reform and the Contradictions of Economic Life.* New York: Basic Books.

—— and —— (1997) *Optimal Parochialism: the Dynamics of Trust and Exclusion in Communities.* University of Massachusetts Working Paper.

—— and —— (1998) *Recasting Egalitarianism: New Rules for Markets, States, and Communities.* London: Verso.

Boyd, Robert and Peter J. Richerson (1985) *Culture and the Evolutionary Process.* Chicago: University of Chicago Press.

—— and —— (1990) Group selection among alternative evolutionarily stable strategies. *Journal of Theoretical Biology* 145: 331–342.

Boyer, Paul and Stephen Nissenbaum (1974) *Salem Possessed: The Social Origins of Witchcraft.* Cambridge, MA: Harvard University Press.

Cavalli-Sforza, Luigi L. and Marcus W. Feldman (1981) *Cultural Transmission and Evolution.* Princeton: Princeton University Press.

Burke, Edmund [1955] *Reflections on the Civil War in France.* New York: Bobbs-Merrill.

Farrell, Joseph (1987) Information and the Coase theorem. *Journal of Economic Perspectives* 1(2): 112–129.

Festinger, Leon (1957) *A Theory of Cognitive Dissonance.* Stanford: Stanford University Press.

Flannery, Kent, Joyce Marcus and Robert Reynolds (1989) *The Flocks of the Wamani: A Study of Llama Herders on the Puntas of Ayacucho, Peru.* San Diego: Academic Press.

Fromm, Erich and Michael Maccoby (1970) *Social Character in a Mexican Village: A Sociopsychoanalytic Study.* Englewood Cliffs: Prentice Hall.

Fudenberg, Drew and Eric Maskin (1986) The folk theorem in repeated games with discounting or with incomplete information *Econometrica* 54(3): 533–554.

Geertz, Clifford (1963) *Peddlers and Princes: Social Change and Economic Modernization in Two Indonesian Towns.* Chicago: University of Chicago Press.

Gintis, Herbert (1975) Welfare economics and individual development: a reply to Talcott Parsons. *Quarterly Journal of Economics* 89(2): 291–302.

—— (1989) The power to switch: on the political economy of consumer sovereignty. In Samuel Bowles, Richard C. Edwards and William G. Shepherd (eds) *Unconventional Wisdom: Essays in Honor of John Kenneth Galbraith.* New York: Houghton-Mifflin.

—— (1997) A Markov model of production, trade, and money: theory and artificial life simulation *Computational and Mathematical Organization Theory* 3(1): 19–41.

Grafen, Alan (1979) The hawk-dove game played between relatives. *Animal Behavior* 27(3): 905–907.

—— (1984) Natural selection, kin selection, and group selection. In J.R. Krebs and N.B. Davies (eds) *Behavioral Ecology: An evolutionary Approach.* Sunderland, MA: Sinauer.

Güth, Werner and Harmutt Kliemt (1994) Competition or co-operation: on the evolutionary economics of trust, exploitation, and moral attitudes. *Metroeconomica* 45(2): 155–187.

Hamilton, W.D. (1975) Innate social aptitudes of man: an approach from evolutionary genetics. In Robin Fox (ed.) *Biosocial Anthropology.* New York: John Wiley and Sons.

Harding, Susan (1978) Street shouting and shunning: conflict between women in a Spanish village. *Frontiers* III(3): 14–18.

Jenness, Diamond (1991) *Arctic Odyssey : the Diary of Diamond Jenness, Ethnologist with the Canadian Arctic Expedition in Northern Alaska and Canada, 1913-1916.* Hull, Quebec: Canadian Museum of Civilization.

Kelly, Raymond C. (1985) *The Nuer Conquest: The Structure and Development of an Expansionist System.* Ann Arbor: University of Michigan Press.

Kohn, Melvin (1969) *Class and Conformity.* Homewood, IL: Dorsey Press.

Kreps, David M. (1990) Corporate culture and economic theory. In James Alt and Kenneth Shepsle (eds) *Perspectives on Positive Political Economy.* Cambridge: Cambridge University Press.

LeVine, Robert A. (1966) *Dreams and Deeds: Achievement Motivation in Nigeria.* Chicago: University of Chicago Press.

Light, Ivan, Im Jung Kwuon and Deng Zhong (1990) Korean rotating credit associations in Los Angeles. *Amerasia* 16(1): 35–54.

Malinowski, Bronislaw (1926) *Crime and Custom in Savage Society*. London: Routledge & Kegan Paul.

Platteau, Jean-Philippe (1996) Traditional sharing norms as an obstacle to economic growth in tribal societies. *Cahiers de la Faculté des Sciences Economiques et Sociales, Facultés Universitaires Notre-Dame de la Paix* 173: 201–223.

Quah, D. (1996) *The Invisible Hand and the Weightless Economy*. Centre for Economic Performance, London School of Economics.

Rousseau, Jean-Jacques [1987] Discourse on the origin and foundations of inequality among men. In Donald A. Cress (ed.) *Basic Political Writings*. Indianapolis: Hackett Publishing Company.

Sen, Amartya K. (1967) Isolation, assurance, and the social rate of discount. *Quarterly Journal of Economics* 81: 1112–1124.

Shapiro, Carl (1983) Premiums for high quality products as returns to reputations. *Quarterly Journal of Economics* 659–679.

Soltis, Joseph, Robert Boyd and Peter Richerson (1995) Can group-functional behaviors evolve by cultural group selection. *Current Anthropology* 36(3): 473–483.

Taylor, Michael (1987) *The Possibility of Cooperation*. Cambridge: Cambridge University Press.

de Tocqueville, Alexis [1958] *Democracy in America*. Volume II. New York: Vintage.

Weber, Eugen (1976) *Peasants into Frenchmen: The Modernization of Rural France, 1870-1914*. Stanford: Stanford University Press.

Weibull, Jörgen W. (1995) *Evolutionary Game Theory*. Cambridge, MA: MIT Press.

Wilson, David Sloan (1980) *The Natural Selection of Populations and Communities*. Menlo Park, CA: Benjamin Cummings.

—— and Elliott Sober (1994) "Reintroducing group selection to the human behavioral sciences. *Behavior and Brain Sciences* 17: 585–654.

15 Cooperation and exclusion in networks

Samuel Bowles and Herbert Gintis

15.1 Introduction

Formally structured nonmarket institutions, such as firms, clubs, partnerships, and families, have been the subject of extensive study by contemporary economists. More diffuse social affiliations, such as those arising from close-knit residential relationships, "old boy" networks, and ethnic or religious identity, have received less attention. We will call these *networks*, defined as sets of agents engaged in relatively frequent, non-anonymous interactions structured by high entry and exit costs.[1] In contrast to economists, biologists have given extensive attention to networks – they are variously called "flocks," "packs," "schools," "bands" or, generically, "groups" – (Wilson 1975, Grafen 1984, Pulliam and Caraco 1984, Kramer 1985, Kramer 1985, Packer and Ruttan 1988), and compelling reasons have been offered for their evolutionary viability based on the advantages that small size and homogeneity may have in promoting group beneficial behaviors (Hamilton 1975, Wilson and Dugatkin 1997). We seek to develop this reasoning for the case of human networks.

Networks support interpersonal interactions that promote the informal enforcement of incomplete contracts. Examples include the management of common pool resources such as fisheries, irrigation, and pasturage (Ostrom, Gardner and Walker 1994, Wade 1987, Baland and Platteau 1997), the regulation of work effort in producer cooperatives (Whyte 1955, Homans 1961, Lawler 1973, Craig and Pencavel 1992, 1995), the enforcement of non-collateralized credit contracts (Hossain 1988, Udry 1993, Banerjee, Besley and Guinnane 1994) the promotion of neighborhood amenities in residential communities (Sampson, Raudenbush and Earls 1997), and the private enforcement of contracts among traders in securities (Baker 1984) and diamonds (Bernstein 1992) markets.

As these examples suggest, we view networks as governance institutions that often provide solutions to otherwise intractable problems of contractual incompleteness. This view contrasts with the more common representation of ethnic, religious, and other groups as expressions of underlying shared values, often termed "particularistic," in contrast to the more "universalistic" values underpinning market transactions and liberal polities (Parsons 1964). According to this conventional view, the exclusionary values that often maintain group boundaries and restrict membership typically also restrict exchange, and thus impose allocative inefficiencies on their members. For this reason, networks and their frequently associated values of loyalty to insiders, close personal interaction, and xenophobia are often seen as vestigial remnants of "traditional" society, whose importance will ebb under the competitive pressures of a market economy.

However, while members of networks typically share some common values, and while these ingroup values often inhibit trade with outsiders, members of exclusionary networks often do quite well economically, counter to the standard prediction. Moreover, far from being inertial remnants of the past, groups that have prospered for generations may disperse rapidly, while newly-formed groups can be quite successful, as the flourishing informal ethnic business linkages among new immigrants to the United States and the United Kingdom attest.[2] For instance, Cambodians run more than 80 per cent of California's doughnut shops. They often raise startup funds by forming credit associations of friends and family to pool resources, the member offering to pay the highest interest rate receiving as a loan the sum of the individual contributions (Kaufman 1995). Similarly, Indians own more than a third of the motels in the United States, frequently raising initial capital through unsecured loans from extended family members (Woodyard 1995).

Among the problem-solving capacities of networks are the powerful contractual enforcement mechanisms made possible by small-scale interactions, notably effective retaliation facilitated by close social ties and the availability of low cost information concerning one's trading partners. This problem-solving capacity allows successful networks to overcome the disabilities imposed by the restricted gains from trade due to small size and exclusionary practices.[3] Members, of course, do not normally express their identification with groups in terms of their economic advantages, typically invoking noninstrumental values, such as religious faith, ethnic purity, the natural order of things, or personal loyalty. These sentiments often support exclusion or shunning of outsiders. We model these practices, which we term *parochialism*, in Section 15.2.

The mechanism for the success of networks explored in this chapter is their ability to promote *trust*.[4] We consider a large population of identical agents who take three types of actions. First, they locate in one of a variable number of networks, or remain outside any network in what we will call the "Walrasian pool" of anonymous traders. Second, they choose strategies that govern their behavior with trading partners. Third, they update these strategies in light of their relative payoff compared to other available trading strategies. Network size and the number of networks are governed by a gravity model in which individuals move according to payoff differentials. We explore the evolution and equilibrium frequency of behaviors within networks, the distribution of population between networks and the Walrasian pool, and the size and number of networks, under the influence of parochial practices.

In Section 15.3 we develop a model with incomplete contracts among self-regarding agents. We use this model to analyze the conditions under which trust may represent an equilibrium strategy. We formalize the effects of variations in network size on such a "trust equilibrium" in Section 15.4. We analyze optimal network size (i.e. that which maximizes the benefits to members) in Section 15.5.

The size and number of networks in equilibrium is then determined by the degree of openness of networks to new members, as well as the rate of creation and dissolution of networks.[5] We show in Section 15.6 that parochial practices resulting in excluding people from networks may implement an optimal network size. We then investigate the conditions under which parochialism remains viable in a competitive economic system, and we conclude by considering the likely future economic importance of networks in light of our results.

15.2 Parochialism

The desire to associate with others who are similar to oneself in some salient respect is a robust behavioral regularity (Homans 1961, Thibaut and Kelly 1959). Homophily, the principle that likes attract, has been documented in a variety of experimental and natural settings (Lazarsfeld and Merton 1954). Among the salient characteristics on which homophily operates are race and ethnic identification, personality characteristics, political orientation, drug use and other forms of deviant behavior, religion and even experimentally induced trivial similarities (Berscheid and Walster 1969, Cohen 1977, Kandel 1978, Tajfel, Billig, Bundy and Flament 1971, Obot 1988). Conversely, people seek to avoid interactions with those who are different from themselves.

Individuals implement their desires to limit social distance in their interactions with friends, neighbors, co-workers, and business associates by means of what we term parochial practices. These practices may take the form of shunning, refusal to trade or to extend friendship, verbal or physical assaults or other behaviors that preclude ongoing interaction. Members of networks often adopt parochial practices with the result that networks are more homogeneous and/or smaller than they would otherwise be.

The restrictions on matching for purposes of trade or production imposed by these exclusionary practices foster allocational distortions that, *ceteris paribus*, lower the returns to members of parochial networks. But in some cases, small size or homogeneity may offer offsetting gains. Highly exclusive communities such as the Pennsylvania Amish and the Canadian Hutterites have expanded their numbers and thrived economically.[6] Among the Amish, for example, distinctive dress, dialect, and technology construct a "cultural moat" around the group and, acting as "armaments of defense, they draw boundary lines between church and world [to] announce Amish identity to insider and outsider alike." (Kraybill 1989: 50,68). Yet the boundaries erected around Amish culture have not prevented economic success and population growth. Further, the record of successful ethnic business affiliations suggests that parochialism may not only foreclose opportunities, but also contribute to the success of groups.[7]

What might these gains be? Suppose, for instance, that individuals with differing ascriptive traits embody complementary productive inputs so that group heterogeneity is favored by the production function, but these positive effects of heterogeneity are partially offset by the increased cost of enforcing incomplete contracts among heterogeneous agents, perhaps due to the lack of a common normative framework, less accurate information transfer, or the reduced sanctioning power of social ostracism. By promoting group homogeneity, parochial exclusion might then enhance the return to group members, despite the losses associated with foregone trade opportunities. Here the key variable would be heterogeneity rather than size, which will play the central role in the model we develop below.

We model parochialism as a filter on given ascriptive traits of those with whom one might interact, a particular form of parochialism excluding those with "objectionable" traits.[8] Individuals who do not exclude those with "objectionable" traits are also objectionable, even if their traits *per se* are not objectionable.[9] Thus any parochialism filter different from one's own is assumed to be "objectionable" so networks will made up of individuals with the same type of parochialism; however different they are in other respects (for example, pursuing different strategies in economic interactions, or differing in a trait not covered by the parochialism filter) they will agree on the common traits for which their parochialism selects.

Suppose in pairwise strategic interactions, agents can condition their actions on whether the other player is an "insider" or an "outsider." Suppose each individual has a certain set of traits (ethnicity, language, physical attributes, cultural or demographic characteristics, and the like), which we take to be fixed. We label these "traits" $j = 1, \ldots, n$, each individual being characterized by a trait profile $a = a_1 \ldots a_n$, where each $a_j = 1$ or $a_j = 0$ according as the individual does or does not possess trait j. Let A be the set of all possible trait profiles. We say an agent with trait profile $a \in A$ is *b-compatible* for $b \in A$ if, for all $j = 1, \ldots, n$, we have $b_j \leq a_j$. We say an agent is *b-parochial* for trait profile $b \in A$ if (a) the agent is b-compatible, and (b) the agent treats another player as an outsider if this player is either not b-compatible, or is b-compatible but treats some non-b-compatible agents as insiders; otherwise the agent consider the other player to be an insider. In effect, b-parochial agents choose a subset of the traits they possesses (the unit-entries in b that are also unit-entries in a), and consider as insiders exactly those agents who have these traits and are "like-minded" in the sense that they have the same criteria for distinguishing between insiders and outsiders.

To simplify our analysis, we assume throughout that if an agent is b-parochial, it is common knowledge that he is b-parochial.

This formalization reflects our view that the immense variety of noticeable individual differences and similarities is the raw material on which parochialism works. A particular b-parochialism makes some subset of these differences behaviorally salient while ignoring others. For instance, suppose the array of traits are ("female,""French speaking"). An agent with characteristics $a = 11$ is a female Francophone. Such an individual could be b-parochial for $b = 11$ (insiders are like-minded female Francophones), $b = 01$ (insiders are like-minded Francophones), $b = 10$ (insiders are like-minded females), or $b = 00$ (insiders are like-minded – i.e. they treat all others as insiders).

We use this representation to model the effects of parochialism on the central problem a group faces: how to solve coordination problems under conditions of contractual incompleteness. We turn now to this problem.

	Inspect	Trust	Defect
Inspect	$b-\delta, b-\delta$	$b-\delta, b$	$c-\delta, c$
Trust	$b, b-\delta$	b, b	d, a
Defect	$c, c-\delta$	a, d	c, c

Figure 15.1 The inspect-trust-defect game

15.3 Trust in networks

To model the population of traders, consider a game G where many agents are randomly paired to play a one-shot prisoner's dilemma in which each receives c if they both defect, each receives b if they both cooperate, and a defector receives a when playing against a cooperator, who receives d. The assumptions of the prisoner's dilemma then require $a > b > c > d$ and $2b > a + d$.[10] The coordination failure underpinning the prisoner's dilemma structure of this interaction arises because some aspects of the goods or services being exchanged are not subject to costlessly enforceable contracts. The Defect strategy, for example could represent supplying shoddy goods where product quality is not subject to contract.

We assume each agent precommits to following one of three available "norms." The first, which we call *Defect*, is to defect unconditionally against all partners. The second, which we call *Trust*, is to cooperate unconditionally against all partners. The third, which we call *Inspect*, is to incur an inspecting cost $\delta > 0$ which reveals whether the agent's partner defects against cooperators, then to defect if the answer is "yes" and cooperate otherwise.[11] The payoff matrix for a pair of agents has the normal form shown in Figure 15.1.

Definition We call a Nash equilibrium a *universal defect equilibrium* if all agents Defect, a *nontrust equilibrium* if some agents Inspect but no agent Trusts, and a *trust equilibrium* if at least one agent Trusts. This classification exhausts all types of Nash equilibria.

Let α_t and β_t be the fraction of the population playing Inspect and Trust at time t, respectively.[12] Let π_I^t, π_T^t, and π_D^t be the return to the strategies Inspect, Trust, and Defect at time t, respectively, against the mixed strategy given by (α_t, β_t). Then we have

$$\pi_I^t = \alpha_t b + \beta_t b + (1 - \alpha_t - \beta_t)c - \delta \quad (15.1)$$

$$\pi_T^t = \alpha_t b + \beta_t b + (1 - \alpha_t - \beta_t)d \quad (15.2)$$

$$\pi_D^t = \alpha_t c + \beta_t a + (1 - \alpha_t - \beta_t)c \quad (15.3)$$

$$\bar{\pi}^t = \alpha_t \pi_I^t + \beta_t \pi_T^t + (1 - \alpha_t - \beta_t)\pi_D^t. \quad (15.4)$$

where $\bar{\pi}^t$ is the average payoff in the game. To reduce notational clutter, we normalize the payoffs so that $d = 0$.

Suppose in every period, with probability $p_i > 0$, an agent using strategy i encounters another randomly chosen agent, compares his strategy with the other's, and changes to the other's strategy if it is perceived to have higher payoff. However information concerning the difference in the expected payoffs of the two strategies is imperfect, so the larger the difference in the payoffs, the more likely the agent is to perceive it, and change. If the probability of perceiving a difference in expected payoffs is proportional to the size of the difference (with proportionality constant q), then the differential equations governing the system follow a *replicator dynamic*, given by

$$\frac{d\alpha_t}{dt} = \gamma_\alpha \alpha_t(\pi_I^t - \bar{\pi}^t) \tag{15.5}$$

$$\frac{d\beta_t}{dt} = \gamma_\beta \beta_t(\pi_T^t - \bar{\pi}^t), \tag{15.6}$$

where $\gamma_\alpha = p_\alpha q$ and $\gamma_\beta = p_\beta q > 0$.[13] We then have

Theorem 3 Taxonomy of equilibrium. *The following hold for the game G:*

(a) There is a locally stable universal defect equilibrium.

(b) In any Nash equilibrium other than universal defect, there is a strictly positive rate of Inspection and a strictly positive rate of Defection.

(c) There exist at most one trust equilibrium.

Proof: The proof of (a), which is intuitively obvious, is in Appendix B. To show (b), note that for any population from which Inspectors are absent, Defect strictly dominates Trust, while for any population from which Defectors are absent Trust strictly dominates Inspect. Thus if any non-Defectors are present in an equilibrium some must be Inspectors, and Defectors cannot be absent. Part (c) is demonstrated in the course of proving of Theorem 4.

Definition We call the inequality

$$\delta < c\left(1 - \frac{c}{b}\right) \tag{15.7}$$

the *efficient inspecting condition* for game G. Notice that for payoff to mutual defect (c) sufficiently close to the payoff to mutual cooperate (b), the efficient inspecting condition fails. The relevance of this condition is clear from

Theorem 4 Trust equilibrium. *The following hold for the game G:*

(a) There is a trust equilibrium if and only if the efficient inspecting condition holds.

(b) The efficient inspecting condition holds if and only if the payoff to the trust equilibrium strategy profile is greater than the payoff in the universal defect equilibrium.

(c) In the trust equilibrium the frequency of Defection is an increasing function of the inspecting cost.

(d) *In the trust equilibrium, the payoff to the agents is a decreasing function of the inspecting cost.*

(e) *The trust equilibrium is locally stable for a sufficiently small inspecting cost.*[14]

Proof: To prove (a), suppose there is a trust equilibrium. Then we know from Theorem 3b that all three strategies are used with positive probability. Since the payoffs to all pure strategies must be equal, using (15.1)-(15.3) we find the equilibrium frequencies of Inspect and Trust, respectively:

$$\alpha = \frac{(a-b)\left(1-\frac{\delta}{c}\right)+\delta}{a-c}, \tag{15.8}$$

$$\beta = \frac{b\left(1-\frac{\delta}{c}\right)-c}{a-c}. \tag{15.9}$$

These equations also give the frequency of defection as

$$1-\alpha-\beta = \frac{\delta}{c}, \tag{15.10}$$

from which $\delta < c$ follows, since there must be a positive level of all strategies. Now $\beta < 1$ also follows from (15.10) and Theorem 3b. Since $0 < \beta$, we must have

$$\delta < c\left(1-\frac{c}{b}\right)$$

by (15.9), which is just the efficient inspecting inequality. Then $\alpha > 0$ follows from (15.8). Thus the existence of a trust equilibrium implies that the efficient inspecting inequality holds. But clearly the above argument can be reversed, which proves Theorem (4a). Note also that as (15.8) and (15.9) uniquely determine α and β, there are no other trust equilibria. This proves Theorem (3c), as promised.

Now equation (15.10) shows that the frequency of Defect in a trust equilibrium is δ/c, which proves (4c).

To prove (4d), note that the expected payoff to Trust is just b, the mutual cooperate payoff, times the probability $\alpha+\beta$ of meeting either a Truster or an Inspector (a Truster meeting a Defector has a zero payoff), so using (15.10), in the trust equilibrium the payoff to all agents must be

$$b(\alpha+\beta) = b\left(1-\frac{\delta}{c}\right), \tag{15.11}$$

which is decreasing in the inspecting cost δ, and is greater than the payoff c to the universal defect equilibrium if and only if the efficient enforcement condition holds, proving (4b). Part (4e) is proved in Appendix B. ■

The left-hand side of Figure 15.2 shows a phase diagram in barycentric coordinates of the equilibrium and dynamic properties of the model for a set of parameters, with a trust equilibrium at T, a nontrust equilibrium at C, and a universal defect equilibrium at D.[15] The basin of attraction for the trust equilibrium

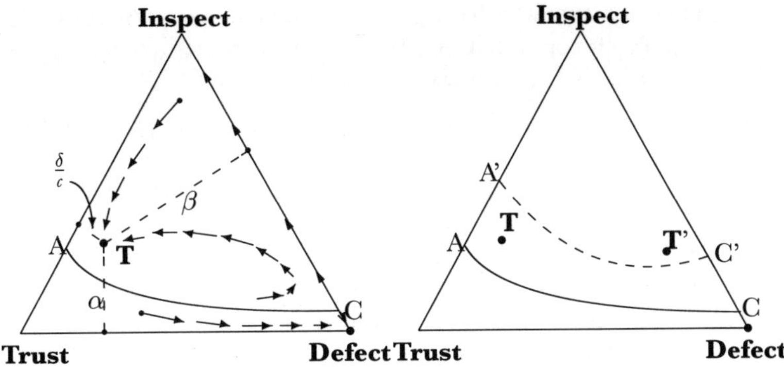

Figure 15.2 Trust and universal defect equilibria (left) and the effects of an increase in the inspecting cost (right). The frequency of Inspect, Trust, and Defect are α, β and δ/c respectively. In the left-hand diagram we have set $a = 1.0$, $b = 0.70$, $c = 0.20$, $d = 0$ and $\delta = 0.02$. The trust equilibrium is at T, with an equilibrium consisting of $\delta/c = 10.0\%$ Defectors, $\alpha = 36.25\%$ Inspectors, and $\beta = 53.75\%$ Trusters. The nontrust equilibrium is at C with $\alpha = 0.04$. The efficient inspection condition holds, as $0.20(1 - 0.20/0.70) > 0.02$. The line AC separating the basins of attraction of the trust and defect equilibria assumes there are no limit cycles and the trust equilibrium is depicted as a stable node, though it could be a stable focus.
In the right-hand diagram we have increased δ from 0.02 to 0.12. The trust equilibrium is now at T', with 60% Defectors, 30% Inspectors, and 10% Trusters. The efficient inspection condition still holds. The nontrust equilibrium is at C', where $\alpha = 24\%$. We continue to assume there are no limit cycles. Note that an increase in the inspecting cost δ moves the trust and nontrust equilibria closer together. It is easy to show that they coincide in the limiting case where the efficient inspecting conditions holds as an equality.

lies above the line AC, and the basin of attraction of the universal defect equilibrium lies below this line. We have indicated two paths to equilibrium in the diagram.

On the right-hand side of Figure 15.2 we show the effect of an increase in the inspecting cost, namely an increase in the frequency of Defect and a reduction in the size of the basin of attraction of the trust equilibrium.[16]

15.4 The benefits and costs of networks

Theorem 4 illustrates an important attribute of the network as a structure of economic governance: the personal and repeated interactions characteristic of networks may facilitate the informal enforcement of contracts. Yet the small-group interactions that permit agents to address problems of contractual incompleteness may limit access to gains from trade that are possible when exchanges are not confined within network boundaries. McMillan and Woodruff's study of trust among businesses in Vietnam suggests the salience of this tradeoff:

> Trading relations in Vietnam's emerging private sector are shaped by two market frictions: the difficulty of locating trading partners and the absence of formal third party enforcement of contracts. . . . firms able to resolve the

> difficulties of more specialized production and/or more distant trade grow more rapidly. By contrast, buying from suppliers managed by family members or friends involves fewer contracting problems.
>
> (McMillan and Woodruff 1966: 23)

We model this tradeoff between the enforcement benefits and foregone gains from trade in this section, extending the results of Theorems 3 and 4 by exploring the effect of the size x on the equilibrium payoff structure.

To do this we consider one (of many) networks in a large population, some members of which belong to no network and trade in the Walrasian pool. Agents trading in the Walrasian pool have no means of informal enforcement and hence receive the defect-defect payoff c, independent of the size of the pool. For agents trading within a network, however, both the cost of inspection $\delta(x)$ and the probability $p(x)$ of meeting a trading partner will be considered increasing functions of network size x. We consider $\delta(x)$ increasing because in a larger network it will be more costly to discover the trading type of one's partners, while $p(x)$ is increasing because a larger number of participants increases the probability of meeting a potentially mutually beneficial trading partner.

To specify the shape of $\delta(x)$, we have

Theorem 5 Network size and inspecting cost. *Consider a network of x individuals each of whom knows the type of κ other members of the network. Suppose member i seeks a member who knows the type of a specific member j of the network. We assume an individual who knows the type of another individual will always reveal it truthfully. Let $\delta(x)$ be cost of learning the type of individual j (the same for all j), which we assume is a convex function of the expected number of individuals that must be queried before encountering a member who knows the type of j. Then $\delta(x)$ is a convex function of x.*

Proof: Let r_x be the expected number of individuals that must be interrogated before an "outsider" encounters a member who knows j's type, when the network size is $x+\kappa \geq \kappa$. We show in Appendix B that $r_x = 1 + x/(\kappa+1)$ for $x \geq 0$. It follows that in a network of size x, an individual will query, on average $r_x - 1 = x/(\kappa+1)$ others to find someone who knows a given individual. Since $\delta(x)$ is a convex function of the increasing linear function $r_x - 1$, it follows that $\delta(x)$ is convex. ∎

To specify the shape of $p(x)$, suppose agents produce goods for trade in the morning, and take them to market for trade in the afternoon. Goods are perishable, and cannot be stored by consumers. Suppose there are x agents in the network, and there are goods $1, \ldots, k$, corresponding to which there are "marketplaces" that have exogenously given relative sizes $f_1, \ldots, f_k$ ($\sum_i f_i = 1$). Marketplace i thus has absolute size $x_i = f_i x$ for $i = 1, \ldots, k$. The members who are to compose this x_i are assigned randomly at the start of the trading period. Each agent decides with equal probability to be a buyer or a seller that period. Buyers and sellers in the same marketplace are randomly paired, and if the number of buyers and sellers differ, a random selection of agents will make no trade at all, and as a result receives a payoff of zero.[17]

At the marketplace for good i, the number ξ_i of buyers and the number χ_i of sellers are independently distributed binomial random variables with mean $x_i/2$ and variance $x_i/8$. The expected number of agents not finding a trade is thus $E[|x_i - \chi_i|]$, where the expectation is with respect to the product distribution. We have

Theorem 6 Gains to network size. *Let $p(x)$ be the probability of making a trade when network size is x. Then $p(x)$ is increasing, concave, and approaches unity for large x.*

The proof is in Appendix B.

These considerations motivate the following

Definition Consider the game G' that differs from the game G in two ways. First, the payoff to the prisoner's dilemma stage game is the payoff in G multiplied by $p(x)$, which is a non-negative, strictly concave, strictly increasing, bounded, differentiable function of network size x. We will assume that $p(\infty) = 1$, and there is a minimum network size, $x_{min} > 0$, below which $p(x) = 0$, while $p(x_{min}) = p_{min} > 0$. Second, we assume the inspecting cost $\delta(x)$ is a nonnegative, convex, strictly increasing, differentiable function of network size. We call the game G' the *variable size network* game.

Appropriately modifying (15.11), we see that the payoff in a trust equilibrium in a network of size x is now

$$\bar{\pi}(x) = p(x)b(\alpha+\beta) = p(x)b\left(1 - \frac{\delta(x)}{c}\right). \tag{15.12}$$

We then have

Theorem 7 Optimal network size. *Suppose the efficient inspecting condition holds for $x = x_{min}$, and suppose $\delta'(x_{min})$ is sufficiently small. Then in the variable size network game we have:*

(a) There is a unique "optimal" network size $x^* > x_{min}$ that maximizes the per-agent payoff.

(b) The optimal network size supports a trust equilibrium.

(c) Optimal network size increases when the payoff to the universal defect equilibrium increases.

Note that at the optimal network size, the trust equilibrium may or may not be locally stable.

Proof: To prove (a), note that since (15.7) holds at $x = x_{min}$, we have $\bar{\pi}(x_{min}) > 0$. Differentiating (15.12), we get

$$\bar{\pi}_x = p'(x)b\left(1 - \frac{\delta(x)}{c}\right) - bp(x)\frac{\delta'(x)}{c}, \tag{15.13}$$

from which we see that $\bar{\pi}(x)$ is strictly increasing at $x = x_{min}$ if $\delta'(x_{min})$ is sufficiently small. Since $p(x)$ is bounded and $\delta(x)$ is increasing and convex, $\pi(x) < 0$ for sufficiently large x. This shows that (15.12) has an interior maximum $x^* > x_{min}$, where the first order condition

$$\bar{\pi}_x = 0 \tag{15.14}$$

holds. The first term on the right hand side of (15.13) is the marginal benefit to increased size and the second is the marginal cost. Equation (15.14) defines the optimal network size as that which equates the two marginal values.

It is easy to check that the concavity of $p(x)$ and the convexity of $\delta(x)$ ensure that $\pi_{xx} < 0$, so this optimum is a maximum and is unique (since two local maxima entail the existence of a local minimum which, given $\pi_{xx} < 0$, cannot exist). This proves (a).

By assumption the efficient inspecting condition holds at x_{min}. Since the efficient inspecting condition is equivalent to the payoff $\bar{\pi}$ in the trust equilibrium being greater than in the universal defect equilibrium, and since $\bar{\pi}(x)$ is increasing from x_{min} to x^*, it follows that the efficient inspecting condition holds at $x = x^*$, which proves (b).

Now differentiating (15.14) totally with respect to c, we get

$$\pi_{xx}\frac{dx}{dc} + \pi_{xc} = 0.$$

Since $\pi_{xc} = bc^2(p'(x) + p(x))/\delta'(x) > 0$, we have $dx/dc > 0$, proving (c). ■

15.5 The demographics of network size and market size

To this point we have explained the effects of exogenous variations in network size. But as agents may "migrate" in response to differential payoffs, we must now let variations in network size reflect the resulting migration flows.[18] To avoid unnecessary complications, we assume the same informational assumptions apply equally to old and new network members. In particular, immigrants know the types of others, and their types are known by others, with the same frequency as less recently arrived network members.

Suppose we have a number of networks, of sizes $x_1, \ldots, x_n$ (n may be variable over time), each in a locally stable trust equilibrium,[19] so the members of a network have payoffs given by (15.12). Suppose all agents not in a network fall into the Walrasian pool of size z. We assume z is sufficiently large that traders in the pool secure transactions with certainty, so all Walrasian traders receive the universal defect payoff c in each period.[20] However agents may migrate from the pool to the various networks according to a demographic dynamic in which the net movement is a function of the pre-migration size of the two populations and the difference between the payoffs to their members. Migration is proportional to the size of the Walrasian pool, and less than proportional to the size of the destination network. Thus net immigration into a network is given by[21]

$$m(x) = \gamma z(\bar{\pi}(x) - c). \tag{15.15}$$

The parameter $\gamma > 0$, which we call the *immigration coefficient*, reflects the sensitivity of immigration to the gains of network membership.[22]

We also assume that network members have a constant probability $\nu > 0$ of migrating spontaneously to the Walrasian pool. We justify this assumption by noting that the stochastic nature of a member's trading partners, and the fact that an agent has a positive probability of not securing a trade, ensure that some agents have a series of payoffs less than c, so such agents may reasonably consider migration to a secure c-payoff region (i.e., the Walrasian pool) to improve their expected future returns. Such agents may in fact be wrong, but they would be using the same adaptive learning mechanism that underlies the replicator dynamic itself – shifting strategies in response to experienced successes and failures. Moreover they may not be wrong, since their experience could equally well reflect that the network has drifted out of the basin of attraction of the trust equilibrium.[23]

The equation governing the expected size of a network is $dx/dt = m - \nu x$, or

$$\frac{dx}{dt} = \gamma z(\bar{\pi}(x) - c) - \nu x. \tag{15.16}$$

Equilibrium expected network size is that for which immigration and emigration are just offsetting, or $dx/dt = 0$, giving

$$\gamma z(\bar{\pi}(x) - c) = \nu x, \tag{15.17}$$

and the condition for stability of a network size equilibrium is that

$$\frac{\partial}{\partial x}\left(\frac{dx}{dt}\right)\bigg|_{\frac{dx}{dt}=0} < 0, \tag{15.18}$$

which requires that

$$\nu > \bar{\pi}'(x)\gamma z. \tag{15.19}$$

The point $\hat{x}$ in Figure 15.3 satisfies (15.17) and (15.19), and represents such a stable equilibrium. Over the interval $x \in (x', \hat{x})$ we have $dx/dt > 0$, with $dx/dt < 0$ for $x < x'$ or $x > \hat{x}$. Note that networks smaller than x' will lose population until they reach x_{min}, and then will disappear (because of our assumption that $p(x) = 0$ for $x < x_{min}$). Also $x = x''$ is the point where $\bar{\pi}(x) = c$. We have

Theorem 8 Equilibrium network size. *Suppose the conditions of Theorem 7 hold. Then there is a minimum immigration coefficient $\underline{\gamma}$ and an optimal immigration rate γ^* with the following properties:*

(a) There is no trust equilibrium with $\gamma < \underline{\gamma}$.

(b) For any $\gamma > \underline{\gamma}$, and for a sufficiently small inspecting cost, there is a trust equilibrium that is stable in the replicator dynamic.

(c) The equilibrium network size for γ^* is x^*, and for $\gamma \geq \gamma^*$ the trust equilibrium is stable in the migration dynamic for network size.

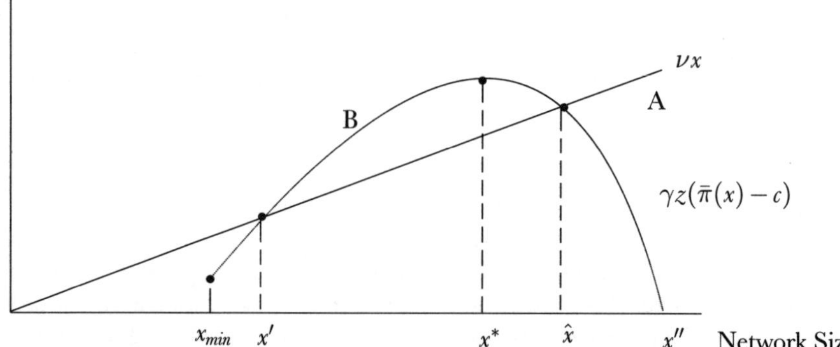

Figure 15.3 Optimal and equilibrium network size. A is the right-hand side of (15.17), and B is the left-hand side. Equilibrium network size is $\hat{x}$, which is stable because A is steeper than B at $\hat{x}$. Also x' is endpoint of the basin of attraction of $\hat{x}$.

The proof is in Appendix B. Intuitively, $\underline{\gamma}$ occurs in Figure 15.3 by shifting down curve B until it is tangent to curve A (or should no such tangency occur for $x > x_{min}$, until A intersects B at x_{min}). For γ less than this value there is no intersection of A and B and hence emigration exceeds immigration for all network sizes, which precludes a trust equilibrium. Increasing γ from $\underline{\gamma}$, curve B crosses curve A at x^*. At that point and for γ greater that this, curve A has a greater slope than the curve B, which means that (15.18) holds, so the equilibrium is stable.

We restrict ν to values such that for networks of optimal size the net migratory flow is inward, or $m(x^*) > \nu x^*$.

To model the dynamics and equilibrium conditions for the size of the Walrasian pool, we now treat the number n of networks as a continuous variable. We assume there is a probability $\tilde{\gamma}(x_k) > 0$ that an individual in network k will return to the pool because network k disbanded, perhaps because the network wandered into the basin of attraction of the universal defect equilibrium or fell below size x'_k through a series of adverse random shocks.[24] We assume $\tilde{\gamma}(x_k)$ is u-shaped, with a minimum at x^*_k, reflecting the fact that a higher expected payoff entails a deeper basin of attraction for x^*_k, thus making the equilibrium more robust in the face of a given series of shocks.

We assume also that random shocks within the Walrasian pool lead to the flow of individuals into newly-formed of networks at the rate $\gamma_z > 0$. Then the equation governing the expected size of the pool is

$$\frac{dz}{dt} = \sum_{k=1}^{n} [(\nu_k + \tilde{\gamma}(x_k))x_k - \gamma z(\bar{\pi}(x_k) - c)] - \gamma_z z,$$

where the first term in the summation represents the migration from networks to the Walrasian pool (by individual emigration and network dissolution), the second term in the summation represents the immigration to networks, and the final term represents new network formation.[25] In demographic equilibrium all networks are at equilibrium size, so from equations (15.17) and (15.22), this expression can be simplified to

$$\frac{dz}{dt} = \sum_{k=1}^{n} \tilde{\gamma}(x_k)x_k - \gamma_z z. \tag{15.20}$$

The equilibrium size of the Walrasian pool is thus given by

$$z = \frac{1}{\gamma_z}\sum_{k=1}^{n} \tilde{\gamma}(x_k)x_k. \tag{15.21}$$

15.6 Optimal parochialism

Theorem 8 shows that there is a close relationship between the viability of networks and the payoff to network membership, on the one hand, and the rate of immigration γ into the network, on the other. In equilibrium, network size is larger than optimal, so members of the network can clearly benefit from refusing membership to a certain fraction ρ of potential immigrants. We formalize this by defining the *degree of exclusiveness* of a network as the fraction $\rho \in (0, 1)$ of potential immigrants who will be excluded. We first assume exclusion is random across character traits, taking up parochial exclusion later. Hence if γ^o is the immigration coefficient assuming no exclusiveness, and if the degree of exclusiveness is ρ, then the immigration coefficient in (15.15) is given by

$$\gamma = \gamma^o(1-\rho), \tag{15.22}$$

and (15.15) becomes

$$m(x) = \gamma^o(1-\rho)z(\bar{\pi}(x) - c). \tag{15.23}$$

We then have

Theorem 9 Optimal exclusiveness. *Suppose the conditions of Theorem 7 hold, that $\nu x^* < m(x^*)$, and let $\hat{x}$ be the equilibrium network size in the absence of exclusiveness. Then there is a degree of exclusiveness ρ^* that maximizes the payoff to network members in a stable trust equilibrium. We call ρ^* the* optimal degree of exclusiveness.

Proof: When the network is in equilibrium without exclusiveness, (15.17) holds with $\gamma = \gamma^o$, so

$$\frac{\nu\hat{x}}{\gamma^o z(\bar{\pi}(x) - c)} = 1,$$

and for $\hat{x} > x^*$ the denominator of the left hand side of this equation is decreasing in x. Now $x^* < \hat{x}$ by our assumption that $\nu x^* < m(x^*)$, so

$$0 < \frac{\nu x^*}{\gamma^o z(\bar{\pi}(x^*) - c)} < 1, \tag{15.24}$$

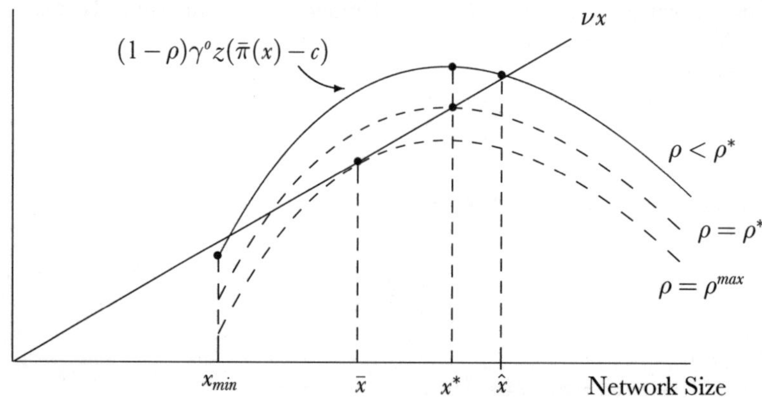

Figure 15.4 Exclusiveness and optimal network size. As the degree of exclusiveness increases from ρ to ρ^*, equilibrium network size falls from $\hat{x}$ to x^*. When the degree of exclusiveness reaches ρ^{max}, the network is no longer of a sustainable size.

so x^* cannot be an equilibrium. However there is some level of restriction on inflows, ρ, so that when we multiply the denominator of (15.24) by $(1-\rho)$, the equilibrium condition (15.17) holds. It can be readily seen that this value, ρ^*, is given by

$$\rho^* = 1 - \frac{\nu x^*}{\gamma^o z(\bar{\pi}(x^*) - c)}, \tag{15.25}$$

then the network is in equilibrium at size $x = x^*$. Because $\bar{\pi}'(x) = 0$ at x^*, (15.19) shows that the optimally exclusive equilibrium is stable. ■

Figure 15.4 depicts network size equilibrium as the equality of the two schedules $(1-\rho)\gamma^o z(\bar{\pi}(x)-c)$ and νx, the two terms in (15.17). An increase in exclusiveness shifts the first curve down proportionately, and the optimally exclusive solution occurs at x^*, so that net migration is negative to the right of x^* and positive to the left of x^*, the condition for stability (15.18) is satisfied.

The welfare properties of a demographic equilibrium for the entire population are explored in:

Theorem 10 A demographic equilibrium. *Suppose the conditions of Theorem 7 hold, networks are identical and they exhibit the same degree of exclusiveness ρ sufficient to sustain a stable trust equilibrium. Then in demographic equilibrium the following hold:*

(a) *The number z of agents in the Walrasian pool is strictly positive.*

(b) *For $\rho < \rho^*$, an increase in exclusiveness increases the payoff to network members, decreases equilibrium network size, and increases the fraction of agents in the population who are in networks.*

(c) *The condition $\rho = \rho^*$ is Pareto efficient in the sense that it jointly maximizes the payoff to network membership and the fraction of the population receiving the trust equilibrium payoff.*

Proof: Part (a) follows directly from (15.20), given that $\tilde{\gamma}(x_k) > 0$ for all k. For part (b), note first that by (15.17) and (15.22), equilibrium network size requires (dropping subscripts, since networks are identical),

$$(1-\rho)\gamma^{o}z(\bar{\pi}(x)-c)=\nu x.$$

Totally differentiating this equation with respect to ρ shows that $dx/d\rho < 0$ for $x > x^*$. This proves the first two assertions in (b). To prove the third assertion, notice that given exogenous variations in ρ and consequent changes in x, stationarity of z is achieved by the entry or exit of networks – that is, by varying n. Increased exclusiveness reduces network size and raise returns to members of networks, thus increasing the attractiveness of networks, while also rendering migration into networks more difficult. The net effect on the fraction of the population in networks is determined as follows.

To obtain an expression for n, we set $dz/dt = 0$ in (15.20), we see that in equilibrium new entrants to the Walrasian pool must be just offset by those exiting, or

$$n(\tilde{\gamma}(x)+\gamma_z)x=\gamma_z\bar{x}. \qquad (15.26)$$

Totally differentiating this expression with respect to ρ, we find

$$\frac{dn}{d\rho}(\tilde{\gamma}(x)+\gamma_z)x+n[(\tilde{\gamma}(x)+\gamma_z)+\tilde{\gamma}'(x)x]\frac{dx}{d\rho}=0.$$

Since $\tilde{\gamma}'(x) > 0$ and $dx/d\rho < 0$, this equation shows that $dn/d\rho > 0$. Also, from (15.26) we know that the number of agents in networks is

$$nx=\frac{\gamma_z\bar{x}}{\tilde{\gamma}(x)+\gamma_z},$$

so

$$\frac{d(nx)}{d\rho}=-\frac{\gamma_z\bar{x}}{(\tilde{\gamma}(x)+\gamma_z)^2}\tilde{\gamma}'(x)\frac{dx}{d\rho}$$

which is positive under the assumptions of the theorem. This proves part (b), from which part (c) is obvious. ■

It follows that barriers to entry may enhance welfare in the population as a whole, and that members of networks erecting barriers to entry may enjoy higher levels of well-being than those not in exclusive networks, thus supporting the persistence of exclusion even in highly competitive environments.[26]

These conclusions assume, of course, that exclusion is random rather than parochial. By contrast, let us suppose that the exclusiveness of a network derives from parochialism, so all newly created networks consist of b-parochial agents for some $b \in A$. The Trust and Inspect strategies analyzed in Section 15.3 now become "trust (resp. inspect) insiders (i.e., agents who are b-parochial) and defect on anyone else." It is clear that the analysis of Section 15.3 applies to this new situation without change. Moreover only b-parochial agents can gain by migrating to a b-parochial network. Hence a b-parochial network will remain uniformly b-parochial throughout its existence.

We can write the immigration coefficient for a b-parochial network as

$$\gamma_b = (1 - \rho_b)\gamma^o, \tag{15.27}$$

where γ^o is immigration coefficient that would obtain in the absence of exclusiveness, and the degree of parochialism ρ_b remains to be determined.

Because b-parochial networks exclude all who are not b-parochial, we have

$$\rho_b = 1 - g_b,$$

where g_b is the frequency of b-parochial agents in the Walrasian pool. Let $\bar{x}$ be the size of the population, so $\mu_z = z/\bar{x}$ is the fraction of the population in the Walrasian pool. Also let μ_b be the fraction of the population consisting of agents in b-parochial networks, and the f_b be the fraction of b-parochial agents in the population. We then have $\mu_b\bar{x} = f_b\bar{x} - g_b z = (f_b - g_b\mu_z)\bar{x}$, so $\mu_b = f_b - g_b\mu_z$. This gives $g_b = (f_b - \mu_b)/\mu_z$, so we have

$$\rho_b = 1 - g_b = 1 - \frac{f_b - \mu_b}{\mu_z}. \tag{15.28}$$

Since the degree of b-parochialism depends not only on the exogenously given fraction f_b of b-parochial agents in the population, but also the distribution of agents between b-parochial networks (μ_b) and the Walrasian pool (μ_z), which are endogenously determined, we must now analyze the population level equilibrium of the system.

We have

Theorem 11 Optimal parochialism *Suppose that there is but a single type of parochialism, b. Then Theorem 10 holds, where $\rho = \rho_b$ is given by (15.28). Moreover, if the frequency of b-types in the population satisfies*

$$f_b = \frac{\gamma_z}{\tilde{\gamma}(x) + \gamma_z} + \frac{\nu x^*}{\bar{x}\gamma^o(\bar{\pi}(x^*) - c)} \tag{15.29}$$

then b-parochialism supports optimal network size. We say that b is optimally parochial *in this case.*

Proof: The condition for equilibrium network size (15.17) can be rewritten

$$\frac{(1 - \rho_b)\gamma^o z}{\nu} = \frac{x}{\bar{\pi}(x) - c},$$

which, using the definition of ρ_b, now becomes

$$\frac{g_b\gamma^o z}{\nu} = \frac{x}{\bar{\pi}(x) - c}.$$

But $g_b z = (f_b - \mu_b)\bar{x}$, so this becomes

$$\frac{(f_b - \mu_b)\bar{x}\gamma^o}{\nu} = \frac{x}{\bar{\pi}(x) - c}. \tag{15.30}$$

Now in equilibrium, from (15.26) we have

$$\mu_b = \frac{nx}{\bar{x}} = \frac{\gamma_z}{\tilde{\gamma}(x) + \gamma_z}, \tag{15.31}$$

where n is the number of b-parochial networks with the trait.

Equations (15.30) and (15.31) yield the equilibrium condition

$$\frac{\bar{x}\gamma^o}{\nu}\left[f_b - \frac{\gamma_z}{\tilde{\gamma}(x) + \gamma_z}\right] = \frac{x}{\bar{\pi}(x) - c}. \tag{15.32}$$

The conclusion follows directly from this equation. ■

The intuition expressed by Theorem 11 is as follows. Consider a b-type who is unselective, say the $b = 00$ of the "female/French-speaking" example above, who excludes nobody as long as they are similarly non-exclusive. Suppose that most members of the population were of this type; then the implied degree of parochialism ρ_b would be insufficient to implement the optimal network size, while a more restrictive filter, say $b' = 01$ (only like-minded Francophones welcome) might do so. The existence of some approximately optimally parochial b is assured if we expand the trait space sufficiently.[27]

15.7 Conclusion

The fact that the exclusionary practices we have called "parochial" may implement a group size or, by extension, a degree of group homogeneity, that maximizes network members' benefits does not imply that these practices – often motivated by racial and ethnic hatred and religious intolerance – are socially desirable, of course. But it may help explain why groups and group identity remains such salient features even of societies whose competitive economies and liberal polities are widely thought to be hostile to parochial sentiment.

We have argued that networks have properties that allow them to persist in a market economy despite their relative inability to exploit economies of scale and the other efficiency-enhancing properties of markets. Among these properties, and the one explored in this chapter, is the capacity of networks to support enforcement of prosocial behavior among network members. Networks have this capacity by virtue of their ability to reduce information costs, thus permitting the emergence of "trusting" Nash equilibria that do not exist, or are unstable, when information costs are high. Our particular model of these relationships could readily be extended to capture other salient aspects of the determinants of network formation, parochial exclusion, and network extinction. For example, because parochialism makes networks not only smaller, but more homogeneous as well, corresponding efficiency enhancing effects of similarity or social affinity with parochial networks may be important.

The value of the informal contractual enforcement capacities of networks, the viability of networks, the optimal network size, and the optimal degree of parochialism all depend importantly on the nature of the goods and services that make up economic exchanges. Kollock (1994: 341) investigated "the structural origins of trust in a system of exchange" using an experimental design based on the exchange of goods of variable quality. He found that trust in and commitment to trading partners as well as a concern for ones own and others' reputations emerges when product quality is variable and non-contractible but not when it is contractible. These experimental results appear to capture some of the structure of actual exchanges. Siamwalla's (1978) study of marketing structures in Thailand contrasts the impersonal structure of the wholesale rice market, where the quality of the product is readily assayed by the buyer, with the personalized exchange based on trust in the raw rubber market, where quality is impossible to determine at the point of purchase. Thus, were technologies to evolve such that quality and quantity of the goods being transacted are readily subject to complete contracting, preferential trading within networks would be of little benefit and would likely be extinguished due to the implied foregone gains from trade. Conversely, were the economy to evolve in ways that heighten the problem of incomplete contracting we would expect to see growing economic importance of networks.

Applying this reasoning to our model, we consider the latter more likely. As production shifts from goods to services, and within services to information-related services (Quah 1996), and as team-based production methods increase in importance, the gains from cooperation will increase as well, because such activities involve relatively high monitoring costs, and hence are subject to costly forms of opportunism. If this is the case the benefits associated with the mutual defect payoff relative to the mutual cooperate outcome (c/b) will decline over time and a wider range of exchanges will thus satisfy the efficient inspection condition.[28] This in turn will support more extensive use of network based trust equilibria as a means of addressing contractual incompleteness.

Further, advances in communications technology arguably increase the number (κ) of acquaintances from whom we can gather information at limited cost, thus by Theorem 5, shifting downwards the inspecting cost schedule $\delta(x)$. The following are consequences: (i) the range of payoff structures for which the efficient inspecting condition holds and for which trust equilibria therefore exist is expanded, (ii) the basin of attraction of a trust equilibrium is expanded, and (iii) by Theorem 4, the average payoffs to members of a network of given size in a trust equilibrium increase compared with the payoffs obtained by traders in the Walrasian pool, and (iv) there is an increase in equilibrium network size (cf. Figure 15.3).

On the other hand the kinds of social exclusion motivating network-based parochialism often violate strongly held universalistic norms and may motivate either legal prohibition or other evolutionary disabilities not considered in this model.

A study of the evolution of parochial sentiments, which could be accomplished by endogenizing the parochialism filter, might yield useful insights, but is beyond the scope of this chapter.

Appendix A: A Non-Trust Equilibrium

Theorem 12 *There is a nontrust equilibrium if and only if the efficient inspecting condition holds. In this case the payoff to the agents is c, the same as in the case of the universal defect equilibrium. Thus in the nontrust equilibrium, all gains from Inspecting are dissipated by the inspecting cost. The nontrust equilibrium is not locally stable.*

Proof: Suppose the Inspect and Defect strategies are used with probabilities α and $1-\alpha$, respectively. The payoff to Inspect against this mixed strategy is $\alpha b+(1-\alpha)c-\delta=\alpha(b-c)+c-\delta$, and the payoff to Defect is c. Equating the two, we get

$$\alpha=\frac{\delta}{b-c}$$

which satisfies $\alpha<1$ as long as $\delta<b-c$. The payoff to Trust must be less than c in this case, so we must have $b\alpha<c$, which an algebraic manipulation shows is equivalent to the efficient inspecting condition. Clearly we can reverse the argument, proving the first statement. The second statement is clear from the fact that the payoff to Defect against the mixed strategy is c, and Defect is used with positive probability.

To check the replicator dynamics of the system, we linearize around $\alpha^*=\delta/(b-c)$, $\beta=0$, getting

$$\begin{aligned}\frac{d\alpha_t}{dt} &= \gamma_\alpha((b-c-\delta)(\alpha_t-\alpha^*)\\ &\qquad +(-(1-b-c)+\alpha^*(1-2b))\beta_t)\\ \frac{d\beta_t}{dt} &= \gamma_\beta((b-\delta)(\alpha_t-\alpha^*)\\ &\qquad +((2c+b-1)+a^*(1-2b))\beta_t+\alpha^*b-c).\end{aligned}$$

Note that $a^*b-c<0$ by the efficient inspecting condition, so in the neighborhood of the nontrust equilibrium the frequency of Trusting is monotonically decreasing to zero. Also $b-c-\delta>0$, since $b-c-\delta=b(1-c/b)-\delta>c(1-c/b)-\delta>0$ by the efficient inspecting condition. Thus when $\alpha_t<\alpha^*$, α_t decreases monotonically to zero, and the system moves to the universal defect equilibrium. When $\alpha_t>\alpha^*$, α_t must increase for small enough β_t by the first equation. Thus in a neighborhood of the nontrust equilibrium (α^*,0), the system always moves away from α^*, so α^* is unstable.

Appendix B: Proofs

Proof of Theorem 3a: Equations (15.5) and (15.6) expand to the system of nonlinear differential equations

$$\begin{aligned}\frac{d\alpha_t}{dt} &= \gamma_\alpha\alpha_t[-\delta+(b-c+\delta)\alpha+(-a+b+c)\beta\\ &\qquad +(c-b)\alpha^2+(a-2b)\alpha\beta+(a-b-c)\beta^2],\end{aligned} \tag{15.33}$$

$$\frac{d\beta_t}{dt} = \gamma_\beta\beta_t[d-c+(b+\delta)\alpha+(-a+b+2c)\beta$$
$$+(c-b)\alpha^2+(a-2b)\alpha\beta+(a-b-c)\beta^2]. \qquad (15.34)$$

We linearize (15.33) and (15.34) around the universal defect equilibrium $\alpha=\beta=0$. This gives

$$\frac{d\alpha_t}{dt} = -\gamma_\alpha\delta\alpha_t \qquad (15.35)$$
$$\frac{d\beta_t}{dt} = -\gamma_\beta c\beta_t \qquad (15.36)$$

for $\alpha_t, \beta_t \geq 0$. The equilibrium (0,0) is then clearly locally stable, since both derivatives are negative. ■

Proof of Theorem 4e: Let α^* and β^* be the equilibrium frequency of Inspect and Trust in the trust equilibrium, given by equations (15.8) and (15.9). We expand the differential equations (15.33) and (15.34) around (α^*, β^*) and take the linear part, which gives

$$\frac{d\alpha_t}{dt} = \gamma_\alpha(q_\alpha(\alpha_t-\alpha^*)+w_\alpha(\beta_t-\beta^*)) \qquad (15.37)$$
$$\frac{d\beta_t}{dt} = \gamma_\beta(q_\beta(\alpha_t-\alpha^*)+w_\beta(\beta_t-\beta^*)). \qquad (15.38)$$

where the coefficients in the above differential equations satisfy

$$(a-c)^2c^2q_\alpha = -c^3(a-b)(b-c)+d_1\delta$$
$$(a-c)^2c^2w_\alpha = -c^3(a-b)(b-c)+d_2\delta$$
$$(a-c)^2c^2q_\beta = c^3(a-b)(b-c)+d_3\delta$$
$$(a-c)^2c^2w_\beta = -c^3(a-b)(b-c)+d_4\delta$$

where $d_1, \ldots, d_4$ are functions of the parameters a, b, and c. The system is locally stable if its eigenvalues have negative real parts in a neighborhood of the equilibrium. The eigenvalues of the system are

$$\lambda_1, \lambda_2 = \frac{1}{2}\left(\gamma_\alpha q_\alpha+\gamma_\beta w_\beta \pm \sqrt{(\gamma_\alpha q_\alpha-\gamma_\beta w_\beta)^2+4\gamma_\alpha w_\alpha\gamma_\beta q_\beta}\right). \qquad (15.39)$$

Notice that for sufficiently small δ we have $q_\alpha, w_\alpha, w_\beta < 0$ and $q_\beta > 0$. It follows that the first two terms in (15.39) are strictly negative, and the quadratic term is either imaginary or less in absolute value than the sum of the first two terms, for sufficiently small δ. Therefore both eigenvalues have strictly negative real parts, proving part (e) of the theorem. ■

Proof in Theorem 5 that $r_n = 1+n/(\kappa+1)$. If there are $\kappa+n$ members of the network, the first queried will know the type of a particular individual with probability $\kappa/(\kappa+n)$, and if not, members of a network of size $\kappa+n-1$, of whom κ know the individual in question, must be queried. Notice that the relationship

$r_n = 1 + n/(\kappa+1)$ is trivially true for $n = 0$. Suppose it is true for some value $n-1 \geq 0$. Then

$$\begin{aligned} r_n &= 1 + \frac{n}{\kappa+n} r_{n-1} \\ &= 1 + \frac{n}{\kappa+n}\left(1 + \frac{n-1}{\kappa+1}\right) \\ &= 1 + \frac{n}{\kappa+1}. \end{aligned}$$

The assertion follows by induction on n. ■

Proof of Theorem 6: We assume x large enough relative to k that the normal approximation to the binomial is sufficiently accurate ($x > 10k$ is enough to ensure this). The difference between the number of buyers and sellers in a marketplace is a random variable ψ_i that is normally distributed with mean zero and variance $\sigma_i^2 = x_i/4$. Then $E[|\psi_i|] = E[\psi_i|\psi_i \geq 0]$ is then given by

$$\begin{aligned} \frac{1}{\sqrt{2\pi}} \int_0^\infty \psi_i e^{-\frac{\psi_i^2}{2\sigma_i}} d\psi_i &= \frac{1}{\sqrt{2\pi}} (-\sigma_i) e^{-\frac{\psi_i^2}{2\sigma_i}} d\psi_i \Big|_0^\infty \\ &= \frac{\sigma_i}{\sqrt{2\pi}} = \frac{\sqrt{x_i}}{2\sqrt{2\pi}} \end{aligned}$$

Thus the probability p_i of finding a trading partner in marketplace i is $p_i = 1 - E[|\psi_i|]/x_i = 1 - 1/2\sqrt{2\pi f_i x}$. Hence

$$p(x) = \sum_{i=1}^{k} f_i p_i = 1 - \left(\sum_{i=1}^{n} \frac{\sqrt{f_i}}{2\sqrt{2\pi}} \right) x^{-\frac{1}{2}}.$$

Clearly $p(x)$ has the asserted properties. ■

Proof of Theorem 8: Define $\phi(x_k) = zx_k(\bar{\pi}(x_k) - c)/\nu_k$, and choose $\underline{\gamma}_k$ as the solution to

$$\frac{1}{\underline{\gamma}_k} = \max_{x_k} \phi(x_k). \tag{15.40}$$

This maximization problem has a solution x_*, since $\bar{\pi}(x_k) - c$ is nonpositive for sufficiently large x_k, and is positive at x_{min} by assumption. Note that if the problem has an interior solution, $\underline{\gamma}_k$ is set so that the two curves in Figure 15.3 are tangent at x_*. Otherwise the equilibrium occurs where the two curves intersect at $x_* = x_{min}$ (since $\phi(x_k)$ has a negative derivative to the right of x^*, because $\bar{\pi}(x_k)$ is concave). By construction there is no network size equilibrium for $\gamma_k < \underline{\gamma}_k$, which proves (a).

Since $\phi(x_k) = 1/\underline{\gamma}_k$ at $x_k = x_*$ and $\phi(x'') = 0$ for x'' such that $\bar{\pi}(x'') = c$, for any γ_k such that $\gamma_k > \underline{\gamma}_k$ there is an x_k such that $1/\gamma_k = \phi(x_k)$. From Theorem 4e, we know this is a stable trust equilibrium for a sufficiently small inspecting cost. To see that this is stable in network size if the equilibrium size $\hat{x}$ satisfies $\hat{x} \geq x^*$, note that

$$\frac{\partial}{\partial x_k} (m_k(x_k) - \nu x_k)|_{x_k = \hat{x}}$$

is strictly negative. This proves (c). ■

Acknowledgments

We are grateful to Katherine Baird, Roland Bénabou, Robert Boyd, Colin Camerer, Jeffrey Carpenter, Vincent Crawford, Steven Durlauf, Marcus Feldman, Edward Glaeser, Avner Greif, David Laibson, Michael Macy, Paul Malherbe, Jane Mansbridge, Corinna Noelke, Paul Romer, Martin Weitzman, Peyton Young, participants in the 1996 NBER Summer Institute, The Santa Fe Institute, the University of Siena, and Yale University for perceptive comments, and to the MacArthur Foundation for financial support.

Notes

1 Our definition is similar to that of "groups" offered by the biologist E.O. Wilson, who (1975: 585) defines them as "any set of organisms, belonging to the same species, that remain together for a period of time interacting with one another to a distinctly greater degree than with other conspecifics." The theory of social exchange, initiated in sociology by Blau (1964) and Homans (1958), and in anthropology by Sahlins (1972) provide insights into the economics of networks. For contributions by economists, see Ben-Porath (1980), Hollander (1990), Iannaccone (1992), Kandori (1992), Wintrobe (1995), Greif (1994), Akerlof (1995), Pagano (1995), Bénabou (1996), Durlauf (1996), Kranton (1996), Taylor (1997), and Glaeser (1997).

2 See Rauch (1996), Granovetter (1985) and Kotkin (1993). The current concern with a "decline of community" typically refers to socially approved aspects of networks thought to be less prevalent in the modern world. Perhaps Jack Hirschleifer (1994: 3–4) exaggerates when he writes: "when people cooperate it is generally a conspiracy for aggression against others . . ." But his remark is a useful reminder that networks as we have defined them often engage in practices that others find offensive. See also Hardin (1995).

3 The advantages of trade with outsiders is a common explanation of the permeability of group boundaries in small scale societies (Adams 1974) and of the extinction of very restrictive groups in favor of more inclusive entities (Gellner 1985, Weber 1976). A particularly well-documented example of this tension is Greif's (1994) account of how the competitive advantages stemming from the superior within-group contractual enforcement capabilities of the tight-knit thirteenth-century community of Maghribi merchants was eventually offset by their lesser ability to engage in successful exchange with outsiders, resulting in their inability to compete with the more individualistic Genovese traders. Yoram Ben-Porath (1980) develops similar reasoning concerning the economic capabilities of families and other face to face groups:

   The transactional advantages of the family cannot compensate for the fact that within its confines the returns from impersonal exchange and the division of labor are not fully realizable (p. 14).

4 Our model develops insights provided by a number of contributions to the sociology of groups. Granovetter (1985) writes:

   ". . . social relations, rather than institutionalized arrangements or generalized morality are mainly responsible for the production of trust in economic life." (pp. 490–491)

   For additional ways in which groups solve coordination problems stemming from incomplete contracts, see Bowles and Gintis (1998).

5 We here use simplified versions of dynamic models developed by Blume (1993), Foster and Young (1990) and Young (1993).

6 See Wilson and Sober (1994) and Kraybill (1989). Hechter (1990) found that two indicators of group homogeneity – common ethnic background and uniform style of dress – were among the few robust predictors of survival of utopian communes established in the late eighteenth and early nineteenth century in the United States. He interprets this finding as in part reflecting variable information costs. See also Longhofer (1996) for a model of the relationship between cultural affinity and monitoring costs.

7 Because the evolutionary viability of what biologists term assortative interactions has been convincingly demonstrated (Hamilton 1975, Axelrod and Hamilton 1981, Wilson and Dugatkin 1997), we know that the mental capacities and psychological dispositions required for parochial practices – such as acute abilities to detect insider/outsider distinctions or discomfort in the presence of those who are socially distant – could well have evolved under the influence of either cultural or genetic inheritance.

8 Iannaccone (1992) analyzes a more active form of parochialism, in which membership in a network subject to participatory crowding is restricted to those who are willing to accept "stigma, self-sacrifice, and bizarre behavioral restrictions."

9 Lazarsfeld and Merton (1954: 26ff) term this second order exclusiveness "value homophily" and present evidence for it with respect to racial attitudes: white "racial liberals" prefer not to associate with white "racial illiberals" and conversely.

10 The latter inequality ensures that mutual cooperation yields higher average payoffs than defect/cooperate pairs.

11 This treatment of inspection and trust is adapted from Güth and Kliemt (1994). There are actually three additional responses available to an agent who pays the inspecting cost δ. One is to defect unconditionally, and another is to cooperate unconditionally. We do not consider these because they are strictly dominated by Defect and Trust, respectively. The final is to cooperate against a "yes" answer from the information technology, and defect otherwise. An agent using either Inspect or Defect will defect against this strategy, since an Inspect players receives a "yes" from the information technology. This strategy is thus also strictly dominated by Defect. Since these strategies cannot be part of a Nash equilibrium, we exclude them from consideration for simplicity.

12 We assume these are continuous variables. This assumption involves an approximation, since there are an integral number of agents each of whom plays a pure strategy.

13 On replicator dynamics in general see Friedman (1991). For a full derivation of the replicator dynamic described above, see Gintis (1997).

14 In Appendix A we prove that there is also a unique nontrust equilibrium if and only if the efficient inspecting condition holds. This equilibrium is not stable.

15 Suppose the height of the equilateral triangle is one. Then each point in the triangle represents a set of relative frequencies of the three strategies Inspect, Trust, and Defect: for any such point (for instance the trust equilibrium T) drop a perpendicular to each of the three sides of the triangle. The length of the perpendicular to a particular side of the triangle is the frequency of the pure strategy associated with the vertex opposite this side. Thus, for instance, the point at Inspect corresponds to $(\alpha, \beta, 1-\alpha-\beta) = (1,0,0)$, and the point equidistant from the three vertices of the triangle corresponds to $(\alpha, \beta, 1-\alpha-\beta) = (1/3, 1/3, 1/3)$.

16 The following considerations account for our depiction of the phase diagrams in Figure 15.2. In the left-hand pane, we have depicted the trust equilibrium as a stable node. In fact, it can be either a stable node or a stable focus. The fact that C is an unstable node implies (*via* the Hartman–Grobman Theorem) the existence of a stable manifold through C, since the unstable manifold through C is the Inspect-Defect face of the phase-space triangle. We have labeled the stable manifold AC. The shape attributed to AC follows from the Poincaré–Bendixson theorem, assuming there are no limit cycles. To see this, note that A cannot coincide with an equilibrium of the dynamical system (since no stable manifold of an equilibrium terminates in C) nor can it lie on the Trust-Defect or Inspect-Defect faces (since no path starting from a point on these faces terminates at C except C itself). Thus the stable manifold through C must exit the

phase space at a point in the interior of the Trust-Inspect face. This does not contradict Poincaré–Bendixson, since the replicator dynamic is not in general continuous along the Trust-Inspect face. If there are limit cycles, the stable manifold of C could wrap around the equilibrium at T with a limit cycle as its α-limit (it must wrap around T since a limit cycle must contain an equilibrium in its interior).

17 Notice that this implies that an agent who does not trade has the same payoff as a cooperator whose partner defects. Our results do not change if we weaken this to a payoff less than the mutual defect payoff c.

18 Here "migration" refers to movement between networks and the pool of Walrasian traders, and need not entail geographic relocation.

19 There is a plausible alternative to the assumption that networks are locally stable at their equilibrium size, in which networks that become too large disintegrate into universal defection because the conditions for local stability of the trust equilibrium fail when the inspecting cost becomes too high. We shall not deal with this case here. Modeling migration dynamics as we do below, we expect that this case will give rise to cycles of growth and dissolution of networks that may be of theoretical and practical interest.

20 Members of networks at the defect equilibrium, should they exist, would receive the mutual defect payoff on the transactions they secure but, as members of networks of limited size, they would fail to secure transactions some fraction of the time, and hence would have expected returns less than those in the Walrasian pool. We thus assume there are no such networks.

21 Our analysis remains valid, it can be shown, if migration varies with the size of the destination network; that is, if (15.15) is replaced by the more general equation $m(x) = \gamma x^{\lambda} z(\bar{\pi}(x) - c)$ for $0 \leq \lambda < 1$.

22 We ignore the possibility that agents may migrate from one network to another. In equilibrium, all networks will have the same payoffs, so no such migration will take place. This is in contrast to flows between the Walrasian pool and networks, which remain positive even in equilibrium.

23 These considerations indicate that the emigration parameter ν could depend on network size and the return to cooperation in the network. However this would complicate the stability analysis and otherwise not change our results, so we treat ν as constant for simplicity.

24 For models of this type, based on the theory of random perturbations of dynamical systems (Freidlin and Wentzell 1984), see Kandori, Mailath and Rob (1993) and Samuelson (1997).

25 We have assumed that networks are sufficiently numerous that the number of networks that appear and disappear in each period can be replaced by their expected values.

26 Where $\hat{x} < x^*$, of course, inducements to entry will have the same effect, though we think this case less likely and have not explored it here.

27 If there are multiple parochialisms which are mutually exclusive in the sense that members of one group are always excluded from the others, this analysis can be readily extended. We have not explored more complicated cases.

28 Reductions in c/b do not make the standard prisoner's dilemma interaction any "easier to solve" of course, but they may enhance evolutionary pressures for the emergence of new rules of interaction that effectively mitigate the dilemma. Wade (1987: 774–775) describes such a process: ". . . a significant number of the villages (in one small part of Upland South India) have institutions for the provision of public goods and services, which are autonomous of outside agencies in origin a and operation. . . . Only a few miles may separate a village with a substantial amount of corporate organization from others with none . . . Why the differences between villages? It is not because of differences in norms or values, for the villages are located within a small enough area for the culture to be uniform. It is rather because of differences in net collective benefit."

References

Adams, R., (1974) Anthropological perspectives in ancient trade. *Current Anthropology* 15: 239–258.

Akerlof, George A. (1995) Social Distance and Social Decisions. Fisher-Schultz Lecture of the Econometric Society.

Axelrod, Robert and William D. Hamilton (1981) The evolution of cooperation. *Science* 211: 1390–1396.

Baker, Wayne E. (1984) The social structure of a national securities market. *American Journal of Sociology* 89(4): 775–811.

Baland, J.M. and J.P Platteau (1997) *Wealth Inequality and Efficiency in the Commons*. CRED, University of Namur.

Banerjee, Abhijit V., Timothy Besley and Timothy W. Guinnane (1994) Thy neighbor's keeper: the design of a credit cooperative with theory and a test. *Quarterly Journal of Economics* May: 491–515.

Ben-Porath, Yoram (1980) The F-connection: families, friends, and firms and the organization of exchange. *Population and Development Review* March: 1–30.

Bénabou, Roland (1996) Heterogeneity, stratification and growth: macroeconomic implications of community structure and school finance. *American Economic Review* 86: 584–609.

Bernstein, Lisa (1992) Opting out of the legal system: extralegal contractual relations in the diamond industry. *Journal of Legal Studies*. 21(1): 115–158.

Berscheid, E. and E. Walster (1969) *Interpersonal Attraction*. Reading, MA: Addison.

Blau, Peter (1964) *Exchange and Power in Social Life*. New York: John Wiley.

Blume, Lawrence E. (1993) The statistical mechanics of strategic interaction. *Games and Economic Behavior* 5: 387–424.

Bowles, Samuel and Herbert Gintis (1998) The moral economy of community: structured populations and the evolution of prosocial norms. *Evolution & Human Behavior* 19(1): 3–25.

Cohen, J.M. (1977) Sources of peer group homogeneity. *Sociology of Education* 15(4): 227–241.

Craig, Ben and John Pencavel (1992) The behavior of worker cooperatives: the plywood companies of the Pacific Northwest. *American Economic Review* 82(5): 1083–1105.

—— and —— (1995) Participation and productivity: a comparison of worker cooperatives and conventional firms in the plywood industry. *Brookings Papers: Microeconomics* 121–160.

Durlauf, Steven (1996) Neighborhood feedbacks, endogenous stratification, and income inequality. In *Dynamic Disequilibrium Modelling*. Cambridge: Cambridge University Press.

Foster, Dean and H. Peyton Young (1990) Stochastic evolutionary game dynamics. *Theoretical Population Biology* 38: 219–232.

Freidlin, Mark I. and Alexander D. Wentzell (1984) *Random Perturbations of Dynamical Systems*. New York: Springer-Verlag.

Friedman, Daniel (1991) Evolutionary games in economics. *Econometrica* 59(3): 637–666.

Gellner, Ernest (1985) *Nations and Nationalism*. Ithaca: Cornell University Press.

Gintis, Herbert (1997) A Markov model of production, trade, and money: theory and artificial life simulation. *Computational and Mathematical Organization Theory* 3(1): 19–41.

Glaeser, Edward L. (1997) Cities and ethics: an essay for Jane Jacobs. University of Chicago Law School.

Grafen, Alan (1984) Natural selection, kin selection, and group selection. In J.R. Krebs and N.B. Davies (eds) *Behavioural Ecology: An evolutionary Approach*. Sunderland, MA: Sinauer.

Granovetter, Mark (1985) Economic action and social structure: the problem of embeddedness. *American Journal of Sociology* 91(3): 481–510.

Greif, Avner (1994) Cultural beliefs and the organization of society: an historical and theoretical reflection on collectivist and individualist societies. *Journal of Political Economy*. October.

Güth, Werner and Harmutt Kliemt (1994) Competition or co-operation: on the evolutionary economics of trust, exploitation, and moral attitudes. *Metroeconomica* 45(2): 155–187.

Hamilton, W.D. (1975) Innate social aptitudes of man: an approach from evolutionary genetics. In Robin Fox (ed.) *Biosocial Anthropology*. New York: John Wiley and Sons.

Hardin, Russell (1995) *One for All: The Logic of Group Conflict*. Princeton: Princeton University Press.

Hechter, Michael (1990) The attainment of solidarity in intentional communities. *Rationality and Society* 2(2): 142–155.

Hirschleifer, Jack (1994) The Dark Side of the Force: Western Economic Association International 1993 Presidential Address. *Economic Inquiry* 32: 1–10.

Hollander, Heinz (1990) A social exchange approach to voluntary cooperation. *American Economic Review* 80(5): 1157–1167.

Homans, George C. (1958) Social behavior as exchange *American Journal of Sociology* 65(6): 597–606.

—— (1961) *Social Behavior: Its Elementary Forms* New York: Harcourt Brace.

Hossain, M. (1988) *Credit for Alleviation of Rural Poverty: the Grameen Bank in Bangladesh*. International Food Policy Research Institute Report 65.

Iannaccone, Laurence R. (1992) Sacrifice and stigma: reducing free-riding in cults, communes, and other collectives. *Journal of Political Economy* 100(2).

Kandel, Denise (1978) Homophily, selection and socialization in adolescent friendships. *American Journal of Sociology* 84(2): 427–436.

Kandori, M.G., G. Mailath and R. Rob (1993) Learning, mutation, and long run Equilibria in games. *Econometrica* 61: 29–56.

Kandori, Michihiro (1992) Social norms and community enforcement. *Review of Economic Studies* 57: 63–80.

Kaufman, Jonathan (1995) How Cambodians came to control California doughnuts. *Wall Street Journal* February 11, 1995: 1, A14.

Kollock, Peter (1994) The emergence of exchange structures: an experimental study of uncertainty, commitment, and trust. *American Journal of Sociology* 100(2): 313–345.

Kotkin, Joel (1993) *Tribes: How Race, Religion and Identity Determine Success in the New Global Economy* New York: Random House.

Kramer, Donald L. (1985) Are colonies supraoptimal groups? *Animal Behavior* 33(4): 1031.

Kranton, Rachel (1996) Reciprocal exchange: a self-sustaining system. *American Economic Review* 86(4): 830–851.

Kraybill, Donald B. (1989) *The Riddle of Amish Culture*. Baltimore: Johns Hopkins Press.

Lawler, Edward J. (1973) *Motivation in Work Organizations*. Monterey: Brooks-Cole.

Lazarsfeld, P.F. and R.K. Merton (1954) Friendship as a social process. In M. Berger *et al.* (eds) *Freedom and Control in Modern Society*. Princeton: Van Nostrand.

Longhofer, Stanley (1996) Cultural affinity and mortgage discrimination. *Economic Review of the Federal Reserve Bank of Cleveland* 32(3): 12–24.

McMillan, John and Christopher Woodruff (1996) *Trust and search in Vietnam's emerging private sector*. La Jolla: University of California.

Obot, I. (1988) Value systems in cross cultural contact: the effect of perceived similarity and stability on social evaluation. *International Journal of Intercultural Relations* 12: 363–379.

Ostrom, Elinor, Roy Gardner, and James Walker (1994) *Rules, Games, and Common-Pool Resources*. Ann Arbor: University of Michigan Press.

Packer, Craig and Lore Ruttan (1988) The evolution of cooperative hunting. *American Naturalist* 132(2): 159–198.

Pagano, Ugo (1995) Can economics explain nationalism? In Albert Breton, Gianluigi Galeotti, Pierre Salmon and Ronald Wintrobe (eds) *Nationalism and Rationality*. Cambridge: Cambridge University Press.

Parsons, Talcott (1964) Evolutionary universals in society. *American Sociological Review* 29(3).

Pulliam, H. Ronald and Thomas Caraco (1984) Living in groups: is there an optimal group size? In J.R. Krebs and N.B. Davies (eds) *Behavioural Ecology*. Sunderland, MA: Sinauer.

Quah, D. (1996) *The Invisible Hand and the Weightless Economy*. Centre for Economic Performance, London School of Economics.

Rauch, James E. (1996) *Trade and Networks: An Application to Minority Retail Entrepreneurship*. Russell Sage.

Sahlins, Marshall (1992) *Stone Age Economics*. Chicago: Aldine Press.

Sampson, Robert J., Stephen W. Raudenbush and Felton Earls (1997) Neighborhoods and violent crime: a multilevel study of collective efficacy. *Science* 277 (August 15, 1997): 918–924.

Samuelson, Larry (1997) *Evolutionary Games and Equilibrium Selection*. Cambridge, MA: MIT Press.

Siamwalla, Ammar (1978) Farmers and middlemen: aspects of agricultural marketing in Thailand. *Economic Bulletin for Asia and the Pacific* 39(1): 38–50.

Tajfel, Henri, M. Billig, R.P. Bundy and Claude Flament (1971) Social categorization and intergroup behavior. *European Journal of Social Psychology* 1: 149–177.

Taylor, Curtis (1997) *The Old Boy Network and the Young-Gun Effect*. Department of Economics, Texas A & M University.

Thibaut, J. and H. Kelly (1959) *The Social Psychology of Groups*. New York: Wiley.

Udry, Christopher (1993) Credit markets in northern Nigeria: credit as insurance in a rural economy. In Karla Hoff, Avishay Braverman, and Joseph E. Stiglitz (eds) *The Economics of Rural Organization: Theory, Practice, and Policy*. New York: Oxford University Press.

Wade, Robert, *Village Republics: Economic Conditions for Collective Action in South India* Cambridge: Cambridge University Press, 1987).

—— (1988) Why some Indian villages cooperate. *Economic and Political Weekly* 33: 773–776.

Weber, Eugen (1976) *Peasants into Frenchmen: The Modernization of Rural France, 1870-1914*. Stanford: Stanford University Press.

Whyte, William F. (1955) *Money and Motivation*. New York: Harper & Row.

Wilson, David Sloan and Elliott Sober (1994) Reintroducing group selection to the human behavioral sciences. *Behavior and Brain Sciences* 17: 585–654.

—— and Lee A. Dugatkin (1997) Group selection and assortative interactions. *American Naturalist* 149(2): 336–351.

Wilson, Edward O. (1975) *Sociobiology: The New Synthesis*. Cambridge, MA: Harvard University Press.

Wintrobe, Ronald (1995) Some economics of ethnic capital formation and conflict. In Albert Breton, Gianluigi Galeotti, Pierre Salmon, and Ronald Wintrobe (eds) *Nationalism and Rationality*. Cambridge: Cambridge University Press.

Woodyard, Chris (1995) Roadside revival by Patels. *Los Angeles Times* Friday, July 14, 1995: 1, A40–41.

Young, H. Peyton (1993) The evolution of conventions. *Econometrica* 61(1): 57–84.

16 Evolution of money

Katsuhito Iwai

16.1 Introduction: Menger, Knapp, Mauss, and the search-theoretic model of money.

> The great thinkers of antiquity, and following them a long series of the most eminent scholars of later times up to the present day, have been more concerned than with any other problem of our science with the explanation of the strange fact that, as civilization develops, a number of goods (gold and silver in the form of coin) are readily accepted by everyone in exchange for all other goods, even by persons who have no direct requirements for them, or whose requirements have already been fully met. A person of the most ordinary intelligence realizes that the owner of a good will give it in exchange for one that is more useful to him. But that every economizing individual of an entire society should be eager to exchange his commodities for small discs of metal, which ordinarily only a few men can use directly, is something that is so contradictory to the ordinary course of events that we cannot be surprised that it appears "mysterious" to even so brilliant a thinker as F. K. v Savigny. The problem that science must solve is thus the explanation of human behavior that is *general* and whose motives do not lie clearly upon the surface.
>
> (Menger 1871: 315)

For centuries economists have advanced two competing theories on the nature of money – the "commodity theory of money" and the "chartal theory of money."[1] Commodity theory asserts that in order for a certain thing to serve as a general means of exchange for commodities, it has to be a commodity itself – a useful thing that has an exchange value independently of its monetary function.[2] Chartal theory, in opposition, asserts that in order for a certain thing to serve as a general means of exchange, it needs not be a commodity itself but its use as a general means of exchange must be approved by a communal agreement, or decreed by the head of a state, or sanctioned by a legal order. These two competing theories on the nature of money have almost always been associated with two competing views on the origin of money, though from a purely logical viewpoint they need not go together. Those who uphold the commodity theory tend to argue that money has evolved naturally from one of the commodities through a long process of barter exchanges, whereas those who uphold the chartal theory tend to argue that money was introduced into the world at a historical moment ("once upon a time") by a communal or political or legal force that is external to the exchange process. The former locates both the nature and origin of money inside of the economic sphere, and the latter its outside. Historians of monetary theory have been busy in classifying past authors on monetary matters into these two camps.[3]

Carl Menger, who, along with Leon Walras and Stanley Jevons, laid out the foundations of what is now known as neoclassical economics, was perhaps the most influential and the most sophisticated advocate of the commodity theory of money in modern times. He believed that the chartalist position was, in spite of the time-honored authority of Plato, Aristotle, and the Roman jurists who espoused it, only an easy way out of the above-mentioned difficulties posed by the "mystery" of the phenomenon of money. True to his intellectual adherence to Adam Smith, what Menger tried to advance was an "invisible hand" account of the evolution of money. He set out to "understand the origin of money by learning to view the establishment of social procedure . . . as the spontaneous outcome, the unpremeditated resultant, of particular, individual efforts of the members of a society . . . ."[4]

The key to Menger's theoretical attempt was the notion of the "salability (Absatzfähigkeit)" of goods. A good is said to have high salability if its "possession would considerably facilitate the individual search for persons who have just the goods he needs." But, not all goods are equally salable. While there is a limited demand for certain goods, that for others may be very general. And when an individual has goods with low salability, it is often difficult to obtain the goods he needs by direct barter. He may therefore find it more economical to exchange his own goods first for a more salable good even if he himself does not need it and use the latter as a temporary medium for obtaining the goods he really needs in later times. Menger then argued that "as *each* economizing individual becomes increasingly more aware of his economic interest, he is led by his interest, without any agreement, without legislative compulsion, and even without regard to the public interest, to give his commodities in exchange for the other, more salable, commodities, even if he does not need them for any immediate consumption purpose," and concluded that "with economic progress, we can everywhere observe the phenomena of a certain number of goods . . . becoming acceptable to everyone in trade," that is, becoming money.[5] Money is thus claimed to be "a natural product of human economy," which has evolved from one of the commodities spontaneously through a long process of barter exchanges among rational individuals, without any intervention of outside authority.

In recent years, we have witnessed a growing number of theoretical works that try to solve the "mystery" of the phenomenon of money once again. They include Jones (1976), Oh (1989), Iwai (1988a, 1988b, 1996), Kiyotaki and Wright (1989, 1991, 1993), Aiyagari and Wallace (1992), Boldrin, Kiyotaki and Wright (1994), and Shi (1995). The first objective of this chapter is to present the essentials of these recent works on money and discuss their implications for the old controversy on the nature and origin of money. What distinguishes them from Carl Menger's is their extensive use of "search theory" in modeling the decentralized exchange process among rational individuals. A century has not passed in total vain. The use of search theory has enabled them to formulate the Mengerian notion of the "salability" of goods in a much more rigorous manner than Menger himself did. If, however, that were all that these recent works have accomplished, there would be no need to present them in this volume. Indeed, what we shall see in the following is an ironic fact that one of the most notable accomplishments of these works, which owe much to Menger, lies in their undermining of his very Invisible Hand account of the evolution of money.

The fundamental proposition of Menger was that when there is a commodity with high salability, every rational individual finds it more economical to use it as a medium of exchange than to seek a direct barter. But this causal order can also be reversed. We shall indeed show that once a certain good has come to be used as a general medium of exchange, the very use of it as a general medium of exchange raises its salability to the maximum at the expense of all the other goods in the economy, thereby creating the very condition for its own use as a general medium of exchange. Because of the inherent increasing-returns-to-scale nature of the decentralized matching process among searching individuals, what Menger called the salability of a good turns out to be not a given characteristic of the good itself, but an endogenous variable whose magnitude is determined by the very exchange structure of the entire economy. Money is money simply because it is used as money. It is nothing but the product of a pure "bootstrap" mechanism.

What are the implications of this bootstrap nature of money for the controversy on the origin of money? In the first place, it calls in question its commodity theory explanation. It is because the high salability of a monetized good, which the commodity theorists have hypothesized as the "cause" of its use as money, may rather be an "effect" of its having already been adopted as money. Money may not have a commodity origin. Does this demise of the commodity theory imply the triumph of its rival chartal theory, which traced the monetary use of a disk of metal or a piece of paper to an "original" act of some authority outside of the sphere of exchanges? Should we accept the 1905 declaration of Knapp that "money is a creature of law"?[6] The answer is, however, "no." The fact that money is able to support itself by its own bootstrap also means that money does not need any outside enforcement for its use as a general means of exchange. Money may not have a chartal origin, either. Knapp must share the same fate with Menger.

It should be hastily added here that I am neither refuting the possibility that money actually evolved from a highly salable commodity nor denying the possibility that money was actually introduced by a communal agreement or an imperial decree or a legislative action. All I am disputing is the belief, the belief that has been espoused by both commodity theory and chartal theory, that the origin of money can be determined by a theoretical consideration alone. Commodity theory and chartal theory may each contain a truth, but it is only a half truth, not the whole truth. No wonder that they have coexisted side by side and competed with each other from time immemorial. Indeed, once a certain thing has started circulating as money, its bootstrap nature erases any trace of its past from itself and imposes a fundamental limit on the power of the theory to explain its origin *ex post facto*.

"History" thus matters; it matters in an essential manner in our understanding of the "mystery" of the phenomenon of money.

In what follows I will present a simple search-theoretic model of decentralized exchange economy, which is able to formalize some of these ideas and claims much more rigorously. The most notable feature of this model is the embarrassment of richness. Indeed, it has a wide variety of decentralized exchange systems as its possible equilibria, such as *barter system*, *commodity money system*, and *fiat money system*. In Section 16.2–16.4 I will introduce the basic ingredients of the search model, and in Sections 16.5–16.8 I will examine the conditions for the existence of each of these different exchange systems as an equilibrium of the economy as well as the possibilities of their natural evolution. I will demonstrate that, while a barter system requires a well-balanced distribution of abilities and needs among individuals (such as the one satisfying the so-called double coincidence of wants) to support itself as an equilibrium, a monetary system, whether it uses a useful commodity as commodity money or a useless token as fiat money, requires no "real" conditions (except what we will call the "connectedness" of the economy) to exist in this world. I will also show that there is a fundamental difficulty in the natural evolution of a commodity money system from a given "real" condition of the economy, in spite of its potential ubiquity. (A fiat money equilibrium is by definition impossible to evolve naturally.)

It turns out that our search model is able to support as its equilibrium another very important form of decentralized exchange system, thus further enhancing our embarrassment of richness. It is a *gift system*, and this will connect us to a scientific discipline wholly distinct from economics.

While economists have been fighting with each other on whether money has the commodity origin or the chartal origin, anthropologist have been elaborating an entirely different story of the origin of money. In *The Gift*, a truly classic monograph in social and economic anthropology, Marcel Mauss argued that there has never existed, either in prehistoric times or in "primitive" societies, anything that might resemble what is called a "natural" economy where people normally live in self-sufficiency and occasionally barter a deer and two beavers.[7] We human-beings are exchanging animals. We have always been exchanging things regularly with each other from time immemorial. What distinguishes "them" from "us" is only the "form" of exchanges. In pre-historic times or in "primitive" societies it is the system of gift-giving and gift-receiving that regulates the whole exchanges of goods and services among people. The system is indeed based on three simple obligations: the obligation to give, the obligation to receive, and the obligation to reciprocate.[8] And it is these three obligations which set up a perpetual cycle of exchanges among individuals, among tribes, and among generations. The most well-known example of such system is *kula* trade of the Trobriand Islands, though we have no space to describe this grandiose circle of inter- and intra-tribal exchanges so beautifully recorded by Malinowski in his *Argonauts of the Western Pacific*.[9] What is important for our study is the claim of Mauss and his fellow anthropologists that the system of buying and selling arose not from autarky or barter but from the gift system.[10] In fact, Mauss suggested that barter should be regarded as a degenerated form of gift-giving and gift-receiving when the time span of these two acts shrinks to zero.[11]

Mauss' description of gift exchange as a system based on the obligations to give, receive and reciprocate must have struck the ears of those who have ever read Axelrod's *the Evolution of Cooperation* as something familiar.[12] Indeed, the second objective of this chapter is to reexamine the evolutionary story of anthropologists – that the system of monetary exchange emerged out of that of ancient gift exchange – from the perspective of game theory, although I am fully aware that it certainly runs counter to the main emphasis of the anthropologists that the gift system is a total social system which encompasses not only economic but also matrimonial, religious, political, sociological, and all the other aspects of human society. Following the lead of Kocherlakota (1998) and Ishihara (1997), two important recent works on the gift system, I will study the possibilities of supporting the gift system as an equilibrium of the economy.[13] There is both good news and bad news to anthropologists. Good news is that, in contrast to the barter system, the gift system requires no "real" conditions to support itself as an equilibrium of the economy, thereby corroborating their claim of its prevalence in "primitive" societies. The bad news is that the gift system can sustain itself as an equilibrium only if every member of the economy can recall every other member's past actions, the past actions of their previous partners, the past actions of those previous partners' previous partners, and so on *ad infinitum*. If he or she has merely a finite-length memory, however long it is, the gift system breaks down as an equilibrium. This is in striking contrast to the system of monetary exchanges which will be shown to require no information about the members' past actions to support itself as an equilibrium. Money transcends itself not only from the "real" structure of the economy but also from its "informational" structure. There thus exists an infinite divide between the system of gift-giving and gift- receiving in "primitive" societies and the system of buying and selling in our modern monetary economy. The anthropologists' story of the evolution of money turns out to be as inconclusive as the economists' two competing stories of the evolution of money.

Yet, we human beings are living in a full-fledged monetary economy. No matter how "miraculous" it might be from a purely theoretical standpoint, money did actually emerge on this planet in the distant past, and has since propagated itself over the entire globe. It is difficult now to find a society which organizes its economy solely by barter exchanges or by gift exchanges. The last section of this chapter is a *postscript* in the double sense of the word. It was added after the conference on "Evolution and Economics," and it is concerned with the fate of the monetary system after its appearance. I will present a very brief account of the propagation process of monetary system. Its main purpose is to emphasize the difference between the logic which governs the emergence of money and the logic which governs the propagation of money – the former is about the internal development of a single economy and the latter is about the processes of selection, imitation and migration across multiple economies.

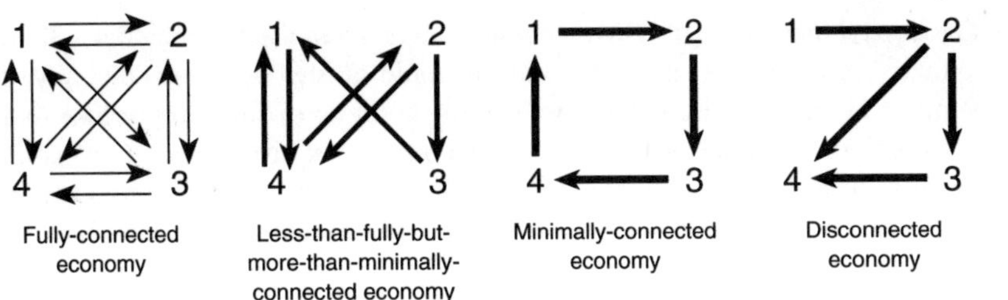

Figure 16.1 Four examples of the "real" structure of the economy

16.2 The basic model of a decentralized exchange economy

Let us consider an economy which consists of a large number of individuals with heterogeneous combinations of abilities and needs. There are n consumption goods, indexed by $i = 1, 2, \ldots, n$, which are indivisible and come in units of size one. Each individual is endowed with a fixed ability to produce one of n goods and a fixed need to consume another one of n goods. Hence, a pair of the indices of goods, (i,j), can be used to identify every member of this economy. (Since no individual corresponds to a twin pair (i,i), we use the convention that whenever a pair of indices (i,j) is referred in this chapter, it automatically excludes the twin pairs (i,i).)

Let us denote the relative frequency of i-producing j-consumers by e_{ij}, and call it *ability- need frequency*. (Note that $\sum_i \sum_j e_{ij} = 1$ by constructions. By convention, the symbol e_{ij} automatically excludes e_{ii}.) Then, the "real" structure of this economy can be summarized by $\{e_{ij}\}$, a set of ability-need frequencies, which represents how "abilities and needs," or more generally, how "technology and preferences" are distributed among its members.

There is an intuitive way to visualize this structure, and Figure 16.1 shows its four examples in the case of four good economy ($n = 4$). In Fig. 1 numerals *1*, *2*, *3* and *4* represent the indices of goods, and *not* the indices of individuals. If there is at least one individual who produces good *2* and consumes good *3*, we draw a gray arrow from *2* to *3*, as is the case in every example. The width represents its frequency. If no producer of good *1* consumes good *3*, or it is the same thing, if no consumer of good *3* produces good *1*, no gray arrow is drawn from *1* to *3*, as is the case in the last three examples.

We now introduce the most crucial characterization of the real structure of the economy. We say that an economy is *connected* if from any index of good i we can visit any other index j by continuously following an one-way chain of gray arrows. Or, more generally, we say that an economy is *connected*, if for any i and j we have a connected sequence of strictly positive ability-need frequencies such that $e_{ih} > 0, e_{hg} > 0, \ldots, e_{lk} > 0$, and $e_{kj} > 0$.[14] Clearly, the first three examples in Figure 16.1 represent three different forms of connected economy – the first one fully connected, the third one minimally connected, and the second one in between. The fourth example represents a disconnected economy.

The importance of the notion of connectedness lies in the following fact. If an economy is connected, an almighty authority could satisfy the real need of any of its members by ordering him or her to give the good he or she can produce to a second individual who needs it, who is in turn ordered to give the good he or she can produce to a third individual who needs it, and so on, until the sequence of the orders reaches an individual who is capable of producing the very good the first individual is in need of. (This divine act has just traced the above sequence, $e_{ih} > 0, e_{hg} > 0, \ldots, e_{lk} > 0$, and $e_{kj} > 0$, in reverse order.) As long as the economy is connected, all of its members could in principle be lifted from the misery of autarky by a centralized exchange coordination. In contrast, if the economy is disconnected, no such coordination is possible even by the almighty authority. The "connectedness" is thus the minimum requirement for an association of individuals to be properly called *an* economy.

The questions we have to pose are: first, whether an autarky-breaking exchange coordination is also possible in a decentralized manner, i.e., without the support of any centralized authority, and second, if that is possible, whether such a decentralized exchange coordination is capable of evolving spontaneously from a historically given "real" structure of the economy, i.e., without the intervention of any outside authority. The first question is concerned with the existence and the second with the evolution of a decentralized exchange system. It is of utmost importance to separate these two questions, at least conceptually.

In order to give some answers to each of these questions, we now have to develop a model of the decentralized exchange economy. In recent search-theoretic works on money, there are at least two different versions of the so-called meeting technology, as is shown in Figure 16.2. Oh (1989), Kiyotaki and Wright (1989, 1991, 1993) and others have supposed that the economy consists of one large trading zone, whereas Jones (1976) and Iwai (1988a, 1988b, 1996) has divided the economy into a number of separate trading zones, each of which is specialized to exchanges between a given pair of goods, and have let people choose trading zones to visit.[15] Both versions, however, assumed that in a trading zone people meet each other just randomly.[16] Since the basic messages of the search theory of money appear mostly independent of the precise specification of the meeting technology, I shall present here the version which is mathematically tractable and yet able to generate the most clear-cut results. It is, not unexpectedly, the one used by myself.

In this economy there are $n(n-1)/2$ trading zones, each of which is specialized to exchanges between a given pair of consumption goods (i,j). (I will later introduce n additional zones, to be used for exchanging real goods for fiat money in Section 16.8 or for giving away goods for nothing in Section 16.9.) Note that (i,j) zone and (j,i) zone are by assumption the same thing and that only those individuals willing to supply good i in exchange for good j and those individuals willing to supply good j in exchange for good i ever visit (i,j) zone. We denote the relative frequency of i-supplying j-demanders by q_{ij} and that of j-supplying i-demanders by q_{ji}, and call them *supply-demand frequencies*. ($\sum_i \sum_j q_{ij} \leq 1$ by construction. In what follows we again use the convention that the symbol q_{ij} automatically excludes

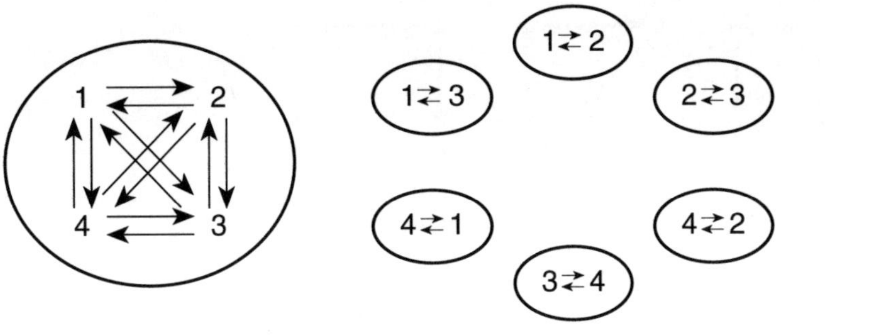

Figure 16.2 Two versions of meetings technology

q_{ii}.) As we shall see later, the most crucial fact about our model of decentralized exchange process is that the set of supply-demand frequencies $\{q_{ij}\}$, which are the main determinants of the searching behaviors of individual members of the economy, in general deviate from the set of ability-need frequencies $\{e_{ij}\}$, which represent the "fundamentals" of the economy.

Now, if each trading zone is large and sparsely populated, the way people meet in it can be reasonably approximated by the so-called Poisson law. We thus assume that the probability that one of i-supplying j-demanders encounters one of j-supplying i-demanders in (i,j) zone during a very short time interval is proportional to q_{ji}, the frequency of the latter.[17] Since we have a degree of freedom in choosing a time unit, we can set this probability equal to q_{ji} per unit of time.

The supply-demand frequency q_{ij} can be regarded as a quantification of what Carl Menger called the "salability" of goods. It is because the possession of a certain good, say m, with high q_{im} would facilitate the individual search for another individual who is willing to supply good i, thereby reducing the search cost. Likewise, a good m with high q_{mi} can be said to have high "purchasability," though Menger himself did not use such notion. It is because its possession would facilitate the individual's search for another individual who is willing to accept good i, thereby reducing the search cost.

16.3 Individual exchange strategies

Now that there is no central authority to coordinate exchanges of consumption goods, every member of the economy must search for exchange partners all by oneself in order to obtain the good in need.

Let us consider an i-producing j-consumer who has a unit of good i in hand. (For the brevity of exposition, we will designate this person as "he.") There are several alternative strategies open to him. (We will consider only pure strategies.) He can stay home and consume his own product. This is an autarky strategy. He can make a direct trip to (i,j) zone and search for a mirror-symmetric individual who is willing to exchange good j for good i. (We assume that exchange ratios

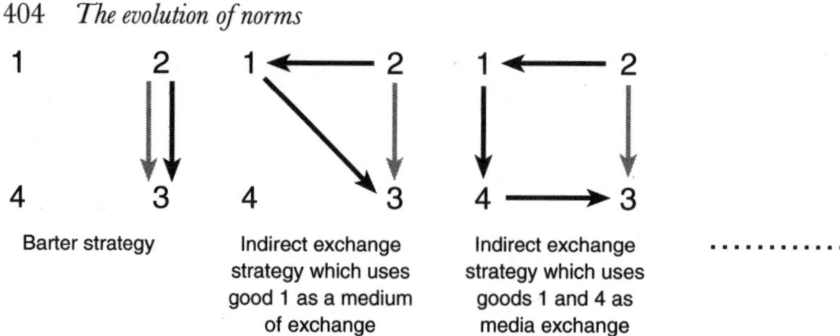

Figure 16.3 Example of search strategies for a 2-producing 3-consumer

are always one to one. In this model of pre-market economy, we believe we can safely leave out the issue of price-formation.) This is a barter strategy. Instead, the same individual may first make a trip to (i,k) zone $(k \neq i)$ and search for another individual who is willing to exchange good k for good i. Having found such a partner and successfully exchanged good i for good k, he then makes a second trip to (k,j) zone and search for another individual willing to exchange good j for good k. This is an indirect exchange strategy which uses good k as a "medium of exchange." Indirect exchange strategies using more than one media of exchange are also possible. Figure 16.3 depicts some of these strategies for a *2*-producing *3*-consumer.

After having acquired a unit of good j, our i-producing j-consumer retires from the economy in order to consume it quietly at home. For the sake of simplicity, we assume that as soon as our i- producing j-consumer has made his exit, a new i-producing j-consumer enters into the economy with a fresh unit of good i in hand. Such instantaneous parent-child succession will keep the whole distribution of ability-need frequencies $\{e_{ij}\}$ constant over time.

Let us now examine the structure of the benefits and costs of each exchange strategy. As an illustration, we first consider the case of barter strategy. Suppose that our i-producing j-consumer has decided to barter his product i for his consumable j. The first thing he does is to visit (i,j) zone and searches for a mirror-symmetric individual. Search is of course time-consuming. Since the probability of encountering a trading partner is q_{ji} per unit of time, his expected search time can be calculated as $1/q_{ji}$.[18] Let us assume that time is money and that its opportunity cost is c per unit. Then, his expected search cost becomes equal to c/q_{ji}. Having found a partner, he has to make a transaction with her. Let us assume that the time expected to conclude a transaction is b. Then, his expected transaction cost becomes equal to cb. Having concluded such transaction, our consumer retires from the economy for consumption. Let us assume that the consumption of a unit of good j gives him a utility u. If we subtract both the search cost and the transaction cost from this utility, we can finally obtain our i-producing j-consumer's (undiscounted) life-time payoff of barter strategy as:

$$u - c(b + 1/q_{ji}). \tag{16.1}$$

Suppose next that our i-producing j-consumer has committed himself to an indirect exchange strategy which uses good $k(\neq i,j)$ as the sole medium of exchange. Then, he is expected to spend a time equal to $1/q_{ki}$ in his first search, b in his first transaction, $1/q_{ik}$ in his second search, and b again in his second transaction, before he can enjoy a utility u of consumption. Subtracting costs from utility, we can calculate the total life-time payoff of this indirect exchange strategy as:

$$u - c(2b + 1/q_{ki} + 1/q_{jk}). \tag{16.2}$$

In general, we can calculate our i-producing j-consumer's total life-time payoff of an indirect exchange strategy which uses goods $k, l, \ldots, g, h$ as media of exchange as:

$$u - c\{(\mu+1)b + 1/q_{ki} + 1/q_{lk} + \ldots + 1/q_{hg} + 1/q_{jh}\}; \tag{16.3}$$

where μ is the number of goods used as the media of exchanges.

To make the story simple as well as complete, let us also assume that our i-producing j-consumer suffers an infinite disutility if he fails to consume good j. Thus, the payoff of staying in autarky is set to $-\infty$.[19]

The determination of the optimal exchange strategy has now become trivial. All that our consumer has to do is to look up the above formulae and choose a strategy that generates the maximum total payoff (or the minimum total cost).[20] If, however, even the maximum payoff fails to exceed $-\infty$, he would rather stay in autarky. Since the number of possible strategies is finite, there is always an optimum. The optimal exchange strategy is determined by the way the supply-demand frequencies $\{q_{ij}\}$ are distributed across trading zones.

Our model of individual search behavior is this simple. Indeed, we will see in the Appendix that even if we extend the life-span of our consumers to infinity and let them solve an infinite-horizon maximization problem (with a positive time discounting), the formal structure of the optimal exchange strategy would retain the same mathematical simplicity.[21]

16.4 Alternative exchange systems

Having thus formulated the individual exchange strategies, let us turn to the decentralized economy as a whole and analyze its possible exchange systems. By an *exchange system* we mean a collection of the exchange strategies adopted by every member of the economy. As was remarked in the introduction, our decentralized economy allows an embarrassingly large number of such systems, ranging from very simple to very complex. But in the present chapter we shall confine our attention only to four relatively simple exchange systems, every one of which should occupy prominent places in any serious study on the nature and origin of money. They are barter system, commodity money system, fiat money system, and gift system. Barter system is perhaps the simplest exchange system, in which everybody exchanges his or her product by direct barter; commodity money system is another exchange system in which everybody, except its producers and consumers, uses one of the real goods as the general medium of exchange, i.e., as a commodity money; fiat money system is an exchange system in which everybody in the economy uses a state-issued fictitious good as the general medium of exchange, i.e., as fiat money; and gift system is a *de facto* exchange system in which everybody gives away his or her product to another as a gift and everybody receives his or her consumable from another as a gift.

One of the fundamental problems we have set ourselves to answer in this chapter is whether an autarky- breaking exchange coordination is possible without any centralized coordinating authority. We now restate this problem in an analytically more tractable manner: whether and under what conditions any of the decentralized exchange systems we listed above can be supported as a Nash equilibrium. We define a (simple) Nash equilibrium as a set of strategies each of which is optimal, taking as given the strategies of all the other individuals in the economy. For the sake of simplicity, we will restrict each member's strategies to pure strategies and be concerned only with steady-states of the economy. Because of the simplicity of the information structure of the first three exchange systems, we do not have to introduce the more sophisticated notion of sub-game perfect Nash until Section 16.9.

Before we proceed, we better record one (trivial) existence theorem here.

Proposition 3 *A complete autarky is a Nash equilibrium in any economy.*

Proof: Suppose no one has shown up in any of the trading zones, so that every q_{ij} is zero. Then, the total search cost of any exchange strategy is infinite. Hence, everyone actually chooses to stay in autarky, and every q_{ij} becomes zero, as is supposed. ■

Though trivial, the above proof shows us in the most skeletal form the general structure of a Nash equilibrium in our decentralized exchange economy. A given set of supply-demand frequencies, $\{q_{ij}\}$, determines the optimal exchange strategies of every member of the economy, whose aggregate outcomes in turn determine the actual values of supply-demand frequencies, $\{q_{ij}\}$. Here is a circular causality, and if there is a set of supply-demand frequencies, $\{q_{ij}\}$, that is consistent with this circular causality, it constitutes an equilibrium in our model.

The autarky is the worst possible situation, from which every exchange system has to liberate itself.

16.5 On the difficulty of barter system

We have defined *barter system* as a decentralized exchange system in which everybody seeks to obtain their consumable by direct barter of their product. Can such system be supported as an equilibrium? Of course it can, and it is possible to write down a non-vacuous sufficient condition for that possibility.[22] But a far more interesting question for the purpose of this chapter is: can the barter system be *always* supported as an equilibrium? The answer is clearly "no"! In fact, ever since the time of Aristotle, every student of the phenomenon of money knows the following non-existence theorem:

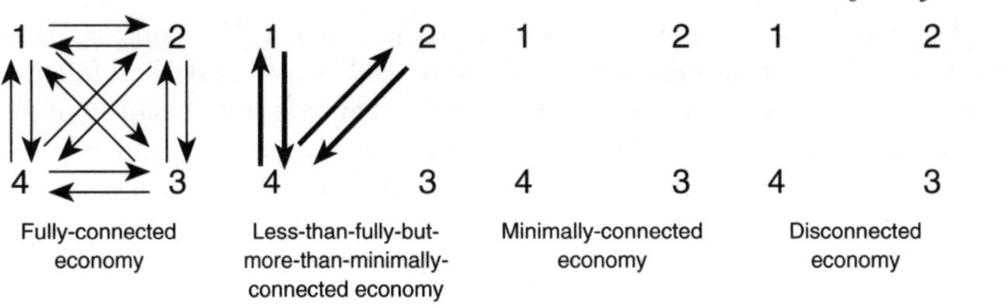

Figure 16.4 The exchange structure in the barter exchange system

Proposition 4 *The barter system cannot support itself as a Nash equilibrium, unless* $e_{ji} > 0$ *for any* i *and* j *such that* $e_{ij} > 0$.

Proof: Suppose, on the contrary, that the barter system is a Nash equilibrium even if $e_{ji} = 0$ and $e_{ij} > 0$ for some pair of i and j. Then, since in a barter system every active member of the economy is by definition seeking a barter exchange, we have $q_{ji} = e_{ji} > 0$ whenever $e_{ji} > 0$ and $q_{ji} = e_{ji} = 0$ whenever $e_{ji} = 0$. This implies that the search cost of barter strategy, c/q_{ji}, becomes ∞ for every i-producing j-consumer, so that they would stay in autarky. Since they are active members of the economy, this is a contradiction. ■

Of course, this is what Stanley Jevons (1875) called the "double coincidence of wants" for barter trade. It says that even if the economy is connected (and is potentially autarky-breaking for everybody), the barter system leaves some of its members forever in a state of autarky, unless the wants of its members coincide doubly, that is, unless its every member can produce the good that is wanted by another member who can produce the good he wants.

Figure 16.4 represents the supply-demand structure of the barter system in each of the four examples of four- good economy in Figure 16.1. A black arrow from, say, good *1* to good *2* now indicates the existence of *1*-supplying *2*-demanders in (*1*, *2*) trading zone. In the case of the barter system, we can draw black arrows only between two goods which were connected both way by two gray arrows in Figure 16.1. This is of course the condition of double coincidence of wants. We also have to check that no indirect exchange strategy is less costly than barter. In the first example of a fully connected economy, we can connect all four goods by two black arrows, which implies that the barter system can liberate everyone from the shackle of autarky. In contrast to this, in the third example of a minimally connected economy, nobody can satisfy the condition of double coincidence of wants, and no black arrows can be drawn in Figure 16.4. The barter system fails to establish itself as a Nash equilibrium. Even though the economy is connected, thereby potentially autarky breaking, none of its members can escape from the misery of autarky. In the second example of a less-than-fully-but-more-than-minimally connected economy, the barter system saves neither *2*-producing *3*-consumers nor *3*-producing *1*-consumers and again fails to establish itself as a Nash equilibrium. Finally, in the fourth example of a disconnected economy nobody can escape from autarky. Economies without barter equilibrium are not the exceptions but the rules.

The barter system is a decentralized exchange system whose supply-demand structure is completely tied down to the given "real" structure of the economy. Indeed, it is this inability to fly over the "reality" that limits the possibility of the barter system to support itself as a Nash equilibrium.

What about our second question on the evolution of the barter system? In the case of the barter system, this question turns out to be redundant. The barter system can never deviate from the "real" structure of the economy, and the condition for its existence is at the same time the condition for its natural evolution.

16.6 The bootstrap nature of the commodity money system

Let us now turn to the analysis of the *commodity money system* – a decentralized exchange system which uses one of the real goods as the general medium of exchange, that is, as a commodity money. Let this particular good be indexed by m. Then, the problem we have to solve first is: under what conditions does everyone in the economy voluntarily come to use this good as the sole medium of exchange (except, of course, the one who produces it and the one who consumes it), even if it would require him to spend search cost and transaction cost not once but twice? We first state the result which answers this question and provide its economic interpretation after.

Proposition 5 *A good m is used as the sole medium of exchange by every member of the economy (except its producer and consumer), if the set of demand-supply frequencies $\{q_{ij}\}$ he daily observes in trading zones satisfy the following set of inequalities for any i and j;*

$$2b + 1/q_{mi} + 1/q_{jm} < \infty; \tag{16.4}$$

$$2b + 1/q_{mi} + 1/q_{jm} < b + 1/q_{ji}; \tag{16.5}$$

$$2b + 1/q_{mi} + 1/q_{jm} < 2b + 1/q_{ki} + 1/q_{jk} \text{ for any } k \neq m; \tag{16.6}$$

$$b + 1/q_{jm} < \infty; \tag{16.7}$$

$$b + 1/q_{jm} \leq 2b + 1/q_{km} + 1/q_{jk} \text{ for any } k \neq m; \tag{16.8}$$

$$b + 1/q_{mi} < \infty; \tag{16.9}$$

$$b + 1/q_{mi} \leq 2b + 1/q_{mk} + 1/q_{ki} \text{ for any } k \neq m. \tag{16.10}$$

In spite of their formidable appearance (and their sheer number), it is trivial to give an economic interpretation to each of the above inequalities. The first three inequalities are concerned with the behavior of those members of the economy who neither produce nor consume the monetized good m at the time of their search for it. Indeed, inequalities (16.4), (16.5) and (16.6) respectively say that it is less time-consuming (hence less costly) to use good m as the medium of exchange than to stay in autarky, than to barter directly, and than to use any other good as a medium. The two inequalities (16.7) and (16.8) in the middle are concerned with the behavior of two groups of individuals – that of those who neither produce

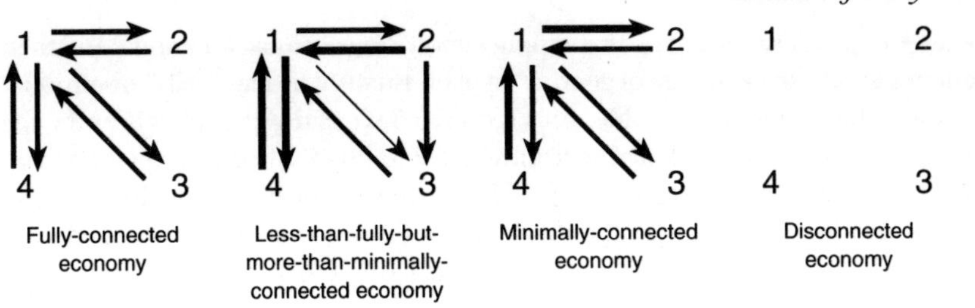

Figure 16.5 The exchange structure in a commodity money exchange system. (When good 1 is used as a commodity money.)

nor consume the monetized good m at the time of their second search for their consumable and that of those who happen to produce the monetized good m. They say that when an individual has good m (either by a previous exchange or by a production) it is less time-consuming to exchange it directly with his consumable than to stay in autarky and than to use some other good as a medium, respectively. And the last two inequalities, (16.9) and (16.10), are concerned with the behavior of the other (lucky) members who can consume the monetized good m. They say simply that when one has a need to consume the good m it is less time-consuming to seek a direct barter than to stay in autarky and than to use some other good as a medium, respectively. The formal proof of Proposition 16.3, which requires some toil and labor, is given in an end note below.[23]

Proposition 16.3 has confirmed the logic of Mengerian theory of money within our search-theoretic framework. What it says is simply that a good m is used as money if its salability q_{im} and purchasability q_{mj} are uniformly higher than those of all the other goods in the economy, $q_{ij}(i,j \neq m)$. We will, however, soon find out that this Mengerian logic can be turned upside down.

Now, our next task is to investigate the question of whether a commodity money system can be sustained as a Nash equilibrium. Since the one half of its circular causality has already been established by Proposition 16.3, we only need to look at the other half and work out the problem of determining $\{q_{ij}\}$ as the very aggregate outcomes of the individual search activities, on the supposition that the economy has already adopted a commodity money system. We provide a heuristic (and yet rigorous) solution in what follows.

Anybody who ever lived in a monetary economy, and that means everybody, knows that "money buys good, goods buy money, but goods do not buy goods," even if he or she has never read a single page of economics textbook. All we need to do here is to translate this famous dictum of Robert Clower (1965) into the determination of $\{q_{ij}\}$ in a commodity money system. We first illustrate this in Figure 16.5 in the case of four-good economy.

For the purpose of the exposition let us choose good *1* as (a candidate for) a commodity money. Then, consider a *2*-producing *3*-consumer who is neither a producer nor a consumer of the monetary good *1*. That such an individual exists is represented in Figure 16.1 by a gray arrow from *2* to *3*. Now, what the second part of Clower's dictum – "goods buy money" and the first part – "money buys goods" – together say is that he first supplies good *2* in exchange for good *1* and then demands good *3* in exchange of good *1*. In plain English, he first "sells" his product and then "buys" his consumable. In Figure 16.5 we can represent his exchange activity by drawing a black arrow from good *2* to good *1* first and then another black arrow from good *1* to good *3*. (If a black arrow has been already drawn there, we only add its width.) Then, the third part of Clower's dictum – "goods do not buy goods" – comes out as a mere by-product. Even if there is a gray arrow from *2* to *3* in Figure 16.1, there is no black arrow going directly from *2* to *3* in Figure 16.5, implying that no *2*-producing, *3*-consumers seek to barter good 2 for good 3. We repeat the same exercise for all the other existing individuals who are neither producers nor consumers of good *1*. As for those lucky individuals who happen to be producers or consumers of the monetary good, they can exchange their product directly for their consumable. Accordingly, if there is a gray arrow from or to *1* in Figure 16.1, we draw a black arrow directly from or to *1* in Figure 16.5. Not every black arrow may survive, however. If it cannot be matched by another black arrow of the opposite direction (or if we can find a less time-consuming indirect exchange route), we have to erase it from the graph (together with the connected black arrow), as is the case in the example of a disconnected economy. It turns out that if the economy is connected, as is the case of the first three examples, we do not have to erase any of the black arrows once they were drawn in Figure 16.5. For instance, in the case of the minimally-connected economy where we can find a continuous sequence of gray arrows which starts from *1*, visits *2*, *3*, and *4*, and then returns to *1* in Figure 16.1, we can draw a continuous sequence of black arrows from *1* to *2*, from *2* to *1* to *3*, from *3* to *1* to *4*, and finally from *4* to *1* in Figure 16.5. Evidently, every black arrow thus drawn is matched by another black arrow with the opposite direction.[24]

Now, let us look at the supply-demand structure of a commodity money system as a whole the picture of which we have just completed in Figure 16.5. In the first three examples of the connected economy, we can find two-way black arrows between *1* and all the other indices in the economy. This implies that the monetary good *1* is constantly demanded and supplied in return for all the non-monetary goods in the economy. Even if no producers of good *2* need good *1* for consumption both in the less-than-fully-but-more-than-minimally-connected economy and in the minimally-connected economy, they nonetheless demand good *1* simply because it is the only good other individuals supply in exchange for good *2*. Even if no consumers of good *3* produce good *1* again both in the less-than-fully-but-more-than-minimally-connected economy and in the minimally-connected economy, they nonetheless supply good *1* they acquired in the previous exchange simply because it is the only good other individuals demand in exchange of good *3*. Note that a black arrow pointing to *1* from, say, *2* represents the salability of good *1* against good *2* (or supply-demand frequency q_{21}) and a black arrow pointing from *1* to, say, *3* represents the purchasability of good *1* against good *3* (or supply-demand frequency q_{13}). Note also that the absence of black arrow between the indices of two non-monetary goods, say *2* and *3*, represents the lack of their salability and purchasability against each other. We have thus succeeded in reversing the causal order of Mengerian theory of money. Both the high salability and the high purchasability of the monetized good against all the other goods in the economy may not be the "cause" of its use as money; they may rather be the "effects" of its use as money!

We now have to formalize the above diagrammatic exposition in the general n-good economy. First, the second and first parts of Clower's dictum – "goods buy money" and "money buys goods" – together imply that once good m is used as a commodity money, any individual who is neither its producer nor its consumer first sells his product $i(\neq m)$ in exchange for it and then buys his consumable $j(\neq m)$ in exchange of it. This implies that each of the i-producing j-consumers spends the first half of his life-time in the (i, m) trading zone as a "seller" of good i, and the second half in the (m, j) as a "buyer" of good j. Since we have supposed that the probability of his encounter with one of the buyers of his product i in (i, m) zone is q_{mi} per unit of time and that the probability of his encounter with one of the sellers of his consumable j in (m, j) zone is q_{jm} per unit of time, his expected search time, or selling time, in the first zone is equal to $1/q_{mi}$ and his expected search time, or buying time, in the second zone is equal to $1/q_{jm}$.[25] He is also expected to spend a time b in his first transaction and another b in his second transaction. Hence, the fraction of the life-time he is expected to spend in the fist zone as a seller is $(1/q_{mi})/(2b+1/q_{mi}+1/q_{jm})$, and the fraction of the life-time he is expected to spend in the second zone as a buyer is $(1/q_{jm})/(2b+1/q_{mi}+1/q_{jm})$. Suppose that the economy has settled down to a steady-state. Then, Ergodic theorem of probability theory tells us that these time-series fractions of an individual i-producing j-consumer can also be identified (with probability one) with the cross-section fractions of all the i-producing j-consumers who are searching in (i, m) zone as sellers and in (m, j) zone as buyers, respectively. Hence, their steady-state frequencies in (i, m) zone and (m, j) zone are respectively equal to $\{(1/q_{mi})/(1/2b+q_{mi}+1/q_{jm})\}e_{ij}$ and $\{(1/q_{jm})/(2b+1/q_{mi}+1/q_{jm})\}e_{ij}$ for any i and $j \neq m$. If we aggregate these frequencies and do not forget to add the frequency of the consumers of good m or the frequency of the producers of good m, we finally obtain the steady-state values of both q_{im} and q_{mi} in a commodity money system. They are

$$q_{im} = e_{im} + \sum_{h \neq m} \frac{1/q_{mi}}{2b+1/q_{mi}+1/q_{hm}} e_{ih}; \qquad (16.11)$$

$$q_{mi} = e_{mi} + \sum_{k \neq m} \frac{1/q_{im}}{2b+1/q_{mk}+1/q_{im}} e_{ki}. \qquad (16.12)$$

Next, the third part of Clower's dictum – "goods do not buy goods" – implies that in a commodity money system no one seeks to barter a non-monetary good for another non-monetary good. Hence, the trading zone for any pair of non-monetary goods becomes completely empty, and we have:

$$q_{ij} = 0 \text{ for any } i \text{ and } j \neq m. \qquad (16.13)$$

Let us take a close look at equation (16.11) which determines the steady-state value of the frequency of those individuals who demand good m in exchange of another good $i \neq m$. This is nothing but the steady-state salability of the monetary good against a non-monetary good. Its first term, e_{im}, is the frequency of i-producing m-consumers, which represents the "real" demand for good m. But the main point of equation (16.11) is that this equation has additional terms which consist of the fractions of all the other producers of good i who are currently demanding good m as the sole medium of exchange. By the same token, equation (16.12) says that the steady-state frequency of those individuals who supply good m in exchange for another good $i \neq m$, or the steady-state purchasability of the monetary good against a non-monetary good, consists not only of its "real" supply e_{mi} but also of the fractions of all the other consumers of good i who are currently supplying good m acquired in his first exchange as the sole medium of exchange. These two equations say that, even if a good has originally very low salability and very low purchasability, once a particular good is accepted as money, the very use of it as money raises its salability and purchasability to the maximum at the expense of all the other goods in the economy. A "bootstrap" mechanism is working here! A totally asymmetric structure of exchange relations has thus emerged within a world of commodities. Or,

> One man is king only because other men stand in the relation of subjects to him. They, on the contrary, imagine that they are subjects because he is king.
>
> (Marx 1867)

Indeed, with some toil and labor relegated to the note,[26] we can now prove the following anti-Mengerian proposition in any connected economy.

Proposition 6 *If a connected economy uses one of its real goods as the sole medium of exchange, then at least in a steady-state all the salabilities and purchasabilites of that good become positive and all the other salabilities and purchasabilities become zero; or if the monetized good is m, we have*

$$q_{im} > 0 \text{ and } q_{mi} > 0 \text{ for any } i, \text{ and } q_{ij} = 0 \text{ for any } i \text{ and } j \neq m. \tag{16.14}$$

We then obtain one of the main propositions of this chapter almost by default.

Proposition 7 *Any connected economy can support a commodity money system as a Nash equilibrium. Indeed, it can use any of its real goods as a commodity money.*

Proof. If we substitute (16.14) into (16.4)–(16.10) of Proposition 16.3, then all the left-hand sides become finite and all the right-hand sides become infinite, thereby satisfying all these inequalities. This implies that every member of the economy, except its producer and consumer, voluntarily uses good m as money. It is also evident that the choice of good m is arbitrary. ■

We have thus succeeded in establishing the "bootstrap" nature of the commodity money system. As long as the economy is connected, and this is no real restriction at all, the very process of monetary circulation creates both the general demand and the general supply (or the general salability and the general purchasability) of the monetary good at least in the long-run. Even if there is little "real" demand (or salability) for it and even if there is little "real" supply (or purchasability) of it, this "bootstrap mechanism" endows any good in the economy with all the characteristics that a money should have. A commodity money system is thus capable of sustaining itself as a Nash equilibrium without any "real" foundation to support it. If we compare Figure 16.5 with Figure 16.1, it is quite striking that the exchange structure of a commodity money system, represented by the configuration of black arrows in Figure 16.5, is all identical in the three examples of the connected economy, in spite of the marked difference in their "real" structure, represented by the configuration of gray arrows in Figure 16.1.

Money is money simply because it is used as money. Indeed, it is because of its transcendence from the "reality" that money is able to overcome the "real" constraints of the economy and make the otherwise impossible decentralized exchanges possible.

16.7 On the difficulty of the natural evolution of a commodity money system

A commodity money system is potentially an ubiquitous system, in the sense that it can be sustained as an equilibrium in any connected economy. But, the "potential" ubiquity should not be confused with the "actual" ubiquity. That it can exist anywhere does not necessarily mean that it does exist anywhere. On the contrary, the very "bootstrap" mechanism which empowers the commodity money system with its potential ubiquity actually works against its "natural" evolution. Its transcendence from the "reality" prevents most economies from reaching it in a spontaneous manner. This may be a self-evident implication of what we have already said in the preceding section, but we at least have to make that implication more explicit here.

Suppose we are witnessing an economy at the time of its historical "beginning." Since the only information each of its members can have is the distribution of ability-need frequencies $\{e_{ij}\}$, we suppose he bases his expectations of the supply-demand frequencies $\{q_{ij}\}$ solely on this "real" structure of the economy. Can this economy evolve into a commodity money system "naturally," as Carl Menger insisted? It can – but only if the "real" structure of the economy, represented by $\{e_{ij}\}$, has the "right" configuration.

To see how restrictive this "right" configuration is, let us look at Fig. 16.1 again. Of course, in the case of a disconnected economy there is no chance for the natural evolution of a commodity money, but the important point is that there is also no chance in both minimally connected and less-than-fully(-but-more-than-minimally) connected economy. For instance, even though there is at least one *2*-producing *3*-consumer in both economies, he never ventures into an indirect exchange which uses either good *1* or good *4* as a medium of exchange, because no one is willing to supply it to him in exchange for his product or demand it from him in exchange for his consumable. We already know that these two economies fail to support the barter system as an equilibrium. But we have now seen that they also fail to develop a commodity money system spontaneously, even though they are potentially capable of supporting it as an equilibrium. What about the fully-connected economy? The answer depends critically on the way ability-need frequencies are distributed among individuals. Since the example given in Figure 16.1 has assumed a uniform distribution of ability-need frequencies, every individual finds it less costly to seek a barter strategy, as we saw in Section 16.5. It is therefore only when the distribution of ability-need frequencies becomes much more concentrated around one particular good that there is a chance for the natural evolution of a commodity money system.

To get a grip of this, suppose that

$$e_{12} = e_{21} = e_{13} = e_{31} = e_{14} = e_{41} = y > e_{23} = e_{32} = e_{34} = e_{43} = e_{24} = e_{42} = x.$$

(We then have an adding-up equation: $6y + 6x = 1$.) This is the most symmetrically asymmetric "real" structure a fully-connected economy can have. It is not hard to see that if $2/y < 1/x - b$, everybody in this economy comes to choose good *1* as the sole medium of exchange, except of course the producers and the consumers of good *1*. (Note that the above inequality corresponds to (16.5) of Proposition 16.3. It is not hard to see that all the other inequalities are already satisfied.) If expected transaction time b is very small, this inequality becomes $y > 2x$. This is already a pretty stringent condition to satisfy. And as soon as b becomes non-negligible, y has to be much larger than $2x$ to satisfy this inequality. Furthermore, as the concentration of ability-need frequencies around good *1* becomes more and more uneven, the condition for the natural evolution of a commodity money system becomes more and more stringent. In fact, we already know that in our examples of both minimally connected and less-than-fully-but-more-than-minimally connected economy there is absolutely no chance for the natural evolution of a commodity money system.

It is true that the above discussions are based on a few examples and many heroic assumptions. But their basic message is clear. Even if "*each* economizing individual becomes increasingly more aware of his economic interest," he is *not* likely to be "led by his interest, without any agreement, without legislative compulsion, and even without regard to the public interest, to give his commodities in exchange for the other, more salable, commodities, even if he does not need them for any immediate consumption purpose."[27] Money is not necessarily a natural product of human economy.

16.8 The "pure" bootstrap nature of the fiat money system

The bootstrap nature of the commodity money system, we demonstrated in Section 16.6, immediately suggests us the possibility of circulating as money a totally useless disk of base metal or a totally useless piece of paper or a mere acknowledgment of the ownership of a large round stone sunken deep in the sea. This then leads us to the third form of decentralized exchange system – fiat money system. We have defined *fiat money system* as a decentralized exchange system in which everybody uses a totally useless token issued by the state as the exclusive medium of exchange.[28]

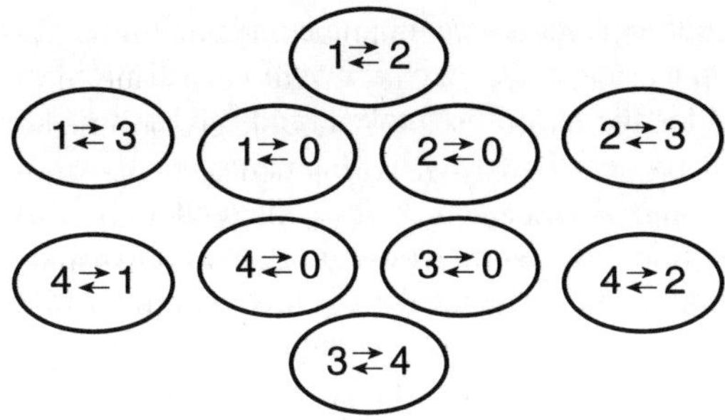

Figure 16.6 Trading zones when the state issues useless tokens

Let us designate the state-issued token by an index *0* and expand the set of goods in the economy to $\{0, 1, 2, \ldots, n\}$. As is seen in Figure 16.6, we also enlarge the set of trading zones by adding (*0*, *1*), (*0*, *2*), . . . , (*0*, *n*) zones, each of which is specialized to exchanges between a useless token and one of the "real" goods. Since the token cannot be consumed by any private individual, we have $e_{i0} = 0$ for any i; since the token cannot be produced by any private individual, we have $e_{0i} = 0$ for any i. Let us suppose that the state sets the value of each piece of token equal to one and fixes its stock level once and for all at the beginning of the history. We denote the level of its "per capita" stock by M. Since the value of money is one, this represents the "real" per capita supply of useless tokens.

The question we now ask is: can the state-issued useless token circulate as "fiat money" – as the exclusive medium of exchange which is handed over from one member of the economy to another and forever staying in the sphere of exchange? In order to answer this question, we again have to go through two complementary exercises. First, we have to deduce the conditions on the supply-demand frequencies, $\{q_{ij}\}$, which induce every individual to use the useless token voluntarily as the sole medium of exchange. Second, we have to determine the values of these supply-demand frequencies as the very aggregate outcomes of all the individuals' search processes, on the condition that they all use the useless token as the sole medium of exchange. Fortunately, we can invoke most of the propositions about the commodity money system, if we add a few obvious modifications.

First, we have:

Proposition 8 *Every member of the economy uses a totally useless token 0 as the sole medium of exchange, if the set of supply-demand frequencies* $\{q_{ij}\}$ *satisfy the following set of inequalities for any i and* $j (\neq 0)$;

$$2b + 1/q_{0i} + 1/q_{j0} < \infty; \tag{16.15}$$

$$2b + 1/q_{0i} + 1/q_{j0} < b + 1/q_{ji}; \tag{16.16}$$

$$2b + 1/q_{0i} + 1/q_{j0} < 2b + 1/q_{ki} + 1/q_{jk} \text{ for any } k \neq 0; \tag{16.17}$$

$$b + 1/q_{j0} < \infty; \tag{16.18}$$

$$b + 1/q_{j0} \leq 2b + 1/q_{k0} + 1/q_{jk} \text{ for any } k \neq 0. \tag{16.19}$$

All the five inequalities have self-explanatory economic interpretations. The first three are concerned with the first stage of the search activity, in which everyone is selling his product in exchange for the state-issued token, and the last two are concerned with the second stage of the search activity, in which everyone is buying his consumable in exchange of the state-issued token. Indeed, inequalities (16.15), (16.16) and (16.17) respectively say that it is less time-consuming (and less costly) to use the token *0* as the exclusive medium of exchange than to stay in autarky, than to barter directly, and than to use any "real" good as a medium. And inequalities (16.18) and (16.19) respectively say that after an individual has acquired the token *0* in exchange of his product, it is less time-consuming (and less costly) to exchange it directly with his consumable than to stay in autarky and than to use any "real" good as a medium.

Next, we can also determine the steady-state values of ability-need frequencies $\{q_{ij}\}$ in the fiat money system in exactly the same way as in the commodity money system. If we keep in mind that no one consumes nor produces the state-issued token, or $e_{0i} = e_{i0} = 0$ for any i, a mere substitution of the index *0* for m leads us to the following expressions in the case of fiat money system:

$$q_{i0} = \sum_{h \neq 0} \frac{1/q_{0i}}{2b + 1/q_{0i} + 1/q_{h0}} e_{ih}; \tag{16.20}$$

$$q_{0i} = \sum_{k \neq 0} \frac{1/q_{i0}}{2b + 1/q_{0k} + 1/q_{i0}} e_{ki}; \tag{16.21}$$

$$q_{ij} = 0 \text{ for any } i \text{ and} j \neq 0; \tag{16.22}$$

Equation (16.20) says that in (*0*, i) trading zone the demand for the state-issued token consists of the fractions of all the producers of good i who are currently demanding the token as money; and equation (16.21) says that in the same (*0*, i) trading zone the supply of the state-issued token consists of the fractions of all the consumers of good i who have acquired the token as money in the previous exchange and are currently supplying it in exchange for good i. Finally, equation (16.22) says that all the zones exchanging a pair of "real" goods are completely vacated. We are again witnessing the work of a bootstrap mechanism! Indeed, the bootstrap mechanism in the fiat money system is much purer than that in the commodity money system. Even if there is no one "really" demanding and no one "really" supplying a state-issued token, that is, even if $e_{i0} = 0$ and $e_{0i} = 0$ for any i, the very decentralized exchange process which uses it as money raises its demands (salabilities) and supplies (purchasabilities) to the maximum at the expense of all the "real" goods in the economy.

In the case of fiat money system, we need one more equation to complete the model. It is the equation which balances the total demand and the total supply of the stock of money. Since each member of this economy holds the state-issue token solely for the purpose of transaction and carries only one piece of it at a time, the existing stock of money M determines the total frequency of individuals who hold

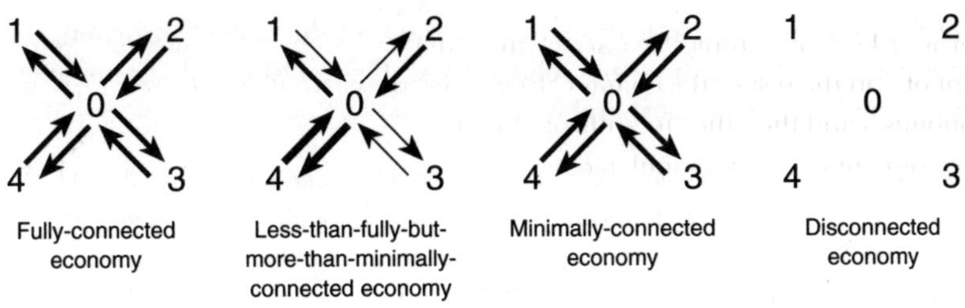

Figure 16.7 The exchange structure in the fiat money exchange system

money and are able to demand their consumables at each point in time. Hence, we have the following "effective demand equation":

$$\sum_i q_{0i} = M. \tag{16.23}$$

Note that in the fiat money system the "goods do not buy goods" equation (16.22) reduces the adding-up equation of supply-demand frequencies: $\sum_i \sum_j q_{ij} = 1$ to a degenerate form of $\sum_i q_{0i} + \sum_j q_{j0} = 1$. Hence, we also have a complementary equation which determines, as a residual, the total frequency of individuals who can supply their products at each point in time:

$$\sum_j q_{j0} = 1 - M. \tag{16.24}$$

Equation (16.23) says that if $M > 0$, at least one member of the economy can appear in $(0, i)$ zone as a supplier of money (or equivalently as a buyer of good i), or $q_{0i} > 0$ for some i. And equation (16.24) says that if $M < 1$, at least one member of the economy can appear in $(0, j)$ zone as a demander of money (or equivalently as a supplier of good j), or $q_{j0} > 0$ for some j.

Figure 16.7 then visualizes some of the above discussions. It has added the index *0* of the state-issued token in the middle of the four indices of "real" goods. We have now inscribed in it the supply-demand structure of the fiat money system. As in the case of a commodity money system, if there is a gray arrow between a pair of real (and hence non-monetary) goods, say, from *2* to *3* in Figure 16.1, we draw a black arrow from *2* to *0* and another black arrow from *0* to *3* in Figure 16.7. (We, however, have to erase them, if one of them is not matched by another black arrow of the opposite direction.) The first black arrow represents the "goods buy money" part, the second black arrow the "money buys goods" part, and the absence of the direct black arrow from *2* to *3*, in spite of the existence of a gray arrow in Figure 16.1, represents the "goods do not buy goods" part of Clower's dictum. It should be evident just by looking at the diagrams that in the first three examples of the connected economy we can draw two-way black arrows between *0* in the middle and all the real goods in the economy. This means that if the stock of the state-issued token is positive (but does not saturate the economy completely), the totally useless token is constantly supplied and demanded in return for all the real goods in the economy at least in a steady-state. In the case of a disconnected economy, we again fail to draw any solid arrows. This quasi-visual argument can be made completely rigorous,[29] and we have:

Proposition 9 *Suppose that the "real" part of the economy is connected and that* $0 < M < 1$. *Then, at least in a steady-state every demand (or salability) for and every supply (or purchasability) of the state-issued token become strictly positive, and all the other salabilities and purchasabilities become zero, or*

$$q_{i0} > 0 \text{ and } q_{0i} > 0 \text{ for any } i, \text{ and } q_{ij} = 0 \text{ for any } i \text{ and } j \neq 0. \tag{16.25}$$

This Proposition has turned Mengerian theory of money completely upside down. Since the fiat money has by definition no "real" demand and no "real" supply, its high salability and high purchasability (relative to those of all the "real" goods in the economy) should be the pure "effect" of its use as money.

As in the commodity money system, once this pure anti-Mengerian Proposition is established, we can prove the "bootstrap" nature – this time, the pure bootstrap nature – of fiat money almost by default.

Proposition 10 *Any connected economy can support a fiat money system as a Nash equilibrium, if the per capita stock of the state-issued fiat money* M *satisfies* $0 < M < 1$.

Proof. Substitute (16.25) into (16.15)–(16.19) of Proposition 16.5. ∎

We can now assert, more forcefully than before, that money is money simply because it is used as money. Fiat money is the product of a pure bootstrap mechanism.

If we compare Figure 16.7 with Figure 16.1, it is quite striking that the exchange structure of fiat money system is, just like that of commodity money system, all identical in the three examples of the connected economy, in spite of the marked difference in their real structure. What is equally striking is, however, that, unlike that of commodity money system represented in Figure 16.5, the exchange structure of fiat money system in Figure 16.7 now shows a complete symmetry with respect to the real goods in the economy, in spite of the marked asymmetry in some of their underlying real structures. Indeed, there remains no trace of the underlying real structure of the economy once it has started circulating the state-issued token as fiat money.

What does this all mean to the controversy on the nature and origin of money? It of course means the complete demise of the commodity theory of money, for the circulation of fiat money severs money from any connections with useful commodities. But the important thing is that it also means the demise of the chartal theory of money as well. Because, as we have now seen, the bootstrap mechanism of money can endow a totally useless token with the power to circulate as money, even without any state legislation and even without any state guarantee of convertibility. In this sense, the term "fiat money" is misleading. It is not the fiat of the state that circulates a useless token as money. The only place the "fiat" enters into the scene is the designation of the material (as well as its quantity) that serves as money.

Before we leave this section, we had better note a way to incorporate macroeconomic policies into our model of fiat money system. If the state controls the level of real monetary balance M, it constitutes the monetary policy of this system. If the state controls the values of e_{0i} and e_{i0} by entering into the economy as a buyer and a seller of the real goods (in exchange of the fiat money it issues), it constitutes the fiscal policy of this system. We can then do an exercise in elementary macroeconomics simply by working out the impacts of these policies on the well-beings of the various members of the economy. Needless to say, however, our search model is still too primitive to do any serious macroeconomics beyond that exercise.

16.9 The gift system and its informational requirement

Let us now cross the traditional boundary of economics and move to the world of anthropologists – the system of gift-giving and gift-receiving.[30] We have defined *gift system* as a *de facto* exchange system in which every member of the economy gives his product as a gift to another member of the economy who needs it and every member of the economy receives his consumable as a gift from another member of the economy who produces it. Although the model of the economy we have so far employed is designed especially for the analysis of real exchange process and by no means the simplest model of gift-giving and gift-receiving process, we keep employing it in this section for the sake of comparability. It needs one alteration in order to serve as a model of the gift-giving process.

Let us remove the state-issued token or fiat money from our picture of the economy. We, however, retain n trading zones associated with it and transform them into "gift-giving" zones. For instance, $(0, i)$ zone now functions as the zone in which individuals give away a unit of good i to anyone who wants it. (Hence, 0 stands literally for "nothing.") The supply-demand frequencies, q_{i0} and q_{0i}, now represent the number of the individuals who are looking for someone to give a unit of good i as a gift and the number of the individuals who are looking for someone who gives them a unit of good i as a gift, respectively.

Our interest in the gift system lies in the following observation. Imagine an economy every member of which feels a strong moral obligation to make a gift to its needy members. This is of course the world of anthropologists. For instance, after having produced a unit of good i, an i-producing j-consumer visits $(0, i)$ zone to meet one of the consumers of good i in order to make her a gift of a unit of his product. After having done such an honorable act, our consumer-producer visits $(0, j)$ zone with a peace of mind and waits for an encounter with a producer of good i who is willing to make him a gift of a unit of good j. If every member of the economy follows such gift-giving and gift-receiving practice, this virtuous economy can extricate itself from the misery of autarky. What should be noted is a fact that as far as the set of supply-demand frequencies $\{q_{ij}\}$ is concerned there is a complete correspondence between the gift system we have just described and the fiat money system we discussed in the preceding section. This leads us to:

Proposition 11 *The gift system and the fiat money system can completely replicate each other's transfers of real goods in the economy.*[31]

An economy we want to model in this chapter is, unfortunately, much baser than the world of anthropologists. We do not want to rely on the sense of obligation to transfer real goods among its members. If there is an act of gift-giving, we want it to be motivated solely by the giver's self-interests. In other words, we want to work in the paradigm of economists. So, the questions we must ask in this section are the same as before. Can a gift system be sustained as a Nash equilibrium? If it can, can it be *always* sustained as an equilibrium? If not, what is the condition for its sustainability? This time, however, our analysis must be more explicitly game-theoretic than in the previous sections, and our equilibrium concept must be that of sub-game perfect Nash. It is not because we are working on the model of a base society, but because the actions taken by each individual in the gift system depend critically on the *information structure* of the economy.

This chapter will deal with only two structures – the case of *perfect information* and the case of *bounded information*. It is, however, possible to incorporate more complex information structures into our model, as Ishihara (1997) has recently done in a different model-setting. In the case of perfect information, any member of the economy is assumed to have a full and true memory of all the past events, i.e. equivalently have an access to an infinite-length record of every other member's past actions, the past actions of their previous partners, the past actions of those previous partners' previous partners, and so on *ad infinitum*. In the case of bounded information, every member is assumed to have only a finite-length record which can trace the previous action of his current partner, the previous action of that partner's previous partner, and so on, but only up to the l-th past partner. We assume $0 \leq l < \infty$. An important limiting case is the case of $l = 0$ – the case where no one has any information about the past acts of even his current partner. In general, a strategy of each member of the economy is a function of the available set of information. A sub-game perfect Nash equilibrium is then defined as a set of strategies such that the action prescribed by each strategy after any possible history of the economy is optimal, taking as given the actions prescribed by the strategies of all the other individuals. As before, each member's strategies are restricted to pure strategies and only the steady-states of the economy are considered.

Now, in this gift system everybody has a temptation to become a beggar. If he could receive a gift without himself giving a gift to another, he would be doubly better off. Because he could then consume his own product (though its utility is assumed to be $-\infty$ in this chapter), and he could save the search cost of finding a person to make a gift. The problem is to find out a decentralized incentive system which can effectively stem off such temptation.

For this purpose, let us consider the following "penal code." "Always give your product to a needy individual who has never broken the penal code in the past, but never give your product to any individual who has broken the penal code at least once in the past." Note that this penal code has a self-referential structure which "ostracizes" those who deviate from the gift-giving practice, those who sympathize with those deviants, those who sympathize with those sympathizers of the deviants, and so on. If every member of the economy follows this penal code as their strategy, we of course have a gift system. First, a good news.

Proposition 12 *If every member of the economy has perfect information, then any connected economy can support a gift system as a sub-game perfect Nash equilibrium.*

Proof. Suppose that everybody follows the "ostracizing" penal code as his strategy and suppose that the economy has already settled down to a steady-state. Then, by Proposition 16.7 the economy replicates the steady-state of the fiat money system, and we have:

$$q_{i0} > 0 \text{ and } q_{0i} > 0 \text{ for any } i, \text{ and } q_{ij} = 0 \text{ for any } i \text{ and } j \neq 0. \tag{16.26}$$

This effectively closes off any kind of exchange activities – barter, monetary, and what not – from everybody's choice set. There thus remain only three strategic options open to each member of the economy – the first one is to make a gift of his product to a needy member who has kept the penal code and then wait for a gift from another, the second to make a gift of his product to a needy member who has broken the penal code and then wait for a gift from another, and the third to consume his own product and then wait for a gift from another. But if every member of the economy except he follows the penal code, the choice of the second and the third option would invite an immediate ostracism and condemn him to the state of autarky. His optimal choice is then to stick to the penal code and enjoys the same payoff as in the fiat money system. Since this is true for any individual and at any point in time, the collection of the penal code strategies by all members of the economy constitutes a sub-game perfect Nash equilibrium. ■

What Proposition 16.10 says is that any connected economy can in principle break the autarky and overcome the difficulty of barter system without any general medium for exchange. What is needed is only a penal code which tells everybody to ostracize deviants and their sympathizers forever from the gift system. In this sense, Proposition 16.10 corroborates the claim of anthropologists that it is not the barter system but the gift system that has universally regulated the exchanges of goods and services in the so-called "primitive" societies. After the now classical work of Axerlod (1984) on the evolution of cooperation, it is not difficult to tell a nice story about the evolution of the gift system.

Does this mean that money is superfluous as a decentralized coordination device? The answer is, however, "no," for we also have the following bad news.

Proposition 13 *If every member of the economy has only a bounded information, then even a connected economy cannot support a gift system as a sub-game perfect Nash equilibrium.*

Proof[32]: First consider the case of $l = 0$. It is then obvious that no one in a gift-giving zone can base his decision on whether an individual he meets there has made a gift or not. Next, consider the case of $l = 1$. Then, no one in a gift-giving zone can base his decision on whether his partner's previous partner has made a gift or not. Knowing that the next partner's decision cannot depend on whether the current partner has made a gift or not, no one can base his decision on whether his current partner has made a gift or not. This then implies that no one can base his decision on whether both his current partner and that partner's previous partner have made a gift or not. We can repeat the same backward-induction type argument for any l as long as it is finite, and show that no one can base his strategy on whether others have made a gift or not in the past. Hence, there is no way to design a system of strategies which can punish a deviant in every possible history of the economy, and everybody succumbs to the temptation to become a receiver of a gift without having made a gift before. (This also implies the breakdown of the configuration of $\{q_{ij}\}$ given by (16.20)–(16.22). But this only strengthens the incentive for deviation.) The gift system cannot be supported as a sub-game perfect Nash equilibrium. ■

The implication of Proposition 16.11 is quite disappointing. Because it says that the gift system can sustain itself among self-seeking individuals only in a tribal society or in a small village or in a closed community, where everybody knows each other (and each other's every ancestor) perfectly well. This is of course the paradigm of anthropologists, although their model human-beings are not necessarily *homo economicus*. As soon as the economy becomes more open, people begin to lose track of each other's past actions. Then, the temptation for deviant behaviors increases, and the tight-network of the gift system is sure to start unraveling. And, once we are in what Friedrich Hayek called the "great society" where everybody is essentially a stranger to each other, there is no chance for the survival of the gift system. We are back to where we started.

Let us look again at the decentralized exchange systems treated in the preceding five sections from the informational perspective. It is now easy to see that none of them – barter system, commodity money system, and fiat money system – depends on the informational structure of the economy. They are consistent even with the extreme $l = 0$ case of the bounded information structure. You do not have to know who your trading partner is when you conduct an exchange by direct barter or through the intermediacy of money; all you have to know is whether your trading partner really has the good or money you want. (It is for this reason that we only needed the notion of simple Nash equilibrium to characterize these exchange systems.) For the sake of completeness, we record here:

Proposition 14 *Neither fiat money system, nor any of commodity money systems, nor barter system requires any member of the economy to know each other's past actions in order to support itself as a sub-game perfect Nash equilibrium.*

Even if the gift system and the fiat money system are alike in their independence from the "real" structure of the economy as well as in their effects on the transfers of real goods, they are totally unlike in their requirement of the informational structure of the economy. While the former needs the help of infinite memory of every member of the economy to support itself, the latter needs none. Indeed, what circulates money as money is not the shared communal memory but the shared expectations of everybody that money will be used as money by everybody else in the economy.

I have no intention to deny the historical possibility that money has actually evolved from some communal mnemonic devices in ancient gift systems. There are indeed some archaeological evidence suggesting that possibility.[33] The important thing is, however, to note that at least from the theoretical standpoint there exists a structural discontinuity between the gift system and the monetary system. It is impossible to fill out this discontinuity by a simple linear causality. History matters than ever.

16.10 On the propagation of the monetary system

This chapter studied four different decentralized exchange systems – barter system, commodity money system, fiat money system, and gift system – as four different forms of Nash equilibrium in a simple model of decentralized economy. It showed that while a well-balanced "real" structure of the economy (such as the double coincidence of wants) is necessary to support the barter system as an equilibrium, no such condition (except what we called the "connectedness") is necessary for the commodity money system or the fiat money system or the gift system to support itself as an equilibrium. It also showed that while infinite memory on the part of all the participants of the economy is essential for the gift system to sustain itself as an equilibrium, no memory, not even finite-length memory, is required for the barter system or the commodity money system or the fiat money system to do so. The monetary system, whether it uses commodity money or fiat money, thus occupies a special position among many an exchange system a decentralized economy can have.

Money is money simply because it is used as money by everybody in the economy. Whether it is made of a useful commodity or of a useless token, money is a pure "social entity" whose existence owes nothing to the "technology and preferences" of the economy nor to the "infinite memory" of its members. And it is for this transcendence from "real" as well as "informational" foundations that money can mediate exchanges between individuals whose abilities and needs fail to supplement each other and whose past actions are unknown to each other. But it is precisely for this transcendence from "reality" as well as "informational" foundations that money has fundamental difficulty in evolving naturally from a historically given "real" structure of the economy or from within a small society with tightly-knit interpersonal relationships. The chapter indeed argued that the origin of money is theoretically "undecidable".

And yet, we human beings are living in a full-fledged monetary economy. No matter how "miraculous" it might be from a purely theoretical standpoint, money did actually emerge on this globe in the distant past, and has since propagated itself all over the globe. It is difficult now to find a society which organizes its economy solely by barter exchanges or by gift exchanges.

In order to conclude this already long chapter on the evolution of money, it is therefore necessary to also talk about the fate of monetary system *after* its appearance on this globe. But the story of the propagation of monetary system is qualitatively different from that of the emergence of monetary system. While the latter is about the internal development of a single economy, the former is about competition, communication and interactions among multiple economies. The former is at least as complex a story as the latter is, and we can only give a brief account of it in the rest of the chapter. In fact, we have to tell two sub-stories – one to economists and the other to anthropologists.

First, imagine a world populated by a large number of economies whose members know only barter exchange,[34] and suppose that one of them has come to be using money. (We of course refrain from delving into the cause of such mutation.) For simplicity, we suppose that money circulating in this mutant economy is fiat money. The question we now pose is: would there be any reason for the use of money to propagate itself, once it has come into being at some tiny corner of a barter world? The answer more or less depends on whether the money-using economy performs better than the rest of the world. Indeed, there are at least three mechanisms that can work for the propagation of a mutant system – *selection, imitation,* and *migration.* The successful economy has a greater chance of survival and a greater momentum for growth than the less successful ones; the system used in the successful economy is often imitated by the leaders of the less successful economies; and the successful economy tends to attract a large number of immigrants from the less successful neighbors. Of course, what we compare here is not individuals but economies, so the notion of "success" is a little murky. But, we can at least say that if the economy with money performs better than the economy without in the sense of Pareto dominance, the use of money is likely to spread out.

Unfortunately, even if the monetary system is autarky-breaking in any connected economy, it is not necessarily Pareto superior to the barter system. For instance, in our examples of the four-good economy depicted in Figure 16.1, the monetary system fails to Pareto-dominate the barter system both in the fully-connected economy and in the less-than-fully-but-more-than-minimally-connected economy.[35] Nonetheless, there is a reason to believe that these cases cannot be regarded as general. Indeed, in the case of minimally-connected economy the monetary system always Pareto-dominates the barter system (because the latter inevitably ends up with complete autarky.) Moreover, it is not difficult to show that even in the cases of fully-connected and less-than-fully-but-more-than-minimally connected economy, if the number of goods n becomes sufficiently large, the monetary system would eventually Pareto-dominate the barter system.[36] All in all, the tendency of the monetary system to propagate itself, once it has come into being in a world originally populated by barter economies, is by no means a necessity but is at least a probability.

Next, imagine another world which is populated by economies whose members exchange their products solely by the system of gift-giving, and suppose that one of them has suddenly come to be using fiat money. We then pose the same question as above: would there be any reason for the use of money to propagate itself, once it has come into being at some tiny corner of this gift-giving world? At first sight, the answer to this question appears to be a simple "no." It is because we know from Proposition 16.8 that both fiat money system and gift system perform just identically with respect to the allocation of real goods! Nevertheless, the case is not entirely hopeless, because we also know from Propositions 16.11 and 16.12 that fiat money system and gift system are totally unlike at least with respect to their requirement on the information structure. We need here a slightly more subtle argument than the one given in the case of barter world.

To begin with, the fact that a gift system requires every member of the economy to know every other member's past actions imposes a limit on the size of the economy adopting it. Even if a gift economy performs well, it cannot expand indefinitely and may soon reach a plateau. In stark contrast, a monetary economy knows no such limit and can expand forever. Hence, there still remains a room for the selection mechanism to work here, and the monetary economy may in the long-run overwhelm the gift economy. That is not all. The differential informational structure between monetary system and gift system also has an important implication for the migration mechanism as well. In order to become a member of a gift economy not only do you have to know the past actions of every other member but your past actions also have to be known to every other member. In stark contrast again, all you have to do to join a monetary economy is to accept the money used there as your money and sell your product in exchange. Your personal identity does not matter there. While the migration from a monetary economy to a gift economy provokes a lot of resistance from the members of the latter, the migration from a gift economy to a monetary economy encounters no such resistance. Hence, the monetary economy is likely to grow relatively larger than the neighboring gift economies by constantly absorbing some of their adventurous or disgruntled members. Furthermore, once the monetary economy has outgrown the neighboring gift economies either by the selection mechanism or by the migration mechanism, all sorts of scale and scope economies start to strengthen these mechanisms and may soon invoke the imitation mechanism as well. Again, the tendency of the monetary system to propagate itself, once it has come into being in the world originally populated by gift economies, is by no means a necessity but is at least a probability.

As the length and complexity of this chapter have indicated, the evolution of money is certainly a long, tortuous process.

Appendix: The optimal exchange strategy for infinitely-lived consumers

The purpose of this Appendix is to show that even if the basic decision units in our decentralized economy are not finitely-lived consumers but infinitely-lived consumers (or infinite-horizon family dynasties), there is no need to change any of the results reported in this chapter.

Consider an infinitely-lived i-producing j-consumer. Let us assume that he receives a positive utility $u(>0)$ from consuming a unit of good j but no utility from any other good, including his own product. We also assume that he discounts future utilities by a positive time discount rate $r(>0)$. For simplicity, we assume that neither production nor exchange takes any time, though they can be easily incorporated into the model. We further assume that his expectations about future parameters are all stationary, so that we can work only on the steady-state strategies. One trivial consequence of these assumptions is that the life-time expected utility of staying in autarky is zero.

Let $Vi\phi j$ denote the expected discounted life-time utility of an i-producing j-consumer with a product i in hand, when he has committed to barter. Then, the method of dynamic programming allows us to calculate its value as follows. Consider a very small time interval $\delta(>0)$. With a probability $q_{ji}\delta$, he meets a trading partner, obtains a unit of good j in exchange of good i, enjoys a utility of u by consumption, produces a unit of good i, and then starts a search activity again with the same utility prospect $Vi\phi j$ as before. His total discounted utility in this case is therefore equal to $(u + Vi\phi j)/(1 + r\delta)$. On the other hand, with a probability $1 - q_{ji}\delta$, he fails to meet a trading partner. His total discounted utility is $Vi\phi j/(1 + r\delta)$ in this case. Hence, $Vi\phi j$ can be expressed self-referentially as: $Vi\phi j = \{q_{ji}\delta(u + Vi\phi j) + (1 - q_{ji}\delta) Vi\phi j\}/(1 + r\delta)$. Solving this, we obtain $Vi\phi j = uq_{ji}/r$: For later convenience, we rewrite this as: $Vi\phi j = u/\{(1 + r/q_{ji}) - 1\}$.

Next, let $Vikj$ denote the expected discounted life-time utility of our i-producing j-consumer with his product in hand, when he is using good $k(\neq i,j)$ as the sole medium of exchange. Let us also denote by $Vikj$, his expected life-time utility when he holds money in hand. Then, the method of dynamic programming again allows us to relate these two life-time utilities during $\delta(>0)$ as: $Vikj = \{q_{ki}\delta\, Vikj, + (1 - q_{ki}\delta)\, Vikj\}/(1 + r\delta)$, and $Vikj = \{q_{jk}\delta(u + Vikj) + (1 - q_{jk}\delta)\, Vikj\}/(1 + r\delta)$. Solving them, we obtain for every $k(\neq i,j)$: $Vikj = u/\{(1 + r/q_{ki})(1 + r/q_{jk}) - 1\}$.

In general, let $Vikl..hj$ denote the expected discounted utility of our i-producing j-consumer with his product in hand, when he has committed to an indirect exchange which uses goods $k, l, \ldots, g, h$ as media of exchange. We can calculate it as: $Vikl \ldots ghj = u/\{(1 + r/q_{ki})(1 + r/q_{lk}) \ldots (1 + r/q_{hg})(1 + r/q_{jh}) - 1\}$.

Note here that all the above expressions have the form of $u/(D - 1)$. Since the maximization of $u/(D - 1)$ is equivalent to the minimization of D or $\log(D)$, and since the non-autarky condition $u/(D - 1) > 0$ is equivalent to $\log(D) < \infty$, we can formulate the optimal search program for our producer- consumer in the form of:

Lemma 1 *The optimal search program for an infinite-living i-producing j-consumer is to choose a set of indices, $k, l, \ldots, g, h$, which minimizes the following summation:*

$$\log(1 + r/q_{ki}) + \log(1 + r/q_{lk}) + \ldots + \log(1 + r/q_{hg}) + \log(1 + r/q_{jh}).$$

If the minimum value is infinite, he rather stays in autarky. If the minimizing set of indices is null (ϕ), he seeks barter exchange. Otherwise, he seeks an indirect exchange which uses the minimizing set of goods, $k, l, \ldots, g, h$, as his media of exchange.

Now, the term $\log(1 + r/q_{kl})$ in the above formula can be regarded as an index of search cost in (l, k) trading zone. (If r is very small, it indeed can be approximated as r/q_{kl}.) Then, our infinitely- lived producer-consumer can determine his optimal exchange program simply by adding this index of search cost in each trading zone and minimizing their total sum. It is as if he had a finite life-time and no time discounting, as in the model of the main text.

Acknowledgments

I would like to thank Hidehiko Ishihara as well as the participants in the workshop on "Evolution and Economics" at Certosa di Pontignano for their comments on an earlier version. This research was partly supported by Suntory Foundation, and this chapter was written while I was visiting Università di Siena, Dipartmento di Economia Politica under the grant of JSPS. I am grateful to the first and the third institution for their financial help and to the second institution for its hospitality.

Notes

1 See Schumpeter (1954), especially pp. 62–64 and 288–322, for the most authoritative account of this debate. See also Monroe (1923) and Vickers (1960). Schumpeter used the terms: metallist theory of money and cartal theory of money, or metallism and cartalism, which he borrowed from Knapp's *State Theory of Money* (1924). Our terms – commodity theory of money vs. chartal theory of money – exactly correspond to theirs.
2 See Schumpeter 1954: 63.
3 According to Schumpeter (1954), the commodity theory began with Aristotle. It was advanced by Bodin, Child, Petty, Locke, Harris, Hume, Turgot, Cantillon, Scaruffi, Davanzati, Montanari, and Galiani during mercantilism, and was made an orthodoxy by classical economists, including Smith, Ricardo, and Marx. On the other hand, Schumpeter found a germ of chartal theory in Plato and saw its full development in the hands of Roman jurists. In modern times it was overwhelmed by the commodity theory and survived only in the writings of Potter, Barbon, Boisguillebert, Berkeley, James Stuart, and John Law. It was the publication of Knapp's *State Theory of Money* in 1905 that chartal theory made a strong revival. (I have, however, two objections to the classification of Schumpeter: first, his characterization of Aristotle as a commodity theorist is an downright misreading of both *Politics* and *Nicomachean Ethics*; second, John Law cannot be classified into either camp, for he is "a class by himself" and came very close to the bootstrap theory of money we will advance in this chapter. I of course need another chapter to elucidate these objections.) It is also interesting to note here that as late as May 1947, *American Economic Review* featured a debate between Benjamin Graham as a commodity theorist and Abba Lerner as a chartal theorist.
4 Menger 1892: 250.
5 Menger 1981: 259.
6 Knapp 1924: 1. The German original appeared in 1905.
7 Mauss (1990).
8 See Mauss 1990: 39.
9 Malinowski (1922).
10 Note that in many of the gift exchange societies, especially among "advanced" ones, anthropologists have found seashells, stones, metals, bones, teeth, mats, clothes, leather, cattle, tea, and many other precious objects circulating among people and tribes. In *kula* trade, for instance, there are a counterclockwise circulation of seashell bracelets and a clockwise circulation of necklaces made of mother-of-pearl among the chiefs of participating of tribes. Many anthropologists, including Mauss, call these circulating objects "primitive money." (Malinowski, however, dissented.) They claim these objects can be called "money" because they often mediate exchanges of goods and services among people and groups. They at the same time concede that these objects are different from the modern form of money, because they are not a mere sign or symbol of value but a sign of honor and wealth, the magical and religious symbol of rank and plenty, and because they are not mere things, but spiritual entities still attached

to the individuality of their original owners, to the history of its past circulation, and to the collective memories of the entire tribes. It may therefore be more accurate to characterize the evolutionary story of anthropologists as a three stage development – a system of gift exchange without primitive money → a system of gift exchange with primitive money → a system of selling and buying with modern money. See, for instance, Quiggin (1949), Dalton (1965), Einzig (1966), Codere (1968), and Grierson (1978), for detailed discussions and analyses on the phenomena of "primitive money."

11 Mauss (1990: 36).

12 Axelrod (1984).

13 Their models have followed an important line of research in monetary theory which emphasizes the record-keeping role of money, such as Ostroy (1973), Ostroy and Starr (1990) and Townsend (1987, 1989, 1990).

14 The notion of connectedness given above is closely related to that of "irreducibility" in the theory of Markov chains (see Feller (1968)) and to that of "resource relatedness" in Arrow and Hahn (1972).

15 To be precise, Jones himself has assumed that each trader commits him- or herself to a simple (and generally sub-optimal) search strategy and meets randomly in a single trading zone. His solution, however, turns out to be formally equivalent to Iwai's specialized trading zones model.

16 However, there is also a variation in the assumption about the meeting probability in a trading zone. While Jones, Oh, Iwai, and the old model of Kiyotaki and Wright have basically assumed that the probability each individual meets another individual increases in proportion to the number of searching individuals, the later models of Kiyotaki and Wright have assumed away such trade externality except at the point of no searching individual. The former implies an increasing returns to scale of the quadratic order in the "aggregate" meeting probabilities, and the latter a constant returns to scale except at the zero point. Note, however, that even the latter model has an increasing returns property at least at the origin.

17 As was suggested in the preceding footnote, this assumption corresponds to what Diamond and Maskin (1979) called the "quadratic meeting technology" in their search model. Diamond later applied this quadratic meeting technology model to the analysis of barter and monetary systems in (1982) , (1984a) and (1984b). The prototype exchange model of Diamond, however, is a single-good barter exchange, and his "monetary economy" model presupposes a monetary transactions technology from the outset. One of the purposes of the present chapter is to deduce the very structure of the monetary transactions technology endogenously on the basis of the search-theoretic analysis of individual exchange behaviors.

18 If the probability of an event is $q\Delta$ for a small time interval Δ, its expected waiting time can be shown to be equal to $1/q$. This is an elementary fact of Poisson process.

19 If we set the payoff of autarky at a finite value, some of the propositions below must be qualified and the chapter's main theses will lose part of their sweepingness.

20 To be rigorous, we need to specify a tie-breaking rule to choose among the exchange strategies which happen to give the same payoff value. The rule we will adopt is a lexicographic-cum-randomizing one which chooses the strategy with the shorter exchange sequence when they have different lengths and tosses a coin when they have the same length.

21 The first version of this chapter presented in the conference employed this infinite-horizon model.

22 The following is a sufficient condition for the barter system to be a Nash equilibrium. Suppose that for any i and j, $e_{ij} > 0$ and for any $k(\neq i,j)$ $b + 1/e_{ji} \leq 2b + 1/e_{ki} + 1/e_{jk}$, the barter system can be supported as a steady-state Nash equilibrium. This is, however, an uninteresting proposition, because it is essentially the condition to prevent everybody from seeking indirect exchanges.

23 The sketch of the proof of Proposition 16.3 is as follows. We first note that inequalities (16.4), (16.7), and (16.9) assure that no one in the economy stays in autarky. We next prove that if (16.8) holds for any j, no holders of good m seek an indirect exchange. This can be done by repeatedly applying (16.8) to its own right-hand side and obtain a series of inequalities: $b + 1/q_{jm} \leq 2b + 1/q_{jk} + 1/q_{km}) \leq 3b + 1/q_{jk} + 1/q_{kh} + 1/q_{hm} \leq \ldots$. They of course imply that the total cost of barter, $b + 1/q_{jm}$, is indeed the minimum total search cost for m-holding j-consumers. In exactly the same manner, we can also prove that if (16.10) holds for any i, no producers of good m seek an indirect exchange either. Finally, we prove that if (16.5), (16.6), (16.8) and (16.10) hold for any i and j, the total search cost of using good m as the sole medium of exchange, $2b + 1/q_{mi} + 1/q_{jm}$, is indeed the minimum total search cost for i-producing j-consumers with i and $j \neq m$. Since (16.5) and (16.6) implies that that expression is smaller than the total search cost of barter as well as the total search cost of using any other good as the sole medium of exchange, what remains to be proved is only that it is also smaller than that of any longer indirect exchange. Suppose not. Then, there is a sequence of $\mu(\geq 1)$ indirect exchanges which uses goods $k, \ldots, h$ as media, such that $2b + 1/q_{jm} + 1/q_{mi} > (\mu + 1)b + 1/q_{jk} + \ldots + 1/q_{lh} + 1/q_{hi}$. Then, by applying (16.5) to the last term in the R-H-S, we have: $> (\mu + 2)b + 1/q_{jk} + \ldots + 1/q_{lh} + 1/q_{hm} + 1/q_{mi}$. But if we apply one of the inequalities we obtained for m-holding j-consumers at the beginning of this footnote to all the terms but the last in the right-hand side, we obtain an inequality: $2b + 1/q_{jm} + 1/q_{mi} > 2b + 1/q_{jm} + 1/q_{mi}$. This is an outright contradiction. ■

24 A proof of Proposition 16.4 given in note 26 merely formalizes this exercise.

25 Recall note 18.

26 An outline of the proof of Proposition 16.4 is as follows. First of all, if the economy is connected, we can easily construct a closed loop of strictly positive ability-need frequencies, $e_{ma} > 0, e_{ab} > 0, \ldots, e_{yz} > 0$, and $e_{zm} > 0$, such that the set of connected indices, $m, a, b, c, \ldots, y, z$ and m, contains all the n indices at least once. Next, if we substitute a for i in (16.12), we have $q_{ma} \geq e_{ma}$. Since $e_{ma} > 0$, we obtain $q_{ma} > 0$. Then, if we substitute a for i in (16.11) and b for i in (16.12), we have $q_{am} \geq \{(1/q_{ma})/(1/q_{ma} + 1/q_{bm})\}e_{ab}$ and $q_{mb} \geq \{(1/q_{bm})/(1/q_{ma} + 1/q_{bm})\}e_{ab}$. Since $e_{ab} > 0$ and $q_{ma} > 0$, we obtain $q_{am} > 0$ and $q_{mb} > 0$ as long as $q_{bm} > 0$. If we repeat the same argument to b and $c, \ldots, y$ and z, we obtain $q_{am} > 0, q_{mb} > 0, q_{bm} > 0, q_{mc} > 0, \ldots, q_{ym} > 0, q_{mz} > 0$, as long as $q_{zm} > 0$. Finally, if we substitute z for i in (11), we have $q_{zm} \geq e_{zm}$. Since $e_{zm} > 0$, we also obtain $q_{zm} > 0$. Hence, $q_{mi} > 0$ and $q_{im} > 0$ for all i. ■

27 Menger (1871).

28 This section draws partly from Iwai (1988b).

29 If $0 < M < 1$, we have by (23) and (24) $q_{0i} > 0$ for at least one i and $q_{i0} > 0$ for at least one i. Then, we can apply the argument in note 26 to (16.20) and (16.21) and prove $q_{0i} > 0$ for any i and $q_{i0} > 0$ for any i. ■

30 This section owes to Kocherlakota (1998) and Ishihara (1997). Their model settings are, however, different from ours. Kocherlakota has examined a Samuelson's overlapping generation model, Townsent's turnpike model, and Kiyotaki–Wright's search model, whereas Ishihara has used a simplified overlapping generation model.

31 This Proposition should be contrasted with Kocherlakota (1998) who finds that in Kiyotaki–Wright model the transfer of goods in the gift system is Pareto-superior to that in the fiat money system. This result is due to the fact that in Kiyotaki–Wright model an option for barter trade remains even in a fiat money equilibrium, thereby weakening the punishment of deviations.

32 The basic idea of this proof owes to Ishihara (1997), part (3) of Proposition 3.

33 We can interpret "primitive money" we discussed in note 10 as such communal mnemonic devices.

34 Note that, as was discussed in Section 16.5, while some of these economies can sustain barter system as an equilibrium, others cannot do so and may end up with partial

barter or complete autarky.

35 For instance, in the case of the four-good fully-connected economy it is not hard to show (in fact, we only have to stare at Figures 16.4 and 16.5) that the total search and transaction time in a barter equilibrium can be calculated as $b + 12$, whereas the total search and transaction time in a steady-state fiat money equilibrium can be calculated $2b + 16$.

36 For instance, in the case of the n-good fully-connected economy the ability-need frequency e_{ij} of the representative individual is given by $1/n(n-1)$, and we can calculate q_{ij} in a barter equilibrium as $1/n(n-1)$ and $q_{i0} = q_{0i}$ in a steady-state fiat money equilibrium as $1/2n$. (In the latter calculation we have to use (16.20) and (16.21).) Hence, the total search and transaction time in the former is equal to $b + n(n-1)$ and in the latter is equal to $2b + 4n$. Hence, if $n(n-5) > b$, the fiat money equilibrium Pareto-dominates the barter equilibrium.

References

Arrow, K. and F.H. Hahn (1972) *General Competitive Analysis*. San Francisco: Holden Day.

Axelrod, R. (1984) *The Evolution of Cooperation*. New York: Basic Books.

Rao Aiyagiri, S. and N. Wallace (1992) Fiat money in the Kiyotaki-Wright model. *Economic Theory* 2: 447–464.

Boldrin, M., N. Kiyotaki and R. Wright (1994) A dynamic equilibrium model of production, and exchange. *Journal of Economic Dynamics and Control* 17: 723–758.

Clower, R.W. (1967) A reconsideration of the microfoundations of monetary theory. *Western Economic Journal* 6(December): 1–9.

Codere, H. (1968) Money-exchange systems and a theory of money. *Man*. 3: 557–577.

Dalton, G. (1965) Primitive money. *American Anthropologist* 68: 44–65

Diamond, P.A. (1982) Aggregate demand management in search equilibrium. *Journal of Political Economy* 90(5): 881-894.

—— (1984a) Money in search equilibrium. *Econometrica* 52(1): 1–20.

—— (1984b) *A Search-Equilibrium Approach to the Micro-Foundations of Macroeconomics*. Cambridge, MA: MIT Press.

—— and E. Maskin (1979) An equilibrium analysis of search and breach of contract I: steady states. *Bell Journal of Economics* 10(Spring): 282–316.

Einzig, P. (1966) *Primitive Money* (2nd edn). New York: Pergamon.

Feller, W. (1968) *An Introduction to Probability Theory and Its Applications: Volume I* (2nd edn). New York: John Wiley.

Graham, B. (1947) Money as pure commodity. *American Economic Review* 37: 304–307.

Grierson, P. (1978) The origin of money. *Research in Economic Anthropology* 1: 1–35.

Ishihara, H. (1997) *Money as a Medium of Information*. Mimeo. Graduate School of Economics, The University of Tokyo.

Iwai, K. (1988a) *The Evolution of Money – A Search-Theoretic Foundation of Monetary Economics*. CARESS working paper 88–3. University of Pennsylvania.

—— (1988b) *Fiat Money and Aggregate Demand Management in a Search Model of Decentralized Exchanges*. CARESS working paper 88–16. University of Pennsylvania.

—— (1996) The bootstrap theory of money – a search-theoretic foundation of monetary economics. *Structural Change and Economic Dynamics* 7: 451–477; *Corrigendum* 9(1998): 269.

Jevons, W.S. (1875) *Money and the Mechanism of Exchange*. London: King.

Jones, R.A. (1976) The origin and development of media of exchange. *Journal of Political Economy* 84(4) pt.1: 757–775

Knapp, G.F. (1924) *The State Theory of Money*. 1905. London: Macmillan.

Kiyotaki, N. and R. Wright (1989) On money as a medium of exchange. *Journal of Political Economy* 97: 927–954.

—— (1991) A contribution to the pure theory of money. *Journal of Economic Theory* 53: 215–235.

—— (1993) A search-theoretic approach to monetary economics. *American Economic Review* 83: 63–77.

Kocherlakota, N. (1998) Money is memory. *Journal of Economic Theory*. 81: 232–251.

Lerner, A. (1947) Money as a creature of state. *American Economic Review* 37: 312–317.

Malinowski, B. (1922) *Argonauts of the Western Pacific*. London: Routledge.

Marx, Karl (1967[1867]) *Capital, Volume I*. Trans by A. Moore and E. Aveling. New York: International Publisher.

Mauss, M. (1990 [1930]) *The Gift – The Form and Reason for Exchange in Archaic Societies*. Trans. by W.D. Halls. New York: Norton.

Menger, C. (1981[1871]), *Principles of Economics*. Trans. by J. Dingwall and B.F. Hoselitz. New York: New York University Press.

—— (1892) On the origins of money. *Economic Journal* 2239–2255.

Monroe, A.E. (1923) *Monetary Theory Before Adam Smith*. Cambridge, MA: Harvard University Press.

Oh, S. (1989) A theory of a generally acceptable medium of exchange and barter. *Journal of Monetary Economics* 23: 101–119

Ostroy, J.M. (1973) The informational efficiency of monetary exchange. *American Economic Review* 63: 597–610.

—— (1990) Transaction role of money. In B. Friedman and F.H. Hahn (eds) *Handbook of Monetary Economics*, Vol. 1. Amsterdam: North-Holland.

Quiggin, A.H. (1949) *A Survey of Primitive Money: The Beginnings of Currency*. London: Methuen.

Schumpeter, J.A. (1954), *History of Economic Analysis*, Oxford: Oxford University Press.

Shi, S. (1995) Money and prices: a model of search and bargaining. *Journal of Economic Theory* 57: 467–496.

Townsend, R. (1987) Economic organization with limited communication. *American Economic Review* 77: 954–971.

—— (1989) Currency and credit in a private information economy. *Journal of Political Economy* 97: 1323–1344.

—— (1990) *Financial Structure and Economic Organization: Key Elements and Patterns in Theory and History*. Cambridge, MA: Basil Blackwell.

Vickers, D. (1960) *Studies in the Theory of Money 1690–1776*. London: Owen.

Index